Sixth Edition

SUBSTANCE USE COUNSELING

THEORY AND PRACTICE

D1568942

Sixth Edition

SUBSTANCE USE COUNSELING

THEORY AND PRACTICE

Patricia W. Stevens

Retired Professor of Counselor Education and Supervision
Transitions Family Counseling, Louisville, CO

Robert L. Smith

Professor & Department Chair
Counseling and Educational Psychology
Texas A&M University, Corpus Christi, TX

330 Hudson Street, NY, NY 10013

Director, Teacher Education & the Helping Professions: Kevin M. Davis

Portfolio Manager: Rebecca Fox-Gieg

Content Producer: Janelle Rogers

Content Project Manager: Pamela D. Bennett

Media Project Manager: Lauren Carlson

Portfolio Management Assistant: Anne McAlpine

Executive Field Marketing Manager: Krista Clark

Executive Product Marketing Manager: Christopher Barry

Procurement Specialist: Deidra Smith

Cover Designer: Melissa Welch

Cover Photo: Frank J Wicker/Moment/Getty Images

Full-Service Project Management: Sudip Sinha, iEnergizer Aptara®, LTD

Composition: iEnergizer Aptara®, LTD

Printer/Binder: LSC Communications

Cover Printer: LSC Communications

Text Font: 10/12 Times LT Pro

Library of Congress Cataloging-in-Publication Data

Names: Stevens, Patricia W. | Smith, Robert L. (Robert Leonard)
Title: Substance use counseling : theory and practice / Patricia Stevens, adjunct faculty, practitioner, and consultant, Boulder, CO, Robert L. Smith, professor & department chair, Counseling & Educational Psychology, Texas A&M University, Corpus Christi, TX.
Description: Sixth edition. | Boston : Pearson, [2018] | Includes bibliographical references and index.
Identifiers: LCCN 2016054858 | ISBN 9780134055930 | ISBN 0134055934
Subjects: LCSH: Substance abuse—Treatment. | Substance abuse—Patients—Counseling of.
Classification: LCC RC564 .S765 2018 | DDC 362.29/186—dc23 LC record available at https://lccn.loc.gov/2016054858

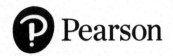

ISBN 10:   0-13-405593-4
ISBN 13: 978-0-13-405593-0

This book is for all the dedicated students and practitioners who strive to make a difference in the lives of their clients and in the quality of life for all. May they continue to find this text to be helpful for them in their personal journey and in their professional career.

—Patricia Stevens

This text is dedicated to the many brave individuals and family members experiencing problems and challenges related to addictions, and to the many professionals devoted to working and conducting research in the field of addictions.

—Robert Smith

ABOUT THE AUTHORS

Dr. Patricia W. Stevens is a retired Counselor Educator currently in clinical private practice in Louisville, CO. She trains student counselors through online teaching. Dr. Stevens also consults with universities in program development and accreditation (CACREP, NCATE/CAEP).

Dr. Stevens is a member of ACA, AAMFT, and served on the CACREP board for eight years. She has held multiple leadership positions in ACA and its divisions, including President of the IAMFC, Board-Member-at-Large of AACD, and Co-Chair of the Professional Standards Committee. Dr. Stevens has also served on several editorial boards of ACA and its divisions. Though retired, she continues to be active in the profession and her clinical work.

Through the years she has delivered more than 70 presentations at the local, state, regional, national, and international levels in the areas of substance abuse, gender implications in counseling, challenges of aging, and ethical/ legal issues in counseling. In the counseling field, she has published more than 50 articles, chapters, and books. Dr. Stevens has prepared and taught more than 26 different courses in the counseling curriculum.

Dr. Stevens is a Fulbright Scholar and works with the Red Cross as a Mental Health Disaster Relief volunteer. She volunteers at her local Red Cross and her local senior center.

Robert L. Smith, Ph.D., FPPR, is Professor & Chair of the Counseling and Educational Psychology Department, as well as the Doctoral Program Coordinator at Texas A&M University–Corpus Christi. He completed his Ph.D. at the University of Michigan. As a licensed psychologist, he has worked as a private practitioner in addition to serving as the chair of three counselor education programs. He is the author of several books and more than 80 professional articles. He serves as the Executive Director and co-founder of the International Association of Marriage and Family Counselors. He is also the founder of the National Credentialing Academy for Family Therapists. His research interests include the efficacy of treatment modalities in individual psychotherapy, family therapy, and substance abuse counseling. He is a Diplomate-Fellow in Psychopharmacology with the International College of Prescribing Psychologists and consultant with the Substance Abuse Program in the U. S. Navy. Dr. Smith as an international lecturer is currently involved in the development and implementation of graduate programs in counseling and psychology in Latin America.

ABOUT THE CONTRIBUTORS

Dr. Robert Dobmeier is an associate professor and Coordinator of the Mental Health Counseling Program at the College of Brockport. Dr. Dobmeier has prior work experience as a mental health counselor, supervisor, and director. He has worked for several Office of Mental Health and Office of Alcoholism and Substance Abuse Services licensed agencies in western New York. Dr. Dobmeier is a Licensed Mental Health Counselor and is a member of the New York Mental Health Counseling Association, and former Co-President of the New York Association of Counselor Education and Supervision. He has advocated for recognition of diagnosis in the scope of practice for mental health counselors in New York State. As President of the Association for Adult Development and Aging, and Chair of their Public Policy and Legislation Committee, he has advocated for Medicare reimbursement for the services of professional counselors. He is also a member of the American Counseling Association, Association for Counselor Education and Supervision, and Association for Spiritual, Ethical, and Religious Values in Counseling. Dr. Dobmeier is a founding member of ACA-NY. He is also a member of the Greater Rochester Chapter of NYMHCA and the North Atlantic Regional Association for Counselor Education and Supervision. Dr. Dobmeier is a member of Chi Sigma Iota and of Nu Chapter. Among the courses Dr. Dobmeier enjoys teaching are several mental health courses, most recently Leadership and Advocacy, Research and Program Evaluation, Measurement and Evaluation, and Spirituality in Counseling.

Dr. Claudette Brown-Smythe is a graduate of Syracuse University, where she completed a doctor of philosophy degree in counseling and counselor education, and a dual masters' degree in rehabilitation and community counseling. Prior to that, she attended the University of the West Indies in Jamaica, where she completed her Bachelor of Science and Master's of Social Work with an emphasis in group and community development. In Jamaica, she worked as a school counselor and later as a college professor training and supervising school counselors. As a social worker, she worked in rural and inner-city communities in Jamaica, educating and doing advocacy around issues of child abuse and child poverty, and later worked on these same issues with the aged in the Caribbean. Dr. Brown-Smythe has worked in various fields in counseling: school counseling, college counseling, and mental health and rehabilitation counseling. With more than 15 years of experience in training and supervision, her current employment is at The College at Brockport State University of New York as a Visiting Assistant Professor in the counselor education department and coordinator of the certificate in advanced studies. She is a Certified Rehabilitation Counselor (CRC), a Nationally Certified Counselor, (NCC), and an Accredited Clinical Supervisor (ACS). Her professional and research interests include addressing diversity issues in counseling and supervision; exploring loss and grief in counseling; supervision in counseling; spirituality, wellness, and well-being; counseling older adults; and training paraprofessionals as mental health and rehabilitation facilitators. Dr. Brown-Smythe is a recipient of the NBCC inaugural Minority Fellowship.

Linda L. Chamberlain, Psy.D., is a licensed psychologist and Coordinator of the Center for Addiction and Substance Abuse (CASA) at the Counseling Center for Human Development, the University of South Florida in Tampa, Florida. She has worked in the addictions field since 1980 as both a clinician and educator with a focus on individual and family recovery from substance abuse and the treatment of problem gambling. Dr. Chamberlain coauthored a book on the treatment of problem gambling entitled *Best Possible Odds* and has written numerous articles and contributed to several books on the dynamics and treatment of addictions and family therapy. Dr. Chamberlain has presented workshops and counselor training through the American Counseling Association and the American Psychological Association, and has been an invited speaker at local, national, and international conferences on addictions.

Ashby Dodge is a licensed clinical social worker with a private practice in New York City that focuses on couples/family therapy, young professionals, LGBTQ issues, sexual assault survivors, and substance abuse. Ashby is currently Clinical Director at The Trevor Project, the nation's leading organization providing crisis intervention and suicide prevention services to LGBTQ youth, ages 13 to 24. Ashby's clinical style is largely strengths-based, helping people find positive and practical solutions to any number of life stressors and problematic relationships.

Dr. Kristina DePue is an Assistant Professor at the University of Florida (UF). She received her doctoral degree in Counselor Education from the University of Central Florida. Before attending UCF, Dr. DePue graduated from Vanderbilt University for both her master's and bachelor's degrees. Helping individuals struggling with addiction has been a personal mission of Dr. DePue's for more than 11 years. She has worked in many roles in treatment settings and was part of Vanderbilt's initiation of the Collegiate Recovery Community (CRC). Dr. DePue's research is focused on substance use in the collegiate population, specifically focusing on student-athletes and mild traumatic brain injury (mTBI), diagnosis, and self-harm. Additional research endeavors involve the trajectory of addiction and recovery, highlighting the relationship between the bottoming-out experience, the turning point, and early recovery. Dr. DePue serves on the editorial boards for the *Journal of Addictions and Offender Counseling* and for the *Annual Review of Best Practices in Addictions and Offender Counseling*. Dr. DePue is actively involved in both the American Counseling Association (ACA) and the International Association of Addiction and Offender Counselors (IAAOC) and has served as the IAAOC Collegiate Addiction Committee Chair for the past two years. She is also on the Board of Directors for UF's CRC. Currently, Dr. DePue is working on funding projects that focus on mTBI and substance use in college athletes, statistical modeling of addiction trajectories, examining the effectiveness of CRCs nationwide, and using technology to assist in harm reduction for college drinkers.

Leigh Falls Holman, Ph.D., LPC-MHSP-S, RPTS, NCC, AMHCA Diplomate and CMHC in Substance Abuse and Co-Occurring Disorders, Trauma Counseling, and Child and Adolescent Counseling, teaches at The University of Memphis. She served as President of the International Association of Addiction and Offender Counselors from 2015 to 2016 and was previously recognized by IAAOC as an Outstanding Counseling Professional in 2013 for her contributions to the profession. Dr. Holman has published and presented at professional conferences on addiction and offender topics and has been a clinician for 20 years.

Melanie M. Iarussi is an assistant professor in the Counselor Education Programs at Auburn University. She earned her Ph.D. in Counselor Education and Supervision from Kent State University. Her clinical background is in substance abuse counseling, college counseling, and private practice. She is a Licensed Professional Counselor and a Certified Substance Abuse Counselor. She is also a member of the Motivational Interviewing Network of Trainers. Melanie's research interests include counselor training in substance use and addiction counseling, college student substance use and recovery, and applications of motivational interviewing.

Davina A. Moss-King, Ph.D., CRC, NCC, CASAC has been a substance abuse counselor for 25 years. Dr. Moss-King is a Certified Rehabilitation Counselor and a National Certified

Counselor, as well as a Credentialed Alcohol and Substance Abuse counselor in New York state. Dr. Moss-King received her doctorate in Counselor Education with honors in 2005 from the State University of New York at Buffalo. Her world-acclaimed dissertation "Unresolved Grief and Loss Issues Related to Substance Abuse" was published as a book, *Unresolved Grief and Loss Issues Related to Heroin Recovery*, in 2009. Dr. Moss-King's research interest is opioid disorders and neonatal abstinence syndrome, which has evolved to writing an internationally accredited online course, "Opioid Dependence during Pregnancy" (2015), along with an article entitled "Neonatal Abstinence Syndrome—the Negative Effects on Our Future" (2015). Dr. Moss-King is an adjunct professor at Canisius College's Counselor Education and Human Services Department, Buffalo, NY. Dr. Moss-King is the founder and president of Positive Direction and Associates, Inc., a consulting company that provides educational seminars focusing on opioid use disorders, women's health, and rebuilding families. Dr. Moss-King is a member of the American Psychological Association and the National Association of Neonatal Therapists.

Summer M. Reiner is an Associate Professor in the Department of Counselor Education, The College at Brockport, State University of New York in Brockport, NY. She served as president of the Association for Adult Development and Aging (AADA), North Atlantic Region Association for Counselor Education and Supervision (NARACES), and the American Counseling Association of New York (ACA-NY). She served as chair of the American Counseling Association North Atlantic Region (ACA-NAR). Dr. Reiner was most recently elected president of the Association for Counselor Education and Supervision (ACES) and to the American Counseling Association Governing Council. She is a National Certified Counselor (NCC), an Approved Clinical Supervisor (ACS), a licensed mental health counselor (LMHC–NY), and a permanently certified school counselor in New York. She teaches courses in career, school counseling, practicum, internship, and human development and provides clinical supervision to students.

Dr. Reiner has authored journal articles on spirituality issues, school counseling issues, and professional counselor identity. In 2010, she received a research grant from the Council for Accreditation of Counseling and Related Educational Programs (CACREP). The research grant resulted in a publication on Professional Counselor Identity and was recognized as one of the top cited articles in the *Journal of Counseling and Development* during 2013. She also has a book chapter in a process addictions text on work addiction.

Dr. Daniel T. Sciarra is Professor of Counselor Education and Director of Counseling programs at Hofstra University. Fluently bilingual in Spanish, he maintains a clinical practice with Latino children, adolescents, and families through the Child Guidance Center of Southern Connecticut. In addition to numerous articles and book chapters on the subject of multicultural counseling, Dr. Sciarra is the author of three books, *Multiculturalism in Counseling* (Peacock, 1999), *School Counseling: Foundations and Contemporary Issues* (Brooks/Cole, 2004), and *Children and Adolescents with Emotional and Behavioral Disorders* (Allyn & Bacon, 2010). His fourth book, *Teaching Difficult Students: Interventions That Work,* will be released in July of 2016. A former bilingual school counselor with the New York City Board of Education, Dr. Sciarra holds a doctorate in Counseling Psychology from Fordham University, a master's degree in counseling from Boston College, and a bachelor's degree in English education from Fairfield University. He is a licensed psychologist, licensed mental health counselor (LMHC), and a national certified counselor (NCC). His research interests include multicultural counseling, racial identity development, and the role of the school counselor in the promotion of academic achievement and educational attainment among students of color.

Dr. Genevieve Weber is an associate professor in the Department of Counseling and Mental Health Professions, School of Health and Human Services at Hofstra University. She is a Licensed Mental Health Counselor in the state of New York, with a specialization in Substance Abuse Counseling. Dr. Weber teaches a variety of courses related to the training of professional counselors, including group counseling, multicultural counseling, counseling the LGBTQ client, psychopathology, and psychopharmacology and treatment planning. She has more than 10 years of experience working in community agencies, where she provides counseling to diverse clients with both substance abuse and mental health concerns. Dr. Weber is a Senior Research Associate with Rankin and Associates Consulting, where she works with institutions to maximize equity through assessment, planning, and implementation of campus climate intervention strategies. In her research and professional presentations, Dr. Weber focuses on the impact of homophobia and heterosexism on the lives of LGBTQ people.

PREFACE

Welcome to the sixth edition of our book. The authors are both proud and delighted to bring you this new edition in a new format with significantly updated and new content. This edition is different in many ways. It has been significantly updated to reflect the changes in the DSM-5 related to the criteria for assessment and diagnosis of substance use disorders. These changes required a complete revision of all terminology within the book to coordinate with the new diagnostic criteria. This edition also addresses the changing face of substance use in our country—from the different demographics of substance users to the substances themselves and how they are used. New effective treatment assessments, methods, and settings are included to assure the student's knowledge of current practice in the field.

There are drugs available and regularly used today that were not even known when we wrote the first edition of this book, and the field of substance use counseling has shifted in response to these changes. Now there are designer drugs—synthetic drugs. Marijuana has been legalized in some states for both medical and recreational use. Synthesized marijuana is now being produced, and it is lethal. Prescription drug use among adolescents has skyrocketed. Meth production is at a pandemic level. Administration of a drug to another person without their consent is becoming more common. In this book, new information has been added and updated information and research references have been included to address these facts. With the addition of gambling as an addiction in the DSM-5 and the prevalence of other dysfunctional behaviors in today's society, the authors felt it was necessary to educate students and clinicians on these behaviors so a chapter has been included on behavioral addictions. New chapter cases in each chapter provide the student with additional critical thinking exercises related to that chapter topic. At the end of Chapters 1 through 13, MyCounselingLab activities allow students to see key concepts demonstrated through video clips, practice what they learn, test their understanding, and receive feedback to guide their learning and ensure that they master key learning outcomes and professional standards.

In the first edition we stated that our goal was to develop a text that was helpful for the general clinician as well as for students in beginning substance use courses, and this goal remains the same. The book is intended to be an adjunct to, not a replacement for, counseling theory and techniques, public policy, and school-specific books and coursework. The text provides you with information specific to the substance use field that must then be integrated with your other counseling knowledge.

As we originally intended, the book is designed to take the reader/student through the process of working with substance use clients and/or behavioral addiction clients from client recognition of need for treatment (in whatever way that is recognized by the client) through the recovery process and beyond. Chapters build on each other as they take you through the process, but each can be used independently for resources or information. Although it is impossible to show you skill sets with a real person, the authors have developed book case studies that are used across the chapters (and therefore represent the process of a client). These case studies provide practical application of the information in each chapter. In addition, each chapter has a case study that specifically addresses the information in that chapter.

We hope that you find the text enjoyable, informative, and a practical read. If so, we have met our goal.

NEW TO THIS EDITION

This new edition has been thoroughly revised. Specific changes include, but are not limited to:

- a new chapter on behavioral addictions
- updated use and cost of use statistics in Chapter 1
- new information in Chapter 2 on ethical issues concerning the Patient Protection and Affordable Care Act and the Health Insurance Portability Accountability Act
- added Integrated Approach as a new theoretical model in Chapter 4
- revised Chapter 6 with new assessment and diagnostic information and information on the Mental Health and Substance Abuse Parity Act and the Affordable Care Act on substance use treatment
- in Chapter 7, the Addiction Society of America diagnostic and treatment criteria and new pharmacotherapy information
- in Chapter 9, re-inclusion of Claudia Black's concept of family roles
- in Chapter 11, substantial changes to the LGBTQ section and new section on counseling military and immigrants with substance use issues
- in Chapter 12, a new section on the socioeconomic impact of substance use
- new terminology to match the DSM-5 criteria for assessment and diagnosis
- ethical codes updated to the latest revision
- updated research references and statistics

ALSO AVAILABLE WITH MYCOUNSELINGLAB®

This title is also available with MyCounselingLab, an online homework, tutorial, and assessment program designed to work with the text to engage students and improve results. Within its structured environment, students see key concepts demonstrated through video clips, practice what they learn, test their understanding, and receive feedback to guide their learning and ensure they master key learning outcomes.

- Learning Outcomes and Standards measure student results. MyCounselingLab organizes all assignments around essential learning outcomes and the professional counseling standards.
- Video- and Case-Based Assignments develop decision-making skills. Students watch videos of actual client-therapist sessions or high-quality role-play scenarios featuring expert counselors. They are then guided in their analysis of the videos through a series of short-answer questions. These exercises help students develop the techniques and decision-making skills they need to be effective counselors before they are in a critical situation with a real client.
- Licensure Quizzes help students prepare for certification. Automatically graded, multiple-choice Licensure Quizzes help students prepare for their certification examinations, master foundational course content, and improve their performance in the course.
- Video Library offers a wealth of observation opportunities. The Video Library provides more than 400 video clips of actual client-therapist sessions and high quality role-plays in a database organized by topic and searchable by keyword.
- MyCounselingLab includes the Pearson eText version of the book, which integrates MyCounselingLab.

ACKNOWLEDGMENTS

We wish to thank, first and foremost, the professors who choose this text and the students who purchase the book, some of whom have let us know how valuable the book has been for them. We appreciate the time and energy the reviewers invested in the reviews for this edition. Their insightful comments assist us in publishing a better text.

Thanks to Kevin Davis for his continued belief in this book. Anne McAlpine has been our go-to person for all manner of issues. She has been accessible and knowledgeable each time we have asked. Thanks, Annie! Pam Bennett, our Project Manager, has been exceptionally patient throughout this process. She has kept us on schedule during some chaotic times. We all thank her for her time and energy.

We wish to thank our contributors. They have all worked diligently to provide a state-of-the-art textbook for training students and clinicians. This edition provided new challenges that they all met with kindness, patience, and professionalism. New contributors have added knowledge and skills to the text and a new perspective that aligns with the changing field. We also wish to thank the reviewers for this edition, who provided us with valuable input for revising this edition: Jeff Blancett, University of Memphis & Victory University; Victor J. Manzon, Western Michigan University; and Martin L. Michelson, University of Illinois at Springfield.

And, again and again, we are grateful to our family and friends who continue to be supportive each time we revise this text.

BRIEF CONTENTS

CONTENTS

Introduction to Substance Use Disorder Counseling

Patricia Stevens, Ph.D.

A lcohol, tobacco, marijuana, prescription drugs, illegal drugs—all are used daily by many in our world today, sometimes with dire consequences. Drugs are used for celebrations, for mourning, for religious rituals, for pain relief, for stress relief, and recreationally. We hear about them daily on the radio, on television, and on the Internet. On the Internet, we can find information about what each drug's composition is as well as how to make many of them ourselves.

Children are beginning to experiment and use at an earlier age, and many of our elders are using a variety of substances, both prescribed and not. Young and old, people use drugs to forget, to feel better (physically and mentally) or not feel at all, to be friendly, to disinhibit, and because of peer pressure. Tobacco, alcohol, and marijuana (in some states) are legal drugs used with social sanction and are easily available. Even if you individually do not use a drug (and this includes alcohol and tobacco), you probably have a user in your family or friend group, or know someone who uses drugs inappropriately.

Consequences of the use of legalized substances (for purposes of this discussion I include alcohol, tobacco, marijuana, and prescription drugs) and illegal substances continue to be disturbing. Many do not understand the far-reaching effects of use. Statistically, for each person who misuses a substance, four or five other people are somehow personally or professionally affected by this use—from minimally to severely—and societal costs reach into the multiple millions. For example, "the average cost for 1 full year of methadone maintenance treatment is approximately $4,700 per patient, whereas 1 full year of imprisonment costs approximately $24,000 per person, usually paid from tax funds" (National Institute on Drug Abuse [NIDA], 2012).

Until the mid-1990s, the tobacco industry denied that there were any physical consequences or addiction from tobacco use even as people were dying from lung cancer. A $145 billion verdict in a 2000 class action suit led by Dr. Howard A. Engle, a Miami Beach pediatrician who smoked and who eventually died of chronic obstructive pulmonary disease, led the way to multiple suits against the tobacco companies; they tried to settle, paying out $10 billion per year in perpetuity. They also placed in the public domain more than 35 million pages of internal documents on the effects of smoking, which included lung cancer and addiction. In 2014, a Florida woman was awarded $23.6 billion in a suit against

R. J. Reynolds Tobacco Company that was filed in 1996, when her husband died at age 36 (Sifferlin, 2014). And while smoking has decreased in the past 10 years, "in 2013, young adults aged 18 to 25 had the highest rate of current use of a tobacco product (37.0 percent), followed by adults aged 26 or older (25.7 percent), then by youths aged 12 to 17 (7.8 percent). Young adults also had the highest rates of current use of the specific tobacco products. Among young adults, the rates of past month use in 2013 were 30.6 percent for cigarettes, 10.0 percent for cigars, 5.8 percent for smokeless tobacco, and 2.2 percent for pipe tobacco" (Substance Abuse and Mental Health Services Administration [SAMHSA], 2014, p. 47).

Other statistics that speak to the use of tobacco and its relationship to other drug use include:

- In 2013, the prevalence of current use of a tobacco product was 40.1% for American Indians or Alaska Natives, 31.2% for persons reporting two or more races, 27.7% for Whites, 27.1% for Blacks, 25.8% for Native Hawaiians or Other Pacific Islanders, 18.8% for Hispanics, and 10.1% for Asians
- Among adults aged 18 or older, current cigarette use in 2013 was reported by 33.6% of those who had not completed high school, 27.7% of high school graduates with no further education, 25.5% of persons with some college but no degree, and 11.2% of college graduates.
- The annual average rate of past-month cigarette use in 2012 and 2013 among women aged 15 to 44 who were pregnant was 15.4%.
- In 2013, past-month alcohol use was reported by 65.2% of current cigarette smokers compared with 48.7% of those who did not use cigarettes in the past month.
- Among persons aged 12 or older, 24.1% of past-month cigarette smokers reported current use of an illicit drug compared with 5.4% of persons who were not current cigarette smokers.

Alcohol, which has been legal in the United States since the 1933 repeal of Prohibition, has multiple consequences—including but not limited to financial loss of work production, increased medical costs for use-related issues, increased intimate partner violence and incest, increased accidents (in all domains), and higher individual risks for a multitude of physical diseases. (SAMHSA, 2014)

According to the SAMHSA 2013 National Survey on Drug Use and Health (SAMHSA, 2014):

- Slightly more than half (52.2%) of Americans aged 12 or older reported being current drinkers of alcohol in the 2013 survey, which was similar to the rate in 2012 (52.1%). This translates to an estimated 136.9 million current drinkers in 2013.
- The rate of current alcohol use among youths aged 12 to 17 was 11.6% in 2013.
- An estimated 8.7 million underage persons (aged 12 to 20) were current drinkers in 2013, including 5.4 million binge drinkers and 1.4 million heavy drinkers. In 2013, an estimated 10.9% of persons aged 12 or older had driven under the influence of alcohol at least once in the past year.
- 1.4 million received treatment for the use of alcohol but not illicit drugs.

- In 2013, 2.5 million persons aged 12 or older reported receiving treatment for alcohol use during their most recent treatment in the past year, 845,000 persons received treatment for marijuana use, and 746,000 persons received treatment for pain relievers (pp. 89, 90, 104).

Further, someone dies in an alcohol-related automobile crash every 51 minutes in the United States (National Highway Traffic Safety Administration, 2013); the annual cost of alcohol-related crashes is $59 billion (Blincoe, Miller, Zaloshnja, & Lawrence, 2010). In 2006, the World Health organization reported that 55% of people involved in intimate partner violence (IPV) believed that their partner/perpetrator had been drinking alcohol before the incident. Although research continues to be complicated on this issue, alcohol use appears to be correlated with IPV, if not cause and effect. Diseases whose risk factors rise with the use of alcohol include human immunodeficiency virus (HIV), hepatitis, and other infectious diseases; cardiovascular complications; respiratory, gastrointestinal, and musculoskeletal effects; kidney and liver damage; neurological and mental health issues; hormonal issues; cancer; and pre- and postnatal complications.

The legalization of marijuana is a recent phenomenon, and studies to document what, if any, effect legalization might have on individual use are in process. SAMHSA's 2013 survey still categorizes marijuana as an illicit drug, as it is on the federal level. Statistics on 2013 use show:

In 2013, marijuana was the most commonly used illicit drug, with 19.8 million current (past-month) users. It was used by 80.6% of current illicit drug users

- In 2013, there were 2.4 million persons aged 12 or older who had used marijuana for the first time within the past 12 months; this averages to about 6,600 new users each day. The 2013 estimate was similar to the estimates in 2008 through 2012 (ranging from 2.2 million to 2.6 million), but was higher than the estimates from 2002 through 2007 (ranging from 2.0 million to 2.2 million).
- In 2013, among persons aged 12 or older, an estimated 1.4 million first-time past-year marijuana users had initiated use before the age of 18. This estimate was similar to the corresponding estimate in 2012. The estimated 1.4 million persons in 2013 who initiated use before the age of 18 represented the majority (56.6%) of the 2.4 million recent marijuana initiates.

In 2012, concentrations of tetrahydrocannabinol (THC), the active ingredient in marijuana, averaged close to 15%, compared to around 4% in the 1980s. This higher concentration creates problems for new and regular users since many times they are not aware of what the concentration may be in each batch.

Marijuana affects the brain areas that influence pleasure, memory, thinking, concentration, sensory and time perception, and coordinated movement. A large long-term study (Meier et al., 2012) showed that people who began smoking marijuana heavily in their teens had a significant decline in their neuropsychological functioning well into adulthood.

Marijuana smoke is an irritant to the lungs causing the same problems that tobacco users experience such as daily cough and phlegm production, more frequent acute chest illness, and a heightened risk of lung infections. Marijuana also raises heart rate by 20-100% shortly after smoking; this effect can last up to 3 hours. NIDA (2014a) reports on a study that estimated that marijuana users have a 4.8-fold increase in the risk of heart attack in the first hour after smoking the drug.

NIDA (2014a) further reported that chronic marijuana use has been linked to mental illness. High doses of marijuana can produce a temporary psychotic reaction in some users and may worsen the course of illness in patients with schizophrenia. Associations have also been found between marijuana use and other mental health problems, such as depression, anxiety, suicidal thoughts among adolescents, and personality disturbances, including a lack of motivation to engage in typically rewarding activities.

The use of prescription drugs for medical misuse or nonmedical purposes is a growing problem, particularly among our youth and elderly populations. For purposes of this discussion we will include the nonmedical use of prescription-type pain relievers, tranquilizers, stimulants, and sedatives. The National Survey of Drug Use and Health reports combine the four prescription-type drug groups into a category referred to as "psychotherapeutics." (SAMHSA, 2014).

These include, but are not limited to:

Opioids
- Fentanyl (Duragesic)
- Hydrocodone (Vicodin)
- Oxycodone (OxyContin)
- Oxymorphone (Opana)
- Propoxyphene (Darvon)
- Hydromorphone (Dilaudid)
- Meperidine (Demerol)
- Diphenoxylate (Lomotil)

Central nervous system depressants
- Pentobarbital sodium (Nembutal)
- Diazepam (Valium)
- Alprazolam (Xanax)

Stimulants
- Dextroamphetamine (Dexedrine)
- Methylphenidate (Ritalin and Concerta)
- Amphetamines (Adderall)

The following statistics on persons aged 12 and older provide a sense of the scope of the problem:

- 4.5 million were using nonmedical pain relievers in 2013 (492,000 were using OxyContin).
- 1.7 million were using nonmedical tranquilizers.
- 1.4 million were using nonmedical stimulants (NIDA, 2014a).

Substance use among the elderly is relatively common but often is undetected or ignored by health and social workers. Psychosocial and health factors related to the aging process are the major contributors to alcoholism and other drug abuse. Although there is much less research regarding elderly prescription nonmedical use or misuse, Medicare's drug program, known as Part D, now covers about 38 million elderly and disabled people and pays for more than one in four prescriptions dispensed in this country.

In 2012, the most recent year for which data is available, Medicare covered nearly 27 million prescriptions for powerful narcotic painkillers and stimulants with the highest potential for abuse (Centers for Medicare & Medicaid Services, 2015). Prescription drug abuse is present in 12% to 15% of elderly individuals who seek medical attention. Of the current population, 83% of older adults, people age 60 and over, take prescription drugs. Older adult women take an average of five prescription drugs at a time, for longer periods of time, than men. And studies show that half of those drugs are potentially addictive substances, such as sedatives, making older women more susceptible to potential abuse issues (Basca, 2008).

Psychoactive medications with abuse potential are used by at least 1 in 4 older adults, and such use is likely to grow as the population ages. It is estimated that up to 11% of older women misuse prescription drugs and that nonmedical use of prescription drugs among all adults aged 50 years or older will increase to 2.7 million by the year 2020 (Simoni-Wastil & Yang, 2006).

Culbertson and Ziska (2008) discuss the lack of screening instrument validity for the elderly populations, even though the elderly use 25% of all prescription drugs. "The prevalence of abuse may be as high as 11% with female gender, social isolation, depression, and history of substance abuse increasing risk" (p. 22).

Much of the foregoing data was collected by the Substance Abuse and Mental Health Services Administration, which is part of the Department of Health and Human Services, one of the premier research organizations in the world. Some data was collected by other national associations and by peer-reviewed published articles. And yet, we still must ask questions about research in the field, due to the very nature of the field. For example, how many of the "current users" meet the criteria for substance use disorder [SUD](American Psychiatric Association, 2013)? How many of them are recreational users? How do we objectively define recreational use? How many of them are physiologically or psychologically attached to the drug? Does this difference in definition lead to problems when comparing data collected? Does self-report affect data collection? Another problem is an outgrowth of the first: the question of how to collect data. Not only do definitions differ, but also substance use may lend itself to isolation and minimization of the facts about the problem.

These issues leave us without a clear idea of the actual number of recreational users and those with more serious problems. In the United States we have waged a "war on drugs" for over a century. In spite of the billions of dollars spent on these efforts in everything from media campaigns to criminal enforcement in an effort to eliminate drug use, virtually every drug that has ever been discovered is available to substance users in the United States, no matter their age or location (Doweiko, 2013).

SOCIETAL COSTS OF SUBSTANCE USE DISORDERS

The impact of use on the quality of life of the individual user and of family, neighbors, and friends cannot be estimated. What we can estimate is the objective costs to society, to the work force, and to medical care. When these economic valuation studies endeavor to incorporate such quality-of-life impacts and costs, the resulting cost, though estimates, are typically several times greater than the objective criteria costs (See Figure 1.1).

Budget Authority in Millions of Dollars.

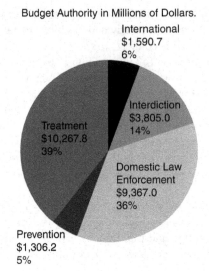

FIGURE 1.1   Cost of Substance Use in Law enforcement.
Surgeon General's, Report, 2004: ONDCP, 2004: Harvard 2000 NIDA
Source: "National Drug Control Budget: FY 2016 Funding Highlights" (Washington, DC: Executive Office of the President, Office of National Drug Control Policy), February 2015, Table 3, p. 18.
http://www.whitehouse.gov///sites/default/files/ondcp/press-releases/ond

---

Estimated Economic Cost to Society Due to Substance Abuse and Addiction:

Illegal drugs:	$181 billion/year
Alcohol:	$185 billion/year
Tobacco:	$193 billion/year
Total:	$559 billion/year

The total costs of drug abuse and addiction due to use of tobacco, alcohol and illegal drugs are estimated at $524 billion a year. Illicit drug use alone accounts for $181 billion in health care, productivity loss, crime, incarceration and drug enforcement.

FIGURE 1.2   Estimated Economic Cost of Substance Abuse and Addiction to Society.

For fiscal year (FY) 2016, a total of $27.6 billion was requested by the president to support 2015 National Drug Control Strategy efforts to reduce drug use and its consequences in the United States. This represents an increase of more than $1.2 billion (4.7%) over the enacted FY 2015 level of $26.3 billion (National Drug Control Budget, 2015, p. 2). This budget provides funds for public treatment facilities, prevention, and so forth.

The estimated total cost of drug use in the United States is $559,000,000,000 (559 billion) (NIDA, 2014c), as shown in Figure 1.2.

The National Drug Intelligence Center includes more modalities in their health cost and estimates. These include the following (reported in thousands of dollars): speciality treatment costs (*$3,723,338*), hospital and emergency department costs for nonhomicide cases (*$5,684,248*),

TABLE 1.1 Admissions to Publicly Licensed Treatment Facilities, by Primary Substance, CY2007-CY2011

	2007	2008	2009	2010	2011
Cocaine	250,761	230,568	186,994	152,404	143,827
Heroin	261,951	280,692	285,983	264,277	278,481
Marijuana	307,053	347,755	362,335	346,268	333,578
Methamphetamine	145,936	127,137	116,793	115,022	110,471
Non-Heroin Opiates/Synthetic*	98,909	122,633	143,404	163,444	186,986

Source: Treatment Episode Data Set (TEDS) 2004 - 2014. Published by Rockville, MD: Substance Abuse and Mental Health Services Administration, 2016.

*These drugs include codeine, hydrocodone, hydromorphone, meperidine, morphine, opium, oxycodone, pentazocine, propoxyphene, tramadol, and any other drug with morphine-like effects. Non prescription use of methadone is not included.

Note: Tennessee included heroin admissions in the "other opiates" category through June 2009. In this report, Tennessee's 2009 heroin admissions are still included in the other opiates category since there is less than a full year of disaggregated heroin data.

TABLE 1.2 Estimated Number of Emergency Department Visits Involving Illicit Drugs, CY2007-CY2011

	2007	2008	2009	2010	2011
Cocaine	553,535	482,188	422,902	488,101	505,224
Heroin	188,162	200,666	213,118	224,706	258,482
Marijuana	308,407	374,177	376,468	460,943	455,636
Methamphetamine	67,954	66,308	64,117	94,929	102,961
MDMA	12,751	17,888	22,847	21,836	22,498
CPD Painkillers	94,448	124,020	146,377	179,787	170,939

Source: Substance Abuse & Mental Health Services Administration (SAMHSA). Published by Substance Abuse & Mental Health Services Administration (SAMHSA).

hospital and emergency department costs for homicide cases (*$12,938*), insurance administration costs (*$544*), and other health costs (*$1,995,164*). These subtotal *$11,416,232*" (p. 3). Tables 1.1 and 1.2 break down some of these costs further.

Productivity

"Productivity includes seven components [costs reported in thousands]: labor participation costs (*$49,237,777*), specialty treatment costs for services provided at the state level (*$2,828,207*), specialty treatment costs for services provided at the federal level (*$44,830*), hospitalization costs (*$287,260*), incarceration costs (*$48,121,949*), premature mortality costs (no homicide: *$16,005,008*), and premature mortality costs (homicide: *$3,778,973*). These subtotal *$120,304,004*" (National Drug Intelligence Center, 2011, p. ix) (See Figure 1.3).

In addition to those just listed, multitudes of other costs are associated with SUD. These include the losses to society from premature deaths and fetal alcohol syndrome; social welfare administration costs, and property losses from substance-related motor vehicle crashes; and costs of related diseases (hepatitis C, HIV/acquired immunodeficiency syndrome [AIDS], cirrhosis of the liver, lung cancer, etc.).

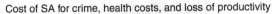

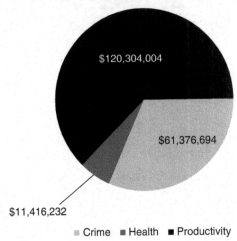

Cost of SA for crime, health costs, and loss of productivity

$120,304,004

$61,376,694

$11,416,232

▪ Crime ▪ Health ▪ Productivity

FIGURE 1.3   Cost of Substance Use for Crime, Health Costs, and Loss of Productivity.

SUBSTANCE-RELATED DISEASES

Although, as mentioned earlier, there are many diseases that may be considered related to substance use, there are three that should be highlighted here.

Hepatitis

Although hepatitis takes multiple forms, we will discuss only two here. Both hepatitis B (HBV) and hepatitis C (HCV) are liver-damaging viruses that are spread through exposure to contaminated blood and body fluids. Hepatitis B is the most common cause of liver disease in the world. HBV is blood-borne and can be transmitted through any sharing of blood. HBV is also found in the semen of infected males, and transmission through sexual contact is likely.

In 2012, a total of 44 states submitted 40,599 reports of chronic hepatitis B to the Centers for Disease Control and Prevention (CDC). The CDC also received 2,895 case reports of acute hepatitis B during 2012. Of these acute cases, 42% did not include a response (i.e., a "yes" or "no" response to questions about risk behaviors and exposures) to enable assessment of risk behaviors or exposures. Of the 1,690 case reports that had risk behavior/exposure information:

60.6% (n = 1,024) indicated no risk behaviors/exposures for hepatitis B.

39.4% (n = 666) indicated at least one risk behavior/exposure for hepatitis B during the 6 weeks to 6 months prior to illness onset (injections, multiple sex partners, household with known HBV individuals) (CDC, 2012)

Hepatitis C (HCV), the most common blood-borne infection in the United States, is a viral disease that destroys liver cells. There are approximately 3.2 million U.S. residents affected by HCV. Mortality from HCV exceeds mortality from HIV/AIDS in the U.S. (CDC, 2012).

In 2012, a total of 145,762 reports of chronic hepatitis C infection were submitted to the CDC by 44 states. In addition, there were 1,778 reported cases of acute HCV—a 75% increase compared with the number of cases reported in 2010. This number represents an estimated 21,870 total acute cases. Some say that the numbers infected are higher than those for HIV/AIDS.

HCV is mostly transmitted through the sharing of needles, and sexual transmission is low. The largest increase of cases was among persons aged 0-19 years. Further, of the acute cases reported with responses to risk behavior questions (63%), 65% indicated at least one risk behavior/ exposure in the 2 weeks to 6 months prior to illness onset. Of those who reported risk information, 513 (75%) indicated injection drug use risk and 86 (13%) indicated recent surgery (CDC, 2012).

People with newly acquired HCV are either asymptomatic or have a mild clinical illness. They may exhibit such symptoms as jaundice, abdominal pain, loss of appetite, nausea, and diarrhea. However, most infected people exhibit mild or no symptoms. HCV RNA can, however, be detected in blood within 1 to 3 weeks after exposure.

About 85% of people with acute hepatitis C develop a chronic infection. Chronic hepatitis is an insidious disease whose barely discernible symptoms can mask progressive injury to liver cells over two to four decades. (CDC, 2012). Chronic hepatitis C, as well as excessive alcohol consumption, often leads to cirrhosis of the liver and liver cancer. Liver cancer is the tenth most common cancer and the fifth most common cause of cancer death among men, and the ninth most common cause of cancer death among women. (American Cancer Society, 2015)

Since the publication of the fifth edition of this book, amazing progress has been made in the treatment and cure of HCV. There are now several antiviral drugs on the market that cure the disease. As well, there are multiple other drugs in clinical trials and in process. This breakthrough will save millions of lives in the coming years.

HIV/AIDS

An estimated 35 million people were living with HIV or AIDS worldwide in 2011, with 2.1 million new cases in 2012. In the United States, about 1.2 million people were living with HIV at the end of 2011, the most recent year for which this information was available. Of those people, about 14% do not know they are infected. An estimated 1.5 million people died from AIDS-related illnesses in 2013, and an estimated 39 million people with AIDS have died worldwide since the epidemic began. (CDC, 2012).

Six common transmission categories are male-to-male sexual contact (MSM), injection drug use (IDU), male-to-male sexual contact and injection drug use (MSM+IDU), heterosexual contact, mother-to-child (perinatal) transmission, and other (including blood transfusions and unknown cause). The highest rate of infection remains male-to-male sexual contact, but injection drug use is second.

African Americans are most affected by HIV. In 2010, African Americans made up only 12% of the U.S. population, but had 44% of all new HIV infections. Additionally, Hispanics/ Latinos are also strongly affected. They make up 17% of the U.S. population, but had 21% of all new HIV infections. In 2010, MSM had 63% of all new HIV infections, even though they made up only around 2% of the population. Individuals infected through heterosexual sex made up 25% of all new HIV infections in 2010.

HIV especially affects young people, aged 13 to 24. They comprised 16% of the U.S. population, but accounted for 26% of all new HIV infections in 2010. Not all young people are equally at risk, however. Young MSM, for example, accounted for 72% of all new infections in people aged 13 to 24, and young, African American MSM are even more severely affected (CDC, 2012).

We would be remiss not to discuss these major diseases along with the other secondary costs of the primary use of substances. At best this information is frightening; in reality, it is terrifying. The cost of SUD and diseases related to SUD, in addition to the monetary and societal costs, is, in many cases, a human life. Many times the life of a person using substances ends in pain and suffering, alone in an unimaginable place.

It is imperative that all counselors have the knowledge to make connections about substance use with their clients' problems—and to remember the frequency with which SUD occurs. It is not unusual for clients to "forget" to let the counselor know about their use, yet this is often the root of the problem they are presenting. And with substance use may come disease information that is relevant to treatment.

Ethical codes and law now give us direction in handling cases of infectious diseases with clients. Read and understand your responsibility to your client, their partners, and yourself. Without thorough knowledge and understanding of the complete context of the client's life, you cannot serve the client ethically or effectively.

A (VERY) SHORT HISTORY OF SUBSTANCE USE

Ever wonder how long humans have been using mind-altering drugs? Did they even realize they were mind altering before we had the technology to ascertain the brain and physiological changes, or did it just feel good? What were they using? Where did they find it?

Well, humankind has used mind- or mood-altering drugs at least since the beginning of recorded history and probably before prehistoric times. Over the centuries, drugs have been used medicinally, religiously, and socially. In tribal societies, mind-altering drugs were commonly used in healing practices and religious ceremonies. Alcohol consumption was recorded as early as the Paleolithic times of the Stone Age culture with the discovery that drinking the juice of fermented berries created a pleasant feeling. Alcohol, cocaine, marijuana, opium, and tobacco have all been used for medical purposes through the years.

An overview of the historical perspective of humankind's use of substances for both analgesic and mind-altering purposes and the multidimensional functions that drugs have played throughout history may provide a context for understanding today's substance use issues and ensuing ramifications. History may also provide some rationale for the treatment methods used with substance users over the past 50 years.

A perusal of some of the early legends that relate to the discovery of substances as well as the development of other drugs may add a perspective to the current view of drug use in our Western society. A complete history would be impossible to provide here, so we endeavor to provide you with the most entertaining and educational historical summary.

Alcohol

It has been documented that early cave dwellers drank the juices of mashed berries that had been exposed to airborne yeast. The discovery of late Stone Age beer jugs established the fact that intentionally fermented beverages existed at least as early as the Neolithic period (ca. 10,000 BCE). When they found that the juice produced pleasant feelings and reduced discomfort, they began to intentionally produce an alcoholic drink.

Beer was the major beverage among the Babylonians, and as early as 2700 BCE they worshipped a wine goddess and other wine deities. Oral tradition recorded in the Old Testament (Genesis 9:20) asserts that Noah planted a vineyard on Mount Ararat in what is now eastern Turkey. (In fact, Noah was perhaps the first recorded inebriate!) Egyptian records give testimony to beer production. They believed that the god Osiris, who was worshipped throughout the entire country, invented beer, a beverage that was considered a necessity of life and was brewed in the home on a regular basis.

Homer's *Iliad* and *Odyssey* both discuss drinking wine, and Egypt and Rome had gods or goddesses of wine. The first alcoholic beverage to obtain widespread popularity in what is now Greece was mead, a fermented beverage made from honey and water. However, by 1700 BCE, wine making was commonplace, and during the next thousand years, wine drinking assumed the same function so commonly found around the world: It was incorporated into religious rituals, became important in hospitality, was used for medicinal purposes, and became an integral part of daily meals. As a beverage, it was drunk in many ways: warm and chilled, pure and mixed with water, plain and spiced.

A 4,000-year-old Persian legend tells the story of the discovery of wine. A king had vats of grapes stored, some of which developed a sour liquid at the bottom. The king labeled these vats as poison but kept them for future use. One lady of the court was prone to severe headaches that no one could remedy. Her pain was so severe that she decided to kill herself. She knew of the poisoned grape juice, went to the storage area, and drank the poison. Needless to say, the lady didn't die but in fact found relief. Over the next few days, she continued to drink the "poison" and only later confessed to the king that she had been in the vats. In the 10th century, an Arabian physician, Phazes, who was looking to release the "spirit of the wine," discovered the process of distillation.

By the Middle Ages, alcohol was used in ceremonies for births, deaths, marriages, treaty signings, diplomatic exchanges, and religious celebrations. Monasteries offered wine to weary travelers who stopped for rest and safety. In Europe, it was known as the "water of life" and considered the basic medicine for all human ailments. Water pollution is far from new; to the contrary, supplies have generally been either unhealthful or questionable at best. Ancient writers rarely wrote about water, except as a warning. Travelers crossing what is now the Democratic Republic of the Congo in 1648 reported having to drink water that resembled horse's urine. In the late 18th century, most Parisians drank water from a very muddy and often chemically polluted Seine. Certainly we can see why wine was the beverage of choice during this time period.

In addition to being used in rituals and for its convivial effect, alcohol was one of the few chemicals consistently available for physicians to use to induce sleep and reduce pain. Alcohol has been used as an antiseptic, an anesthetic, and in combinations of salves and tonics. As early as 1000 CE, Italian winegrowers were distilling wine for medicinal purposes.

When European settlers brought alcoholic beverages in the form of wine, rum, and beer to the Americas, native cultures were already producing homegrown alcoholic beverages. The *Mayflower*'s log reports, "We could not take time for further search or consideration, our victuals having been much spent, especially our bere." Spanish missionaries brought grapevines, and the Dutch opened the first distillery in 1640. American settlers tested the strength of their brews by saturating gunpowder with alcohol. If it ignited, it was too strong; if it sputtered, too weak.

In 1760, President Adams wrote in his diary that taverns were

> becoming the eternal haunt of loose, disorderly people . . . . These houses are becoming the nurseries of our legislators. An artful man, who has neither sense nor sentiments, may, by gaining a little sway among the rabble of the town, multiply taverns and dram shops and thereby secure the votes of taverner and retailer and of all; and the multiplication of taverns will make many, who may be induced to flip and rum, to vote for any man whatever. (Cherrington, 1920, p. 37)

Then in 1790 federal law provided that each soldier receive one-fourth pint of brandy, rum, or whiskey per week. In the Civil War, army regulations prohibited the purchase of alcohol by enlisted men, and soldiers who violated the rule were punished, but men on both sides found ways around it. Members of a Mississippi company got a half-gallon of whiskey past the camp guards by concealing it in a hollowed-out watermelon; they then buried the melon beneath the floor of their tent and drank from it with a long straw. If they could not buy liquor, they made it. One Union recipe called for bark juice, tar water, turpentine, brown sugar, lamp oil, and alcohol.

World War I, which took place primarily in Europe between 1914 and 1918, saw foot soldiers as well as commanders imbibing. With the advent of Prohibition (1920–1933), when the U.S. Constitution outlawed the manufacture, transport, and sale of alcoholic beverages, many returning soldiers were none too happy. The Eighteenth Amendment prohibited the sale of alcoholic beverages, but the federal Volstead Act, which became law during the Prohibition era, enforced the amendment.

During Prohibition, alcohol continued to be made and used (sometimes called bathtub gin because it was made in bathtubs). Data for the era shows that alcohol consumption may have actually increased during Prohibition, instead of decreasing as the moral entrepreneurs had hoped. "*Per capita* consumption of alcohol increased during Prohibition, according to the federal Wickersham Commission. More specifically, it increased over 500% between 1921 and 1929, according to a study published by Columbia University Press. It's important to point out that *per capita* consumption dropped dramatically between 1910 and the imposition of Prohibition in 1920. So Prohibition reversed a downward trend in alcohol consumption" (Hanson, n.d.).

Groups such as the Anti-Saloon League believed drinking alcohol was amoral, deviant, and counter to Christianity. As one of the most effective groups to lobby for Prohibition, the Women's Christian Temperance Union (WCTU) was founded in 1874 in the United States. The WCTU began as a group of housewives in Ohio concerned about their husbands drinking away household income. They blamed alcohol for a majority of societal problems and considered the lack of willpower to resist as the individual drinker's problem. The WCTU grew in membership from 22,800 in 1881 to a reported 344,892 in 1921.

After 13 years, Prohibition was repealed, alcohol became legal again, and its legal use continues today. To date, alcohol is the only mind-altering substance to have been fully legalized by Federal and State governments after a period of prohibition. In fact, the Eighteenth Amendment to the Constitution remains the only one to have been repealed.

It is of interest to note the remarks of the founding director of the National Institute on Alcohol Abuse and Alcoholism (NIAAA): "Alcohol has existed longer than all human memory. It has outlived generations, nations, epochs and ages. It is a part of us, and that is fortunate indeed. For although alcohol will always be the master of some, for most of us it will continue to be the servant of man" (Chafetz, 1965, p. 223).

This (very) brief history provides context for the use of alcoholic beverages throughout time as well as the complexity of opinions about their worth. Is it the "demon" or the "servant of man"?

Cocaine

Like alcohol, coca has been around for thousands of years. South American Indians have used cocaine as it occurs in the leaves of *Erythroxylum coca* for at least 5,000 years. In traditional Indian cultures, Mama Coca was considered a benevolent deity. She was regarded as a sacred goddess who could bless humans with her power. Before the coca harvest, the harvester would have sexual intercourse with a woman to ensure that Mama Coca would be in a favorable mood. Typically, a mixture of coca and saliva was rubbed onto the male organ to prolong erotic ecstasy for both partners.

Traditionally, the leaves have been chewed for social, mystical, medicinal, and religious purposes. Coca has even been used to provide a measure of time and distance. Native travelers sometimes described a journey in terms of the number of mouthfuls of coca typically chewed in making the trip.

The active ingredient in cocaine was not isolated until 1860 by Albert Neiman. Cocaine was then added to wine and tonics in the mid-19th century as well as to snuff, and advertised as a cure for asthma and hay fever. Sigmund Freud experimented with cocaine as a cure for depression and digestive disorders, hysteria, and syphilis. He also recommended cocaine to alleviate withdrawal from alcohol and morphine addiction. He and his friends experimented with every method of introducing cocaine into the body. Freud himself used cocaine daily for a considerable period of time. In fact, in 1884, he published a hymn of praise to cocaine entitled *Uber Coca* (Public Broadcasting System, n.d.).

During this time, the mid- to late-1800s, the medical profession was blissfully ignorant of the addictive qualities of cocaine. So, not surprisingly, by the late 1800s, more than half the scientific and medical community had developed healthy "coke" habits. As more was learned about cocaine's addictive properties, these individuals discontinued their own use and also stopped prescribing it to patients to alleviate all types of medical problems.

An American named John Stith Pemberton developed his own version of a European drink that included extract of coca leaves and kola nuts. He advertised this product as an "intellectual beverage" or "brain tonic." This product, later known as Coca-Cola, contained about 60 milligrams of cocaine in an 8-ounce serving. It was only a moderate hit, and after the cocaine and alcohol ingredients were banned in Atlanta, GA, Pemberton sold the company to Asa Griggs Candler for a paltry $2,300.

In the 20th century, cocaine grew in popularity as it decreased in cost. However, as people began to see the rise of violence among abusers of the drug in the lower socioeconomic stratum and a rise in the awareness of cocaine's harmful physical effects, anti-cocaine legislation began. The first federal legislation regarding cocaine was the 1906 Pure Food and Drug Act that required manufacturers to precisely label product contents. In 1914, the U.S. Congress passed the Harrison Narcotics Act, which imposed taxes on products containing cocaine. Soon, drug enforcement officials transformed the law to prohibit all recreational use of cocaine. By the 1930s, synthetic amphetamines were available and began to take the place of the now-illegal cocaine. By the early 1980s, the use of freebase cocaine became popular again among those searching for the "highest" high. Freebase is a form of cocaine produced when the user takes cocaine hydrochloride and mixes liquid with baking soda or ammonia to remove the hydrochloric acid and then dissolves the resultant alkaloidal cocaine in a solvent, such as ether, and heats it to evaporate the liquid. The result is pure, smokable cocaine. The conversion process in freebasing was dangerous and time-consuming and was not suitable for mass production. The danger and volatility of the process led to drug dealers developing a more potent, less volatile form of cocaine: crack.

In the conversion process for crack, the drug is similarly cooked down to a smokable substance, but the risky process of removing the impurities and hydrochloric acid is taken out. Thus, all that is required is baking soda, water, and a heat source, often a home oven. As this process allowed people essentially to get more bang from their buck by delivering the drug more efficiently, cocaine became available to the lower socioeconomic stratum. This development gave rise to the "crack epidemic," and American society was drastically affected by the increase in availability.

Morphine, Heroin: The Opioids

Opium is a derivative of the poppy plant, and early humans learned that by splitting the top of the *Papaver somniferum* (poppy) plant, they could extract a thick resin. Later it was discovered that the dried resin could be swallowed to control pain. By the Neolithic Age, there is evidence that the plant was being cultivated for this purpose (Doweiko, 2013).

As long ago as 3400 BCE, the opium poppy was cultivated in lower Mesopotamia. The Sumerians refer to it as *Hul Gil,* the "joy plant." In 460 BCE, Hippocrates, "the father of medicine," dismissed the magical attributes of opium but acknowledged its usefulness as a narcotic and styptic in treating internal diseases, diseases of women, and epidemics. In 129–199 CE, there were reports of opium cakes being sold in the streets of Rome. Ships chartered by Queen Elizabeth I in

1601 were instructed to purchase the finest Indian opium and transport it back to England. In 1729, China found it necessary to outlaw opium smoking because of the increasing number of opium addicts. The Chinese railroad workers brought opium smoking to the United States, and by the beginning of the 19th century, opium dens were common throughout the nation.

Friedrich Sertürner of Paderborn, Germany, made a startling discovery in 1806. He found the active ingredient of opium by dissolving it in acid and then neutralizing it with ammonia. The result: alkaloids—"principium somniferum," or morphine. Physicians believe that opium had finally been perfected and tamed. Morphine was lauded as "God's own medicine" for its reliability, long-lasting effects, and safety. Morphine was freely used in the Civil War and in other wars for pain as well as for dysentery. The resulting addiction was known as "soldier's disease."

When Dr. Alexander Wood of Edinburgh in 1843 discovered a new technique of administering morphine, injection with a syringe, he also found that the effects of morphine on his patients were instantaneous and three times more potent. C. R. Alder Wright originally synthesized a new drug in 1874 by adding two acetyl groups to the molecule morphine. In 1895, Heinrich Dreser, who worked for the Bayer Company in Elberfeld, Germany, found that this drug did not produce the common morphine side effects. Bayer began production of diacetylmorphine and coined the name "heroin."

From 1895 until 1914, opium, morphine, and heroin were available without a prescription. Tonics and elixirs were available throughout the 19th century at most drugstores and were consumed mostly by women. In pharmacological studies, heroin proved to be more effective than morphine or codeine. The Bayer Company started the production of heroin in 1898 on a commercial scale. The first clinical results were so promising that heroin was considered a wonder drug. Indeed, heroin was more effective than codeine in respiratory diseases. It turned out, however, that repeated administration of heroin resulted in the development of tolerance, and the patients soon became heroin addicts. In the early 1910s, morphine addicts "discovered" the euphonizing properties of heroin, and this effect was enhanced by intravenous administration with the hypodermic syringe. Heroin abuse began to spread quickly.

However, on December 17, 1914, the Harrison Narcotics Act, which aimed to curb drug abuse (especially of cocaine, as discussed earlier, but also of heroin) and addiction, was passed. It required doctors, pharmacists, and others who prescribed narcotics to register and pay a tax. This one law created a significant change in the use and availability of opioids.

During the 1930s and '40s, heroin was associated with the jazz cultural identity, then in the '50s with the Beatnik generation and in the '60s with the hippie movement. During the Viet Nam war, there was a 10% to 15% addiction rate among soldiers (Public Broadcasting System, n.d.) With improvements in the quality of street heroin in the '80s and '90s, it became possible to snort or smoke heroin as well as inject the drug. Currently, heroin appears to be increasing in use, particularly among youth (see SAMHSA, 2014).

Heroin, illegally available on the street, is usually diluted to a purity of only 2% to 5% but purity can differ widely. It is usually mixed with baking soda, quinine, milk sugar, or other substances. The unwitting injection of relatively pure heroin is a major cause of heroin overdose, the main symptoms of which are extreme respiratory depression, deepening into coma and then into death. Aside from this danger, heroin addicts are prone to hepatitis and other infections owing to their use of dirty or contaminated syringes. Scarring of the surfaces of the arms or legs is another common injury, because of repeated needle injections and subsequent inflammations of the surface veins.

Another drug, oxycodone, is a semisynthetic opioid agonist derived from thebaine, a constituent of opium. Oxycodone tests positive as an opiate in available field-test kits.

Pharmacology of oxycodone is essentially similar to that of morphine in all respects, including its abuse and dependence liabilities. Pharmacological effects include analgesia, euphoria, feelings of relaxation, respiratory depression, constipation, papillary constriction, and cough suppression. Oxycodone abuse has been a continuing problem in the United States since the early 1960s. It is administered orally, rectally, nasally, or by IV injection. Considered a controlled prescription drug (CPD), oxycodone is one of the most abused drugs in the United States today (see SAMHSA, 2014).

Marijuana

Marijuana (or cannabis) has been used recreationally and medicinally for centuries. The earliest account of its use is in China in 2737 BCE. In Egypt, in the 20th century BCE, cannabis was used to treat sore eyes. From the 10th century BCE up to 1945 (and even rarely to the present time), cannabis has been used in India to treat a wide variety of human maladies. In ancient Greece, cannabis was used as a remedy for earache, edema, and inflammation.

In colonial times, hemp, the plant from which marijuana is derived, was an important crop. Our forefathers used it to produce paper, clothing, and rope. It was so important in those early days of America that Virginia introduced legislation in 1762 that exacted penalties on farms that did not produce it. In 1793 the invention of the cotton gin made the separation of cotton fiber from the hull easier and far less expensive than it had been previously. Hemp, however, remained a cash crop until well after the Civil War because of its availability and the ease with which it could be made into clothing. Eventually, the price dropped until it was no longer profitable, and many hemp growers switched to tobacco.

In 1850, the *United States Pharmacopeia* (*USP*) recognized marijuana (hemp) for its medicinal value. It was used to treat lack of appetite, gout, migraines, pain, hysteria, depression, rheumatism, and many other illnesses. Nothing is mentioned about the "high" that marijuana is famous for in the early reports on the herb, but that omission seems appropriate in contexts where its medicinal aspect is stressed. Dosage problems due to different plant strengths kept it from being continued as a "legitimate" drug, and it has been removed from the *USP,* but adherents still point to marijuana's medicinal value as a major point for legalization.

The continued primary interest in this drug has been for its euphoric effects. In November 1883, "A Hashish-House in New York" by H. H. Kane, was published in *Harper's Monthly*. He carefully describes the wonders of the hashish (a cannabis derivative) house and writes a vivid description of his trip to "Hashishdom." He enjoys the experience but is grateful for the sights and sounds of the "normal" world upon exiting the house of dreams. In mid-19th century Europe, members of the French romantic literary movement used cannabis extensively. Through their writings, American writers became aware of the euphoric effects attributed to the drug.

With the beginning of Prohibition, individual use of marijuana increased in the 1920s as a substitute for alcohol. After Prohibition, its use declined until the 1960s, when it gained significant popularity along with LSD and "speed." It has been used as an analgesic, a hypnotic, an anticonvulsant, and recently an antinausea drug for individuals undergoing chemotherapy for cancer. Advocates of marijuana for medicinal use cite it as a treatment for asthma, depression, drug withdrawal, epilepsy in children, glaucoma, and nausea, and as an antibiotic.

On October 27, 1970, the Comprehensive Drug Abuse Prevention and Control Act was passed. Part II of this act is the Controlled Substance Act (CSA), which defines a scheduling system for drugs. This schedule places most of the known hallucinogens (LSD, psilocybin, psilocin, mescaline, peyote, cannabis) in Schedule I. Despite all the years of conflict about whether marijuana was medicinal or not and the history of its medicinal use, in 1988 administrative law judge Francis Young of the Drug Enforcement Administration (DEA) found after thorough hearings that marijuana has clearly established medical use and should be reclassified, as a prescriptive drug (DEA, 1988).

Twenty-three states and Washington, DC, have now legalized marijuana for medicinal use, and four states have legalized the drug for recreational use. Even in these states, the controversy continues about the value of the drug as a viable medication for certain conditions, as well as the financial implications of legalization and the abuse of that legalization. The state of Colorado currently has four lawsuits pending to repeal the recreational and medicinal use of marijuana.

Amphetamines

Amphetamines were discovered in 1887 and used in World War II by U.S., British, German, and Japanese soldiers for energy, alertness, and stamina. In the late 1920s, they were seriously investigated as a cure or treatment for a variety of illnesses and maladies, including epilepsy, schizophrenia, alcoholism, opiate addiction, migraine, head injuries, and radiation sickness.

Amphetamines were also prescribed to treat depression, induce weight loss, and heighten capacity for work. Misuse increased in the 1930s with the sale of Benzedrine over the counter. In the 1950s came the beginning of injection use, with capsules broken open and their contents injected into the body with a syringe to heighten the effect of the drug. By the early 1960s, "mainlining" was a major problem in America. In 1962, San Francisco pharmacies were selling injectable amphetamines, and law enforcement began to close these shops. This drew national attention and led to the beginning of the home-based "speed labs."

Methamphetamine (meth), more potent and easy to make, was discovered in Japan in 1919. The crystalline powder was soluble in water, making it a perfect candidate for injection. In Japan, intravenous methamphetamine abuse reached epidemic proportions immediately after World War II, when supplies stored for military use became available to the public. In the United States in the 1950s, legally manufactured tablets of both dextroamphetamine (Dexedrine) and methamphetamine (Methedrine or meth) became readily available. College students, truck drivers, and athletes regularly used these drugs to energize and to prolong awake time.

Meth is produced as pills, powders, or chunky crystals called *ice*. The crystal form, nicknamed *crystal meth,* is a popular drug, especially with young adults who frequently go to dance clubs and parties. Swallowed or snorted (also called *bumping*), methamphetamines give the user an intense high. Injections create a quick but strong, intense high, called a *rush* or a *flash.* Methamphetamines, like regular amphetamines, also take away appetite.

Meth labs are now a major problem across the country—in every type of neighborhood, rich and poor. Meth labs turn up in houses, barns, apartments, trailers, campers, cabins, and motel rooms—even the backs of pickups. The equipment for a meth lab can be small enough to fit in a duffel bag, a cardboard box, or the trunk of a car. It is important to be alert about the possibility of a lab near your home, as the fumes from the product are lethal (Weisheit & White, 2010).

One of the newer hallucinogens, Ecstasy, or Molly (an abbreviation for "Molecule" and generally refers to a "purified" form of Ecstasy), is also classified as an amphetamine. Ecstasy is referred to as the chemical MDMA (methylenedioxymethamphetamine). MDMA was first synthesized in 1912. The Merck Company patented it in 1914 Germany after Merck stumbled across MDMA when trying to synthesize another drug. MDMA was an unplanned by-product of this synthesis. It may have been tested by Merck and also by the U.S. government over the next years to treat a variety of symptoms. However, it was never found to be effective.

As a street drug, Ecstasy was originally most popular with the White population but now has a broader range of ethnic users. These drugs are used to enhance the user's feeling of well-being while providing more energy/arousal. However, MDMA users may experience symptoms such as muscle tension, involuntary teeth clenching, nausea, blurred vision, faintness, and chills or sweating, especially with multiple doses.

At high doses, MDMA can interfere with the body's ability to regulate temperature. On rare but unpredictable occasions, this can lead to a sharp increase in body temperature (hyperthermia), which can result in liver, kidney, or cardiovascular system failure or even death (NIDA, 2014d).

Essentially Molly and Ecstasy have two types of action: a psychogenic effect, plus an amphetamine or "speed"-like effect. Molly is more potent than Ecstasy, hence increasing the psychedelic and amphetamine-like component. Molly may be "cut" or mixed with pure amphetamine or methamphetamine since there is no quality control on the manufacture of these illegal drugs. The amphetamine component of Molly can be very potent.

All amphetamines are addictive. They are considered Schedule II drugs (use potentially leading to severe psychological or physical dependence); except for Ecstasy and Molly, which are Schedule I drugs, the most dangerous drugs of all the drug schedules, with potentially severe psychological or physical dependence) (Drug Enforcement Administration, 2014).

Hallucinogens

Hallucinogens have been around for about 3,500 years. Central American Indian cultures used hallucinogenic mushrooms in their religious ceremonies. When the New World was discovered, Spanish priests, in an effort to "civilize" the Indians, tried to eliminate the use of the "sacred mushrooms." This continued until the American Indian Religious Freedom Act in 1978, and its amendment in 1994, provided Native Americans with the right to use peyote in religious services.

In 1938, the active ingredient that caused hallucinations was isolated for the first time by a Swiss chemist, Albert Hofmann. He was studying a particular fungus in bread that appeared to create hallucinations. The substance he synthesized during this research was LSD (lysergic acid diethylamide). Between 1950 and the mid-1970s, LSD was well researched by the U.S. government in the hope that it could be used to understand the psychotic mind and to view the subconscious. It was called "the truth drug." LSD has been used in the treatment of alcoholism, depression, epilepsy, cancer, and schizophrenia. Before the early 1960s, the drug had limited availability, but as researchers, clinical practitioners, research participants, and physicians used the drug and shared it with friends, it became more popular. Because LSD was easy and inexpensive to make (at that time, the formula could be purchased from the U.S. Patent Office for 50 cents), a black market began to emerge.

Hallucinogens were a primary drug in the 1960s. Dr. Timothy Leary, a Harvard professor and icon of the 1960s counterculture of music, made the term "turn on, tune in and drop out" popular. Then the "Summer of Love" in 1967 in San Francisco firmly linked LSD to this movement.

After losing popularity in the 1970s and '80s, LSD began to resurface in the 1990s with the rave culture but has since seemed to decline in use.

Tobacco

It is believed that tobacco was growing in the Americas around 6000 BCE. As early as 1 BCE, Indians in the New World were using tobacco for medicinal and religious purposes.

In 1492, natives in the New World offered Columbus dried tobacco as a gift. Sailors carried tobacco back to Europe, where it began to be cultivated. In the 16th century, it was believed that tobacco could cure many illnesses, and in the 1600s, it was used as money. By 1632, in the Americas, it was illegal to smoke tobacco in public in Massachusetts. Smoking became quite popular in Europe and Asia, but it faced harsh opposition from the church and government. Public smoking was punishable by death in Germany, China, and Turkey and by castration in Russia. Despite this early response, people continued to smoke and eventually were at least moderately accepted into society.

The first tobacco company in the United States, P. Lorillard, was founded in 1760 in New York City and remains open today. With the Industrial Age came the invention of machinery to make the cigarette a smaller, less expensive, neater way to smoke, making the price affordable to almost everyone. Laws were passed that allowed the decrease in price, and after 1910, public health officials began to campaign *against* chewing tobacco and *for* smoking tobacco. Smokers also realized that, unlike cigars, cigarette smoke could be inhaled, entering the lungs and the bloodstream, creating a more intense feeling. World War I brought a dramatic increase in smoking and in World War II, cigarettes were included in soldiers' rations. In the 1940s and '50s, smoking was seen as sophisticated.

Nicotine is one of the most addictive drugs. In the mid-19th century, when the pure form of nicotine was extracted, it was deemed a poison. A few hours of smoking are all that is needed for tolerance to begin to develop. The body immediately begins to adapt to protect itself from the toxins found in tobacco. As this process begins, it creates a rapid physiological development that requires smoking again to return to a normal feeling.

By the mid-1950s, however, research began to show the negative effect of tobacco. The highly addictive nature of nicotine was acknowledged as a health hazard by the Surgeon General of the United States in his 1964 report on tobacco. In his report, the Surgeon General outlined the various problems that could be related to, or caused by, smoking tobacco. Since then, the relationship between smoking and cancer has continued to be researched and substantiated. Our view of tobacco smoking and chewing has changed dramatically since that 1964 report. Many cities now ban smoking in public areas/buildings. Government offices and most private companies and businesses do not allow tobacco smoking in their facilities.

This has been a (very) brief overview of the most popular drug categories available. It is easy to see the context in which these drugs have existed through history, often back to prehistoric times. Seeking an altered state of consciousness through the use of these plants is a sociological imprint. Although the drugs themselves may have important medical uses, the problem becomes misuse of these drugs and the impact on the whole of society.

THE IMPORTANCE OF TERMINOLOGY IN SUBSTANCE USE DISORDER COUNSELING

The terms *substance use, misuse, abuse,* and *addiction/dependency* have been in the popular and clinical vocabulary for as long as most of us can remember. With the publication of the *Diagnostic and Statistical Manual of Mental Health Disorders, Fifth Edition* (DSM-5) (American Psychiatric Association, 2013), the mental health community language and criteria for diagnosing substance use has significantly changed.

The DSM-5 no longer uses the terminology just listed; it uses updated terminology in the criteria for diagnosis. Drug craving has been added to the list of criteria but law enforcement issues have been deleted. Gambling has also been added in the section as the only condition of behavioral disorder. Caffeine use has been deleted.

Substances for which a person can be diagnosed with a substance use disorder include:

- Alcohol
- Cannabis
- Phencyclidine
- Other hallucinogens
- Inhalants
- Opioid
- Sedative, hypnotic, or anxiolytic drugs
- Stimulant: Specify amphetamine or cocaine
- Tobacco
- Other (unknown)

In an effort to view substance use on a continuum, the DSM-5 now includes all substance use under "substance use disorder." Each substance has its own listing of criteria, but basically, for example; if a person meets 2 of the 11 criteria for alcohol use, they are diagnosable as having a substance use disorder. The degree of the disorder (mild, moderate, or severe) is based on the number of criteria met beyond the two. As a general estimate of severity, a *mild* substance use disorder is suggested by the presence of 2 or 3 symptoms, *moderate* by 4 or 5 symptoms, and *severe* by 6 or more symptoms.

This text uses the DSM-5 terminology throughout to assist you as a new professional to become familiar with the new language and criteria for diagnosis. In historical context, we have used the terminology of that time period if necessary for clarity.

We have used the term *substance* or *chemical* to include alcohol, nicotine, tobacco, prescription drugs (CPD), and illegal drugs. We may, however, at times refer to alcohol and other drugs when the distinction is necessary to maintain clarity or when the majority of the research has focused on alcohol. It is, of course, relevant to acknowledge that alcohol, nicotine, and tobacco (and in some states marijuana) are legal and societally accepted drugs. This fact lends a different dynamic to the use issues related to these substances that do not exist for illegal drugs. It is imperative, however, to acknowledge that these drugs, legal or not, represent a major threat to a person's biological, psychosocial, and familial health. Further, the definition of *drug* is one that changes with fluctuations in social mores as well as with shifts in the law. Cultures also differ considerably on classification of substances as foods, poisons, beverages, medicines, and herbs.

In this text, *drug* is defined as any nonfood substance whose chemical or physical nature significantly alters structure, function, or perception (vision, taste, hearing, touch, or smell) in the living organism. Legality of a substance has no bearing on whether it is defined as a drug. Alcohol, nicotine, tobacco, prescription drugs, and marijuana are legal but are considered drugs in the same way as are hallucinogens and narcotics. A *drug user* is a person who intentionally takes legal or illegal drugs to alter his or her functioning or state of consciousness. A drug might be instrumental but still abused. Instrumental (prescribed) drugs are used to reduce anxiety, induce sleep, reduce pain, stay awake, and so on. However, instrumental drugs are often abused and may serve as an entry to other drugs.

A term that is closely associated with drug use is *drug of choice*. A person's drug of choice is just that: Of all the possible drugs available—of all the drugs a person may have used over the years—which specific drug(s) would this person use if given the choice? This concept is of particular importance as the number of polydrug users increases. In assessment, diagnosis, and treatment, drug of choice may play an important role.

Looking at substance use on a continuum allows the counselor to design individualized treatment plans. An adolescent who begins to use drugs may need only facilitation in good decision-making skills. An adult who is using a substance to cope with a recent loss may need facilitation in improvement of coping skills as well as support in a new life stage. These individuals need significantly different clinical intervention than do users with a severe SUD diagnosis.

THE PROFESSION IN THE 21ST CENTURY

The field of substance use counseling is continually evolving. Where once confrontation was the norm, now a collaborative approach that fits the client's life is being used. Research-based programs are being adopted that show more efficacy than previous programs based in opinion and ideology.

SAMHSA's Evidence-Based Program and Practices site (nrepp.samhsa.gov, 2015) shows the commitment to research-based treatment that is the standard for today's treatment world. Evidence-based practices have been subjected to randomized clinical trials and other experimental research designs and have been found to be the more effective treatment protocols.

The use of motivational interviewing (MI) is another example of a new effective, collaborative, and positive treatment skill. Motivational interviewing is a process to elicit change in the client through skillful questioning. Further, MI recognizes that change comes from within the client and that the client-counselor interaction is the most powerful aspect of the treatment process.

AN OVERVIEW OF THIS TEXT

The authors of this text endeavored to thoughtfully bring you the process of working with clients in this field. We have tried to make this text mimic that process from the beginning of your work with the client in out- or in-patient treatment to ending with relapse planning for continued recovery. It is our hope that this progression will assist you in understanding how to work effectively with your clients—and also how to care for yourself in the process.

We have attempted to organize the material in this text in a manner that presents a logical progression of knowledge about substance use disorder counseling. As a supplement to the knowledge base, we have incorporated the following three brief cases throughout the text to illustrate concepts discussed in each clinical chapter. The cases assist in understanding the process of assessment and diagnosis, treatment, and relapse prevention planning. Because a "live" case was not an option, the written cases will allow you to integrate the many concepts presented in the text. Authors have also developed and presented cases in each chapter as appropriate.

Case 1: Sandy and Pam

Presenting Problem

Sandy, a White female, age 52, and Pam, her biracial daughter, age 29, came into counseling to examine their relationship with each other as well as their relationships with men. They have noticed patterns in their interactions that are similar and create conflict between them and with partners that they choose. When asked to rate their problem on a scale of 1 to 10 (with 10 being the best), Sandy stated it was a 1 while Pam chose 4.

Family History

Sandy (mother) was the child of two alcoholic parents. Her parents divorced when Sandy was 10 years old, and her father basically "was never seen again." Her mother dated throughout her adolescence and finally married Harry when Sandy was 17. Harry was a heavy drinker, and Sandy is sure that he "ran around on her mother" until he died. Sandy is the oldest child and has a younger brother and sister. She reports feeling like she had to take care of her siblings throughout her life. However, she took on the role of the rebellious child from an early age, drinking, sneaking out of the house, and finally getting pregnant at 18. Sandy's mother died in an automobile accident while drinking when Sandy was 30 years old.

Sandy married Jim, an African American and Pam's father, who was an alcoholic and abusive to both Sandy and Pam. Sandy had two children with Jim: Pam and Albert. Albert is two years younger than Pam. When Pam was 7 years of age, her parents separated. Pam has had a distant and often disappointing relationship with her father. Her relationship with her mother has been close but conflictual.

Sandy admits to continuing to abuse alcohol. She remembers leaving Pam and her brother at home when she thought they were asleep so that she could go to bars. After her separation, she brought home numerous men and would be sexual with them. Pam remembers hearing her mother in the bedroom with strangers and feeling frightened and alone. Sandy stopped drinking two months ago and has been trying to make amends to Pam. Pam stated, "There is nothing to forgive. Mother was doing the best she could do." Pam admits to "following in her mother's footsteps"—sneaking out of the house when she was younger, using alcohol and "downers" from her mother's medicine cabinet. She also admits having sex with many partners since she was 12 or 13.

Pam states she drinks "too much" but "not as much as a couple of years ago." She was living with a cocaine abuser, Sam, who abuses alcohol and is emotionally and verbally abusive to her. She has used cocaine on "several occasions" with him but says she prefers to drink alcohol. She has not been using "downers" as much since living with Sam. Pam says she is tempted to "sleep around to get even" with Sam.

Pam recently moved out of Sam's house and back in with her mother. She is attempting to stay away from him, but he is pursuing her. She states that she "feels drawn to him and wants to make it work." She believes he will not be abusive if they both stop using alcohol and cocaine.

Education/Work History

Sandy did not complete high school, nor does she have any technical training. She has worked various jobs throughout her life as well as being on welfare for the past five years. Pam is a bright young woman with a high school degree and two years of study at a community college. Her career counseling indicated that her best fit was in a people-oriented position, but she has been uninspired by any job she has held. Like her mother, her job history is sporadic, with Pam holding jobs for an average of about three months as a waitress, receptionist, and bank teller. She then quits her job because she "hates it" and usually drinks and uses drugs heavily for several weeks before "getting it together" and finding another job. She is currently employed as a cashier in a convenience store and works the night shift.

Pam believes her problem is her inability to commit to anything. Sandy says that this issue is her problem also, so Pam must have "learned it from me." Pam has recently begun to experience anxiety attacks that she attributes to her fear of being alone. She has been prescribed an anti-anxiety drug but still drinks alcohol along with it.

Medical Information

Sandy is on Medicare and Social Security disability for back problems that prevent her from working. She has been disabled for the past five years. Sandy reports that she has been in pain for over 10 years. The pain level varies but she takes prescribed narcotics for the pain. She says that "sometimes" she mixes the drugs with alcohol when the pain is "really bad."

Pam is in fairly good health but was prescribed an antidepressant and an anti-anxiety medication about six months ago.

Support Systems

Sandy and Pam have both been in Alcoholics Anonymous (AA) but only occasionally. They both state that they don't really know anyone who doesn't drink or use drugs.

Counseling Goal(s)

Both women admit that they drink and use drugs to "help them with life's stresses" but would like to learn other ways of handling life. Sandy appears to be less willing to abstain but seems to be willing to "drink in moderation." They also want to understand why they continue to seek out bad relationships that "just get them back into using again."

Case 2: The Martinez Family: Juanita and Jose

Presenting Problem

Jose and Juanita are in their mid-40s, with a daughter from Juanita's first marriage, Sarita, age 15, and their birth daughter, Karen, age 4. The family comes into therapy due to conflict between Jose and Sarita. The parents described the chaos and hatred that ensues when Sarita blows up at Jose, using Sarita's phrase that Jose "is not my real father." When asked to describe the problem on a scale from 1 to 10 (scale of 1 being worst to 10 being best), Jose and Juanita chose 3 and 4 respectively, while Sarita chose 1.

Family History

Juanita and her family came to the United States from Mexico when she was 5 years old. Her father was not able to find steady employment and was very bitter about being away from his home in Mexico and the disappointment of his life in the United States. Juanita states, "I only wanted to be like the other children in my school. I resented my father for his continued use of Spanish, his rigid rules, and his drinking." Her mother died when Juanita was only 5 months old. She has a brother, Alberto, who is seven years older than Juanita. She left home at age 14 and was placed in a foster home with an American family that was loving and supportive. Juanita states that she is grateful for the four years she had in the foster home. She states that she has made peace with her father and forgiven her brother, both of whom she continues to have a relationship with as an adult.

At age 19, she married Hector, a traditional Hispanic male. She was married for less than two years and reports he was just like her father and "that it was too difficult to be what he wanted me to be." Sarita is the child of this marriage, and her father is still involved in her life, according to Sarita, "as much as Mother will allow." Hector drinks only socially and does not use drugs. Juanita states that he is "very concerned about Sarita." Juanita divorced Hector when Sarita was 10 and married Jose shortly thereafter, having met him at the bar where she worked.

Jose is the oldest of five children and had to parent the younger children from about age 10. Both parents drank "a lot," but Jose does not see them as alcoholics. Jose's parents came from Ecuador before he was born. They acclimated well to their life in the States, and Jose and his siblings were raised as "Americans" with no sense of their own culture or heritage. Jose also left home at an early age but has had no relationship with his parents or siblings as an adult. He chooses to share no other information regarding his family of origin.

Sarita has been raised with the conflicting values and messages from the Spanish culture that her mother knows and her birth father supports, and the American culture that is her stepfather's. She is beginning to act out both at home and in the classroom. Her grades are dropping, and she is sneaking out of the house at night. She admits to yelling and screaming at Jose and turning up the stereo too loud "just to bug him." She also says he drinks too much, and when he is drunk, he tells her how much he loves her and how he hates that they fight all the time. Sarita says he then yells at her, tells her to get out of his face, and calls her friends "dummies." Jose's response to Sarita's acting out behavior when he is sober is to tighten the rules.

Karen, the younger daughter, is not present at the session. Juanita reports that she is "visibly sad." She is "quiet and withdrawn" from the family fights. She spends lots of time in her room playing with her stuffed toys.

Trauma, Domestic Violence, Substance Abuse

Juanita reports a traumatic childhood with an alcoholic and abusive father. She recalls being sexually abused by Alberto, her older brother, beginning at around age 9 or 10 and going on until she left the house.

Both have abused alcohol for approximately 20 years. Juanita stopped drinking five years ago for health reasons and remained sober for one year before beginning to drink beer and then wine again. She states that she drinks only after the children are in bed and does not think that Sarita or Karen have ever seen her drunk. She states that she uses cocaine only at work—never at home. Jose drinks mostly beer every evening after work, many times with his friends, and smokes some "pot" on the weekends. He admits to drinking in front of the girls but not smoking pot until they are in bed or not around.

Both Jose and Juanita admit that quitting the use of drugs and alcohol would be difficult but express a desire to stop. Juanita particularly believes this is a problem in the family. The longest they have been able to stop (except for Juanita's one year) was 14 days. When they started again, both drank alcohol and used drugs to intoxication. Juanita is somewhat reluctant to give up her "uppers." She says she feels more socially upbeat when she "does a line or two" and, since she gets it for free and has "no ill effects," sees no reason to abstain. She states it really helps at work.

Jose does not like that she gets drugs from "friends" at the bar, and he says he would like to stop using pot and for Juanita to stop using cocaine completely. Both admit that their use may be part of the problem with Sarita—and with Karen—but are not sure what to do about the problem. They believe that Sarita "just needs a stronger hand" and that she is "just acting her age and will get over it soon."

Medical Information

None reported.

Education/Work History

Juanita currently works as a bartender and receives free cocaine from her patrons. Jose worked as a bartender at the same place for almost two years but has changed professions. He is currently working as a contractor and is fairly successful. Both state a sporadic work history with many different jobs as they moved quite frequently before marriage. Neither has kept a job more than two years. Jose was incarcerated as a teenager for theft and illegal drug possession.

Sarita works after school at a local shop. She reports that she really likes it and loves to be out of the house.

Support Systems

Both parents share mutual couple friends (Jane and Marta; Fernando and Marie), whom they describe "as close to the family, like uncles and aunts." These are friends who live in the same neighborhood as the family does. Jose talks loosely about his friends that he hangs out with after work but does not identify a significant male friend outside of the neighborhood. Jose reports no close ties to church or cultural organizations. Juanita attends church with Karen and Sarita "when she will go." Sarita says that her aunts are her support and also her friends at school.

Counseling Goals

Both parents report that they would like to learn different parenting skills. Their goals for alcohol and drug use is to continue use on a moderate basis. Jose, Juanita, and Sarita would like a better relationship among themselves but differ in how to achieve this. Juanita has indicated that the girls might be interested in learning more about their culture. She thinks this might help Sarita to understand herself in a deeper way.

Case 3: Leigh

Presenting Problem

Leigh, age 16, has been referred because of problems at school and a shoplifting charge. Leigh and her mother moved to this area about eight months ago. She is currently in 11th grade and is attending a new school this year. She is dressed in black with pierced ears, nose, eyebrow, and lip. Her appearance is disheveled and her hygiene poor. She appears to be overly thin. She has previously admitted to "smoking some dope" every now and then and having a drink or two with her friends. When asked to rate her problem on a scale of 1 to 10 (with 10 being no problem), Leigh replied "9" but said her mom's problem was a –5. Leigh says the shoplifting charge is a mistake; that she intended to pay for the makeup and just forgot it was in her purse. She doesn't understand why everyone is making such a "big deal out of it."

When directly asked about her drug and alcohol use, Leigh admits that she has been smoking, drinking, and using Ecstasy, cocaine, and pot at parties for the past four months. She also implies that some of her friends have a meth connection, and she has "tried meth" on a couple of occasions but denies steady use. She says "maybe" she raids her mother's medicine cabinet "like all the other kids." She also admits to multiple sex partners at these parties. She states that she sees nothing wrong with any of this and that she is "tired of everyone trying to tell her what to do." She says that running away with her friends seems to be the best solution for her.

When asked about why she believes running away is the best solution, she describes a series of losses that she has had over the past 10 years. Leigh's parents divorced when she was 5 years old. When she was a young child she had a close relationship with her brother, who is two years older, but now they do not speak. Both children lived with their mother after the divorce. Until eight months ago they lived in the same town as their father. Leigh and her brother saw him frequently, although she says he was "always busy with work" and she could never talk to him about much of anything. Leigh states that her mother was also busy but would "sometimes" stop and listen. She reports that her mother has a temper and is stressed all the time about money and work. She also reports that her mom and dad still fight about money and "us kids." She feels like she is in the middle and is always being asked to choose.

Family History

Leigh's father and brother have "disappeared from her life." Although her brother is attending college about one hour from their new home, he infrequently comes to visit. He is moody and withdrawn and either goes out to "party" or sleeps most of the time. Her father now lives about four hours away, and she has not seen him since they moved, although he calls her on occasion.

Leigh's mother is working as a real estate salesperson at a new office and dating Hank, whom she met in their old town and who moved to be close to her in the new town. Leigh says that Hank is "OK" but that she misses her father and never sees her mother now that she is dating as well as working all the time.

In addition to the changes in her family life, she reports missing her old school and friends. At her previous school she received excellent grades and good conduct reports. She was involved in several extracurricular activities and had many friends. Her grades have dropped significantly this year, and her new friends are "different" from her old friends but "accept her for what she is." Leigh states that her new friends are more fun than her old friends but that she sometimes misses her old school and friends.

Medical Information

Leigh recently went to the doctor for her school physical and reports that the doctor said she was in good health. She is underweight and her menses have not been regular. She denies any eating disorder but some of her comments reflect that behavior. She discusses her mother's struggle with weight and how she never wants to be "fat." She also says she "knows different ways to zone out besides drugs and sex when she needs to do that." Further, she is taking an antidepressant prescribed by the new doctor two months ago.

Leigh reports that her mother is diabetic and she has lots of mood swings. Sometimes she gets really angry and manic. Leigh is worried about her mother's health and states that she drinks alcohol with Hank every night. The mother is on an anti-anxiety drug as she is "very stressed" at her new job according to Leigh. Her blood pressure is high and she is "on some drug" for that problem. Leigh expresses worry about where she would live if something happened to her mother.

Trauma, Domestic Violence, Substance Abuse

Leigh says the divorce and moving was a very big trauma and that she did not want to move and that now she never sees her father. When they lived in the previous town, at least she saw him sometimes. She also reports that Mom and Hank fight a lot when they are drinking.

Support Systems

Leigh's only current support system is her new friends. She does stay in touch (text, email) with one of her best friends from her old school, Kathy. She says Kathy is worried about her but that is "crazy; I'm doing fine." She wants Kathy to visit. When asked about her mother as a support system, she states, "No way!"

Counseling Goals

Leigh states that her goal is just to "get this done." We did agree that she will attend at least five more sessions and that we would discuss her grades as well as her drug use.

Conclusion

Substance use creates multifaceted problems that vary across cultures and families as well as with individuals. It is an issue that affects everyone directly, indirectly, or as a societal cost from these individuals. And the costs at all levels are staggering. The complexity of the problem has resulted in no single treatment method evolving as *most* effective for health-distressed individuals experiencing the consequences of substance use. However, current research does find that some approaches are more effective than others and that family treatment approaches for substance users and their families may be one of those approaches.

All counselors, whether they specialize in the field of substance use disorders or work in the general field of psychotherapy, will encounter issues of substance use with many of their clients. Considering the economic costs and the price in human suffering of substance use, it seems imperative that counselors be trained in all aspects of substance use intervention and prevention. It is essential that all mental health professionals understand the process of use; the etiology of use; the individual, family, and societal costs; and available treatment modalities. The professional must also be aware of the psychological and physiological effects of drugs on the human brain and thereby on human behavior. *Substance Use Counseling* has been written to guide mental health professionals in their recognition, assessment, and treatment of substance use disorders in their clients.

MyCounselingLab for Addictions/Substance Use

Try the Topic 1 Assignments: *Introduction to Substance Use Disorder Counseling.*

CHAPTER 2

Ethical and Legal Issues in Substance Use Disorder Counseling

Summer M. Reiner, Ph.D.

Ethical and legal issues facing substance use disorder (SUD) counselors are complex and stem from many sources. SUD counselors are recruited from a variety of health and mental health professions. Each profession has its own representative organizations and licensing and certification requirements. These representative, certifying, and/or licensing entities offer their own distinctive ethical codes. In addition, there are conflicting federal and state laws, as well as agency regulations, that influence ethical decision making. This chapter briefly reviews the legal and ethical issues that impact the SUD counselor.

Because of the variety of professions that offer substance use disorder counseling and space constraints, this chapter is presented from the perspective of a SUD counselor from a counseling background. The narrowed scope exemplifies the conflicting laws and ethical issues within the SUD counseling field, bringing to light the issues that SUD professionals in general may face despite their background. It is imperative that SUD professionals be aware of the federal, state, and local laws, regulations, and codes of ethics that apply to them and their profession.

It should be noted that entire books are devoted to reviewing the ethical and legal issues that affect SUD counselors; this chapter is meant to provide an introduction and awareness of the complexity of legal and ethical issues in SUD counseling. The complexity of legal and ethical issues will be illustrated by the review of laws and standards of this decade. Laws, standards, requirements, and ethical codes continually change in response to societal needs. It is the responsibility of the SUD counselor to be aware of the current federal and state laws, workplace regulations, and ethical codes governing his or her profession.

EDUCATION AND TRAINING OF MENTAL HEALTH PROFESSIONALS WORKING WITH SUBSTANCE USE DISORDER

The SUD counseling field comprises counselors with an array of educational and experiential differences. Historically, the SUD counseling community embraced the counselor who had experienced a substance use disorder and recovery process, accepting successful recovery rather than education as a qualifier for professional counselor status (Doukas & Cullen, 2010). Recovering counselors were believed to be able to empathize with and assist their clients simply through personal experiences and the ability to relate (Hagedorn, Culbreth & Cashwell, 2012). Today personal experience is not considered adequate preparation for SUD counselors as most states and organizations require some coursework in SUD counseling for those who will be working in the clinical field. However, there is still a discrepancy in academic requirements between SUD counselors and mental health counselors. Mental health counselors typically need to complete a master's degree to be credentialed, whereas associate-level SUD counselors have as little as an associate's degree and 2,000 hours of supervised training, and entry-level SUD technicians need to earn a minimum of 150 hours of education and training beyond a high school diploma/GED (National Association of Alcoholism and Drug Abuse Counselors [NAADAC], 2011a).

As described earlier, state licensing boards contribute to the confusion, because states vary on formal education and supervised experience requirements for addiction counselors (Astramovich & Hoskins, 2013). As of 2014, only 35 states offered credentials for SUD mental health professionals with some states (i.e., Alabama, New York) requiring only a high school diploma or GED and experience (National Addiction Technology Transfer Center, 2010). In contrast, all 50 states required mental health counselors to hold a master's degree and to pass an examination for license eligibility (American Counseling Association [ACA], 2010).

In response to the inconsistency of educational and experiential requirements, the National Board for Certified Counselors (NBCC), an organization affiliated with ACA, in conjunction with the International Association of Addictions and Offenders Counselors (IAAOC), developed a Master's of Addiction Counseling (MAC) certification (NBCC, 2011). To earn an NBCC MAC certification, counselors must complete a master's degree; earn 12 credits of graduate-level course work in addiction counseling or 500 continuing education hours in substance abuse issues, which may include 6 credits in group and/or family counseling; pass the Examination for Master Addictions Counselors (EMAC); and complete 3 years (36 months, 24 of which must occur after earning a master's degree) of experience in SUD counseling under the supervision of a master-degreed counselor, psychologist, psychiatrist, marriage and family therapist, or clinical social worker (NBCC, 2011). The content of the EMAC includes questions on assessment, counseling practices, treatment process, treatment planning and implementation, and prevention specific to addictions. Nationally Certified Counselors (NCC) who hold the MAC credential are eligible to seek Substance Abuse Professional status through the U.S. Department of Transportation (USDOT).

The National Association of Alcoholism and Drug Abuse Counselors (NAADAC) also developed a Master Addiction Counselor (MAC) credential. The criteria for the NAADAC MAC includes holding a master's degree in a "healing art" or related field with an emphasis in addiction counseling; having a current state license in your profession or certification as a substance abuse counselor; having 3 years (6,000 hours) of supervised SUD counseling; documenting 500 clock hours of education in alcoholism and drug abuse counseling matters, with at least 6 hours of HIV/AIDS training and 6 hours of ethics training; signing the NAADAC ethical statement; and passing the written Master Addiction Counselor examination (NAADAC, 2015). The content of the exam focuses on pharmacology and psychoactive substances, counseling practices, and professional issues. NAADAC also offers certifications to professionals with less than a master's degree (see Table 2.1). In addition to the certifications options, NAADAC offers specialty endorsements.

The U.S. Department of Health and Human Services, Substance Abuse and Mental Health Services Administration (SAMHSA) expressed concern about the inconsistent educational and experiential requirements of substance abuse counselors (Broderick, 2007). In their report to Congress, SAMHSA identified five needs. One need focused on the educational standards and

TABLE 2.1 NAADAC Addiction Counselor Certification

| Title | License/Certificate Requirement | Education Contact Hours | | | Supervised Experience | Degree Requirement | Exam |
		SUD Counseling	Ethics	HIV/AIDS			
Nationally Certified Peer Support Specialist	None, but must attest to 1 year recovery from SUD	125	6	6	1 year	High school diploma or GED	Pass Peer Support Specialist
National Certified Addictions Counselor, Level I (NCAC I)	SUD counselor	270	6	6	3 years/6,000 hours	None	Pass Level I
National Certified Addictions Counselor, Level II (NCAC II)	In your profession	450	6	6	5 years/10,000 hours	Bachelor's	Pass Level II
National Certified Adolescent Addiction Counselor	In your profession	450 + 100 contact hours in adolescent treatment	6	6	5 years/10,000 hours in SUD, of which 5 years or 6000 hours working with adolescents with SUD	Bachelor's	Pass National Certification Examination for Adolescent Addiction Counselors
Nationally Endorsed Student Assistance Professional	SUD professional	100, of which 70 are student assistance focused	6	6	3 years/4,500 hours in SUD, of which 3,000 must be in a school setting	Bachelor's	Pass National Student Assistance Professional

Nationally Endorsed Co-Occurring Disorders Professional	SUD Professional	70 hours of co-occurring disorders	0	0	5 years/10,000 hours, half of which must be in co-occurring disorders	Bachelor's	Pass Co-Occurring Disorders Professional
Master Addictions Counselor	SUD or in other healing art	500	6	6	3 years/6,000 hours	Master's	Pass MAC
Master Addictions Counselor with Co-Occurring Endorsement Component	In your profession	500	6	6	3 years/6,000 hours	Master's	Pass Master Addiction Counselors with Co-Occurring Endorsement Component
Nicotine Dependence Specialist	In a helping profession	270 in health care, of which 40 must be tobacco or nicotine focused	0	0	3 years/ 6,000 hours	Bachelor's	Pass Certification Exam for Nicotine Dependent Specialist

credentialing of the SUD professionals. The report specifically called for a national set of core competencies for all SUD professionals (physicians, nurses, counselors, social workers, psychologists, etc.), an adoption of a national accreditation for addictions education programs, and an increase in salaries for individuals who work in the SUD field. Despite such concerns being raised nearly a decade ago, the inconsistencies persist.

Clearly there are different avenues for entering the SUD counseling profession. No matter which avenue SUD counselors have taken, they must adhere to professional ethical codes, laws, and work site regulations. The professional SUD counselor must know and understand these codes, laws, and regulations—and, even more important, how they interact, as this can affect the SUD counselor's ethical decisions and legal responsibility.

ETHICS

As previously mentioned, ethical codes are written and revised by most mental health organizations. Ethical codes are intended to be the minimum standard counselors abide by when working with clients. The purpose of the ACA *Code of Ethics* is to set the ethical obligations of professional counselors and counselors-in-training and serve as the basis for processing ethical complaints of violation of ACA members (ACA, 2014).

Many ethical codes of mental health organizations are based on moral principles (see Table 2.2) such as autonomy, nonmaleficence, beneficence, justice, fidelity, and veracity (Remley & Herlihy, 2013).

Upon reviewing ethical codes of several mental health organizations including ACA, the American Mental Health Counseling Association (AMHCA), NAADAC, and NBCC, it is clear that despite the fact that the ethical codes offer differing principles and focus on varied ethical issues, they also have many similarities (see Table 2.3). The commonalities between the ethical codes embrace principles aimed at protecting client welfare; avoiding harm and the imposition of personal values; professional qualifications and competence, and knowledge of standards; consultation and counselor supervision with other counseling professionals; competence to administer, use, or interpret assessment instruments; and knowledge of and adherence to the laws and ethical codes (ACA, 2014; American Mental Health Counseling Association [AMHCA], 2010; International Association of Marriage and Family Counselors [IAMFC], 2011; Hendricks, Bradley, Southern, Oliver, & Birdsall, 2011; NAADAC, 2011b; NBCC, 2012). One important

TABLE 2.2 Moral Principles and Definitions

Moral Principle	Definition
Justice	Fair, equitable, and nondiscrimination.
Beneficence	Promote mental health and wellness.
Nonmaleficence	Do no harm.
Autonomy	Foster self-determination.
Fidelity	Fulfilling the responsibility of trust.
Veracity	Truthfulness and honesty.

Source: Remley, T., & Herlihy, B. (2013). *Ethical, legal, and professional issues in counseling* (4th ed.). Upper Saddle River, NJ: Pearson Education.

TABLE 2.3　Organizational Ethical Codes' Content

ACA Code of Ethics 2014, Sections A–I

A. The Counseling Relationship
B. Confidentiality and Privacy
C. Professional Responsibility
D. Relationships with Other Professionals
E. Evaluation, Assessment, and Interpretation
F. Supervision, Training, and Teaching
G. Research and Publication
H. Distance Counseling, Technology, and Social Media
I. Resolving Ethical Issues

NAADAC Code of Ethics 2011, Principles 1–10

1. The Counseling Relationship
2. Evaluation, Assessment and Interpretation of Client Data
3. Confidentiality/ Privileged Communication and Privacy
4. Professional Responsibility
5. Working in a Culturally Diverse World
6. Workplace Standards
7. Supervision and Consultation
8. Resolving Ethical Issues
9. Communication and Published Works
10. Policy and Political Involvement

NBCC Code of Ethics 2012, Directives

NCCs take appropriate action to prevent harm.
NCCs provide only those services for which they have education and qualified experience.
NCCs promote the welfare of clients, students, supervisees or the recipients of professional services provided.
NCCs communicate truthfully.
NCCs recognize that their behavior reflects on the integrity of the profession as a whole, and thus, they avoid actions, which can reasonably be expected to damage trust.
NCCs recognize the importance of and encourage active participation of clients, students, or Supervisees.
NCCs are accountable in their actions and adhere to recognized professional standards and practices.

AMHCA Code of Ethics 2010, Principles 1–6

1. Commitment to Clients
2. Commitment to Other Professionals
3. Commitment to Students, Supervisees, and Employee Relationships
4. Commitment to the Profession
5. Commitment to the Public
6. Resolution of Ethical Problems

commonality that exists in all five of the highlighted ethical codes is the emphasis on confidentiality and client rights. As shown in the Table 2.3 for the NBCC and NAADAC ethical codes, confidentiality is actually embedded in the NBCC "Counseling Relationship" section and the NAADAC "Client Welfare principle." The following sections focus on confidentiality standards regarding counselors in general and as they apply to SUD counseling, as well as group settings and working with minors.

CONFIDENTIALITY

Clients seeking counseling often reveal information and emotions that are potentially embarrassing or damaging to their reputation; they do so with an understanding that the counselor will not share it with others. This promise of keeping information private is called *confidentiality*. Confidentiality is considered the core value of mental health professionals and is intended to reduce stigma, foster trust, protect privacy, and allow clients to discuss their issues without fear of future repercussions (Remley & Herlihy, 2013). It is the counselor's responsibility to protect client confidential information. It is important to note that the right or privilege of confidentiality belongs to the client, even the deceased client (ACA, 2014), not to the counselor. Confidentiality is not only an ethical principle; law often protects it. In fact, clients receiving SUD treatment have their confidentiality strictly protected by federal laws—specifically, the laws 42 CFR Part 2, HIPAA, and the Patient Privacy and Affordable Care Act, which are discussed later.

Because the privilege of confidentiality belongs to the client, the client has the right to waive confidentiality and/or to consent to the transmission of confidential information (Remley & Herlihy, 2013). Typical client consents include information being shared with third-party payers, other health or mental health professionals, and family or loved ones. The counselor should involve the client in the disclosure decision-making process and obtain written consent to release confidential information (ACA, 2014). Counselors should release only the essential information that was discussed with the client. It is also the counselor's responsibility to ensure information that is transmitted via fax, email, telephone, or another method maintains the client's right to confidentiality (ACA, 2014; AMHCA, 2010), because technology can often lead to unintended breaches of confidentiality and to an increase in the number of people with access to information (Remley & Herlihy, 2013). The protection of client information during the transmission process has been especially relevant since the passage of the following legislation: Health Insurance Portability and Accountability Act (HIPAA, 1996), HITECH Act (2009), and the Patient Protection and Affordable Care Act (2010). These laws require the sharing of patient information through encrypted systems, with significant penalties for failing to sufficiently protect client information.

There are, however, imposed limits to confidentiality, and it is the counselor's responsibility to inform the client of these limits at the onset of the counseling relationship. Aside from the possible risks associated with technology, counselors may be ethically or legally obligated to break confidentiality, without client consent, in limited situations (see Table 2.4).

Some of the limits to confidentiality are a result of the *Tarasoff v. The Regents of the University of California* court decision in 1976. This case imposed a *legal* duty on therapists to warn people who may become victims of a violent act by a client, and the phrase "duty to warn" was set in motion (Herbert & Young, 2002). The case was redecided in 1976, changing the language to "duty to protect"; the language change reflects the therapist's responsibility to protect or lessen the threat by contacting either authorities or the targeted person, not necessarily both.

TABLE 2.4 Common Limits to Confidentiality

If client intends to:
- Harm self
- Harm an identifiable third party
- Transmit a communicable, life-threatening disease to an identifiable third party

If client is the victim or perpetrator of:
- Child abuse/neglect
- Elder abuse/neglect or domestic abuse (depending on state law)

If client receives a valid court order

Any emergency situation in which information would be necessary

Although this case technically applies only in California, other states' laws and ethical codes were adopted to reflect the *Tarasoff* decision. *Lipari v. Sears, Roebuck & Co.* was a federal case that further extended the duty of counselors to warn *and* protect unknown *and* identifiable victims (Remley & Herlihy, 2013).

The *Tarasoff* decision also contributed to the legal and ethical obligations of counselors to notify a third party if the third party is at high risk for contracting a communicable disease from the client (ACA, 2014; American School Counselor Association [ASCA], 2010). With that being said, however, not all states legally allow this information to be shared; therefore, it is important to refer to the valid state laws and consult with an attorney. Finally, the *Tarasoff* decision influenced the requirement of counselors to break confidentiality in the event that a client intends to commit suicide (ACA, 2014; AMHCA, 2010). Another situation that may constitute a counselor sharing confidential information is in the event that the counselor is presented a valid court order (ACA, 2014; AMHCA, 2010). If a court orders a counselor to release confidential information, the counselor should first attempt to obtain the client's written consent to share information, but they must obey the court order.

Many ethical codes and state laws also indicate that counselors are responsible for reporting indications of abuse or neglect of children, the elderly, and/or persons not competent to care for themselves. SUD counselors need to be aware of their state laws regarding the reporting of abuse; as indicated in other chapters, there is a higher incidence of child and/or domestic abuse in SUD families (Macy & Goodbourn, 2012). States differ slightly on which forms of abuse and the minimum age of victims required to be reported.

It is important to note that counselors may discuss client cases with treatment team members; however, the counselor must inform the client of the type of information that will be shared with the team, as well as describe the purpose of sharing information. Counselors may also consult with other counselors and supervisors about clients, as counselor supervision and consultation is necessary for counselors to monitor their effectiveness and to receive guidance with ethical issues; counselors receiving supervision or consultation, however, must protect the identity of the client (ACA, 2014).

Code of Federal Regulations 42, Part 2

The previous section discussed common confidentiality issues pertaining to counselors in general. Counselors providing substance use screening or treatment services are legally bound to additional confidential restrictions under the federal law known as *Code of Federal Regulations (CFR) 42, Part 2*. *CFR 42* strictly protects the confidentiality of "records of the identity, diagnosis, prognosis, or treatment of any patient" that are maintained by a program that provides screening or treatment of drug or alcohol abuse and receives funds (directly or indirectly) from the federal government (*CFR 42, Part 2*). The purpose of *CFR 42* is to encourage individuals with substance use disorder to seek treatment without fear of discrimination, legal ramifications, or fear of losing one's job. The information shared in this section is only a summary of the federal regulation; SUD counselors need to review and follow the *entire* law.

According to *CFR 42, Part 2*, confidential client and former client information can be disclosed in only a few instances: (a) to medical professionals in the event of an emergency; (b) to qualified individuals for the purpose of conducting research, audits, and program evaluations—but such personnel may not directly or indirectly identify any individual patient; (c) with an appropriate court order indicating the extent of the necessary disclosure; and (d) with client consent. The federal confidential regulations, however, do *not* apply in the following circumstances: (a) members or veterans of the armed forces under the care of military facilities, (b) communications within a program, (c) qualified service organizations (e.g., blood work laboratories conducting drug testing), (d) crimes on program premises or against program personnel, and (e) reports of suspected child abuse and neglect. The law *does not* permit the disclosure of information for the purpose of preventing imminent danger to a third party, preventing the transmission of communicable diseases, or reporting elder abuse or domestic violence. It is important to note that CFR 42, Part 2 supersedes state laws regarding reporting abuse of adults or warning a third party about imminent danger.

The most common disclosure of information under *CFR 42, Part 2* is as a result of client consent. Clients consenting to a disclosure of information must do so in writing. A legal written consent must contain the following elements:

- The name of the person or program permitted to make the disclosure
- The name of the person or program receiving the disclosed information
- Patient name
- The purpose of the disclosure
- How much and nature of information
- Patient or authorized person's signature
- Date of consent
- A statement indicating that consent can be revoked at any time, including through verbal indication
- The date, event, or condition on which the consent will expire

In addition to the written consent of disclosure, a written statement, indicating that further disclosure of information is prohibited and that confidential information cannot be used to investigate or prosecute any alcohol or drug patient, must also accompany each disclosure. Any person who violates *CFR 42* shall be fined no more than $500 for the first offense and up to $5,000 in each subsequent case.

CFR 42 stipulates that clients be made aware of the federal confidentiality requirements "at time of admission or when patient is capable of rational communication." A sample notice is as follows (*CFR 42; 2.22 [d]*):

Confidentiality of Alcohol and Drug Abuse Patient Records

Federal law and regulations protect the confidentiality of alcohol and drug abuse patient records maintained by this program. Generally, the program employees may not say to a person outside the program that a patient attends/attended the program, or disclose any information identifying a patient as an alcohol or drug abuser unless:

1. The patient consents in writing; or,
2. The disclosure is allowed by a court order; or,
3. The disclosure is made to medical personnel in a medical emergency or to qualified personnel for research, audit, or program evaluation.

Violation of the federal law and regulations by a program is a crime. Suspected violations may be reported to appropriate authorities in accordance with federal regulations. Federal law and regulations do not protect any information about a crime committed by a patient either at the program or against any person who works for the program or about any threat to commit such a crime. Federal laws and regulations do not protect any information about suspected child abuse or neglect from being reported under State law to appropriate State or local authorities.

HEALTH INSURANCE PORTABILITY AND ACCOUNTABILITY ACT OF 1996 (HIPAA)

As with most federal regulations, the Health Insurance Portability and Accountability Act of 1996 (HIPAA) is complex and can only be summarized in this chapter. Service providers, however, need to read and adhere to the entire rule. The information shared in this section is not a thorough explanation of HIPAA but is rather outlined to illustrate how HIPAA and *CFR* 42 often conflict.

The purpose of HIPAA is to protect individually identifiable health information while increasing the flow of information between health care providers, health plans, and health care clearinghouses. *Health care providers* are defined as any provider, or third party on behalf of the provider, who *electronically* transmits health information for the purpose of claims submissions, inquiries about patient eligibility benefits, and authorizing referrals. *Health plans* refer to health insurance companies, health maintenance organizations (HMOs), Medicare, Medicaid, and other health carriers. Health care clearinghouses often refer to billing services, community health management information systems, and other processing systems.

The individually identifiable health information that is protected by HIPAA includes demographic data regarding an individual's past, present, or future physical or mental health condition and payment for the health care provided to the individual. It also protects information related to the provision of health care to the individual. HIPAA does not apply to health information contained in employer records or in educational records. Personally identifiable health information may only be disclosed to a covered entity as the privacy rule permits or at the discretion of the client (or personal representative who is legally authorized to make health care decisions on behalf of the client), which must be consented to in writing. A covered entity must disclose information when requested by the client or in compliance investigations conducted by the U.S. Department of Health and Human Services. The privacy rule permits, but does not require, covered entities to disclose protected health information without client authorization in the following circumstances: (a) to the individual; (b) to treatment, payment, and health care operations; (c) as part of an opportunity to agree or object (informal permission or in instances where the client is incapacitated, or in emergency situations); (d) incident to an otherwise permitted use and disclosure; (e) for public interest and benefit activities (e.g., reporting communicable diseases or keeping employers informed in the event of a work-related injury); and (f) as part of limited data sets for research activities related to public health or health care operations. It should be noted that private information disclosures must be limited to necessary information.

Permitted disclosures of protected health information, without client consent, under the *public interest and benefit activities* circumstance also includes the reporting of abuse, neglect, and domestic violence of victims; the release of information with a court order; the release of information for law enforcement purposes; health oversight activities; in the event of the death of the client to funeral directors and medical examiners; and to facilitate organ, eye, or tissue donation. Personal health information may also be disclosed if there is a serious threat to health or safety to the client or other persons. Finally, information may be disclosed without client permission for "assuring proper execution of a military mission, conducting intelligence and national securities activities that are authorized by law, providing protective services to the President, making medical suitability determinations for US State Department employees, protecting the health and safety of inmates or employees in a correctional institution, and determining eligibility for conducting enrollment in certain government benefit programs" (Office for Civil Rights [OCR], 2003, p. 8).

Health care providers must furnish a privacy practices notice to clients no later than the first service encounter, and they should make every attempt to obtain a written acknowledgment from the client. Covered entities must also supply the notice to anyone on request. Health plans must inform all new enrollees of the privacy notice at enrollment, and they must send reminder notifications every three years.

Patient Protection and Affordable Care Act

The purpose of the Patient Protection and Affordable Care Act is to provide affordable health care to uninsured Americans, to better detect mental health issues, and to provide better integration of health care (Pearlman, 2013). An essential component of the Affordable Care Act is the consolidation and integration of health records through the use of electronic health records (EHR) systems. Information that is shared across providers can improve care, reduce costs, provide critical information during emergency situations, and allow for the analysis of aggregate health data (Hu, Sparenborg, & Tai, 2011). The consolidated health record and its transmission over the Internet, however, increase the risk for potential breaches of privacy, security and confidentiality.

Given that many individuals with SUD issues are already wary of the risk of confidential breaches, they may avoid seeking treatment or sharing of accurate information (Hu et al., 2011). Furthermore, the potential for unintended disclosure of private client information exposes counselors to the penalties associated with HIPAA and *CFR* 42. To help protect client privacy, a *Consent Directive* could be offered to clients seeking SUD and or mental health services, whereby this information would be masked from view of health providers who have not been identified as having permission to access the information. Consent Directives, however, do not reduce the risk of exposure via electronic transmissions. Furthermore, Consent Directives could prevent optimal health care as they are in direct opposition to the benefits of health care integration. Counselors will need to discuss with clients the benefits and risks inherent with the EHR and Consent Directives.

The previous two sections described federal laws protecting confidentiality; they also delineated the limits to confidentiality related to these laws. The next two sections focus on confidentiality issues in specific settings or with specific populations, particularly group settings and school settings, and working with minors and diverse clients.

Confidentiality in Group Counseling or 12-Step Groups

Group counseling and 12-step-type groups are popular treatment/support options for clients in recovery from drug or alcohol abuse. Despite the legal and ethical regulations that apply to professional counselors, confidentiality cannot be ensured in group settings. In group counseling, the leader may be a certified/licensed professional who is bound by confidentiality, but the group members are not legally bound to confidentiality, even if they signed an agreement at the onset of the group experience (Olivier, 2009). Confidentiality does not protect 12-step-type groups that are not run by licensed, credentialed professionals. In fact, group members can actually be forced to testify against another group member. Such an instance occurred in the *Cox v. Miller* appellate case when Paul Cox admitted to killing two people while under the influence (Coleman, 2005). Group members were subpoenaed and forced to testify against Cox by divulging the information that he revealed during group. On the other end of the spectrum, the District of Columbia imposes civil and criminal penalties for group members who disclose confidential information shared in a group counseling setting. Clearly the disparity between these policies highlights the importance of SUD counselors having an awareness and understanding of federal regulations and their state regulations.

The limits to confidentiality in group settings may seriously undermine the SUD recovery process. Clients with substance use disorders need to be assured of and are legally entitled to confidentiality when disclosing personal information—or at least when working with a substance abuse professional. It is therefore important that, when a client is referred to group therapy or 12-step groups, they be made aware of their rights and the limits to confidentiality and privileged information prior to attending group support. Unfortunately, many insurance companies require clients to attend a 12-step group for eligibility for SUD treatments. Professional counselors must consider that not all clients are appropriate for group counseling settings, as many clients have coinciding mental health conditions. Counselors are obligated to screen clients for group appropriateness for the safety and benefit of all clients (ACA, 2014). If group counseling is an inappropriate course of treatment for the client, it is the counselor's responsibility to communicate this with the insurance company.

Confidentiality of Minors

Understanding the privilege and limits of confidentiality of minors can be difficult, particularly because there are several conflicting laws that govern confidential information of minors, including *CFR* 42, HIPAA, the Family Educational Rights and Privacy Act of 1974 (FERPA), the Individuals with Disabilities Education Act of 1997 (IDEA), and the 1994 Protection of Pupil Rights Amendment Act (PPRA). Generally, parents have legal authority over their minor children with few exceptions. FERPA, IDEA, and PPRA ensure parental authority, whereas *CFR* 42 and HIPAA restrict information that can be shared with parents.

This section will discuss the confidentiality issues that both SUD counselors and school counselors may face when working with minors. School counselors will usually not be providing SUD counseling to students; however, they may become aware of a student's substance use disorder and will be responsible for providing appropriate referrals and support. In addition, there has been a push for school-based drug and alcohol prevention, in which students are identified and referred to in-school or contracted staff SUD counselors (Burrow-Sanchez, Jenson, & Clark, 2009). SUD counselors working in a school assistance program, or under contract of a school district, would be responsible for understanding the education laws such as FERPA, IDEA, and PPRA that regulate the confidentiality of minors and parental rights. Furthermore, community

SUD counselors working with minors may use the school counselor as a resource for information and as a support for preventing relapse. Having an awareness of the education laws governing school counselors may be useful to the SUD counselor partnering with a school counselor; the SUD counselor will have an understanding of the laws that school counselors need to follow and how the laws conflict with *CFR* 42, Part 2. SUD counselors may also need to educate school counselors about *CFR* 42, Part 2, as some school counselors will be unaware of the regulations and may unintentionally break the law and be subject to litigation.

According to the ASCA *Code of Ethics* (2010), the professional school counselor has a primary obligation to the student and is knowledgeable of laws, regulations, and policies aimed at protecting students' rights. These laws, regulations, and policies affect the confidentiality that can be assured to the student. Confidential information gained through the counseling relationship should not be revealed to others without the informed consent/assent of the student. The exceptions include applicable limits to confidentiality based on federal and state laws, written policies, and ethical standards. Unfortunately, counselors working with minors are faced at the outset with the issue of informed consent; *informed consent* refers to the legal and ethical requirement of counselors to inform the client of the potential risks and benefits of counseling. Although the primary client is the minor, minors often do not have the legal right to give consent; only their parents have this right (Hanson, 2009). Typically school counselors do not need the consent of the parents to work with students, simply the minors' assent (Remley & Herlihy, 2013). Some scholars, however, recommend that school counselors seek both minor assent and parental consent if working with a particular student for more than three sessions.

Minor clients must also be informed of the limits of confidentiality in understandable language. Typical limits to confidentiality reflect the same limits imposed on adult clients, including consulting with other professionals, preventing imminent danger to the client or others, court orders, and preventing a third party from contracting a communicable disease from the student/client. In the event that the counselor must disclose confidential information, it is recommended that the counselor inform the student before disclosing the information and remind the student of the limits of confidentiality that were outlined at the onset of the relationship. The counselor should also describe the purpose of the disclosure and the type of information that will be shared.

In regard to the school counselor's obligation to the parent, the ASCA *Code of Ethics* (2010) states that although the counselor's primary obligation is to the student, counselors "recognize that working with minors in a school setting requires school counselors to collaborate with students' parents/guardians to the extent possible" (B.2.b). The ethical code also indicates that it is the counselor's responsibility to inform parents of the counselor's role and the confidential nature of a counseling relationship that is afforded to the student. Students should be informed that the school counselor would contact the parent(s) or guardian(s) in the event that the student indicates a clear and imminent danger to self or others. *Imminent danger* refers to an immediate serious threat, but it is often the counselor's values and beliefs that influence the perception of danger (Hanson, 2009). Finally, although school counselors are ethically bound to keep student information confidential, possibly from parents, school counselors must adhere to the Family Educational Rights and Privacy Act (FERPA)/Buckley Amendment, IDEA, and PPRA, using any exceptions to those laws that serve confidentiality.

FAMILY EDUCATIONAL RIGHTS AND PRIVACY ACT OF 1974 (FERPA)   FERPA gives parents the right to inspect school records; when the student reaches the age of majority or attends an educational institution beyond high school, the right is transferred to the student

(Remley & Herlihy, 2013; U.S. Department of Education, 2009). Parents and eligible students may also request corrections to inaccurate records. Student records can be disclosed only with written parental permission or under the following conditions: (a) to school employees with legitimate educational interests; (b) to a school to which the student is transferring; (c) in connection with financial aid for the student; (d) to organizations conducting studies on behalf of the school; (e) in health and safety emergencies; (f) to comply with a judicial order; or (g) to appropriate authorities in connection with the juvenile justice system in accordance to state laws. Schools may also make directory information available without parental consent, provided the school informs and offers an opportunity for the parent/student to request that directory information not be disclosed. It is the school's responsibility to inform parents and students at the age of majority of their rights protected under FERPA.

A parent or eligible student may request any and all school records, including digital data contained on computer servers and email. Often this raises the question as to whether the counselor's personal counseling notes are considered school records. Personal counseling notes would be considered a school record the moment anyone other than the counselor knows of their existence, including students, parents, other counselors, or any other person. Because of the accessibility afforded to parents, school counselors should be careful about what information is placed or retained in a school record, keeping in mind that student confidentiality needs to be protected (ASCA, 2010).

INDIVIDUALS WITH DISABILITIES EDUCATION ACT OF 2004 (IDEA) IDEA was intended to ensure that students with disabilities receive a free appropriate public education (FAPE) with accommodations in the least restrictive environment (LRE). In 2008, it was expanded to ensure that students with disabilities enrolled in private schools would have access to accommodations and be placed in the LRE. Essentially, an Individual Education Plan (IEP) is developed for every child with an identified disability that would qualify the student for special education services (U.S. Department of Education, 2009). Fortunately, educational records and the disclosure of confidential information of special education students fall under FERPA regulations, effectively eliminating conflicts between the two federal regulations. School districts need to inform parents when the district intends to destroy student records. Parents may decide and are entitled to keep their child's records, as they may need the records for other purposes, such as to file for Social Security benefits.

PROTECTION OF PUPIL RIGHTS AMENDMENT OF 1994 (PPRA) PPRA has been referred to as the Hatch Amendment, the Grassley Amendment, and the Tiahrt Amendment after authors of the amendments to the Goals 2000: Educate America Act. It was further revised in 2001, by the No Child Left Behind Act (Illinois State Board of Education, n.d.). Essentially, PPRA states that information collected from students through surveys, analyses, or evaluations funded by the U.S. Department of Education must be available for parental inspection (Protection of Pupil Rights Amendment, 1994). PPRA also requires state and local entities to obtain consent from parents prior to collecting information from students concerning the following items: (a) political affiliation; (b) mental and psychological problems; (c) sexual behavior and attitudes; (d) illegal or self-incriminating behavior; (e) clinical assessments of other individuals or family members; (f) privileged information shared with lawyers, physicians, or ministers; (g) religious practices, affiliations, or beliefs; and (h) income, other than what is required by law for program eligibility. Obviously this regulation could complicate screening, referral, and treatment of minors seeking SUD counseling without parental consent.

HIPAA   Although HIPAA was discussed earlier, there are regulations that are specific to minors and parental access to confidential information. This section is particularly targeted to SUD counselors who are considered "covered entities." HIPAA states that parents can access medical records on behalf of their child, except in cases where the parent is not considered the personal representative; in this case, the privacy rule defers to the state and local laws to determine parental access to the minors' records. If state and local laws do not address this issue, a covered entity (licensed health care professional) has the discretion to deny parental access to the minor's records if the professional determines that the access is not in the minor's best interest. In states where the minor can consent to treatment, and there are no other laws that state otherwise, the minor can decide whether the parents are entitled to confidential information.

CFR 42, PART 2 IN REGARD TO MINORS   *CFR* 42, Part 2 warrants a special discussion in regard to minors as it contributes to the complexity of working with minors. According to the federal regulation, counselors must maintain the client's confidentiality, with few exceptions. In fact the counselor may not be able to share information with the parents of a minor. The entire *CFR* 42, Part 2, law applies to any person, regardless of age. The law protects any information about a minor who has received any SUD-related services or referrals from a program that receives any federal funding. This would include public schools. Information may be shared with parents if the minor provides written consent. The written consent must have all of the elements that *CFR* 42 requires (as described earlier in the chapter), including the minor's signature. The minor may verbally revoke this consent at any time. The exception is if the counselor believes that the minor lacks the capacity to disclose or if there is a substantial threat to the minor's life or well-being.

When a minor seeks treatment for SUD, a counselor is faced with a confusing situation. On one hand, the student's confidentiality must be maintained; on the other hand, some state laws restrict the minor from entering a treatment program without parental permission. It is imperative that the counselor know the appropriate legal age in his/her state for which a minor can seek treatment without parental consent. Fortunately the Internet provides quick and easy access to the current state and federal laws.

Froeschle and Crews (2010) suggested that, when working with minors in school settings, counselors should adhere to the following ethical strategies:

- Act in the best interest of students.
- Prior to the onset of a counseling relationship, inform students of limitations of the relationship.
- Have awareness of personal values, attitudes, and beliefs and when they affect the counseling relationship.
- Work to understand the backgrounds of diverse clients and know how personal biases affect the counseling relationship.
- Have an awareness of personal skill levels and limitations and function only within the boundaries of professional competence.
- Practice from a theoretical perspective and use decision-making models when faced with dilemmas.
- Encourage family involvement in sensitive and controversial matters.
- Follow written job descriptions.
- Read and adhere to applicable ethical codes.
- Consult with peers.

- Hold memberships in appropriate professional organizations.
- Keep up-to-date with laws and regulations, especially as they relate to working with minors.
- Consultation should be solely focused on benefitting the client, not the counselor.
- Consult with an attorney when needed.

ETHICAL CONFLICTS SPECIFIC TO SUBSTANCE USE DISORDER COUNSELORS

Dual Relationships

Counselors in smaller communities, particularly recovered SUD counselors, are at risk for developing dual relationships (Oser, Biebel, Pullen & Harp, 2013; Schank, Helbok, Haldeman, & Gallardo, 2010). Small communities create opportunities for increased interactions between individuals. Picture a small town; the only pharmacist in town comes to the only counselor for SUD treatment. They likely know each other well. Clearly, the counselor is faced with an ethical dilemma: if the counselor treats the pharmacist, they will have a dual relationship, if the counselor refuses treatment and refers the pharmacist, the pharmacist may not find appropriate treatment. In addition to the dual relationship, there may also be a power differential, because the pharmacist could know personal information about the counselor.

Also as described earlier in this chapter, many SUD counselors entered the profession through recovery. For many SUD counselors, abstinence from drugs or alcohol is attributed to ongoing support such as 12-step groups. However, SUD counselors are at risk for developing dual relationships if the recovered counselor participates in the local meetings and former, current, or future clients also attend the meetings (Doukas & Cullen, 2010).

Situations like this complicate the counseling relationship and quite possibly detract from the effectiveness of the 12-step-support meeting. First, the counselor is faced with a dilemma as to whether to acknowledge the client/former client. Acknowledging the client creates legal and ethical problems, as it suggests that the individual was or is in treatment, which threatens the confidentiality of the client. However, not acknowledging the client/former client may damage rapport. In regard to the content of the meeting, the counselor may feel compelled to guard the information that he or she shares in order to protect him/herself, the client, or both. The self-imposed restrictions placed on the counselor may make the ongoing support less effective for all, including the counselor, perhaps increasing the chance of relapse. In the event that the counselor does relapse and shares this information with the group, it may affect the former client, perhaps increasing the likelihood that he or she will also relapse. Furthermore, this situation may create a power differential, as the client may gain personal information about the counselor that changes the client's view of the counselor; or, in the case of the former client, the counselor may exploit the lingering power differential that was created during the counseling relationship. Finally, some counselors may attempt to get their own needs (e.g., friendships, addressing one's own emotional or substance use problems, rescuing others) met through their clients (Doukas & Cullen, 2010). White (2008) also raised concerns about therapist counter-transference, and impairment should the therapist relapse. Clearly, the recovering SUD counselor is faced with a myriad ethical decisions.

SUD counselors who are faced with dual relationships are encouraged to seek supervision, find alternate support for ongoing recovery, look for support from recovery designed for SUD professionals, review ethical codes, and use common sense when engaging in situations that create dual relationships.

Clients and Criminal Activity

SUD counselors are often faced with a dilemma when their clients have or are currently engaged in criminal activities. Aside from the legal and ethical issues that may arise from knowledge of criminal activities, counselors may be torn by their moral values. Because of the nature of the confidential relationship between a counselor and a client, some clients will reveal past criminal acts such as rape and murder. Most ethical codes that apply to counselors indicate that it is ethical to breach confidentiality only if an individual is presently in danger, with the exception of child and/or elder abuse. In other situations, given that the victim has already been victimized, the counselor will not be able to breach confidentiality, as a third party is not currently in danger. Despite state and local laws, or moral obligations, according to *CFR* 42, Part 2, counselors providing SUD counseling are not permitted to report these past crimes. The exception, as previously stated, is when it becomes clear that a client has engaged in activities that are considered child abuse. Counselors are ethically and legally mandated to report child and/or elder abuse.

When clients are currently engaged in criminal activities SUD counselors may be concerned that there is a duty to warn a third party about the client's current or planned acts. Clients dealing illegal drugs are potentially placing others at risk for death. According to the ethical codes and state laws presented earlier, if a third party is in imminent danger, it is the counselor's duty to protect that individual. Also as described earlier, imminent danger is often perceived through the counselor's values and beliefs. Some counselors may believe that the people purchasing the illegal substances are in danger and may feel as though this activity should be reported. Some counselors may feel the need to report based on the illegality of the activity itself. Counselors may also feel that they are faced with a dilemma if a client admits to "lacing" the drugs with toxic substances, either to increase their customers' addiction or to thin out the product to increase the amount that can be sold. In this instance, the counselor may believe that the purchasers are in imminent danger and feel compelled to report the client. However, if the SUD counselor works in a setting that is covered under *CFR* 42, Part 2, the counselor may not be able to report this crime or danger. In fact, the regulation states that the information gained through SUD counseling cannot be used to convict a person of a crime. There are, however, a few instances in which the counselor may be able to report this danger. If the drugs are being sold to identifiable children, this activity could constitute child abuse. Drugs sold on the school premises are a reportable crime as well. This is especially important to recognize in school settings; students who are receiving SUD counseling in a school setting, who also sell drugs to their peers on school grounds, could be reported for committing a crime on the premises.

Conflicting Laws

There are many conflicting federal and state laws that leave counselors in legal and ethical dilemmas. It is the counselor's responsibility to be aware of all the laws and to follow the most stringent law, whether it is a federal or state law. For example, *CFR* 42, Part 2 conflicts with state laws and ethical codes that indicate that counselors have a duty to warn a third party of foreseeable or imminent harm. *CFR* 42 has very strict guidelines for breaking confidentiality; warning a third party is not one of the permissible reasons. A counselor in this situation has four options: (a) obtain a federally sanctioned court order allowing the disclosure, (b) make a disclosure that does not identify the client's status as seeking treatment for SUD, (c) make a limited report to medical personnel, or (d) obtain written informed consent from the client.

Ethical Code Conflicts

Differences among ethical codes can be problematic because some counselors are actually responsible for knowing and adhering to several codes simultaneously. For example, a SUD counselor may belong to ACA and AMHCA and be MAC certified. In this instance, the SUD counselor must follow all three ethical codes associated with these organizations. Although all of these codes are similar, they do vary as well, and therefore the counselor must follow the most restrictive statements across all ethical codes. For example, the ACA *Code of Ethics* (2014) requires that at least 5 years must pass since the termination of counseling services before a counselor can engage in a sexual or romantic relationship with a former client, whereas the NAADAC *Code of Ethics* states that it is never ethical to enter into a sexual or romantic relationship with a former client (NAADAC, 2011b).

ETHICAL DECISION MAKING

In a study of counselor ethical violations, professional competence was identified as the leading violation at 27.6% (Even & Robinson, 2013). Professional competence included practicing outside the training and education of the counselor or practicing while impaired (due to substance use or mental health issues). Professional boundaries, including dual relationships, represented 22.3% of the violations, and breach of confidentiality accounted for 10%. While the aforementioned study included counselors of various specialties, the outcome is reflective of the sorts of issues (i.e., practicing impaired, dual relationships, confidentiality issues) that SUD counselors face. Preventing ethical violations involves the use of ethical decision-making models.

A number of ethical decision-making models are available, but counselors must first determine if they are actually faced with an ethical dilemma. Rubin, Wilson, Fisher, and Vaughn (1992) identified the four characteristics of an ethical dilemma: (a) a choice between two courses of action must be made, (b) there are significant consequences for selecting either course of action, (c) each decision is supported by ethical principles, and (d) the ethical principle of the non-selected action will be compromised.

One decision-making model (Corey, Corey & Callanan, 2011) has eight steps to assist the practitioner in making ethical decisions:

1. Identify the problem.
2. Identify the potential issues involved.
3. Review relevant ethical guidelines.
4. Know relevant laws and regulations.
5. Obtain consultation.
6. Consider possible and probable courses of action.
7. List the consequences of the probable courses of action.
8. Decide on what appears to be the best course of action.

For SUD counselors working in conjunction with a school district, the ASCA ethical code (ASCA, 2010) suggests the use of Stone's (2001) Solutions to Ethical Problems in Schools:

1. Define the problem emotionally and intellectually.
2. Apply the ASCA Ethical Standards and the law.
3. Consider the students' chronological and developmental levels.
4. Consider the setting, parental rights and minors' rights.
5. Apply the moral principles.

6. Determine your potential courses of action and their consequences.
7. Evaluate the selected action.
8. Consult.
9. Implement the course of action.

The decision-making models described here can be slightly altered to assist the SUD counselor with decision making; as an example, we use the ACA *Code of Ethics* decision-making model. Step 1 involves determining if the problem is legal, ethical, professional, or clinical. The second step is to apply to the ACA *Code of Ethics*; however, it might be better stated as consulting the applicable laws and applicable ethical codes, and/or seeking supervision. Often, reviewing the applicable laws and/or ethical codes will reveal a proper course of action. Step 3 involves applying the moral principles of autonomy, nonmaleficence, beneficence, justice, veracity, and fidelity; it also calls for reviewing relevant professional literature and seeking supervision. Step 4 involves brainstorming courses of action with at least one colleague. Step 5 involves reviewing the potential consequences for the generated courses of action and eliminating less useful and/or negative options. Step 6 involves evaluating the selected course of action for ethical or legal dilemmas. Step 7, the final step, is to actually implement the course of action. Using a decision-making model and seeking supervision will ensure that the counselor has considered the legal and ethical issues related to the situation and the best interests of the client, and it will provide a justification for his or her course of action.

When ethical decision making is rooted in a values conflict (Francis & Dugger, 2014; Kaplan, 2014) counselors can use the Counselor Values-Based Conflict Model (CVCM; Kocet & Herlihy, 2014). The CVCM encourages counselors to examine the conflict and determine if it is based on personal values (e.g., cultural, religious, moral) or professional values (e.g., lack of skills or training). The second step involves asking counselors to reflect on the core of the issue and potential barriers to servicing the client. In the third step, counselors need to seek remediation in an effort to provide quality care. The fourth step involves determining and evaluating the available courses of action. Finally, the proposed actions are examined for ensuring that they promote client welfare.

CASE DISCUSSIONS

The three case studies presented in Chapter 1 of the text assist in highlighting potential ethical and/or legal issues facing SUD professionals. At the onset of the counseling relationship, the counselor should have described the client's right to and the limits of confidentiality. Furthermore, the counselor should be aware of the state laws, federal laws, and ethical codes that are applicable to the counseling relationship. Each time we encounter an ethical dilemma, using the criteria described earlier, we will use a decision-making model. To determine whether the ethical concerns are in fact an ethical dilemma, the counselor must answer four questions:

1. Is there a choice between two courses of action?

2. Are there significant consequences for selecting either course of action?
3. Can each decision be supported by ethical principles?
4. Will the ethical principles of the non-selected action be compromised?

Case 1: Sandy and Pam

Possible ethical concerns:

- Pam is emotionally abused by her boyfriend Sam.
- Pam is biracial.

Ethical concern dilemma test:

1. Yes, there is a choice between two courses of action: the counselor could report the emotional abuse or not report the emotional abuse.
2. Yes, if the abuse is reported, Pam may endure more emotional abuse, as she feels "drawn" to Sam and already endures the abuse; if the abuse is not reported, Pam's self-esteem could suffer further, complicating her abuse of drugs and alcohol.
3. Yes, reporting may support beneficence, or doing what is in the best interest of the client; not reporting respects client autonomy.
4. Yes, both beneficence and autonomy are important moral principles at the heart of the counseling profession, but there may have to be a trade-off in this instance.

Now that we have determined that we are faced with an ethical dilemma, we can apply the steps of ethical decision making.

1. Identify the problem:
Her boyfriend is emotionally abusing Pam.
2. Identify the potential issues involved:
Pam may continue to be emotionally abused by her boyfriend, which can be harmful to her emotional well-being.
3. Review relevant ethical guidelines.
Given that SUD professionals may be drawing from any number of ethical codes, it may be helpful to generalize to the principles from which the codes were developed. In this situation, the counselor is faced with the choice to protect client autonomy or to prevent maleficence.
4. Know relevant laws and regulations.
Does the emotional abuse require mandatory reporting or allow the reporting? This question can be thoroughly answered only through a series of questions. Before asking the questions, it is important to note that although Sandy and Pam entered into counseling to repair their relationship with each other and with men, they actually received at least a drug/alcohol abuse screening, possibly

protecting their confidentiality under *CFR* 42, Part 2. The first question in this case is: does the counselor work for an entity that is covered under HIPAA or *CFR* 42, Part 2? If so, it is unlikely that the emotional abuse could be reported without Pam's express written consent. If the answer is no, then is emotional abuse considered abuse under state law? If the answer is no, then the emotional abuse does not have to be reported. If the answer is yes, then the counselor will want to remind the client of the limits of confidentiality and inform Pam that the abuse must be reported. The counselor should clearly state the process and how much information will be revealed. However, if the counselor determined at the onset that this information could not be disclosed to the authorities, due to *CFR* 42 or HIPAA, the dilemma is resolved. The options are limited to (a) not reporting the abuse or (b) obtaining Pam's written consent to report the abuse. If the counselor determines that the client is not covered under *CFR* 42 or HIPAA, the decision needs further review.

5. Obtain consultation.
A colleague may suggest that your best option is to encourage the client to provide consent for reporting Sam with the intention of connecting him with appropriate support. Another colleague may suggest that the counselor respect Pam's autonomy, but provide the client with assurance of support in the course of her relationship.
6. Consider possible and probable courses of action.
 • Report Sam with client consent.
 • Report Sam without client consent.
 • Do not report Sam.
7. List the consequences of the probable courses of action.
 • If the counselor reports Sam with client consent, the counselor will need to provide support to Pam and be aware that the abuse could get worse.

(Continued)

(Continued)

- If the counselor reports Sam without client consent, the counselor risks losing Pam's trust, and the counselor will need to provide support to Pam and be aware that the abuse could get worse.
- If the counselor does not report Sam, Pam's self-esteem could suffer further, possibly increasing her use of drugs/alcohol.

8. Decide on what appears to be the best course of action.

Clearly, this is a complex series of questions. Because of the limits of this chapter, we will assume that each ethical concern described from here on meets the ethical dilemma test.

The other ethical concern for the counselor working with Sandy and Pam is whether the counselor is competent to work with them. Multicultural counseling competence (Arredondo et al., 1996; Sue, Arredondo, & McDavis, 1992) will be ethically necessary to work most effectively with Sandy and Pam, as Pam is a biracial client—her father is African American, and her mother, Sandy, is White. It will be important for the counselor to have an understanding of the values that both Sandy and Pam have regarding counseling, substance use, and treatment.

Case 2: Juanita and Jose

Possible ethical concerns:

- Multicultural issues: Juanita is Mexican, Sarita is Mexican and Hispanic, Jose is Ecuadorian but was raised with American values, and Karen is Mexican and Ecuadorian. Sarita complains of receiving mixed cultural messages.
- Sarita, age 15, and Karen, age 4, are minors.
- When Jose is drunk, he tells Sarita he loves her and is upset that they fight so much. When sober, he yells at her and calls her friends dummies.
- Jose and Juanita think that Sarita needs a stronger hand.

- Karen is visibly sad and withdrawn.
- Jose and Juanita drink alcohol or use drugs when they believe the kids are sleeping.

Based on these ethical concerns, it will be necessary for the counselor to be multiculturally competent. Also, ethically, the counselor will have to follow up on whether Jose is sexually, physically, or emotionally abusing Sarita or Karen. If so, this activity will likely have to be reported. If the counselor is planning to report the abuse, he or she should remind Jose of the limits of confidentiality, and what exactly will be reported, in an effort to maintain the trust of the clients and the counseling relationship. The counselor would also want to explore whether Jose or Juanita become intoxicated when the girls are "sleeping." If they were intoxicated, they would likely be unable to appropriately respond to an emergency situation (e.g., fire), and therefore may be reported for child neglect of their 4-year-old daughter.

Case 3: Leigh

Possible ethical concerns:

- Leigh is a minor, age 16.
- Mom has a temper.
- Leigh is considering running away.

In this situation, it will be important for the counselor to determine whether *CFR* 42 or HIPAA are factors. Because Leigh is a minor, her parents could be entitled to her personal information under HIPAA regulations, but they would not be privy to information under *CFR* 42, without Leigh's written consent. Determining what may or may not be disclosed to the parents will be particularly important if Leigh runs away, as the counselor may know her whereabouts but would be unable to tell her parents. The counselor will also want to explore what Leigh means by Mom having a temper. If Leigh were being abused, this would have to be reported to authorities.

Conclusion

Clearly the SUD counselor is faced with a number of legal and ethical issues. Although many of the codes and laws are similar and support analogous principles, there are important differences, even conflicts. SUD counselors should be aware of applicable laws, codes, and regulations, as they are all designed to protect the client. Lack of awareness can potentially lead to infringement of client rights, harm of the client, or malpractice lawsuits. Ethical decision-making models, such as the ones presented, offer a methodical structure

for reasoning through dilemmas. Using a decision-making model ensures that all options are reviewed, that the counselor consults with other counselors, and that all applicable laws and ethical principles are considered.

Finally, it is important that the SUD professional remain abreast of contemporary laws and ethical codes, as they reflect the current needs of society. Doing so can often be accomplished through participation in continuing education opportunities and organizational affiliations.

MyCounselingLab for Addictions/Substance Use

Try the Topic 13 Assignments: *Ethical and Legal Issues in Substance Use Disorder Counseling.*

Case Study: Jamaal

Jamaal, a 19-year-old college student and Division 1 athlete, scheduled an appointment with a counselor in the College Counseling Center. His intake form reveals that he grew up in a single-family home in an inner-city environment. He describes himself as multiracial. He begins the session by reporting that he is experiencing some anxiety. He describes that he has had a really successful football season thus far, and that his coach has stated that professional football team scouts are expected to be attending some of his upcoming games. Jamaal indicates that he is really excited about the prospect of playing for a professional football team, as that has always been his dream. His excitement, however, is diminished by fears of not performing well enough to be drafted by a professional football team.

He tells the counselor that he has been working out for additional hours each day and is watching his diet carefully, but is concerned that his actions are still not sufficiently preparing him for impressing the team scouts. As he becomes more comfortable with his counselor, he states "on the down-low" that his coach has been supplying him with "something to enhance his performance." Jamaal indicates that he is concerned

that if he does not use the "performance enhancers" that he will not be at the top of his game. On the other hand, he is concerned that if he is caught using the performance enhancers, his professional sports career will be over before it even begins. He further explains that he feels pressured by the coach to use performance enhancement drugs. He does not want to let the coach down and states that the coach probably knows what is in Jamaal's best interest. At times Jamaal wonders if the coach is really looking out for him, or if he is looking to gain team wins to improve his coaching status. After sharing his concerns, Jamaal indicates that his thoughts are consumed with these worries and that he just wants to learn how to not worry.

As the counselor probes Jamaal further, Jamaal reveals that if he does not take the provided performance-enhancing drugs, his coach has suggested that Jamaal will not be "fit enough" to be a starter for all of the games. Jamaal is concerned that if he does not get sufficient field time, he will not be able to impress the scouts. He reports feeling stuck between knowing that it is unacceptable to use performance-enhancing drugs in collegiate and professional football, and being able to perform at the top of his game, and wanting to keep his coach satisfied. He has considered telling someone "in power" that he feels coerced by the coach to use performance-enhancing drugs, but is terrified that he will lose his opportunity for a professional football career. He does not want to lose field time, and does not want his drug use to be revealed. He is also concerned that if he reported the coach, it would be his word against the coach's word, and that he would have to admit to using performance-enhancing drugs. Furthermore, he believes that his teammates would never forgive him and would consider him a snitch. Finally, he is concerned that he would lose his athletic scholarship and that he would need to drop out of college and return home, to a place where he feels that he has a bleak future.

Critical Thinking Questions

1. What are the possible legal issues in this situation?
2. What are the possible ethical issues in this situation?
3. What impact does *CFR* 42 have on the counselor's obligations to the client?
4. What are the personal implications that the counselor may face in this situation?
5. Using the ethical decision-making model, how could this case be resolved?

CHAPTER 3

The Major Substances of Use and Their Effect on the Brain and Body

M. Kristina DePue, Ph.D., NCC and Robert L. Smith, Ph.D., NCC, CFT, FPPR

Drugs are chemicals that affect the brain and the processing of information. When drugs enter the brain, they disrupt its normal processing and change how its internal mechanisms work. These changes can lead to mild to severe substance use with tolerance and dependence. As the result of scientific research, neuroscience, it is realized that severe substance use is a disease that affects both the brain and behavior. The cause or causes of substance use mild to severe, however, are complex, as indicated in the case studies of Leigh, Juanita and Jose, and Sandy and Pam in Chapter 1. We do know that the long-term use of substances does affect the brain and most parts of the body, in many cases leading to an early death.

Research has demonstrated (Licata & Renshaw, 2010) that drug use affects neuronal health, energy, metabolism and maintenance, inflammatory processes, cell membrane turnover, and neurotransmission. These changes are believed to be the neuropathology that leads to the cognitive and behavioral impairments related to drug use. Despite evidence of the effects of substance use on the brain and the body, people's overall attraction to these chemicals remains strong.

Changes in the substances that are used as well as how they are used are consistent themes in the study of substance use. As an example, there continues to be a tendency to inhale rather than to inject substances such as heroin. There has also been a reduction in traditional cigarette use, but an increase in electronic cigarette use. Drug users seek out the easiest access to their system, whether it be an inhalant, an injection, smoking, or in pill form. Trends in both use and creative manufacturing of substances continue, particularly with the club drugs Ecstasy, Rohypnol, and methamphetamine. Over-the-counter drug use and access to and use of prescription drugs are becoming more of an issue in today's world.

All drugs have an effect on the body and brain. This chapter explores some of the physical factors in use—the chemical makeup of the commonly used substances and their effects on the body and brain, including symptoms of tolerance, withdrawal, and overdose. Neuroscience research findings are providing us with more defined information on the damage caused to the brain as the result of substance use. It is also noteworthy that the DSM-5 includes both tolerance and withdrawal as criteria for substance abuse disorders (SUDs); therefore, we highlight these physical effects of substance use in this chapter.

THE BRAIN

The human brain is the command center of the body. After hundreds of millions of years of evolution, the brain possesses various centers or systems that process different kinds of information. The complexity of the brain and its interactions with other systems of the body (e.g., endocrine, muscular, vascular) continue to challenge researchers as they attempt to find causes and more effective treatments for substance use. Neuroscience, the branch of biology that focuses on the body's nervous system including the brain, attempts to shed light on the effects of drug use on the brain and how brain chemistry is changed (Campbell, 2010). The National Institute on Drug Abuse (NIDA) Neuroscience Consortium (NIDA, 2015a), through its research efforts, has established that substance-related use is a brain-based disease. Research findings have focused on identifying the brain mechanisms that underlie drug cravings and reward systems, vulnerabilities to severe use, and the consequences of overusing substances (Gilpin, 2014).

Neuroscience Research

Neuroscience research findings continue to provide evidence of how the brain works and how substances affect the brain (NIDA, 2015a). Technological advances using modern imaging findings on computed tomography (CT), magnetic resonance (MR) imaging, and conventional angiography have allowed researchers to identify the damage to the brain when drug use is present (Geibprasert, Gallucci, & Krings, 2009). The consequences of persistent drug use have become evident and convincing as the result of neuroscience research. Leading the charge in researching drug use is NIDA, with its establishment of the Neuroscience Consortium (2015a). The consortium provides a forum to facilitate the development of neuroscience research programs to understand, prevent, and treat drug use. The goals in basic neuroscience of the NIDA Neuroscience Consortium include:

- Continue and expand molecular structure-function studies to improve definition of molecular sites of used drug action and possible therapeutic targets.
- Determine neurobiological events underlying vulnerability factors in drug taking (environmental, physiological/genetic, and cognitive).
- Determine the neurobiological bases of use as a possible manifestation of learning or memory.
- Extend the mapping of the neuroanatomy and neurochemistry of the brain reward system as it relates to reward, dysphoria, withdrawal, and craving.
- Determine the effects of drug use on neuroendocrine, immune, and autonomic systems.

Throughout this chapter the most recent neuroscience research findings are cited, providing the reader with an update on the effects of drug use and how those effects change the makeup of the brain. Neuroscience research provides us with an understanding of how substances affect brain structure, but also, more importantly, the parts of the brain that have shown the ability to repair themselves following abstinence from substance use.

The Structure of the Brain

The brain itself is a 3-pound mass of gray and white matter, divided into two sections called *hemispheres*. The body of the corpus callosum forms the fissure dividing them and connects them with fibers. The corpus callosum serves as the communication vehicle between the left and right sides of the brain. The left hemisphere controls the right side of the body and is basically concerned with thinking and intellectual functions. It is the site of logic and verbal ability, producing and understanding language. The right hemisphere controls the left side of the body and is considered to be the creative side, involving intuitive and creative processes. The right hemisphere is involved with temporal and spatial relationships, analysis of nonverbal information, and communicating emotion. It uses pictures, while the left hemisphere uses words. The sex of an individual, which is determined hormonally in the brain before birth, influences the development, organization, and basic shape of the brain (Schore, 2014).

As you see, the brain consists of three basic parts: the *hindbrain*, which contains the cerebellum and lower brain stem; the *midbrain*, which houses relay areas from the upper brain stem; and the *forebrain* (see Figures 3.1 and 3.2) (Doherty, Millen, & Barkovich, 2013). Although substance use affects the brain overall, the forebrain houses the mechanisms that most often interact with substances that can cross the blood–brain barrier. The forebrain includes the cerebral hemisphere and the rind or outer covering (about 2 mm thick) called the *cortex*. Activities of a higher state of consciousness take place in the cortex, including thought, perception, motor function, sensory data processing, and vision. Neuroscience research (e.g., Xue, Lu, Levin, Weller, Li, & Bechara, 2009) has used magnetic resonance imaging (MRI) to investigate functional specificity in the medial prefrontal cortex regarding decision making. Results have consistently demonstrated that the relative strengths of signals in the brain indicate the behavioral decisions one makes involving risk and uncertainty. It is noteworthy that neuroscience studies

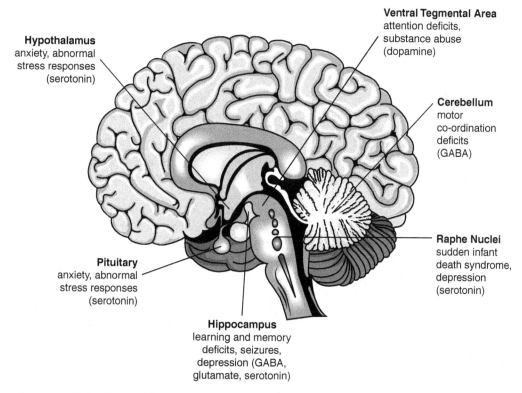

FIGURE 3.1 *Major Parts of the Brain.*

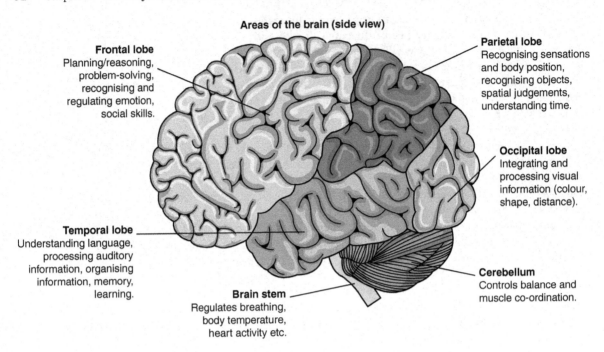

Areas of the brain (side view)

Frontal lobe
Planning/reasoning, problem-solving, recognising and regulating emotion, social skills.

Parietal lobe
Recognising sensations and body position, recognising objects, spatial judgements, understanding time.

Occipital lobe
Integrating and processing visual information (colour, shape, distance).

Temporal lobe
Understanding language, processing auditory information, organising information, memory, learning.

Brain stem
Regulates breathing, body temperature, heart activity etc.

Cerebellum
Controls balance and muscle co-ordination.

FIGURE 3.2 Side View of Brain.

(e.g., Fukunaga, Bogg, Finn, & Brown, 2013) indicate a strong relationship between risky decision making and substance use.

The brain also includes the *limbic system* and the structures of the *diencephalon*, which contains the *thalamus* and the *hypothalamus*. The limbic system lies just below and interconnects with the cortical area. It is involved in emotional behavior and long-term memory, while the hypothalamus regulates more basic, autonomic (primitive) functions such as hormonal activity, thirst, hunger, temperature, sex drive, and sleep. The complexities of the brain's structural and functional systems are becoming better understood through brain imaging and graph theoretical analysis (Kamali et al., 2015).

All these systems of the brain interface in a space about the size of a grapefruit. It accomplishes this through *neuronal* (nerve cell) networking. The brain is composed of an estimated 100 billion neurons (see Figure 3.3), with an astounding range of structural variations and functional diversity found in brain cells that in complex ways are important to cognition, behavior, and psychopathology (NIDA, 2014a). It has long been believed that, unlike most other cells, neurons cannot regrow after damage (except neurons from the hippocampus). This belief is now being challenged (Lau, Yau, & So, 2011). Studies on the regrowth of cells, called neurogenesis, are growing, and evidence suggests that the neuroplasticity of the brain does allow for neuron growth and development after damage. Although previously thought to be stable, adult brains continue to produce neurons in specific areas throughout life and are able to regrow after damage (Fernández-Hernández & Rhiner, 2015).

About one tenth of these neurons are nerve cells that have actual or potential links with tens of thousands of others. Signals are processed by groups of neurons called nuclei areas

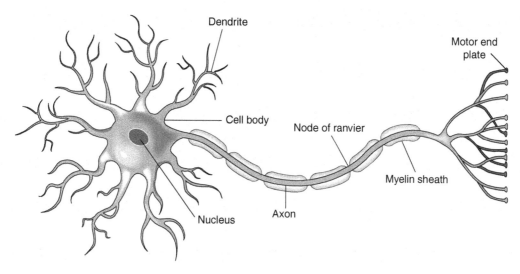

FIGURE 3.3   Diagram of a Neuron.

(Johnson & Kenny, 2010). These groups are cellular clusters that form highly specialized centers. These centers are interconnected by bundles of nerve fibers called *tracts*, which link up the different switchboards of the brain.

The tracts all conduct information in much the same way. Chemical messengers (molecules) called *neurotransmitters* are released by electrical impulses (action potentials) that reach the presynaptic membrane of a given synapse. These pathways can send thousands of electrochemical messages per second and yet work in harmony, because each cell in a tract responds like a complex, microscopic information processor (NIDA, 2014a). It is this process of electrical "blipping" and chemical "dripping" that allows the brain to communicate. Newly sensed experiences (*imprints*) are sifted, rejected, or passed on to appropriate pathways. These imprints are matched to ones already encoded in the data banks directing conscious and unconscious feelings, thoughts, and actions. The bulk of this encoding is stored at an unconscious level.

It is believed that most neurons contain multiple transmitters. The chief chemical messenger may be a neurotransmitter (amine/amino acid), but it acts in conjunction with a neuropeptide to modulate the transmission and/or with a neurohormone to prolong the transmission.

There are several main neurotransmitters involved in substance use: *acetylcholine* (Ach), *dopamine* (DA), *norepinephrine* (NE), *epinephrine* (E), *serotonin* (5-HT), *histamine* (H), and *gamma-aminobutyric acid* (GABA) (see Table 3.1) (Cui et al., 2013; el-Guebaly, Mudry, Zohar, Tavares, & Potenza, 2012). These neurotransmitters discharge from the terminal of one neuron (presynaptic), cross a small gap called the *synapse*, and find their way into "receptor" sites on the adjoining neuron (postsynaptic) (see Figure 3.4). Each neurotransmitter or hormone has a particular shape that allows it to fit into the appropriate receptor site, much like a key fitting into a lock. If the key fits the lock, it will turn on a message in the adjoining neuron. The receptors exhibit a self-regulatory capacity, changing their sensitivity during excessive or infrequent use. The classic neurotransmitters tend to have more than one receptor.

TABLE 3.1 Drugs Related to Neurotransmitters

Drug	Neurotransmitter
Alcohol	Gamma-aminobutyric acid (GABA), serotonin, metenkephalin
Marijuana	Acetylcholine
Cocaine/amphetamines	Epinephrine (adrenaline), norepinephrine (noradrenaline), serotonin, dopamine, acetylcholine
Heroin	Endorphin, enkephalin, dopamine
Benzodiazepines	GABA, glycine
LSD	Acetylcholine
PCP	Dopamine, acetylcholine, alpha-endopsychosine
MDMA (Ecstasy)	Serotonin, dopamine, adrenaline
Nicotine	Adrenaline, endorphin, acetylcholine
Caffeine	Dopamine, norepinephrine

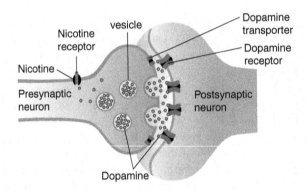

FIGURE 3.4 Diagram of Receptor Cells.

The neurotransmitter interaction functions for the well-being of the individual, ensuring the basic survival of that organism. Survival is accomplished by the recall of memory imprints that have been stored in the neocortex of the brain. These survival skills become more sophisticated as the organism develops and uses them repeatedly in day-to-day functions.

The human brain has many abilities. One of these is the ability to conceptualize and formulate future possibilities, including dangers. In early childhood, the brain forms pathways based on the raw data it receives from the environment. The mind wires up these pathways quickly so that it can avoid or survive potential dangers. For instance, if a child is repeatedly exposed to "fight or flight" situations, whether real or perceived, the association to this stimulus will cause the mind to strengthen developing excitatory pathways. This allows the organism to be more vigilant and foster its survival.

The feeling of pleasure is considered one of the most important emotions connected to survival. Closely connected to this feeling is the brain's reward system, found to be highly associated with drug use (SAMHSA, 2010; Volkow & Baler, 2015). It is produced and regulated by a circuit of specialized nerve cells in a limbic structure called the *nucleus accumbens*. Dopamine-containing neurons relay pleasure messages through this part of the brain via a circuit that spans the brain stem, the limbic system, and the cerebral cortex. Scientists consider this feeling of pleasure or reward to be a strong biological force. If something elicits strong pleasure within the brain, then because of how it is wired, its owner will develop behaviors that will reinforce this good feeling. Basic drives such as eating, sexual activity, and the need for power are activities that evoke rewards in the brain. We learn quickly to reproduce events that bring us pleasure, and such rewards become one of the brain's most powerful learning mechanisms (NIDA, 2014a).

After an overview of brain structure and functioning, the remainder of this chapter focuses on classification systems of substances and the impact that they have on the brain and body. After an introduction on how psychoactive substances affect the brain, the chapter highlights aspects of the following substance classification systems: (a) depressants, (b) stimulants, (c) cannabis, (d) cannabicyclohexanol/Spice/K2, (e) hallucinogens, (f) club drugs, (g) volatile substances/inhalants, and (h) anabolic steroids. It is important to note that some substances fit into more than one category, but we have attempted to explain the substances in an easy-to-understand manner for counselors.

Psychoactive Substances and the Brain

For centuries, the brain has been the recipient of psychoactive substances, often allowing human beings to cope with both internal and external stressors. Substances have offered the user a variety of effects, including pain relief, pleasure, mystical insight, escape, relaxation, stimulation, and ecstasy, as well as a sense of social and spiritual connectedness. It has been proposed that the pursuit of intoxication is as powerful a drive in human beings (and many animal species) as the innate survival drives of hunger, thirst, and sex.

The blood–brain barrier acts to keep certain substances in the blood away from brain cells. Although not well understood, a factor in the barrier is the nonpermeability of capillaries in the brain. Brain capillaries have no pores, preventing water-soluble molecules from passing through capillary walls. Only lipid-soluble substances can pass through the lipid capillary wall. The blood–brain barrier is not completely developed in humans until age 1 to 2 and can be damaged by head trauma or cerebral infection.

Substances are considered psychoactive when they can cross the blood–brain barrier and create changes in the brain and, therefore, in the thinking and behavior of the user. The primary use of psychoactive substances is to change the neurochemistry of the brain and alter one's consciousness. Substances accomplish this by exciting, quieting, or distorting the chemical and electrical state of the brain. Substance use can include intoxicating substances such as ethanol (ethyl alcohol; ETOH), marijuana, crack cocaine, heroin, caffeine, Ecstasy, cannabis, and LSD, which produce rapid neurochemical shifts (8 seconds to 20 minutes), or non-intoxicating substances such as nicotine. Even some foods, such as sugar, act on similar neural pathways as psychoactive substances and can produce feelings of euphoria (Fortuna, 2010).

Specific sites in the brain demonstrate a possible neurochemical basis for the ongoing use of substances. These sites include the *medial forebrain bundle* (MFB), the *ventral tegmental area* (VTA), the *nucleus accumbens*, the *hypothalamus*, and the *locus coeruleus* (LC) (Cui et al., 2013). The hypothalamus houses multiple nerve centers that are necessary for the maintenance of life. Among them is the "pleasure center" that converges with the MFB as well as the nucleus accumbens and the VTA. There is a profuse convergence of cell bodies, axons, and synaptic terminals among these systems. The MFB region has been associated with the positive reinforcement associated with substances of use by the release of dopamine (DA). Likewise, it has been found that several categories of substances have a *synergistic* or an enhancing effect on the brain stimulation reward thresholds that involve the DA system. This includes all major substances of use except some of the hallucinogenics.

Neuroscience studies have clearly shown that abnormalities in the brain are produced by substance use. As an example, Tobias and colleagues (2010) found microstructural abnormalities in white matter underlying and interconnecting prefrontal cortices and hippocampal formation as the result of methamphetamine use.

Of particular interest is the effect of substances on *plasticity*. Plasticity is the ability of brain cells to remember. It is thought, for example, that repeatedly stimulated synapses are changed in function (i.e., they learn; Giedd, 2015). The changes seem to be maintained for extended periods of time. This phenomenon is known as *long-term potentiation* (LTP). *N*-Methyl-D-aspartate (NMDA) receptors are thought to be pivotal in LTP, plasticity, and long-term depression. Repeated exposure to substances create a condition called *excitotoxicity*, which damages and eventually kills NMDA neurons, thus altering plasticity, especially in the developing brains of children and adolescents (Giedd, 2015). With the findings regarding substance damage to the brain, we are also beginning to unlock the secrets of its adaptability or plasticity, with implications for reversing damage as the result of substances and other phenomena (Doidge, 2007).

CONTROLLED SUBSTANCES SCHEDULES

In an effort to stem the growing consumption of both the types and quantity of substances that were being abused in the 1960s, the U.S. Congress passed the Comprehensive Drug Abuse Prevention and Control Act in 1970, establishing the Drug Enforcement Agency (DEA) within the Department of Justice in order to enforce drug policy. Another provision of the act established a schedule of controlled substances that, by federal law, regulates the sale of certain substances. They vary from low potential for abuse with currently accepted medical use (Schedule V) to those with a high potential for moderate to severe substance use and no currently acceptable medical use (Schedule I). Schedule V substances include some over-the-counter medications, whereas Schedule I substances are not generally accepted for medical purposes and include substances such as heroin, LSD, and cocaine. The remainder of the chapter discusses specific classifications of substances that fall into multiple areas of the drug scheduling system. Substances in each classification are presented with their properties, effects, and withdrawal symptoms.

DEPRESSANTS

Depressants of the central nervous system (CNS) include *ethanol, barbiturates, methaqualone* (a prescription depressant that is no longer legal in the United States), *meprobamate* (Librium, sometimes used in alcohol detoxification and a forerunner of Valium), and all *benzodiazepines* (e.g., Valium and Xanax). At usual doses, depressants dampen CNS activity while displaying a weak analgesic effect. CNS depressants such as ethanol are sometimes referred to as "top-down" CNS depressants, because their action begins in the cerebral cortex and works its way "down" to the core or reptilian brain. This action explains why the course of intoxication starts with disinhibition and impaired judgment, moves on to emotional changes and loss of motor skills, and, in cases of severe intoxication referred to as *alcohol poisoning*, ends with coma or death. In the last case, virtually the entire CNS has been put to sleep by the substance, so breathing and heartbeat simply cease.

All substances in this class can cause physical symptoms of tolerance (criterion 10 in the DSM-5) and withdrawal (criterion 11 in the DSM-5), can be lethal in overdose, and demonstrate cross-tolerance and potentiation of one another. *Cross-tolerance* refers to the ability of one classification of substances to produce a tolerance to the effects of another pharmacological classification, and *potentiation* to the ability of the combined action of some substances used together to be greater than the sum of the effects of each substance being used alone. Potentiation is sometimes referred to as *synergistic effect*. Depressants also have the ability to induce severe depression as well as promote extreme anxiety during withdrawal.

Alcohol

Ethyl alcohol (ethanol; ETOH) is a clear liquid with a bitter taste. It can be used as an anesthetic, a poison, a foodstuff, an antiseptic, or a surface blood vessel dilator. It is an unstable CNS depressant that produces euphoria and disinhibition. These well-known side effects, together with the fact that its use is legal for U.S. adults, undoubtedly account for alcohol's popularity. Without question, alcohol is the most used psychoactive substance in existence (SAMHSA, 2014).

INCIDENCE   The National Survey on Drug Use and Health (NSDUH) estimates the prevalence of alcohol use by reporting on participation at three levels. The NSDUH report defines a "drink" as a can or bottle of beer, a glass of wine or a wine cooler, a shot of liquor, or a mixed drink with liquor in it. According to the *Monitoring the Future 2015* report, the prevalence rates of alcohol use were 5% in 8th graders, 11% in 10th graders, and 17% in 12th graders (Johnston, O'Malley, Miech, Bachman, & Schulenberg, 2016). In adults, over 50% of the population engages in alcohol use, with almost 38% of young adults (ages 18–25) engaging in binge drinking (SAMHSA, 2014).

PSYCHOACTIVE EFFECTS   ETOH is a small organic molecule consisting of only two carbon atoms surrounded by hydrogen atoms, with a hydroxyl group attached to one of the carbons (CH_3-CH_2-OH). This molecular arrangement provides ethanol with water-soluble properties as well as lipid- (fat-) soluble properties, which allow it to be more readily absorbed in the bloodstream (Paton, 2015). As it passes the blood–brain barrier after ingestion and affects the cerebral cortex, most people feel their inhibitions quickly disappear and sense a more relaxed social attitude concerning their interactions with others (Sayette et al., 2012). Contrary to the belief of some, alcohol does not improve mental or physical capabilities. Individuals who continue to drink for an extended period of time (two to three drinks per hour for several hours) often disregard their own pain, exhibit poor judgment, and endanger their own or others' safety.

As a depressant, alcohol has a relaxing effect, but also releases one's inhibitions and clouds judgment. Many people erroneously assume that alcohol is a powerful aphrodisiac and a sexual stimulant. The assumption is based on observing people who appear to have a heightened sexual response when drinking. This reaction is due to the disinhibiting factor of ETOH and its immediate influence on the frontal lobes of the brain where the neurochemical mechanisms for exercising judgment are located. This can cause a desire to perform, but a lack of ability to act with sound decision making (i.e., drunk driving, bar fights).

Early thinking was that the primary action of alcohol in the brain included the activation of the endorphin reward system. More recently it has been demonstrated that ethanol has a more complex mechanism.

One issue is the report by many that alcohol stimulates them. This could be caused by the *biphasic* action of ETOH, whereby low levels of the substance activate some neurons.

This notion is consistent with reports that the stimulation of the drinker occurs in the beginning of the drinking cycle. At higher levels of ETOH concentration, the effect on the same nerve cells is reversed. However, biphasic action is only one theory of alcohol mechanism. Evidence has been highlighted in a review article by Volkow, Koob, and McLellen (2016) on the three fundamental neurological effects of alcohol on the brain: (a) a diminished ability to feel pleasure and motivation, (b) an increase in cravings due to conditioned reflexes (i.e., learned responses from the stimulus of alcohol and response of pleasurable feelings) and stress levels (i.e., stress increases when the cravings are not met) in the brain, and (c) negative effects on cognitive functioning, such as decision making. This neuroscience research has begun to help us better understand the effects of alcohol, particularly with reward and pleasure channeling.

Of particular interest is alcohol's effect on two amino acid neurotransmitters, glutamate (Glu), an excitatory transmitter, and gamma-amino butyric acid (GABA). GABA is the major inhibitory transmitter in the brain. The amino acid transmitters are thought to be the major transmitters in the mammalian CNS, but others—serotonin, dopamine, and norepinephrine—have received more attention. Recently, however, the importance of alcohol's effect on Glu and on GABA has been demonstrated. These advances have led to the discovery that alcohol increases the inhibitory activity of GABA and decreases the excitatory activity of Glu receptors, two major ways of suppressing brain activity. The increase in GABA is likely to be a major factor in the general sedation characteristic of alcohol.

Alcohol's effect on glutamate may impair the formation of new memories by suppressing activity at NMDA receptor sites. It is responsible as well for impairing complex thought and judgment while intoxicated. Suppression at NMDA sites may explain alcohol-related memory deficits.

EFFECTS ON THE BODY   A standard drink contains approximately 0.5 ounce of ethyl alcohol. It makes no difference whether that drink is served in a 12-ounce can of beer, a 4- or 5-ounce glass of wine, or a single shot (about 1.5 ounces) of 80-proof, distilled spirits (Friedmann, 2013). A standard drink is the measure used to compute blood alcohol levels.

Blood alcohol level (BAL) or blood alcohol concentration (BAC) is measured in milligrams per 100 milliliters of blood (e.g., 80 mg/100 mL), but it is more often expressed as a percentage of blood ethanol (0.08 BAC). Either of the foregoing examples represents the level of legal intoxication in most states and requires the consumption of roughly three standard drinks within 1 hour to achieve this status.

One ounce of pure ethyl alcohol contains about 210 calories that can convert to energy at the cellular level, but it contains no nutrients to nourish the cell. It can pass through every tissue cluster in the brain and body if enough is consumed. Immediately after drinking, the mouth and esophagus begins to absorb small amounts via the mucous membranes. The stomach will rapidly assimilate about one-quarter of a dose, followed by complete absorption through the walls of the small intestine within 20 to 30 minutes.

The cardiovascular system is affected by low doses of alcohol through the dilation of peripheral blood vessels, whereas severe alcohol intoxication will create a depression of the entire cardiovascular system. Alcohol irritates the gastrointestinal tract through direct contact, as well as by stimulating the secretion of stomach acid and pepsin, which can cause gastritis and injury to the mucous membranes of the stomach lining. The presence of food can modify these effects to some extent and also slows the absorption rate of alcohol. Because alcohol is a diuretic, it overstimulates the production of urine in the kidneys.

The liver, the body's largest glandular organ, is associated with dozens of processes of body chemistry and metabolism. It is the primary organ of alcohol detoxification. This 3-pound organ is the central filter for the blood and is the site of 90% of alcohol metabolism. The major pathway for such conversion involves the enzyme *alcohol dehydrogenase* and occurs in two phases in the liver. The first phase produces the metabolite *acetaldehyde*, and the second converts acetaldehyde to *acetic acid*. With continued heavy intake of alcohol, the liver cells begin to accumulate fatty deposits that destroy the cells and produce scarring called *cirrhosis*. This disease occurs in, and is fatal to, about 10% of chronic alcoholic patients.

Nearly every organ in the body is affected by heavy use of alcohol. Gastritis, diarrhea, and gastric ulcers are commonly associated with heavy drinking. A single heavy drinking episode can cause the pancreas to hemorrhage. The consumption of large amounts of alcohol can depress the respiratory center in the medulla, causing death. Alcohol can be deadly for individuals with epilepsy because it can promote convulsive seizures due to a hyperexcitable rebound condition in the brain after drinking has ceased.

Strong evidence indicates links between alcohol and cancers that occur in the upper digestive tract, respiratory system, mouth, pharynx, larynx, esophagus, and liver (Nelson et al., 2013). There is a possible link between alcohol and cancer of the pancreas, stomach, large intestine, rectum, and breast (Nelson et al., 2013). Alcohol ingested with cocarcinogens such as tobacco is believed to account for some of the cancer deaths that occur in the United States (American Cancer Society, 2010).

Besides liver damage (cirrhosis), alcoholics may develop pathology of the nervous system due to vitamin deficiencies, as well as experience neurological complications such as the Wernicke-Korsakoff syndrome (Hermens et al., 2013). This chronic brain syndrome is the result of thiamin deficiency from poor absorption, metabolism, and storage of the vitamin in the prolonged presence of alcohol, as well as poor diet while drinking. It has as its most striking feature a dementia characterized by permanent short-term memory loss coupled with filling in the blanks of memory with exaggerated stories.

TOLERANCE AND WITHDRAWAL   In the presence of repeated drinking, tolerance to the effects of alcohol begins as the body adapts to try to maintain its normal functioning in the continual presence of a foreign chemical. The liver becomes more efficient in detoxifying alcohol, the cells of the brain become less and less sensitive to the intoxicating effects of the chemical, and the chronic drinker exhibits fewer of the behavioral effects of intoxication. However, while brain cells may be less sensitive, damage continues unabated to the brain and organs such as the liver.

Risk of severe alcohol substance disorder, both physically and psychologically, is moderate to high. The etiology is complicated and appears to be affected by such factors as genetics, biological changes, brain reward systems, and stress relief mechanisms. It is suggested that the younger the onset of drinking, the greater the chance of that person developing a clinically defined alcohol disorder (Scott-Sheldon, Carey, Elliott, Garey, & Carey, 2014).

The acute withdrawal syndrome generally appears within 12 to 72 hours after drinking has ceased. The earliest signs of withdrawal are associated with *hyperarousal* and can include anxiety, irritability, insomnia, loss of appetite, tachycardia (rapid heartbeat), and tremulousness. An "eye-opener" (i.e., a drink first thing in the morning) is a common solution to hyperarousal for the problem drinker. Hence, alcohol use interviews commonly include a question concerning morning drinking. *Alcoholic hallucinosis* occurs in about 25% of withdrawal episodes, usually within the first 24 hours. It includes true auditory and visual hallucinations, illusions, and misperception of real environmental stimuli. *Convulsive seizures*, or "rum fits," can occur with acute alcohol withdrawal. These seizures are most often of the grand mal variety, in which the eyes roll back in the head; body muscles contract, relax, and extend rhythmically and violently; and loss of consciousness occurs. About a third of alcoholics who have seizures in withdrawal develop delirium tremens. *Delirium tremens*, or DTs, is the most serious form of withdrawal. Without medical intervention, mortality rates are as high as 20%. With medical help, there still remains a 1% to 2% death rate. Benzodiazepines have worked as a prophylactic for DTs. In addition, these medications can mitigate the anxiety and irritability of hyperarousal. However, because of the potential for cross-addiction, they must be prescribed judiciously. Chlordiazepoxide (Librium), which was the prototype for benzodiazepines, has been used to manage acute withdrawal, because it has a lower potential for mild to severe use than other substances of its type. It is also noteworthy that toxic and lethal effects can occur with alcohol use. For example, comas can occur at BALs of 0.40%. Alcohol becomes lethal in higher concentrations by depressing the respiratory center in the medulla.

GENDER DIFFERENCES   Early studies on the effects of alcohol had only men as subjects, based on the assumption that their findings could be generalized to women. However, it has been found that, under standard conditions, BALs in women can reach higher levels, for several reasons. First, men have a greater average body water content (65% ± 2%) than women (51% ± 2%). Since alcohol is absorbed into total body water, a standard dose of alcohol will be therefore more concentrated in women. Second, women have a lower level of gastric alcohol dehydrogenase (ADH), thus metabolizing significantly less than men under standard conditions (Baraona et al., 2001). Women have fewer alcohol-related deaths than men, which occur from brain damage, diabetes, cirrhosis, and cancers (Rehm & Shield, 2010). Women also have lower levels (i.e., frequencies) of alcohol use disorders than men, although the exact nature of this relationship is relatively unknown, as gender does not predict alcohol use disorders in statistical analyses (Goldstein, Smith, Dawson, & Grant, 2015).

FETAL ALCOHOL SYNDROME   Alcohol ingested during pregnancy easily passes through the placental barrier and can result in fetal alcohol syndrome (FAS). Doctors first recognized and reported FAS in 1973 as a pattern of birth defects emerged in children born to alcoholic mothers, and before that time, drinking during pregnancy was not viewed negatively (Warren, 2015). Since that time, numerous reports (e.g., Alvik, Aalen, & Lindemann, 2013; Huebner, Tran, Rufer, Crump, & Smith, 2015; Memo, Gnoato, Caminiti, Pichini, & Tarani, 2013) have established ethanol as a *teratogenic* agent, producing defects in utero. The intellectual disabilities associated with FAS are preventable; however, current cases of FAS are costing up to $5.4 billion per year in health and education services in the United States (Popova, Stade, Bekmuradov, Lange, & Rehm, 2011). In fact, more than 2 million U.S. women are at risk for pregnancies resulting in FAS (Cannon et al., 2015). FAS is characterized by distinct symptoms that can generally be observed in the newborn. The child will exhibit fetal growth retardation and is at risk for craniofacial deformities, central nervous system damage, and major organ malformations. A high percentage, 80% to 90%, will exhibit cognitive delays, which are permanent (Memo et al., 2013). The symptoms can range from gross *morphological* defects (defects to the structure or form of the body) to subtler cognitive–behavioral problems.

Fetal alcohol effects (FAE) have been associated with moderate prenatal drinking. The typical symptoms of hyperactivity, distractibility, impulsiveness, and short attention spans are similar to attention deficit hyperactivity disorder (ADHD). However, children with FAS or FAE are more intellectually impaired than ADHD-diagnosed children. Technology continues to improve to help identify and assess children with fetal alcohol spectrum disorder (FASD) (Drake, 2009).

Benzodiazepines: Prescription and Over-the-Counter Medications

Benzodiazepines, sometimes called tranquilizers or psychotherapeutics and include substances such as diazepam (Valium), chlordiazepoxide HCl (Librium), and alprazolam (Xanax), are the most widely prescribed group of substances in the treatment of anxiety, acute stress reactions, and panic attacks. Unfortunately, these prescription substances often lead to substance use disorders (SAMHSA, 2014). After about 4 to 6 months of daily use, users of benzodiazepines are at high risk of a substance-related disorder diagnosis (Doweiko, 2014). Sedating benzodiazepines, such as triazolam (Halcion) and estazolam (ProSom), are prescribed for short-term treatment of sleep disorders. Although commonly prescribed and considered less lethal than the barbiturates, they are supposed to be used only for brief periods of time (Hood, Norman, Hince, Melichar, & Hulse, 2012). Many are capable of achieving a daytime anxiolytic response without excessive drowsiness. However, substances from the benzodiazepine family can interfere with the normal sleep cycle, and upon withdrawal after prolonged use, the patient may experience rapid eye movement (REM) rebound, with a greatly increased need for REM sleep, often accompanied by vivid, frightening dreams.

Xanax, as a CNS depressant, remains the most popular adult prescription drug that ends up being used by children and adolescents (Johnston et al., 2016). *Xanbars*, *french fries*, and *footballs* are terms used to describe individual doses of Xanax by youthful users who favor the drug because of its portability, ease of access and concealment, and its euphoric effect. Like many prescription drugs, Xanax has been a prescribed drug that can be easy for youngsters to obtain from parents' medicine cabinets or friends.

INCIDENCE The incidence of benzodiazepine use depends partly on the definition of substance use. If the criterion is any nonmedical use (i.e., without a prescription), then benzodiazepine use is common. In 2013, there were 1.7 million users (ages 12 or older) of benzodiazepines, also called tranquilizers in many reports (SAMHSA, 2014). The prevalence of these psychotherapeutics peaked in 2001 and 2002 and has progressively decreased in 8th, 10th, and 12th graders, with current use levels at 1.7%, 3.9%, and 4.7% of the population (Johnston et al., 2016). Among adults, nonmedical use of prescription drugs is the second highest illicit substance used, and past-year use prevalence equated to about 4.8% of the population in 2013 (SAMHSA, 2014).

It is known that taking these substances beyond how they are prescribed can affect the body and brain. Neuroscience research has demonstrated the effects on the brain through altering the reward system and thus increasing a craving for over-the-counter drugs (Tan et al., 2010).

PSYCHOACTIVE EFFECTS There are more than a dozen varieties of benzodiazepines. The most notorious and controversial are diazepam (Valium), chlordiazepoxide (Librium), and triazolam (Halcion). Benzodiazepines have been prescribed for a number of reasons. Alprazolam (Xanax) has been found effective in the treatment of panic attacks. Benzodiazepines are considered effective in the short-term treatment of anxiety, regardless of the cause. Short-term effects can include a "sleepy" and uncoordinated feeling during the first few days, as the body becomes accustomed to the substance. Long-term use has the potential for both tolerance and withdrawal (DEA/OD/ODE, 2013).

A very potent benzodiazepine, flunitrazepam (Rohypnol), manufactured by Hoffman La Roche, which also manufactures Librium and Valium, has a rapid onset. Although not approved for sale in the United States, flunitrazepam looks like a legal prescription drug because it is typically distributed in the manufacturer's bubble pack. A 2-mg standard dose of Rohypnol is approximately equivalent to 20 mg of Valium. It produces a dreamy stupor. A characteristic of Rohypnol is that it can be added to a drink without affecting the taste, but compounding the effect of alcohol and producing a comatose state of anterograde amnesia (Baldwin et al, 2013). Rohypnol quickly gained a reputation as a "date rape" drug.

EFFECTS ON THE BODY   Gamma-aminobutyric acid (GABA) is considered the most important inhibitory neurotransmitter in the brain (Baldwin et al., 2013). CNS depressants slow brain activity through actions on the GABA system and, therefore, produce a calming effect. Benzodiazepines produce CNS depression by enhancing the effects of gamma-aminobutyric acid, and thus decreasing brain activity (Drug Enforcement Administration, 2013). Receptor sites become more sensitive to GABA. This inhibitory action produces anxiolytic, anticonvulsant, and sedative effects, useful in treating seizures, short-term insomnia, preoperative sedation and anesthesia, and anxiety disorders.

Benzodiazepines are lipid-soluble and absorbed into the gastrointestinal tract after oral ingestion. They can also pass the blood–brain barrier and the placental barrier. Peak effects from use occur within 2 to 4 hours. By virtue of their specific recognition sites, the benzodiazepines act by potentiating the action of GABA, which increases neural inhibition (Drug Enforcement Administration, 2013).

The half-life of benzodiazepines can vary from 1.5 to 5.5 hours (Halcion) to 18 to 30 hours (Klonopin). Faster-acting compounds tend to promote a conditioned response in the brain by positively reinforcing through the rapid onset of the effect, whereas a shorter half-life contributes to this response by negatively reinforcing avoidance of withdrawal (Allain, Minogianis, Roberts, & Samaha, 2015). Benzodiazepines are classified by their duration of action that ranges from less than 6 hours to more than 24 hours. Some of the benzodiazepines have active metabolites that can prolong their effects (Drug Enforcement Administration, 2013).

TOLERANCE AND WITHDRAWAL   Benzodiazepines, like alcohol and barbiturates, are CNS depressants. Frequent chronic use can cause tolerance and withdrawal syndromes (Doweiko, 2014). Yet, benzodiazepines are not as reinforcing as many other substances; that is, they do not produce the euphoric effect that is the main attraction of substances use for most people. A history of substance use disorders increases risk for benzodiazepine use disorders (McCabe, Cranford, & West, 2008)). Benzodiazepines are often misused along with alcohol. In addition, early nonmedical use of medications has been found to predict later substance use disorders involving prescription drug use (McCabe, West, Morales, Cranford, & Boyd, 2007).

Withdrawal symptoms from low dosages of benzodiazepines can allow symptom reemergence (a return of the symptoms, such as anxiety or panic attacks, for which the benzodiazepines were originally prescribed). For others, including those on higher doses, withdrawal symptoms may include anxiety, mood instability, sleep disturbance, agitated depression, seizures, or schizophrenia (Baldwin et al., 2013). It is important for treatment to differentiate between symptom reemergence and withdrawal symptoms. Over time, withdrawal symptoms gradually subside. Despite the half-life of some of these, withdrawal symptoms may persist for weeks. In addition, chronic consumers of high doses of benzodiazepines may be at risk for severe, perhaps life-threatening, withdrawal symptoms.

Although benzodiazepines are most commonly used for reduction of anxiety or sleep induction, on the street they are often self-administered by individuals with SUDs to reduce symptoms of withdrawal from heroin, alcohol, and other substances or to lessen the side effects of cocaine or methamphetamine intoxication (Maldonado, Nguyen, Schader, & Brooks, 2012).

Individuals can also use benzodiazepines to enhance the effects of heroin, alcohol, or marijuana because of the potentiation effects with these substances.

GENDER DIFFERENCES A growing number of individuals aged 12 to 25 of both genders are using benzodiazepines. However, incidence rates indicate that males are more likely to struggle with tranquilizer use disorders than females (Lev-Ran, Le Strat, Imtiaz, Rehm, & Le Foll, 2013).

Barbiturates

"Street people" first viewed barbiturates as substances of use. However, benzodiazepines (e.g., Halcion, Librium, Valium, Xanax, Rohypnol) have largely replaced short-acting barbiturates (e.g., Amytal, Nembutal, Luminal, Surital) in therapeutic medicine, as well as on the streets. Furthermore, controls have been placed on the availability of barbiturates, listing them as II, III, or IV on the DEA Controlled Substances Schedule. They are still present in today's society, however, and deserve a cursory look.

INCIDENCE From 1950 to 1970, barbiturates were second only to alcohol as substances of use, with a prevalence rate of 10.7%. From 1975 to 1992, there was a significant decline in barbiturate use, dropping to a prevalence rate of 2.8%, and a continued decline has been observed since then (Johnston et al., 2016). Although abuse of barbiturates has decreased significantly as benzodiazepines have largely replaced them in medical use for insomnia and anxiety, certain populations continue to use them. Among individuals 40 and older, subgroups became severe users when they were younger, sometimes through prescribed barbiturates.

PSYCHOACTIVE EFFECTS Barbiturates are used medically for their anesthetic, sedative, hypnotic, and anticonvulsant effects. They are short-acting sedative-hypnotics that can be administered as recreational substances orally or by injection to produce intoxication similar to that of alcohol. This intoxicated state produces "disinhibition," elevated mood, a reduction of negative feelings and negative self-concept, and an increase in energy and confidence. The euphoric mood can shift quite suddenly to sadness. Someone who is intoxicated on barbiturates may possess an unsteady gait, slurred speech, and eye twitching and may exercise poor judgment.

The most commonly used barbiturates include thiopental (sodium pentothal), amobarbital (Amytal), pentobarbital (Nembutal), secobarbital (Seconal), amobarbital in combination with secobarbital (Tuinal), butabarbital (Butisol), and phenobarbital (Luminal). On the street, the drug may be assigned a name that correlates with the color of the capsule, such as *yellow jackets* (Nembutal), *red birds* (Seconal), or *rainbows* (Tuinal).

Barbiturates are a lipid-soluble compound, which allows them to pass the blood–brain barrier. They are also capable of passing the placental barrier and affecting the fetus. Barbiturates depress the CNS and inhibit neuronal activity, ranging from anxiety reduction to coma. This depressant action is achieved by potentiation of GABAergic transmission, which creates a diminished calcium ionic channel action resulting in a decreased state of neurotransmitters. Barbiturates also reverse the action of glutamate, which induces depolarization and adds to the CNS depression. Barbiturates and any of the other CNS depressants, such as narcotic-based analgesics, benzodiazepines, or alcohol, potentiate each other's effects, causing dangerous combinations or even death. In potentiation, each substance interferes with the biotransformation of the other chemical by the liver, allowing for the toxic effects of each substance to be at a higher level than expected from each substance alone.

As noted earlier, barbiturates, being mostly replaced by sedative-hypnotics and benzodiazepines, have declined in use. Research on barbiturates use has waned over time, with studies examining side effects of other medications containing this substance. Some studies have found that a number of medications containing barbiturates or narcotics used to relieve migraine headaches actually made migraines worse, particularly when there is an overdose (Staff, 2009).

NONBARBITURATE SEDATIVE-HYPNOTICS   Other sedative-hypnotics that have a potential similar to barbiturates include Quaalude, chloral hydrate, and meprobamate. Methaqualone (Quaalude) is chemically distinct from the barbiturates but is an example of a substance approved by the U.S. Food and Drug Administration (FDA) that became a severe social hazard. Through its depression of the CNS, a dramatic reduction in heart rate, respiration, and muscular coordination may result from its use.

TOLERANCE AND WITHDRAWAL   Like all sedative-hypnotic substances, barbiturates can create tolerance in the user with a single dose. Although tolerance to barbiturates builds quickly, it is not uniform to all of its actions. For example, those taking a barbiturate for control of epileptic seizures may develop tolerance to its sedative effects but not to the anticonvulsant effect.

Withdrawal symptoms generally begin 12 to 24 hours after the last dose and peak in intensity between 24 and 72 hours. These symptoms include anxiety, tremors, nightmares, insomnia, anorexia, nausea, vomiting, delirium, and seizures. Death from overdose can occur through respiratory arrest when centers of the brain that control oxygen intake are severely depressed.

GHB (Identified as a Club Drug)

GHB (gamma-hydroxybutyrate) is a metabolite of GABA, an inhibitory neurotransmitter, and a naturally occurring depressant. Dr. Henri Labroit, a French researcher, synthesized GHB in 1960. With the ability to rapidly produce a deep coma, GHB became popular in Europe as an over-the-counter sleep aid. However, GHB seemed to cause neurological problems. That, coupled with its failure to alleviate pain, prevented GHB from being marketed for its original intended use as a surgical anesthetic. GHB acts on at least two sites in the brain: the GABAB receptor and a specific GHB binding site (NIDA, 2014c).

GHB can be produced in clear liquid, white powder, tablet, and capsule forms. It is typically marketed as a liquid in a small, sometimes brightly colored plastic bottle. The cap is used for dosing. GHB has over 80 street names. Some of the more popular are *liquid Ecstasy, easy lay, grievous bodily harm, soap, salty water,* and *Georgia home boy.* Other names associated with GHB include *Bedtime Scoop* and *Cherry Meth.* Analogs, such as GBL (gamma-butyrolactone), are marketed as blue nitro, gamma-G, renewtrient, or reviverent. GHB has been increasingly involved in poisonings, overdoses, date rapes, and fatalities.

INCIDENCE   GHB has been used predominantly by adolescents and young adults, along with other party drugs like Ecstasy and ketamine when attending nightclubs and raves. It is often manufactured in homes with recipes and ingredients found and purchased on the Internet. Because of its rapid resolution in the body and limited testing capabilities, along with its sedative effect accompanied by anterograde amnesia, GHB use is believed to be underreported. However, GHB and its analogs, GBL and BD (1,4-butanediol), have gained popularity as a club drug. The typical user is an 18- to 25-year-old White (94%) male (79%) and either a bodybuilder or someone attending a rave or party. GHB use has been on the decline. The 2015 *Monitoring the Future* report stated the 2011 prevalence of GHB use in 12th graders to be 1.7% of the population, and 2015 prevalence to have decreased to 0.7% in 12th graders (Johnston et al., 2016).

PSYCHOACTIVE EFFECTS   GHB is a precursor of the GABA that acts on the dopaminergic system. GBL and BD, ingredients in GHB, can also be converted by the body into GHB. These ingredients are found in a number of dietary supplements available in health food stores and gymnasiums to induce sleep, build muscles, and enhance sexual performance. GBL is widely available as an organic solvent used for cleaning circuit boards, stripping paint, or flavoring soy products.

GHB is a central nervous system depressant. Intoxication, increased energy, happiness, talking, desire to socialize, feeling affectionate and playful, mild disinhibition, sensuality, and enhanced sexual experience are reported effects at low doses. At higher doses it can slow breathing and heart rate to dangerous levels. GHB's intoxicating effects begin 10 to 20 minutes after the drug is taken. The effects typically last up to 4 hours, depending on the dosage.

EFFECTS ON THE BODY   GHB is unpredictable and dose-sensitive. At lower doses, GHB can relieve anxiety and produce relaxation. It can also produce blurred vision, stumbling, dizziness, and loss of gag reflex. As the dose increases, the sedative effects may result in unconsciousness within 15 minutes and coma within 30 to 40 minutes. Severe cases present a triad of symptoms: coma, bradycardia (slowing of the heart rate), and myoclonus (brief, involuntary twitching of a muscle or a group of muscles) (Brunt, Koeter, Hertoghs, van Noorden, & van den Brink, 2013). Anterograde amnesia is common, thus making GHB a dangerous date rape drug along with Rohypnol and ketamine.

TOLERANCE AND WITHDRAWAL   GHB is difficult to detect and is often taken with other substances that produce similar symptoms. One can develop a tolerance where individuals need more of the substance to produce the desired high. Withdrawal includes profuse diaphoresis (sweating), anxiety attacks, dangerously elevated blood pressure, and rapid pulse (van Noorden, van Dongen, Zitman, & Vergouwen, 2009). Often, these symptoms subside after 3 days or in response to medical treatment. Hallucinations and an altered mental state may be delayed until day 4 or 5, often after a seemingly well patient has been released from medical care.

TOXIC AND LETHAL EFFECTS   Other effects of GHB include nausea and vomiting (Brunt et al., 2013). These can be especially dangerous when the user is comatose, as the gag reflex is also depressed. Adverse effects are potentiated by alcohol, ketamine, and benzodiazepines, and methamphetamine use increases the risk of seizure. Overdose can result in death by itself or as a complication of a number of factors.

Opiates

Opium is derived from the poppy flower (*Papaver somniferum*). It possesses a variety of pharmacological activities that have been studied by scientists for years. The main active ingredient is *morphine alkaloid*, which is widely used because it is the most effective and most powerful painkiller (analgesic) available. Besides pain relief, other effects and signs of use include euphoria, drowsiness, constricted pupils, nausea, possible respiratory distress, coma, and death. Derivatives include heroin, codeine, hydromorphone (Dilaudid), hydrocodone (Hycodan), oxymorphone (Numorphan), and oxycodone (Percodan), as well as a number of synthetic medical compounds, including meperidine (Demerol), methadone (Dolophine), fentanyl (Sublimaze), and propoxyphene (Darvon). At least 20 substances are available in the United States whose opioid actions may differ in the way they are absorbed, metabolized, and eliminated from the body. An extended-release version of oxycodone (OxyContin) was created in the 1990s that produced widespread use and resulted in many opioid use disorders—to the extent that, in 2010, an abuse-deterrent formulation (ADF; pills that were difficult to crush) was created (Cicero & Ellis, 2015). Although some reports (e.g., Cicero & Ellis, 2015) argued that the ADF version reduced the levels of OxyContin use in the United States, SAMHSA (2014) survey results have remained stable since 2004 with the use of OxyContin in individuals ages 12 and older.

INCIDENCE   In 2013 there were 169,000 persons aged 12 and older who had used heroin for the first time within the past year (SAMHSA, 2014). This was significantly greater than the average annual number from previous years. The 2015 *Monitoring the Future* report marked prevalence rates for heroin use in 8th, 10th, and 12th graders as 0.2%, 0.2%, and 0.3%, with significant declines observed in 8th and 10th graders (Johnston et al., 2016). Heroin appears to be gaining in popularity again, especially among the young, who may be lured by inexpensive, high-purity heroin that can be sniffed or smoked instead of injected. Use of OxyContin, an opioid prescribed for pain, among adolescents is a concern because of its ability to develop rapid tolerance in the user. In 2013 the number of new nonmedical users of OxyContin aged 12 or older was 436,000, with an average age of first use at 22.3 years. These estimates are similar to those reported from 2004–2012 (SAMHSA, 2014).

PSYCHOACTIVE EFFECTS   Injection continues to be the predominant method of heroin use, with intravenous injection providing the greatest intensity and most rapid onset of euphoria (7 to 8 seconds). The taking of heroin via a needle has revealed a small, but statistically significant decrease since the 1990s (Johnston et al., 2016). Intramuscular injection produces euphoria in 5 to 8 minutes, whereas sniffing or smoking requires 10 to 15 minutes for peak effects to occur. Although nasal ingestion does not produce as intense or as rapid a rush, all forms of heroin administration are subject to rapid tolerance and dose increase.

Recent scientific demonstration of receptors in the central nervous systems of both animals and humans, followed by the discovery that the body makes its own opiate-like substances, has greatly enhanced the understanding of the action of opioids (Dacher & Nugent, 2011; Zhang & Pan, 2010). Administered opioids are thought to act at the neuronal synapses, either by acting as a neurotransmitter decreasing the transsynaptic potential or by modulating the release of a neurotransmitter postsynaptically. This appears to be the basis of their analgesic effect and may be similar to the action of the body's endogenous opioids.

EFFECTS ON THE BODY   It is believed that chronic morphine use produces marked structural changes in the dopamine neurons in the brain's ventral tegmental area (Liu et al., 2013). In research studies with rats, injections that targeted opioid stimulation produced effects of increased wanting and liking of the cue/stimulation. Thus, the opioids cause an effect in the brain that increases the desire to use the substance, which leads to continuing substance use (Peciña & Berridge, 2013).

TOLERANCE AND WITHDRAWAL   Users of opioids have a high risk of severe substance-related disorders. Physiological tolerance results from brain changes after prolonged use, while psychological tolerance is a result of linking learned associations between substance effects and environmental cues. These phenomena of tolerance (neuroadaption) to opioids appear to be receptor site–specific. Endogenous molecules have been identified with opioid activity, and at least 12 peptides have been discovered, including the beta-endorphins and dynorphins. These long-chain peptides are believed to bind to their own specific opioid receptors. Stimulation of opioid receptors located in critical cells, such as those located in the locus coeruleus, produces a decrease in cell firing, ultimately causing the cells to become hyperexcitable. Markers for potential dependence have been recently investigated. An article titled "Naloxone 'Reboots' Opioid Pain-Relief System" (2010) identified self-reported craving as a potential marker for individuals at risk for opioid medication misuse.

Tolerance to opioids can develop quite rapidly in frequent users, and experiments have verified that a clinical dose of morphine (60 mg a day) in an individual can be increased to 500 mg per day in as little as 10 days. Over time, the brain substitutes administered chemical opiates for natural endorphins, causing effects such as euphoria to become less intense. As the body accommodates to the presence of chemical opioids, long-term use produces a "threshold effect," after which time the chronic opioid user will use the substance just to function in a normal state, no longer getting high.

The symptoms of withdrawal from opioids include feelings of dysphoria, nausea, repeated yawning, sweating, tearing, and a runny nose. It is during this period that subjects experience craving or "drug hunger" for repeated exposure to the drug. The symptoms of opiate withdrawal are the result of interactions between the opioid and other neurotransmitter systems.

OVERDOSE   Mortality figures indicate that death by overdose of heroin/morphine is highly prevalent throughout the nation (Lopez-Quintero et al., 2015). This phenomenon occurs because an important effect of narcotics is to depress the respiratory center's response to blood levels of carbon dioxide. In addition, this effect is additive with alcohol or other sedative-hypnotics, which increases the danger of fatal overdose. Naloxone (Narcan), a narcotic antagonist, is administered for emergency medical treatment of overdose. Overdose on narcotics may be diagnosed by observation of the *narcotic triad*: coma, depressed respiration, and pinpoint pupils. In addition, the number of users of opioid analgesics increased 4,680% from 1996 to 2011, with oxycodone increasing 146% (Atluri, Sudarshan, & Manchikanti, 2013). The increased availability of this pain medication is correlated with an increase in its use. The number of admissions for opioid detoxification, particularly oxycodone, at medical centers has increased 87% over the past few years, with physician prescriptions identified as the main source for obtaining this opioid (Atluri et al., 2013). Comorbid pain, psychiatric symptoms, and use of other substances complicate the treatment of oxycodone users. This schedule II compound produces effects similar to morphine. Researchers state that excessive use can produce cognitive and psychomotor impairment (Højsted, Ekholm, Kurita, Juel, & Sjøgren, 2013). Hassan and colleagues (2010) studied gene expression in brain tissues of rats treated with high doses of oxycodone. Based on their findings, they believe that global changes in gene expression in the brain may be possible with the excessive use of this opioid by humans.

STIMULANTS

This section focuses on substances of arousal, which include all forms of cocaine, amphetamine, prescription weight-reducing products, amphetamine-like substances such as methylphenidate (Ritalin), some over-the-counter (OTC) weight-reducing substances, and the minor stimulant substances nicotine and caffeine. The potential difficulties with frequent use of these substances include possible overdoses, tolerance, psychoses, severe depressions, and all anxiety syndromes, including panic attacks and obsessions. Stimulants were historically used to treat asthma (respiratory problems), obesity, and neurological disorders and to increase alertness, attention, and energy. They also elevate blood pressure and increase heart rate and respiration. Stimulants, such as Dexedrine, Adderall, and Ritalin, that are often prescribed for attention deficit disorder (ADD) and attention deficit hyperactivity disorder (AHDH) have been frequently misused by people other than the one for whom they were prescribed.

Minor psychoactive stimulants include caffeine and nicotine. These substances are considered minor because they can induce and exacerbate anxiety but usually are not capable of producing the more intense psychiatric syndromes such as psychosis and major depression.

Cocaine

Cocaine is an alkaloid drug compound that creates intense CNS arousal. It is a powerful stimulant that is processed from an organic source, the coca leaf. The natural source for the leaf (*Erythroxylum coca*) comes from two varieties of flowering coca shrubs, the *huanuco* and *truxillo*, which can exist only in the fertile soil of South America. They are grown and cultivated in the mountainous regions of South America (NIDA, 2013a).

To convert the coca leaf into a substance that can be used as a psychoactive, various chemical processes involving mixtures of alcohol, benzol, sulfuric acid, sodium carbonate, and kerosene or gasoline baths combined with several shaking and cooling segments convert the coca leaf into a paste. The final product is a precipitate of crude cocaine called *basuco or bazooka*. With the addition of acetone, potassium permanganate, and hydrochloric acid, this pasty sulfate becomes powdery flakes or rocks of nearly pure *cocaine hydrochloride*. At this point it is a white, odorless, crystalline powdered substance that is a member of the tropane family. Most bazooko is converted into cocaine hydrochloride in the jungle laboratories around Colombia and then smuggled out through the networks of organized crime to various destinations including the United States, Europe, and Asia. While en route, it is diluted several times ("stepped on") with various additives such as lactose or dextrose (sugar), inositol (vitamin B), mannitol (baby laxative), and even cornstarch, talcum powder, or flour to stretch the quantity. This "stretching" process increases profits as the now-diluted cocaine finds its way onto the streets of major cities throughout the world (NIDA, 2013a).

Drug dealers have developed marketing strategies by processing cocaine hydrochloride (powder) into a potentiated form of prefabricated, freebase cocaine called *crack*. Crack cocaine that has been neutralized by an acid to make the hydrochloride salt now comes in a rock crystal that can be heated and its vapors smoked. The term *crack* refers to the crackling sound made when the substance is heated and smoked. This inexpensive method of psychoactive stimulant conversion can be accomplished in one's own kitchen by applying heat to cocaine cooked in a mixture of water, ammonia, baking soda, or liquid drain opener. Cocaine is listed as a Schedule II drug on the DEA Controlled Substance Schedule (NIDA, 2013a).

INCIDENCE   Cocaine use in the United States peaked in 1985 at 5.7 million (3% of the population 12 or older). Since that time use among 8th, 10th, and 12th graders has declined (Johnston, O'Malley, Bachman, & Schulenberg, 2011). SAMHSA (2014) reported that the number of past-year cocaine initiates was 601,000, which averages to 1,600 initiates per day, and that 1.5 million people (ages 12 or older) in the in the United States had used cocaine within the past year. Although crack cocaine is still considered a serious problem, the number of initiates has declined from 337,000 in 2002 to 94,000 in 2009 and has remained similar each year since then. The 2015 *Monitoring the Future* report stated that cocaine use among 12th graders is at an all time low of 2.5%, with 8th graders at 0.9% and 10th graders at 1.8% (Johnston et al., 2016). The number of young adults who had used cocaine within the past year in 2013 equated to about 1.1% of the population, which was similar to previous years (SAMHSA, 2014).

PSYCHOACTIVE EFFECTS   The quality of the cocaine experience depends on a number of variables, such as the strength of the substance, the setting, the circumstances under which it is taken, and the user's attitude, emotional state, substance-taking history, and expectation of what the substance should produce. Most users will experience at least a mild euphoria, an increased heartbeat, and a subtle sense of excitement. Some may get little or no reaction from using the substance. This occurs most frequently as tolerance builds and cocaine is required to maintain the body in a relatively normal state.

Cocaine is a tremendous mood elevator, filling the user with a sense of exhilaration and well-being due to molecules binding to dopamine transporters and blocking the reuptake of catecholamine, thus flooding the brain with dopamine (Mariani & Levin, 2012). It melts away feelings of inferiority while loosening inhibitions and evaporating tensions. It relieves fatigue and imparts the illusion of limitless power and energy. Many users "treat" themselves for obesity, lack of energy, depression, shyness, and low self-esteem. High doses may be associated with rambling speech, headache, tinnitus, paranoid ideation, aggressive behavior, disturbances in attention and concentration, auditory hallucinations, and tactile hallucinations (coke bugs). Users of cocaine have reported feelings of restlessness, irritability, and anxiety. The use of cocaine in a binge, at which time the substance is taken repeatedly at increased dosage levels, can result in a period of full-blown paranoid psychosis, with the user losing touch with reality and experiencing auditory hallucinations.

Cocaine can be ingested through inhalation through the nose, commonly called *snorting* or *tooting*; injection under the skin into a muscle or a vein; and smoking freebase or crack. Death can and has occurred with the use of all forms of cocaine ingestion. Cocaine use may also indirectly lead to the user's premature death through suicide resulting from cocaine-induced depression or from aggressive or risk-taking behaviors. Individuals who use cocaine are 4 to 8 times more likely to die than their peers of the same age who do not use cocaine (Degenhardt et al., 2011).

When cocaine is snorted, the moist nasal membranes quickly dissolve the powder into microscopic molecules that flood the circulatory system within 1 to 2 minutes. These molecules encounter and pass through the protective blood–brain barrier, penetrating the cortical tissue that surrounds the deeper layers of the brain. The molecules find their way into stimulatory pathways in the limbic system, which regulate emotion and connect to primitive pain/pleasure centers deep within the brain. These pathways are normally indirectly activated by pleasurable activities such as eating, drinking, and sex. So powerful is the reward/pleasure stimulus from cocaine that responsibilities, family, job, morality, sleep, and safety may be ignored in its pursuit.

EFFECTS ON THE BODY   Cocaine acts directly on the heart muscle, causing the heart to beat inefficiently and its vessels to narrow, restricting the oxygen needed for peak performance. The heart has to work harder to keep up with the restricted blood flow in the rest of the body. Heavy use can cause angina, irregular heartbeat, and even a heart attack. As cocaine constricts blood flow, it can injure cerebral arteries. The acute hypertension brought on by cocaine use has been known to burst weakened blood vessels or produce strokes in young people.

It is not uncommon for severe users to experience seizures that result in a constant tingling sensation of the jaw and neck region. The seizures are a result of neurons firing in bursts, creating uncontrollable electrical storms in the brain. They can cause a general diminution of alertness and mental functioning and can induce epilepsy, even in those with no previous signs of it. Cocaine users exhibit loss of laterality of motor-cortical recruitment (Hanlon, Wesley, & Porrino, 2009; Hanlon, Wesley, Roth, Miller, & Porrino, 2009). In other words, chronic cocaine users have alterations in brain chemistry that affect their movement.

Many other potential difficulties, both physical and psychological, may ensue with the continued use of cocaine. Physical dangers include possible overdose, tolerance, and withdrawal symptoms; psychological effects may manifest themselves as severe depression, paranoid psychosis, and anxiety syndromes including panic attacks and obsessions. The most common causes of death from cocaine are heart attacks, strokes, respiratory failure, paralysis, heart rhythm disturbances, and repeated convulsions, usually from massive overdoses or at the end of a binge.

TOLERANCE AND WITHDRAWAL   Smoking cocaine as coca paste, freebase, or crack has the highest potential for severe cocaine use disorders. An intense high, described by some as a "full-body orgasm," occurs within 8 to 10 seconds after inhaling the smoke. Effects of the substance last only 5 to 10 minutes, and the symptoms of withdrawal (anxiety, depression, and paranoia) are in proportion to the high obtained, leading to intense craving. The intense high occurs when cocaine blocks the reuptake of dopamine, greatly increasing the availability of the neurotransmitter. This flooding allows dopamine to stimulate the receptors more intensely, acting directly on the reward pathways of the brain. In addition, both serotonin and norepinephrine levels are also increased (Zaniewska, Filip, & Przegaliński, 2015). The pattern of rapid onset of intense euphoria, followed in a few minutes by intense dysphoria that can be quickly relieved by another self-administered dose of more cocaine, establishes a highly destructive cycle (Chapy et al., 2015). This neurochemical response creates a rapid tolerance (drug hunger) for almost anyone who uses this drug. Each time the effects of cocaine wear off, dopamine levels drop, sending the user into a serious state of withdrawal. Normally, the brain replenishes dopamine from proteins in food, but in cocaine addicts, dopamine is quickly depleted, partly because of poor diet and partly because cocaine blocks the mechanism that recycles the neurotransmitter for future use. Chronic cocaine use can deplete the normal stores of dopamine in the brain, causing serious depression, not infrequently leading to suicide. Many individuals depress the action of the central nervous system with alcohol or benzodiazepines to temporarily counter the loss of the brain's dopamine supply. In the long run, this only heightens the need for more cocaine. Neuroscience studies have demonstrated that individuals with continued use of cocaine have different responses to cholinergic probes in areas of the brain relevant to craving, learning, and memory (Adinoff et al., 2010).

EFFECTS ON THE FETUS   It is estimated that 4.6 million women of childbearing age use cocaine regularly, with prenatal cocaine exposure rising from 300,000 annually in 1992 to 750,000 annually in 1995 (SAMHSA, 2013). However, the abnormalities that have been identified in the offspring of pregnant cocaine users, including low birth weight, are probably more related to the lifestyle of the substance user than to the pharmacological effects of cocaine. There is no doubt, however, that the substance constricts the blood vessels of the placenta, reducing the supply of blood and oxygen that reaches the fetus. Cocaine is also thought to contribute to premature birth and stillbirth, because of both vasoconstrictive effects on the developing fetus and its ability to induce intrauterine contractions. Babies born to cocaine-using women may have persistently elevated cocaine levels for days, and the possibility exists that the enzymatic pathway for conversion of cocaine into metabolites may not be fully developed in the newborn. Predictions were made that the 1980s would produce a generation of crack babies (Dow-Edwards, 2010). Currently it is believed that many of the effects of prenatal crack use appear to be largely the result of poor nutrition related to the lifestyle of the mother, use of multiple substances, lack of prenatal care, and premature birth. The exact effect of cocaine itself on the developing fetus is still unknown (Meyer & Zhang, 2009).

Amphetamines

Amphetamines are psychomotor stimulants that were first proposed as a treatment for asthma. Their actions on the CNS were not reported until 1933, followed by reports of amphetamine abuse (Rasmussen, 2009). The most commonly prescribed amphetamines include Adderall, a mix of amphetamine salts, and methylphenidates Ritalin and Concerta. Although these medications were first prescribed for the treatment of hyperactive (attention deficit disordered) children, they are currently frequently used without a prescription. Amphetamines can be orally ingested, intravenously injected, snorted, or smoked, creating intense CNS arousal and a rapid increase of dopamine (NIDA, 2014f). Amphetamines and methamphetamines have a similar but slightly different molecular structure.

In past decades, "speed" epidemics were reported in Japan, Sweden, and the United States. In the United States, this situation led to a change in laws when amphetamines were restricted to medical use by the Controlled Substances Act of 1970. They are listed as Schedule II drugs on the Controlled Substances Schedule, and their use is strictly enforced by the DEA. In recreational use, amphetamines can be "snorted," smoked, administered by injection, or taken orally. In recent years, the explosive increase in use of methamphetamines by men who have sex with men (MSM) is of grave concern, as the disinhibiting and sexually stimulating effects of the substance place homosexual male users at even higher risk for infection with human immunodeficiency virus (HIV) (Clark, Marquez, Hare, John, & Klausner, 2012; Knight et al., 2014).

The underground production of amphetamines in North America is largely accomplished through small, clandestine laboratories. They produce more than $3 billion worth of illegal amphetamines per year with a huge profit margin. Law enforcement officials believe these "speed labs" are often financed by motorcycle gangs who distribute the final product mainly in Australia (Shukla, Crump, & Chrisco, 2012). In the United States, less than half of the counties in a large, nationwide study reported zero meth lab seizures by the police, and the majority of locations only had one to three meth lab seizures. However, a very small number of counties had the majority of all meth lab seizures (varying from 20 to 100 lab seizures by police), indicating that the meth house problem varies widely by geographical location (Weisheit & Wells, 2014).

Methamphetamine is the most potent form of amphetamine. As a Schedule II stimulant it has a high potential for chronic use. Illicit forms of methamphetamine sold on the street may be called *ice, crystal (meth), crank, Btu, slate,* or *glass* (NIDA, 2014e). Ice is an odorless, colorless form of crystal methamphetamine, up to 100% pure, resembling a chip of ice or clear rock candy. It is taken orally, intravenously (snorting the powder), or by needle injection. Neuroscience research has demonstrated the effects of long-term use of methamphetamine on the brain, particularly with white/gray matter distortions (Tobias et al., 2010).

INCIDENCE   Amphetamine abuse in the United States peaked in the late 1960s or early 1970s, and then declined to a low in the late 1980s or early 1990s. SAMHSA (2014) reported past-year nonmedical use of prescription stimulants, such as Ritalin, at 2.7% for ages 12 and older.

Amphetamines as a group ranked third among 12th-graders for past-year illicit drug use, with Adderall the drug being mainly used.

Methamphetamine spread from Japan to Hawaii after World War II and has remained endemic there. Methamphetamine has long been the dominant substance problem in the San Diego area and has spread to other sections of the West and Southwest, as well as to both rural and urban sections of the South and Midwest. As it has spread from the traditionally blue-collar user to a more diverse user population, SAMHSA (2014) reported that methamphetamine users equaled 595,000 (0.2%) in 2013. These numbers have remained consistent since 2011 after rising from 2010.

EFFECTS ON THE BODY   Amphetamines cross the blood–brain barrier easily after oral ingestion. Once the amphetamine molecules pass through the stomach, they are absorbed via the intestines into the blood, where they are able to reach peak levels within 1 hour. After absorption, the lipid-soluble molecules are distributed into the brain, lung, and kidneys. Brain levels reach about 10 times the levels in blood, which accounts for the intense CNS effect. Some of the metabolites are active and, if present in sufficient quantity, can cause high blood pressure and hallucinations.

In the CNS, amphetamines mimic cocaine, acting on the neurotransmitters dopamine, and norepinephrine. They cause a tremendous release of newly synthesized dopamine from the presynaptic neuron to bind and stimulate the postsynaptic neurons (2014e, 2014f). The nerve endings (terminals) of dopamine and serotonin-containing neurons are damaged, and new growth is limited. According to NIDA, heavy use of methamphetamine produces alterations in the activity of the dopamine system, reduced motor speed, impaired verbal learning, and possible structural and functional changes in the brain affecting emotion and memory. Amphetamines also inhibit the action of monoamine oxidase (MAO), the enzyme that ends the action of these neurotransmitters, allowing them to remain active in the synapse for a longer time. They act on the sympathetic nervous system (SNS) through the stimulation and release of norepinephrine while blocking the reuptake of norepinephrine back into the presynaptic terminal. This action elicits a "fight or flight" response. Thus, the psychostimulants are called *sympathomimetic* drugs and have been said to mimic the action of the SNS. These substances are identified as sympathomimetic since they produce physiological effects resembling those caused by the sympathetic nervous system. They can increase cardio action and blood pressure. High doses of amphetamines have a direct effect on serotonergic receptors. Electroencephalogram (EEG) recordings have shown that amphetamine accelerates and desynchronizes neuronal firing rates in the brain, a possible explanation for some of the behavioral effects of amphetamines (NIDA, 2014e, 2014f).

With large doses of amphetamines, extreme symptoms may occur, including rapid heartbeat, hypertension, headache, profuse sweating, and severe chest pain. This generally occurs when dosages exceed 50 to 100 mg per day on a continuous basis, and the user may appear psychotic or schizophrenic. Severe intoxication also can produce delirium, panic, paranoia, and hallucinations. Murders and other violent offenses have been attributed to amphetamine intoxication, and studies (e.g., Blanco-Gandía et al., 2015) have shown increased aggression in humans after ingestion of amphetamines.

TOLERANCE AND WITHDRAWAL   Tolerance develops to specific actions of amphetamines, including euphoria, appetite suppression, wakefulness, hyperactivity, and heart and blood pressure effects. Physical dependence on amphetamines is possible, and the risk of psychological dependence is high.

During withdrawal, there is a reduction of available neurotransmitters due to depletion and reduced reuptake, causing a period of depression, fatigue, increased appetite, and prolonged sleep accompanied by REM (dream sleep) following the cessation of use. Death occurs from extreme heat elevation, convulsions, and circulatory collapse.

Tobacco

Nicotine is not listed as a controlled substance on the DEA's Controlled Substances Schedule. However, nicotine has had its share of controversy. It has come to light that cigarette manufacturers have long known that the psychoactive agent in cigarettes is nicotine and that they have often viewed cigarettes as little more than a single-dose container of nicotine (U.S. Department of Health and Human Services, 2014). Lawsuits won by several states have held tobacco manufacturers liable for health problems caused by tobacco use because of their awareness of the addictive nature of nicotine and the effects of smoking on the nonsmoker (FDA commissioner testified, 2009; U.S. Department of Health and Human Services, 2014).

INCIDENCE Tobacco smoking has been prevalent for thousands of years. Modern use in the United States peaked in the mid-1960s, as research has increasingly shown the dangers of tobacco use (U.S. Department of Health and Human Services, 2014). Following the Surgeon General's report on the health hazards of smoking, published in 1964, the incidence of smoking in the United States began to drop. SAMHSA (2010) estimated in 2009 that 69.7 million Americans aged 12 or older were current (past-month) users of a tobacco product. In 2013, 66.9% of the U.S. population aged 12 or older reported tobacco use within the past 12 months, which was a decline since the 2010 statistics (SAMHSA, 2014). An estimated 58.7 million persons (23.3%) were current cigarette smokers; 13.3 million (5.3%) smoked cigars; 8.6 million (3.4%) used smokeless tobacco; and 2.1 million (0.8%) smoked tobacco in pipes. Between 2002 and 2009, past-month use of any tobacco product decreased from 30.4% to 27.7%, with cigarette use declining from 26.0% to 23.3%. The Centers for Disease Control and Prevention (CDC; U.S. Department of Health and Human Services, 2014) indicated that tobacco use is the leading preventable cause of death in the United States.

EFFECTS ON THE BODY Nicotine is both a stimulant and a sedative to the central nervous system. The absorption of nicotine is followed almost immediately by a "kick" because it causes a discharge of epinephrine from the adrenal cortex. This, in turn, stimulates the CNS and other endocrine glands, producing a sudden release of glucose. As the effects of the sudden release of epinephrine and glucose wear off, depression and fatigue follow, leading the abuser to seek more nicotine. Research has also shown that nicotine, like cocaine, heroin, and marijuana, increases the level of the neurotransmitter dopamine, affecting the brain pathways that control reward and pleasure (NIDA, 2015b).

Nicotine is readily absorbed in the body from every site with which it comes into contact, including the skin. It is both water- and lipid-soluble, allowing it to cross the blood–brain barrier quickly to reach the brain and virtually every other blood-rich tissue in the body. Inhaled nicotine reaches the brain within 7 to 19 seconds of puffing. Once in the bloodstream, a portion is carried to the liver, where it is metabolized into cotinine (90%) and nicotine N-oxide (10%). It has a wide range of effects on the peripheral and central nervous systems, including increased blood pressure and heart rate, cardiac output, coronary blood flow, and cutaneous vasoconstriction. Women who smoke tend to have an earlier menopause, and those who also use oral contraceptives, particularly those older than 30, are more prone to cardiovascular and cerebrovascular diseases than are other smokers (Sherman, 2006; Buttigieg et al., 2008; U.S. Department of Health and Human Services, 2014).

Cigarette smoking is a profound contributor to mortality. Cigarette smoking and smoke-less tobacco use claim thousands of lives every year in the United States (U.S. Department of Health and Human Services, 2014). Tobacco-related health problems include cardiovascular disease, cancer, chronic obstructive lung disease, and complications during pregnancy. Nonsmokers exposed to environmental tobacco smoke (passive smokers) also are at increased risk for the same diseases as smokers. They breathe in a mixture of chemicals including formal-dehyde, cyanide, carbon monoxide, ammonia, and nicotine. These carcinogens increase the risk of developing heart disease by 25% to 30% and lung cancer by 20% to 30% (NIDA, 2015b).

TOLERANCE AND WITHDRAWAL   Tolerance is believed to occur as the body becomes accus-tomed to the presence of nicotine that appears to be linked to the number of binding sites. Nicotine accumulates in the body, and regular use causes it to remain in body tissues 24 hours a day. Nicotine has a high potential for chronic use, and cessation is difficult.

When chronic smokers are deprived of cigarettes for 24 hours, they experience increased anger, hostility, aggression, and loss of social cooperation. They take longer to regain emo-tional equilibrium following stress. During periods of craving or abstinence, smokers experience impairment across a wide range of cognitive and psychomotor functioning. Neuroscience research, through the use of positron emission tomography (PET) ligand imag-ing, has demonstrated nicotine receptor changes during acute and prolonged cigarette absti-nence, concluding that these changes may contribute to difficulties with tobacco cessation (Cosgrove et al., 2009).

Caffeine

Caffeine belongs to a chemical class of alkaloids known as *xanthine derivatives*, and it was chemically isolated more than 170 years ago. It is found in coffee, tea, cocoa, chocolate, and a number of soft drinks, as well as hundreds of prescription and OTC drugs. Caffeine is not listed as a controlled substance on the Controlled Substances Schedule.

INCIDENCE   Caffeine is the most widely consumed psychoactive agent in the world. About 80% of adults in the United States use caffeine regularly (Bergin & Kendler, 2012), a per capita intake of 220 to 240 mg per day (American Psychiatric Association, 2013). Caffeine has been included in the DSM-5, and chronic overuse would be considered to be a caffeine use disorder.

EFFECTS ON THE BODY   Caffeine is rapidly absorbed into the gastrointestinal tract, and peak plasma levels occur within 30 to 45 minutes after ingestion. It crosses the blood–brain barrier very quickly and concentrates in brain plasma relative to the amount that is ingested.

Caffeine and other xanthines block the brain's receptors for adenosine, a neuromodulator. Adenosine has sedative, anxiolytic, and anticonvulsant actions. When caffeine occupies adenosine-binding sites, these actions cannot occur, and there is a stimulating or anxiogenic effect. Two hundred milligrams of caffeine (the equivalent of two cups of coffee) will activate the cortex of the brain, showing an arousal pattern on an EEG. At this level, caffeine acts directly on the vascular muscles, causing dilation of the blood vessels. The CNS stimulation is also responsible for "coffee jitters" and increases the time it takes to fall asleep.

At higher dose levels (500 mg and above), autonomic centers of the brain are stimulated, causing increased heart rate and respiration and constriction of the blood vessels in the brain. Caffeine increases heart rate and contraction, physiologically creating arrhythmias and mild tachycardia. It increases gastric acidity and is contraindicated for patients with ulcers. Caffeine directly acts on the kidneys to increase urine output and also increases salivary flow.

Caffeine is generally not considered a toxic substance. Approximately 15% of circulating caffeine is metabolized an hour, with a half-life of 3.5 to 5 hours. A lethal dose for an average adult male would be 5 to 10 g, the equivalent of 50 to 100 cups of regular coffee, probably necessitating ingestion in a non-beverage form.

TOLERANCE AND WITHDRAWAL   The key reinforcing factor for caffeine may be its effects on the pleasure and reward centers found in the hypothalamus and the median forebrain bundle. Stimulation of the brain's reward center might be the most powerful reason that people move from a controlled phase of caffeine ingestion to the stage of caffeine use disorder.

Children do not seem to possess an innate craving for caffeine, and most people in our society seem to be exposed to it gradually as their intake eventually progresses to a pattern of frequent or daily use. Moreover, there appears to be an age-related rate of metabolism of caffeine, leaving newborns, infants, and small children more vulnerable to its effects.

The potential for brain conditioning responses, neural changes in the brain, and tolerance symptoms of caffeine is small. However, a large number of variables make it difficult for researchers to determine users' responses to varying doses of caffeine intake. These include a subject's age, body mass, other psychoactive substances in use, amount of stress, level of fatigue, sleep disorders, and varying degrees of sensitivity to the substance. Furthermore, the acute use of caffeine produces very different biological consequences when compared with chronic use (Dubroqua, Yee, & Singer, 2014).

Caffeine withdrawal may precipitate such symptoms as craving for caffeine, headache, fatigue, nausea or vomiting, or marked anxiety or depression. There have been a number of reports on caffeine withdrawal. For example, caffeine withdrawal symptoms can include low alertness, sleepiness, poor performance, mood disturbances, nausea, flulike symptoms, and headaches (Juliano, Huntley, Harrell, & Westerman, 2012; Rogers, Heatherley, Mullings, & Smith, 2013).

Cannabis

Cannabis or marijuana is the most widely abused illicit substance in the United States, and with increased social and legal acceptance of the substance, the rates of its use are expected to rise. Marijuana is also the substance with the highest level of illicit SUDs. In 2013 there were 19.8 million past-month users of marijuana among individual 12 years of age and older (SAMHSA, 2013). The percentage of users in 2013 (7.5%) was higher than in 2009 (6.1%). In 2013, 2.4 million individuals ages 12 and older reported using marijuana for the first time within the past 12 months, with 1.4 million individuals who recently started using marijuana before age 18. Most disturbing is the fact that high rates of marijuana use during teen and preteen years, as the brain continues to develop, place users at risk for SUDs.

Marijuana and hashish are produced from the hemp plant, cannabis. As a psychoactive agent, it is used primarily to produce euphoria followed by relaxation. Cannabis is known by many names—*Indian hemp, marijuana, hash, pot, herb, weed, grass, widow, ganja,* or *dope*—and is a controversial substance in U.S. society (NIDA, 2015b). The major chemical in marijuana that produces the "high" is tetrahydrocannabinol (THC), which acts on the cannabinoid receptors in the brain. Cannabis is usually smoked as cigarettes (joint, nail) or in a pipe (bong) or eaten as edible food products. Vaping marijuana through products similar to electronic cigarettes is also growing in frequency. The strength of the end product that comes from the hemp plant vary, owing to the climate and soil in which it is grown and the method of cultivation and preparation. Its potency and quality depend mainly on the type of plant that is grown. Experienced growers identify potency by grading the plant with East Indian names. *Bhang* is identified as the least potent and cheapest and is made from the cut tops of uncultivated plants that have a low resin content. *Ganja* is derived from the flowering tops and leaves of selected plants that have been carefully cultivated to have a high content of resin and, therefore, are more potentiated to the user. *Charas* is the highest grade and is produced from the resin itself, obtained from fully mature plants. This highly potentiated source is generally referred to as *hashish*.

The potency of marijuana, a Schedule I substance on the Controlled Substances Schedule, has drastically increased in the United States, as growers have been able to legally cultivate the plant. Additionally, clandestine laboratories have developed a method of producing a butane "hash oil," also called "dabs," which has been found to have more than 70% to 90% THC content, compared with an average of 30% in regular hashish, and is considered to be the "crack" of cannabis because of its high rate of absorption in the body (Loflin & Earleywine, 2014). It is noteworthy that one of the reasons marijuana use is controversial in the United States is due to its classification as a Schedule I substance, meaning there are no accepted medicinal purposes for the substance. The word "accepted" is significant. A segment follows on medicinal uses of marijuana in this section.

INCIDENCE   As stated earlier, marijuana is the most frequently used illicit substance in the United States, with rates increasing. In 2013, there were 19.8 million users (age 12 or older) of marijuana, as compared to 16.7 million in 2010 and 14.5 million in 2007 (SAMHSA, 2011, 2014). Marijuana was thought to have reached its peak in the 1970s. However, marijuana use began rising, particularly among teens from 2008 forward. Marijuana use in 2013 increased for all prevalence periods studied (lifetime, past year, past 30 days, and daily in the past 30 days). Reports indicate that about 1 in 16 12th graders in 2013 used marijuana on a daily or near-daily basis. One explanation is that over the past several years the perceived risk and the level of disapproval have declined in society. In contrast to 2.4 million initiates in 2009, there were 4.8 million marijuana users in 2013 who initiated use within the past year. These trends of incidence again are disturbing, particularly as we learn more about the habitual use of this substance as the result of neuroscience research findings (Konopka, 2014; Quickfall & Crockford, 2006; Rais et al., 2008).

PSYCHOACTIVE EFFECTS   Smoking of cannabis can produce relaxation following euphoria, loss of appetite, impaired memory, loss of concentration and knowledge retention, and loss of coordination, as well as a more vivid sense of taste, sight, smell, and hearing. Stronger doses cause fluctuation of emotions, fragmentary thoughts, disoriented behavior, and psychosis. It may also cause irritation to the lungs and respiratory system and cancer. The short-term effects of marijuana include problems with memory and learning, distorted perception, difficulty in thinking and problem solving, loss of coordination, and increased heart rate (Konopka, 2014). Long-term marijuana use indicates some changes in the brain similar to those seen after long-term use of other major substances (Quickfall & Crockford, 2006; Rais et al., 2008).

EFFECTS ON THE BODY   In the United States, cannabis is generally smoked in a cigarette called a *joint* or a *doobie*. A marijuana cigarette contains 421 chemicals before ignition. There are 61 cannabinoids, including delta-1-tetrahydrocannabinol, which is the psychoactive agent. Neuroscience research findings have indicated the effects of this psychoactive agent on the prefrontal cortex (involved in cognitive complexity), as well as the dorsal and ventral striatal (part of the reward system) functions of the brain (Hurd, Michaelides, Miller, & Jutras-Aswad, 2014). There are also 50 different waxy hydrocarbons, 103 terpines, 12 fatty acids, 11 steroids, and 20 nitrogen compounds, as well as carbon monoxide, ammonia, acetone, benzene, benzanthracene, and benzoprene. When ignited, these chemicals are converted into more than 2,000 other chemicals. As these are metabolized by the body, they are converted to about 600 chemical metabolites. Cannabinoids have a half-life of 72 hours in the human body. When ingested, effects appear to be dose-dependent. Cannabinoids are lipid-soluble and are stored at microscopic levels for indefinite periods of time in the body (Bhattacharyya et al., 2009).

Recent neuroscience research using structural imaging findings on CT or MR imaging, and conventional angiography clearly indicates that excessive use of cannabis leads to functional or structural impairment of the central nervous system (Geibprasert et al., 2009). Chemicals found in marijuana and hashish are believed to interfere with the cell's ability to manufacture pivotal molecules, which grossly affects the supply of substances necessary for cell division, including DNA, RNA, and proteins. This causes an "aging process" in particular clusters of cells found in the brain, liver, lungs, spleen, lymphoid tissues, and sex organs.

Many of the early studies on the effects of long-term use of cannabis were conducted at a time when the THC content of cannabis was extremely low (0.05% to 4%). With some strains of the substance reportedly now reaching THC content that extends into the teens (sinsemilla, 14%) and even the 20s (neiterweit, 27%), there is increasing evidence that cannabis is doing more damage than previously realized (Konopka, 2014).

One well-confirmed danger of heavy, long-term use is damage to the lungs due to the fact that it burns 16 times "hotter" than tobacco and produces twice as many mutagens (agents that cause permanent changes in genetic material). Biopsies have confirmed that cannabis smokers may be at an extremely high risk for the development of lung diseases including bronchitis, emphysema, and cancer (Kim, Hung, Lee, Oh, & Chung,, 2013). NIDA (2015c) reports research results that include people who smoke marijuana frequently have breathing problems, increased heart rates, problems with child development before and after birth, and mental illnesses (e.g., depression and anxiety). It is believed that some of marijuana's adverse health effects may occur because THC impairs the immune system's ability to fight disease. There is a prevalence of studies supporting the biological association of marijuana smoking with lung cancer (Kim et al., 2013).

It is believed that long-term marijuana use causes mental or emotional deterioration. Amotivational syndrome, which includes symptoms of passivity, aimlessness, apathy, uncommunicativeness, and lack of ambition, has been attributed to prolonged marijuana use (Bartholomew, Holroyd, & Heffernan, 2010). Marijuana has the potential to cause problems in daily life or make a person's existing problems worse—depression, anxiety, and personality disturbances can be exacerbated with chronic marijuana use. One still needs to ask whether these symptoms result from the use of marijuana, or from the personality characteristics of heavy substance users—bored, anxious, depressed, listless, cynical, and rebellious—or a combination.

Marijuana has also been looked on as a "gateway drug" or precursor to use of other, more dangerous substances. Research identifies that individuals who use marijuana "before the age of 17 are five times more likely to abuse other substances later in life" than their peers who do not use marijuana (Konopka, 2014, p. 282). In fact, there is an undeniable link between early mari-juana use and later substance use, and animal models show that early adolescent marijuana use does increase susceptibility to opiate use in adulthood (Hurd et al., 2014). Although specific brain-based causal results of marijuana use are still being understood, there are various environ-mental and psychological explanations. For example, marijuana use in youth has been linked to cognitive developmental delay or impairment. This impairment could cause poor decision mak-ing and decreased motivation throughout life, both of which have connections to substance use in adults. Also, users of one substance often find themselves in the company of users of other substances, making them readily available. Last, anyone who uses one substance may be inter-ested in others for similar reasons.

TOLERANCE AND WITHDRAWAL   Research is being continuously developed on the tolerance issues with marijuana use. Recently, chronic marijuana use in rats with increased tolerance to THC was shown to increase habit memory; this implies that individuals who use marijuana regu-larly and have developed a tolerance may be more likely to continue to use marijuana because of the increased activity of habit memory formation (Goodman & Packard, 2015). Many individu-als who develop marijuana use disorder are susceptible to other disorders because of anxiety, depression, or feelings of inadequacy. Further, there is evidence linking marijuana use to cross-tolerance of other substances.

Signs of possible mild to severe use of marijuana include animated behavior and loud talk-ing, followed by sleepiness, dilated pupils and bloodshot eyes, distortions in perception, halluci-nations, distortions in depth and time perception, and loss of coordination. An overdose of marijuana can cause fatigue, lack of coordination, paranoia, and psychosis. Withdrawal can cause insomnia, irritability, anxiety, and a decrease in appetite.

Studies have shown that withdrawal symptoms from marijuana include decreased appeti-tive, marijuana cravings, sleep disorders, aggression, irritability, and anxiety in early treatment (Lee et al., 2014). In the same study by Lee and colleagues, most marijuana withdrawal symp-toms decreased over time; however, sleep issues, including bad dreams and difficulty sleeping, actually increased over time. Although the reason for this is unknown, a persistent withdrawal symptom that could affect lasting abstinence is sleep disturbance. A 1999 study conducted at Harvard Medical School confirmed higher levels of aggression in marijuana users during with-drawal when compared with the infrequent or former marijuana user (Bartholomew et al., 2010). However, more recent work has focused on the individual differences between substance users and withdrawal symptoms. Specifically, aggression withdrawal symptoms are typically found in individuals who had histories of aggression, whereas marijuana users without histories of aggres-sion did not have aggression as a withdrawal symptom (Smith, Homish, Leonard, & Collins, 2013). Therefore, clinicians should be mindful of clients with histories of aggression, as this symptom might occur during withdrawal for that population. Research also reported by Bartholomew and colleagues (2010) indicated that cannabinoid (THC or synthetic forms of THC) withdrawal in chronically exposed animals led to an increase in the activation of the stress-response system and changes in the activity of nerve cells containing dopamine. It should be noted that dopamine neurons are involved in the regulation of motivation and reward and are directly or indirectly affected by all substances of abuse, including cannabis. (See Chapter 4 for more information on the reward system of the brain and substance use.) Last, attempts to cease or regulate use of marijuana have been found to be most frequent among users with serious psy-chological disorders and depressive disorders (Shi, 2014). Thus, withdrawal symptoms and comorbidity with psychological disorders and depression are needed to help individuals cease using marijuana. Some possible reasons for this relationship include self-medication, avoidance of withdrawal symptoms, and vulnerability of this population to substance use.

MEDICAL USE   Cannabis use for treatment of some medical ailments has held interest for a number of years, particularly in obtaining relief from glaucoma, asthma, and epilepsy, as well as from the side effects of chemotherapy used to treat some types of cancer. Some have experimented with its usefulness in treating the physical wasting that can occur with advanced acquired immunodeficiency syndrome (AIDS). Its effectiveness compared with other methods of treatment remains controversial, partly because of legal complications involved in doing such research. Typically, the following common conditions would allow for someone to receive medical marijuana: terminal or debilitating illness, glaucoma, HIV infection, AIDS, or pain disorders (Kaplan, 2015). Additional illnesses and ailments vary from state to state and change as research grows.

Although some states have legalized marijuana for medicinal purposes, and some also for recreational use, there continues to be political discussion over legalization, particularly for medical use (Fairman, 2016). However, parts of the medical community remain skeptical of its medical value compared with other substances, and research supporting each position is scarce (e.g., Mathern, Beninsig, & Nehlig, 2015). Recent neurological research findings have provided evidence that long-term use of cannabis creates structural abnormalities in the hippocampus and amygdala and is associated with brain abnormalities and later risk of psychosis (e.g., Hurd et al., 2014; McQueeny et al., 2011; Welch et al., 2010; Yucel et al., 2008).

Cannabicycohexanol/Spice (K2)

Cannabicyclohexanol, also known as Spice, *K2, or synthetic marijuana (SM)*, is a relatively new category of designer drug consisting of laboratory-made chemicals that function similarly to THC, the primary psychoactive ingredient in marijuana (Egan et al., 2015; Ukaigwe, Karmacharya, & Donato, 2014). Around 2004, Spice became available in specialized shops selling paraphernalia for cannabis. Later on, as its popularity increased, tests were conducted and synthetic cannabimimetic agents were identified as JWH-018, JWH-073 (named after medicinal chemist John W. Huffman), and CP 47 497 C8. These cannabinoids produce intoxication similar to that of marijuana. JWH-018 ((1-pentyl-1*H*-indol-3-yl)-1-naphthalenyl-methanone) was one of the most studied synthetic cannabinoids with high pharmacological activity (Brents & Prather, 2014; Zawilska & Wojcieszak, 2013).

The DEA classified the active chemicals as controlled substances because of the high potential for continued use. Disadvantages to substance screening are that the cannabinoids in Spice have a longer duration and low detection on traditional substance screens. Spice is sold under brand names such as *K2, Yucatan Fire, Bombay Blue, K2 Blueberry, Black Mamba*, and *Ultra Chronic*. The synthetic substances found in Spice can be classified as JWH compounds, cyclohexylphenols, benzoylindoles, classic cannabinoids, and other compounds. To differentiate Spice from other products, observe for variations in core structure of the synthetic cannabimimetics, the inter- and intravariability in smoke mixtures, and variations in composition.

Manufacturers dissolve the synthetic cannabinoids into a solvent that is used to spray onto dried plants. It is then labeled as unfit for human consumption and distributed in either loose leaf, pre-rolled, or powder form. Spice can be smoked using a cannabis or water pipe, or rolled in cigarette paper. Although users may consume Spice as a tea, it is uncommon. One of the key reasons Spice products can be combined with various substances is due to Spice having up to

15 different vegetal compounds, including large quantities of vitamin E. It is common for Spice products to have a pleasant aroma and taste.

INCIDENCE   Spice is the second leading illicit substance behind marijuana, with an estimated street value of $5 billion per year. Spice originated in Europe around 2004, where it was sold over the Internet and in head shops. By 2008, synthetic cannabinoids entered the U.S. market and were legally available in retail stores. In December 2008 came the first official report of Spice distribution in the United States (Spaderna, Addy, & D'Souza, 2013). The growing popularity of Spice results from the expectation of a better high, avoiding detection in drug tests, and easy access. However, there is also growing concern by members of the public about the physical and psychological effects of Spice consumption. In 2011, approximately 11.4 % of 12th grade students in the United States used Spice. Spice was reported as the second most widely used substance among 10th and 12th graders. However, among 8th graders it is the third most widely used substance following marijuana and inhalants.

The 2015 *Monitoring the Future* (Johnston et al., 2016) survey indicated that there has been a significant decline in high school seniors (11.3% in 2012 to 5% in 2015), 10th graders (8.8% in 2012 to 4% in 2015), and 8th graders (4.4% in 2012 to 3% in 2015) who reported a history of Spice use. Male adolescents and young adults are the primary population using Spice. Based on the results from a 2013 self-reported study with 14,966 participants from various countries worldwide, 16.8% reported lifetime use of Spice. Reports also indicate increased exposure to synthetic cannabimimetics among the military and athletic population (Zawilska & Wojcieszak, 2013). Spice users also admit to using marijuana (Egan et al., 2015). It is important to note that the phenomenon of Spice use and its contents change over time. The recent decline in Spice use has been argued to be due to lower availability and policy change making the substance more difficult to obtain.

The American Association of Poison Control Centers (AAPCC) reported an increase in K2 related calls from approximately 53 in 2009 to 2500 in 2010. In 2010, 11,406 emergency department visits were reported as a result of Spice use. This number increased to 28,531 reported visits in 2011. In the 12- to 17-year-old age group, emergency visits increased from 3,780 in 2010 to 7,584 in 2011. In users aged 18 to 20, visits increased from 1,881 in 2010 to 8,212 in 2011. Male users accounted for the majority of emergency department spice-related visits, specifically accounting for 79% of all spice-related visits in 2011 (SAMHSA, 2014).

PSYCHOACTIVE EFFECTS   Although reports of the prevalence of psychosis among Spice users have been inconsistent, the psychosis that some users experience is important to understand and document (Durand, Delgado, Parra-Pellot, & Nichols-Vinueza, 2015). Because psychoactive chemicals are added to Spice, its effect is stronger than that of marijuana, leading to a higher risk of experiencing adverse effects such as a psychotic episode. Psychoactive effects include alteration of perception, euphoric feeling, relaxation, transient hallucination, and impairment of memory and attention. Users can become very irritable, angry, and agitated. Anxiety, paranoia, delusions, panic attacks, and general mood alteration can also develop as a result of using Spice. Users may also experience suicidal ideation and suicidal attempts (Harris & Brown, 2013).

Psychotic symptoms may resolve without medical intervention; however, some symptoms are more severe, causing the user to seek medical attention. Psychotic symptoms may last from a few hours to a prolonged time, in some cases weeks or months. The symptoms of Spice use may be worse than those produced by marijuana and can produce similar effects in the brain, causing both tolerance and dependence in users (Harris & Brown, 2013). Symptoms of Spice use can start immediately after use or hours after, depending on the user.

EFFECTS ON THE BODY   Some presenting symptomology in Spice use is similar to that for cannabis. The differences may be accounted for when considering the difference between synthetic and non-cannabinoid components. Effects of Spice include neurological, cardiovascular, and gastrointestinal changes. Because of the extended time that Spice is stored in the body, the long-term effects are difficult to estimate. Although there are few human studies on the effects of Spice, data has shown that the cannabinoid compound in Spice acts on the same cell receptors as the psychoactive ingredient in marijuana, THC (Seely, Lapoint, Moran, & Fattore, 2012). The significant difference in physiological effects results from a strong receptor bond in the brain. This leads to effects that are unpredictable but powerful (NIDA, 2015d).

Spice users can experience increased heart rate, vomiting, nausea, and seizures. Anticholinergic effects such as dry mouth and dehydration can also result from Spice use (SAMHSA, 2014). Spice compounds may be excreted from the body at a slower pace, and renal damage may occur in previously healthy men. Users may also experience a change in appetite, dry skin, dry mouth, dizziness, tremors, and nystagmus. Other effects include reddened conjunctiva, blurry vision, light sensitivity, and pupillary changes. In some rare cases, death may occur.

TOLERANCE AND WITHDRAWAL   Symptomology is similar to the effects of THC from marijuana use. Regular use may result in tolerance and the need for more of the substance to reach the same effect. Therefore, Spice use can meet the criteria for SUDs. However, there is little information on the long-term use of synthetic marijuana. Thus, much data about long-term use is hypothesized from available research and data on long-term marijuana use (Seely et al., 2012).

Withdrawal symptoms from Spice use may include vomiting, internal restlessness, hyperventilation, diarrhea, somatic pain, tremors, hypertension, headaches, and depressive symptoms. Severe withdrawals may last for about a week.

MEDICAL USE   Although cannabinoid compounds, through pharmacological preparation, can be used as a therapeutic intervention for headaches, there is no supporting data that Spice has medicinal benefits.

HALLUCINOGENS

Hallucinogens, as the name implies, cause hallucinations and profound distortions in a person's perception of reality. When using hallucinogens, individuals report seeing images, hearing sounds, and feeling sensations that seem real but do not exist. Some users report emotional mood swings. Hallucinogenic compounds from plants and mushrooms have been used for centuries. Most hallucinogens contain nitrogen and have chemical structures similar to those of natural neurotransmitters such as serotonin (NIDA, 2014d). Hallucinogenic substances include the *indoles*, which include (a) lysergic acid derivatives and (b) substituted tryptamines such as dimethyltryptamine (DMT), psilocybin, and psilocin. All of the indole-type hallucinogens have a structure similar to that of the neurotransmitter serotonin, whereas the substituted phenylethylamine-type hallucinogens are structurally related to the neurotransmitter norepinephrine. It is believed that the mechanism of action occurring in the indole-type hallucinogens involves the alteration of serotonergic neurotransmission (NIDA, 2014d). It should be noted that the serotonin system is involved in the control of behavioral, perceptual, and regulatory systems, including mood, hunger, body temperature, sexual behavior, muscle control, and sensory perception. The four most common types of hallucinogens include LSD (D-lysergic acid diethylamide, manufactured from lysergic acid), peyote (a small cactus with an active ingredient of mescaline), psilocybin (a mushroom containing psilocybin), and PCP (phencyclidine, manufactured for anesthetic use).

Lysergic acid diethylamide (LSD) is probably the best known of the indole-type hallucinogens and has been most used by white males between the ages of 10 and 29 years. LSD is also often viewed as a club drug. A few of the indole-type hallucinogens such as psilocybin and psilocin are found in nature, whereas mescaline is a naturally occurring hallucinogen derived from the peyote cactus.

The overall effects of many of the hallucinogens are similar, although there is a multitude of variability involving the rate of onset, duration of action, and the intensity of the experience. This is due to the wide range of potency available and the amount of the substance that is ingested relative to its specific dose–response characteristics. Because the goal of this text is to give an overview of the topic of substance use, a discussion of LSD and PCP (phencyclidine) will represent the hallucinogenic substances used for recreation.

Lysergic Acid Diethylamide (LSD; Identified as a Club Drug)

LSD is between 100 and 1,000 times more powerful than natural hallucinogens, but weaker than synthetic chemicals such as 2,5-dimethoxy-4-methylamphetamine (DOM), also known as Serenity, Tranquility, and Peace (STP) (NIDA, 2014d). Confiscated street samples of LSD can range from 10 to 300 micrograms in a single dose. LSD is listed as a Schedule I substance on the Controlled Substances Schedule.

INCIDENCE   In 2013 more than 1.1 million individuals aged 12 or older reported that they had used LSD for the first time within the previous year (SAMHSA, 2014). There was no change reported from 2010 in the number of new initiates of LSD. The 2015 *Monitoring the Future* survey reported a sharp decline in LSD use from 2001 to 2003 in 8th, 10th, and 12th graders. In 2013, 482,000 Americans aged 12 and older had initiated use of LSD in the past 12 months, which is consistent with the trends seen in 2008, 2010, and 2012 (SAMHSA, 2014). However, since 2013 there has been a slight increase in LSD use in the upper grade levels (Johnston et al., 2016).

PSYCHOACTIVE EFFECTS   LSD triggers behavioral responses in some individuals after doses as low as 20 micrograms. Psychological and behavioral effects begin about an hour after oral ingestion and generally peak between 2 and 4 hours. There is a gradual return to the pre-drug state within 6 to 8 hours. The subjective effects can be somatic with symptoms of dizziness, weakness, and tremor, followed by perceptual changes of altered vision and intensified hearing, which gradually change into visual distortions, dreamlike imagery, and synesthesia that includes "seeing" smells and "hearing" colors. LSD is metabolized mainly at the site of the liver to various transformation products, and very little is eliminated as an unchanged product.

TOLERANCE AND WITHDRAWAL   There appears to be no potential for physical withdrawal from LSD, as it does not lead to compulsive drug-seeking behavior. Yet, LSD does affect tolerance, with regular users needing to take progressively higher doses to achieve the sought-after effect of the substance.

Phencyclidine (PCP; Identified as a Club Drug)

Phencyclidine (PCP, "angel dust") is considered a hallucinogenic substance. It was originally developed as a general anesthetic for human application but was found to be unstable. It was then offered as an anesthetic for veterinary applications but was soon placed in the classification of Schedule I substances under the Anti–Drug Abuse Act. Currently there are extreme penalties for trafficking or manufacturing PCP.

In its pure form, PCP is a lipid-soluble white powder. It is often adulterated or misrepresented as a variety of other substances, including THC, cannabinol, mescaline, psilocybin, LSD, amphetamine, or cocaine. On the street, it can be found in powder, tablet, and liquid form. A typical street dose (one pill, joint, or line) is about 5 mg, but confiscated street samples have revealed that purity can run from 5% to 100% depending on the form. This wide variance can create tremendous risk for the user.

INCIDENCE   PCP use peaked, reaching epidemic proportions, between 1973 and 1979, and again between 1981 and 1984. In 1979, 14.5% of 18- to 25-year-olds had ever used PCP, compared with 9.5% in 1976. By 2015, only 1.4% of 12th graders had used PCP in the past year (Johnston et al., 2016). Considering a broader perspective, in 2013, 32,000 Americans age 12 and older had initiated PCP use within the past year (SAMHSA, 2014). Whites are more likely to use PCP than other groups, followed by Hispanics and African Americans.

PSYCHOACTIVE EFFECTS   PCP can be ingested orally, smoked, snorted, intravenously injected, and even inserted vaginally. The mode of administration can drastically alter the onset of effects. Smoking and injection create a rapid onset of effects that usually peak within 30 minutes. The highs last from 4 to 6 hours. For typical chronic users, PCP is generally the primary substance of choice, whereas users of other substances may occasionally combine PCP with other substances they are using. Staying high on PCP may last 2 to 3 days, during which time the user remains sleepless. Chronic users may also exhibit persistent cognitive and memory problems, speech difficulties, mood disorders, weight loss, and decrease in purposeful behavior for up to a year after cessation of use. Coma can occur at any time during intoxication. When used in this fashion, many of these chronic users may need emergency room treatment to overcome the residual effects of the substance (NIDA, 2014d).

PCP is a potent compound and extremely lipid-soluble. Its psychological/behavioral effects are dose dependent. The dose range for PCP's effect on brain stimulation reward enhancement is relatively narrow. At low doses, it produces reward enhancement or a "good trip"; at high doses, it inhibits the brain reward system and may produce a "bad trip." It is believed that PCP binds to specific sites in the human brain and blocks the reuptake of several major neurotransmitter systems. It also disrupts electrophysiological activity by blocking the ionic exchange of sodium and potassium. These serious actions on major brain systems probably account for PCP's symptoms of dissociative anesthesia and its ability to create coma and lethal complications. Currently, there is no PCP antagonist available to block its effects, and treatment for overdose must address the symptoms of toxicity. Close observation of the PCP-toxic patient must continue for days, as PCP levels may continue to vary unevenly for hours or days.

TOLERANCE AND WITHDRAWAL   Repeated use of PCP can lead to craving and compulsive PCP-seeking behavior (NIDA, 2014d). As such, there exists a high potential for development of an SUD.

Ketamine (Identified as a Club Drug)

Ketamine is known on the street as *special K, vitamin K, cat valium, super K, ketalar, green,* or simply *K*. It has become a favorite of young people at raves, dance parties and nightclubs. Ketamine was approved for use in human and veterinary medicine (Veterinary Practice News, 2010).

INCIDENCE   Ketamine is usually taken with other substances, making data on incidence of use difficult to verify. According to the Drug Abuse Warning Network, data on ketamine has been too imprecise to predict use rates accurately. It is popular because of its hallucinogenic effect and its availability over the Internet and for legal purchase in many countries, including Mexico. In the United States, ketamine is a Schedule III drug used in veterinary medicine. Break-ins at veterinary practices have increased as a source for obtaining the drug for illegal use. As with a number of other illicit substances, U.S. use of ketamine has significantly declined in 8th, 10th, and 12th graders since 2011, with a 2015 prevalence rate of ketamine use at 1.4% in 12th graders (Johnston et al., 2016).

PSYCHOACTIVE EFFECTS   Ketamine is a dissociative anesthetic with effects similar to PCP's but less potent. It is available in liquid and powder forms. As a liquid, it is ingested orally and has a bitter taste. It is most frequently insufflated (snorted) as a powder. An insufflated dose is known as a *bump*. When a user experiences the desired hallucinations and visual distortions, he or she is said to be in *K-land*. At high doses, dissociation is at a level of producing a sensation of near-death, known as the *K-hole*.

EFFECTS ON THE BODY   Tachycardia, hypertension, impaired motor function, and respiratory depression are all physiological consequences of ketamine ingestion. Dissociation, depression, recurrent flashbacks, delirium, and amnesia are psychological consequences (Liu, Zerbo, & Ross, 2015). There is an added risk of unintentional injury because a person under the influence of ketamine feels little or no pain. Long-term effects in humans are unknown, but long-term brain damage has been noted in animal studies (NIDA, 2014c).

A FURTHER LOOK AT CLUB DRUGS

The term *club drug* refers to one of a variety of psychoactive drugs that are grouped not by effect but by the milieu in which they are typically used (e.g., raves, dance parties, and nightclubs). They include amphetamine and methamphetamine, MDMA (most commonly known as *Ecstasy*), LSD, PCP, ketamine, GHB, and benzodiazepines such as flunitrazepam (Rohypnol) and alprazolam (Xanax). As you can see, these substances often fit into other classifications already discussed in this chapter, but the popularity of these substances in the dance and music scene gives rise to the need to explain their use in these settings for clinicians. They are the same substances previously discussed in this chapter, but their grouping here is due to their common use within social, party-based settings.

Many club drugs were introduced in response to the scheduling of controlled substances. Black market chemists began manufacturing *designer drugs*, which are essentially synthetic substances that are used for their psychoactive properties. MDMA (Ecstasy), MDEA (Eve), and several others either surfaced or gained in popularity between 1970 and 1986, when the Controlled Substances Analogues Enforcement Act was passed. The act placed onto Schedule I or II those synthetic substances "substantially similar" to the chemical structure of a substance already listed under those categories in the Controlled Substances Act.

Club drugs have gained in popularity in recent decades because of their ease of manufacture, availability of precursors of the final chemical compound, and ease of sale. New club drugs have continued to surface. A form of methamphetamine was introduced from Southeast Asia called *ya ba*, which means "crazy drug." Gas chromatography analyses have determined that the methamphetamine pills were adulterated with a variety of substances, ranging from caffeine to morphine, making the effects unpredictable and dangerous.

Many, if not most, club drugs are anything but pure. Drugs are nearly always adulterated, sometimes with extremely unhealthy substances, making dance floor pharmacology a very risky business. Many are analogs of the drug that customers believe they are buying. MDMA, MDEA, GHB, and other drugs are often substituted for the most popular club drug, Ecstasy.

The use of club drugs in conjunction with alcohol, cocaine, and marijuana—which is highly likely—is even more dangerous because of potentiation. In an attempt to minimize adverse reactions, club drug users frequently use a quasi-scientific approach to dose administration during a drug-using episode. Partygoers, often with the aid of information gained from the Internet, measure doses with crude devices such as teaspoons or bottle caps. Often, a companion will monitor the drug use of a raver or club hopper. These attempts at safe drug use frequently end in a trip to the emergency room or, for the most unfortunate, to the morgue.

MDMA (Ecstasy)

Ecstasy (3,4-methlenedioxymethamphetamine, or MDMA or Molly), is a unique club drug, possessing aspects of both an amphetamine and a mild hallucinogen. But the effect of MDMA that makes it unique and the one every consumer of the drug desires is called *empathogenesis*—the ability to open up and feel affection and connectedness for everyone around them. MDMA was legal for a number of years and was used in psychotherapy, but it was outlawed in 1985. MDMA is most common in oral pill form, but is sometimes crushed and smoked or snorted as well. As noted for other substances, MDMA also increases neurotransmitter activity, producing a euphoric feeling for the user (NIDA, 2013b).

INCIDENCE   Popularity of MDMA spread from the United States to England in the 1980s and rapidly throughout Europe, becoming a feature at rave dance parties. After 1994, the use of Ecstasy skyrocketed. Between 2007 and 2010, incidence reports identified increases in the numbers of individuals using MDMA; however, the numbers have fallen and remained stable since 2011. In 2013, 751,000 Americans initiated Ecstasy use within the past 12 months, which was a decline from use levels in 2008 (SAMHSA, 2014). A drop in the use of Ecstasy by high school students appeared from 2001 to 2004, as its use began to be perceived as a high risk. However, a rebound has taken place in 2010 with Ecstasy use increasing for 8th, 10th, and 12th graders, with significant increases for 8th and 10th graders. As of 2015 there has been a decline in use at all three grade levels (Johnston et al., 2016).

PSYCHOACTIVE EFFECTS   MDMA has both stimulant and hallucinogenic effects. It is a synthetic, psychoactive drug chemically similar to the stimulant methamphetamine and the hallucinogen mescaline (NIDA, 2013b). Animals who were trained to recognize amphetamines have also recognized Ecstasy.

When MDMA is first used, the primary effects are elevated mood, euphoria, and a feeling of closeness with others. At lower doses (40 to 80 mg), MDMA also produces high self-esteem, intensified senses of touch and taste, intensified colors, and a feeling of insight into one's self. Doses of 120 mg produce panic, depression, confusion, and anxiety.

The behavioral and psychological effects of MDMA use appear to result from an acute depletion of serotonin in the brain. Animal studies have suggested that damage to the serotonergic system may be reversible in rats. However, studies with primates are not as encouraging.

Neuroscience research has identified that dopamine systems can be affected by MDMA abuse. Although low doses produce few side effects, larger doses, particularly when taken with alcohol or other substances, have produced fatalities. Cardiovascular events (heart attacks) have occurred, as have cerebrovascular accidents (strokes). Liver disease, hyperthermia, panic disorder, paranoid psychosis, and depression have been reported to be precipitated by MDMA use (NIDA, 2013b).

Some evidence indicates that people who take MDMA, even just a few times, may be risking permanent problems with learning and memory. Animal studies found that serotonin neurons in some parts of the brain, specifically those that use the chemical serotonin to communicate with other neurons, were permanently damaged (Rio, 2011). Areas particularly affected were the neocortex (the outer part of the brain where conscious thought occurs) and the hippocampus (which plays a key role in forming long-term memories).

Research has linked MDMA use to long-term damage to those parts of the brain critical to thought, verbal memory, and pleasure (Raj et al., 2009). All indications are that MDMA is toxic to the brain. R. Cowan and colleagues at Vanderbilt University (2006) revealed altered activation in motor-system brain regions in Ecstasy users. Their research findings were consistent with the MDMA-induced alterations in basal ganglia-thalamocortical circuit neurophysiology demonstrated by earlier studies.

EFFECTS ON THE BODY   MDMA is readily absorbed, and effects can be noticed approximately 30 minutes after ingestion. Peak effects are noticed in 1 to 5 hours. Consumers take a dose or "roll" at designated intervals to prolong peak effects. MDMA is metabolized in the liver and eliminated by the kidneys as an active metabolite in about 24 hours.

Ogeil, Rajaratnam, and Broadbear (2013) found that female Ecstasy users report more psychological symptoms after each use and males experience more physiological symptoms. Short-term side effects include dizziness, nystagmus, jaw clenching, and hallucinations. More severe effects include dehydration, hyperthermia, hyponatremia, seizures, and arrhythmia. With prolonged use, euphoria and empathy effects are diminished and replaced by a jittery amphetamine-like experience. Long-term effects include dysphoric mood and cognitive dulling.

MDMA has implications for sexual activity. It has been reported to cause impotence in men. At the same time, some men have reported sustained erection but an inability to achieve an orgasm. MDMA users report decreased sexual interest when intoxication effects are highest, followed by a rapid switch to intensified sexual desire. When effects of disinhibition and social openness are factored in, it is very likely that unsafe sex practices are increased.

VOLATILE SUBSTANCES OR INHALANTS

This group contains several chemicals that can be "sniffed," "snorted," "huffed," "bagged," or inhaled. Current use includes volatile organic solvents, such as those found in paint and fuel; aerosols, such as hair sprays, spray paints, and deodorants; volatile nitrites (amyl nitrite and butyl nitrite); and general anesthetic agents, such as nitrous oxide (NIDA, 2012a). Volatile substances, as ordinary household or medical items, are not listed on the DEA Controlled Substances Schedule.

INCIDENCE   Abuse of inhalants is a much larger problem than most people realize. The National Survey on Drug Use and Health reported in 2008 that 2 million Americans age 12 and older had abused inhalants, and in 2013 there were 563,000 persons aged 12 or older who had used inhalants for the first time (SAMHSA, 2010, 2014). The 2015 *Monitoring the Future* report revealed that inhalant use has been on the decline in 8th graders since 2015, significantly declining in 10th graders since 2007, and considerably declining in 12th graders since 2005. For the three grades combined, the annual use of inhalants has declined significantly in both 2012 and 2013, held constant in 2014, and slowly started declining again in 2015 (Johnston et al., 2016).

PSYCHOACTIVE EFFECTS   Inhalants are widely available, readily accessible, inexpensive, and legally obtained, making them attractive to adolescents (Oklan & Henderson, 2014). The toxic vapors make users forget their problems as they obtain a quick high with a minimal hangover (Howard, Bowen, Garland, Perron, & Vaughn, 2011). Short-term effects are similar to those of anesthetics (Ahern & Falsafi, 2013). Disruptive and antisocial behavior as well as self-directed aggression is associated with individuals who use inhalants. However, it is not clear whether there is a cause-and-effect relationship—that is, whether inhalant use promotes antisocial and self-destructive tendencies or, conversely, whether those youths who have antisocial or self-destructive tendencies tend to use inhalants.

EFFECTS ON THE BODY   Acute symptoms associated with the use of inhalants include excitation turning to drowsiness, disinhibition, lightheadedness, and agitation (Garland & Howard, 2011). With increasing intoxication, the user may develop ataxia, dizziness, and disorientation (Cairney et al., 2013). Extreme intoxication may create signs of sleeplessness, general muscle weakness, nystagmus, hallucinations, and disruptive behavior. After the high wears off, the user may sleep, appear lethargic, and experience headaches. Chronic users may experience continual weight loss, muscle weakness, general disorientation, inattentiveness, and lack of coordination. These physical conditions can be complicated by the use of other substances (mainly alcohol, cigarettes, and marijuana), malnutrition, and respiratory illness.

TOXICITY   Neurotoxicity is predominantly related to the type of substance inhaled and the dose and duration of exposure. Because of the extreme neurotoxicity of these volatile substances, death and permanent neurological damage with lasting neuropsychological sequelae, from which individuals often do not recover, can be seen just after one use (Dingwall & Cairney, 2011). Acute, high-level exposure to solvents will induce short-term effects on brain functioning, but appear to be reversible. Chronic, high-level exposure over a longer time slowly produces irreversible neurological syndromes. Severe damage to the brain and nervous system can occur, and prolonged use can cause death by starving the body of oxygen or forcing the heart to beat more rapidly and erratically. There is concern over the number of deaths caused by the direct toxic effects of inhalants, particularly in young people. Harmful irreversible effects including loss of hearing, central nervous system damage, peripheral neuropathies, and bone marrow damage can be caused by inhalation of spray paints, glues, dewaxers, dry-cleaning chemicals, correction fluids, or gasoline (NIDA, 2012a; Volkow, 2005).

ANABOLIC-ANDROGENIC STEROIDS

Anabolic-androgenic steroids (AASs), although strictly not psychoactive or mood-altering substances, are included in this chapter because of their incidence of use and their effects on the body. The use of AASs to enhance athletic performance and muscular appearance has been widespread in world-class athletes and in non-athletes, such as adolescents, law enforcement and corrections officers, and physical fitness devotees. They are listed as Schedule III drugs on the DEA Controlled Substances Schedule. AASs are human-made substances related to male sex hormones. Steroids refer to a class of drugs that are legal only by prescription (NIDA, 2012b).

The use of anabolic steroids can lead to serious health problems including risk of liver and heart disease, stroke, hepatitis, and infections from contaminated needles (Volkow, 2006).

INCIDENCE   Use of AASs has been viewed as a silent epidemic in the United States. However, there is a lack of data on the prevalence of AAS use in the population (Pope et al., 2014). A SAMHSA report in 1995 showed 1,084,000 Americans as having used AASs, with 312,000 (29%) using in the previous year, compared with a lifetime heroin use of 2,083,000 Americans and 281,000 (13%) having used in the previous year. The *Monitoring the Future* survey has reported that steroid use among young adults has remained mostly consistent since 1989 (Johnston et al., 2016). Additional researchers have made an attempt to aggregate databases to predict the current number of lifetime steroid users in the United States. They found that an estimated 2.9 million to 4.0 million people aged 13 to 50 in the United States have used steroids in their lifetime, with 1 million of those users having met the criteria for steroid use disorder (Pope et al., 2014). It has been reported that use of steroids in 2015 was only 0.5%, 1.0%, and 2.5% for boys in grades 8, 10, and 12 compared to 0.5%, 0.4%, and 0.7% for girls in the same grades, respectively (Johnston et al., 2016). However, these numbers are on the low end of estimates, and even with this data, the study by Pope and colleagues (2014) still predicted the current population to include 2.9 to 4.0 million lifetime users of steroids.

Factors that can motivate individuals to use to AAS include a desire for increased muscular strength, improved physique, improvement in athletic performance, and increased self-confidence. Some coaches and parents of young athletes exert pressure to use AASs to become more competitive. In addition, certain groups or personality types seem more associated with AAS use. It has been suggested that histrionic, narcissistic, antisocial, and borderline personality disorder groups have a higher incidence of use, as do those dissatisfied with their body image (NIDA, 2012b).

EFFECTS ON THE BODY   *Anabolic* describes the action of this category of substances to increase the speed of growth of body tissues, whereas *steroids* refers to their chemical structure. Anabolic-androgenic steroids are only one in the classification of steroids produced naturally in the body. Testosterone and similar altered steroids are androgenic, having masculinizing effects on the body, increasing muscle mass, aggression, and self-confidence. Testosterone has the disadvantage of having a brief elimination half-life, making it available to the body only for short periods of time.

Administration of AASs is commonly by injection, but they can be taken orally, typically in cycles of weeks or months (referred to as "cycling"). Dosing is usually done with a pyramid-dosing schedule, in which a cyclic building to a peak followed by a gradual reduction in dosage is maintained. Cycles typically run 4 to 18 weeks on AASs, with 1 month to 1 year off the substances. Alternatively, up to eight AASs may be used concurrently.

AASs affect many body systems. Unwanted effects may include cardiovascular conditions, such as myocardial infarction, myocarditis, cardiac arrest with enlargement of the heart and death of heart cells, cerebrovascular accident (stroke), and severe restriction of blood flow to the lower limbs of the body. Liver changes may also occur. Testosterone and other AASs are metabolized in part by estrogen antagonists, such as estradiol. The estrogen antagonists can cause breast pain in men and gynecomastia (enlargement and development of breast tissue) requiring medical or surgical intervention. Testicular atrophy in men is common, as is voice deepening, clitoral hypertrophy, shrinking of breasts, menstrual irregularities, and excessive growth of hair in women. These changes are largely irreversible in females, whereas the sexual side effects in males are often reversible. The masculinizing effects of testosterone are achieved by its binding to intracellular receptors in target cells. This forms an androgen-receptor complex that binds to chromosomes, leading to increases in proteins and RNAs within the chromosome (NIDA, 2012b). Mood disturbances of hypomania, mania, irritability, depressed mood, major depression, elation, recklessness, feelings of power and invincibility, and both increased and decreased libido have been reported during use of AASs.

The first reports of what was considered at the time as "psychological dependence" on AASs emerged in the late 1980s. Loss of control and interference with other activities has been reported during use. Withdrawal symptoms include the desire to take more AASs, fatigue, dissatisfaction with body image, depressed mood, restlessness, anorexia, insomnia, decreased libido, and headache. Suicidal thoughts have been reported after cessation of use.

CASE DISCUSSIONS

Case 1: Sandy and Pam

Both Sandy and Pam exhibited depressant use, using alcohol and "downers." As noted in this section, depressants have a tendency to decrease inhibitions, and users can engage in poor decision making. Considering this, the actions of both Pam and Sandy under the influence of depressants with regard to risky sexual behaviors align with using this class of substances. What else in the case of Sandy and Pam might be occurring that is a direct influence of depressant use?

Case 3: Leigh

Leigh has been shoplifting and using many substances, including specific stimulants. Remember that stimulants can elevate mood. Leigh has been struggling with a series of losses, including missing her father, old school, and friends. The adjustments in Leigh's life may have influenced depressant symptoms in Leigh; thus, her stimulant use could be viewed as an attempt to increase feelings of happiness and decrease any depressive symptoms.

Conclusion

The human brain is the major site for all psychoactive substance interactions. All psychoactive substances manipulate the biochemistry of the brain and change the neuron's process of communication within its existing structural framework. Substances affect the brain's communication system and interfere with the way nerve cells normally send, receive, and process information. These changes alter the user's perceptions, emotions, thoughts, and behaviors over time. In addition, substances have effects on many other body organs. Neuroscience research is making significant strides in determining the biological actions that make people reliant on substances and how over time they affect the makeup of the brain. Research involving the neurosciences, psychopharmacology, and new therapeutic strategies with chemically dependent populations is producing new insights into successfully identifying the effects of illicit substance use on the CNS, particularly the brain, and strategies to repair some of the damage. Several recent findings in neuroscience research have been reported in this chapter.

MyCounselingLab for Addictions/Substance Use

Try the Topic 2 Assignments: *Substance Use and the Body*.

Case Study

The background of this client follows: He is a 63-year-old White male. He is currently financially stable with an income exceeding $250,000 annually. He has worked for 30 years in the oil and gas industry. He has been married for 35 years and has two married children and five grandchildren, aged 5 to 17 years old. He has provided minimal information regarding his family of origin.

The presenting issue of this client is polysubstance abuse. He is physiologically dependent on opiates as a result of taking medication as originally prescribed by his medical doctor for pain management. Prescriptions include hydrocodone, oxycodone, and fentanyl. Along with abusing these meds daily for 13 years, the client has been a regular user of cocaine. In fact, his cocaine habit at times

affected his family's economic stability. He was referred by his employer for treatment with the goal of total abstinence as a condition for continued employment.

Critical Thinking Questions

1. What additional information would you need from this client in order to properly assess damage potentially caused by the long-term use of substances?
2. What would you expect to find through neuroscience brain imaging considering cocaine and prescription substance use?
3. Is it possible for the brain to repair itself under these circumstances of long-term polysubstance use?

CHAPTER 4

Etiology of Substance Abuse: Why People Use

M. Kristina DePue, Ph.D., NCC

Theories about what causes substance use disorders (SUDs) are varied and controversial. For instance, does a weak moral character cause substance use, or is it a disease? Is substance use a learned behavior? Or, is substance use a result of heredity or caused by environmental factors? This chapter addresses these questions by examining theories used to explain why individuals begin and continue to use alcohol, tobacco, and other drugs. Understanding the theoretical foundation of use may be important when developing a treatment plan for individuals and their families. Theoretical understanding of SUDs provides a useful roadmap for understanding and directing treatment. Although professionals no longer believe that some early theories are valid, they provide the reader with an understanding of the foundation, progression, and advancements in the field. In my discussion of etiology, I will use the language that is associated with the specified theory. The DSM-5 has significantly changed the language of diagnosis in the field, but to understand theories, I believe it is important to keep their language. Additionally, there may be times when the research uses "alcoholism" or "addiction," and I may use those terms as well. Chapter 5 provides the current criteria and explanation for the DSM-5 language for diagnosis.

UNDERSTANDING THEORY

In common usage, people often use the word *theory* to express an opinion or a speculation. In this usage, a theory is not necessarily based on facts and is not required to provide true descriptions of reality. However, for research purposes, Faulkner and Faulkner (2009) define a *theory* as ideas or a group of ideas used to explain a phenomenon based on experiments and/or observations. These ideas or groups of ideas are often shared by most experts in a particular field. Therefore, in research, the terms *theory* and *fact* do not necessarily stand in opposition. For example, it is a fact that an apple dropped from a tree can be observed to fall toward the earth, and the theory used to explain this phenomenon is the theory of gravitation.

This chapter addresses the question of why people begin to use drugs, continue to use drugs, and develop severe substance use disorders based on the following theories: (1) moral theory, (2) disease/medical theory, (3) genetic theory, (4) behavioral theory, (5) sociocultural theory, and (6) an integrated approach. The etiological theories are also considered as models; therefore, the terms *theory* and *model* are used interchangeably.

OVERVIEW OF SUBSTANCE USE DISORDER THEORIES

Moral Theory

For centuries, alcohol consumption was considered a natural part of daily living. It was used at mealtimes, celebration times, mourning times, for pleasure, and for controlling pain. Only at certain periods in time did alcohol use create problems in societies. For example, during the early industrial revolution in England, gin was so cheap that alcohol consumption became problematic among both adults and young children. But at the same time, in the United States the consumption of alcohol was largely considered to be a personal choice, and those who could not "hold" their liquor were considered to have a lack of willpower and, in some cases, were judged to be morally corrupt. This attitude, with its roots in the Puritan belief system, prevailed through much of the 18th and 19th centuries.

During the Civil War, the temperance movement began to gain momentum. The growing sentiment among many people was that alcohol and its uncontrolled ingestion (alcoholism) was a sin—even while alcohol was being used as a sedative on the battlefield. Any individual who "took to drink" and who could not control his or her drinking was morally corrupt. This attitude prevailed and gained momentum until it reached its apex with the passage of the Eighteenth Amendment to the United States Constitution: *Prohibition of Intoxicating Liquors* (National Prohibition Act, 1919). This amendment made the sale, manufacture, or transportation of alcoholic beverages illegal; however, Prohibition did not stop the use of alcohol. The Eighteenth Amendment was repealed in 1933, and once again alcohol could be bought and sold legally in the United States.

It is of note that some prohibitionist themes continue even today, including both user and supplier defined as "fiends" and drug use viewed as "contagious" (an epidemic) (White, 2009, p. 18). But perhaps the best evidence of the popular beliefs that moralize SUDs is the cultural "stigma" attached to it (Barry, McGinty, Pescosolido, & Goldman, 2014). This includes drug users being stigmatized by outsiders as well as the stigmatization of classes of users (alcoholics/ drug users/needle users) for having less "control" of their drug use and prevention and educational campaigns that still portray the drug user as "physically diseased, morally depraved, and criminally dangerous" (White, 2009, p. 20).

Aspects of Use Addressed by the Moral Theory

CONTINUUM OF USE   Moral theory views addictive substance use and behavior as sinful and morally wrong. In this theory, people begin using because they are bad people with little moral strength. Because moral theory considers addictive substance use and behaviors to be a choice, people continue these behaviors because they choose to continue them. So, essentially, continued use occurs because bad people are making bad choices. Individuals have full control over their substance use, and because of a lack of willpower and moral regulation, people choose to continue addictive substance use or behaviors. The moral theory views substance use solely as the fault of the person using and categorizes people with addiction as evil.

CHANGE   The notion of change in moral theory is rarely considered; therefore, "treatment" based on moral theory would consist primarily of punishment. Because the person with addiction is considered evil and morally decrepit, rehabilitation is not the goal of treatment. Instead, the goal is to lock away the "antisocial" individuals and rid society of such addicts. Arguably, recovery would take place only if the person chose to stop using and changed their moral belief system.

At that point, the individual would be "cured" of addiction. Consequently, relapse occurs when the individual chooses to forgo moral choices and use addictive substances or behaviors again. Relapse is the result of a lack of willpower and moral standards.

CONCLUSION   The moral view of addiction is a mostly historical theory that is rarely found in treatment centers today. Because of strengths in research, considering addiction as a moral deficiency based on individual choices seems illogical. In some ways, the idea of choice resonates with many individuals; however, a major pitfall of this theory is that it focuses exclusively on individual ability (willpower) and characteristics to control or quit addictive substances and behaviors and ignores the compounding factors of genetics, neuroscience, and the environment.

DISEASE/MEDICAL THEORY

In 1935 an organization known as Alcoholics Anonymous (AA) was founded based on the statement that addiction was a progressive and chronic disease. AA shifted responsibility away from the alcoholic as morally deficient with the concept that alcoholics suffer from an illness. AA retained some elements of the moral model, believing that the help of a Higher Power is needed to achieve and maintain sobriety and individuals are responsible for seeking their own recovery. However, AA was a shift in philosophy from the moral model in that the individual was not held responsible for "having the disease" of alcoholism, but was responsible for seeking help to arrest the disease. This shift toward the disease model (also known as the medical model) gained validity when the American Medical Association recognized alcoholism as a disease in a 1966 policy statement (American Medical Association, 1966). It is this shift in paradigms that allowed alcoholism and other substance abuse to be scientifically studied. These research studies precipitated the development of new theoretical models for causality and treatment.

Historically, the notion of the disease model has been thought of in linear terms, indicating that addiction follows a trend of worsening symptoms, bottoming out, and then an upward pathway of recovery once substance use has ceased. For example, a physician, Dr. E. M. Jellinek (1946), provided the first theoretical description of the predictable progression of alcoholism as a disease. In his book titled *The Disease Concept of Alcoholism* (1960), he described five types of drinking behaviors identified by the first five letters of the Greek alphabet—alpha, beta, gamma, delta, and epsilon. This information suggested that there were distinct signs and symptoms of alcoholism, an important criterion if it is to be termed a disease. These symptoms were clustered into developmental stages of alcoholism: early, middle, and late. In 1975, M. M. Glatt expanded on Jellinek's developmental model of alcoholism by adding additional addictions: drugs, gambling, food, and smoking. Glatt (1975) also created a visual representation of Jellinek's ideas, which is often incorrectly referred to as the "Jellinek Chart" (Figure 4.1). Glatt's V-chart expanded on Jellinek's phases to include descriptive pathways to hitting "rock bottom" as well as locations for intervention. On this chart, the disease progresses downward on the left side and recovery progresses upward on the right side of the chart.

A caveat: It is important to keep in mind that Glatt's V-chart is still widely used in treatment settings (Venner & Miller, 2001), but there is little to no empirical support for the chart (DePue, 2013; DePue, Finch & Nation, 2014). Jellinek founded his theory using unsound methods with only male participants, and Glatt's additions were also based solely on theory and observations (Jellinek, 1946; Glatt, 1975).

In the traditional disease theory, the disease of addiction rested on the assumption that substance use was a primary disorder and not the underlying cause of other psychological or

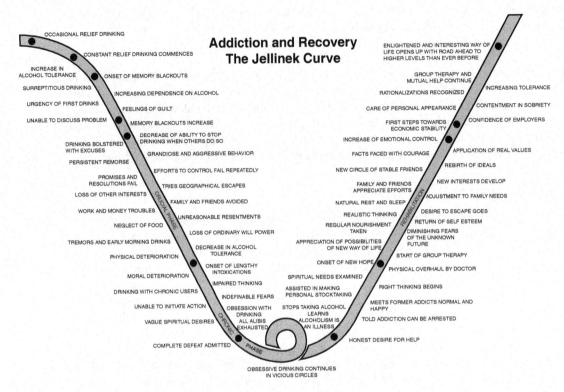

FIGURE 4.1   Jellinek curve.

Source: Indiana State Government. Retrieved from http://www.in.gov/judiciary/ijlap/jellinek.pdf

moral issues. Today, the disease/medical model is the most prevalent of all treatment models of SUDs and has received increasing attention from the research community, as medical research has found extensive evidence that SUDs are indeed comparable to a disease. AA was founded on disease theory; however, research has evolved the disease theory into a complex, multifaceted approach to understanding SUDs. You will learn more about AA in Chapter 10.

Once substance use, abuse, and dependency began to be viewed as a progressive disease, this led to the epidemiology of alcohol abuse and alcohol dependence published in the American Psychiatric Association's *Diagnostic and Statistical Manual of Mental Disorders* (*DSM*). A review of the history of the DSM criteria by the National Institute on Alcohol Abuse and Alcoholism (1995) notes that the DSM-I and DSM-II categorized alcoholism as a subset of personality disorders, homosexuality, and neuroses. However, the evolution of diagnostic criteria for behavioral disorders involving alcohol reached a turning point in 1980 with the publication of the DSM-III. For the first time, the term *alcoholism* was dropped in favor of two distinct categories labeled "alcohol abuse" and "alcohol dependence." These criteria have continued through several revisions and editions. The current DSM-5 combines abuse and dependence into a single disorder called substance-use disorder (e.g., alcohol-use disorder, nicotine-use disorder, cannabis-use disorder, amphetamine-use disorder, etc.) (American Psychiatric Association, 2013).

A caveat: Twelve-step programs agree that SUDs are a chronic, relapsing disease, but messages of the linear models are found within the 12-step narrative. For example, the notion of rock bottom was included with the original, linear models of addiction. AA also considers hitting rock bottom to be a necessary requirement for sustained recovery but considers rock-bottom experiences to be unique to the individual. Considering the chronicity of addiction, there may be many rock bottoms or bottoming-out experiences (BOEs; DePue, Finch, & Nation, 2014) in the trajectory of addiction. In fact, rock bottom can be thought of as a subjective experience that helps individuals claim a negative experience as the end of their use. When working with clients, the idea of rock bottom might be harmful before a person enters recovery; however, helping clients formulate their individual rock-bottom experience/s to avoid a lower BOE can be an extremely useful tool helping client stay sober.

The Neurobiology of Substance Use Disorders

Modern approaches to disease theory state that SUDs are not linear, but in fact, chronic in nature (Dennis & Scott, 2007; Volkow, Fowler, & Wang, 2004). The *chronicity of SUDs* means that instead of SUDs following an identifiable stage-based pathway, the course of addiction may look more like a roller coaster with many ups, downs, twists, and turns (McLellan, Lewis, O'Brien, & Kleber, 2000; Silverman, DeFulio, & Sigurdsson, 2012). Therefore, SUDs are more closely associated with chronic, incurable medical conditions such as diabetes and asthma, which need lifelong attention to maintain stability. This does not mean that recovery cannot be a straight path for some, but that change might involve several attempts. Since the disease model has shifted its focus to a chronic view of SUDs, the following section highlights current trends explaining this disorder according to the medical model.

A Look at Brain Function Reward

The medical model notes that SUDs are a brain disease and increase in severity over time if left untreated. As noted in Chapter 3, addictive substances and behaviors affect the reward center of the brain by causing a powerful release of dopamine, which is the neurotransmitter involved in experiences of pleasure. Over time, the brain needs more of the chemical or behavior to achieve the same amount of pleasure, thus perpetuating continued use of the substance. Under normal circumstances, dopamine interacts with another neurotransmitter (glutamate) to imprint an association of the experience of pleasure with survival necessities, such as eating, into our memories. With increasing exposure to addictive substances and behaviors, dopamine tells the brain that it not only wants the addictive substances or behaviors, but also needs them for survival. The brain was never meant to handle the amount of dopamine released by addictive substances and behaviors; therefore, the brain is tricked into thinking it needs that amount of dopamine to survive. These unconscious brain mechanisms cause tolerance and craving in individuals, thus perpetuating continued use and causing addiction. Disease theory notes that people continue to use addictive substances and behaviors because they are unaware that they have the disease until it is problematic.

CHANGE   Because SUDs affect multiple layers of functioning, the disease/medical model takes a multidimensional approach to treatment. The medical model considers SUDs to be a lifelong, chronic, and relapsing condition. Therefore, a person with an SUD is never considered cured, only "in remission," "recovering," or a "nonpracticing" person with an SUD. One early Alcoholics Anonymous–approved brochure (1976) titled *Is There an Alcoholic in Your Life?* states:

> The alcoholic is a sick person suffering from a disease for which there is no known cure; that is, no cure in the sense that he or she will ever be able to drink moderately, like a nonalcoholic, for any sustained period. Because it is an illness—a physical compulsion combined with a mental obsession to drink—the alcoholic must learn to stay away from alcohol completely in order to lead a normal life. (p. 8)

Recovery is, therefore, focused on abstinence. After abstinence, the medical model postulates that relieving underlying psychological issues, such as the guilt and shame felt by individuals experiencing the consequences of their disease, through the AA Twelve Step or counseling process might make them more amenable to treatment.

Initial detoxification, if necessary, is often followed by counseling and AA 12-step support groups to make lifestyle changes that eliminate being around the drug(s) of choice and "using" friends. Twelve-step programs are a major part of many professional treatment plans, and treatment staff often recommend that clients attend "90 meetings in 90 days." A 12-step "home group" is identified by the person with an SUD, and a recovering "sponsor" is obtained to provide ongoing social support for sobriety. Sayings such as "If you don't want to get shot, don't go where the shooting is" reinforce behavioral changes to eliminate exposure to temptation.

However, by claiming to have a disease, some people believe they can deny responsibility for change, especially since denial is a primary symptom of substance use. Some may refuse treatment with the attitude of "What do you expect from a person with a disease?" The medical models encourages individuals to take responsibility for their actions caused by their disordered substance use.

Once clean and/or sober, the person with an SUD may begin to feel confident that s/he can now be in control of the use. Further, underlying or confounding problems may have been ignored during recovery. There are some adherents to disease theory that consider relapse to be a "failure" for someone working a recovery program. Modern approaches to the medical model take a more accepting stance on relapse because disordered use of substances is a chronic, relapsing condition. This modern view normalizes the concept of relapse for clients and can be a useful tool to facilitate clients' work through the guilt and shame associated with a return to use. AA also considers relapse to be a part of the process for many individuals and warns that relapses often send people back to using as severely and heavily as before sobriety. Although research does not support this notion, the fear of a return to previous use may be both a deterrent and a cause of relapse (see Chapter 10).

In today's treatment world, all substance use disorders are often treated in the same way. When this occurs, there is minimal recognition of the complex accompanying factors such as polydrug use, gender, and age. There is a lack of drug- and gender-specific treatments for SUDs; ignoring these factors could be related to relapse. Research is growing in each of the aforementioned areas as federal funding has increased for both drug-specific and gender-specific studies in SUD research, thus leading to more clearly defined relapse prevention models.

CONCLUSION   Viewing alcohol dependence as a disease caused a major paradigm shift in social perception and treatment approaches of disordered substance use in this country. The belief that there is no cure for alcoholism but that it can be brought into remission through sobriety is one of the strengths of the disease theory. People with SUDs were no longer blamed for their disease (much as one would not blame someone for having cancer or diabetes).

Having a disease also removed some of the social stigma of being an "alcoholic," thus making it easier and more palatable for someone to seek treatment. Categorizing an SUD as a disease created opportunities for scientific research and the study of genetic influences, as discussed in the next section.

A limitation of the disease theory is that it does not address the individuals who seek to reduce their alcohol consumption as opposed to abstaining. In fact, some argue that the disease concept disables an individual into being "sick," with no control over their own actions (Henden, Melberg, & Røgeberg, 2013), and that the "ill" person is disempowered (Graham, Young, Valach, & Wood, 2008). Regardless of this debate, the medical theory remains the prominent etiology for diagnosing substance disorders.

A final note of consideration in the therapeutic community is that a recovering counselor is viewed as an asset—people with SUDs are more likely to believe recovery is possible if the person telling them so has "been there." Recovering people commonly work as paraprofessional staff members or peer mentors in treatment programs. This is reinforced by the 12th step of *The Twelve Steps of Alcoholics Anonymous*: "Having had a spiritual awakening as the result of these steps, we tried to carry this message to alcoholics, and to practice these principles in all our affairs" (Alcoholics Anonymous, 2002, p. 106). Although personal experiences are empowering for clients, additional professional training and/or education in treatment techniques and skills strengthen the possibility of client recovery. It is noteworthy that new outcome research is focused on the therapeutic alliance, and more studies need to be done on the relationship between the client–counselor alliance and counselor recovery status. Nonetheless, according to the medical model, just as a physician would not need to have cancer to effectively treat cancer, mental health professionals do not need to have used substances to treat a substance use disorder.

A caveat: It is noteworthy that the remaining theories in the chapter are often considered as complementary theories with the medical model. This chapter presents them separately for reasons of clarity.

GENETIC THEORY

Research involving intergenerational studies, twin studies, adoption studies, biological research, and a search for genetic markers of alcohol and substance dependence are currently underway in an attempt to further explain alcohol and drug dependency. Heritability studies on families, adoption, and twins have demonstrated that genetic factors contribute between 50% and 60% of the variance of risk for alcoholism (Foroud, Edenberg, & Crabbe, 2010). Dependence on illicit drugs has recently been studied in twins, and heritability estimates range from 45% to 79% (Dick & Agrawal, 2008). Twin studies compare the rates of SUDs for both monozygotic twins (twins developing from one egg and one sperm—commonly referred to as identical twins) and dizygotic twins (twins developing from two separate fertilized eggs—commonly referred to as fraternal twins). Evidence from longitudinal twin studies reveal several childhood genetic risk factors that are predictive of substance abuse in adolescents (Hicks, Iacono, & McGue, 2012).

In addition to twin studies, adoption studies have also examined the influence of genetics and environment that address the ongoing debate of nature versus nurture (genetics vs. environment). Adoption studies compare the disease status of adoptees with their birth parents and their adoptive parents with whom they have no genetic relationship. If SUDs were influenced by genetic factors, then we would expect to find a high rate of SUDs in children of parents who were addicted regardless of whether they were raised by their substance-abusing parents or someone else. If a disease (such as alcoholism) is genetically transmitted, then monozygotic twins should both exhibit that disease (because they are genetically identical).

To date, adoption studies consistently indicate a relationship between biological parent substance use and the adopted child (Agrawal & Lynskey, 2008). A study conducted by King and colleagues (2009) compared the effects of alcoholism history on offspring in 409 adoptive and 208 nonadoptive families. The results showed exposure to parental alcoholism to be a risk factor for a child using alcohol. Although scientists have found that there are indeed genetic influences on SUDs, the exact nature of these influences is unclear. Scientists have not been able to identify specific genes responsible for SUDs, but adoption studies have provided strong evidence for the contribution of genetic influences to vulnerability to alcoholism, somatization, criminality, anxiety, and depressive disorders. Identifying specific genes responsible for SUDs is difficult. For example, multiple genetic variants can predict SUDs in twins, and a single genetic variant is also predictive (Ducci & Goldman, 2012). Therefore, being able to identify the primary genetic variant causes of SUDs becomes quite complex. If you are interested in learning more specifics about genetic variants of SUDs, we encourage you to read Ducci and Goldman's 2012 article "The Genetic Basis of Addictive Disorders."

CLASSIFICATION SYSTEMS AND TYPOLOGIES   Biological research on SUD classification subtypes consists of single domain (e.g., age of onset) and/or multidimensional classification schemes (Babor & Caetano, 2006; Ducci & Goldman, 2012). Although there have been studies indicating as many as five classification systems for alcoholism (Lynskey et al., 2005), researchers have consistently identified two basic subtypes of people with alcoholism, or binary topologies (Babor & Caetano, 2006; Ducci & Goldman, 2012). In a foundational cluster study consisting of 321 alcohol-addicted male and female participants, Babor and colleagues (1992) found two typologies and labeled them Type A and Type B. Type A alcoholics are characterized by later onset, fewer childhood risk factors, less severe dependence, fewer alcohol-related problems, and less psychopathological dysfunction. Type B alcoholics are characterized by childhood risk factors, familial alcoholism, early onset of alcohol-related problems, greater severity of dependence, polydrug use, a more chronic treatment history, greater psychopathological dysfunction, and more life stress.

Another binary topology was discovered as the result of studying the behavior of a large birth cohort of children born in Stockholm that had been separated from their biological parents at birth and reared in adopted homes. Cloninger, Bohman, and Sigvardsson (1981) found evidence of two subtypes of alcoholism: Type 1 and Type 2. Type 1 alcoholics, it is believed, transmit cross-gender (from mothers to sons or grandfathers to granddaughters). Type 2 alcoholics transmit the disease to the same gender (fathers to sons or grandmothers to granddaughters). Type 1 alcoholics tend to have less criminal behavior, have less dependent personality traits, be less violent when they drink, and have a later onset of the disease (most often after age 25). Type 2 alcoholics, on the other hand, tend to exhibit more violent behaviors when they drink, show signs of compulsive drinking (blackouts, for example), and have more dependent personality traits. What was once considered to be a normal part of the alcoholic drinking pattern (fighting and argumentative behavior) is now seen as germane to Type 2 alcoholics. These original findings were later confirmed by the same researchers in a replication study using the same methods (Sigvardsson, Bohman, & Cloninger, 1996). Binary/dichotomous typology models have been demonstrated repeatedly in the literature over time (Ducci & Goldman, 2012). Continued research is needed to standardize accepted typologies to aid in assessment and treatment modalities for the mental health profession (Leggio, Kenna, Fenton, Bonenfant, & Swift, 2009).

Aspects of Use Addressed by Genetic Theories

CONTINUUM OF USE   There are many factors that influence the motivation to engage in substance use (Hayatbakhsh, Williams, Bor, & Najman, 2013; Urbanoski & Kelly, 2012). For example, a history of parental drinking, smoking, or drug use and the degree of life stability are important factors in determining initiation of substance use (Hayatbakhsh et al., 2013; Park, Kim, & Kim, 2009; Urbanoski & Kelly, 2012). Exactly how genetics influences alcohol use initiation is unclear, partially because of the difficulty in measuring the substance use–genetics relationship (Urbanoski & Kelly, 2012). Initiation of both alcohol and drug use is likely to be environmental (King et al., 2009; Smirnov et al., 2013). For example, Ecstasy initiation is related to having many peers who also use Ecstasy (Smirnov et al., 2013), and alcohol use initiation significantly co-occurs with tobacco and marijuana use (Komro, Tobler, Maldonado-Molina, & Perry, 2010). Therefore, initiation of substance use increases with exposure to environmental influences and social forces, such as peer-related events where drugs are used and a high level of sensitivity to peer pressure exists. With the use of other drugs (such as heroin, cocaine, methamphetamines, etc.), genetically influenced factors such as personality types (e.g., borderline personality, high impulsivity) have been linked with alcohol and drug dependence (Kienast, Stoffers, Bermpohl, & Lieb, 2014; Walther, Morgenstern, & Hanewinkel, 2012) and other individual factors such as coping strategies (Dolan, Rohsenow, Martin, & Monti, 2013; Giordano et al., 2015).

The decision to continue using a drug may involve a complex combination of social and biological factors. Genetically influenced factors may be important in how the effects are experienced. For instance, the individual's personality, level of anxiety, rate of metabolism, and nervous-system sensitivity to the drug (e.g., coughing, nausea, and vomiting) may all contribute to the final balance between a positive and negative experience of the first ingestion of a drug that will influence the individual's decision to try it again. Social and psychological factors that interact with biological reactions—including peer pressure, the desire to assume an adult role, the need to copy parental models, and society's general attitude about the drug—may induce an individual to repeat the drug use despite a negative effect.

Research on the genetics of tolerance found a gene (*hangover*) that contributes to the development of rapid tolerance to alcohol in fruit flies and has been correlated with alcohol dependence in Irish populations (Pietrzykowski & Treistman, 2008; Riley, Kalsi, Kuo, Vladimirov, Thiselton, & Kendler, 2006). When Scholz, Franz, and Heberlein (2005) announced the discovery of the *hangover* gene in August 2005, the press had a field day. The researchers claimed to have isolated a mutant strain of flies (AE10) that lacks the ability to acquire ethanol tolerance. Even when exposed to ethanol 4 hours earlier, AE10 flies, referred to as *hang*, require the same amount of ethanol to become intoxicated as in instances when they were not previously exposed to ethanol vapors. Thus, this particular mutant strain apparently fails to produce the protein product (the P-element inserted into gene CG32575) called *hangover*. Scholz and colleagues (2005) cited their previous work that demonstrates when normal flies are exposed to ethanol 4 hours prior to a second exposure, the flies require more ethanol in repeated ethanol exposures to reach the same effects as in the first event (Scholz, Ramond, Singh, & Heberlein, 2000). In other words, just like humans, fruit flies have the capacity to develop tolerance to alcohol when repeatedly exposed to the drug.

The greatest impact of genetics might hypothetically occur in the process from first use to SUD development (Chastain, 2006). In this theoretical framework, a variety of genetically influenced factors create a predisposition toward SUDs. Based on family and twin studies, multiple genes are involved (i.e., a polygenic inheritance) or one major gene that acts differently in different circumstances (i.e., incomplete penetrance). This genetic predisposition, or "heritability," has the greatest impact in explaining why many individuals between their mid-20s to 30s might decrease their drinking while others maintain or increase their use (Agrawal & Lynskey, 2006, 2008; Dick & Agrawal, 2008; Foroud et al., 2010; Nurnberger & Bierut, 2007; Schlaepfer, Hoft, & Ehringer, 2008). Genetic variables could be *protective factors,* such as the gene encoding protein ALDH resulting in an acute reaction to alcohol that leads to facial flushing (Ducci & Goldman, 2012). Or, they could be *risk factors,* such as a high tolerance leading to more ingestion of the drug to obtain the pleasant effects related to the gene encoding the protein (ADH) that affects how alcohol is metabolized.

More recently, personality traits have been reexamined (i.e., neuroticism, extraversion, agreeableness, conscientiousness, openness) using a five-factor model (FFM) and are considered in identifying risk factors for substance use disorders (Andreassen et al., 2013; Harakeh, Scholte, de Vries, & Engels, 2006; Hopwood et al., 2007; Kornør & Nordvik, 2007; Luo, Kranzler, Zuo, Wang, & Gelernter, 2007; Terracciano, Löckenhoff, Crum, Bienvenu, & Costa, 2008). Based on the FFM or "Big Five," the NEO Personality Inventory was developed by Costa and McCrae (1985) and revised in 1992 as the NEO PI-R to include additional characteristics (six characteristics under each factor for a total of 30 characteristics). One factor, Neuroticism, measures anxiety, hostility, depression, self-consciousness, impulsiveness, and vulnerability, all of which could be risk factors for use of alcohol, tobacco, and other drugs. Current research on personality focuses on specific phenotypes that are predictive of later substance abuse and dependence. More specifically, impulsivity and elevated risk-taking phenotypes have been clearly associated with SUDs (Walther et al., 2012; Schneider et al., 2012). Sex/gender differences exist in risk taking, with men more likely to engage in risky decision making than women (Daughters, Gorka, Matusiewicz, & Anderson, 2013; Rolison, Hanoch, Wood, & Liu, 2014). The neural and genetic mechanisms behind these personality types are currently being studied in many areas of SUD research.

Comorbidity is high with SUDs, and arguments can be made that genetics are an influence. Mental health disorders, such as antisocial behavior disorder, attention deficit–hyperactivity disorder, and borderline personality disorder, are also linked with SUDs, although the causality is unclear (Carbaugh & Sias, 2010; Demetrovics, 2009; Ducci & Goldman, 2012; Hasin et al., 2006). Possibilities include (a) mental health disorders and SUDs may share risk factors, (b) mental health disorders may be caused by SUDs, or (c) SUDs may result from mental health disorders (Ducci & Goldman, 2012; Moos, 2007). Considering the role of neural mechanisms in SUDs, genes that are involved with the reward circuitry of the brain are of high interest in the SUD research field and considered to play a role in the comorbidity of SUDs and mental health disorders (Ducci & Goldman, 2012). Further research is needed to determine any link to cause and effect or association by risk factors.

SUDs also have a high comorbidity rate with polydrug use (Le Moal & Koob, 2007). In fact, concurrent use of alcohol with other substances is commonly found to be a part of relapse in both adolescents and adults (Ciesla, 2010; Staiger, Richardson, Long, Carr, & Marlatt, 2013). The high incidence of concurrent multiple drug use may be a result of addiction-like patterns of behavior (e.g., reaching for a cigarette and/or an alcoholic drink when under stress) or may be the result of the effects of one drug on another (Hasin et al., 2006). Further, the vulnerability to comorbid conditions may be from a common genetic liability that has been conceptualized as a general predisposition (Dick & Agrawal, 2008). Therefore, as with any disease or pathology, multiple and coexisting conditions may create more complexity in the stabilization and recovery process.

CHANGE   Genetic factors may play a role in temporary remission as metabolism or tolerance changes over time or organ damage leads to an illness that motivates the user to take a "break" from using. A thorough physical examination and family history are important parts of the assessment protocol to identify genetic predisposition. Genetic factors also interact with environmental influences that may encourage the person to stop (at least temporarily) to salvage a marriage or job or avoid legal prosecution. Crisis situations include any compromised ability to maintain adequate personal health or self-care and may prompt the user to seek treatment.

   Conclusion.   A review of the literature reveals a consensus that children of alcoholics run a higher risk of developing alcoholism than children in the general population. The results of several studies suggest a genetic predisposition to alcoholism. Others point to environmental dynamics of the family in predicting the intergenerational transmission of SUDs. Recent studies point to the possibility that there may be several distinct types of genetic conditions, each with its own pattern of heritability and susceptibility, that increase the risk of dependency. Further, recent studies examine the interaction between the genetic conditions and environmental conditions that relate to abuse and dependency. The finding of associations between genetically determined personality traits and disorders and substance use may shed more light on the risk factors involved in determining which individuals may be more vulnerable to the development of alcoholism and other substance abuse.

BEHAVIORAL THEORIES

Behavioral theories have their beginnings in psychology with behavioral psychologists such as Pavlov, Thorndyke, Watson, and Skinner (Gurman and Messer, 2003). They postulated that all behavior is learned thus lending credence to an environmental perspective. Yin (2008) highlighted the three modes of behavioral control identified in studies that are important for understanding substance use disorders: the Pavlovian approach (e.g., approaching environmental stimuli associated with reward), goal-directed action (repeat of stimulation that leads to increased activity), and habit (continued behavior regardless of consequences).

Aspects of Use Addressed by the Behavioral Theory

CONTINUUM OF USE   *Social Learning Theory*, published by Albert Bandura (1977), also forms a part of the behavioral theory about substance abuse. Cognitive, genetic, and sociocultural factors are thought to predispose individuals to or influence experimentation with alcohol or drugs as well as subsequent use. In social learning theory, substance use is a function of the person and environmental interaction, including a focus on positive norms, expectations, value systems, cognitive factors, and modeling from family members and peers who engage in obtaining and using them (Kouimtsidis, 2010).

   However, the drug of preference is more likely to be a function of availability and affordability (e.g., caffeine, alcohol, nicotine). Drug experimentation might be viewed by behaviorists as a function of undesirable behaviors caused by weak or absent social controls such as deviant friends or lack of supervision (Moss, 2007). For instance, a rebellious child takes a puff of a cigarette even though he or she has been told never to smoke. In addition, individuals might try a drug to succumb to the perceived rewards of drug use—for example, a teenager who drinks alcohol for the first time as an initiation to be a part of a peer group. Therefore, initial use of a drug may occur when an individual's coping abilities, through the interaction of personality sets, learned responses, and current circumstances, are overwhelmed.

Although continued use is generally seen as dependent on a positive experience or other reward (such as group inclusion or relief from anxiety), researchers are beginning to examine whether the chemicals themselves act to reinforce the continued use of the drug. For example, a review of the literature on SUDs and dose response by Calabrese (2008) suggests that psychomotor stimulation (the arousal or acceleration of physical activity), based on Skinnerian operant reinforcement theory, is a predictor of whether a drug will be reinforcing (i.e., addictive). Considerable support for this conclusion was found in caffeine, nicotine, alcohol, and pentobarbital (a short-acting barbiturate).

Further, neuroscience research contributes to the efficacy of behavioral theory by focusing on neural mechanisms that underlie behavioral actions, specifically the reward circuitry of the brain. The release of dopamine acts as a positive reinforcement for drugs (especially opiates) because many drugs have the ability to increase dopamine in synapses made in various parts of the brain (as you previously read in this chapter). Essentially, substances can cause a person to feel good because of the dopamine release, thus resulting in both a positive reinforcement and a positive association between feeling good and the substance. This works on several levels, not just within the brain but behaviorally. For example, if an individual is naturally shy and withdrawn and then becomes talkative and outgoing after using a particular chemical, it is a natural occurrence that this person will continue to use that chemical to achieve mastery over shyness.

A characteristic of positive reinforcement is when an individual continues to engage in a behavior long after negative consequences are experienced—simply because of the rewarding characteristics. In other words, the substance user will continue to use even though it is clearly causing problems (legal, familial, problems with work, etc.). A characteristic of social learning is when the user is engaging in compulsive behavior because it is a "habit" that has become a part of daily functioning, sometimes tied to certain times of the day (e.g., first thing in the morning or after 5:00), events (e.g., clubbing or entertaining), or rituals (while cooking or talking on the phone) (Wise & Koob, 2014). However, Sjoerds and colleagues (2014) point out that habituation may vary and can resemble SUDs, but that enhanced habits are not always the same as addictive habits. Research results indicate that the loss of control over substance use separates habit from SUDs. This loss of control is not experienced by all people, and those with a high behavioral impulsivity trait might accelerate from action to habit to substance use disorders more frequently than those without the high impulsivity trait (Everitt, 2014).

Addictive behavior is maintained by reinforcement (i.e., the rewarding aspects of drug consumption and the social setting). Several principles of reinforcement are active in behavior formation and maintenance, including addictive behaviors. Some examples are as follows:

1. The more rewarding or positive an experience is, the greater the likelihood that the behavior leading to that experience will be repeated. Thus, an individual who is depressed and becomes "the life of the party" after using cocaine will want to re-create that experience by using again.

2. The greater the frequency of obtaining positive experiences through drug consumption, the more likely that drugs will be consumed again.

3. The more closely in time that the behavior (drug consumption) and consequences of the behavior are experienced, the more likely it is that the behavior will be repeated. Conversely, the further in time that a consequence of the behavior is experienced, the less the likelihood that the consequence will affect future behavior. For example, a lonely man who finds companionship in the bar drinking with others is likely to remember the camaraderie associated with the drinking, and the hangover the next day is more easily attributed to "overdrinking" than to drinking with certain friends. It is this reinforcing association of the two events that increases the likelihood of his drinking when feeling lonely or isolated.

CHANGE   Recovery involves a behavior change to break the cyclical pattern of substance abuse and may include replacing the rewards gained by continued use. One way to break a habit is to present the drug (stimulus) to the individual until a negative effect results—or aversive conditioning. An example would be giving an individual a cigar (stimulus) to smoke until he or she becomes ill (negative response). However, this would be a dangerous approach to use in SUD treatment and could lead to multiple physical problems or death.

A second way to break a habit is to introduce the drug (stimulus) selectively until the user learns over time not to respond in a habitual manner. There is much controversy over the use of "controlled drinking" as a form of therapy, and no longitudinal studies have indicated this approach works. However, some treatment approaches have included introducing the drug in the presence of the user to *desensitize* the effect. An example of this would be watching drug-related television programs or commercials over time until the "urge to use" subsides.

Finally, the last way to break a habit is to replace it with a new habit. "Switching drugs" is commonly reported by individuals in recovery and may include overeating, a relationship dependency, sexual compulsions, or even use of another drug. In this case, treatment would focus on searching for rewards that are nondestructive, such as hobbies, exercise, education, support groups, and spirituality.

The drug user's whole life is dominated by drug-related activities: planning the use, talking about using, and being with other users. Therefore, it is not surprising that treatment is difficult. Personality, motivation, and habit are particularly important in bringing about a relapse to drug usage. There is a spontaneous recovery of behaviors learned in the past when motivation to abstain becomes weaker than the motivation to use drugs.

Results of heroin-induced brain changes, such as sleep disturbances and problems with bladder control, require months to reverse themselves, whereas it takes only a few minutes to get a high. Unable to feel good without drugs for months during withdrawal, an individual gets immediate reinforcement from drug-taking behavior.

Situational antecedents, such as time of day, place, and association with certain people or emotional states, are all important when analyzing the cause of the behavior. For example, drinking with friends at the local bar three to four times a week to blow off steam, snorting cocaine at parties with friends once a week, and shooting heroin alone would be evaluated for behavioral and situational antecedents, associations, and situational settings. Each of these factors is analyzed so that the maladaptive behavioral sequences can be restructured and changed.

Cognitive behavior processes involved in substance abuse originate with the interaction between the person and his or her environment (Kouimtsidis, 2010). Anticipating the desired effects of the drug, remembering past pleasant associations with the behavior, and modeling the behavior by others are all important as reinforcements of substance use (Burrow-Sanchez, 2006).

According to Becker (2008), events that can trigger relapse fall into three categories: drinking a small amount of alcohol; exposure to alcohol-related (conditioned) cues; and stress. Studies show that alcoholics are more sensitive to the effects of these three categories of stimuli, which elicit craving and other negative effects that can increase the risk of relapse (Fox, Bergquist, Hong, & Sinha, 2007; Sinha, Fox, Hong, Bergquist, Bhagwagar, & Siedlarz, 2009).

Conclusion.   Behaviorists approach substance abuse as they approach all behavior—as the product of learning. Recent theories add cognitive factors and brain reward mechanisms as mediating variables to the learning patterns believed responsible for SUDs. These disorders are seen as the result of learning patterns, and antecedent actions and situational factors are analyzed to determine the sequence of these patterns. In treatment, goals are easily formulated because behaviors are easily observed and measured.

A major disadvantage of the behavioral approach is that intergenerational, family, and biological factors are not directly addressed. Critics would claim that, although the present behavior of the individual might be changed, long-lasting change requires a shift in family patterns and attention to the biological changes involved in SUDs, as well as the genetic differences in addicts. Behavioral approaches may not supply the total answer to causal factors in abuse of alcohol and other substances, but they do have certain advantages. Relationships between antecedent actions and addictive behavior can be clearly viewed and measured, as can social conditions associated with that behavior.

SOCIOCULTURAL THEORIES

Just as with the debate that exists about behavior (is it shaped strictly by environment or strictly by genetics?), these theories look at social and cultural factors that can lead to substance abuse. Environmental support for heavy drinking is an important sociological variable contributing to alcohol use disorder. Attitudes toward alcohol consumption and abuse vary from culture to culture and greatly affect the amount and context of the alcohol consumption. In general, solitary, addictive, pathological drinking is more associated with urbanized, industrial societies than with societies that remain largely rural and traditional. However, there are additional sociocultural factors to consider in the etiology of addiction. This section highlights some of the major sociocultural influences on SUDs and their impact on clients.

GENDER As in the past, the rates for both illicit drug use and alcohol use are higher in men than women (SAMHSA, 2014). As the focus on women is increasing in alcohol studies, researchers have identified risk factors for women that differ from those of men. The National Institute of Health and the National Institute on Alcohol Abuse and Alcoholism (U.S. Department of Health and Human Services, 2008) compiled a collaborative summary of research on women and alcohol. Findings include the following: women and adolescents are more vulnerable to being a victim of sexual violence; drinking over a long term causes more health problems than for men even if the amount is less; individual risk factors include stress, childhood sexual abuse, and depression; and there are social risk factors such as biological relatives with drinking problems or a partner who drinks heavily.

However, gender differences in alcohol use disorders have decreased over the past 80 years (Keyes, Li, & Hasin, 2011). Subgroups of women with elevated rates of heavy drinking include younger women, those lacking social roles or occupying unwanted social status, women in nontraditional jobs, cohabiting women, and ethnic minority women experiencing rapid acculturation (Schuckit, Smith, & Danko, 2007). Interestingly, most of these factors are associated with the rapidly changing societal conditions for women in this country.

RACE/ETHNICITY Sociocultural differences exist in the rates of illicit drug use based on race/ethnicity. In 2013, Asian populations demonstrated the lowest rates of illicit drug use, followed by Hispanics, Whites, and then Blacks (SAMHSA, 2014; Johnston, O'Malley, Bachman, & Schulenberg, 2011; SAMHSA, 2014; Wu, Swartz, Brady, Blazer, & Hoyle, 2014). The highest rates of illicit drug use in the United States were seen in multiracial adults. A study found that multiracial adolescents are at an even greater risk for substance use (Jackson & LeCroy, 2009). In the United States, Whites are most likely to report heavy alcohol use, followed by multiracial adults, and then Blacks (SAMHSA, 2014). Asians were again the group least likely to report alcohol use.

Research findings also highlight differences in illicit drug use by race/ethnicity when looking at urban (metropolitan) and rural (nonmetropolitan) counties. For instance, marijuana use among Blacks, Hispanics, Whites, and American Indian/Native Americans is lower in nonmetropolitan (rural) counties than in small or large metropolitan counties (urban), whereas the converse is true for Asians (i.e., marijuana rates are higher for Asians in rural areas than urban areas) (SAMHSA, 2014).

SOCIOECONOMIC STATUS Social inequality is a strong predictor of alcohol and drug use, especially related to lower social class and drug use (Room, 2005). Although SUDs are represented in all socioeconomic statuses, low income and poverty levels have an over-represented number of individuals that abuse drugs, For instance, the levels of use for illicit drugs decreased as education levels increased (SAMHSA, 2014). In addition, the rates of illicit drug use are related to unemployment, with individuals who are unemployed more likely to engage in illicit drug use (SAMHSA, 2014). As unemployment is a predictor of poverty, the association between substance use and SES is undeniable. Looking further at the relationship between socioeconomic status (SES) and drug use, the literature has shown that adolescents with lower SES are more likely to engage in substance abuse, as are adults with high SES (Humensky, 2010). However, research is growing in this area demonstrating that high SES also predicts high substance use for adolescents (Kendler, Ohlsson, Sundquist, & Sundquist, 2014). The correlation between SES and substance use in adolescence is quite complex and perhaps a changing phenomenon.

Alternately, the patterns in alcohol use and SES differ. One study noted that alcohol use increased with income for White men, but for Black men alcohol use decreased with higher levels of income (Akins et al., 2010). SAMHSA (2014) noted that as education and employment increased, the likelihood of alcohol use also increased. Unemployment rates are highest for minorities; therefore, the trends in high illicit drug use for the unemployed and high alcohol use for those employed are of notable interest.

SOCIALIZATION The socialization and cultural environment of the adolescent creates factors that influence drug and alcohol experimentation and continued use that may differ from those of adults. Practices of peer groups, such as fraternities, have a great influence on whether an adolescent within that group will or will not use drugs. It may be "cool" to experiment with or continue to use drugs, or it may be considered "in" to abstain. Moreover, the peer group can facilitate substance use by providing the social structure within which use is part of the culture, as well as providing the substances to use. Club drugs, such as Ecstasy, are a good example. Developmentally, adolescents not only feel omnipotent and invulnerable to life's tragedies, but also are attracted to risk-taking behaviors. They often feel a rise in self-esteem when accepted by a group that approves of drug use.

Aspects of Use Addressed by Sociocultural Theories

CONTINUUM OF USE Social factors can contribute to the first use of a drug. Factors that appear to protect youngsters from initiating substance use and progressing toward abuse include bonding, goal direction, and monitoring from family, peers, religion, and other societal processes; participating in rewarding activities and prosocial behaviors; selecting and emulating individuals who model temperance or shun substance use; and increased self-confidence and coping skills (Moss, 2007).

A cultural trend is that newly introduced drugs may influence the rise in the use and abuse of chemicals. Key findings from Johnston and colleagues (2011) state that "generational forgetting" involves the fading use of current drugs and reintroduction of older drugs. This then increases the risk of initiation because "word of the supposed benefits of using a drug usually spreads faster than information about the adverse effects" (p. 6).

Cultural beliefs may be attributed to the use of alcohol. Some protective factors, such as Hispanic communities' strong cultural prohibitions among women, and Confucian and Taoist philosophies, may contribute to the low consumption rate among Hispanic women and Asians. Risk factors influenced by culture include drinking as a business practice among Chinese and Japanese men, and experiences of oppression and discrimination among Native American groups (National Institute on Alcohol Abuse and Alcoholism, 2005). There is also a wide variety of literature on Hispanics that finds that acculturation is a key predictor of substance use (Salas-Wright, Clark, Vaughn, & Cordóva, 2015).

Family factors, such as the cultural attitudes previously discussed, customs of the family involving alcohol and other substances, tolerance toward public intoxication and drug use, and childhood exposure to alcohol and drug use models, form a background for adolescent attitudes toward substance use. Additionally, several types of parenting have been associated with an increase in substance use in offspring. Four common types used in research are authoritative parenting (clear and direct parenting with a high degree of warmth); permissive/indulgent parenting (warm but free of discipline or structure); authoritarian parenting (lacks warmth but demands unquestioning obedience); and neglectful/uninvolved parenting (free from discipline or structure and lack of warmth). Both authoritative and permissive parenting have been related to lower substance use, whereas the neglectful and authoritarian parenting styles had the opposite effects (Calafat, García, Juan, Becoña, & Fernández-Hermida, 2014; Stafström, 2014). In addition, high parental monitoring and supervision were found to be protective factors for drinking control (Clark, Shamblen, Ringwalt, & Hanley, 2012).

General sociological studies give expected conclusions: Those who continue drug use report having a positive initial experience. However, a positive reaction to a drug does not always occur with the first use. The circumstances or inadequacies that drove a person the first time may encourage him or her to try again, hoping to capture the desired psychological effect or social acceptance. Existence of a drug-using peer group appears important to the continuing use of drugs. Adolescents who are exposed to negative/delinquent peers are more likely to use substances than adolescents not exposed to delinquent peer groups (Ferguson & Meehan, 2011).

Pressure can be great to conform and to "fit in." Peers and parents show how and where to drink. In fact, having friends who use drugs is predictive of alcohol abuse for Whites, Blacks, and Hispanics; however, having parents with substance abuse problems is not a predictor among Blacks. This indicates that pathways to alcohol use are different among racial/ethnic groups (Akins et al., 2010), and these findings may have application for prevention and intervention in Black communities. To refuse to comply with cultural expectations to drink heavily or continue drug use may mean turning away from friends and changing relationships with one's family. Another concern is the growing evidence that adolescents with high SES are at risk for substance abuse (Humensky, 2010). For instance, higher parental education is associated with higher rates of binge drinking and marijuana and cocaine use in early adulthood, and higher parental income is associated with higher rates of binge drinking and marijuana use.

Substance use can also be seen as being both system maintained and system maintaining. For instance, reactive changes in family dynamics usually occur when substance use is introduced into the family. Once the family assimilates these changes and reorganizes around the disordered use of a substance, these changes actually support the SUD (Saatcioglu, Erim, & Cakmak, 2006). For example, if a 10-year-old child begins to watch over a 3-year-old sibling because their mother is high on crack, family function is preserved, if imperfectly. However, this assumption of parental roles by the child also makes it easier for the mother to continue with her crack use, causing a circular pattern of reinforcement. When a family attempts to reorganize itself in the face of a prolonged crisis such as alcoholism, changes in roles, rules, and boundaries of the family occur in an effort to stabilize the system. Behavior of family members within the family system, observed from the outside, can appear strange or abnormal, whereas, when viewed within the context of the addictive family, they can be seen as being adaptive or an integral part of maintenance of family *homeostasis*. This often places children in these families at greater risk for SUDs (Doweiko, 2011).

Sociocultural theories suggest that a confluence of sociological and cultural factors contribute to the proliferation of SUDs. For example, diagnosis of an alcohol disorder shows some variation in pathways between other racial/ethnic groups. When looking at age, marital status, gender, level of strain, and emotional status, age is a predictor for Whites and Blacks (younger) but not for Hispanics; negative emotions are a predictor for Whites and Hispanics but not for Blacks; marital status is a predictor for Whites and Hispanics (unmarried) but not for Blacks; and, rural status is a predictor for Hispanics but not for Whites and Blacks. Common predictors across all three races were high levels of strain and being male (Akins et al., 2010). In Chapter 12, you will learn more about the multicultural aspects of SUDs. Being culturally sensitive during all aspects of prevention, assessment, and treatment is critical for treatment providers.

CHANGE Drug subculture theory was first developed based on a framework of deviant acts. However, drug use trends indicate that in today's society, the widespread recreational drug use across ethnicity, gender, and social class suggests that the behavior is being accommodated into the larger society (Gourley, 2004). These "cohort effects" are observed when use rates, along with attitudes and beliefs about various drugs, increase and decrease over time (Johnston et al., 2011). Therefore, although replacing prodrug-socialized peers with nonusing peers is an important goal in recovery, social and cultural tolerance may be a limiting factor to maintaining recovery.

Within the sociocultural model, if the broader systems of the individual are not addressed or changed, the chances of relapse are increased. Therefore, relapse occurs because users return to familiar patterns within a group, family, job, or other social, cultural, or environmental setting. An addict who ceased drug use because of an involuntary intervention may never have truly left the drug subculture and will quickly revert to old drug-using patterns on completion of treatment.

Conclusion. Several components of culture and the environment affect the likelihood that an individual will become involved with substance abuse (see the example illustrated in Figure 4.2). The racially segregated inner city has encouraged the growth of substance abuse as an industry (Draus, Roddy, & Greenwald, 2012). In 2009, the U.S. economy had the highest unemployment rate since World War II (Sum, Khatiwada, McLaughlin, & Palma, 2011). The low number of labor-intensive jobs, and the residential segregation of low-skilled and high-skilled workers, has caused unskilled laborers to sink further into poverty (Sum et al., 2011). At the same time, the increased cost of adequate housing has created a sizable population who have inadequate or no housing. Inner-city youths face internal and external barriers that cause them to be less likely to finish high school or to have marketable skills (Samel, Sondergeld, Fischer, & Patterson, 2011). As households experience severe crises concurrently, many are socialized into deviant behavior, such as antisocial acts, child abuse or neglect, or criminal activity. In such settings, families may also experience learned helplessness and feel disenfranchised from society as a whole (Moos, 2007).

Treatment that changes an individual also affects that person's interpersonal system. Therefore, in order for drug abuse treatment to be successful, the social and cultural context of the abuser must be considered. For instance, finding family environment patterns that predispose children for alcoholism and other substance abuse may enable counselors to prevent these conditions in children considered to be at risk. Dysfunctional family patterns can be changed through family therapy and parent training. In general, environmental forces, cultural context, and peer and family relationships that influence the development and maintenance of an SUD should be considered under this theory.

AN INTEGRATED APPROACH: SUBSTANCE USE DISORDERS IN THE 21ST CENTURY

New research and schools of thought are moving toward an integrated, multidisciplinary theoretical approach (du Plessis, 2012; Kovac, 2013). Integrated theories combine elements of existing theories into a working model. Researchers are beginning to view SUDs as more than a one-dimensional process that can be explained by a single theory. Integrated ways of viewing SUDs synthesize several of the models listed earlier. Further, the existing theories are not mutually exclusive of one another. For example, there are strong comparisons between the disease theory and genetic/biological theories. Sociocultural theories also pull ideas from the behavioral, genetic, and psychological models.

One such integrated approach is the bio/psycho/social/spiritual (BPSS) approach. BPSS considers SUDs as stemming from varying combinations of biological/genetic, psychological, spiritual, and sociological factors. BPSS argues that a single theory cannot explain the complex nature of the disordered use of substances, and that any one theory would exclude fundamental aspects of the process. For instance, although AA most closely aligns with the disease theory, AA's spiritual approach to treatment is not fully explained by the model. AA considers addiction as a spiritual disease or illness. Infused in 12-step literature is the notion that the addicted person's spirit must be filled with a Higher Power or the search for gratification will continue. Addiction is the result of an attempt to try and fill a spiritual void that can be satisfied only through spiritual means. Therefore a person must strive to heal wounds that inhibit the spirit from having a true connection. Doweiko (2011) offers philosophies on spiritual models of disordered use, explaining that an SUD is a disease of the spirit. As with AA, this notion is based on the idea that a spiritual void exists in the person that they try to fill through substances. This void may exist due to emotional wounds and pain, and substance use only temporarily fills it. Spiritual considerations are frequently part of a mental health professional's work with addicted individuals, yet strict adherence to one model may not fully explain the cause of SUDs. Using the BPSS approach, one can see how the notion of a spiritual void may relate to biological, psychological, and social factors. A purely psychological approach to etiology may not consider the notion of only a "void" and see this disordered use as the result of trauma or mental health comorbidity.

Current research cites many factors contributing to, or having an effect on, substance abuse: genetics, family environment and structure, and brain changes from use of substances expressed in behavioral ways and within a social context (Bryson & Silverstein, 2008). Further, spirituality is viewed as a significant aspect of successful recovery for many people (Doweiko, 2011). An integrated theory, taking all of these factors into consideration, conceptualizes behavior as a function of mutual determination and reciprocal effects of an individual, the environment, and behavior. It assumes that many influences combine to create the conditions under which an individual will abuse, or not abuse, alcohol or other substances. Integrated rather than eclectic, it weaves all of the influences and components of dependency into holistic concepts with contributing parts, rather than being a collection of ideas and concepts. This approach also accounts for differences in addictive substance and behavior use and abuse, based on individual differences in genetics, personality, family, and social environment.

Careful consideration of the material presented in this chapter will lead to the conclusion that the origins of substance use disorders are much more complex than any one theory can explain. An integrated approach such as BPSS offers a wider range of considerations in explaining why SUDs occur and is growing in popularity in the treatment community. As one considers the multifaceted and complex nature of SUDs, it becomes difficult to imagine treating a client without considering the environment or the neural pathways involved in substance use. Further, how does a clinician effectively work with clients without learning about family backgrounds, coping skills, and psychological histories?

CASE DISCUSSIONS

Case 1: Sandy and Pam

As you may recall, Sandy was the child of alcoholic parents and also had an alcoholic stepfather. Therefore, both genetic and environmental influences existed in Sandy's life to predispose her to SUDs. Sandy has struggled with alcohol abuse, and also married an alcoholic, who is Pam's father. Consequently, Pam

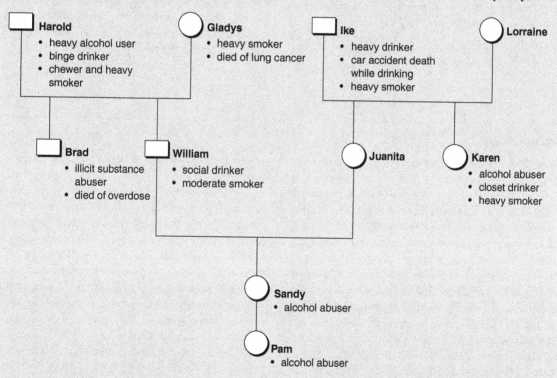

As indicated above, the genogram of Pam and Sandy reveals that alcohol and other substances have been abused for four generations, causing family problems and death throughout the family's history.

FIGURE 4.2 Genogram: Sandy and Pam

(Continued)

(Continued)

also had both genetic and environmental predispositions to SUDs, which led to her substance abuse. Pam's childhood was unstable, as her parents separated when she was 7, and this was followed by Sandy bringing home multiple sexual partners. Considering the rate of comorbidity and SUDs, it is likely that there are additional mental health concerns for both clients.

Both Sandy and Pam could be considered to have begun using substances as a result of social learning theory. By watching their parents drink alcoholically, they learned the behavior of alcoholism. Further, Sandy admits that Pam's lack of commitment was learned from her. In addition, reinforcements must be considered. Sandy's drinking and bar-hopping behaviors may have given her positive reinforcement from men, perpetuating the behavior of drinking. What other types of reinforcements do you notice with Sandy and Pam?

Case 3: Leigh

According to the moral theory, Leigh's behavior with shoplifting, sexual activity, running away from home, and substance abuse would be the result of a lack of morals. It might be argued that Leigh's parents neglected to instill upstanding moral values in her. Because Leigh is 16 years old, a moral theorist might suggest a spiritual or religious intervention to try and strengthen her value systems and willpower.

In contrast to moral theory, the disease/medical theory would take the approach that Leigh's behaviors are symptomatic of an underlying disorder of the brain—she is sick. As Leigh began to experiment with substances and risky behaviors, she altered the reward pathways in her brain, thus causing both craving and continued use over time. Treatment would be focused on abstinence and increasing sober support systems based on the medical approach.

Conclusion

There has been a progression of theories of substance use, ranging from a view that alcoholism is a result of personal choice to an integration of several possible factors that contribute to initiation, continuation, then the recovery/relapse/recovery cycle. Sociocultural influences appear to offer mitigating factors in the development of alcohol abuse. It is uncertain whether these sociocultural differences are due to genetic predispositions, socioeconomic conditions, or cultural attitudes toward drinking, but the overall effect remains clear: some ethnic groups have more problems with alcohol consumption than others (Moore, Montaine-Jaime, Carr, & Ehlers, 2007; Scott & Taylor, 2007). Psychological factors that may interact with a genetic or biological predisposition and sociocultural factors include the effects of growing up in an alcoholic home, learned

or conditioned drinking behavior, and cognitive deficiencies.

All of the preceding factors—personal choice, medical epidemiology, sociocultural factors, and psychological/behavioral factors—may be present, yet an individual may not become addicted to alcohol or other substances. Therefore, perhaps the most promising research is identifying genetic and neural pathways that can help explain why some people develop substance use disorders but others do not in similar circumstances. This chapter has offered a broad range of etiological models that explain how SUDs occur. No one model completely encompasses the complexity of a client; therefore, use this chapter in your practice as a guide and reference for comprehensively understanding what a client brings with him/her into the session.

MyCounselingLab for Addictions/Substance Use

Try the Topic 3 Assignments: *Etiological Theories of Substance Use Disorders.*

Case Study: Tom

Tom is a 28-year-old man born to Japanese immigrants. His parents immigrated to the United States after World War II and are proud to be American. However, they have held on to many traditional customs and beliefs (such as the value that the family is all-important, and to act in ways that brings shame on the family disgraces the entire family). Recently, Tom attended a party with friends—the party was hosted by friends of friends, and he did not know the people well. While at the party, Tom admits to smoking marijuana. Later that night, he was arrested for acting strangely in a local supermarket. Tom was approached by the police when the manager saw him wandering up and down the aisles aimlessly taking items off of the shelves. Tom was arrested for public intoxication and spent the night in jail.

The judge sent him to you for an evaluation. When questioned, Tom admits to trying marijuana in the past, but never with these results. He also admits to occasional use of other drugs (such as alcohol and cocaine). He reports that he is not particularly fond of the drugs he uses; he only partakes to fit in with his friends who seem to enjoy getting high. Tom is very embarrassed by his arrest and the shame it has brought on his family and seems eager to comply with your recommendations.

Critical Thinking Questions

1. How would you apply the moral theory to Tom's case?
2. How would you apply both the behavioral theory and sociocultural theory to Tom's case?

CHAPTER 5

Assessment and Diagnosis

Robert A. Dobmeier, Ph.D., LMHC, CRC, Claudette Brown-Smythe, Ph.D., ACS, NCC, CRC, Linda L. Chamberlain, Psy.D.

Accurate assessment and diagnosis in the treatment of substance use are crucial for adequate treatment planning and delivery of services. Improper assessment and faulty diagnosis can lead counselors to create ineffective treatment plans, have inappropriate expectations for therapy, and instill an overall sense of frustration in both the client and the therapist. You cannot treat what you do not recognize or understand. As with other diseases and disorders, the earlier a therapist diagnoses a substance use problem, the better the prognosis for the client.

This chapter presents a theoretical and practical framework for assessment and acquaints clinicians with several methods and tools that can aid in the diagnosis of a substance use disorder (SUD). Guidelines for conducting an assessment interview and obtaining a reliable history are provided. Several major assessment instruments generally available to clinicians are reviewed. The issue of diagnosis and the problems related to differential and dual diagnosis are explored. It is the intent of this chapter to give counselors a pragmatic orientation to making an accurate diagnosis of a substance use problem.

ISSUES IN ASSESSMENT

It may be helpful to note at the outset that the assessment and diagnosis of substance use disorders (SUD) are not exact sciences. Currently, there is no single medical or psychological test that can determine with absolute certainty that a person has a substance use disorder. Also, the inconsistency in social attitudes about substance use often complicates a clinician's awareness and attitudes about a client's substance use. The stigma associated with substance use often leads to denial or avoidance by the user, their family, and many health professionals (Earnshaw, Smith, Cunningham, & Copenhaver, 2015; Kulesza, Ramsey, Brown, & Larimer, 2014; Livingston, Milne, Fang, & Amari, 2012; Mattoo et al., 2015; Stone, 2015; van Weeghel, van Boekel, Garretsen, & Brouwers, 2013).

The beginning therapist must be aware of several problems that may interfere with the diagnostic process. First, the therapist may have developed some biases about individuals with substance use problems. Beliefs that substance users are uncaring, irresponsible, untrustworthy, dangerous, or untreatable are concepts that are certain to interfere with a clinician's ability to conduct an accurate and sensitive diagnostic interview. As Lewis, Dana, and Blevins note (2015), "It is vital that clinicians avoid preconceived notions about the client and that they make treatment determinations based only on data collected during the initial evaluation" (p. 82). Second, the client's attitude about substance use, and his or her sense of shame in seeking help from a mental health professional, may create a barrier to accurate assessment. It is not unusual for clients to seek help from clinicians for problems such as depression, anxiety, or behavioral problems that may be secondary to their substance use. The stigma of being labeled a "drunk" or "addict" is still a powerful deterrent to disclosing a pattern of substance use for many people, especially women. Finally, it is important for clinicians to be aware of cultural and ethical bias when assessing substance use disorders. Diagnostic criteria should reflect a sensitivity to cultural variations in behavior, emotional expression, and accepted patterns of substance use within that group. Practitioners must be aware of the prejudice and stereotyping they hold (Substance Abuse and Mental Health Services Administration [SAMHSA], 2013).

In large part, a clinician's awareness of common factors and problems related to substance use is of great importance. An understanding of the dynamics of denial, tolerance, loss of control, and the diverse medical consequences associated with different drugs is an essential prerequisite for accurate diagnosis. A familiarity with common medical, behavioral, cognitive, social, and emotional symptoms associated with alcohol and drug use can help guide the clinician in the assessment process (American Psychiatric Association, 2013). Materials that delineate the progression of symptoms for use of alcohol and other drugs can help guide the clinician in the assessment process. Later in this chapter, the behavioral and social characteristics associated with substance use are described in greater detail.

Previous chapters have acquainted you with some of the symptoms, effects, and dynamics that should serve as "red flags" for pursuing more formal diagnostic procedures. Assessment, however, is still somewhat a process of "skunk identification," meaning that if it looks, smells, and walks like a skunk, it's probably a skunk. Any one or two symptoms of disordered substance use don't necessarily constitute a clear diagnosis. An isolated or occasional experience of intoxication does not constitute a diagnosis of a substance-related disorder. Just as we suggest moderation in substance use, we encourage moderation in assessment and diagnoses as well. It is important to be thorough, ask all the necessary questions, know the symptoms and patterns of problematic substance use, and not jump to conclusions without evidence of a pattern of problematic use. Not everyone who uses cocaine, alcohol, heroin, or any other drug has a substance use disorder.

The process of conducting an assessment and diagnosing substance use problems is perhaps most complicated by the phenomenon of denial. Denial and minimization of the severity of a drug use problem are often an essential part of how individuals who misuse a substance learn to function in their world. For the substance user, denial is a coping mechanism, albeit one with a negative outcome, that protects them from facing the increasing consequences of their behavior. As a result of denial, the substance user is often the last to acknowledge that they have a problem. Without the mechanism of denial, the user could not continue the pattern of substance use. Although not all who use a substance exhibit patterns of denial, many minimize or avoid facing the consequences of use on both themselves and others. Those with substance use disorders are often motivated to "avoid the consequences of substance use such as legal sanctions by not admitting to the use of certain chemicals" (Doweiko, 2015, p. 408). Denial or minimization serves to keep reality at arm's length and allows the individual to believe that no one is aware of his/her excessive drug use and the negative impact it is having on his/her life. Doweiko (2015) notes that denial operates through a "process of selective perception of both the past and the present" so that users can avoid painful realities about themselves (p. 349). The use of denial to delude both the individual and others tremendously complicates the assessment process. Establishing some standardized format for assessment and diagnosis is essential in helping clinicians maintain consistency in providing appropriate detection and treatment for their clients. Importantly, counselors must be wary of developing an aggressive or combative reaction to obvious denial or minimization when assessing clients. Rather, the counselor's efforts to empathize with the client's thoughts and feelings as she or he considers pros and cons of substance use is more likely to evoke openness about its consequences (Myers & Salt, 2013). Accusing clients of lying, or implying that they are doing so, whether they suffer from a SUD or other disorders is never a productive strategy.

A critical part of beginning an assessment with substance users is to encourage them to be honest and forthright in their responses and interactions with the evaluator or counselor. It may be helpful to assure them that the assessment process is primarily for their benefit, to help them in making decisions about whether they have a problem and, if so, what actions they might take. Even with clients who are mandated for assessment through the courts, referred through employers, or brought in by family members, it is important to focus the diagnostic interview and assessment on addressing the needs of the substance user.

THE DIAGNOSTIC INTERVIEW

The most important aspect of any assessment of substance use is the diagnostic interview. A carefully planned and conducted interview is the cornerstone of the diagnostic process. The initial contact with someone for the assessment of a substance use disorder may occur within the context of individual, family, group, or marital counseling. The clinician may be aware of the possible problem by the nature of the referral, or it may be discovered within the context of a family or marital problem. Referrals from physicians, other clinicians, or the legal system may be clearly defined as a referral for the purpose of assessing a drug or alcohol problem. Many assessments, however, will initially be undertaken as a part of the clinician's normal interviewing procedure. It is striking how many mental health professionals do not include at least some questions about a client's substance use history in their standard intake format. A routine clinical interview should include questions about clients' habits of using both prescription and illicit drugs, alcohol, tobacco, and caffeine (Mancini, 2013). Clinical training programs are often lacking in coursework or opportunities for practical experience that expose medical and mental health professionals to the dynamics and treatment of addictions.

If there is reason to suspect significant minimization or denial on the part of the person being assessed for substance-related problems, it may be important in the first interview to request permission to also interview family members, friends, employers/co-workers, medical professionals, and/or others who may be able to provide more objective information about the client's pattern of substance use and related behaviors. Collateral interviews often help to give a more complete picture of both the user and the impact they are having on others in their environment. Partners and family members of alcoholics and drug addicts often want to be helpful in the user's treatment (Mancini, 2013).

An important part of the diagnostic interview is an assessment of the client's readiness for change (see Motivational Interviewing information in Chapter 7). The transtheoretical model developed by Prochaska and DeClemente (1982, 1984) offers clinicians very useful guidelines and information to assist in evaluating where the client is in the process of change. This model describes a series of six stages people experience in making changes, whether the changes are in therapy or not: precontemplation, contemplation, determination, action, maintenance, and relapse. By determining the stage that the client is in, therapists can focus treatment on helping that client proceed through the various stages of change.

Miller and Rollnick (1991) incorporated the transtheoretical model into their principles of motivational interviewing with substance use clients. Their work further elaborates on targeting specific questions and responses to the stage of change, which can be enormously helpful in the process of diagnostic interviewing. A clinical interview that incorporates motivational interviewing techniques can set the stage for a successful counseling relationship and help with treatment planning. Therapists who plan to work with substance use clients benefit greatly from familiarity with the model and techniques of interviewing described by these authors. Given the frequency of denial and minimization encountered with clients who are experiencing substance use problems, having a supportive, respectful, effective strategy for interviewing is essential.

Initially, it is still important to ask the client directly about his or her use of substances. A useful question is "Do you believe that your use of alcohol or other drugs has caused problems in your life?" Many clinicians find it helpful to assure the client that they are not asking questions about substance use in order to make judgments. Often, people will respond less defensively if they are reassured that "I'm not here to tell you that you do or do not have a problem. I simply need to understand as much about your life as I can and to help you (and your family) determine whether your substance use may be playing a role in the current situation." Also ask significant others in the client's life about his or her use in order to get information on whether they view the client's problems as related to substance use. If either a substance user or family member is describing examples of domestic violence, legal problems, financial problems, medical complications, or other issues that are often related to substance use, it can be helpful to ask if they believe the problem would have occurred if use of substances were not a factor. Families can be engaged in the assessment to shed light on relationships within the family system that are affected by and that contribute to substance use among family members (Bender, Tripodi, & Rock, 2013).

An interview format that gathers information specific to substance use should be a standard part of the assessment process. An example of a structured interview format is the Substance Use History Questionnaire (Appendix A: Substance Use History Questionnaire at the end of this chapter). It may be given to the client to complete, or the questions can be asked during the interview. The information from this procedure will help in determining what additional assessment instruments to use. Information regarding work habits, social and professional relationships, medical history, legal history, and previous psychiatric history is also necessary for the assessment. Questions related to each of these areas should be included as a part of the standard intake interview.

It is important to note that family members and significant others may be unaware of or reluctant to divulge information about the client's substance use patterns. Like the client, they are often experiencing denial or avoiding a confrontation with the user. Common misinformation about substance use may divert the focus of the problem to other factors that are then presented as the primary problem. For example, a spouse may describe the partner as using alcohol to relieve feelings of depression rather than identifying the substance use as a causal or maintaining factor in the partner's emotional turmoil. Because of the shame and embarrassment that frequently accompany the admission of substance use, the clinician may need to reassure everyone involved in the assessment that appropriate help can only be made available if an understanding of the problem is accurate and complete.

DSM-5 DIAGNOSIS

One of the primary difficulties encountered in diagnosing substance use problems may lie in the inadequate definitions commonly used. In an attempt to provide a more comprehensive, specific, symptom-related criteria for diagnosis, the American Psychiatric Association (APA) (2013) developed categories for "Substance-Related and Addictive Disorders" in the Diagnostic and Statistic Manual, Fifth Edition (DSM-5). This marks a significant change in the diagnostic lexicon with the change of terminology to "substance use" and the inclusion of the term "addictive disorders" (Dawson, Goldstein, & Grant, 2013). In previous editions of the DSM (American Psychiatric Association, 2000) the diagnostic categories were restricted to substance-based disorders. The DSM-5 (2013) expanded the criteria for substance-related disorders to include gambling disorder. Gambling addiction activates reward systems in the brain and produces behavioral symptoms similar to those shaped by substance use (APA, 2013). It is likely that future editions of the DSM will include other "behavioral addictions" such as sex addiction, Internet addiction, and shopping addiction if there is sufficient research to justify those inclusions (APA, 2013).

In the DSM-5, the term *substance* refers to alcohol, a misused legal drug—for example, a prescription, a medication or a toxin that is used in a manner incongruent with medical treatment—or an illegal drug. It is not the substance itself but the manner in which it is employed and the behavioral changes that are produced that provide the critical information for a diagnosis of a substance use disorder (Dailey, Gill, Karl, & Barrio Minton, 2014). The DSM-5 states that, "the essential feature of a substance use disorder is a cluster of cognitive, behavioral, and physiological symptoms indicating that the individual continues using the substance despite significant substance-related problems" (APA, 2013, p. 483). Lack of clarity around the meaning of the term substance *dependence* in the previous edition of the DSM resulted in elimination of the terms substance "dependence" and substance "abuse" in the DSM-5. Rather, the tem "substance use disorder" represents a continuum of severity of cognitive, behavioral, and physiological problems associated with misuse of a substance. It is important to note that the basis for a diagnosis of SUD is based on a problematic pattern of behaviors related to the substance, not a single incident of abuse or intoxication.

In the DSM-5 substances are grouped into 10 classes: "alcohol; caffeine; cannabis; cocaine; hallucinogens; inhalants; opioids; sedatives, hypnotics, and anxiolytics (tranquilizers and anti-anxiety medications); stimulants (amphetamine, cocaine, caffeine and similar substances); tobacco; and other (or unknown) substances" (APA, 2013, p. 481). The Substance-Related Disorders are divided into two basic groups: the Substance Use Disorders and the Substance-Induced Disorders, including substance intoxication, substance withdrawal, and other substance/medication-induced mental disorder.

DSM-5 Criteria for Substance Use Disorders

There are a total of 11 criteria that represent a continuum of severity on Criterion A, which includes "impaired control, social impairment, risky use, and pharmacological conditions":

Impaired Control

Patterns of behavior characteristic of impaired control relate to the degree of impairment an individual experiences in relation to duration, regulation, and intensity. Substance users are unable to control their use, imbibing more than was intended; are unable to cut down use; are preoccupied with obtaining, using, or recovering from a substance; or suffer from cravings that are typical of individuals who meet criteria for impaired control.

Social Impairment. Social impairment is marked by an inability to maintain and satisfy key responsibilities in the home, work, or school. An example of social impairment due to substances is a college athlete who has been reprimanded several times for problem drinking, has been suspended from the team, and who continues to engage in drinking.

Risky Use. Risky use is demonstrated by substance users who have suffered bodily harm due to use and persistent using despite knowledge of adverse health or psychological conditions.

Pharmacological Criteria. Pharmacological criteria include increased tolerance and withdrawal. Tolerance is characterized by increased dosage requirements after prolonged substance use. Withdrawal is a physiological response occurring after the decline in substance use, resulting from a reduction of the concentration of substance in the blood and tissue.

Clinicians should be acquainted with the physiological and psychological manifestations of both acute drug or alcohol intoxication and withdrawal symptoms (Substance Intoxication and Substance Withdrawal) as outlined in the DSM-5 (APA, 2013). Certain drugs, such as barbiturates, can have serious medical complications associated with withdrawal, and clients must be under a physician's care in order to ensure they will safely complete the detoxification period.

BEHAVIORAL CHARACTERISTICS

Substance use almost always occurs within the context of other problems. Common presenting problems related to substance use are marital and family conflict, child abuse or neglect, unemployment, financial problems, multiple medical problems, anxiety, depression, suicide, and problems with aggression and violence. In assessing the role of substance use within the context of other problems, the clinician needs to understand the dynamics of other behavioral problems and how they may be exacerbated by the substance use. It is estimated that most domestic violence occurs during periods when one or both parties are using some substance and that as many as two-thirds of homicides and serious assaults involve alcohol (Hart & Ksir, 2013). Criminal behavior such as child abuse or sexual molestation may be committed when the perpetrator is under the influence of substances. It is estimated that alcohol is implicated in two-thirds of all cases of family violence (Kinney, 2015) and frequently in military sexual assaults (Connell, 2015). Although there is some disagreement about the exact nature of the relationship between substance use and violence, clearly a strong correlation exists between the two.

An important question for the clinician during a first interview is "Did all or any of these problems occur while you were using a substance?" If the answer is yes, one can then begin to gather information to determine if a pattern of use is causing or contributing to the client's behavioral symptoms. Again, given the nature of denial, this query should also be made to significant others who are participating in the assessment.

As a general rule, a substance use problem exists and requires treatment if the use of the substance continues despite significant interference in any one of the six major areas of a person's life:

- Job or school
- Relationships with family
- Social relationships
- Legal problems
- Financial problems
- Medical problems

Behaviorally, disordered use of a substance can be considered any use of a psychoactive substance that causes damage to the individual, family, and/or society.

Severe substance use involves interactions among biological, psychological, and social factors. Severe substance use is a process that occurs over differing periods of time for different individuals and varies with the use of different substances. Physical craving for dependence on alcohol may take several decades to develop, whereas physical craving for dependence on cocaine, especially crack cocaine, may occur within days or weeks. There are, however, certain phases that individuals are likely to pass through as their reliance on a substance increases. An old proverb regarding alcoholism outlines the progression of addiction: "The person takes a drink, the drink takes a drink, and the drink takes the person." The journey from controlled use to being controlled by the use is the nature of overreliance. No one begins using substances with the goal of becoming a severely disordered user. A more in-depth, definitive review of the behavioral symptoms will provide a basis for recognizing the path that many individuals with severely disordered substance use travel.

Phase 1: The Prodromal Phase

The first phase of disordered use can be labeled the prodromal phase. In the prodromal phase, casual or social use of a substance begins to change and the first signs of disordered use can be recognized. In this early phase, the following behavioral changes generally occur:

- Increase of tolerance
- First blackout or loss of significant time to drug use
- Sneaking drinks or drugs
- Preoccupation with drinking or drug use
- Gulping drinks or hurried ingestion of chemicals
- Avoiding reference to drinking or drug use

The first symptom noted in the prodromal phase is an increase in tolerance. Tolerance can be defined as a "physiological condition where the body requires an increased amount of a given substance in order to achieve desired effects" (Vaughn, 2013, p. 36). Physiologically, the brain and central nervous system adapt over time to the effects of almost any psychoactive substance. Therefore, the user must increase over time the amount of the substance or the frequency of use in order to achieve the sought-after effect. Counselors should ask about any changes in the amount or frequency of substance use in order to establish the symptom of tolerance.

The second symptom in this phase is the onset of blackouts or loss of significant amounts of time due to drug use. Not all substances cause blackouts; it is primarily a symptom associated with central nervous system depressants like alcohol, benzodiazepines, barbiturates, and narcotics. A blackout isn't unconsciousness; the user remains awake and active but later does not remember what was said or done while s/he was using. It is an indication that the user was able to ingest enough of the substance to "anesthetize" the part of the brain that processes short-term memory. Blackouts are a prominent feature of disordered alcohol use, particularly with binge drinkers.

The third behavioral symptom is sneaking drinks or drugs. This often means that the user will "pre-use" by using the substance before a social gathering in order to ensure that they have enough. It also means that the user is "stockpiling" their substances or hiding them from others who might share them. The user typically experiences discomfort or irritability with others who are not keeping up with the user's rate of substance use.

The fourth symptom involves a cognitive change in which the user becomes more preoccupied with time spent using. Behaviorally, it is manifested by making social plans that increasingly focus on the opportunity to use, such as leaving work early in order to have extra time to use, becoming irritable if there is any interruption in the time set aside to use, and spending an increased amount of time and effort in ensuring that the user has plenty of alcohol or drugs available.

The fifth symptom, a more hurried ingestion of substances, is an extension of the development of tolerance. Users become concerned that they will not have enough of the substance to relax or "get a buzz" and use more quickly in order to get a higher level in their system. Nearly all of the behaviors in the first stage are summarized by describing the user who might develop a serious problem as the one who must have a drink (or drug), and have it fast.

The final symptom in the prodromal phase sets the stage for denial. The user begins to feel uncomfortable with others' comments or questions about the changes in pattern of substance use and avoids confrontation. The user begins to estrange others who might express concern about use and avoids questioning about the changed relationship with the substance.

Phase 2: The Crucial Phase

In the middle or crucial phase, the individual experiences some of the more obvious and pronounced behavioral changes associated with severely disordered substance use. This phase is labeled "crucial" because it offers the most hope for an intervention in the growing physical and psychological reliance before some of the more severe medical and social consequences enter the picture. It is also during this phase that family and significant others usually become more aware of the user's growing reliance on substances. In this second phase, the following behavioral symptoms generally occur:

- Loss of control of substance use
- Denial and minimization of use
- Confrontation by others
- Behavioral loss of control
- Guilt and remorse
- Periodic abstinence or change in patterns of use
- Losses
- Medical and psychological interventions
- Growing alienation and resentment
- More frequent substance use

The first symptom, loss of control of the substance, is often misunderstood and poorly defined. Loss of control can be thought of as a loss of predictability. For example, an individual who uses alcohol begins to experience times when they drink more than they intend. On one night, they may have only the three beers they planned to drink after work. On the following night, the same plan falls apart, and the person drinks until they pass out. The user cannot predict with any certainty when they will be able to stick to the plan and when they will use more than intended.

The next set of behavioral symptoms (Denial and Minimization through Loss) will be considered together because they usually occur as part of a pattern of confrontation and denial. At this point, changes in the user's behavior related to drugs or alcohol are generally more obvious. While intoxicated or recovering from a binge, the user is more likely to become aggressive, impulsive, extravagant, or otherwise unpredictable in behavior. If confronted, the user is likely to insist that they can control it and stop any time. In fact, the user may quit for a brief period of time to "prove" control. Guilt feelings may begin when the user is confronted with the result of some harmful behavior that occurred while intoxicated (e.g., missing a child's birthday because the user was drinking with buddies at the bar instead of picking up the birthday cake and going home as promised). Fear sets in, followed by flashes of remorse, and sometimes aggressiveness or isolation to keep others at a distance. The consequences of the user's actions while using are increasingly difficult to minimize, rationalize, or deny and have a more pronounced impact on relationships.

The final group of symptoms in the crucial phase represents some of the more overt consequences that users experience as the severity of use progresses. These include loss of friends, divorce, loss of a job or financial setbacks, loss of other interests such as hobbies or leisure pursuits, and loss of a normal, daily routine that does not revolve around substance use. Other, less clearly observable losses include a loss of ordinary willpower, loss of self-respect, and an abandonment of moral or spiritual values. Often during this phase, the user experiences some acute medical consequences related to substance use and will seek medical intervention for specific symptoms (problems that are secondary to the drug or alcohol use). For example, a cocaine user may experience periodic heart arrhythmias (irregular heartbeat) and seek a doctor's advice for the heart problem, but not for the cocaine use that is causing the difficulty (the primary problem). Denial creates and perpetuates a vicious circle. Because the user denies a substance problem, he cannot go to anyone else to talk about it and so may use more to overcome the guilt or anxiety that results from the loss of control of his behavior. As the user becomes further trapped in the cycle of guilt, resentment and blame help externalize the fears but lead to increased alienation.

Phase 3: The Chronic Phase

The final or chronic phase of severe substance use is typified by a more profound loss of behavioral control and by the physical manifestations that accompany chronic disordered use of substances. In the last phase, the following symptoms appear and often continue in a vicious cycle until the user either dies or finds help. The general symptoms are as follows:

1. Continuous use of the substance for longer periods
2. Indefinable fears and vague spiritual desires
3. Impaired judgment and irrational thinking
4. Tremors, malnutrition, overdoses, decreased tolerance, and/or other physiological problems associated with the substance
5. Obsessive use of the substance until recovery or death

Binges, benders, daily use, and the inability to stop without help are characteristic of this phase. The user engages in prolonged, continuous use and is unable to function without using the drug of choice on some regular basis. The addict neglects daily needs to the point of not eating or caring for self or others. Attempts to control usage are abandoned as the periods of intoxication and withdrawal encompass most of the user's time.

Symptoms 2 and 3 reflect the loss of ability to function that accompanies brain deterioration associated with prolonged use of psychoactive drugs and alcohol. The user cannot think clearly and will make outlandish claims that are obviously irrational. For example, one will claim and believe that someone broke into the house and took all the cocaine while s/he was asleep. As the fears increase, one may experience a vague yearning for some miracle or "divine intervention" to stop the continuation of the downward spiral that is the course of severely disordered use.

The final two symptoms comprise the absolute deterioration of the individual prior to death. Especially with severely disordered use of alcohol, the individual may experience a "reverse tolerance" in which he once again becomes very intoxicated by a smaller dose of alcohol.

This is an indication that overuse of alcohol has resulted in deterioration of one's physical ability to process the alcohol quickly enough to remove it from the body. Obsessive use, if unbroken, ultimately leads to death by suicide, homicide, accident, or medical complications. Here, the drug truly "takes the person" by becoming the solitary focus of life. The individual becomes obsessed with using not to get high but to feel normal and avoid the consequences of withdrawal.

ASSESSING THE BEHAVIORAL SYMPTOMS OF USE

The following questions are suggested for helping the clinician evaluate the behavioral symptoms of substance-related use. In Figure 5.1 they are classified under the headings Preoccupation, Increased Tolerance, Rapid Intake, Using Alone, Use as a Panacea (Cure-all), Protecting Supply, Non-premeditated Use, and Blackouts (for alcohol).

The more *yes* answers a client gives, the greater the likelihood of severely disordered substance use. In assessing the behavioral components of a client's substance use, it is important to remember that each individual will experience some diversity in the pattern of use. Some individuals who are severe users of cocaine will experience periods of profound depression following a binge, and some will not. Not all alcoholics will experience a reverse tolerance even in the chronic stage of severely disordered use. The symptoms certainly overlap and present in many varieties and time frames depending on the individual situation. The description of the behavioral characteristics and questions about behavioral changes are meant to serve as guidelines and directions for further exploration with the client.

Social Characteristics

It is through the investigation of a client's social and family life that evidence of substance use is often initially detected. As the user continues to become more heavily involved in severely disordered use of a chemical, the primary relationship in life eventually becomes the relationship with the substance. As the use becomes increasingly important and central to the person's life, it is inevitable that other social relationships will suffer.

Individuals who use a substance often develop clear patterns over time of focusing one's life on social activities that afford opportunities to indulge in substance use. Especially with the use of illegal substances, in order to be protected from detection, one becomes increasingly involved in socializing with others who use similar drugs in a similar manner. Users prefer to use with others who use like them. Family members or friends who are sober and do not use become excluded from a significant part of the user's life. As a person's "affair" with a substance grows and the barrier of denial is fortified, the chasm in important relationships with family and friends deepens. Increasing family conflict related to the substance use, a very constricted social life, lack of involvement in activities that do not afford an opportunity to use, and general withdrawal from sober friends are signals that the involvement with a substance is well under way. The more advanced the reliance on the substance, the more alienated the user becomes from others who don't indulge.

Patterns of behaviors that are found in families of disordered users are well established (Lewis et al., 2015; Mattoo et al., 2015). The strength of the reliance on the substance is easily evidenced when users fail to make attempts to prevent family breakups or isolation from significant others in order to maintain their substance use. Intimate relationships that endure a user's increasing disordered using become distorted through the denial or "enabling" behaviors exhibited by the user's family.

1. Preoccupation

Yes	No	
_____	_____	Do you find yourself looking forward to the end of a day's work so you can have a couple drinks or your drug of choice and relax?
_____	_____	Do you look forward to the end of the week so you can have some fun getting high?
_____	_____	Does the thought of using sometimes enter your mind when you should be thinking of something else?
_____	_____	Do you sometimes feel the need to have a drink or "hit" at a particular time of the day?

2. Increased Tolerance

Yes	No	
_____	_____	Do you find that you can sometimes use more than others and not show it too much?
_____	_____	Have friends ever commented on your ability to "hold your alcohol or drugs"?
_____	_____	Have you ever experienced an increased capacity to drink or use drugs and felt proud of this ability?

3. Rapid Intake

Yes	No	
_____	_____	Do you usually order a double or like to drink your first two or three drinks fairly fast, or use your drug of choice in a way it works the fastest to get you high?
_____	_____	Do you usually have a couple of drinks before going to a party or out to dinner or use a drug before going out in order to "get a head start"?

4. Using Alone

Yes	No	
_____	_____	Do you routinely stop in a bar alone and have a couple of drinks or go home and get high by yourself?
_____	_____	Do you sometimes use alone when no one else with you is using?
_____	_____	Do you usually have an extra drink by yourself when mixing drinks for others or have extra drugs of your own when using with others?

5. Use as a Panacea (Cure-all)

Yes	No	
_____	_____	Do you fairly routinely drink or get high to calm your nerves or reduce tension or stress?
_____	_____	Do you find it difficult to enjoy a party or social gathering if there is nothing to drink or use?
_____	_____	Do you often think of relief or escape as associated with your use?
_____	_____	When encountering any physical or emotional problems, is your first thought to use?
_____	_____	Does life seem easier knowing your drug of choice will help you out?

FIGURE 5.1 Questions for assessing behavioral symptoms.

6. Protecting the Supply

Yes   No

____   ____   Do you sometimes store a bottle or drug away around the house in the event you may "need" to use or do you fear you may run out?

____   ____   Do you ever keep a bottle or substance in the trunk of your car or office desk or stashed in the house "just in case" you might need it?

7. Non-premeditated Use

Yes   No

____   ____   Do you sometimes start to have a drink or two or use just a little and have several more drinks or hits than you had planned?

____   ____   Do you sometimes find yourself starting to use when you had planned to go straight home or do something else?

____   ____   Do you sometimes use more than you think you should?

____   ____   Is your use sometimes different from what you would like it to be?

8. Blackouts (for Alcohol)

Yes   No

____   ____   In the morning following an evening of drinking, have you ever had the experience of not being able to remember everything that happened the night before?

____   ____   The morning after a night of drinking, have you ever had difficulty recalling how you got home or who you were with and what you did?

FIGURE 5.1   *(Continued)*

Family Characteristics

Family members, like the user, progress through different phases in their journey with the user. Substance-related use is often classified as a "family illness" because the effects of the disordered use on those who are in a close relationship with the user mean that they experience symptoms that, while different, are frequently as serious as those suffered by the user. Essentially, everyone in the user's family and social system suffers. Several evidence-based treatment approaches emphasize that the user's behavior cannot be viewed in isolation from the family (Marsiglia & Booth, 2013; SAMHSA, 2015b).

Four stages in the family system of the severely disordered user can delineate the dynamics that are often seen in families of severely disordered users (Lewis et al., 2015). Although these stages represent common patterns of family interaction with substance users, not all families can be defined or described using these criteria. These are not discrete stages; it is likely that there will be some overlap or that several stages will be in evidence simultaneously. Also, not every family will experience the same intensity or exact set of responses in each stage. Some families may stay in a prolonged state of denial, even to the point of the user's death. The description of the stages, however, can provide some guidelines for assessing the dynamics in the user's family and provide a basis for treatment planning with both the user and other family members.

1. *Denial.* In this stage, family members deny that there is a substance use problem. They try to hide the problem both from other family members and from those outside the family. Excuses are made, members "cover" and make excuses for the user's behavior, other explanations are offered, and the family begins to isolate from others who might suspect "something is wrong."

2. *Home Treatment.* Family members try to get the user to stop using. Hiding drugs or bottles, nagging, threatening, persuasion, and sympathy are attempted. Home treatment, or the family's effort to stop the user from using without seeking outside help, may fail because the focus is on controlling the behavior of someone else. The roles in the family often change significantly, usually with deleterious effects. Children may try to care for a parent, coalitions among family members are formed, and family members ignore or minimize their own problems by keeping the focus on the substance user.

3. *Chaos.* The problem becomes so critical that it can no longer be denied or kept secret from those outside the family. Neighbors and friends become aware of the severely disordered substance use. Conflicts and confrontations escalate without resolution. The consequences for family members become more pronounced and a child or partner of the user may experience serious emotional or physical problems. Threats of divorce, separation, or withdrawal of family support are often made but not acted on. There may be domestic violence or abuse or neglect of children in the family that must be carefully assessed in order to intervene if needed.

4. *Control.* A spouse or family member attempts to take complete control of and responsibility for the user. If still living within the family, the severely disordered user becomes an emotional invalid who exists outside the "normal" functioning of the family. Control is often exercised through divorce, separation, or a total emotional alienation from the family. The family, like the disordered user, exists in a state of suspended animation, trapped in a cycle of helplessness and futile attempts to control the user's behavior.

ASSESSING THE SOCIAL AND FAMILY-RELATED SYMPTOMS

As previously noted, it is important to have access to family members, friends, and/or important others in the user's life in order to adequately assess a substance use problem. If a severely disordered user has somehow entered the mental health system, through a doctor's referral or employer's recommendation, it is highly likely that the situation has become unmanageable enough for significant others to break the barrier of denial. Many clients report that their "entrance into treatment was the result of an intervention" (Lewis et al., 2015, p. 183). As with the user, it is critically important to undertake the assessment in a supportive, caring, nonjudgmental manner. Many family members experience a high degree of guilt or shame about the user's behavior and feel that the continuation of the severely disordered use is somehow their fault. They may feel that they have not been a good enough spouse, child, or parent or that they have created so much stress in the user's life that they have promoted the severely disordered use.

Other social and familial factors appear more frequently in substance-using groups. Genetic factors clearly play a role as a predisposing factor for the development of severely disordered use of alcohol. Experiences of loss and grief can contribute to the onset of substance-related problems (Creighton, Oliffe, Matthews, & Saewyc, 2016).

The questionnaire in Figure 5.2 can be given to family members or friends in order to gain important information about the user's pattern of substance use. Information gathered from others can be compared with the responses given by the client in order to assess the degree of

Questionnaire: Do You Have a Spouse, Friend or Loved One Who Has a Drinking or Drug Use Problem?

1. Do you worry about how much they use drugs or drink?
2. Do you complain about how often they drink or use?
3. Do you criticize them for the amount they spend on drugs or alcohol?
4. Have you ever been hurt or embarrassed by their behavior when they are drinking or using?
5. Are holidays in your home unpleasant because of their drinking or drugging?
6. Do they ever lie about their drinking or drug use?
7. Do they deny that drinking or drugs affect their behavior?
8. Do they say or do things and later deny having said or done them?
9. Do you sometimes feel that drinking or drug use is more important to them than you are?
10. Do they get angry if you criticize their substance use or their drinking or drug using companions?
11. Is drinking or drug use involved in almost all your social activities?
12. Does your family spend almost as much on alcohol or drugs as it does on food or other necessities?
13. Are you having any financial difficulties because of their use?
14. Does their substance use keep them away from home a good deal?
15. Have you ever threatened to end your relationship because of their drinking or drug use?
16. Have you ever lied for them because of their drug use or drinking?
17. Do you find yourself urging them to eat instead of drink or use drugs at parties?
18. Have they ever stopped drinking or using drugs completely for a period of time and then started using again?
19. Have you ever thought about calling the police because of their behavior while drunk or high?
20. Do you think that alcohol or drugs create problems for them?

FIGURE 5.2 Questions to determine patterns of substance use.

minimization or denial that may be present. A *yes* response to any of the questions indicates some possibility of substance use; a yes response to four or more indicates a substance use problem.

In addition to gathering information from others who are familiar with the user, counselors must be alert to some of the common social consequences that frequently appear in a user's life. Frequent job loss, a driving under the influence (DUI) or driving while impaired (DWI) or driving under the influence of drugs (DUID) arrest or other legal problem (particularly domestic violence or child abuse), the breakup of important relationships, a series of moves (also called "the geographic cure"), a history of psychological or medical problems that are unresolved, and a lack of interest in activities that were once important to the individual are all indicators of severe substance use. Several of the assessment devices discussed in the next part of the chapter will assist the clinician in gathering information related to the symptoms and social characteristics of substance use disorder.

SCREENING AND ASSESSMENT INSTRUMENTS

To assist in the diagnosis and assessment of substance use, psychometric instruments are often very helpful. It is estimated that there are at least 100 different screening tests for substance use. A variety of specific psychometric instruments are generally available to counselors. Standardized assessment materials, however, have several benefits. They provide data about clients compared to a normative population, help maintain objectivity, assist in treatment planning, and provide a way to communicate with other professionals (Laux, Perera-Diltz, Calmes, Behl, & Vasquez, 2016).

The primary benefit of assessment is to accurately and efficiently determine the treatment needs of the client. Assessment results and diagnostic data are essential for research as well as clinical purposes. Assessment can be defined as the "act of determining the nature and causes of a client's problem" (Lewis et al., 2015, p. 82).

Material from the initial interview should help the clinician select appropriate measures that will enhance understanding of the exact nature, dynamics, severity, and effects of the client's substance use. For example, several tools are focused on alcohol use only, while others include abuse of additional or other substances.

The assessment measures reviewed in this text are only a sample of those that are available. They were chosen based on their widespread use and availability, ease of administration and scoring, and reliability and validity. The assessment devices that are included in this segment include the Michigan Alcoholism Screening Test (MAST) and the Short Michigan Alcoholism Screening Test (SMAST); the Drug Abuse Screening Test (DAST-20); the CAGE Questionnaire; CAGE-AID; the Alcohol Use Disorders Identification Test (AUDIT); the Substance Abuse Subtle Screening Inventory-3 (SASSI-3 and SASSI-A2); Tolerance, Worried, Eye-Opener, Amnesia, K/Cut-down (TWEAK); Problem Oriented Screening Instrument for Teenagers (POSIT); Screening, Brief Intervention, and Referral to Treatment (SBIRT); and the Addiction Severity Index (ASI). Many of these screening devices are available to clinicians and researchers free of charge and are accessible online. Project Cork (https://web.archive.org/web/20160325172357/http:/www.projectcork.org/clinical_tools/index.html) provides clinicians and researchers access to the AUDIT, CAGE, DAST, and MAST along with a few of their adaptations and several other tests. In addition, those who are trained to use the Millon Clinical Multiaxial Inventory (MCMI-II) and/or the Minnesota Multiphasic Personality Inventory (MMPI-2) may use information from those tests to help with diagnostic and treatment considerations. State licensure laws must be consulted for training requirements for use of assessment instruments in various states (e.g., New York State Education Department [NYSED], 2014, Mental Health Practitioners; NYSED, 2015, Psychology).

The Michigan Alcoholism Screening Test (MAST)

The most researched diagnostic instrument is the self-administered Michigan Alcoholism Screening Test (MAST; The MAST's questions can be located at the following website: http://www.integration.samhsa.gov/clinical-practice/sbirt/Mast.pdf), which was created in 1971 by M. L. Selzer). The 25-item MAST correctly identifies up to 95% of severe alcohol users, and the SMAST, an even shorter 10-question form of the MAST, has also been shown to identify over 90% of the severe alcohol users entering general psychiatric hospitals. The MAST was originally validated with treatment-seeking alcoholics. Numerous studies have used it to assess both adolescent and adult populations in a variety of settings. The MAST may realistically and effectively be used with virtually any population (Shields, Howell, Potter, & Weiss, 2007).

The MAST is simple to administer; clients are instructed to answer all questions either yes or no. After clients complete the test, the points assigned to each question are totaled. A total of 4 points is presumptive evidence of severe alcohol use; a total of 5 or more points makes it extremely unlikely that the individual is not a severe alcohol user.

The Drug Abuse Screening Test (DAST-20)

The DAST-20 is a 20-item self-report inventory designed to measure aspects of substance use behavior, not including alcohol. It was derived from the Michigan Alcoholism Screening Test

(MAST) and reflects similar content. DAST-20 scores are computed by summing all items positively endorsed for drug use. Higher scores indicate a greater likelihood of severe drug use. The DAST-20 is designed for use with adult male and female drug users.

The DAST-20 is a useful tool for helping to differentiate between several categories of substance users. In clinical trials, the DAST-20 scores demonstrated significant differences between the alcohol, drug, and poly-substance use groups. DAST-20 scores were also found to correlate highly with other drug use indices.

The DAST-20's questions can be located at the following website:

https://web.archive.org/web/20160325172655/http://projectcork.org/clinical_tools/html/DAST.html

The CAGE Questionnaire

The CAGE is a four-item questionnaire that includes questions related to a history of attempting to cut down on alcohol intake (C), annoyance over criticism about alcohol (A), guilt about drinking behavior (G), and drinking in the morning to relieve withdrawal anxiety, sometimes known as an "eye-opener" (E). Most questionnaires duplicate information by using different phrases or words to detect similar patterns of behavior. The CAGE condenses the essential diagnostic questions into a brief, but powerful, tool for assessing severe alcohol use. This is also an extremely useful questionnaire to use with family members or others that are participating in the assessment.

The CAGE was originally developed and used with adult alcoholics presenting for treatment. Like the MAST, the CAGE may be used to screen for severe alcohol use in a variety of health care settings. The CAGE effectively discriminates severe alcohol users from mild alcohol users 90 percent of the time.

The CAGE is generally administered verbally as part of the diagnostic interview. Instructions for administering the CAGE include observing the client's attitude in responding to the questions. The counselor should ask them to explain any yes answer and watch for signs of rationalization, denial, projection of blame, and minimization. The first question deals with the user's common problem of repeatedly trying to get the drinking under control only to lose control again and again once they resume drinking. The next question detects sensitivity to criticism of the drinking behavior. The third question taps into the personal sense of guilt, and the fourth looks at the tendency to use morning drinking as a remedy for excessive drinking the night before. It is recommended that the CAGE be supplemented with the first three questions from the AUDIT, that is, checking for quantity, frequency, and evidence of alcohol dependency, thereby screening for alcohol use disorder. As with the SMAST, the CAGE questions can be adapted as an assessment tool for other substances.

Variations of the CAGE Questionnaire that offer alternative questions to assess use of substances other than or in addition to alcohol are also available. Sullivan and Fleming (2008) recommend that clinicians ask specific questions about the use of street drugs, especially with adolescents and individuals who have not had negative effects as a result of drug use. For example ask the client if they have used any street drugs more than five times. A positive answer to this question may indicate a drug problem and the need for more in-depth screening, like the CAGE-Adapted to Include Drugs (CAGE-AID), that explores a lifetime of use.

The CAGE-AID consists of the same four questions in the CAGE with "or drug use" added to each question. For example, the first question asks about repeatedly trying to get the drinking "or drug use" under control. If a client responds positively to any one of the questions, further assessment is required. Another version of the CAGE for Youth and Adolescents is help-ful in assessing substance use problems with clients in this age range. The CAGE Questionnaire is available online for researchers, clinicians, and students to access.

The CAGE can be located at the following website: https://web.archive.org/web/20160325175454/http://projectcork.org/clinical_tools/html/CAGE.html/

Tolerance, Worried, Eye-Opener, Amnesia, K/Cut-down (TWEAK)

TWEAK was the first instrument developed to assess at-risk drinking during pregnancy (Russell, 1994) and is now used on a wider scale to assess harmful drinking in the general population. The acronym stands for (T), tolerance, asking about the quantity of drinks the person consumes before showing signs of impairments; (W), worried, are significant others worried or concerned about the individual's drinking habits; (E), eye opener, consuming alcohol in the morning to rouse oneself or to relieve withdrawal anxiety; (A), amnesia, has the individual experienced blackout or is unable to recall events while drinking; (K), k/cut down, does the individual feel the need to cut down on the drinking. The instrument is simple to use and takes two minutes to com-plete. It can be self-administered or be used as part of the clinical interview. Maximum scoring for TWEAK is 7 points. The first two questions—Tolerance and Worried—receive 2 points each, and subsequent questions 1 point each. A score of 2 or more indicates harmful drinking and requires further evaluation. This instrument has high sensitivity in detecting alcohol use with pregnant women and White women and is less sensitive with minority populations (Bones, Bailey, & Sokol, 2013). TWEAK is accessible online at www.http://adai.washington.edu/instruments/pdf/TWEAK_252.pdf

The Tolerance, Annoyed, Cut down, Eye opener (TACE) and its modification TACER3 are also useful screening tools to detect alcohol use in pregnant and perinatal women (Bones et al., 2013). TACE can be downloaded from the Internet at http://pubs.niaaa.nih.gov/publications/arh28-2/78-79.htm

The Alcohol Use Disorders Identification Test (AUDIT)

The AUDIT is an internationally used screening tool developed by the World Health Organization (WHO) to assess for risky or harmful alcohol use as well as for alcohol use disorder (Hodgson et al., 2003). It is a very simple, quick to administer, 10-question tool that provides information on the quantity and frequency of alcohol consumption, evidence of alcohol dependence, and the nega-tive consequences of alcohol use. The AUDIT is particularly useful in detecting less severe alcohol consumption in persons who might be in the early stages of developing an alcohol use disorder. A study with college students exiting bars produced good reliability and validity esti-mates among persons whose alcohol use was mild to moderate (Celio et al., 2011). It is a useful screening tool with adolescent and young adult clients who may not have developed a severe use of alcohol. For counseling purposes, it can help advise and educate less severely impaired drink-ers and provide guidance in encouraging behavior change to reduce the possibility of severe alcohol use in the future.

The AUDIT-Consumption (AUDIT-C) is a shortened version of the AUDIT used to assess binge drinking. This shortened version has three questions assessing frequency and quantity of alcohol consumption as well as frequency of binge drinking (Lundin, Hallgren, Balliu & Forsell, 2015). Questions on both the AUDIT and the AUDIT-C are coded 0 to 4, and the score for each item is summed to provide the total score. Total score of 8 or more for the AUDIT and 4 or higher for the ADUIT-C indicates hazardous drinking.

The AUDIT manual can be downloaded from the WHO at the following website: http://apps.who.int/iris/bitstream/10665/67205/1/WHO_MSD_MSB_01.6a.pdf. An online version of the AUDIT is available at: testandcalc.com/etc/tests/audit.asp

The Substance Abuse Subtle Screening Inventory (SASSI-3 and SASSI-A2)

The Substance Abuse Subtle Screening Inventory-3 (SASSI-3) for adults and the Adolescent SASSI-A2 for adolescents (Miller, 1997) are single-page, paper-and-pencil questionnaires. On one side are 52 true/false questions that generally appear unrelated to chemical use; on the other side are 26 items that allow clients to self-report the negative effects of any alcohol and drug use. Clients can complete the SASSI in approximately 10 to 15 minutes. It is easily scored, and training is available in interpretation and use of the SASSI as a screening tool for identifying substance use. The SASSI is available only to therapists who have met certain criteria and completed some training in its use. Information, training, and materials are available through the SASSI Institute, P.O. Box 5069, Bloomington, IN 47407.

The primary strength of the SASSI is in identifying substance use patterns that are hidden by the more subtle forms of denial common to substance users. Items on the SASSI touch on a broad spectrum of topics seemingly unrelated to chemical use (e.g., "I think there is something wrong with my memory" and "I am often resentful"). The questions are designed to be non-threatening to users to avoid triggering the client's defenses and denial. The SASSI is resistant to faking and defeats efforts to "second-guess" the "right" answer. As a result, the SASSI is effective in identifying clients who are minimizing or in denial about their substance use. It is also effective in identifying substance use regardless of the drug of choice. Both of the SASSIs are adapted for either male or female clients.

The data from research with the SASSI indicates approximately a 90% accuracy in identifying substance use patterns in clients. Further, SASSI-3 was found to be useful in helping clients acknowledge substance use regardless of their readiness for change (Laux, Piazza, Salyers & Roseman, 2012). Thousands of test items were designed or considered, then given to samples of severe alcohol users, other drug users, and controls (non-substance-using people). The inventory was tested over a period of 16 years and is still being adapted and updated. In 1997, the Adult SASSI-3 replaced the adult SASSI-2. Two scales from the original test were dropped and three new scales were added. Counselors have used the SASSI as a screening tool for court-ordered substance use programs (Huber, Keferl. Lazowski, Heinemann, & Moore, 2011; Hupp & Jewell, 2010), employee assistance programs (Heinemann, Moore, Lazowski, Huber, & Semik, 2014), illegal behaviors (Burck, Laux, Ritchie, & Baker, 2008), and in general mental health settings. Information about the SASSI and how to purchase it is located on the following websites: psychscreen.com/epiphanyWeb/FlexPage.aspx?ID=27 or https://www.sassi.com/products/

The Addiction Severity Index (ASI)

The Addiction Severity Index (ASI; Fureman, Parikh, Bragg, & McLellan, 1990) provides basic information that is useful both for the clinician and the clients. The ASI manual gives clear instructions for administering, scoring, and using the data in planning treatment strategies. The current ASI is designed for use with adults, but variations for use with adolescents are being developed. A particular strength of the ASI is its utility with dual diagnosis populations. For treatment planning purposes, the ASI is especially helpful in determining the severity of the client's drug use and the need for additional or extended treatment.

The ASI is administered as a structured interview with specific questions that cover several basic areas of treatment needs, including medical, employment/support, drug/alcohol use, legal, family/social relationships, and psychiatric. The drug/alcohol subscale includes an extensive history of all drug and alcohol use, the longest period of abstinence, and previous drug treatment history. Administration of the ASI relies on fairly basic clinical interviewing skills. Counselors can adjust questions to use terms that are familiar to the client and fit with his or her level of education and "sophistication." In some treatment settings, the ASI questions can also be given as writing projects for the client to further examine their history of drug/alcohol use and its impact on their lives.

The client uses a 0- to 4-point scale to rate how "bothered" they have been in the past 30 days by problems in the different areas of assessment. This serves to give a clearer picture from the client's perspective of how they rate the severity of the problem and gives some indication of the desire for treatment. These ratings are then compared with the counselor's ratings on the same scales. With the influence of denial or minimization on the client's perceptions, it is common for the interviewer to perceive a higher severity of problems than the client.

A final benefit of the ASI is its usefulness as a training tool for counselors. It can greatly facilitate training in substance use and dual diagnosis work, particularly when clients are somewhat resistant or evasive. The structured format of the ASI gives the counselor a direction when clients are not forthcoming. Understanding the content of each scale of the ASI assists the clinician to recognize the interaction of substance use with other areas of the person's life (Kessler et al., 2012).

Problem Oriented Screening Instrument for Teenagers (POSIT)

POSIT (Rahdert, 1991) is a multidimensional screening tool for substance use problems and other areas of functioning needing in depth assessment in adolescents aged 12 to 19 years. There are 139 true/false questions organized around 10 scales. The instrument can be self-administered and requires approximately 20 to 30 minutes for administration and review. The 10 scales are substance use and abuse, physical health status, mental health status, family relationship, peer relationships, education status, vocational status, leisure and recreation, social skills, and aggressive behavior and delinquency. The substance use subscale assesses severity of use and psychosocial risk factors associated with substance use. The questions fall into three categories: general, age related, and red flagged. A positive score on any item indicates a potential problem and that further assessment is needed in that area.

One of the strengths of this instrument is that it screens for substance use and concurrent mental health problems. Negative behavior in any one of the other functioning areas can potentially be seen as contributing to, facilitating, or maintaining the substance use. Another strength is its utility, as different professionals working with adolescents can use this instrument without the need for extensive training. The results can begin the discussion around risk and problem behavior regarding substance use with the adolescent (Kim, 2009). The POSIT is not copyrighted and can be accessed at http://www.emcdda.europa.eu/html.cfm/index4439EN.html. or copies of POSIT with scoring template can be requested from the Adolescent Assessment/Referral System Manual, DHHS Publication No. (ADM) 91-1735, from: National Clearinghouse for Alcohol and Drug Information, P.O. Box 2345, Rockville, MD, 20847-2345, 1-900-729-6686.

Screening, Brief Intervention, and Referral to Treatment (SBIRT)

SBIRT is designed to provide universal screening, secondary prevention, early intervention, and timely referral to treatment for individuals who may have substance use disorder, or those who may be at risk (Babor et al., 2007; SAMHSA, 2013). SBIRT is viewed as a transtheoretical model using motivational interviewing techniques to screen for substance use and perform brief intervention. Screening is done through interviewing as well as using screening tools to identify individuals who may have a substance use problem and those who are at risk, as well as those who do not use any substance.

Screening is followed by brief intervention. This brief intervention will differ for clients based on the risk assessed. For example, an intervention for individuals who report no problem or minimal substance use may involve prevention education and activities to help them maintain non-risky use or abstinence. An intervention for someone identified to be at moderate risk for substance use may involve education and awareness around substance use, consequences, and behavioral changes. This can be done in one session or multiple sessions. Brief treatment is aimed at facilitating change in the individual. SAMSHA (2013) noted that "The goal of brief treatment is to change not only the immediate behavior or thoughts about risky behaviors, but also address long-standing problems with harmful drinking and drug misuse and help patients with higher levels of disorder obtain intensive care" (p. 9). This treatment can be done on site, depending on the agency, or it can be by referral to substance use treatment facilities.

The SBIRT is comprehensive, as it is useful in detecting substance use disorders as defined by the DSM-5 (APA, 2013) and provides prevention as well as early intervention strategies. These services can occur in multiple settings: for example, in public health settings; in medical settings such as emergency rooms and primary care physician offices; in educational settings in the school counselor or college counseling offices; and in other non–substance use treatment settings. The SBIRT has strong research to support this model, and grants and training are available to agencies to implement this approach to diagnosing and treating substance use disorder. More information on the SBRIT is available at http://www.samhsa.gov/sbirt.

The Millon Clinical Multiaxial Inventory (MCMI-II) and Minnesota Multiphasic Personality Inventory (MMPI-2)

Although both the MCMI-II and the MMPI-2 are primarily designed for the assessment of personality, they are often used to assess a full range of psychopathology, including substance use. Both are copyrighted, protected evaluation instruments that require additional training to administer, score, and interpret. Both have elaborate computer-scoring programs available through the resources that sell the tests. Incorporated into both the MMPI-2 and MCMI-II are validity scales that may help to identify clients who are "attempting to look good" or answering randomly. It is not in the scope of this text to provide the reader with an in-depth understanding of either of these instruments.

There is, however, some information that can be used in a basic assessment. The MCMI-II is useful in identifying several aspects of personality functioning: clinical syndromes (e.g., depression, anxiety), changing symptoms, and personality styles or disorders. It is certainly a useful addition to any evaluation in which there is a question of dual diagnosis. It is a simple, true/false, 173-question self-report regarding the client's behavior and experience. Given the difficulty of hand scoring, it is generally scored by a computer program.

The symptom scales on the MCMI-II are useful in corroborating a clinical impression of the types or patterns of symptoms experienced by the client. The personality scales may help a clinician understand the relationship between the client's substance use and their typical pattern of managing their experience and relationships. For example, someone with a score indicating a Narcissistic Personality style may use substances to establish or maintain a particular image.

Understanding a client's basic personality can be very useful in planning treatment to address specific character traits that may either support or undermine recovery.

Like the MCMI-II, the Minnesota Multiphasic Personality Inventory-2 (MMPI-2) is useful in identifying behavioral and personality patterns and clinical symptoms. These tests are generally used as part of a comprehensive personality or behavioral assessment. The MMPI-2 is a self-report questionnaire that consists of 567 true/false questions. There is also a version of the MMPI-2 for adolescent populations, the Minnesota Multiphasic Personality Inventory—Adolescent (MMPI-A).

The MMPI has been used extensively for over 20 years in the evaluation of alcohol-related disorders. There is a common pattern in MMPI scores among these individuals. Elevations on scales 2, 4, and 7 represent a combination of personality characteristics commonly found in male severe users. These scores reflect depressive, sociopathic, and obsessive-compulsive features. They also reported symptoms of anxiety, marital discord, financial problems, insomnia, and tension that were reflected in the MMPI profiles of these individuals. In addition to the basic clinical scales, both the MMPI-2 and MMPI-A contain items that indicate the possibility of substance use problems. A subscale of both tests, the MacAndrew Alcoholism Scale—Revised (MAC-R), was developed using items from the original MMPI and became widely used as a method of screening for substance use problems. The revised MAC (MAC-R) deleted several questions and added others to further refine the content of the scale. The MAC-R has been an effective tool for identifying substance use problems in both adults and adolescents (Graham, 1990), and is about 85% accurate in the detection of SUDs (Craig, 2004).

Two other subscales on both MMPIs are the Addiction Acknowledgement Scale (AAS) and the Addiction Potential Scale (APS). Persons who obtain a high score on the AAS are usually acknowledging a substance use problem, and additional assessment of the nature of their substance use would be indicated. The APS may help discriminate between persons who use substances and those who do not. Both the APS and AAS are still in the process of being validated and evaluated for their reliability in assessing substance use problems. Particularly with the APS, high scores should be corroborated with other data and information.

Additional information about the MMPI-2 is available through: http://www.pearsonclinical.com/psychology/products/100000461/minnesota-multiphasic-personality-inventory-2-mmpi-2.html.

ASAM Criteria for Patient Placement

The American Society of Addiction Medicine (ASAM) provided specific criteria as a multidimensional approach to determine the biopsychosocial severity of a client's condition and provide guidance for placement through assigning one of the four levels of care (Hoffman, Halikas, Mee-Lee, & Weedman, 1991). In clinical settings for substance use, the ASAM guidelines were the most widely used criteria to define intensity of medical necessity and associated evaluation of level of required services and structure, ranging from standard outpatient care to intensive inpatient facilities for those with more severe problems (Klein, di Menza, Arfken, & Schuster, 2002; Shepard et al., 2005). Later, the early criteria were more specifically applied in the Treatment Mix Index (TMI), a questionnaire to assess the needed level of care (Shepard et al., 2005).

The four levels of care, reflective of the strength of services needed by a client, include (a) outpatient treatment; (b) intensive outpatient/partial hospitalization; (c) medically monitored intensive inpatient, such as residential treatment; and (d) medically managed intensive inpatient treatment, seen in hospitalization. The particular level would be identified along biopsychosocial assessment dimensions: (a) acute intoxication and/or withdrawal potential, (b) biomedical conditions and complications, (c) emotional/behavioral conditions and complications, (d) treatment acceptance/resistance, (e) relapse potential, and (f) recovery environment (Magura et al., 2005).

Further clarification was offered when ASAM (2007) published a revised second edition of the guidelines, ASAM PPC-2R, with two sets of criteria, one for adults and another for adolescents. The newest criterion published by ASAM for the Treatment of Substance-Related Disorders is the "most comprehensive set of guidelines for assessment, service planning, placement, continued stay and transfer/discharge of individuals with addiction and co-occurring conditions" (Mee-Lee, 2014, p. 2).

DIAGNOSIS

Professionals who have to make decisions about the presence or absence of a substance use disorder for their clients must make a series of complex judgments. An adequate conceptualization of SUD emphasizes the interaction among the individual user, the physiological effects, and the social context in which the user functions. A useful general thesis is that a SUD exists when drug or alcohol use is associated with impairment of health and social functioning. It is important to note that the goal of a diagnostic assessment is not to "label" a client with a SUD. The purpose of assigning a diagnosis is to aid in treatment planning and to assist clients in making a determination of what steps they might decide to take to address a substance use problem if one is detected. Clinicians should be cautioned to avoid telling clients they have a SUD and instead share assessment results with the understanding that it is the client's decision whether they have a problem or not based on the information gathered.

Inconsistent attitudes and imprecise standards for what constitutes an "addiction" in the past have complicated the diagnosis of a substance use disorder. Inadequate definitions of SUDs have often been cited as the primary reason for a lack of success in developing adequate epidemiological, diagnostic, and prognostic assessment tools. With many medical illnesses, the etiology, prognosis, and treatment are known, and no biases, misinformation, or stigma interferes with the identification of the disease. In the past this has not been the case with the diagnosis of a substance use disorder. Here, much of the information needed to establish a diagnosis is based on self-reports from a population that is often unreliable, given the preponderance of denial and minimization along with possible cognitive impairment. Long-standing prejudices and moral attitudes further complicate making an adequate diagnosis. Although the DSM-5 (APA, 2013) offers seemingly clear, behavioral descriptions of symptoms that constitute Substance-Related and Addictive Disorders, exceptions to the rule are always a possibility.

Differential Diagnosis

It is frequently the case that one of the most challenging aspects of diagnosing a substance use disorder is its interplay with other mental disorders. Counselors who effectively treat individuals with a primary diagnosis of SUD may be faced with treating additional psychological disorders. Other diagnostic categories, such as personality disorders, posttraumatic stress disorder, mood disorders, and thought disorders, are common differential or dual (co-occurring) diagnoses. Symptoms related to other disorders may be accentuated or mollified by a client's substance use.

It is important that clinicians working with substance users be trained in diagnosing other mental disorders as well as SUD. Many symptoms of intoxication or withdrawal from certain substances mimic the behaviors seen in psychiatric disorders. Clinicians who are untrained in the recognition of such problems as depression, mania, psychosis, and dementias may risk misdiagnosing a client. For example, if a client arrives in the counselor's office with symptoms of slurred speech, difficulty with coordination, and difficulty focusing his attention, the counselor might assume that these behaviors are evidence of a substance use problem. These symptoms, however, are also associated with certain neurological diseases such as multiple sclerosis or medical disorders such as diabetes. Differentiating between a bipolar disorder and the highs and lows experienced by one experiencing disordered substance use is often a complicated diagnostic process.

Generally, a longitudinal approach is useful in differentiating between psychiatric and substance use–related symptoms. Many symptoms of substance intoxication and withdrawal improve or are alleviated within days or weeks. It is not unusual for those with disordered substance use to appear far more disturbed when initially assessed than they will after a period of abstinence. Family or others who can be consulted regarding a client's behavioral history prior to the onset of disordered substance use can also be invaluable in accurately diagnosing and planning for treatment.

A standard rule of practice for counselors working with individuals presenting with disordered substance use is to refer for a thorough physical as an early part of the assessment process. Establishing a good working relationship with a physician who is familiar with disordered use of substances is an essential step in providing appropriate and adequate services. Also, a clinician who is trained in differential diagnostic techniques for assessing substance use disorders and other psychological and neuropsychological problems should be a part of the counselor's assessment referral network. For example, licensed psychologists have a broad range of standardized evaluation techniques that they can administer to help differentiate among emotional, characterological, or psychological disorders and alcohol- or drug-related problems.

Dual Diagnosis

Many individuals diagnosed with substance abuse problems also meet the criteria for other psychological disorders. Sometimes the *term co-occurring disorders* is used to describe this feature. This happens when clients can be diagnosed with one or more mental illnesses as identified by the DSM-5 as well as meeting the criteria for a substance use disorder. The Substance Abuse and Mental Health Services Administration (SAMHSA, 2015a) estimates that almost 7.9 million adults in the United States meet the criteria for both serious mental health and substance-related disorders. Serious mental illness is defined as "any mental, behavioural, or emotional disorder that substantially interfered with or limited one or more major life activities" (SAMHSA, 2015a, p. 3). Schizophrenia and mood disorders such as major depression, anxiety, and bipolar disorder are the most common co-occurring mental illnesses with substance use disorder. There is growing recognition of self-medication among adults with attention deficit hyperactivity disorder (ADHD; Huntley & Young, 2014). It is important to discover whether symptoms of a psychological problem either preceded the onset of the problems or persist after the substance use has been treated and a period of abstinence has been maintained for several months. For example, psychoactive drugs may initially offer some relief to individuals who suffer from mood disorders. As a result, some clients may self-medicate or use substances to cope or relieve distress and mental health issues such as depression and anxiety. In this case, depression, the mental health diagnosis, would have preceded the substance use.

On the other hand, substance use can lead to mood disorders or other mental health issues. Clients with alcohol use disorders can typically exhibit a high rate of depressive symptoms due to the depressant effects of their chronic use of alcohol and the associated consequences. Sleep and appetite disturbances, feelings of helplessness and hopelessness, and loss of pleasure and motivation are symptoms of depression and are also part of the pattern of alcohol use disorder. The deterioration of a severe alcohol user's lifestyle and health, the loss of significant relationships, and other problems related to excessive drinking along with the basic chemical effects of alcohol make it nearly inevitable that the client will appear depressed while actively drinking. In this case the depression is a consequence of the alcohol use (APA, 2013). This depression is usually reactive and should decrease significantly with abstinence and efforts to resolve life problems that accumulated during the period of substance use. Psychotic behaviors can also result from alcohol use and withdrawal.

Dual diagnosis can be difficult to detect. It is helpful for clinicians to question clients carefully about their psychological history before they used drugs or alcohol and seek information regarding a family history of psychological problems. A biopsychosocial assessment is also recommended. The learning theory of substance use in fact proposes that the concept of anxiety reduction related to drug or alcohol use is the basis for many severe substance-related disorders (Lewis et al., 2015).

With dual diagnosis, both the mental health and the substance use disorders need to be treated as separate entities, as both have unique symptoms. In most cases when the mental health diagnosis is not treated, it will exacerbate the substance use, and when the substance use is left untreated the mental health disorder will worsen. Integrated treatment is found to be effective in treating dual diagnosis of severe mental health and substance use disorders (Wusthoff, Wall, & Grawe, 2014).

In a national study of the prevalence of co-occurring substance use and mental disorders based on race and ethnicity, it was discovered that among those with a substance use disorder, 35.8% had a depressive disorder, 40.0% had an anxiety disorder, and 53.5% had another mental disorder, which would include schizophrenia and personality disorders. Among those with a substance use disorder, 55.4% of those who were White had a mental disorder, followed by 50.1% of Asian, 47.8% of Black, and 46.4% of Latino participants (Mericle, Park, Holck, & Arria, 2012). Among individuals with an arrest history who were receiving public mental health services for a diagnosis of schizophrenia or a related psychosis, 48.0% of the males and 41.0% of the females had a co-occurring substance use disorder. Among the 1,538 participants, 74.5% of the males and 79.1% of the females were White (McCabe et al., 2012). In a study comparing dually diagnosed individuals who had a personality disorder along with a substance use disorder with individuals without a substance use disorder, it was discovered that the occurrences of antisocial personality disorder and not otherwise specified personality disorder were significantly greater among those with a substance use disorder (Di Pierro, Preti, Vurro, & Madeddu, 2014). This information can be useful for clinicians who are working with clients presenting with these disorders and for substance use professionals who are detecting symptoms of any of these disorders in addition to symptoms specific to drug and alcohol use.

There is also a frequent relationship between substance use and suicide (Doweiko, 2015). In a global meta-analytical study of suicide risk, mental and substance use disorders were responsible for 62.1% of total years of life lost due to suicide. Of the loss of life due to suicide attributable to mental and substance use disorders, major depressive disorder was responsible for 46.1%, alcohol dependence for 13.25%, anxiety disorder for 7.4%, bipolar disorder for 5.4%, schizophrenia for 4.7%, and dependence on amphetamines for 2.4%, opioids for 1.9%, cocaine for 0.9%, and anorexia nervosa for 0.2%. Of the 10 leading classes of diseases included in the 2010 Global Burden of Disease, mental and substance use disorders increased from the fifth to the third leading class of disease burden, exceeding the burden due to neoplasms and neonatal conditions, but trailing cardiovascular and circulatory diseases (Ferrari et al., 2014).

As suggested in these findings, clients may be using alcohol or other drugs to treat the symptoms of depression or other disorders. In these clients, it is essential to provide an accurate diagnosis and initiate treatment as soon as possible. Involvement of a qualified clinician to assist in diagnosing and providing treatment for these clients at an early stage is critical.

CASE DISCUSSIONS

Case 1: Sandy and Pam

Effective assessment and diagnosis in the case of Sandy and Pam would begin with the diagnostic interview. Using the Substance Use History Questionnaire (see Appendix), information would be gathered regarding each of their histories of substance use and abuse. Significant factors to consider about Sandy's substance use are as follows:

- She has a history of alcohol use dating back to junior high.
- By self-report, Sandy admitted to continuing to abuse alcohol into adulthood.

In assessing Sandy's substance use, it is apparent that her alcohol use has affected her family life and social relationships. She reports that she had married Joe, a violent alcoholic, and that during her drinking days, she left the children at home so she could go to bars and pick up numerous men. This behavior would clearly indicate that Sandy's alcohol use affected her judgment and ability to care for herself and her children.

With the information from the Substance Use History Questionnaire, it is possible to assess the phase of alcohol use that Sandy is experiencing. The crucial phase is characterized by obvious and pronounced behavioral changes. Sandy reported behavioral loss of control coupled with guilt and remorse about her actions while using alcohol.

In diagnosing Sandy's substance use, additional information is needed. The MAST and the CAGE Questionnaire would be useful in deciding whether Sandy meets the criteria for a substance-related disorder in the DSM-5. Sandy's childhood history is indicative of the potential for a personality or mood disorder. Her marriage to Joe may indicate that she has suffered some type of physical or emotional abuse. Posttraumatic stress disorder (PTSD) is also a diagnostic possibility. Differential or dual diagnoses must be considered when evaluating Sandy's substance use. After a period of sobriety, additional psychological testing would be indicated to assess whether Sandy needed treatment for other disorders.

Pam's history of substance use included cocaine and alcohol. In assessing Pam's substance use, the significant factors are her

- employment history,
- unstable relationships, and
- report of anxiety symptoms.

In addition to the diagnostic interview using the Substance Use History Questionnaire, use of the Substance Abuse Subtle Screening Inventory-3 (SASSI-3) (https://www.sassi.com/products/) would be useful in identifying treatment issues and potential diagnoses. Clearly, Pam's substance use has also affected her judgment regarding relationships. The history with her live-in boyfriend seems to indicate intense conflict resulting in potential negative outcomes. Pam's history of unsuccessful employment indicates that she may be in the crucial phase of the progression of a severe substance use disorder. This pattern of substance use after a loss is a clear indicator of the overt consequences of the progression.

Other factors that need to be explored are the periodic abstinence or changes in Pam's pattern of substance use. The information from the SASSI-3 may be helpful in determining a SUD with a focus on polydrug use. Pam's childhood and recent conflicts with her boyfriend may indicate a possible personality disorder or mood disorder. Pam's statement regarding her boyfriend—that she "feels drawn to him" and wants to "make it work"—could indicate tendency to be dependent in a relationship. Pam's increasing anxiety could be indicative of either periodic withdrawal from the substances or an underlying anxiety disorder.

In summary, additional information gathered through an assessment would be needed in both cases in order to make accurate diagnoses and assist in planning treatment. Contacting other family members or significant others to gather information would be useful. Once each woman had established abstinence of at least two months, further assessment would help with answering questions about dual diagnoses.

Case 2: Juanita and Jose

In this case, Jose and Juanita's substance use is of primary importance and must be addressed. It is important to note that Juanita and Jose admit to severe alcohol use for 23 years and to recent use of cocaine. Both continue to have ample access to both substances through contacts at work.

In assessing substance use, some psychometric instruments may be valuable in gaining more information. Using the Substance Use History Questionnaire and the Drug Abuse Screening Test (DAST-20) would help in evaluating the degree of substance use. In addition, the questionnaire for families should be given to Sarita, and Karen should be interviewed on an age-appropriate level. This would provide further information regarding the parents' substance use and its impact on the family.

In assessing Juanita's substance use, some significant factors are her

- attempt to stop drinking for health reasons;
- reluctance to give up drugs completely; and
- traumatic childhood history with an alcoholic/abusive mother, sexual abuse by a brother, foster home placement, and cultural assimilation issues.

Juanita's substance use indicates that she is in the crucial to chronic phase of severe substance use evidenced by her denial and minimization of her cocaine use and her five years of periodic attempts at abstinence from alcohol. Juanita's traumatic childhood history needs to be evaluated as to the impact that these factors have in her substance use.

Diagnostically, Juanita would meet the criteria for both Alcohol Use Disorder and Stimulant Use Disorder in the DSM-5. Her history may indicate that other diagnoses such as a personality disorder, depression, and/or posttraumatic stress disorder are likely.

In assessing Jose's substance use, the significant factors are his

- frequent substance use,
- family history, cultural messages, and assimilation issues, and
- increasing conflict with Sarita over his drinking.

Jose's history of alcohol use every day and marijuana use on the weekend, and his behavioral changes when drinking, are indicative of the crucial phase of substance use. It is clear that when Jose drinks, he loses control and acts inappropriately toward Sarita. In addition, Jose's longest period of abstinence was nine days, and after that, he drank to the point of intoxication. This pattern indicates a tolerance for alcohol, as well as minimization and denial.

Diagnostically, Jose would meet the criteria for Alcohol Use Disorder in the DSM-5. In addition, diagnoses of depression and personality

(*Continued*)

(Continued)

disorder need to be investigated. Additional information about Jose's childhood experiences should be gathered.

In summary, it is clear that Juanita and Jose's substance use is a major factor to be considered in treatment of this family. Sarita's increasing and escalating behavioral problems may be indicative of her response to her parent's drinking and drug use. Sarita may also be at risk for using substances. The patterns of both children should be evaluated using information about typical coping styles or roles adopted by children in response to substance use problems in the parents.

Case 3: Leigh

Leigh's substance use needs to be evaluated in the context of her developmental stage. Coupled with her reported substance use, other factors such as problems at school, shoplifting, parental conflict, parental divorce, and relocation to a new area are issues that need to be examined.

During the diagnostic interview, the adolescent version of the Substance Abuse Subtle Screening Inventory (SASSI-A2), the Adolescent Diagnostic Interview (ADI), and the Alcohol Use Disorders Identification Test (AUDIT) can be administered, along with other instruments to determine a general level of functioning. More information from parent interviews and school assessment needs to be gathered.

In assessing Leigh's substance use, the significant factors include

- her development stage (adolescence),
- loss of parental support,
- increased conflict with her mother, and
- ambivalent feelings toward the conflict between her mother and father.

Leigh's acting-out behavior may be indicative of substance use, or the substance use may be an "outlet" for her problems. This possibility needs to be evaluated before treatment interventions can be implemented. It is clear that Leigh's behavior at school and in the community must be addressed. Her appearance of being "overly thin" must be investigated so that a possible eating disorder can be assessed. Referral to a physician for a thorough physical would be indicated. In order to diagnose a substance use disorder with Leigh, more information needs to be gathered. Family members should be interviewed to assist in obtaining this information. Family conflict and Leigh's feelings of isolation must be addressed. Parent–child conflict, adjustment disorder, and eating disorder are potential dual diagnoses.

In summary, Leigh may be experiencing some prodromal-phase symptoms related to her substance use. It will be important, however, to more carefully evaluate her previous functioning to determine whether her substance use is a temporary, reactive response to conflict and changes in the family.

Conclusion

The use of substances such as alcohol and medications often serves a positive purpose when used in moderation and for therapeutic purposes. Unfortunately, sometimes people overuse a substance for a host of possible reasons with harmful consequences to their bodies, relationships, and performance of societal roles such as work and family. When substance use undermines one's health, the quality of one's relationships, and one's ability to fulfill social responsibilities, often the person needs help to recognize the effects of use in his or her life. Assessment refers to the professional's working with the individual to identify the negative consequences of substance misuse. A range of assessment instruments are available to help identify risks associated with substance misuse and to provide a direction for intervention. The DSM-5 looks at substance use on a continuum and in its interaction with other parts of the person's life. Co-occurring disorders of substance use with mental illness are common and require the clinician to

pay attention to their interactive effects. Accurate assessment provides the individual with information about the risks associated with misuse of a substance and can result in greater awareness of resources available within oneself, one's network of relationships, and the community to overcome harmful substance use.

MyCounselingLab for Addictions/Substance Use

Try the Topic 4 Assignments: *Assessment and Diagnosis.*

Case Study: Tania

Tania is a 19-year-old single woman, sent for assessment and diagnosis of a possible substance-related disorder by her college counseling center. She was arrested by campus police for resisting arrest approximately one month prior to the time of the assessment. Tania reported that she and three friends were celebrating the end of the college semester by partying for three straight days. Tania used cocaine continuously; she did not sleep through the entire binge. On the third day of use, Tania began to experience thoughts that she was a vampire, that others identified her as such, and that they meant to do her harm. She was running through the campus when spotted by the police. In an attempt to escape, she ran into the college bookstore, frightened some of the customers, and the police apprehended her. She resisted arrest and the police report indicated that Tania was speaking incoherently and was clearly "out of touch with reality."

In the interview, Tania reported a history of cocaine use starting at 16 years of age. She uses cocaine by snorting, usually only on the weekends. The incident leading to the arrest was the only time she used in a binge manner. Tania began using alcohol at age 14, getting intoxicated nearly every weekend. She does not use alcohol much except to help her

sleep after using cocaine. Tania smokes one to two packs of cigarettes per day. She is in college with a B to C average but feels she could do better if she tried. She reported no previous psychiatric treatment and no prior symptoms like those experienced on the day of the arrest. There was no reported history of a family substance use problem or of psychiatric treatment.

Tania did not present with any bizarre or unusual behavior and was completely free of psychotic or other psychiatric symptoms since a day or so after the arrest. She does not feel that she has a severe substance use problem but does appear distressed by the arrest and subsequent problems related to her education (her college was notified about the arrest because it occurred on campus, and she was placed on probation). Her family was notified about the arrest.

Critical Thinking Questions

1. Identify the primary problem areas and issues that need to be assessed and which assessment tools/methods might you use to get more information.
2. Do you believe that there might be a dual diagnosis? What mental health diagnosis is possible with Tania?
3. Would you consider a diagnosis of a substance use disorder? Why? To which substances?

Substance Use History Questionnaire

1. What substances do you currently use? (Check all that apply.)

_____ alcohol   _____ amphetamines (uppers)

_____ cocaine   _____ barbiturates (downers)

_____ marijuana   _____ nicotine (cigarettes)

_____ narcotics (heroin, methadone)

_____ prescription medication (specify)_____

_____ "bath salts," "incense," or other over-the-counter substance (specify)

_____

_____ other (specify) _____

2. What are your present substance use habits?

_____ daily use   _____ social use (with friends or at parties)

_____ weekend use only   _____ occasional heavy use (to point of intoxication)

_____ occasional light use (not to point of intoxication)

3. How many days ago did you last take a drug or drink? _____ days

4. Have you used daily in the past 2 months? _____ yes _____ no

5. Do you find it almost impossible to live without your drugs or alcohol? _____ yes _____ no

6. Are you always able to stop using when you want to? _____ yes _____ no

7. Where do you do most of your drinking or drug use? (Check all that apply.)

_____ home

_____ friends

_____ bars, restaurants, or other public places

_____ parties or social gatherings

_____ other

8. Do you drink or use during your work day? _____ yes _____ no

9. Do most of your friends use like you do? _____ yes _____ no

10. With whom do you use or drink or use drugs? (Check all that apply.)

_____ alone _____ neighbors

_____ family _____ coworkers

_____ friends _____ strangers

11. Do you consider yourself to be a

_____ non-user _____ recreational/occasional user

_____ moderate user _____ heavy user

_____ nonuser

12. Do friends or family think you use more than other people? _____ yes _____ no

13. Have any family or friends complained to you about your drug or alcohol use? _____ yes _____ no

14. Do you feel you use more or less than other people who use? _____ yes _____ no

15. Were your drug use or drinking habits ever different from what they are now? _____ yes _____ no

If yes, please explain what changed:

16. Has your drinking or drug use ever caused you to (check all that apply):

_____ lose a job or have job problems

_____ have legal problems (DUI, arrest for possession)

_____ have medical problems related to your use

_____ have family problems or relationship problems

_____ be aggressive or violent

17. Have you ever neglected your obligations, family, or work for 2 or more days in a row because you were drinking or using drugs? _____ yes _____ no

18. Because of your alcohol or drug use, have you felt (check all that apply):

	Often	Sometimes	Seldom	Never
Tense or nervous	_____	_____	_____	_____
Suspicious or jealous	_____	_____	_____	_____
Worried	_____	_____	_____	_____
Lonely	_____	_____	_____	_____
Angry or violent	_____	_____	_____	_____
Depressed	_____	_____	_____	_____
Suicidal	_____	_____	_____	_____

19. Do you ever feel bad about things you have done while using? _____ yes _____ no

If yes, please specify:

20. People use alcohol and/or drugs for different reasons. How important would you say that each of the following is to you?

	Very	Somewhat	Not at all
It helps me relax.	_____	_____	_____
It helps me be more sociable.	_____	_____	_____

(*Continued*)

I like the effect. _____ _____ _____

People I know use drugs or drink. _____ _____ _____

I use when I get upset or angry. _____ _____ _____

I want to forget or escape. _____ _____ _____

It helps cheer me up. _____ _____ _____

It makes me less tense or nervous. _____ _____ _____

It makes me less sad or depressed. _____ _____ _____

It helps me function better. _____ _____ _____

I use to celebrate special occasions. _____ _____ _____

Are there other reasons you use drugs or alcohol? Please specify:

21. Have you tried to stop using drugs or alcohol in the last 2 months? _____ yes _____ no

    If yes, did you experience any medical or physical problems when you stopped? Please explain:

22. Have you ever gone to anyone for help about your drinking or drug use? _____ yes _____ no

    If yes, please explain:

23. Have you ever attended a meeting of Alcoholics Anonymous (AA), or any other self-help group because of your drug or alcohol use? _____ yes _____ no

24. Do you feel that you have an addiction to alcohol or drugs? _____ yes _____ no

25. Do you want help with a drug or alcohol problem at this time? _____ yes _____ no

Treatment Planning and Treatment Settings

Leigh Falls Holman, Ph.D., LPC-MHSP-Supervisor, RPTS, NCC, LSC

Methods for developing accurate assessments and diagnoses for substance use behaviors are described in Chapter 5 of this text. The DSM-5 is used to diagnose and identify level of severity (*mild, moderate,* or *severe*) of substance use at the point the client is being evaluated. This essential first step provides a practical foundation for making future decisions regarding development and organization of effective individualized treatment plans and choice of treatment settings for the client.

WHAT IS TREATMENT PLANNING?

Treatment plans are written documents that detail how problems are defined and treatments are formulated. Plans provide a map for how treatment should progress. Treatment plans should be designed to benefit all participants in treatment, from the client to the treatment providers and the administration. Treatment planning serves to:

- Focus the issues for the client
- Assist the multidisciplinary team in their assessments and suggestions
- Provide clarification for insurance reimbursement
- Provide documentation for counselor, client, and accrediting agencies

It can be easy for the counselor and client to lose sight of the issues that initially brought the client into treatment. The treatment plan serves to focus and structure the therapeutic sessions. A treatment plan is considered to be a dynamic document designed to evolve and change, reflecting the client's progress and changing treatment needs. Therefore, these plans should be reviewed on a regular basis and updated to reflect a client's progress or regression in treatment. The documentation of a sound treatment plan provides evidence supporting the client's need for services and ultimately documents necessary elements for reimbursement by third-party payers (grant-funding sources, insurance companies, etc.). Following each session, the counselor will document the client's progress in the medical record as it relates specifically to the treatment plan goals and objectives.

Treatment plans are helpful when multiple service providers (e.g., psychiatrist, social worker, individual counselor, family counselor, and nutritionist) are working as a multidisciplinary treatment team with one client. This document is one method enabling effective and efficient focused treatment that identifies which treatment team member is responsible for each element of the client's treatment plan. Treatment plans may identify targets, identify interventions, suggest resources, clarify provider responsibilities, and provide indicators of progress. The treatment plan and progress notes are crucial methods used by individual treatment team members to communicate with one another about the client's progress so that subsequent interventions are informed by the client's recent progress or regression, which is documented in the client's medical record. This is one reason that documentation of the treatment plan and the client's progress toward treatment goals and objectives need to be written in a timely manner.

How to Develop a Treatment Plan

The foundation of any treatment plan is the data or information gathered in a thorough assessment. Assessment data and diagnosis including co-occurring disorders and level of severity of the substance use disorder inform treatment planning so that it is individualized for each client. The format of treatment plans may be slightly different from one setting or treatment program to the next. The American Society of Addiction Medicine's *ASAM Criteria* (ASAM, 2016) is a standardized guide for developing a treatment plan, including determining appropriate level of care based on the client's assessment. Various editions of *The ASAM Criteria* have been used in programs throughout the United States since 1991; it is now in its third edition (ASAM, 2015). The guiding principles of the ASAM Criteria are summarized here:

- Use a multidimensional approach to assessment and treatment.
- Design treatment for the individual patient need, including choice of goals, objectives, and length of treatment that match the client's current treatment needs.
- Relapsing behavior or unsuccessful completion of a previous treatment program should not be used to determine the client's current needed level of care.
- A continuum of care is used to provide appropriate services for the client's current needs, as informed by the current ASAM definition of addiction.

Following assessment, a counselor needs to consider the client's motivation for change, their goals for treatment, and treatment needs as informed by the counselor's training and experience related to the client's presenting issues. There are six life areas or "dimensions" that are considered in treatment planning (ASAM, 2015).

Dimension 1: Acute Intoxication and/or Withdrawal Potential: Consider the client's substance abuse history and current presentation.

Dimension 2: Biomedical Conditions/Complications: Consider physical and medical issues including nutrition and exercise.

Dimension 3: Emotional/Behavioral/Cognitive Conditions and Complications: Consider the client's thoughts, emotions, and mental health issues assessed, including co-occurring disorders.

Dimension 4: Readiness to Change: Consider the client's level of motivation for engaging in treatment in a meaningful way.

Dimension 5: Relapse/Continued Use/Continued Problem Potential: Consider risks related to co-occurring mental health issues, relapse history and current environmental triggers, and current severity of the substance use disorder.

Dimension 6: Recovery Environment: Consider where the client is living and working and the people that are in his/her life with regard to risks to relapse or potential supports for recovery.

The intensity of services the client needs is determined based on the assessment of these six dimensions.

According to Magellan Health Services (2016), treatment plans should be specifically (S) individualized to the client's diagnosis and current functioning, measurable (M), achievable (A), relevant (R) to diagnosis or presenting issue, and time limited (T). The acronym SMART is used for this model. Each goal should have objectives, which are specific tasks that are small steps that need to be completed to achieve the goal. The following provides more description of SMART goals and objectives:

- *Specific:* Targeted behaviors need to be observable so the client, different providers involved in treatment, or even third-party payers can easily assess the client's progress. If the target is too conceptual (e.g., self-esteem), different people may perceive it to mean something different. So concepts like self-esteem need to be operationalized with specific observable behaviors (e.g., articulating positive self-statements) so that anyone evaluating the target knows what is being measured. Also, the goal should be specific about who is responsible (e.g., the client will articulate positive self-statements).
- *Measureable:* How will you be able to evaluate progress without some way to measure the behavior? For example, "the client will articulate three positive self-statements in each counseling session" makes the goal measurable because the client and the counselor both know when the goal is met.
- *Attainable/Achievable:* You want to challenge the client to grow without frustrating her. You need to consider what a specific client is capable of at this point in time. Remember that you can modify the goal to increase the expectations as the client achieves success with the current goal. Is the client capable of three positive self-statements within one hour? Does the client demonstrate this now, or would it be a challenge?
- *Relevant:* How is the goal relevant to the presenting issue? You may say that working on self-esteem is irrelevant to addiction treatment, but let's say that the assessment revealed that a trigger for this client's substance use is experiencing low self-esteem in relationships resulting in binge drinking in social situations. Documenting the identifying trigger in the assessment provides support for including it as a treatment goal.
- *Time-Bound:* Ultimately when do you know that the client has met the goal so that it can either be modified or removed from the treatment plan? Does the client need to articulate three positive self-statements in one session to achieve the goal? Do you think they should do this more consistently in order to improve the likelihood that they have incorporated this new behavior? For example, "the client will articulate three positive self-statements in session each week for four consecutive weeks" might strengthen the goal.

To continue with the same example, you now have a goal that "the client will articulate three positive self-statements in session each week for four consecutive weeks." Now what are the objectives to reach this goal? Remember, objectives are tasks to be accomplished that lead to the goal being met. You will want to identify two to four objectives. For instance: (a) the client will acknowledge in session when s/he articulates negative self-statements; (b) the client will consistently complete a thought journal documenting when s/he has negative self-statements (as thoughts or verbalizations), what was occurring when it happens, and feelings and behaviors associated with the thoughts; and (c) the client will begin substituting positive self-statements for negative self-statements when s/he becomes aware of them and document or verbalize (if in session) how this impacts his or her feelings and behaviors. These are examples of objectives that you might use for this particular goal.

These objectives clearly reflect a cognitive–behavioral theory orientation. In other words, your theoretical perspective or evidence-based practice may also be a consideration in determining objectives. Notice that each objective identifies who is responsible for the task. What if one of the objectives was that the counselor will teach the client how to use a thought journal? That would be another reasonable objective, but the counselor, rather than the client, would be responsible for completing the task. Therefore, treatment objectives may identify the client, the counselor, the doctor, or some other member of the treatment team as responsible for the task.

Treatment plans should be devised in collaboration with the treatment team and the client so that everyone knows what needs to occur during treatment. Each team member who facilitates the client's progress in treatment needs to document the intervention and the client's response in a progress note. Progress notes should reflect the date of the intervention (e.g., 2/16/16), the length of time (e.g., 45 minutes), the modality (e.g., Individual Therapy, IT), and documentation related to the client's progress (or lack thereof) toward treatment objectives or goals. There are several standard formats for writing progress notes. Most treatment programs will dictate which format you need to use. The following are examples of standard progress note formats:

- *SOAP:* **Subjective** (the client's subjective perception using quotations or summarizing the themes of the session), **Objective** (the counselor's objective observation of affect, mood, behavior, etc.), **Assessment** (the general content and process of the session, the counselor's working hypotheses or conceptualization of the problem, results of formal assessments), **Plan** (goals and objectives addressed in the session, what the counselor will do next, next session date, and any treatment plan revisions needed).
- *BIRP:* **Behavior** (the client's subjective perception; the counselor's objective observation of affect, mood, behavior, etc.), **Intervention** (the general content and process of the session, the counselor's working hypotheses or conceptualization of the problem, results of formal assessments), **Response** (the client's response to the treatment plan currently and any treatment plan revisions needed), **Plan** (goals and objectives addressed in the session, what the counselor will do next, and the next session date).
- *DAP:* **Data** (the client's subjective perception; the counselor's objective observation of affect, mood, behavior, etc.; the general content and process of the session), **Assessment** (the counselor's working hypotheses or conceptualization of the problem, results of formal assessments, and the client's response to the treatment plan currently), **Plan** (goals and objectives addressed in the session, what the counselor will do next, next session date, and any treatment plan revisions needed).
- In the documentation you should identify whether the client has progressed or not by using the client's words or your observations of the client's behavior as supportive evidence for their level of progress. If a treatment goal has been met, then it should be reviewed to determine if the goal should change to be more challenging (e.g., the client will articulate six positive self-statements in session each week for four consecutive weeks) or if it should be removed from the treatment plan. The progress notes are used to document the client's need for services and the need for the current level of care. (Level of care is discussed further in the later section on treatment settings.)

There are several things to consider when writing a progress note, regardless of the format. The most important is to make sure the note reflects a connection with the client's individualized treatment plan goals and objectives. Make certain to identify both strengths and challenges the client possesses related to treatment progress. Any changes in the client's level of functioning or the level of severity of the substance use disorder needs to be documented with evidence of the client's words or the counselor's description of observable behaviors. Would someone unfamiliar with the case, such as an auditor, be able to read the note and understand what has occurred in treatment? Some other important documentation items to tend to may seem picky, but they are crucial to writing a note, such as using only approved abbreviations in the chart, having the client's name and identifier on each page, documenting risk assessment and referral information, signing the note with your credentials (and having your supervisor sign if necessary), and finally noting any non-routine calls, missed sessions, or professional consultations.

Finally, it is important to consider the fact that someone other than the treatment staff may have access to the notes at some point. For instance, clients, attorneys, and auditors with accreditation agencies might read notes. Therefore it is important to write notes in a neutral tone so that they do not sound pejorative. An example would be commenting on a client's "poor insight" or "poor judgment." These are value statements that the client or his attorney could consider biased. It is important to use evidence to support these types of statements. For instance: "The client acknowledges driving while intoxicated with his children in the car with him on numerous occasions. He stated, 'I only drank a sixpack after work on the days I picked them up from school.'" This type of evidence supports the conclusion that the client demonstrates poor judgment because he is driving while intoxicated, made more concerning by the fact that his children were in the car. It also supports the conclusion that the client demonstrates poor insight because he indicates by saying he "only drank a sixpack" on the days he picks his kids up that he believes this is not a problem. You might state that the client demonstrates poor insight as evidenced by … (fill in the example), or you might just state the client's acknowledgment and quote it as written above, which basically makes the same point without sounding biased because of pejorative language.

Notes that do not directly relate to the client's assessment of functioning or treatment plan should be kept as process notes. Only the counselor has access to process notes, which she uses as memory aids to facilitate treatment. These process notes are not "discoverable," so they cannot be subpoenaed. They must be kept in a secure location, such as a locked file cabinet or password-protected computer file. They cannot be placed in the medical chart at any time. If they are placed in the medical chart, then other people have access to them, and they become part of the client's medical record and consequently discoverable.

When an individual has reached his/her goals in a treatment setting and a less restrictive setting becomes more appropriate, discharge occurs. Discharge/recovery planning, particularly in inpatient or residential settings, is a crucial component of substance use counseling because it will serve as a road map for the client's ongoing recovery, particularly during transitions from inpatient or residential to outpatient settings. Most discharge planning emphasizes abstinence, investigating self-help and peer support groups, and management of coping skills for relapse prevention. However, discharge or transfer to a different level of treatment may occur if a client is unable to resolve the presenting problem at his or her current level of care or the problem has increased in intensity. When this occurs, a different level of care may be indicated as more helpful to the client's resolution of the problem. Levels of care coincide with treatment settings, discussed next.

WHAT IS A TREATMENT SETTING?

A treatment setting is the environment where treatment happens. Treatment settings vary based on the level of restriction placed on the clients who are receiving treatment. Restriction refers to the degree of physical and social structure and/or freedom provided by the professional staff. As previously mentioned, the client's use is assigned a severity level based on the DSM-5 diagnostic criteria. A more highly restrictive environment indicates that the client needs more external supports to be successful in treatment (severe), whereas a less restrictive environment would reflect a client's ability to internally manage potential relapse triggers with less external support (mild). Selection of a treatment setting should fit the diagnosis, meeting the needs of the client and the presenting problems. This rationale suggests that clients need settings that match their diagnosis and severity level for treatment to be effective.

A DSM-5 descriptor of severe would indicate the need for a highly restrictive environment such as an inpatient hospital setting where the client would live and receive treatment for a defined period of time. For those clients with a moderate descriptor, a partial hospitalization program (PHP) or an intensive outpatient program (IOP) environment may provide additional external supports while allowing the clients to have more freedom in where they live and whether they participate in certain treatment opportunities. For clients who are able to manage their substance use issues with minimal external supports, those with a mild descriptor, weekly outpatient treatment, the least restrictive environment, would be most appropriate.

The goal is to provide treatment in the least restrictive setting that will support a successful treatment outcome based on each client's needs at a particular point in recovery. Additionally, the heterogeneity of clients demands consideration of other client factors such as resources available to the client, necessity of medical or psychiatric monitoring, specialization and characteristics of available facilities, clients' capacity and willingness to cooperate with treatment, clients' social and financial support, and insurance coverage (Galanter, Kleber, & Brady, 2014).

Effective treatment planning requires appropriate considerations of client transitions between levels of care (Mee-Lee & Shulman, 2011; Mee-Lee, 2016). Clients can move between settings depending on their progress (or regression/relapse) in treatment and the resulting recommendations of treatment staff. This approach ensures respect for the client's autonomy. It embraces the client's self-determination skills, which are essential in initiating and maintaining recovery. This treatment system is referred to as a "continuum of care," in which treatment levels appropriately match the needs of clients.

The American Society of Addiction Medicine (ASAM, 2015) conceptualizes the levels of care along a continuum. The ASAM model has five levels of care with decimal numbers used to indicate gradations of intensity (ASAM, 2015, 2016). Early Intervention (level .5) is used for assessment and psychoeducation for people who exhibit risk for substance use disorders (SUDs) but do not meet the diagnostic criteria for a SUD. Outpatient services (level 1) are recommended for people who may have mild withdrawal symptoms and are likely to complete detox and continue treatment or recovery with little supervision. Less than nine hours of services per week for an adult or less than six for an adolescent are expected at this level, with the treatment provider using motivational interviewing methods to engage the client in treatment.

Level 2 includes intensive outpatient and partial hospitalization services. Intensive outpatient (2.1) services are recommended if the client needs nine or more hours of service per week for adults or six or more hours per week for adolescents. This occurs when clients are not stable enough in their recovery to follow through with outpatient services, unless they are more closely monitored, but they do not need hospitalization. Partial hospitalization services (2.5) are indicated for clients who are minimally stable in their recovery, such that they do not need clinically managed 24-hour care, but they do need more intensive supervision than intensive outpatient services. Partial hospitalization is 20 or more hours of services per week.

Level 3 includes clinically managed low-intensity residential services (3.1), clinically managed population-specific medium-intensity residential services (3.3), clinically managed high-intensity residential services (3.5), and medically monitored intensive inpatient services (3.7). Clinically managed low-intensity residential services have 24-hour structured care with trained personnel and at least five hours of clinical services per week. Clinically managed population-specific (e.g., low cognitive functioning) medium-intensity residential services include 24-hour care with trained counselors focused on stabilizing behaviors creating imminent danger related to more than one of the life dimensions discussed previously. In these situations, services use an inpatient therapeutic milieu and group treatment for those individuals with cognitive impairment that makes full participation in the therapeutic community impossible.

Level 3.5, clinically managed high-intensity residential treatment, provides 24-hour care with trained counselors similar to medium-intensity settings, but these individuals are able to fully participate in the therapeutic community. Clinically monitored intensive inpatient settings provide 24-hour nursing care with a physician available for significant problems in the first three dimensions, such as physical withdrawal symptoms, and counseling available for 16 hours each day. Often these programs are located in private psychiatric hospitals.

Medically managed intensive inpatient services (level 4) provide 24-hour nursing care and daily physician care for severe and unstable clients. Instability is generally due to acute intoxication or withdrawal potential; biomedical conditions and complications; and/or emotional, behavioral, or cognitive complications. Medical management of withdrawal is the primary focus of treatment, with counseling available to engage the patient in the initial stages of treatment. These services often occur in a medical facility where psychiatric treatment is an adjunct rather than the focus.

Client progress or regression in treatment should be consistently monitored to determine if the current level of care is the most appropriate based on the client's current needs (ASAM, 2015). Services should continue in the current setting if the client is progressing toward treatment goals and it is reasonable to expect they will be successful at their current level of treatment. However, when clients are not able to achieve their goals in the current setting, or they have developed new goals that indicate a different level of treatment intensity is needed, then they may be transferred to a different setting that will better meet their needs. When clients complete their treatment goals and no other services are needed, they are ready to be discharged from treatment.

The efficacy of the treatment setting is necessarily impacted by client autonomy and motivation. Clients may voluntarily decide to enter treatment, or they may be involuntary participants in treatment. This means that within any one setting, some participants may be court ordered or mandated, while others enter treatment without legal requirements. Generally, the treatment setting does not consistently reflect the client's voluntary or involuntary status. An exception would be prison-based substance use treatment and DUI diversion programs where either all have been court ordered to treatment or they will earn a reduced sentence or have adjudication for their DUI removed from the legal record if they successfully complete treatment. Treatment for substance use disorders is dominated by court referrals, rather than self-referral, which is different from other health care areas. According to the Substance Abuse and Mental Health Services Administration (SAMHSA), 33.9% of all substance use treatment admissions in 2012 were criminal justice referred. Of these 72.1% were alcohol related, 34.9% related to opiates, 51.6% related to marijuana, 62.9% related to cocaine, and 47.2% to methamphetamine (SAMHSA, 2016). Many substance use treatment professionals argue that most "voluntary" clients entering treatment have an involuntary element to their decision to enter treatment. These "voluntary" clients can often feel pressured by co-workers, family members, and/or physicians. Fisher and Roget (2009) report that coerced treatment, although popular and successful for some, may have little benefit, adding that self-motivation is essential for long-term success. Clients' treatment success or failure involves quality and effectiveness of the treatment program, their relational supports, and their commitment to treatment goals. Given that most clients are mandated to treatment, whether by the court, a boss, or a family member, their level of motivation for treatment and their readiness for change is generally an important issue that needs to be accounted for in all aspects of treatment planning and intervention.

TYPES OF TREATMENT SETTINGS

Several different types of treatment settings may be available. However, the types of settings may vary from one part of the country to another because of a variety of factors such as the amount of resources a community has and what is dictated by the entity paying for the treatment. Following is a description of some of the more common treatment settings.

Medical Detoxification and Stabilization

When clients with substance use disorders stop using, it can be dangerous, resulting in medical complications and even death. Therefore, these clients may need to go through medically supervised detoxification and be medically cleared (approved for a less restrictive environment by a medical doctor) before being placed in a setting that focuses primarily on therapeutic interventions for their substance use disorders. Research published by the U.S. Department of Health and Human Services, Substance Abuse and Mental Health Services Administration Center for Substance Abuse Treatment (SAMHSA, 2016) describes a medical model and social model of detoxification in the *Detoxification and Substance Abuse Treatment Training Manual*. The medical model uses medical staff, including doctors and nurses, who administer medication to safely assist people through withdrawal. The social model, on the other hand, rejects the use of medication and relies on a supportive, non-hospital setting to help the client through withdrawal. Admittedly, there is no "pure" model for detoxification treatment, as both models use concepts from the other in their respective programs with success.

Medical models establish medical necessity before admission and refer to the risk of medical problems (e.g., seizures) or psychiatric difficulties (e.g., suicidal ideation) the client exhibits. In substance use detox facilities, doctors use medication to lessen the often uncomfortable and sometimes brutal side effects of drug withdrawal, while preparing the client for counseling (Grohsman, 2009). This process includes gradual tapering of the drug(s) over a period of several days or weeks. For example, heroin can be weaned from an individual and substituted with a longer-acting opioid such as methadone. Other medications may be administered to lessen physical and psychological symptoms associated with withdrawal.

There are three approaches to using medications to assist treatment for substance use disorders, including the following:

- Aversion therapy, where a client is given a drug that produces a negative physical reaction if the client also uses the target substance. An example would be Antabuse that, if coupled with alcohol use, can result in headaches, fatigue, nausea, or even severe vomiting.
- Craving reduction therapy, which helps clients control urges to use a substance. Topamax, for example, reduces dopamine levels, which results in less pleasure gained from using a substance such as alcohol. Baclofen increases GABA thereby creating a relaxing effect, thus aiding craving reduction. And naltrexone, an opioid antagonist, blocks the brain's ability to feel pleasure from using. Zofran and neurontin are two more medications that are used to help reduce cravings.
- Replacement therapy, which provides legal substances as substitutes for more harmful substances, such as giving methadone or suboxone to heroin users.

Although medications may be used during detoxification, they may also be used at other points in treatment to improve the client's successful treatment outcomes.

The length of stay in a unit like this is usually less than two weeks. Detoxification should be considered only the beginning of treatment. Although medical detoxification is an effective method of intervention during the initial phase of treatment, it is rarely sufficient to help clients achieve long-term sobriety by itself (Grohsman, 2009). It is important to establish a treatment plan that will outline the client's goals and necessary interventions to reach those goals well past the point of detoxification. Ideally, treatment planning, including discharge plans and long-term goals, should be developed upon client admission to the detox unit (Baron, Erlenbusch, Moran, O'Conner, Rice, & Rodriguez, 2008). The discharge plan should continue to be updated during the course of the client's treatment.

According to the ASAM Criteria (ASAM, 2016), detoxification settings provide:

- screening for presence of withdrawal symptoms and/or psychiatric conditions
- on-site medical and psychiatric care that promotes safe and complete withdrawal
- staff who structure and nurture the environment
- staff who protect clients from self-harm or harm to others
- staff who educate and counsel clients about substance abuse and dependency

Dual-Diagnosis Inpatient Hospitalization

Usually located in psychiatric hospitals, dual-diagnosis programs are designed to treat clients with the presence of both serious psychiatric illness (e.g., posttraumatic stress disorder [PTSD], bipolar disorder, or schizophrenia) and an SUD and/or behavioral addictive disorder (e.g., gambling disorder). Individuals may reside in these hospital units from several days to several weeks. Programs are designed for either adult or youth treatment.

Often people struggling with substance use disorders use the substance to manage symptoms of a co-occurring mental illness. For example, a war veteran who has PTSD symptoms of hypervigilance, exaggerated startle response, and nightmares may use alcohol or barbiturates to dull these symptoms so that he can sleep (Allen, Crawford, & Kudler, 2016; U.S. Department of Veterans Affairs, 2016). Alternatively, severe substance use may result in alterations in neurochemistry such that clients may develop mental health issues as a result of their SUD. For instance, a client who has used alcohol for 15 years may demonstrate symptoms of depression that could be resulting from his chronic alcohol use because alcohol is a depressant.

Another type of co-occurring mental illness may involve cross-addictions, where someone who is diagnosed with a substance use disorder is found to have gambling disorder and bulimia co-occurring, both considered behavioral addictions (Jazeri & Habil, 2012). Severe and persistent mental illness such as bipolar disorder or schizophrenia may also co-occur with a substance use disorder (Lieb, 2015). Treatment for these can be quite complicated, given the delicate and unique neurotransmitter balance that needs to occur to treat these mental illnesses. Stabilizing the equilibrium of these neurotransmitters can be made significantly more difficult by the use of substances that alter certain neurotransmitters such as dopamine, which is etiologically indicated in both bipolar disorder and schizophrenia. Services are provided to diagnose and treat substance use disorders as well as symptoms attributable to psychiatric illness. Each condition must be assessed independently and in relation to the other presenting conditions or symptoms. This is done to withdraw the affected client safely from substances, stabilize the client emotionally and physically, and identify and treat the concomitant disorders. Some treatment programs treat the co-occurring disorders concurrently, and others attempt to treat them consecutively (Dom & Moggi, 2015). Generally, in SUD treatment settings conducting consecutive treatment, the substance use disorder is treated as primary, and once it is controlled, treatment for the co-occurring mental illness becomes the focus. However, some approaches treat the underlying mental illness as primary, in the belief that if that is resolved, the substance use will no longer be necessary for the client to manage the symptoms of mental illness. More contemporary approaches involve concurrent treatment of the addictive behavior(s) and the co-occurring mental illness (Dom & Moggi, 2015). This perspective asserts that the dual disorders are intertwined and cannot be neatly separated and treated one at a time. The belief is that the underlying mental illness may trigger relapse behaviors and that the SUD may result in a worsening of the underlying mental illness, in cyclical fashion.

Dual diagnosis programs rely on an interdisciplinary treatment team of psychiatric and psychotherapy staff working together to manage the unique needs of these clients. It is crucial that the treatment staff in these programs have training and supervised experience working not only with substance use disorders but also with other mental illnesses. Specialized training in dual diagnosis requires staff and counselors to understand how concomitant disorders can interact and manifest in the clients' lives.

Dual-diagnosis hospital inpatient settings provide:

- on-site medical and psychiatric care that includes 24-hour nursing and milieu supervision and locked units with limited access to family and friends
- personnel with specialized knowledge in dual diagnosis
- 7-, 14-, or 28-day stays in a protective, restricted environment
- psychiatric and substance use crisis stabilization
- more intensive assessment and diagnostic services
- daily intensive group contact with other clients and staff

REHABILITATION PROGRAMS Rehabilitation programs are usually freestanding facilities that are not hospitals. For most rehabilitation programs, psychiatric evaluations are conducted off site, but some may have their own staff psychiatrists. This obviously depends on the site, personnel, and available resources. Doweiko (2015) maintains that the well-recognized Minnesota Model of SUD treatment has been the dominant model for rehabilitation programs in the United States since its inception.

According to Owen (2000, 2016), the Minnesota Model's primary goal is for the person with a substance use disorder to remain abstinent from mood-altering chemicals for life. Secondarily, there is a long-term goal for personality change, including the client's changing his/her thinking, feelings, and actions. The approach relies heavily on the 12-step model. Proponents of this model view a substance use disorder solely as a primary, chronic, and progressive disease that cannot be attributed to intra-psychic, interpersonal, or sociocultural or economic circumstances. The typical length of treatment is 28 days for inpatient treatment and 5 to 6 weeks of intensive outpatient therapy (3 to 4 nights a week, 3 to 4 hours per session) followed by 10 or more weeks of weekly aftercare sessions. Most of the therapy under this model occurs in a group setting, with individual therapy used to address issues that are deemed too sensitive or complex to address in a group setting (Owen, 2016).

Moore, Rothwell, and Segrott (2010) describe the 12 steps as so important to the ongoing recovery that behavioral health professionals developed a series of parallel therapeutic approaches that maintained consistency with the steps themselves. This consistency helps clients transition from treatment to external social support (AA, NA, CA, etc.) relatively easily. Involvement in self-help groups like these is considered critical for long-term abstinence (Owen, 2016). The Hazelden program (Owen, 2016) describes the ideal counselor as being a recovering addict who understands and practices the 12-step philosophy. However, Dr. Lance Dodes (2014) of Harvard University analyzes the scientific evidence supporting the 12-step model in his book *The Sober Truth* and concludes that programs built on this model do not offer a universal solution for culturally competent treatment of SUD and/or behavioral addictions. His analysis reveals methodological flaws in the studies that undermine their reliability as evidence-based practice.

Under the Minnesota Model, counselors assume the role of educator and coach; therefore many counselors may have only an associate's degree with little or no education in psychological or neurobiological issues related to co-occurring disorders, which is another criticism of this model of treatment. Ideal personal characteristics of a counselor include "being tolerant and nonjudgmental of client diversity; collaborative when working with clients and able to elicit and use input from other professionals; flexible in accepting job responsibilities; having good verbal and written communication skills; having personal integrity; and conveying compassion to clients" (Owen, 2016, paragraph 4.4).

One strength of the model discussed by Doweiko (2015) is that it takes a multidisciplinary approach. Staff members from diverse disciplines, such as psychiatry, psychology, social work, and counseling, work together to direct the treatment planning process and its implementation. This includes enforcement and maintenance of facility rules; providing treatment recommendations and evaluations of client progress; and educating clients about substance use disorders. The multidisciplinary treatment approach helped make the Minnesota Model a dominant treatment program model for over 40 years, and it is an element that has been used in other treatment programs.

Residential programs are intermediate-care facilities that allow individuals to live within a residential setting, be employed during the day, and receive comprehensive treatment, including individual, group, and family therapy as well as education and relapse prevention services. Average stays can range from four months up to a year. Residential programs, like rehabilitation programs, are designed for either adult or youth populations.

Residential programs are often used as a bridge between the more restrictive dual-diagnosis inpatient and rehabilitation programs and the less restrictive outpatient programs. Many use a level system similar to the Minnesota Model. Residential treatment programs are designed for long-term treatment stays. Sometimes residential programs are used as an alternative to outpatient programs with lower-income clients because of clients' lack of housing resources.

These programs tend to be expensive to maintain, so insurance companies often do not pay for them. However, there are residential treatment centers for teens that juvenile court or Medicaid will pay for, particularly if the client is involved with the juvenile justice system or foster care system. Additionally, much of the "residential" treatment for substance use disorders that occurs in the United States actually occurs within specialized treatment units in prison settings.

Partial Hospitalization Programs

Partial hospitalization programs (PHP), occasionally referred to as day treatment, offer comprehensive substance use treatment in a semi-restrictive program where clients live at home and attend treatment during the day. According to the Commission on Accreditation of Rehabilitation Facilities (CARF, 2016), PHP programs are "time limited, medically supervised programs that offer comprehensive, therapeutically intensive, coordinated, and structured clinical services" (p. 15). These settings are for clients who need a level of restrictiveness between hospital inpatient/rehabilitation/residential and intensive outpatient. They do not need 24-hour care, but they generally need intensive treatment beyond traditional outpatient counseling. PHPs may be freestanding facilities or part of a larger continuum of care. Services can range from 3 to 12 hours per day for 3 to 7 days a week. PHPs may offer services during half-day, weekend, or evening hours. This environment is an intensive and highly structured treatment program. The services generally are a time-limited solution to stabilize acute symptoms or to transition level of care (step-down) from inpatient or residential treatment into outpatient treatment. They generally last only between one and six weeks based on the client's needs. Similar to other more restrictive treatment settings,

PHPs require the client to be medically cleared by completing a detox program. Only clients without medical or psychiatric complications that require inpatient care are admitted.

The goal of a PHP is to help clients successfully transition to an even less restrictive environment. Linking clients with outpatient counseling, supportive housing, and other services may be part of the PHP treatment plan. Ideally, family is involved during this time, unless clinically contraindicated. Clients are encouraged to access appropriate social, family, and vocational or educational activities that will support their recovery post-discharge. Continued support and weekly counseling are generally recommended when stepping down from PHP to outpatient services. This may include individual, group, and/or family counseling. This type of treatment may be effective for many people because it combines the best parts of inpatient treatment (intensive care and strict goals) and outpatient treatment (the ability to continue working, being with family, a flexible schedule, and lower cost).

Partial hospitalization offers:

- a cost-effective level of care between full hospitalization/rehabilitation and intensive outpatient
- a professionally staffed structured environment providing treatment services

Temporary Recovery or Halfway Homes

A recovery/halfway house is usually a community-based home or a building near a rehabilitation or residential facility. Resident clients rely on the safe and supportive group social structure of a transitional living arrangement with less monitoring than a more restrictive environment. Requirements for residence in these homes typically are abstinence, employment, attendance of 12-step recovery meetings, and possible random urine testing to evaluate recovery progress and to maintain a safe, sober house. Staff members are usually considered "paraprofessional," and most often are in recovery themselves. Stays can vary ranging from several weeks to several months.

Recovery or halfway homes provide:

- a minimum structured transitional living in a recovering environment
- an opportunity to save money to live independently
- help in maintaining a connection with a recovering community while dealing with day-to-day trials

Intensive Outpatient Programs

Intensive outpatient programs (IOPs) consist of substance-free treatment that can range from daily all-day activities to once-a-week meetings. In traditional comprehensive "intensive outpatient" programs, clients are initially enrolled to attend three evenings of three hours of group therapy with one hour of family therapy per week. In addition, clients are expected to attend a certain number of AA/NA 12-step meetings.

Group therapy meetings can range in theme from managing stress to handling dysfunctional family patterns. Random urine testing is usually an integral part of these programs. Continued participation is based on abstinence as evidenced by self-report, family report, and/or urine testing. Completion is usually determined by documented behaviors such as length of abstinence, attendance in groups, and keeping scheduled counseling appointments. Intensive outpatient programs are typically 90- to 120-day commitments.

Weekly or biweekly outpatient settings are often for those clients who have successfully completed the intensive portion of treatment and demonstrated sustained abstinence, employment, and a sober/clean lifestyle (e.g., staying away from high-risk substance-using friends).

Intensive outpatient treatment provides:

- comprehensive treatment with off-site living arrangements while establishing or maintaining employment
- graduated treatment services
- possibly longer-term, intensive treatment than hospitals and rehabilitation settings

This setting typically includes group therapy meetings three times per week. Homework is given to extend learning into home and work environments. Clients maintain their place of residence and employment while committing to a program of recovery that includes abstinence. If a client is unable to maintain sobriety and/or is not making sufficient progress, a more restrictive environment such as inpatient rehabilitation might be recommended.

OUTPATIENT DUI/DWAI/DUID PROGRAMS   Driving under the influence (DUI), driving while ability impaired (DWAI), and driving under the influence of drugs (DUID) are some of the titles used by state legislatures to address the problem of driving while intoxicated or drug impaired. States have well-defined penalties and treatments for impaired drivers that vary from state to state.

Beginning in the mid-1970s, large institutions such as the National Institute on Alcohol Abuse and Alcoholism began funding pilot projects known as alcohol-driving countermeasures (ADC) programs. These were most often administratively placed under motor vehicle divisions or highway safety departments. In the late 1970s and early 1980s and with the onset of action groups such as Remove Intoxicated Drivers (RID), Mothers Against Drunk Driving (MADD), and Students Against Drunk Driving (SADD), treatment programs and citizen advocacy groups collaborated to influence the development of more formal mandated programs targeting impaired drivers. Despite the involuntary mandated nature of the clients attending DUI/DWAI/DUID programs, they are considered the least restrictive treatment setting. Typical alcohol/drug education track programs last for 12 weeks with 90-minute group meetings, the basics of which include:

- describing the physiological effects of alcohol and drugs
- describing the possible psychological consequences of use/abuse of drugs
- defining the legal limits of blood alcohol levels
- presenting current theories of substance use disorder
- developing alternatives to impaired driving

SPECIAL ISSUES IMPACTING TREATMENT PLANNING

There are several issues affecting treatment planning for substance use disorders. These include several landmark pieces of legislation including the Mental Health Parity and Addiction Equity Act (MHPAEA; Public Law 110-343, 2008) and the Patient Protection and Affordable Care Act (42 U.S.C. § 18031, 2010). Additionally, external reviewers such as accrediting agencies and insurance companies often impact treatment planning. Here we give a general overview of these issues.

Federal Legislative Changes and Implications for Treatment

The ratification of the Patient Protection and Affordable Care Act (42 U.S.C. § 18031, 2010) brings about major improvements in addressing access to care for mental health and substance use disorders. Since coverage provisions have taken effect, millions of uninsured people have gained health insurance coverage (Kaiser Family Foundation, 2015). Intended to assist with the rising cost of health care and expanding insurance coverage, the ACA builds on the Mental

Health Parity and Addiction Equity Act (MHPAEA; PL 110-343, 2008) and contains several provisions that bring focus onto wellness, prevention, and access to quality care. Among these provisions, some expand access to treatment, including ensuring dependent coverage until age 26, inclusion of preventive services, improving provider networks, excluding annual and life-time limits, and flexibility in expanding Medicaid to childless adults (Beronio, Glied, & Frank, 2014).

Probably the most significant impact of the ACA is the importance of insurance reform measures place on treatment of substance use disorders. Most notable is that treatment for sub-stance use disorders is included as one of 10 essential health benefits for Medicaid enrollees, and most individual and small-group health plans mandate coverage for substance abuse treat-ment. An estimate from a policy strategist group indicates that the MHPAEA and the ACA together will allow over 32 million people to access substance use treatment for the first time (Carnevale Associates Strategic Policy Solutions, 2013). However, the scope of substance use services offered varies by state. An increased need for substance use treatment providers is expected in order to meet the needs of the newly insured who have not had access to treatment in the past.

Integrated substance use care within primary care settings is another trend associated with the ACA. Although the ACA does not require that substance use treatment be integrated into primary care, the act does encourage it. SAMHSA has implemented several programs to increase the numbers of both substance use treatment providers and integrated care networks. Substance use screening and treatment will increasingly occur within primary medical care settings. Coordinated care integrated into existing primary care is thought to improve the provider's abil-ity to identify clients who need substance use treatment earlier through regular screening. Additionally, proponents of this trend believe that client follow-through with continued treat-ment will be improved. However, because integrated care is a new phenomenon, its impact on substance use treatment efficacy is too new to evaluate.

External Reviewers: Health Care Accreditation Organizations and Managed Care

Clinics, hospitals, and freestanding treatment agencies seeking to qualify for third-party reim-bursement must attain and maintain accreditation from entities such as the Joint Commission (JC). The JC's main purpose is to give its stamp of approval to substance abuse treatment pro-grams (SATPs) and facilities that are providing respectful, ethical assessment, care, and educa-tion to clients and their families.

Acceptable care consists of a continuum of services that can provide a range of services extending from pretreatment to treatment to follow-up. To evaluate the adequacy of a program's continuum of care, Joint Commission surveyors (evaluators who site-visit settings to ensure compliance) expect evidence that the program affords access to an integrated system of treat-ment environments, interventions, and care levels.

When evaluating SATP functions, accreditation visitors/surveyors examine the structures and processes that are used in six areas of performance:

1. Do structures and processes improve the SATP system and care provision?
2. Are leaders providing the structure and program administrative activities that are critical to developing, delivering, and evaluating good health care?
3. Are there safe and supportive environments for clients and staff?
4. Is the atmosphere conducive to staff self-development for the purpose of improving care?

5. What is the quality of the processes by which health care providers communicate and document?
6. Are there appropriate and effective surveillance and infection prevention and control?

SATPs that are accredited and those considering accreditation consider accreditation visits very important. They are taken very seriously and can determine the viability of the organization and its ability to provide care to substance abusers. The Joint Commission requires care standards that are divided into five major areas: treatment planning, medication use, nutrition care, rehabilitation care and services, and special treatment services.

The Joint Commission *requires* that SATP clinical staff write treatment plans. Its guidelines for treatment planning are the following:

- Use diagnostic tools such as the DSM-5 to identify complex treatment needs of each client.
- Design a program intervention tailored to meet those needs.
- Develop treatment objectives that are reasonable, attainable, and written in measurable and objective terms.
- Determine patient goals for treatment and involve patients in developing their own treatment plans.

It is important to remember that the Joint Commission is only one of several accrediting bodies, and each has its own set of treatment planning standards. Clinicians should know the accrediting body that guides and monitors their facility and understand all aspects of this increasingly important element of delivering substance abuse treatment.

Insurance companies and managed care companies are insisting that counselors move quickly through assessing the problem, formulating treatment plans, and implementing interventions. Managed care companies function as health care "gatekeepers of services" for the people participating under their particular plans. The "gate" is the point at which insured individuals can begin to access their mental health and/or substance use treatment benefits. It is common today for counselors to interact with managed care professionals such as preauthorization specialists, care reviewers, primary care physicians, and employee assistance professionals. A written treatment plan with complete progress notes can help when accountability for one's services is demanded. If a plan has uniformity, detail, and is written/signed it will gain credibility with lawyers, administrators, regulatory agency workers, and managed care case reviewers. These important nonclinical professionals are very much involved in the treatment of substance use. They rely on the written word for documentation of treatment.

Helpful Hints for the Substance Abuse Counselor and Managed Care:

- Know the various problem domains for substance use.
- Know the behavioral symptoms of substance use disorders.
- Know DSM-5 diagnostic criteria and terminology.
- Know the limits and strengths of your treatment setting.
- Develop strong treatment planning skills.
- Know the language of managed care and know the procedural requirements of each managed care company with which your facility interfaces.
- Use detailed standardized forms when possible.
- Communicate using behavioral language.
- And above all, document all interactions for your own liability and for the sake of your clients.

CASE DISCUSSIONS

Case 1 (Sandy and Pam)

The appropriate treatment setting for Sandy and Pam should be determined by evaluating the assessment and diagnosis information. Setting selection will depend on the answers to such questions as these: What is the severity of chemical dependency or phase of abuse for Sandy and Pam? What psychiatric symptoms or disorders might be present? Does Pam need detoxification? What DSM-5 diagnosis might be appropriate? What descriptor category would be appropriate if diagnosed with a substance use disorder? What previous substance abuse and/or psychiatric treatment have the mother and daughter had? If Pam's substance use is considered *severe,* would she be willing to attend treatment? If not, would involuntary procedures be necessary?

Both clients volunteered for family counseling and do not seem to be a danger to themselves or others. The extent of Pam's alcohol and drug use is uncertain, but if she attempts to stop using substances, she might be at risk medically and psychologically. A detoxification program might be necessary to ensure her safety. Pam's diagnosis and her willingness to attend treatment will help direct the setting. If psychiatric problems also exist for Pam, a dual-diagnosis program may be appropriate.

Treatment planning would identify several important problem areas for each family member such as substance abuse/dependency, enabling, and transgenerational patterns of coping. Modalities might include individual, family, and group counseling. Methods emphasizing solution-oriented approaches might incorporate "the miracle question," scaling questions, and discussions of previous attempts at abstinence. Pam and Sandy might also benefit from 12-step meetings and the development of a sober peer network.

Case 2 (Juanita and Jose)

Jose and Juanita reportedly have a long history of substance abuse (alcohol, cocaine, and marijuana). Such long-standing polysubstance abuse can be difficult to treat. Abstaining from all mind- and mood-altering substances might be overwhelming for such dependent individuals. Intensive, simultaneous inpatient or outpatient treatment would be recommended for both partners.

The logistics for arranging treatment for both partners could be complex. What if their diagnosis suggested that they *both* needed separate, freestanding rehabilitation programs? Would the spouses enter treatment voluntarily? What if one partner was willing and the other was not? Who would care for their daughters Sarita and Karen if both attended rehabilitation programs? Does the family have health insurance that would cover such extensive treatment?

Depending on their diagnoses, this couple may benefit from intensive outpatient programs that would enable them to live at home and attend treatment. Family therapy should be reconsidered in light of both parents possibly being diagnosed with the severe category of a substance use disorder. Should family therapy continue while Jose and Juanita attend their treatment programs? What would be the benefits or concerns of continuing family therapy? Is it effective to continue family therapy while both parents may be abusing substances? How would the children be involved in their parents' substance abuse treatment?

Treatment planning would be very important for such a complex counseling scenario. Coordinating two separate treatments, while maintaining individual confidentiality, requires considerable planning and ongoing assessment and evaluation. The potential for confusion among treatment providers and family members is high when many individual and family services are used at once. Providers would need to decide who gets what kind of information. Written documentation would be critical for providing clear, responsive, and effective substance abuse treatment. Getting everyone "on the same page" while respecting individual differences in treatment progression would be a focus for the treatment providers of this family.

Case 3 (Leigh)

To illustrate the concept of treatment settings, let us extend Case 3 and imagine Leigh, a 16-year-old marijuana and alcohol user who has run into trouble with her substance use. Her problems intensified one evening when she and her friends were taken into custody for questioning by police. Leigh was partying with some new friends in a wooded area close to the high school she attends. Police, responding to a complaint initiated by neighbors in the area, confronted the adolescents and found alcohol and marijuana. Officials were concerned about the underage drinking, illegal use of marijuana, and in particular Leigh's emotional state, which was hostile, disoriented, and apparently intoxicated.

Police contacted Leigh's mother and discussed the possibility of charging Leigh with possession of marijuana and disorderly conduct. After several unsuccessful attempts by police to persuade Leigh to seek immediate medical care, she was evaluated to be at risk to herself and was involuntarily admitted to medical detoxification. She spent several days in detoxification and getting "clear headed," and then she voluntarily agreed to attend a rehabilitation program. When she had 28 days of successful treatment, her counselors recommended an intensive outpatient program to continue her recovery.

This scenario illustrates that treatment settings are not stagnant environments but integrative opportunities to move clients toward recovery and health. The reverse is also possible. Leigh might have a relapse (or slip) and need a temporary, more restrictive setting to regain her hard-won progress.

Moving up and down this continuum of care provides a multitude of treatment services designed to fit the client's unique needs. The effectiveness of treatment settings comes from their flexibility, adaptability, and responsiveness to the client's current recovery needs.

Conclusion

The substance use treatment industry is a diverse collection of team members who have organized themselves (e.g., research, clinical, administrative, and financial) to provide strategies for those who struggle with substance use disorders. Treatment settings described in this chapter provide an overview of the diversity of how treatment is delivered.

An understanding of federal legislation and its impact on newly insured users and their ability to seek treatment is important to providing competent care. Treatment planning and its place with accreditation bodies and managed care companies continue to play an important role in the changing health care system—a system that has expanded in significance and sophistication. This chapter presented guidelines to promote analytic thinking about treatment planning decisions, including treatment placement that meets the client's current needs. Substance use treatment, the diagnostic classification system for substance use disorder from dichotomous to a continuum, and the severity level of use based on the DSM-5 diagnostic classification system have recently changed, requiring vigilance in modifying and adapting treatment plans and settings.

MyCounselingLab for Addictions/Substance Use

Try the Topic 5 Assignments: *Treatment Setting and Treatment Planning.*

Case Study: Robert

Biopsychosocial Assessment and Treatment Plan

Orienting Information and Presenting Issue

Robert Lopez is a 38-year-old Hispanic man currently residing with his spouse and three children. He was referred to treatment after a conversation with his probation officer (PO) about his struggles with abstaining from marijuana. The client reports feeling "exhausted by [his] current drug use and the chaos it causes in [his] life."

History of Presenting Problem

Mr. Lopez stated that he began using alcohol and marijuana with friends when he was 10; however, over time he began to use every weekend. This occurred for about eight years. Currently, he reports consuming 8 to 12 beers three or four times each week. He added that he "avoids all liquor." The client acknowledged using cocaine two or three times and meth once, but he stated, "I didn't like the way it made me feel. It made me jittery." He acknowledged that he has been drinking regularly for the past 20 years, although he stated, "I don't think I have a problem with drinking. I just need to cut back on weed."

The client stated that his marijuana use progressed quickly from occasional use with friends when he was 10 to seeking out fellow drug users and smoking alone if he could not find someone to "get high with." He reported using marijuana daily for 28 years, acknowledging that it is a significant part of his life. Currently he smokes on average 20 to 25 joints per day, before, during, and after work (when employed) as well as before bed. He acknowledged his marijuana use is a problem that he has attempted to quit unsuccessfully several times over the years. While discussing his "frustration" with trying to stop using, he became tearful and appeared defeated because it has negatively impacted his ability to find and keep jobs, resulting in both economic stress and family fights.

He is in the second year of a five-year probation sentence for possession of a controlled substance (marijuana, personal use). He submits to random drug screens as part of his court order, and he has failed several of these in the past year. Although he found it very challenging, he has maintained abstinence from marijuana use for one month. Because it has been a struggle, he stated that he sought help and is willing to go to an inpatient facility if necessary because he is worried what will happen to him and his family if he continues to use.

Mental Status and Psychological Functioning

Mr. Lopez was dressed casually but appropriately when he arrived on time for his appointment. He was oriented to time, place, identity, and situation. Intelligence and general functioning level appeared within the average range. There was no evidence of current or past thought disorders or psychosis. Mr. Lopez appeared to be cooperative, openly answering questions and expanding on answers with additional information most of the time. He also demonstrated no obvious signs indicating problems with understanding, concentrating, or memory. He was able to communicate in a clear, organized manner that indicated he was sober and lucid during the interview. However, often the client looked at his feet rather than the counselor and spoke in a soft voice.

When asked about his mood, he described feeling "depressed," "anxious," and "tense," which was consistent with my observation of affect. He attributed his depression partially to the fact that he has not engaged in marijuana use in the past month but still struggles daily with both the desire to use and the consequences of his continued use. He reported a belief that he is not certain if he can do anything to change at this point in his life, and added that he is so concerned about it that he has started having trouble going to sleep and has lost an unspecified amount of weight because he worries about what will happen to him. His facial expressions and posture contributed to his withdrawn appearance.

He further displayed his distress by becoming tearful when stating that he simply does not know what to do to change his life. When asked, Mr. Lopez reported he had no suicide attempts or current ideation, although he acknowledged "thinking about it sometimes."

Although he appeared to sincerely want treatment for marijuana use, he clearly indicated that he does not believe his alcohol use is a problem, stating, "I can drink without hurting anyone." When prompted to expand on this statement, Mr. Lopez reported when he uses marijuana he sometimes has physical altercations with his wife or friends. He acknowledged that when he is "high" he "just can't keep it together," thus indicating potential issues with controlling behavior that may lead to family or community violence. He reported no specific or general threats of intent to harm anyone else, stating, "I just can't control it when I'm high. I don't mean to hurt anyone."

Legal History

Mr. Lopez has been on probation for one year of a five-year sentence, after being charged with possession of marijuana. During the past year, Mr. Lopez has had several positive random drug urine tests. His court papers indicate that he had an arrest for possessing a weapon (brass knuckles) six years ago, which was dismissed. He acknowledged having marijuana at the time of the current arrest, stating, "I know this is on me." When asked, he reported he uses drugs but does not sell them. Mr. Lopez appears to perceive his legal problems as very serious and stated his belief that counseling is important to help him stay out of jail. He reported his understanding that if he continues to use, he will be at risk for further legal issues, which he stated he wants to avoid. He acknowledged that drugs have been a consistent part of his life despite the fact that this is his first documented drug charge.

Developmental and Medical History

Mr. Lopez reported that he was born a month early and that he "wasn't wanted" because his parents were "too young and stupid to know what they were doing." He consistently reported that he was not aware of any early developmental issues when asked about these during the assessment. The client reported no significant accidents or injuries or hospitalizations in his past. He reported no ongoing medical treatment for any chronic medical issues. He appears to be in good physical condition; however, he stated that he does not have health insurance, so he does not go to the doctor. He reported his last medical exam was five years ago when he had a physical as requirement for a job he was doing on a construction site and that "it was fine."

Mental Health History

The client reported he has never received counseling for substance use or any other issues. He was court-ordered to go to a drug education program before his probation officer referred him here. He stated that he came to treatment "because I want help and want to stop." However, he also indicated several times that he would need a "letter" from the treatment center stating that he was "successful" in treatment.

Educational/Vocational/Financial History

Mr. Lopez reported dropping out of school when he was told he would repeat his freshman year for the third time, stating that it was "because of peer pressure" and "not really [being] into school stuff." He acknowledged spending much of his time skipping classes to smoke with friends and consequently did not learn a great deal. He stated that he has not attempted to pursue either his GED or any other type of vocational training. However, he indicated a belief that at this point in his life he would like to obtain his GED because it would improve his employment opportunities.

Mr. Lopez described his employment as working irregular hours mostly at part-time jobs. He reported he has worked 15 of the past 30 days. Mr. Lopez stated he "paints houses for a living." His employment history has primarily consisted of construction work and odd jobs. History of employment appears to be extremely unstable, which he stated was largely due to his drug use. He stated that when he smokes "weed" he is not interested in working or getting trained for a new skill. He acknowledged that his use of marijuana has prevented him from securing employment because he "can't pass the drug test to get the job."

As a result of his unstable employment history and the money he spends on drugs, Mr. Lopez and his family consistently experience financial problems. He reported that his wife's job as a convenience store clerk supports the family. He added that she works "long hours" 8 to 14 hours a day, six or seven days a week. Mr. Lopez rejected his probation officer's recommendations for employment counseling because he stated his belief that if he obtains treatment for his marijuana problem, the rest of his life will "fall into place."

Social History

The client provided the following history during a clinical interview. Mr. Lopez, the oldest of seven, grew up with his maternal grandparents until he left home at 19, although his siblings (two brothers and four sisters) lived with their parents. When asked, he explained that his parents were teenagers when he was born and could not care for him. At different points in the interview he reported that he was "happy" but also "lonely" during his childhood. He demonstrated difficulty expanding on his feelings when prompted to do so. He reported that since his grandparents were elderly, he was able to do what he wanted to as a kid. He said he was a loner and that his grandparents gave him "too much freedom." He stated that it was "their fault I was able to go out and party with friends all the time." He reported that he has two close friends that he has known since he started school, but he added that they "like to smoke, too," which makes being with them hard.

Mr. Lopez stated he was close with his mom but that she was more like a sister and close to his siblings even though he did not live with them. When asked about his father he scoffed and said, "He's an asshole who's always on my case even though he couldn't even take care of his own responsibilities."

When prompted to explain further, he stated, "My dad's not even in my life, so I don't think he has anything to do with this." He reported having a five-year relationship when he was a teenager that ended because he got violent when he was high. He reported that he "picked up women" when he wanted to have "company" but avoided relationships until he met his wife 10 years ago. She was 19 and had two children. He stated that she was "sweet like my mom" and that he knew her boys (Carlos, 14, and Trevor, 12) needed a man in the house, so they got married. They had a child a year later (Eliana, 11). He reported that he loves his family but knows that he "cause[s] a lot of problems because of my drug use and because I can't keep a good job." He has had arguments with his mom, several siblings, and his wife because of these issues. He added that recently he had a physical fight with his son when Carlos said his dad was "a no-good freeloader that didn't treat his mom right." The client reported that he got "really angry mostly because I know it's true ... I'm pretty much useless." He added that different family members have urged him to get help for his substance use disorder on numerous occasions over the years.

Mr. Lopez's family history is positive for substance use disorders including a maternal uncle and a paternal uncle, both of whom had legal issues related to their use. He indicated his father may have a problem but avoided discussing this further at this time. He reported that all of the men in his family (brothers and brother-in-laws) drink and smoke marijuana at least weekly and that one of his brothers "had a drug problem." He identified this as a barrier to quitting his substance use, although he also stated that he spends most of his time alone because he "like[s] it that way." No one in his family has ever received any type of counseling services because "we don't like to share our business out on the street."

He reported that he usually likes to fish, play soccer, and "hang out with family and friends." He acknowledged that alcohol and marijuana are part of all of these activities, adding that he does not really like doing any of them anymore. When asked, he reported he grew up Pentecostal but added that he does not believe in God and is not interested in that "higher power crap." He stated that his wife and mom both think that if he went to church more often that he would be "cured of these demons that have possessed" him.

Assessment

Mr. Lopez was informed of his rights and responsibilities as a client. The informed consent was explained including limits to confidentiality, Mr. Lopez's questions were answered, and then he signed the consent for treatment. He also signed a general release of information for the treatment staff to provide written and oral updates on his attendance and progress with his probation officer and for his PO to provide information to the treatment staff about his legal history and a copy of his court order,

drug education class notes, and past urine screens. He also signed a release for the treatment staff to talk with both his mother and his wife. A clinical interview was conducted with Mr. Lopez. He was given the SASSI-2, which indicated a substance use disorder, and a Beck Depression Inventory that indicated a moderate level of depression. A review of the data gathered from the formal assessments, collateral information, and clinical interview along with the staff's clinical judgment resulted in a determination that Mr. Lopez meets the DSM-5 criteria for Substance Use Disorder, Severe and Major Depressive Disorder, Moderate. Since he did not exhibit physical withdrawal symptoms or other issues that might indicate a need for 24-hour nursing care, he was medically cleared to participate in a 60-day residential program focused on treating his co-occurring substance use disorder and depression.

Treatment Plan

Client Strengths and Challenges	
Strengths	• Able to acknowledge he has a problem with marijuana use
	• Stated desire to stop using marijuana
	• Verbalized willingness to engage in treatment
	• Able to identify problems in functioning that result from marijuana use
	• Willing to verbally take responsibility for consequences of his substance use disorder most of the time
	• Support and encouragement of wife, mother, and children
	• Probation officer and court order provide an incentive for engaging in treatment
	• Average intelligence and no apparent cognitive deficits
Challenges	• Depression makes it more difficult to get clean and stay clean
	• Preference for isolation over social support
	• Social relationships and hobbies revolve around using substances
	• Unwilling to explore alcohol use as a potential problem
	• Attachment relationship wounds that appear to be triggers for using coupled with the client's guarded presentation regarding discussing distressing family history
	• Rejection of traditional 12-step support
	• Lack of education or job training coupled with a felony conviction make it difficult to gain work
	• Anger and resentment of some family members being fed up with his use and the consequences to the family

Treatment Plan Goals and Objectives

Goals	Objectives
1. Client will successfully manage withdrawal symptoms and cravings for 2 continuous weeks.	1. Nurse will administer Benadryl to help client with anxiety and problems sleeping on a PRN basis, as approved by doctor. 2. The client will inform the nurse on duty when he is having trouble going to sleep. 3. The psychoeducational group leader will teach the Distracting, Delaying, De-Catastrophizing, and De-Stressing Method of managing withdrawal and cravings. 4. The counseling staff will provide instruction and practice in thought restructuring, deep breathing, and meditation exercises to assist with managing withdrawal and cravings. 5. The client will practice thought restructuring, deep breathing, or meditation when he experiences withdrawal symptoms or cravings. 6. The recreational therapy staff will teach the client physical activity interventions for managing withdrawal or craving symptoms. 7. The client will participate in approved recreational activities to help manage withdrawal and craving symptoms.
2. Client will identify specific ways that he can avoid triggers or high-risk situations for using substances.	1. The counselor will teach the client what triggers and high-risk situations are. 2. The client will identify at least 10 people, places, and things that trigger use. 3. Client will generate a list of at least 10 strategies to avoid triggers. 4. Client will generate a list of at least 10 ways to manage high-risk situations that cannot be avoided.
3. Client will earn level four by consistently demonstrating recovery behaviors in the therapeutic milieu, treatment planning meetings, and in individual, group, and family counseling sessions, as determined by the treatment team.	1. The client will demonstrate necessary behaviors to work through the level system. 2. The client will verbally identify triggers and actively employ methods identified in treatment for intervening to avoid addictive behaviors. 3. The client will identify high-risk situations and use identified strategies to avoid them in the therapeutic milieu, treatment team meetings, and in counseling. 4. The client will seek out support rather than isolating when experiencing emotional distress. 5. The client will demonstrate no more than two times where he does not follow relapse plan within a 2-week period.

Residential Treatment Modalities:

- Psychiatric Nurse and Medical Doctor, PRN
- Therapeutic Milieu Community Meetings two 30 minute meetings daily
- Psychoeducational Group 1 hour daily
- Recreation Therapy Groups 2 hours daily
- Process Groups 3 hours daily
- Family Therapy 2 hours per week
- Individual Therapy 1 hour 2 times per week

Critical Thinking Questions

1. Mr. Lopez's history indicates a number of sociocultural issues that may need further exploration or attention in planning treatment. Identify three issues and discuss how you would approach dealing with them as his counselor.

2. Mr. Lopez's family history indicates some issues that may have contributed to his substance use issues. Discuss three potential family issues impacting the client's treatment and how the treatment plan can help address these.

3. Using the DSM-5 and review of the client's biopsychosocial history, what is your understanding of Mr. Lopez's alcohol use in relationship to his view of his drinking, and how does this impact treatment and how will you address it therapeutically?

CHAPTER 7

Individual Treatment

Davina A. Moss-King, Ph.D., C.R.C., C.A.S.A.C., N.C.C.

This chapter presents an overview of individual treatment and the current strategies that are being used in the field of substance use disorders (SUD). The individuals who are using drugs attend individual treatment for various circumstances. Regardless of the reasons for individual treatment, clinicians are aware that the changes in health care and the approaches to treatment are different than in the past (Smith, Lee, & Davidson, 2010). In the past, insurance providers allowed an individual to receive inpatient treatment for 28 days and possibly an unlimited amount of time for outpatient treatment as well. Currently an individual obtains permission from the insurance provider for a specific amount of time for inpatient or outpatient treatment that will need to be reviewed and renewed to lengthen treatment time. This time is usually significantly less than the 28 days of the former treatment approval (Walker, 2009).

Because of the shortened treatment times, the counselor who assists the client through the recovery process will need to provide creative, swift, and efficient counseling techniques (Fields & Roman, 2010). For a counselor in training or for a seasoned counselor, new and more efficient techniques are imperative to assist the client toward recovery and to accompany the changes in health care. This chapter provides information for the counselor to assist the client in the treatment process. Other chapters explore group, family, and recovery treatment strategies. It is important to note that individual treatment is most successful when group and family treatments are incorporated and evidenced-based treatment strategies are used. Therefore, this chapter focuses on current evidenced-based treatment strategies.

BEGINNING INDIVIDUAL TREATMENT

The first step for individual treatment is the individual's mental and emotional readiness for treatment (Ekendahl, 2007; Redko, Rapp, & Carlson, 2007). Readiness is the process of mentally and emotionally preparing to detach oneself from substance use (Cihan, Winstead, Feit, & Feit, 2014). The person who uses substances has an emotional attachment to his or her drug despite the duration of use. This attachment revolves around the individual using the drug of choice to cope with life's difficulties and missing the drug of choice when it is not available. Individual treatment addresses the issue of grief and loss in relation to the attachment (Moss-King, 2009). The individual must cease the use of his or her substance and be willing to make a change in lifestyle (Ekendahl, 2007; Lewis, Dana, & Blevins, 2015). Research has shown that substance use is a coping mechanism that has become a debilitating crutch to manage life's daily stressors. The attachment occurs when there becomes an emotional bond that lingers long after the substance is absent physically (Fowler, Groat, & Ulanday, 2013). The emotional bond has become significantly vital and will psychologically impede the individual's ability to be ready for an appropriate therapeutic relationship.

Previous research has illustrated that there are four components of the substance use relationship that must be severed. Moss-King's (2009) research on heroin recovery describes a person who stated there were significant components that interfered with the success of individual therapy: heroin (love affair), heroin culture, heroin lifestyle, and finally needle obsession. The psychological attachment to the components of use will impede the counseling therapeutic relationship. Each of the four components must be addressed, especially the paraphernalia obsession, after the recovery process has begun.

The substance user must stop using the substance and be willing to make changes in his or her lifestyle. These changes include the community in which an individual resides as well as the individual's acquaintances/associates. Evaluating and eventually detaching can escalate to grief and loss issues that can be compared to death, as described in Kübler-Ross' (1969) grief stages: (1) denial, (2) anger/sorrow/despair, (3) depression, (4) bargaining, (5) acceptance. According to Moss-King (2009), when a relationship with a substance has officially ended, the recovering person may have (1) loss of self-esteem, (2) loss of identity, (3) loss of living structure, (4) loss of friends, and (5) loss of ambition. These losses may overwhelm the individual in the beginning of treatment; however, therapeutic outcomes improve if the counselor addresses these issues as they arise. As mentioned earlier, as the substance users are navigating the recovery process, their readiness needs to be assessed. One assessment that might be used is DiClemente's Stages for Change, along with other screening and assessment instruments such as the Alcohol and Drug Consequences Questionnaire, Readiness to Change Questionnaire, Stages of Change Readiness, and Treatment Eagerness Scale (Substance Abuse and Mental Health Services Administration [SAMHSA], 2012).

According to Norcross, Krebs, and Prochaska (2011), an individual transitioning from an SUD into treatment encounters five stages of change: (1) precontemplation (not considering change); (2) contemplation (weighing all options for change and possibly ambivalent); (3) preparation (trying to change); (4) action (changing behaviors); and (5) maintenance (commitment and planning). To make changes and to be mentally prepared for treatment at any level, the substance user must be at the stage of preparation, which is the stage at which the individual is attempting to change.

The preparation stage is interrupting the drug use as the individual begins counseling, whether in an inpatient or an outpatient treatment facility. The individual must be willing to separate from the drug itself along with any associations. These associations can include but are not limited to the emotional bond with using partners and the paraphernalia associated with the drug of choice (Moss-King, 2009).

The type of treatment the substance user will receive depends on a variety of factors: the initial assessment, the resources available in the community, the individual's resources, and insurance. The American Society of Addiction Medicine (ASAM) released an updated version for treatment criteria during the fall of 2013. This new release includes changes that occurred within the DSM-5 (American Psychiatric Association, 2013). The ASAM (2013) revised criteria continue to include guidelines for assessing the appropriate level of care for SUD individuals. The level of care is determined by an assessment that is separated in six dimensions: (1) acute intoxication and/or withdrawal potential; (2) biomedical conditions and complications; (3) emotional, behavioral, or cognitive conditions or complications; (4) readiness to change; (5) relapse, continued use, or continued problem/potential; and (6) recovery/living environment. ASAM lists five levels of continuum care (level of care, LOC), which helps physicians and therapists to appropriately refer the substance user.

Once the assessment is complete, the clinician will need to decide the continuum of care for the SUD individual. Before discussing care, it is important that the differences among medically monitored, clinically managed, and medically managed care be defined. According to ASAM, "medically monitored" means that the substance user will be under the direct supervision/care of a licensed physician and a quality assurance program for the length of stay for detoxification (ASAM, 2013). Monitoring includes but is not limited to the multidisciplinary team reviewing the case daily, and face-to-face contact with the client. "Clinically managed" is facilities that are appropriate for those individuals who are ready to change, but their primary issue is behavioral or emotional, cognitive concerns, and there are no major issues existing such as acute intoxication/withdrawal or biomedical issues (ASAM, 2013). Last, "medically managed" involves intense medical care where diagnostic and treatment services are directly provided and/or managed by appropriately trained staff and under the supervision of a licensed physician.

The continuum of care is as follows:

Level of continuum	Explanation
.5	Early intervention
1.0	Outpatient services
2.0	Intensive outpatient/partial hospitalization
2.1	Intensive outpatient
2.5	Partial hospitalization services
3.0	Residential/inpatient services
3.1	Clinically managed low-intensity residential services
3.3	Clinically managed population-specific, high intensity/residential services
3.5	Clinically managed high-intensity inpatient services
4.0	Medically managed intensive inpatient services

(ASAM, 2013 pg. 2)

The level of treatment is normally chosen by the insurance carrier using the initial assessment information via the medical model as a basis for their decision (Smith et al., 2010). Once the decision is made for the level of care, the counselor will need to begin treatment in a timely and effective manner with particular regard for the participant's needs within the constraints of the length and type of program chosen.

In some cases, drug courts strongly encourage individuals to attend treatment. These drug courts were developed to give individuals with SUD the opportunity to become clean and sober with the help of treatment facilities. Mandated treatment has proven to be successful (Patra et al., 2010). In other cases, people are forced to the preparation stage because of ultimatums given by family, friends, employers, or significant others. Sometimes the ultimatum is structured as a formal intervention, and other times the intervention is in the form of informal threats to job or family life.

Intervention

An intervention is an action or occurrence that causes an individual to try to stop the use of substances. An "informal" intervention may happen in several ways. For example, an individual stops smoking because of the educational materials he or she has read, an individual's employment is in jeopardy because of continuous drug and alcohol use, or a spouse threatens to leave if the individual does not stop using. Another example may be individuals who have been mandated into treatment by the court system and required to cease all forms of substance use.

The process of a formal intervention can involve all significant people in the individual's life: the partner, children, siblings, parents, friends, supervisors and co-workers, minister, medical professionals, and any other support people in the person's world. To be successful, interventions are structured to acknowledge the care and concern for the user but also to emphasize that continued use of substances has both limits and significant consequences.

Although it is possible to complete an intervention successfully without professional assistance, the level of emotional intensity usually requires that the planning and completion be performed under the supervision of a SUD counselor who is trained in the process of intervention. Significant others may need the assistance of a professional in planning and completion of this intense situation to stay focused, and to remember that there is no malice in this process even though a confrontation is occurring (Doweiko, 2012).

Individuals involved in the intervention decide to "break the silence" concerning the individual's behaviors and the effect of these behaviors on everyone involved. It is important to have as many significant people as possible involved in the intervention. Anyone who has ever tried to challenge a person using substances one-on-one knows the frustration and power of the user's excuses, rationalizations, anger, projection, and denial. Therefore, the strength of the caring group becomes powerful. Each individual should bring specific situations or incidents involving the individual to the intervention, with a focus on facts or firsthand observation of behaviors. Owing to the emotions involved and the seriousness of the situation, participants may want to write down what they wish to express. With a large and well-prepared group of people present at the intervention, it becomes very difficult for the individual to manipulate the facts of any situation or to discount the seriousness of the situation (Doweiko, 2015).

ETHICAL AND LEGAL CONCERNS OF INTERVENTION: A WORD OF CAUTION In today's litigious society, it behooves the SUD counselor to proceed with caution. As early as 1988, Rothenberg addressed the concern for a thorough diagnosis of a substance use disorder before an intervention began. Should this be an independent diagnosis? Are there any legal sanctions for a SUD counselor who supervises an intervention without this diagnosis? It is possible that some families may use the intervention as a tool to control behavior (Doweiko, 2012). This raises some ethical issues, including the individual's right to leave at any time. What if the person being confronted decides to exercise this right? What are the ethical considerations if the individual is not fully informed of this right? It is imperative that all rules and actions should be stated at the outset. In addition, it is vital that all participants be fully aware of their rights and responsibilities before any intervention begins. Once the intervention has been completed, the desired effect is for the individual to seek treatment immediately in the appropriate setting.

In summary, no matter what path the individual takes to reach treatment, once the decision is made, effective treatment needs to take a holistic approach. All aspects of the individual's life—physical, emotional, behavioral, familial, and social—have been impacted by the ingestion of substances, and to be successful, treatment needs to address these same areas. To facilitate this process, a variety of methods should be incorporated into the treatment planning. Effective treatment should include individual therapy, group therapy, family therapy, physical exercise, healthy nutritional plan, and a supportive environment. This chapter focuses on individual treatment approaches that directly impact substance use and that augment the direct impact therapeutic work.

The next section discusses the direct impact individual therapies and the importance of a therapeutic alliance between the individual seeking counseling and the therapist/counselor.

DIRECT IMPACT INDIVIDUAL THERAPY

An assortment of approaches have been used in individual therapy with clients who use substances, including cognitive–behavioral therapy (Courbasson & Nishikaway, 2010), social skills training (Lewis et al., 2015), behavior therapy (Carroll & Onken, 2007), solution-focused therapy (Lightfoot, 2014), and aversion therapy (Verendeev & Riley, 2012). One concept is central to therapeutic interventions: the counselor/client relationship, also referred to as the therapeutic alliance. So before we examine some of these theoretical approaches in depth, it is important to discuss this central issue.

The Therapeutic Alliance

The therapeutic alliance, or the relationship between the client and counselor, is an essential component of therapy. The fundamental principle of the therapeutic alliance is listening to the individual without passing judgment verbally or nonverbally. The relationship is the variable for predicting client response and the counseling outcome. Duff and Bedi (2010) concluded that validation was an important part of the therapeutic alliance, and that nonverbal communication and positive regard were both effective in enhancing an individual's self-efficacy and bringing about a positive outcome. Another part of the therapeutic alliance is the language used by the counselor to create motivation toward behavioral changes in recovery. There are five core skills to create a positive therapeutic relationship during an individual counseling session: asking open questions (invites the substance user to consider elaborating on their answers and thoughts); affirming (depends on the substance user's inner strengths and amazing efforts toward the recovery process); reflective listening (the counselor continues to engage the substance user by allowing exploration and consideration of previous statements made in the session); summarizing (presenting material discussed before and encouraging more conversation on a deeper level to explore the substance user's statements); and informing as well as advising (the counselor will provide information and advice only by request of the substance user; Miller & Rollnick, 2013).

DIRECT EFFECT THEORIES Some strategies/theories have a direct effect on the discontinuation of substance use. Therapies that have been employed in the past for individual therapy were psychodynamic therapy, aversion therapy, psychopharmacology alone, solution-focused therapy, and reality therapy (which was later replaced by choice theory). Research continues to be controversial as to the effectiveness of these treatment models. Currently, the SAMHSA National Registry of Evidence-Based Programs and Practices (NREPP) mentions motivational interviewing, cognitive–behavioral therapy, mindfulness therapy, and psychopharmacology as four of their endorsed methods of working with SUD (SAMHSA, 2013). Therefore, this chapter focuses on these theories.

Motivational Interviewing

Motivational interviewing (MI) was developed in Norway in 1982 and published in 1983 by William Miller and Stephen Rollnick (2009, 2013). Motivational interviewing can be used during individual therapy because it is client centered and directed as demonstrated in the past by Carl Rogers (Miller & Rollnick, 2013). MI is a way to motivate an individual toward recovery where there is resistance, along with resolving ambivalence by increasing internal motivation and self-efficacy (Miller & Rollnick, 2009, 2013). The individual may be contemplating recovery, and the spirit of MI evokes healing and encourages the client to bring forth positive ideas toward the treatment process. These positive ideas are the results of a therapeutic relationship that is goal directed and client centered and increases self-efficacy (Lewis et al., 2015). The therapeutic relationship consists of the counselor having empathy and unconditional positive regard to assist the individual to facilitate change. This change is the result of a required respectful exchange of ideas between the counselor and the client during the sessions (Miller & Rollnick, 2013). The flow of motivational interviewing is combining MI methods and the MI spirit to elicit motivation and plans toward change along with strengthening commitment for change while rolling with resistance.

The Method of Motivational Interviewing

There are four processes used in the method of MI, and they need to follow in sequence (Miller & Rollnick, 2013). The four processes are engaging, focusing, evoking, and planning. It is important to recognize that the first step is the engaging process, which lays the foundation for focusing on the goals regarding the presenting problem. Once trust is established and the environment is safe, the individual can focus on developing goals that are evoked by change talk, and planning for change can begin.

1. *Engaging:*   The beginning of the MI process is the engaging phase, which is the moment that the counselor and the client connect and make a decision to work together toward change in a therapeutic relationship.
2. *Focusing:*   The counselor will begin to focus on the presenting problem and begin to provide direction for the client. The counselor will use MI to identify the goals that the client may have toward change and will use the therapeutic relationship to focus on the change.
3. *Evoking:*   The counselor will draw out arguments toward change, allowing clients to discuss their feelings about change and move quickly toward planning.
4. *Planning:*   The planning stage is also key to being ready for change. This is the balance between talking and thinking about change, where actual steps develop for change (Miller & Rollnick, 2013; Lewis et al., 2015). The planning process stage will have a combination of commitment to change and creating a specific plan. The counselor will discuss the plans and encourage the client's autonomy to make a decision, and thus change talk emerges.

The motivation to change is definitely in the spirit of MI. The next section focuses on the components of the MI spirit that the counselor brings to the therapeutic relationship.

The Spirit of Motivational Interviewing

Motivational interviewing is a partnership between two experts, the counselor and the counselee. The counselor who embraces the spirit of MI finds success with his or her client accomplishing goals toward recovery. The counselor has a complementary therapeutic relationship with the client that is an honest and collaborative effort, with the counselor forfeiting the leadership role in the session. The counselor will encourage the client to have autonomy and be the expert while the counselor continues to guide. As this system works toward goals of behavioral changes, the client's confidence level is elevated to make independent decisions about his or her recovery and appropriate lifestyle changes. The spirit of MI is therefore used to awaken the client's motivation and the resources they have available for change. This is done by incorporating the four spirits of MI: acceptance, compassion, evocation, and collaboration (Miller & Rollnick, 2013).

ACCEPTANCE In the spirit of MI and the belief that the client is also an expert in the therapeutic relationship, the counselor accepts the individual's thoughts and his or her contributions to the session. This resurfaces the work of Rogers in the aspect of absolute worth, autonomy support, accurate empathy, and affirmation (Miller & Rollnick, 2013).

In the spirit of MI, the counselor is consistently working through ambivalence by demonstrating during the session that there is trust between the two experts and there is respect for each other's worth. The counselor also has respect, without judgment, for the client's ability to choose direction(s), thus providing autonomy support for the client. The act of accurate empathy is illustrated by understanding the client's worldview along with affirming the client's strong points and intentions toward change.

COMPASSION The counselor is intentionally working with the client to show that the client's needs take priority and to promote the client's welfare. This characteristic in the MI counselor will create a welcoming environment where the client feels important and therefore will begin to feel comfortable about discussing change.

EVOCATION The spirit of evocation is the counselor's interest and understanding of the client's perspective and wisdom toward change. It is the belief that the clients have the power within themselves to rationalize and to promote change by consistent encouragement from the counselor to extract these ideas.

COLLABORATION The combination of evocation, compassion, and acceptance with the assimilation of empowerment to the client from the counselor is a movement toward change. The sense of empowerment that the clients have is embodied in the knowledge that their thoughts are valued and their decisions are respected. In the true sense, the counselor and the client are working together to overcome ambivalence by increasing motivation toward change.

The role of collaboration is impossible without the development of a positive therapeutic relationship between the counselor and the client. Counselors use the five core skills mentioned in the therapeutic alliance section with a client-centered approach to encourage change talk (Lewis et al., 2015). The change talk that is spoken by the individual becomes a microcosm outside of the therapeutic environment as the individual works through the ambivalence. The counselor works through ambivalence by evoking change talk, keeping in mind that ambivalence can be toward change or toward sustaining the precipitating problem.

CHANGE TALK

Miller and Rollnick (2013) define change talk as a self-expressed language that is an argument for change. The language that the client is speaking is self-motivating and illustrates commitment toward change. The client that is speaking change begins with *preparatory change talk* and gradually transitions to *mobilizing change talk.*

PREPARATORY CHANGE TALK Preparatory change talk has four components: desire, ability, reasons, and need (Miller & Rollnick, 2013). The first component is desire, which illustrates an individual's wishes and hopes toward recovery. The second is ability, which is the individual's

Advantages of lifestyle change in sobriety	Advantages of lifestyle change with continued use
Disadvantages of lifestyle change in sobriety	Disadvantages of lifestyle change with continued use

FIGURE 7.1 Decisional balance.
Source: Miller & Rollnick, 2013.

self-perception toward being clean and sober and the intrinsic motivation to acknowledge and envision sobriety as an actual possibility. These are the sentences that have "could" and "would" as part of the change talk (Miller & Rollnick, 2013). The third is reasons. These are statements that support or do not support the ability statements. If the counselor recognizes that the individual is struggling with ambivalence toward sobriety in relationship to lifestyle changes and has stated reasons that were for change or against, the counselor could do a decisional balance as suggested by Miller and Rollnick.

The fourth component is need, which expresses the immediacy toward change. Once the counselor observes the change in language, the individual is now moving toward *mobilizing change talk.*

MOBILIZING CHANGE TALK Mobilizing change talk is moving toward resolving the presenting problem by hearing the language of commitment and activation. The language of commitment is the intent to change with minimal hesitation. Such statements from the client can be, "I promise to attend self-help meetings to maintain my sobriety." These statements demonstrate that activation is the next step toward accomplishing the sobriety goal, and the client is willing to give direction toward the goal (Miller & Rollnick, 2013).

Activation is the language the counselor will hear in the session, and it is direction-motivated along with taking steps toward change. Previously, our example was "I promise to attend self-help meetings to maintain my sobriety." The client can be more concrete with this action and take steps by stating: "I will be attending self-help meetings three times per week." Not only was the client moving toward action, but also the client illustrated the steps that will be taken toward maintaining sobriety (Miller & Rollnick, 2013).

In conclusion, MI is effective because it allows the client to be the expert and also encourages positive thinking and talking, which then allows an active plan to take place. The client creates this action plan at the same time the counselor uses the methods and the spirit of MI effectively, developing a safe environment for strength and growth and creating a microcosm to implement goals toward recovery.

Motivational Enhancement Therapy

Motivational enhancement therapy (MET) incorporates feedback from structured assessments and using MI to provide feedback for the personal findings. MI is used to have a productive conversation regarding the assessments in a directive approach intended to strengthen the client's commitment to change and increase self-efficacy (Lewis et al., 2015; SAMHSA, 2013). The use of the structured assessments helps the client to develop intrinsic motivating goals along with increasing self-efficacy while working with ambivalence. The method of motivational interviewing and the spirit of motivational interviewing are used during the MET sessions, with the ultimate goal of change talk for the client to set goals and to be successful. Burlew, Montgomery,

Kosinski, and Forcehimes (2013) compared African American substance users who were administered MET and other African Americans who were administered counseling as usual (CAU). Both measured readiness to change. The results were that the individuals with MET reported fewer days of substance use per week and were ready for change more than the participants that had CAU. Also according to Korte and Schmidt (2013) the Anxiety Sensitivity Index was administered and MET was used to discuss the results of the evaluation along with developing goals. The results were in favor of MET reducing anxiety sensitivity and creating goals to reduce symptoms. Both of these empirically researched studies have supported the fact that MET, with the spirit of MI, encourages intrinsic motivation toward change talk and goal planning for success and increasing self-efficacy (Burlew et al., 2013).

Cognitive-Behavioral Therapy

Cognitive–behavioral therapy (CBT) is another direct effect theory. It is based on two forms of psychotherapy combining cognitive therapy and behavioral therapy (SAMHSA, 2013). CBT is also known as a cost-effective treatment that examines the relationship between thoughts and feelings having a direct result on the substance user's behavior (LeBeau, Davies, Culver, & Craske, 2013). In order to reach the goal of changing behavior, the therapist has the substance user vividly recount the traumatic event and then give homework to motivate change in thoughts and feelings (Shapiro, 2014). According to LeBeau and colleagues (2013), homework is the most important compliance measure for treatment to be successful. Homework also fosters continued engagement in treatment while allowing the substance user to be keenly aware of the thoughts as well as emotions that are impacting behavior or possibility of a relapse.

CBT has the substance user recount trauma in a vivid manner before working toward the behavior change. The use of eye movement desensitization and reprocessing therapy (EMDR) concentrates on the bodily sensations that the traumatic event caused rather than reliving the traumatic event in a detailed manner (Shapiro, 2014).

Eye Movement Desensitization and Reprocessing Therapy

Eye movement desensitization and reprocessing therapy is the third direct effect theory, developed by Dr. Francine Shapiro in 1988. According to Shapiro (2014), EMDR is an effective therapy for trauma victims and is recognized by the American Psychiatric Association and the U.S. Department of Defense. This type of therapy is known as a comprehensive and integrative psychotherapy approach and can also be eclectic, because it could be used in combination with cognitive–behavioral therapy as well as mindfulness (Shapiro, 2014). EMDR was created to discover and to identify traumatic feelings that create negative emotions. These emotions can lead to anxiety and/or depression, which can be masked with addiction to control the overwhelming emotions. Self-medicating is the long-term result of the substance user not addressing the underlying issues that are creating negative emotions from a past experience. Some underlying issues could be a traumatic event such as childhood sexual abuse or an event that resulted in posttraumatic stress disorder (PTSD) (Asberg & Renk, 2012).

The goal for using EMDR with the SUD individual is to gently reach into the negative emotions and process as well as confront these emotions in relation to the SUD. Asberg and Renk (2012) state in their study that negative events are at times buried and can be the driving force behind the substance use disorder. The negative events require processing followed by coping skills training in conjunction with self-help groups that assist the individual through the treatment process.

The procedure of the EMDR treatment could include eye movement with focusing on a light or focusing on tones or taps through earphones. While the individuals are concentrating on the stimulus, they are attending to the memory that is painful/traumatic and identify current triggers for the memory that may be suppressed, along with discussing the anticipated future experience that may have resulted in the negative feeling (Shapiro, 2013).

The EMDR has eight phases of treatment. Phase 1 (history taking) includes the therapist taking a history and discussing the reason for attending therapy. In phase 2 (preparation), the therapist evaluates the individual's readiness to handle emotional distress and whether the individual has appropriate coping skills. Phase 3 (assessment) is organizing the groundwork for the EMDR sessions with three specific goals: (1) to explain where the trauma took place, including the emotions or physical sensations attached; (2) to discuss any negative beliefs related to self as a result of the trauma; and (3) to discuss the positive belief of the substance user associated with the present. Phase 4 (desensitization) is the substance user's opportunity to focus on the negative self-beliefs and disturbing emotions, along with physical sensations associated with the trauma. In phase 5 (installation phase), the substance user focuses on the positive self-beliefs that will eventually replace the negative beliefs surrounding the traumatic event. Phase 6 is the body scan, in which the substance user focuses on the physical sensations that are negative, eventually replacing these with positive thoughts that will resolve the negative stimulation. The goal of phase 6 is for the substance user to discuss the trauma without negative physical sensations that will retraumatize the user. Phase 7 is the closure area, in which the counselor practices coping techniques and relaxation exercises with the substance user to increase a healthy balance. Finally, phase 8 is the reevaluation period, in which the counselor reviews the substance user's responses and progress (Shapiro, 2014).

According to Shapiro (2014), the majority of EMDR participants state that the stress associated with the memory is greatly diminished or eliminated totally. Because the memory now produces minimal negative emotions, the individual will begin to have positive life changes that eventually affect behavior by using guided imagery and mindfulness technique training.

The Mindfulness Technique

According to Brewer et al. (2009), the mindfulness technique is an avenue to effectively control stress and undesirable feelings that could result in a relapse. Individuals who are in early recovery have continual impulsive thoughts that can lead to using the drug of choice if the individual gives in to them. Witkiewitz, Bowen, Douglas, and Hsu (2013) examine mindfulness in terms of controlling craving. Their study indicates that mindfulness is effective in lowering self-reported cravings on scales of acceptance, awareness, and lack of judgmental feelings. An individual who uses substances is learning, through the language of the therapist, to "live in the moment" of the experience by using all senses, including the mind. O'Connell's (2009) study examined the use of mindfulness in an inpatient setting, in which the patients would "sit" with their emotions. This entailed focusing on a certain part of the body and meditating. The result of the study was that the participants were able to regulate their thoughts. This regulation included, but was not limited to, the participant being aware of his or her disorder and the thought process of compulsivity. Although this study was completed in an inpatient residential facility, mindfulness can be an adjunct to treatment at all levels of care mentioned earlier in the chapter.

Brewer and colleagues (2009) conducted a study comparing the effects of mindfulness and cognitive–behavioral therapy on participants' responses to personalized stress. The results showed that mindfulness techniques were more effective than cognitive-behavioral therapy in reducing patients' response to psychological and physiological stressors.

Pharmacotherapy

Regardless of the therapeutic treatment used, some individuals who are involved in individual therapy will require an additive to maintain abstinence so they are able to focus on and commit to change. Certain medications can be prescribed or administered to aids in detoxification, increase the quality of therapy, and even assist with relapse prevention.

Medications can be used in conjunction with individual therapy in three ways. The first way is to safely withdraw from a substance and increase the quality of counseling; the second is during treatment; and the third is to aid in maintaining sobriety. This section discusses the three uses in relationship to treatment of alcohol, opiate, tobacco, and cocaine use.

DETOXIFICATION Medications may be prescribed to provide safe detoxification for an individual attempting to withdraw from a substance. Individuals who are withdrawing from heroin are given methadone, suboxone, or buprenorphine (Subutex), and sometimes also clonidine (trade name Catapres). A more recent form of detoxification being used in England for heroin addiction is rapid opiate detoxification, for which the individual is given lofexidine. More research, and approval by the U.S. Food and Drug Administration with studies authorized by the appropriate government agencies, is needed before this form of detoxification can be used in the United States (National Institute on Drug Abuse [NIDA], 2012).

Individuals who are detoxifying from alcohol are given benzodiazepine or phenobarbital to ease the discomfort of the withdrawal symptoms and decrease the chance of seizures. The physician who is medically managing the detoxification process can also prescribe acamprosate, which decreases withdrawal symptoms such as insomnia and anxiety (NIDA, 2012).

Medication During and After Treatment

After detoxification has been completed at a medically managed facility, an individual may continue taking medications to remain abstinent. These medications are measures for relapse prevention and maintenance while engaging in individual therapy.

Substance users who are recovering from opioid use can maintain sobriety by using methadone to reduce symptoms of craving. Methadone is taken orally on a daily basis. The use of methadone is monitored by a physician as well as the substance use counselor assigned to the substance user. Other forms of maintenance for opioid use are buprenorphine (Subutex), or suboxone (buprenorphine and naloxone) and naltrexone (Vivitrol). These medications are useful for substance users who are motivated toward treatment and are compliant with outpatient treatment (NIDA, 2012).

Substance users who are motivated toward treatment for alcohol use are prescribed disulfiram, which will cause unpleasant physical symptoms when alcohol is consumed (NIDA, 2012). The drug topiramate is not yet approved by the FDA, but has been used in studies that have shown positive drinking outcomes when compared with a placebo (NIDA, 2012; Anton et al., 2006).

Many outpatient treatment providers have encouraged substance users to decrease their use of tobacco products to increase the treatment success rate. Some nicotine replacement therapies include bupropion and varenicline (NIDA, 2012). Other nicotine replacement therapies that are sold over the counter (OTC) include Nicorette gum and Nicorette Lozenge, NicoDerm, Nicotrol spray, and Nicotrol Inhaler (American Academy of Family Physicians, 2014).

Substance users in treatment for cocaine use can be prescribed the anti-epileptic drug topiramate (Topamax). When compared to a placebo there were more non-cocaine use days with the drug than the placebo when urinalysis was collected. Topamax was also associated with cravings.

For the opiate population, suboxone, buprenorphine, and methadone are used as maintenance to sustain recovery (Finch, Kamien, & Amass, 2007). Individuals recovering from opiate addiction may choose to enroll in a methadone maintenance clinic, or they could receive suboxone or buprenorphine from a physician in an office-based setting. Methadone maintenance is primarily administered in a clinic setting and has been in existence for many years as a treatment to end opiate use. Research has proven that abstinence is associated with higher doses; as the doses decrease, there is risk for depression and using other substances such as alcohol, cocaine, and benzodiazepine (Senbanjo, Wolff, Marshall, & Strang, 2009). Suboxone is another alternative that may be administered in an office setting prescribed by a physician. Suboxone is a pharmacotherapy treatment that is a combination of buprenorphine and naloxone. It can be used for detoxification but is intended for abstinence from the use of opiates, mainly to control cravings (Fareed, Vayalapalli, Casarella, Amar, & Drexler, 2010; Orman & Keating, 2009). Orman and Keating report that participants who received suboxone had negative urinalysis for opiates. Suboxone is usually recommended for recovering individuals who are fully committed to treatment and a lifestyle change as well. It can also be a physician's recommendation for pregnant women (Wesson & Smith, 2010).

Buprenorphine can also be administered as a pharmacological treatment option for opioid-dependent individuals and is administered in the office of a physician. According to Wesson and Smith (2010), participants who received buprenorphine had negative urine tests and were retained in 28- and 90-day treatment. Buprenorphine has been used successfully on the opiate population. According to Ciccocioppo and colleagues (2007), the administration of the drug also reduces alcohol intake among a special breed of rats, so research has yet to determine whether it can be a successful type of pharmacotherapy for alcohol use.

In addition to these and other direct-effect theories, strategies that augment the discontinuation of substance use are required to help individuals gain improved living skills and quality of life after the discontinuation of the substance that the user was given treatment for.

BEYOND DISCONTINUATION OF USE

In this section we examine harm reduction, coping skills training, life-skills training, relationship skills, and prevocational readiness training. The purpose of incorporating these strategies into individual treatment is to approach the client holistically while addressing concerns that could hinder individual treatment and continued recovery.

Despite the model that motivates individuals toward change, they will be challenged with handling life stressors without the use of their drug of choice and will need to continuously develop appropriate coping strategies. This next section discusses coping skills training as well as life skills training.

Coping Skills Training/Life Skills Training

There is a need for teaching coping skills for successful recovery during individual therapy. Therapists have often stated that substance users do not have appropriate coping strategies. These strategies involve structured living situations and the substance user making decisions that promote wellness and balance (Cleveland & Harris, 2010). The fact is that the substance user has been using coping strategies that have "worked" for them for many years. The coping mechanisms include and are not limited to the drug of choice. The drug/alcohol had been the substance user's way of balancing a situation to make it acceptable, and was also a strategy for of handling unfamiliar and uncertain situations. Because the substance user is now learning to live life without their usual coping mechanism, it is imperative that healthy coping strategies be explored during the early recovery stage.

The coping mechanisms that are taught by the therapist continue to be an evolving tool that manages changes in the life of the substance user. Some of these changes are welcomed, and others are a complete surprise. The changes that are welcomed can be appropriately managed in various ways. However, regardless of the change, there is an emotional feeling of stress that plays a key role in experiencing triggers that can lead to relapse. *Stress* is problems or strains that individuals may encounter throughout life that may cause a disruption in daily living (Hassanbeigi, Askari, Hassanbeigi, & Pourmovahed, 2013). *Coping* is a behavioral or cognitive response that individuals use to manage stress. Stress has a dual role for the substance user for the development of substance use behavior and a major cause of relapse after short or long periods of abstinence (Ungless, Argilli & Bonci, 2010). Stress has a relationship to substance use, and the use does not occur without a trigger or a craving. Ames and Roitzsch (2000) stated that individuals who have daily stressors have a high probability of experiencing cravings to use the drug of choice. According to Hassanbeigi et al. (2013), there is a direct relationship between stress and substance use. Their research with participants who were opioid dependent indicated that stress is one of the strongest predictors of using a drug as a coping mechanism to handle stress. The therapist teaches important skills such as life skills, stress prevention/management and appropriate strategies to handle high-risk situations. Stressful events that a therapist will need to be aware of are grief and loss, familial crises, occupational difficulties, and personal problems. Askari, Hassanbeigi, and Fallahzadeh (2011) stated that opioid clients experience stressful events more often than normal subjects and often lack appropriate coping mechanisms to survive the stressful event. Some of the ways that clients can support their coping skills include attending a support group, such as an Alcoholics Anonymous or Narcotics Anonymous meeting The frequency will depend on the needs of the individual and how they are able to handle their fears of being incapable of continuing sobriety. The individual may begin his or her therapy by investigating the various situations that trigger use/relapse along with identifying situations when cravings appear. Once these triggers are identified, strategies to cope with the relapse triggers are mandatory. These are addressed by journaling and recognizing the triggers from the journal and creating a strategy for each (Cleveland & Harris, 2010).

Dolan, Rohsenow, Martin, and Monti (2013) identify strategies for coping with stressful situations, triggers, and cravings during periods of abstinence. The strategies that are significantly successful include (1) negative consequences, (2) spiritual coping, (3) resolving conflict with a family member, (4) relaxation or meditation, (5) substituting a cigarette, (6) imagery, and (7) leisure activities. The act of spiritual coping includes meditating and the act of reflecting on a positive self. This contributes to increased awareness and the ability to depend on a higher power for guidance, which is discussed in Narcotics Anonymous or Alcoholics Anonymous self-help groups. Mindfulness skills are relevant at this point also.

The substance user who is going through the process of recovery has differences in lifestyle that can be a challenge. Lifestyle skills training can be an effective part of the individual sustaining abstinence. Some lifestyle skills training that is imperative to a successful recovery include learning to manage personal finances, eating healthy food, and understanding how to use a calendar and organize the day. These lifestyle skills are important to prevent stressful situations from becoming overwhelming to the point of a possible relapse. According to Dolan and colleagues (2013), helpful lifestyle change strategies included (1) healthy food, and appropriate hours of sleep; (2) work toward future goals; and (3) avoid tempting situations.

Completing lifestyle and coping training is important to sustain abstinence and to avoid or appropriate managing stress. Improved coping mechanisms increase an individual's self-efficacy to handle stress in various areas. The next section examines the importance of transitioning social skills training to prepare the substance user for vocational readiness.

Vocational Readiness

Research has shown that recovery is more successful if an individual is gainfully employed post-treatment (DeFulio, Donlin, Wong, & Silverman, 2009; West, 2008). According to Melvin, Davis, and Koch (2012), research has shown that employment is an important factor to maintaining abstinence. West (2008) also acknowledged that family support and support groups in conjunction with employment helped an individual continue with sobriety successfully. An individual who is involved with competitive employment has an increased sense of self-worth, which helps him or her in developing clean and sober relationships. Other positive benefits include gaining independence, an increase in self-esteem and self-confidence, and community connection (Webster, Dickson, Stanton-Tindall, & Leukfeld, 2015; West, 2008).

Counselors recognize that vocational issues may be in the forefront of the substance-abusing individual's mind, and if the vocational issues are not addressed, those individuals are more likely to discontinue treatment. Most treatment agencies, however, address vocational issues on a limited basis, if at all (West, 2008).

In West's study (2008), mail surveys were collected throughout the United States. She concluded that 73% of the treatment agencies did not conduct vocational assessments for the individuals in treatment and did not provide vocational counseling as a standard practice. The success of maintaining recovery relies heavily on the substance user's ability to work and to fill the day with positive activities; therefore, working becomes beneficial to recovery.

There are barriers that need to be addressed and coping skills put into place to decrease the possibility of disappointment, which could lower self-confidence and decrease the motivation to find employment or training. Some of these barriers include lack of education, lack of training, prejudice from potential employers, physical or mental health issues resulting from substance use, and finally the fear of losing social service benefits or Social Security benefits (Melvin et al., 2012).

SUD individuals may say that their skill level and educational level are limited and because of that and possible legal issues, their career development is compromised. The counselor may able to provide direction and encouragement by referring the individual to local vocational services such as a Diagnostic Vocational Evaluator, who is a specialist located at a local private or state vocational rehabilitation agency. The specialist will provide the individual with a Diagnostic Vocational Evaluation (DVE) to assess his or her interests, skills, and academic ability for approximately 3 to 5 days. The assessment will include comprehensive learning/academic assessments to gauge the academic level, a situational work assessment, and career exploration from the results (Zarrin, Baghban, & Abedi, 2011). Once all of the information has been collected, a vocational goal is created, and the therapist can continue individual therapy combining the treatment issues and the vocational plan. Some treatment issues that are already being addressed include relapse as well as coping skills. For example, at this point in treatment, the user may discuss how working in a specific environment triggers relapse emotions. Coping skills will be needed to avoid such traps. If the combination of substance use and vocational rehabilitation is discussed early during individual treatment, the individual has a good chance of success with work and will continue with recovery with fewer limitations.

In addition to filling his or her day with employment, the client will also need to identify another means of developing a clean and sober social network. Family and friends who have not been associated with the use need to be encouraged to participate with the recovering individual. Another excellent way to do this is to become involved in a group for recovery. Such groups are Alcoholics Anonymous, Narcotics Anonymous, Cocaine Anonymous, and other self-help groups. These groups are discussed in detail in Chapter 10.

Harm Reduction

Harm reduction has been used in the substance use field since the 1920s. Its success has been mostly with the opiate intravenous user and the human immunodeficiency virus (HIV) population in association with syringe exchange programs in the United States, Canada, Great Britain, Australia, New Zealand, Switzerland, Spain, France, and Germany (Des Jarlais, McKnight, Goldblatt, & Purchase, 2009). Most recently, harm reduction has been associated with other substances such as marijuana and cocaine (Hathaway, Callaghan, Macdonald, & Erickson, 2009). Harm reduction includes education about the drug of choice, along with counseling to encourage a decision in favor of abstaining or reducing harm. Some therapies that work well were mentioned earlier, such as motivational interviewing and cognitive–behavioral therapy. Harm reduction is not limited to substances; it also includes any activity that can cause harm to an individual, such as unsafe sexual contact, HIV, and gambling, as well as other behaviors that may result in public health risks (Marlatt, 1998). Harm reduction offers an alternative during individual therapy for individuals with a substance use disorder who are not ready to separate from their drug of choice, to reduce their risky behaviors.

An organization that specializes in this approach is the Harm Reduction Coalition (HRC), a national advocacy and capacity-building organization that promotes the health and dignity of individuals and communities affected by drug use. HRC advances policies and programs that help people address the adverse effects of drug use, including overdose, HIV, hepatitis C, SUD, and incarceration. The mission of the HRC states, "We recognize that the structures of social inequality impact the lives and options of affected communities differently, and work to uphold every individual's right to health and well-being, as well as in their competence to protect themselves, their loved ones, and their communities" (harmreduction.org/section.php?id=63). The HRC posts the Principles of Harm Reduction:

> Harm reduction is a set of practical strategies that reduce negative consequences of drug use, incorporating a spectrum of strategies from safer use, to managed use to abstinence. Harm reduction strategies meet drug users "where they're at," addressing conditions of use along with the use itself.
>
> (harmreduction.org/about-us/principles-of-harm-reduction/)

The overall goal of harm reduction programs is also to help the individual faced with harmful events to identify coping strategies and reduce risky behaviors. In order for these principles to be effective, the therapist must be a strong supporter of harm reduction and must develop a therapeutic alliance with the substance user that is nonjudgmental. The next section discusses the therapeutic relationship and harm reduction.

Harm Reduction from the Therapist's Perspective

The harm reduction model favors the individual making positive changes in his or her life. The individual who uses substances can make positive changes with the assistance of the therapist and the possible therapeutic interventions chosen. The therapeutic relationship is vital to move the client toward positive changes using the harm reduction model. According to Marlatt (1998), motivational interviewing, solution-focused counseling, and cognitive–behavioral therapy are compatible with the harm reduction model. Motivational interviewing has an impact because its main goal is to motivate the person toward change. Cognitive–behavioral therapy is helpful because it processes the individual's behavior in an attempt to change harmful thinking patterns. Finally, solution-focused counseling is useful because its purpose is to focus on a problem and to create attainable solutions and goals. Solution-focused counseling is also beneficial because some of the individuals involved with a harm reduction program may not be involved in individual therapy, but will seek recommendations from harm reduction staff while using their services.

Within the therapy session, goal setting is part of the relationship. One of the principles of harm reduction is to "meet the client where he or she is at." Setting long-range goals not only defeats the purpose of reducing harm, but discourages the individual. A more effective procedure is setting proximal goals. Seminal work conducted by Bandura and Schunk (1981) found that short-term goals were effective in self-motivating users toward long-term goals. Therefore, in a harm reduction model, proximal goals (short-term goals) may be developed with the individual during the therapy session or during a brief encounter based on the individual's stage of change or motivation.

Now that we have the salient information related to individual therapy, the next section is a case study using motivational interviewing, EMDR, coping skills, harm reduction, vocational skills, and pharmacotherapy. Imagine that you are a substance use counselor, and you have Jodi for a client.

APPLY MOTIVATIONAL INTERVIEWING

As mentioned at the beginning of the chapter, motivational interviewing is a counseling technique that can be used to motivate an individual toward a positive lifestyle change. This includes positive regard and language from the counselor addressed to the substance-using individual in the session. The result of this positive regard is "change talk." After the initial assessment, you as Jodi's counselor are aware of her desire to be abstinent; however, you also acknowledge her resistance. As you counsel Jodi and give her the opportunity to discuss her substance problem, she reveals to you her fear of change and the uncertainty of the outcome as well as all the benefits of abstinence. As her counselor, you give positive regard by commending the strides that Jodi is currently making by attending sessions and recognizing her current difficulties, but you also encourage her to continue with treatment and self-help groups. You and Jodi have made a treatment plan to abstain from heroin that is visited each session. Imagine that you are on your fourth session with Jodi and she is still clean and sober. You acknowledge that this is a milestone and continue with encouragement and positive regard. Jodi is now beginning "change talk," because at this point she is recognizing her commitment and plan to change by self-initiation and expressing optimism toward recovery. During the sessions, you and Jodi are both able to witness the "change talk" and the commitment to change. This commitment will allow Jodi to begin recovery and to maximize her sessions toward reaching her long-term goal of abstinence and obtaining custody of her daughter.

APPLYING EMDR

Jodi has been through trauma because of a rape, and her home life has not been conducive to her recovery. The trauma that she has experienced in her past can cause her to continue to live in the past and continue to use the substance. The EMDR treatment will use all eight phases as discussed earlier in this chapter. You will know that the treatment is working when Jodi is able to discuss the rape and the loss of the relationship with her father without bodily sensations that may cause cravings as well as triggers to use heroin. You include imagery as well as mindfulness as coping mechanisms to continue with treatment and reach Jodi's proximal goals.

COPING SKILLS

You plan to incorporate some coping mechanisms to improve Jodi's end-of-treatment results. Some strategies include Jodi journaling her thoughts when she is missing her substance-using friends and when she is having difficulty balancing motherhood with adapting to the community. Some other plans for coping could be meditating and implementing lifestyle changes to avoid relapse. One such change would be for Jodi to seek medical attention for the abscess. This will increase her chances for successful treatment without pain and discomfort, which is the number one reason a substance user will relapse. Another lifestyle change to cope with treatment is to be involved with other individuals who are attempting to cope with life's stressors without the use of heroin or other substances.

VOCATIONAL READINESS

Jodi will be administered the Self-Direct Search vocational assessment to identify the careers that would be appropriate with her equivalency high school diploma and some of the Certified Nurse Assistant coursework that she started. You have advised Jodi to obtain employment or training that will be a low-stress environment conducive to continued successful treatment.

APPLYING HARM REDUCTION

Because Jodi is attempting treatment, and as her counselor you are aware of her attachment issues to heroin and her inability to recover successfully in the past, it is important to include the harm reduction model. You will give her information regarding addiction issues in families and the long-term effects, which will be directly related to her daughter, Natalie. You will also provide Jodi with educational information regarding heroin and its long-term physical and psychological effects. Jodi will also be given information on syringe exchange programs in her area, along with information on sexually transmitted infections because of past prostitution behaviors.

APPLYING SUBOXONE TREATMENT/SELF-HELP GROUP

Jodi had attempted suboxone treatment in the past; however, she was not successful. Now that she has committed herself to obtaining custody of her daughter and will use individual counseling to reach her goal, suboxone treatment can be considered. As discussed earlier, an individual may be recommended for suboxone treatment when there is a commitment to treatment and it is used to minimize the craving for using opiates. This form of treatment, because it reduces cravings, also helps the individual to concentrate on treatment goals during the individual sessions. Jodi states that she is motivated, and as a result she will be referred to a local physician who administers and monitors the medication in the office setting. As mentioned earlier in the chapter, the administration of medication and individual counseling is successful if a self-help model is available to support the substance user in recovery. Therefore, you recommend that Jodi attend a Narcotics Anonymous meeting at least once a week to provide added support while she is making new lifestyle changes.

CASE DISCUSSIONS

Case 2: Juanita and Jose
Possible Treatment Planning

Because Jose and Juanita have not been able to stay sober for the past 14 days, it is imperative to introduce them to the benefits of pharmacotherapy with regard to relapse prevention. The two admit that once they return to drinking, they continue until they are intoxicated. At this point, it would be appropriate to discuss disulfiram and educate them about the adverse effects if they decide to drink while taking the medication. The discussion would continue with Juanita that disulfiram can be safely administered to individuals addicted to cocaine as well as alcohol.

Case 3: Leigh
Possible Treatment Planning

While working with Leigh in recovery planning, a harm reduction model would apply for her protection during multiple sexual encounters at various parties. Leigh does not recognize that being with multiple partners is inflicting self-harm as well as exposing her to sexually transmitted diseases and HIV, which constitute both a long-term and a short-term problem. Therefore, harm reduction education is salient to her safety and well-being. Leigh would be given the option of female and male protection as well as instructions on proper use.

Conclusion

Individual therapy consists of creating an environment where lifestyle changes can begin. The beginning is the therapeutic relationship with the counselor and the substance user. This therapeutic relationship is a partnership in which moving toward lifestyle changes can begin without the use of the individual's drug of choice. Treatment goals are created in session with collaboration of the individual and the counselor, gradually moving toward change to effectively begin recovery. This must begin with the individual making a commitment to abstinence or reduction of use. The client must be aware of attachment as well as grief and loss issues to eventually develop coping skills without the substance to provide security. Once the individual is ready to commit to change regardless of the counseling theory chosen by the counselor, they will gain self-efficacy toward maintaining abstinence. Along with the confidence gained during the individual sessions, in combination with the augmentations of social skills and relationship training and vocational assistance, the individual will acknowledge their self-worth and move toward self-actualization in recovery.

MyCounselingLab for Addictions/Substance Use

Try the Topic 6 Assignments: *Individual Treatment*.

Case Study: Jodi

Jodi is a 22-year-old Hispanic female who has been addicted to heroin for five years. While on a binge three years ago, Jodi was raped and became pregnant. She gave birth to her daughter Natalie three months prematurely. Natalie is 2 and is currently involved in the foster care system because she was born addicted to heroin and there were no family members available to care for her. She lives with a foster family that has four other children. Jodi is able to visit her daughter weekly; however, for the past year she has visited only three times because she has been in active addiction.

Jodi uses heroin five to six times per day intravenously. She has attempted recovery twice. Jodi attempted an outpatient detoxification program but did not complete the treatment. Jodi then decided to try an inpatient detoxification program, but she left treatment on the second day. Next, she began suboxone treatment but discontinued after one month. Jodi then returned to using heroin and has been actively using for the past nine months. She is currently using heroin daily, is working as a prostitute to supply her habit, and is homeless. Jodi has not been honest with her counselors about where she sleeps at night.

Jodi has no contact with her parents. She states that her mother is currently in active addiction using crack cocaine and can't take care of Jodi's 15-year-old sister and 13-year-old brother. Jodi states that her father lives in another town but has had some problems with addiction in his past and is clean and sober now. She states that he went to a halfway house and has never returned to their hometown and has not corresponded with her since she was 15. Jodi states that she was so sad that her father would not contact her that she began smoking marijuana daily at the age of 15 and then began using alcohol at age 17. She reports that she graduated to heroin at the age of 17 with a friend out of curiosity and became dependent very quickly.

Jodi received her GED at age 20 and had started a Certified Nurse Assistant training program at her local educational opportunity center, but did not finish because of substance use. She explained that she had time and attendance issues because of experiencing withdrawal.

Jodi has been arrested for prostitution in the past. She is not on parole or probation and has never been involved with drug court, but states that she fears the legal system.

Jodi says that she feels depressed all of the time because she misses her daughter and her siblings. When she is not using heroin, she misses the drug as well as her friends.

Jodi says that recently she attempted suicide by taking pills she purchased from a friend. Jodi states that her friends called the ambulance and she was taken to the hospital. She is very angry with her friends for saving her life. She does not foresee recovery in her future and feels that she cannot make changes fast enough to obtain custody of her daughter and assist her siblings.

Jodi had been diagnosed with posttraumatic stress disorder (PTSD) because of being raped three years ago. Jodi has never been officially treated for the PTSD in a group setting or individually.

Jodi has had past employment as a waitress and a telemarketer. She reports that she does not keep a job for a long period of time because of the substance use. Her long-term goal is to be employed as a certified nurse assistant.

Jodi has not seen a physician for a physical since she was in an inpatient facility. At the time of her medical examination she was underweight and had irregular menses. Jodi has been treated in the past month at the emergency room for an abscess on her left forearm. The abscess was packed and an antibiotic was prescribed. Jodi stated that she did not take the full prescription and has noticed some redness and swelling.

Jodi's support system consists of her friends who are actively using. She has not attended a Narcotics Anonymous group since she was at the inpatient detoxification facility for two days.

Jodi has been referred to counseling from the Department of Family and Youth Services because her daughter is in foster care and she has agreed to attend counseling sessions biweekly.

Jodi states that she would like to begin a relationship with her daughter, and to develop better coping strategies when dealing with negative emotions.

CHAPTER 8

Group Counseling for Substance Use Disorders

Melanie M. Iarussi, Ph.D., LPC

G roup counseling is one of the most common treatment modalities for individuals recovering from substance use disorders, as it is both clinically effective and cost effective (Brook, 2015). In 2013, 95% of treatment programs for substance use disorders reported offering group counseling as part of treatment. The majority of clients who enter treatment will engage in group counseling (Substance Abuse and Mental Health Services Administration [SAMHSA], 2014). Group counseling is conducted across the levels of care, including inpatient, residential, partial hospitalization, intensive outpatient, and outpatient treatment settings. Such groups are led by a professionally trained leader who applies specific knowledge and skills to facilitate the group members learning from each other and progressing toward mutual goals specific to substance use (Schimmel & Jacobs, 2015).

Group counseling typically comprises individuals who are biologically unrelated to each other. However, family group counseling can also be a valuable component to treatment in which several families make up the group (see Chapter 9 for full description of family counseling). In group counseling, members experience mutual support and understanding with others who also have substance-related issues, and they create the environment of trust necessary to members to share and explore their concerns (Corey, 2016). In addition to giving and receiving social support, group counseling can provide opportunities for clients to learn information about substance use and addiction, as well as social and coping skills needed to reduce risk of relapse. Group members can acquire new information and change thoughts and behaviors through observational and vicarious learning.

In courses and books specific to group counseling, students learn about the therapeutic factors in group work, characteristics and skills of effective group leaders, and the stages of group development (for full descriptions related to general group counseling, see Corey, 2016; Yalom & Leszcz, 2005). In this chapter, we explore how each of these components applies specifically to group counseling for the treatment of substance use disorders, starting with a description of the different types of groups and how the therapeutic factors pertain to substance use groups. Next, the importance of matching clients with appropriate group counseling is discussed, followed by a description of effective group leaders. The stages of group development are then described, including specific considerations for groups that focus primarily on substance use. This chapter provides a description of three evidence-based practices applied to group counseling, and finally, the efficacy of group counseling for substance use disorders is presented. This information is followed by case studies.

TYPES OF GROUPS

Group counseling for substance use disorders can be *open or closed*, with open groups having ongoing admissions and terminations and closed groups having all members beginning and terminating at the same time. Two basic types of group formats are common: psychoeducational and counseling/psychotherapy groups, both of which are led by a professionally trained helper. Psychoeducational groups are typically brief and can be offered to a larger group compared to counseling or psychotherapy groups. The group format is efficient in that a single leader can transfer information to a number of clients simultaneously, which is ultimately cost effective. These groups emphasize didactic instruction and use planned, structured activities to achieve the group's goals, which are typically defined by the group leader (Brown, 2011). The lecture offers information that is expected to be useful to all members in attendance, on topics such as the prevention of substance use issues or relapse prevention. Other examples include groups focused on the psychological and physiological effects of substance use and addiction, information about standard drinks, patterns of substance use, the impact of substance use on interpersonal and occupational functioning, and education about the recovery process and resources.

The terms "counseling" and "psychotherapy" are commonly used interchangeably, as both formats use specific interventions to address personal and interpersonal problems; however, distinctions can be made in that counseling groups have a specific focus with preventative as well as remedial objectives, whereas psychotherapy groups focus on chronic issues and restructuring personality (Corey, 2016). For the purpose of this chapter, I use the term "group counseling." In group counseling, the leader is trained in a specific method of counseling, such as cognitive behavior therapy, motivational interviewing, or Twelve Step facilitation (a description of these specific methods employed in group counseling is provided later in this chapter). Group members have opportunities to interact, and group process is an important factor in the effectiveness of the group. Common goals of counseling groups include establishing and maintaining abstinence, learning and improving coping skills, identifying and managing emotions, and developing healthy relationships.

There is a common misperception that mutual-help groups such as Alcoholics Anonymous, Narcotics Anonymous, or Al-Anon are counseling groups. Although many treatment providers in the United States encourage 12-step programming as an adjunct to treatment and/or incorporate 12-step work in group counseling (i.e., Twelve-Step Facilitation), there is a clear distinction between the mutual help offered by 12-step meetings and the professional interventions and methods provided in group counseling. In mutual-help groups, leadership is shared among group members. Mutual-help group members relate to one another based on shared concerns and characteristics associated with substance use disorders, and they strive to remain abstinent and move toward states of serenity and well-being through spiritual disciplines and participation in mutual help meetings. In this chapter, we focus on the components of counseling groups, which are led by a professionally trained leader who uses specific methods to help members pursue their goals.

THERAPEUTIC FACTORS IN GROUP COUNSELING FOR SUBSTANCE USE DISORDERS

Groups counseling is unique in that it offers therapeutic factors not available in other treatment modalities. The group itself is the agent of change, which is particularly important in the treatment of substance use disorders, as the majority of group members enter treatment feeling isolated and experience chronic issues with relationships (Roth, 2004). Yalom and Leszcz (2005) outlined the therapeutic factors, or specific human experiences, that account for the effectiveness of group counseling. Here, they are described as they pertain to group counseling for substance use disorders:

- *Instillation of hope:* Group members often present for treatment feeling hopeless. They commonly have a trail of wreckage in their lives as a result of the substance use disorder, and they have difficulty understanding a life without substance use. The road to recovery is a difficult journey, and having hope for a positive future can be unfathomable. Contact with group members who have made healthy changes in their lives instills hope in clients that they can make changes as well. The group leader can further instill hope by believing in and treating each client as though he or she is capable of making positive changes and helping to build client self-efficacy.

- *Universality:* Group members often feel relieved after coming into contact with other members who experience similar issues with substance use and with life. Universality can counteract the feelings of isolation and loneliness that are commonly associated with severe substance use disorders. By coming together to discuss experiences and grow, group members learn firsthand that they are indeed not alone, and that others have been affected by substance use in similar ways.

- *Imparting information:* Educational information and direct advice provided among members are common components of groups for substance use disorders. Educational information is often provided about effects of substances, recovery, coping skills, and so on. It is common for clients with substance use issues to be skeptical of information imparted by "experts" or a person holding a position of authority (i.e., the group leader). Therefore, clients with substance use concerns may be more inclined to receive information when it is imparted by their peers, and they are more likely to successfully confront each other's deceptions to be able to move toward growth (Milgram & Rubin, 1992).

- *Altruism:* Clients with severe substance use disorders often perceive themselves as having nothing positive to offer others or as being a burden in others' lives. When group members recognize that they can be helpful to others, it provides them with an alternative perspective that they can have a positive impact on another member's life, and in turn the group members gain greater self-esteem (Center for Substance Abuse Treatment [CSAT], 2005).

- *Corrective recapitulation of the primary family group:* When the group members mimic a family, similar dynamics occur. This phenomenon presents opportunities for members to become aware of, relive, and correct conflicts experienced in the past with their primary family groups, especially related to substance use patterns and issues. Yalom and Leszcz (2005) emphasized the importance of correcting, not just reliving, experiences while engaged in group work, as it can be harmful to relive an experience in the group without a correction. Thus, it is important for the group leader to be aware of therapeutic process and foster corrective experiences for group members.

- *Development of socializing techniques:* People often use substances in social situations to manage perceived deficits in this area. Hence, many group members will lack basic social skills and confidence in social situations. In group counseling these skills can be developed formally, such as when communication skills are the content of the group session, as well as informally, such as when group members learn to communicate and interact socially with one another even when such skills are not the topic of the group.

- *Imitative behavior:* Group members commonly mimic the behaviors of the group leader and of other (typically senior) group members. As such, the group leader can model appropriate communication skills and offer support and understanding to group members to help members develop these skills as well as to help create the culture of the group. Further, group members' self-efficacy related to their recoveries can be increased by witnessing the vicarious experiences of other members being successful in recovery. Bandura (1994) noted that when individuals witness others who are similar to them put forth effort and succeed, their beliefs that they too are capable of such behaviors and success increase.

- *Interpersonal learning:* Weegmann (2004) emphasized that addiction is a "lonely business" (p. 36) in which the afflicted individuals have a difficult time developing and maintaining healthy relationships. Ideally, group members become aware of and take responsibility for their interpersonal tendencies, and then make changes inside and outside of the group to form healthy relationships.

- *Group cohesiveness:* Groups with strong cohesion "feel warmth and comfort in the group and a sense of belongingness; they value the group and feel in turn that they are valued, accepted, and supported by the other members" (Yalom & Leszcz, 2005, p. 55). The relationships between group members are essential to foster healing and recovery, especially among persons with substance use disorders who have struggled with feeling worthy and accepted in their interpersonal relationships. Khantzian, Golden-Schulman, and McAuliffe (2004) noted that although it is natural for group cohesion to initially develop surrounding the common experience of being "an addict," it is important for this cohesion to mature to other common experiences in order for group members to begin to associate with the "human mainstream." They state that sharing ordinary life events that are not related to addiction can offer group members a channel into the ordinary world.

- *Catharsis: Emotional* expression is linked with the ability to cope, and thus group members begin to develop alternative coping strategies in group counseling (i.e., talking about emotions as opposed to avoiding them with substance use). Catharsis permits group members to share their experiences of shame and guilt in a safe, accepting environment.

- *Existential factors:* The presence of a substance use disorder can be perceived as an unjust circumstance. After all, very, very rarely does an individual intend to become reliant on a substance. However, now that the substance use disorder is present, group members are in the position to take responsibility for how they are living their lives under the given circumstances.

Yalom and Leszcz (2005) identified clients' perceptions of the most helpful curative factors in group psychotherapy by conducting Q-sort research with successful group members. The four highest-ranked factors in descending order were interpersonal input, catharsis, *cohesiveness*, and interpersonal learning. The therapeutic factors individually and cumulatively foster the development of a group climate in which meaningful choices and changes arise. These factors arise in groups emphasizing warmth, empathy, and support (Johnson, Burlingame, Olsen, Davies, & Gleave, 2005). The working alliance and self-esteem building possible in cohesive group process contributes to collective well-being and creates a climate for growth and change (Marmarosh, Holtz, & Schottenbauer, 2005).

MATCHING CLIENTS TO APPROPRIATE GROUP COUNSELING

In addition to the presence of the therapeutic factors, group counseling for substance use disorders is most effective when group members are provided treatment that matches their readiness to change and includes culturally appropriate interventions. Attrition is a fundamental concern in that members who terminate prematurely, similar to those who do not engage fully in the treatment process (e.g., those who "go through the motions" but do not engage in treatment sincerely), are unlikely to receive benefits or make meaningful changes. Motivation or readiness for treatment can impact attrition and the benefits clients experience from group counseling. Mandated treatment and involuntary clients raise special concerns regarding matching clients with appropriate group counseling interventions. In this section, we explore matching clients according to their readiness to change, as well as providing culturally appropriate interventions.

Matching Readiness to Change

Given the ongoing criminalization of persons with substance use disorders, the justice system continues to produce a large number of mandated clients who seek treatment for substance use. For example, persons who receive consequences for driving under the influence (DUI) of alcohol intoxication may be required to attend psychoeducational and motivational enhancement groups specific to DUI offenses (Miller, Curtis, Sønderlund, Day, & Droste, 2015), and physicians who have substance-related disorders are often required by physician health programs or their regulatory boards to participate in various forms of mandated treatment as a requirement for ongoing licensure (DuPont, McLellan, Carr, Gendel, & Skipper, 2009). As a result of these systems, it is very common for group members to lack readiness for behavior change when entering treatment.

Before any type of treatment plan can be implemented, the client's readiness for change must be taken into consideration. The stages of change model (Prochaska, DiClemente, & Norcross, 1992) has long been applied to the treatment of substance use disorders (described in further detail in Chapter 10). The five stages include precontemplation, contemplation, preparation, action, and maintenance, and the following change processes explain how shifts in readiness occur: consciousness raising, self-reevaluation, self-liberation, counterconditioning, stimulus control, reinforcement management, helping relationship, dramatic relief, environmental reevaluation, and social liberation (see Prochaska et al., 1992). Tailoring treatment to clients' stages of change is essential to enhance the effectiveness of group counseling, especially given the various degree of readiness to change with which clients present to substance use treatment. For example, treatment providers can expect about 40% of clients to enter treatment in the precontemplation stage, 40% in contemplation, and 20% in preparation or action (Norcross, Krebs, & Prochaska, 2011). Norcross et al. (2011) describe the stages as "a period of time as well as a set of tasks needed for movement to the next stage" (p. 143). The CSAT (2005) described ways in which group leaders can attend to the specific needs of group members in the early, middle, and late stages of treatment, and the authors emphasized that as clients progress through the stages of change and mature in their recoveries, treatment must evolve with them, which requires the group leader to adjust his or her methods. Velasquez, Crouch, Stephens, and DiClemente (2016) developed the stages of change manual for group treatment of substance use disorders with the purpose of tailoring treatment to clients' readiness to change and assisting them in moving through the stages to alter their substance use behaviors.

Velasquez and colleagues (2016) begin their treatment model with 17 group sessions designed to increase motivation for change for clients who present to group as precontemplative, contemplative, or in preparation. In the early stages of treatment, clients are typically ambivalent about stopping substance use, and they might experience cognitive impairment and difficulty problem solving as a result of substance use (CSAT, 2005). Further, they are often mandated to treatment by some outside entity (e.g., correctional system, family member, employer) and experience intense emotions such as guilt, shame, and anger. Initially, the group leader strives to decrease the level of resistance and denial among group members. Most treatments for substance use disorders recommend the use of motivational interviewing (MI) (Miller & Rollnick, 2013) to decrease resistance and enhance clients' motivation for treatment and for change. The application of MI to group counseling is discussed in greater detail later in this chapter. In the 2016 model proposed by Velasquez et al., interventions such as assessment, psychoeducation, values clarification, decisional balance, evaluations of one's environment (i.e., relationships, roles), functional analysis, problem solving, and goal setting are implemented in the MI style in order to assist with the change processes of conscious raising, self and environmental reevaluations, social liberation, building self-efficacy, and making a commitment to change (Velasquez et al., 2016). The group leader seeks to engage members and create an accepting and empathic environment in which members can acknowledge the harm caused by their substance use and the conflict between using and their goals and desires (CSAT, 2005), which can help members move through the stages of change.

Norcross et al. (2011) encouraged treatment providers to "treat precontemplators gingerly" (p. 151) because of the reality that if the counselor attempts to push these clients into action prematurely, they are more likely to terminate or further resist treatment. They also recommended that the counselor and client set realistic goals, including perceiving a client moving from precontemplation to contemplation as evidence of progress. Witkiewitz, Hartzler, and Donovan (2010) found empirical support for matching clients who presented with lower levels of motivation with motivational interventions. Some group treatments for substance use disorders rely heavily on confrontation. However, overly directive and confrontational approaches have been linked to poorer outcomes in substance abuse counseling (Karno & Longabaugh, 2005; Miller, Benefield, & Tonigan, 1993), and their use in group work for substance use disorders has been cautioned against (Matano & Yalom, 1991). Brook (2015) suggested the use of "supportive confrontation," in which the leader creates empathic "holding" in the group, characterized by understanding and acceptance, as a member explores difficult emotions or dysfunctional behaviors (p. 465). Further, the leader might avoid using confrontation, but facilitate group members' confrontation of one another, as they are more likely to receive this information from their peers as opposed to an authority figure (e.g., Morgan, Romani, & Gross, 2014).

When clients are ready for action, they have made a commitment to change their behaviors, and they may have taken small steps in the preparation stage. The interventions employed when clients are in action are often cognitive–behavioral in nature and focus on change processes such as building self-efficacy, self-liberation, stimulus control, counterconditioning, reinforcement management, and helping relationships (Velasquez et al., 2016). Interventions used in group sessions include identifying and avoiding or altering triggers for substance use, learning and practicing healthy relaxation techniques, using positive reinforcement for successes in recovery, developing social skills including practicing through role play, cognitive restructuring, enhancing social support, and relapse prevention planning. In the maintenance stage of change, social liberation is emphasized as well as helping clients understand how to manage a relapse, should one occur. It is not uncommon for clients to recycle through the changes of change, and many clients will experience relapse. Therefore, continuous assessment of clients' readiness to change and meeting them with appropriate interventions is an ongoing process. Group leaders are encouraged to include relapse prevention content in group sessions and, should relapse occur with a group member, to address the shame and guilt that often accompany relapse. In addition, the member's stage of change should be reassessed upon returning to treatment, as it is common for clients to recycle through the stages after relapse (Connors, DiClemente, Velasquez, & Donovan, 2013).

Matching Culturally Relevant Treatment

A major contributing factor to attrition may be failure to attend to the specific needs of diverse clients. For example, Guerrero et al. (2013) found that women who were African American and Latina completed substance use treatment at significantly lesser rates, compared to women who were White. When looking at treatment for both genders, Marsh, Cao, Guerrero, and Shin (2009) found that clients who were White were more commonly matched to appropriate treatment compared to African American and Latino clients, who were more likely to have limited social and financial resources and receive fewer and lower quality substance use treatment services. As match with appropriate interventions has an important impact on client outcomes, treatment should be tailored to meet the specific needs of various cultural, racial, and ethnic groups.

Providing culturally relevant interventions promotes maximum client outcomes from group counseling for substance use. For example, women tend to have greater success and treatment retention when participating in women-only groups compared to mixed-gender groups (Cummings, Gallop, & Greenfield, 2010; Stevens, Arbiter, & Glider, 1989), and resources are available for treatment providers to tailor treatment for substance use disorders to the specific needs of women (CSAT, 2009b). Further, LGBT individuals often benefit from an LGBT-affirming group, and such resources are also readily available for clinicians' use (CSAT, 2009a). Veterans are another specific cultural group who often benefit from homogenous counseling groups. Veterans often relate better to other veterans compared to civilians who have not had similar experiences, allowing for therapeutic factors such as cohesion and universality to be enhanced in veterans-only groups. However, according to SAMHSA's 2013 National Survey of Substance Abuse Treatment Services (SAMHSA, 2014), substance use treatment groups specific to veterans were offered by only 13% of substance use group treatment providers, and only 12% of providers offered groups specific to LGBT individuals. Groups for women were the most popular, as 44% of providers reported offering them. Only 12% of providers reported offering groups for older adults. These findings are promising in that gender-specific groups are more commonly offered, and yet other groups for those who would likely benefit from a more homogeneous group, such as veterans, LGBT individuals, and older adults, are sparsely offered.

McNair (2005) offered recommendations for *co-occurring mental health and substance use disorders* in African Americans, which may also apply for other cultural groups. McNair recommended that treatment professionals determine the cultural contexts and meanings associated with substance use. In addition, it would be important to examine the contributions of racism and discrimination in the initiation of substance use and development of a substance use disorder. Prejudice and discrimination can present barriers to accessing effective treatment as well as triggers for relapse. African Americans and members of other minority groups may have comorbid health concerns that demand concurrent attention. Group interventions for substance use disorders should be based on the matching model of treatment specific to the clients' needs, affording opportunities for clients and counselor to explore meanings associated with substance use and recovery.

Generally speaking, if a client is a minority member in a heterogeneous group, the group leader must be sensitive to this and maintain a person-centered approach to foster seeing each client as an individual and as the expert on him- or herself (Miller, Forcehimes, & Zweben, 2011). No group member should be in the position of having to be the spokesperson for their greater racial or cultural group. Yalom and Leszcz (2005) cautioned that group members who are of a cultural minority might feel excluded, limiting the therapeutic factor of universality. To mitigate this possibility, group leaders are encouraged to acknowledge cultural differences, but then move past the differences to the common human—or transcultural—experiences. Group leaders must strive for multicultural competence when leading any group, as every group experience will be multicultural.

THE GROUP LEADER

Leaders of group counseling for substance use must possess competence in group work as well as treatment for substance use disorders. Licenses and other credentials are available to demonstrate sufficient preparation to offer treatment services for substance use disorders. For example, NAADAC offers various national certifications (www.naadac.org/ncc-ap) and state boards offer state certifications and licenses. Training in group work typically includes educational and supervised experience in selecting members, facilitating groups, and evaluating progress. The American Group Psychotherapy Association (www.agpa.org) and the Association for Specialists in Group Work (www.asgw.org) offer training and educational resources specific to group counseling, and most professional counseling degree programs include courses devoted to group counseling. For instance, the Council for Accreditation of Counseling and Related Educational Programs (2016) standards for accreditation include group work as one of the eight core curricular areas for all types of counseling programs. Further, group leaders should demonstrate multicultural and social justice competencies (Singh, Merchant, Skudrzyk, & Ingene, 2012).

Historically, counselors and other helpers providing treatment identified as being in recovery from substance use disorders themselves. In contemporary treatment, however, professional helpers, including group leaders, do not need to be in recovery to offer effective services. Group leaders should demonstrate the common factors known to enhance any counseling process, including empathy, genuineness, acceptance, active listening skills, and the ability to establish a strong therapeutic alliance (Miller et al., 2011; Yalom & Leszcz, 2005). In general, group leaders should avoid behaviors that would elicit resistance from members, such as blaming, criticizing, labeling, and shaming (Miller et al., 2011). According to Corey (2016), effective group leaders possess the following characteristics: being emotionally present for members; personal power including having confidence in and an awareness of the influence the leader has on members; courage to take risks, be vulnerable, and share power with members; willingness to enhance self-awareness; sincerity and authenticity; a strong sense of identity including awareness of strengths and limitations; belief in group process; inventiveness and creativity; stamina; and commitment to self-care.

There are also basic skills involved in facilitating counseling groups for substance use disorders. CSAT (2005) suggested that group leaders be able to adjust their methods to meet the needs of the group, facilitate communication among group members, and be able to motivate clients with substance use disorders. They must also maintain safety in the group, including ensuring emotional safety of members, managing emotional contagion, and curtailing emotion when it becomes too intense for members. The leader should model appropriate behavior, including acting ethically and resolving ethical dilemmas that arise in group. Group leaders should avoid multiple roles (e.g., attending 12-step meetings with group members) and also avoid rigid roles of members within the group (e.g., one member is the "caretaker" while another is the "comedian"). Group leaders must also be able to terminate group work effectively.

Self-awareness and monitoring are essential tasks of the group leader to ensure that she or he is staying focused on the group and treating group members appropriately and respectfully. Group leaders are especially effective when they model proper behavior, as well as being able to describe it. Group leaders should therefore be self-aware of their characteristics and skills they bring to the group (Corey, 2016). Further, as all groups will be multicultural, group leaders must strive to be multiculturally competent to be able to effectively work with diverse group members and have an awareness of how social oppression and privilege can impact group process (Singh et al., 2012) and how ethnicity and culture can affect substance use and group engagement (CSAT, 2005). Concerning the tasks of the group leader, according to Yalom and Leszcz (2005) the leader is responsible for (a) creating and maintaining the group, (b) building a group culture, and (c) activating and illuminating the here-and-now (p. 118), all of which are described in the stages of the group's development.

STAGES OF GROUP DEVELOPMENT

The stages of group development as described here reflect what is known about the group process in general (Corey, 2016; Yalom & Leszcz, 2005) applied to the specific needs of counseling for clients with substance use disorders. Corey (2016) described the development of counseling groups in terms of early stages and later stages. The early stages consist of attending to issues of forming the group, the initial stage of orientation and exploration, and then a transition stage that includes dealing with reluctance. The later stages comprise a working stage that includes cohesion and productivity and the final stage of consolidation and termination. After termination, the leader attends to evaluation and follow-up.

FORMING THE GROUP   Group leaders must consider several clinical and logistical issues when forming a group to address substance use. Such considerations include the type of group, time and location of group meetings, the goal of the group and its members, the composition of the group, and processes for screening group members. Ideally, group members have the opportunity to attend successive group meetings with the same members in order to develop maximum cohesiveness to provide members with the greatest possible benefit of group work (CSAT, 2005). Group meeting times and places are ideally set to enhance members' abilities to access the group meeting. For example, the leader should avoid establishing a group counseling meeting that might conflict with a popular 12-step group meeting, especially if self-help or mutual help group attendance is a required or encouraged component of the treatment program. Concerning location, groups should meet in an accessible location taking into account various degrees of ability (e.g., accessible for clients who use assistive technology) and means (e.g., accessible by public transportation). Further, social issues should be taken into consideration, such as offering excuses for time off work, providing bus passes or parking validations, and child care considerations. Issues of literacy and potential clients' first language should be taken into consideration when developing print materials to advertise the group (e.g., providing materials about group services in Spanish in a community that is majority Latino).

In treatment for substance use disorders, abstinence is often a prescribed goal either by virtue of the treatment program or by the referral source (e.g., probation or parole, a drug-free workplace employer, etc.). Although not fully embraced by many treatment providers, harm reduction, or continued use in a non-harmful way, can also be identified as a treatment goal (Faragher & Soberay, 2014). The goal of the group, whether it is abstinence or harm reduction, should be made clear to potential group members before they join. In terms of goals and group compositions, the group leader decides whether or not all members must have the same goal upon entering the group or if goals can vary. If goals can vary, it is important to consider how one member who has a harm reduction goal and who is continuing to use might influence another member who is pursuing abstinence. As discussed previously in this chapter, some treatment protocols assign clients to counseling groups based on their readiness to change, and therefore, members are more likely to have compatible goals. As for the duration of the group, some groups may be ongoing whereas others have a fixed number of sessions. Research has shown better client outcomes as a result of longer duration in group treatment (Brook, 2015). Make-up policies and procedures should be established and implemented whenever a member misses a group session.

Another consideration concerning treatment goals is whether or not goals can extend beyond substance use into broader life issues (Miller et al., 2011). As severe substance use disorders can affect all of life's facets, group members will likely have concerns beyond the substance use itself, such as mental health concerns (e.g., depression, anxiety), relationships issues, or vocational difficulties. The parameters of the group should be described to prospective group members, including a description of what will be included beyond substance use.

The size of a group can vary contingent on the purpose of the group. For example, a psychoeducational group with the primary purpose of imparting information might be a large group. On the other hand, a group that focuses on cognitive–behavioral skills training with the purpose of group members learning and trying out new skills, and then receiving feedback during group sessions, might include no more than 10 members. In addition to the size of the group, the group leader must consider the impact of having a homogenous group versus a heterogeneous group related to specific member characteristics. Differences based on gender, age, race, ethnicity, or culture should be considered. As discussed previously in this chapter, group interventions and treatment should be matched to clients' cultures as much as possible to enhance treatment outcomes.

Once the goals and the group composition are determined, selecting group members is an important task of the group leader. Not every client will be appropriate for group counseling. Individuals who are suicidal, homicidal, or acutely psychotic, who experience antisocial personality disorder, or who deviate from the group are typically not appropriate for group work (Brook, 2015; Yalom & Leszcz, 2005). The leader might also consider another form of treatment if the individual refuses to attend the group or expresses a lack of interest, expresses strong discomfort in groups, has impulse control or anger management problems, is disrespectful of the group rules, has language barriers, or is a young person who may be negatively influenced by other group members (Miller et al., 2011). The leader must also match group members to the appropriate group based on ability to function, maturity, level of motivation to change, and phase of recovery (Brook, 2015). Recommendations for member screening include the group leader meeting with each prospective group member individually to assess for appropriateness for the group (Miller et al., 2011), as well as to observe prospective members in the group setting (Yalom & Leszcz, 2005). Individual meetings with group members can also be used to answer any questions the member might have about the group and to enhance the member's motivation to engage in the group to help prevent premature termination (Brook, 2015; Miller et al., 2011).

INITIAL GROUP STAGES After the group is formed, group orientation and exploration involve the efforts of the group leader to provide necessary information and engage members in the emerging group process. In these stages, the group leader provides the initial structure for the group and helps members focus on goals. In the orientation to the group, whether this occurs with the group as a whole (common in a closed group) or on an individual basis (common in an open group), the details, expectations, and rules of the group should be presented and agreed upon by each member to facilitate a group culture that promotes recovery. A written form can be helpful to clearly provide the rules and expectations of the group and to have a written commitment from group members to abide by these protocols (Margolis & Zweben, 2011). In open groups, how the new member will be introduced and assimilated into the ongoing group should be considered. Miller and colleagues (2011) suggested that existing members share how long they have been part of the group and some of the benefits they have experienced as a result of their attendance. In a closed group, all group members can be oriented together during the first group meeting.

Norms of the group are important to consider when building the culture of the group. Yalom and Leszcz (2005) described norms as "an unwritten code of behavioral rules . . . that will guide the interaction of the group" (p. 120). Yalom and Leszcz encouraged group leaders to establish norms derived from the therapeutic factors of acceptance and support, universality, imparting information, interpersonal learning, altruism, and hope. By doing so, group leaders will foster a group culture that will maximize the group as an agent of change. For example, the group leader might encourage and reinforce members' providing spontaneous support to each other when describing their struggles to remain abstinent. The leader can also model nonjudgmental acceptance and genuine care and concern of members. In another example, the group leader might model a certain skill (e.g., refusal skills, relaxation skills) prior to asking members to try out the skill themselves. In this way, the leader models taking risks without adverse effects (Yalom & Leszcz, 2005). The group leader is responsible for activating the here-and-now in group work (Yalom & Leszcz, 2005). In doing so, the leader reinforces the culture of the group by attending to the group process and fostering group cohesion.

The rules of the group are typically established by the group leader; however, in some cases group members might collaborate on the group rules. The rules affect the culture of the group and should aim to facilitate the goals of the group, including the growth and development of the group members. The group leader reinforces and enforces the rules throughout the group to maintain group structure. Structure is especially important in group counseling for substance use disorders as a result of the lack of structure in the lives of the group members upon entering treatment (Brook, 2015). Further, by setting appropriate limits, the group leader fosters safety within the group setting.

Confidentiality is often included in the rules of group counseling, meaning that members will not discuss the identities of group members or other group members' experiences outside of the group. Compared to individual counseling, confidentiality in group counseling is not as well safeguarded, as group members are not bound to the same confidentiality limits as the professional group leader. However, the NAADAC (2013) ethical code states that "Confidentiality standards are established for each counseling group by involving the addiction professional and the clients in setting confidentiality guidelines," and the American Counseling Association (ACA) ethical code (ACA, 2014) states, "counselors clearly explain the importance and parameters of confidentiality for the specific group" (p. 6). Confidentiality among members should be discussed and agreed upon by each member. This rule is essential for group counseling for substance use disorders to create the safe environment needed to promote trust and group cohesion. Trust issues among members are significant, as substance use is often associated with shame and secrecy. Group members who are mandated to attend group are often particularly concerned with the degree to which they share information and how confidential that information will be kept. Such clients may require additional reassurance regarding rules and norms, especially the practice and limits of confidentiality.

In addition to confidentiality, group rules can include guidelines pertaining to group members' contact with each other outside of the group. Given the nature of substance use disorders, group members' convening outside of the group could possibly lead to intimate or romantic relationships and perpetuating unhealthy relationship patterns, including engaging in substance use. Margolis and Zweben (2011) suggested group leaders emphasize the norm of the group to provide support in recovery and invite group members to consider and discuss the possible risks of engaging with group members outside of group counseling sessions.

Another common group rule pertains to group participation and intoxication. Most treatment groups for substance use disorders prohibit clients from participating in group when they are under the influence of a substance. This is under the premise that individuals who are intoxicated will not benefit from the group and can cause possible harm to other group members. Group members will likely benefit from an open discussion about such situations (Margolis & Zweben, 2011).

TRANSITIONAL STAGE Following orientation and exploration, the transitional stage of group development addresses reluctance to change, expression of emotion, emergence of conflicts among members, and ambivalence or perceived lack of commitment. Addressing denial is a common issue in groups for substance use disorders (CSAT, 2005). Facilitating group members' confrontation of one another's denial can be a powerful component of the transitional stage. As noted by Milgram and Rubin (1992), confrontation from members as opposed to the leader is likely to be better received by members because of the negative reactions people with substance use disorders often have to persons of authority. Motivational interviewing is commonly used to reinforce a strong therapeutic alliance and address clients' reluctance to change, and is therefore a natural fit for this stage of a substance use group. There may be a struggle for control of the group process and even a confrontation or challenge of group leadership, especially if the leader is not perceived as having credible personal experience with substance use and treatment (Miller, 2005). The group leader must be self-aware, resilient, well prepared, and focused on group goals in order to navigate through this difficult stage (Corey, 2016).

WORKING STAGE The working stage emerges from the conflicts and difficulties to afford an enhanced sense of cohesiveness. Group members work together in mutually beneficial transactions. They share an identity and invest in one another. A higher degree of cohesion prepares members for meaningful disclosure, existential relatedness, and emotional exploration (Yalom & Leszcz, 2005). Brooks and McHenry (2015) emphasized the importance of facilitating group in the here and now, especially related to emotional exploration. Altruism and interpersonal learning can also be emphasized in this stage (CSAT, 2005). The working stage often consists of skill building in order for members to able to sustain their recoveries within and beyond their engagement in treatment. Pooler, Qualls, Rogers, and Johnston (2014) encouraged leaders to ask members to discuss what they are learning from each other and how they are aiding each other's recoveries, as well as to share their experiences of being in the "flow" of recovery in order to help others develop self-efficacy that they can also achieve this (p. 327). In addition, issues such as shame and loss can be addressed in the working stages, depending on the members' readiness to address these issues (Pooler et al., 2014). The working stage will be time-limited in some groups (e.g., a closed 10-week prevention group for adolescents), and in other groups, it can continue over months in open groups (e.g., an ongoing aftercare group at a halfway house).

FINAL STAGES As the working stage closes, it is important to consolidate learning, transfer gains to natural settings outside the group experience, and prepare for termination. In working toward termination, group members will examine progress, share feedback, and offer near-future goals. Various aspects of the group should be evaluated, and ideally there should be opportunities for follow-up.

When members complete group counseling or terminate by some planned process, it is useful to evaluate the impact of the group, including an assessment of the outcomes and client experiences (Harris, Underhill, & Hill, 2011). For example, Harris, Underhill, and Hill (2011) suggested evaluating members' satisfaction with the group, the effectiveness of specific activities or interventions used in the group, progress made on specific goals (e.g., substance use, self-efficacy in recovery, readiness to change), and the process of the group. Such evaluations can be especially important for passive or minimally involved members, who may need referrals for follow-up care or additional treatment.

Ideally, termination is a process that transpires over several group sessions. As a general rule of thumb, the longer the group is together, the more time they will need to process termination (CSAT, 2005). Termination can be a difficult stage for many clients with substance use disorders because of profound losses they experienced in their lives prior to group counseling (Pooler et al., 2014). Termination has the potential to initiate discomfort among group members and the group leader as it stirs up "good-byes" in their past. Therefore, the group leader must be self-aware to ensure that he or she is not avoiding issues related to termination, and to implement specific methods to bring the group to a healthy conclusion (Miller et al., 2011). Unfortunately, oftentimes termination cannot be predicted in substance use counseling, such as in the case of a client's premature termination or the need to terminate a client from group for rule violation or other issue that might be harmful to the client or the group (e.g., suicidal or homicidal ideation). In some forms of group counseling for substance use disorders (e.g., residential treatment, intensive outpatient programs), members will terminate by "graduating" from an open group. The prospective graduate may apply for discharge, discuss progress and aftercare plans, and receive input from the group. After the completion of group counseling, there may be planned follow-up or booster sessions. Upon completion of a higher level of care (e.g., inpatient, residential, intensive outpatient), group members should be provided information about follow-up or aftercare treatment.

SPECIFIC METHODS FOR GROUP COUNSELING FOR SUBSTANCE USE DISORDERS

In this section, you will read about three empirically supported group counseling methods: Twelve Step Facilitation (TSF), cognitive behavior therapy (CBT), and motivational interviewing (MI). All of these interventions are acknowledged as evidence-based practices for the treatment of substance use disorders in SAMHSA's National Registry of Evidence Based Programs and Practices (http://nrepp.samhsa.gov), and all have demonstrated effectiveness in group counseling.

Twelve Step Facilitation Counseling Groups

In Twelve Step Facilitation (TSF), a professionally trained leader uses a structured, manualized treatment to facilitate clients learning and participating in the 12-step approach (Kingree, 2013). By applying the 12-step conceptions and philosophy, the group leader helps clients pursue two goals: (a) to achieve and maintain abstinence, and (b) to increase participation in 12-step mutual help organizations, such as Alcoholics Anonymous or Narcotics Anonymous. The manual commonly used in TSF originated for Project MATCH, which described 12 individual counseling sessions, including the session topics, the order to be addressed, purpose of the sessions, and suggested activities (Kingree, 2013). TSF emphasizes the first three steps of AA, which are designed to facilitate acceptance and surrender of addiction/alcoholism (Kaskutas, Subbaraman, Witbrodt, & Zemore, 2009). Facilitators of TSF groups must be very familiar with 12-step groups (Kingree, 2013), and even be members of a 12-step group themselves (Kaskutas et al., 2009).

Several adaptations of TSF for group counseling have been empirically investigated. One program, Making Alcoholics Anonymous Easier (MAAEZ), applies TSF in a group format with the specific aims to help group members move past their opposition to 12-step groups, to facilitate group members' interactions with AA members at mutual help group meetings, and to offer an introduction to the 12-step culture (Kaskutas et al., 2009). MAAEZ consists of six 90-minute group counseling sessions delivered weekly. Kaskutas and colleagues (2009) found that outcomes of the MAAEZ included higher rates of abstinence from alcohol and drugs compared to treatment as usual, especially for group members who attended all six of the sessions. MAAEZ was found to be especially helpful for group members who experienced mental health concerns and for those who had been in treatment for substance use disorders prior to this treatment.

STAGE-12 is a manualized program based on TSF for people with stimulant drug use disorder (Donovan et al., 2013). This intervention consists of five 90-minute group counseling sessions plus three individual sessions. Findings of a recent investigation found that clients who participated in STAGE-12 reported greater abstinence from stimulant drugs during treatment, attended more 12-step meetings, and engaged in more recovery-related activities compared to the treatment-as-usual group. However, the findings were mixed in that clients who did not achieve abstinence during treatment reported more stimulant drug use with the STAGE-12 program (Donovan et al., 2013).

Cognitive Behavior Therapy and Skill Building

From a behavioral perspective, problematic substance use can be considered learned behavior under the functional control of contingent consequences. According to these models, substance use emerges initially because intoxication produces euphoria and other powerful, rewarding effects. In addition, substances may be used in excess to reduce anxiety, alleviate depression, or bolster deficient social and coping skills. Over time, tolerance and withdrawal effects increase the likelihood that larger or more frequent doses of mood-altering substances may be required to produce the anticipated positive effects (i.e., positive reinforcement) or avoid aversive consequences (i.e., negative reinforcement). Additionally, substance use disorders are often maintained by dysfunctional cognitions, or errors in thinking. As such, CBT treatment seeks to help clients counter-condition the effects of substances and identify their cognitions, understand how these thoughts affect their emotions and behaviors, gain insight into the dysfunction of the cognitions, and work to alter their belief systems and thought processes (Doweiko, 2015; Velasquez et al., 2016).

In addition to thought restructuring, skill development is common in groups for substance use disorders. Such skills can include relaxation training, assertiveness training, communication skills, refusal skills, problem solving and decision making, job searching, emotional regulation, behavioral self-control, and coping with urges and cravings (CSAT, 2005; Marinchak & Morgan, 2012; Miller et al., 2011). Such training is fitting for the group format as clients benefit from witnessing a range of skills among members and vicariously learning through each other (Miller et al., 2011). The process of skill development typically begins with the group leader describing the skill and how it can be useful, then demonstrating how to execute the skill. By demonstrating the skill, the group leader also models taking risks for the sake of growth and development and cultivates a group culture of embracing vulnerability. Group members then try out the new skill and receive feedback from the group leader and members (Miller et al., 2011). Homework derived from the group session, such as implementing skills learned, is typically assigned toward the end of each group meeting to help members progress toward their goals in between sessions (Wenzel, Liese, Beck, & Friedman-Wheeler, 2012). With these skills in place, group members are better prepared to cope with challenges in healthy and productive ways and avoid substance use. CBT skills training groups are the most empirically "support" type of group in the treatment of substance use disorders (Miller et al., 2011).

Motivational Interviewing

MI can be implemented as a precursor to or integrated into group treatment for substance use disorders. Research on MI in groups has found that this approach can increase clients' perceived autonomy and self-efficacy; enhance their readiness to change, including intentions to change specific behaviors; and increase treatment engagement and retention, including participation in aftercare. MI groups have also been found to increase problem recognition and reduce social isolation and negative group processes (Wagner & Ingersoll, 2013). (See Chapter 7 for more details on MI.)

When MI is used in a group setting, the group leader is non-confrontational and draws on the power of members' intrinsic motivation. As previously discussed, strategies used to enhance motivation are employed in the style of MI, providing an environment grounded in compassion and empathy (Miller & Rollnick, 2013). Group leaders use skills that encourage clients to engage in the group process, such as open questions, reflections and paraphrases, and summarizations (Krejci & Neugebauer, 2015). Krejci and Neugebauer (2015) proposed the following suggestions when using MI in group counseling for substance use disorders:

- Listen carefully rather than talk. Your primary role is to facilitate rather than to teach. Model empathetic listening within the group.
- Focus on process change rather than specifics of issues that arise.
- Focus on the dynamics of group process. Be willing to address in an open-minded and respectful manner negative responses such as conflict, boredom, and anger.
- Within the group always highlight the stength of particpants, affirming effort, strength, courage, honesty, etc.
- Avoid providing quick solutions or making suggestions for quick resolution, and encourage others in the group to also avoid doing so.

The method of MI consists of four overlapping phases: engaging, focusing, evoking, and planning (Miller & Rollnick, 2013). Mitcheson and Grellier (2011) cautioned that using MI in the group setting can be extremely complex, especially as each group member may present with varying levels of motivation that fluctuate within and across group sessions. As such, group leaders can be mindful of these phases to ensure that each group member is involved in treatment. The first phase, *engaging*, involves establishing an effective therapeutic alliance, including diminishing any resistance that might be present in the relationship initially. The leader uses specific skills (e.g., reflective listening, "rolling with resistance," affirmations) to establish effective relationships, even with "difficult" or "resistant" clients. MI is remarkable in that it offers skills to build therapeutic alliances in situations when this relationship might be more challenging to cultivate, such as with mandated clients. The group leader may need to take extra care and time to engage silent members or those who present as disengaged from the group process. In the second phase of

MI, *focusing*, the clients and leader establish a clear direction for their work together. In group counseling, all members should share a common goal. The focusing phase of MI can be useful to emphasize the common goal of members to be sure all members are prioritizing this focus during group sessions. Next, the leader seeks to help members explore and resolve their ambivalence about change and enhance motivation to proceed with change in the *evoking* phase (third phase). In this phase, the group leader evokes *the client's* arguments in favor of change (termed "change talk") and against the status quo and helps guide clients to further develop these arguments based on the client's personal beliefs, values, and goals. In the group setting, members benefit from hearing each other's change talk and capitalize the therapeutic factors of universality and vicarious learning. One of the primary goals of MI is the resolution of ambivalence. One way to work toward this is to have the group develop discrepancies between their present behavior and their values or their goals. This aids in the development of change talk and enhances motivation for change, and group members can challenge each other to further develop discrepancies compared to what the counselor could do alone in individual counseling (Mitcheson & Grellier, 2011). In the final phase of MI, *planning*, the counselor and clients collaboratively develop plans for change. This plan includes actions to be taken by the clients and can include engagement in a specific treatment (e.g., cognitive behavior therapy). Further, consistent with the therapeutic factors, group members can offer each other advice and encouragement when developing their plans to implement specific behavioral changes (e.g., attending 12-step meetings, engaging in healthy relaxation techniques as opposed to using substances), as well as challenge unrealistic or seemingly unproductive plans.

An Example: Cannabis Youth Treatment: Integrating MI and CBT

Both MI and CBT have been successfully applied to group work and can be used together in sequence or integrated in a single treatment to have a synergistic effect to enhance treatment outcomes. In other words, MI can be used prior to a CBT group to enhance motivation for change and engagement in treatment, and MI and CBT can be integrated together in that the group leader uses MI and CBT with group members. The Cannabis Youth Treatment (CYT) series is a prime example of how these two methods can be combined. The CYT is an evidence-based program that consists of two phases of manualized treatment: the first phase employs motivational enhancement therapy (MET; based on MI) and the second phase uses CBT interventions. The MET sessions are used to enhance clients' motivation to address their cannabis use and to engage in CBT group counseling. Strategies used include expressing empathy, developing rapport, reviewing personalized assessment feedback, goal setting, and introducing a functional analysis. The CBT interventions are then used to help clients develop skills to diminish or stop cannabis use. Such interventions include learning and practicing refusal skills, developing a social network that is supportive of recovery, increasing healthy, non-using recreational activities, and coping with high-risk using situations and possible relapse. Although MI and CBT are two separate phases of the treatment, their integration is encouraged and expected in all five sessions. For example, Sampl and Kadden (2001) stated, "It is expected that therapists will make effective use of MET interventions, to some extent, across all five treatment sessions" (p. 17).

Research on CYT has consistently shown that it produced outcomes similar to or better than those for other treatments, as well as being more cost-effective compared to other approaches (Dennis et al., 2004; Hunter et al., 2012; Ramchand, Griffin, Suttorp, Harris, & Morral, 2011). The first volume of the CYT series offers a five-session treatment model (Sampl & Kadden, 2001); the second volume offers seven sessions (Webb, Scudder, Kaminer, & Kadden, 2002).

Both volumes include information about the rationale for the program, overview of the program, detailed descriptions of each approach (MI and CBT), session guidelines and exercises, worksheets, and information to assist with challenges in treatment. The CYT is available for free download at the SAMHSA store (http://store.samhsa.gov).

Family and Couples Group Counseling

Family group counseling involves several families of persons experiencing substance use disorders; couples group counseling involves several couples. Both have the purpose of examining relationship dynamics. The most common form of relational counseling in treatment for substance use disorders is multifamily groups. The multifamily group is a logical extension of the group counseling processes. It involves combining family members of clients into a recovery community where clients and family members receive support. Multifamily groups give patients and families a sense of universality and cohesiveness and the feeling that they are not alone in their experiences.

Family programs in residential treatment centers, which are usually several days in duration, can be quite intensive. Lectures, counseling, and extracurricular activities are often planned. In addition, family members may need transportation from their accommodations and other forms of assistance. The scheduling of family week evokes considerable anxiety among clients and family members who may not have seen one another for weeks. High degrees of structure in such programs can help minimize anxiety, potential conflicts, and acting-out behavior.

One or more multifamily groups will likely involve each family system having the opportunity to reduce shame and embrace reality by addressing the reality of the family member's substance use disorder. Shame, control, and denial are associated with families affected by substance use disorders, and family members often experience difficulties with managing emotions, resolving conflicts relating to others, and balancing care of self with the care of others (Kelly, 2016).

The multifamily group and other family program treatment components attempt to prepare the family for the reentry of the client and to support the involvement of all family members in treatment and recovery groups. Most couple and family groups are conducted through a large organization such as a hospital or residential treatment center. However, some community programs (e.g., the community mental health center) are able to offer couple and family groups, psychoeducational groups, and workshops. Couples groups can be offered within the context of a larger family program (e.g., "family week" at a residential treatment center), a self-contained intervention (a "weekend couples retreat"), or an adjunct to ongoing treatment (e.g., an intensive outpatient codependency group). Whatever the schedule and setting, care should be taken to select couples who will benefit from the group format and process. Each member of the couple should be adequately prepared, including individual consultation if needed, and free to provide informed consent. Because family and couples group work is demanding, the group leader should be competent in group counseling, family and/or couples counseling, and the treatment of substance use disorders.

GROUP TREATMENT IN THE CONTINUUM OF CARE

Group counseling can take many forms depending on the setting in which it is offered and the placement in the continuum of care. In Chapter 6, you read about the levels of care for the treatment of substance use disorders. Group counselors must provide appropriate treatment based on the members' needs and time in the group. For example, group counseling in an inpatient setting, where group members are initiating their recoveries and will be in group for only a few days or weeks, will look different compared to group counseling in an outpatient aftercare setting, in which members have been in recovery for months and will remain in the group for 6 to 12 months (CSAT, 2005). In this section, we briefly examine group counseling approaches in each level of care.

In the highest level of care, detoxification occurs in an inpatient setting. This is the first stage of treatment for persons who require medical management of acute withdrawal symptoms (National Institute on Drug Abuse [NIDA], 2012). Withdrawal from substances such as opioids, benzodiazepines, alcohol, barbiturates, and other sedatives can be medically managed with medication. As a result of the medical nature of this treatment, client stays tend to be brief and group counseling opportunities are often limited. However, this level of care represents the beginning of treatment and should lead to additional treatment, as detoxification alone is not sufficient to change chronic substance use disorders. Therefore, motivational enhancement approaches should be used in this setting to increase clients' likelihood of engaging in subsequent treatment (NIDA, 2012).

In the next level of care, residential and inpatient settings, the client is removed from the demands and contingencies of daily life, as well as from family members and other relationships that could contribute to relapse, and is placed in an environment with a high degree of structure. The residential treatment center becomes the safe haven for intervening in an overlearned lifestyle or chronic course of deterioration. Group counseling is used extensively over a period of months or weeks to help clients alter dysfunctional beliefs, self-concepts, and behaviors and to adopt healthy ways of interacting with others (NIDA, 2012). As groups occur throughout the day in inpatient and residential treatment, content from morning groups can be transferred into afternoon groups, creating powerful continuity of treatment (Brooks & McHenry, 2015). Family issues are often addressed during residential treatment, and family and/or couples groups can be part of treatment. In addition to multifamily groups, psychoeducational and support groups are offered for partners, parents, and other family members.

Similar to residential treatment, partial hospitalization or day treatment predominantly uses groups for service delivery. As the name implies, the groups are conducted within the hospital setting. There is a high degree of structure with respect to scheduling and goal setting, but less monitoring than the surveillance associated with inpatient treatment. Groups are conducted during the work day, which typically overlaps the day shift of the hospital. Staff and resources may be shared with an inpatient unit, or the day treatment program may be self-contained.

Inevitably, graduates of highly structured levels of care return to the community settings in which they engaged in substance use. Some hospitals and residential treatment centers provide outpatient aftercare group counseling in the facilities in which the client received treatment. Having follow-up group sessions helps in transfer and generalization of gains realized during treatment. Some graduates of structured programs will benefit from referral to "halfway houses" or "sober living" environments in which recovering persons reside together in an environment supportive of recovery and personal growth. In addition, not all clients will need higher levels of care (i.e., detoxification, residential treatment), and some will be placed in intensive outpatient or outpatient treatment from the start. These groups can range from 90 minutes to 3 hours and meet up to three times per week (i.e., intensive outpatient) (Brooks & McHenry, 2015). Clients engaging in these levels of care are learning to live in their lives without substances (CSAT, 2005). Brooks and McHenry (2015) recommended that group leaders debrief and explore group members' emotions at the close of each group session before members return to their homes.

Relapse is frequently associated with stressors at home or work and through associations with persons who continue to abuse substances or engage in addictive behaviors (Donovan & Witkiewitz, 2012). These groups therefore often focus on skill building to help clients develop tools to sustain their recoveries in spite of challenging environments and circumstances. Relapse prevention groups are outpatient groups found to be beneficial to clients who may susceptible to relapse, despite being abstinent for some time (CSAT, 2005).

The continuum of care described so far represents efforts to assist persons experiencing substance use disorders. However, groups can also be used in prevention efforts on each of the three tiers of prevention. Universal prevention involves all individuals receiving the intervention, such as all eighth graders at a middle school. Selective interventions target populations perceived to be at a greater risk for the development of a substance use disorder, such as middle school students who have experienced a significant loss, who come from a substance-using or otherwise dysfunctional family, or who lack social skills. Finally, indicated prevention efforts target those who demonstrate risk-taking behaviors, such as middle school students who were caught using substances on one occasion (LeNoue & Riggs, 2016). Group size should decrease as the prevention interventions become more targeted. Schools are commonly the source of such prevention, as the classroom lends itself to ready-made groups for prevention interventions. Several prevention programs delivered in group formats have gained empirical support for preventing substance use issues, such as the Life Skills program for dissemination in schools (Botvin & Griffin, 2015) and the PRIME for Life program for court-referred adults with substance-related driving offenses (Beadnell, Nason, Stafford, Rosengren, & Daugherty, 2012). (See Chapter 13 for more details on prevention models.)

GROUP TREATMENT EFFICACY

In spite of its widespread clinical use, there is a need for recent outcome research on group counseling for the treatment of substance use disorders. Past research has consistently found group counseling to be as effective as other modalities (e.g., individual and family counseling) in reducing substance use with advantages related to cost-effectiveness and client retention. For example, Sobell, Sobell, and Agrawal (2009) conducted a randomized controlled trial (RCT) comparing the group and individual applications of a CBT+MI intervention. Findings from this RCT showed no significant differences in the outcomes between the individual and group modalities, as both resulted in significant reductions in alcohol and drug use during treatment and at a 12-month follow-up. However, additional analysis found that the group format consumed 41.4% less time to treat clients, making it a significantly more cost-effective treatment over the individual format.

One of the largest and most rigorous clinical trials examining the effectiveness of treatment for alcohol use disorders was conducted by the Project MATCH Research Group (Allen, Babor, Mattson, & Kadden, 2003; Kelly, Magill, & Stout, 2009). Project MATCH (Matching Alcoholism Treatments to Client Heterogeneity), sponsored by the National Institute on Alcohol Abuse and Alcoholism (NIAAA), conducted a randomized clinical trial, with a central focus of assessing the hypothesis that using client characteristics and matching them to specific treatments would enhance outcomes (Allen et al., 2003). Project MATCH compared the effectiveness of cognitive–behavioral therapy (CBT), motivational enhancement therapy (MET), and Twelve Step Facilitation (TSF). The study consisted of 1726 patients (n = 774 inpatient; n = 952 outpatient) diagnosed with alcohol use disorder. The results of this study concluded that all three interventions yielded similar outcomes in relation to alcohol consumption, alcohol-related problems, and depressive symptoms. These symptoms were reduced across all three treatments. The TSF condition, however, produced higher abstinence rates (at the three-year follow-up), more AA meeting attendance, and greater AA-related activities in comparison to the CBT or MET groups (Project MATCH Research Group, 1997, 1998).

Methodological differences across studies create challenges for meta-analytic research in this area. For example, variations in member recruitment and retention, group structure (e.g., closed vs. open enrollment), interdependence of members, and lack of measures and data-analytic approaches impose barriers to gathering logical conclusions (Morgan-Lopez & Fals-Stewart, 2006; Weiss, Jaffee, de Menil, & Cogley, 2004). Nevertheless, the evidence available continues to support group counseling as an efficient and effective treatment option. For example, Weiss and colleagues (2004) examined outcome studies comparing group with individual counseling modalities, treatment as usual, and no treatment. The reviewers found evidence in 24 sufficiently rigorous, prospective treatment outcome studies that group counseling was effective when compared to no treatment and "treatment as usual" conditions. There were no consistent significant differences between group counseling and individual counseling. No particular type of group counseling (e.g., skills training versus process-oriented groups) emerged as superior to others. Groups varying in duration and intensity (e.g., 6 hours per week in intensive outpatient vs. 12 hours per week in day hospital treatment) produced similar positive results. Although the findings were encouraging, the mixed results identified the need for ongoing research.

The findings of outcomes studies evaluating the effectiveness of group treatment established some benefits from TSF, CBT, and MET group interventions. Group modalities are more effective than no treatment or treatment as usual. There is no conclusive evidence that group therapy is more effective than individual therapy. However, the observed lack of differences argues for the efficiency and cost-saving features of group counseling. There is no clearly superior model or type of group approach. Ongoing research is needed to continuously assess the efficacy of groups in the treatment of substance use disorders.

CASE DISCUSSIONS

The case studies in Chapter 1 and considered in other chapters illustrate the relevancy and utility of group counseling for substance use. The case discussions explore application of several types of groups.

Case 1 (Sandy and Pam)

Group work could be a powerful treatment modality for Sandy and Pam. They might benefit more from a women's group compared to a mixed-gender group, as women have been found to have greater success and treatment retention when participating in women-only groups. The interpersonal dynamics involved in group would present opportunities for Sandy and Pam to address their problems with boundaries and relationships, while simultaneously addressing their substance use. Interpersonal learning in group work would facilitate Sandy and Pam becoming aware of and modifying unhealthy patterns in their relationships. Further, the group members would offer them interpersonal support from others who are not using alcohol or drugs or who are changing their own using behaviors. This would help promote a sober social support network to encourage initial and sustained behavior changes. Sandy and Pam would also benefit from an assessment related to sexual addiction and group work that included sexual and intimate behavior as a primary focus along with substances. The group modality would provide the opportunity to interact with group members who are successfully pursuing recovery, which will instill hope and enhance their self-efficacy that they can change their using and problematic behaviors.

Concerning group methods, MI could be used with Sandy and Pam individually before engaging in group as well as during group sessions to create a compassionate and accepting environment that is based on empathy, which would help all group members feel accepted and unjudged as they shared their experiences. By using MI, the group leader would assess Sandy and Pam's readiness to change and employ appropriate interventions. If they were ambivalent about engaging in group or about changing their behaviors related to substance use or unhealthy relationships, the counselor would use MI to explore and resolve their ambivalence, leading to stronger engagement in treatment and commitment to change. CBT interventions could be used in group counseling to help Sandy and Pam learn healthy coping skills to "help them with life's stressors" without turning to alcohol or unhealthy relationships. They could also learn skills to enhance their success in recovery (e.g., relapse prevention), improve their relationships (e.g., communication skills), and address distorted beliefs that are contributing to unhealthy substance use and relationship patterns, as well as anxiety. The group format would enable Sandy and Pam to learn from other group members, practice new skills in a safe and accepting environment, and receive feedback.

Case 2 (Juanita and Jose)

For this family, each member would likely benefit from engaging in separate group work, to address his and her own issues of substance use as well as other concerns, and then coming together to engage in couple and family counseling. Juanita would likely benefit from treatment to address her substance use as well as her trauma history. A women-only group would be most appropriate to facilitate a

supportive network of other sober trauma survivors. Her ambivalence about ceasing cocaine use should be addressed using MI in individual sessions prior to engaging in group work. Jose would attend a group in an outpatient setting to address his frequent alcohol and marijuana use and its impact on his familial behaviors. Once Juanita and Jose have a handle on their substance use, they would also likely benefit from attending a parenting skills group. Such a group would provide them with psychoeducation on healthy, positive parenting skills and then the opportunity to try out and practice new skills before taking them home to use with their daughters. Couples and family counseling would likely be the next step to help the parental and couple subsystem work smoothly as well as help repair the strained family dynamics between the parents and daughters.

Sarita (and possibly Karen) would likely benefit from an adolescent group that is culturally relevant and even specific to Latina Americans to help her navigate her confusion in the conflicting values and messages from the Latino and American cultures. If the group is specific to Latino Americans, the therapeutic factor of universality will help Sarita feel less alone in her dilemma and provide her with a group of people who have an understanding of the conflicts to support her in reaching her own cultural synthesis. Within this context, she would be able to address her experiences of having two using parents in her household and her behavior concerns.

Case 3 (Leigh)

Developmentally, Leigh is going to be influenced by her peer group. In her current situation, she is surrounded by peers who routinely use a variety of substances. Group treatment for substance-using adolescents could be a good option for Leigh, given that the group consists of members who are engaged and invested in treatment. If this was the case, the group modality would provide Leigh with the opportunity to interact with group members who are successfully changing their substance use behaviors,

(Continued)

(Continued)

which will instill hope and enhance her self-efficacy that she, too, could change her behaviors. The group modality could also provide Leigh with the start of developing an alternative social network. CBT group methods would allow Leigh to address self-esteem and self-concept issues that often plague adolescence, receive psychoeducation about healthy sexual behaviors, and enhance her social skills. MI

would be an excellent fit for Leigh initially in order to develop a working therapeutic relationship and enhance her motivation to change her using behaviors. In addition to group counseling for substance use, Leigh would also benefit from a referral to a specialist in eating disorders who can complete an in-depth assessment and make treatment recommendations if indicated.

Conclusion

Discussions of the case studies and reviews of published research confirm that group counseling can be effective in addressing substance use disorders. When the needs of particular clients are matched with group interventions, therapeutic gains are realized in an efficient manner. The therapeutic factors and group dynamics are shared by the various types of groups across the continuum of care, and groups can be specialized according to population, problem, or setting. Group counseling is conducted in prevention, inpatient, residential, day treatment, and outpatient settings. Group counseling practices such

as TSF, CBT, and MI have established empirical support and require specific training for implementation. Qualities of the leader, opportunities for meaningful interaction, group climate, and ongoing group development contribute to the eventual outcomes of group counseling, regardless of the underlying philosophy, theory, or model. Nevertheless, the future of group counseling may depend upon innovation of measurement techniques that fit the complexities of group process and ongoing efforts to conduct rigorous trials of integrative treatment packages in specific settings.

MyCounselingLab for Addictions/Substance Use

Try the Topic 7 Assignments: *Group Treatment*.

Case Study: Rodney

Rodney is a 36 year-old African American male veteran who was recently released from prison on parole. He was mandated to complete a substance use assessment. During his assessment, Rodney described a history of cocaine and alcohol use. He reported he drank alcohol most days for 10 or more years before being arrested, and he used cocaine daily for about a year. Rodney experienced increasing irritably and aggressiveness when using cocaine, which contributed to his arrest and incarceration. He was in prison for four years, and he was released three weeks ago. He has used alcohol every day since being released, and he drank to heavy intoxication,

including experiencing blackouts and vomiting, three times in the past three weeks. He has not used cocaine, and he is trying to avoid it, but he has increasing thoughts of using.

Rodney served in the Marines for six years and was discharged five years ago. While on deployment in Afghanistan, two of his closest friends died when coming into contact with an improvised explosive device (IED). He has never talked about the event, but he has nightmares about it often. Rodney was recently hired as a laborer, and while he is grateful for the work, he is struggling to cope with long days of difficult labor for minimum pay. In addition, he was recommended to the intensive outpatient group for substance use treatment, which will impact his work schedule, and he is concerned about his finances and meeting the requirements of his parole.

Rodney is divorced. His wife of six years left him two months before he was arrested due to his increased cocaine and alcohol use and aggression. He was verbally abusive toward her and physically abusive on one occasion, which he deeply regrets and attributes to the cocaine use because it made him "a monster." Rodney has a four-year-old daughter who is extremely important to him and who he "would do anything for." He does not drink when he is with his daughter. Rodney and his ex-wife have been getting along well and are working on how to co-parent their daughter. He is currently renting a room from a landlord, and he has little communication with his family. His father drank alcohol daily and was physically abusive to Rodney and his brother. Rodney's brother died in a car accident five years ago, and his father died while he was in prison. Rodney's mother was married to his father until his father's death, and she now spends most of her time gambling at bingo and in casinos. They speak sporadically, and the last time they spoke, Rodney's mother was upset that he could not lend her some money to help pay her bills.

Rodney suffered from severe depression, including thoughts of suicide when he was using cocaine before prison. Currently, he is experiencing some insomnia and anxiety, but no thoughts of suicide.

After nights of drinking heavily, he feels embarrassed and ashamed of his behavior, and yet he is struggling to stop it from happening again. He drinks with his friends, who are the same friends he had before he went to prison. They all drink heavily and use various drugs.

Critical Thinking Questions

The case of Rodney introduced some complexities that are increasingly common in the treatment of substance use. His case emphasizes the importance of matching client needs and stage of change to type of intervention. In order to develop your case conceptualization of Rodney, reflect on the following questions.

1. What are the possible advantages and disadvantages of Rodney participating in group counseling?
2. What considerations might you have for Rodney's veteran status? What other cultural considerations would you have when matching Rodney to appropriate treatment?
3. What counseling approaches might be useful to Rodney in the group modality? How would you apply specific approaches to help him in the group setting?
4. What are some reasonable treatment goals for Rodney? What would be a logical course of action if Rodney is unable to make progress toward his goals in the intensive outpatient level of care?

CHAPTER 9

Family Counseling with Individuals Diagnosed with Substance Use Disorder

Patricia W. Stevens, Ph.D.

Through the years, systems theory and the substance use field have often been at odds with one another. Much of this disagreement has focused on whether substance use disorder (SUD) is an individual or a family problem—the old nature-versus-nurture argument. Is the SUD secondary to the dysfunction in the family (i.e., a result of it) or the primary cause of the dysfunction (i.e., the result of the individual's dysfunction)? Although how the clinician views the problem determines the primary focus of treatment, both conceptualizations are important factors in the success of treatment.

The power of the family system to impact the behavior of its members cannot be denied. On the cause/result debate, this author takes the position, like even early family therapy theorists such as Bateson (1971) and others, that it is not an either/or proposition but a "both/and" problem. Basing this position on the stated philosophy that the etiology of substance use disorder is "biopsychosociofamilial," it makes sense to incorporate all aspects of the client's life with special attention to the family into the treatment model. Furthermore, it may be less important for the counselor to determine the etiology of the problem than it is for the counselor to determine how the problem continues to maintain itself within the client's and family's life.

Over the years, research in the use of family therapy in the substance use disorder field has been delineated into two separate tracks: working with the "alcoholic family" and working with the families using "other drugs." Research in the area of alcoholism has tended to focus on families of White middle-class males in their mid-40s. Research on families with substance-use disordered individuals whose primary drug is not alcohol has tended to focus on adolescents or young adults. Therefore, researchers may unknowingly study the same family but from two different perspectives: a parent with an alcohol problem and an adolescent who is using other substances that are currently in vogue. As clinicians begin to assess individuals in treatment, we find that many young adults who are drug users have alcoholic parents. This further substantiates the need to address multigenerational patterns that support chemical use along with individual issues as treatment plans are developed (Acheson et al., 2014; Söderpalm Gordh & Söderpalm, 2011).

As the SUD field has expanded its research base, it has become increasingly apparent that family structure and dynamics play an important role in the continuation of substance use within a family (Doweiko, 2015; McCrady, 2011; McNeece & DiNitto, 2011). Also, substance use increases other dysfunctional patterns of behavior in families, such as domestic violence, child abuse, incest (Duke, Giancola, Morris, Holt, & Gunn, 2011; Livingston, 2011), increased criminal behavior, and accidental injuries (Cherpitel, Yu Ye, Brubacher, & Stenstrom, 2012; Hughes, Payne, Macgregor, & Pockley, 2014). Further, many substance-use disordered individuals and/or family members have dual-diagnosis issues (National Alliance on Mental Illness, 2015) that further compound the treatment variables needed for success with the client and the family. Research supports that substance use in families impairs a child's physical, social, and psychological development in a way that may lead to an adult with mental illness or substance use issues (Cleaver, Unell, & Aldgate, 2010; Mares, van der Vorst, Engels, & Lichtwarck-Aschoff, 2011).

Although biological factors have been proven to be a factor in predisposition for substance use disorder (SUD), new brain research called system biology further evidences the effect of the brain on drug use (see Chapters 3 and 4; National Institutes of Health, 2014). However, even this brain model includes the impact of environment on the brain system. So we can safely assume that nurture (or lack thereof) explains a significant portion of the development and substance use issues (Erickson, 2007). Dramatic statistics have been gathered about substance-abusing families and the impact of childhood experiences on adult substance use (Anda et al., 2009; Doweiko, 2015). Felitti's (2004) early work, which is supported by later studies, states that there is a significant correlation between adverse childhood experiences (ACEs) and a substance use disorder diagnosis (e.g., child abuse, alcoholic or drug-abusing parents). He states that a "male child with a score of 6 ACE as compared with a male child with an ACE of 0 has 46-fold (4600%) likelihood of becoming an injection drug user sometime later in life" and "a 500% increase in adult alcoholism is related in a strong, graded manner to adverse childhood experiences (in other words, the more ACEs the more likely the person is to be an alcoholic)" (pp. 6, 7). The National Survey on Drug Use and Health (Substance Abuse and Mental Health Services Administration, 2014a) states that more than 7.5 million children currently live in a household with at least one adult who is using alcohol. Further, these children are 4 times as likely to develop an alcohol problem themselves. Of Americans 12 and older, 24.6% have used illicit drugs in the past month. Approximately 17 million U.S. adults (18 and older) had an alcohol use disorder in the past year, and 52.6% of individuals 12 and over in the United States reported using alcohol (SAMHSA, 2014a).

With these few statistics, it is not difficult to understand how many people are affected by the use of alcohol or illicit drugs—not only the active user, but also family, friends, and community. It is a commonly held belief that for each substance user, five other people in their life circle are significantly affected by the use. This information clearly supports the need to work from a systems perspective, which declares that as the individual influences the family, so the family influences the individual in feedback loops that are always connected, never-ending, and system-maintaining.

Family therapy with addicted families strives to stop the present, active use and to mitigate the multigenerational transmission process noted in these statistics. No matter what your belief about the etiology of substance use disorder—biological, sociological, or psychological—it clearly passes from generation to generation.

This chapter discusses the general concepts underlying all systemic theories. It is beyond the scope of this chapter to detail the numerous and diverse theories available to the systems practitioner. Furthermore, the theory one might choose to use to work with clients varies with the individual's beliefs, values, philosophy, and personality. To choose a particular systemic theory, the reader is referred to the vast literature available on these theories, which includes but is not limited to experiential/symbolic family therapy (Satir, 1967), structural family therapy (Minuchen, 1974), strategic family therapy (Jackson, 1960; Napier & Whitaker, 1988), Adlerian family therapy (Adler, 1927; Lowe, 1982), and transgenerational/Bowenian family therapy (Bowen, 1974). Goldenberg and Goldenberg (2012), Nichols (2012), and Gladding (2014) present excellent overviews of these systemic theories. The author hopes that the student will have access to classes whose primary focus is to detail these theories for use in general counseling as well as with substance users.

DEFINING FAMILY

Understanding the terminology used in the field of substance use is difficult enough, but in today's society, with so many different combinations of individuals, we find that we must also define the word *family*. It is essential to understand and integrate that the definition of family varies from culture to culture but may also vary from individual to individual in the same culture. Much of the research in the family therapy field, as well as in the SUD field, has been focused on the White Anglo-Saxon Protestant definition of family as an intact nuclear family in which lineage (blood line) is important in tracing one's ancestry. However, because we know that ethnicity is no prerequisite for use, it behooves us to acknowledge the different cultural/personal definitions, expectations, and structures of families as we begin to work in this field (see Chapter 12).

One definition of family would be the traditional term *nuclear family*, which has been defined as the individuals with whom the person is currently living. Individuals in relationships come together from their respective "nuclear families" of origin (birth) to create this nuclear family. It is impossible to examine the roles, rules, rituals, boundaries, and subsystems in the current "nuclear family" without examining its interrelatedness with the family of origin. The present nuclear family becomes the family of origin for the next generation, shaping the multigenerational transmission process of behavioral patterns (Gladding, 2014).

The definition of family in our current society, however, takes on many forms and structures. Therefore, for the purpose of this chapter the definition of family includes any combination of nuclear, extended, single-parent, reconstituted, gay and lesbian couples, friends, and/or any other form of family life. A family is composed of the people—regardless of their actual blood or legal relationship to the client—whom clients consider to be members of their family. In other words, if your client considers someone "family," it is best that you as a clinician accept this person as family. Although this definition complicates the treatment plan that includes the family, it is truer to the client's view of the world, and therefore more effective, than a family that is artificially defined by the treatment program or the social system values by which the provider lives.

GENERAL SYSTEMS CONCEPTS

A *system*, as defined by *Merriam-Webster's Online Dictionary* (2014), is "a regularly interacting or interdependent group of items forming a unified whole and/or a group of interacting bodies under the influence of related forces."

The foundation of all family systems work comes from the literature by Bertalanffy (1968) on the functioning of all systems in the universe. Some of the original general systemic concepts of functioning need to be discussed to understand this idea of interdependence that Bertalanffy assigned to all systems—which, for our purposes, we will assign to families with whom we are counseling. The systems theory framework is based on several underlying concepts:

- All systems seek *homeostasis*.
- All systems incorporate *feedback loops* to function.

- *Hierarchy* is an integral part of systemic functioning, including all the *roles*, *rules*, and *subsystems* necessary. *Boundaries* are necessary to facilitate the existence of roles, rules, and subsystems.
- The system cannot be understood by reductionism but must be examined as an entity, synthesizing the component parts into a *whole*.
- *Change* in one part of the system creates change in all parts of the system.

And, when we define and conceptualize systems as families, counselors add a final concept that is consciously specific to humankind: values. *Values* are passed down from one generation to another, affecting the dynamics of the family system.

To understand family functioning adequately, the individual's behavior must be examined within the context of the family interactions.

Virginia Satir (1967) first described this interaction using the example of a mobile or wind chime. All pieces are connected yet independent to the extent that the mobile/wind chime hangs in balance with pieces not touching. However, if moved, for example, by a breeze, the parts are shown to be interdependent because when one piece moves, it causes the other pieces to move as well. Each breeze may cause the pieces to move and "interact" in different ways. As the breeze diminishes and finally ceases, the pieces also stop moving and return to their original place or balance. This seminal example in the field still describes the interactiveness of family in a simple yet multifaceted manner.

As the basis for all systems work, a closer examination and understanding of these concepts in relationship to families is crucial. These concepts are highly interrelated in all systems. They do not exist independently, and therefore the discussion of one may overlap the other.

Homeostasis

The term *homeostasis* is used to define the natural tendency of families to behave in such a manner as to maintain a sense of balance, structure, and stability in the face of change (Gladding, 2014; Goldenberg & Goldenberg, 2012). Homeostasis is *not* equivalent to healthy functioning, but represents a psychological and emotional comfortable/stable position for the family. Inherent in this definition is the assumption that change in one family member will create change in all other family members (Lewis, Dana, & Blevins, 2014).

There will be times when change requires the family to adjust. Systems (in this case families) have a natural resistance to change, which serves as a mechanism to avoid complete chaos during the change process. During these times, families will need to renegotiate their roles, rules, and boundaries to fashion a new, more functionally balanced structure to manage these changes. An example of this is the changing rules for children as they get older. If families are too resistant to change, they become rigid and decline into entropy. Conversely, too much flexibility produces chaos. Substance-using families demonstrate too much flexibility when the person is using. When the using stops, the roles, rules, and boundaries in the family must be renegotiated, and this scenario creates a crisis state for the family. Many times the family becomes very rigid. This cycle can continue ad infinitum in alcohol, tobacco, and other drug (ATOD) families, creating a surreal lifestyle for all of the family members.

Feedback Loops

The essence of systems is feedback loops. Feedback loops provide the communication that enables the system to continue functioning and to maintain homeostasis, to promote or resist change. They are the system's method of self-regulation and self-maintenance—or, in simple terms, the communication between parts of the system or members of the family. Feedback serves two purposes: to move the system toward change, and to bring the system back into balance.

Reinforcing feedback moves the system toward change. Sometimes called *positive feedback*, this interaction can be thought of as "heating up" the system. As feedback continues, it increases, sometimes exponentially, the system's move from the original balance. Just as a snowball gains size as it rolls downhill, so reinforcing feedback moves the system rapidly away from its first point of balance. Balancing feedback (sometimes called *negative feedback*), in contrast, brings the system back into balance. This represents the "cooling down" of the system. Balancing feedback brings the system back to its goal. How dissonant the system is from its goal determines how much feedback is necessary to regain homeostasis. A good example of balancing feedback is being thirsty. Your body begins in fluid balance, but loses that balance as you exercise or sit in the hot sun. As a result, you experience the sensation of thirst, drink water, and your body then regains fluid balance. How thirsty (or out of balance) you are determines the amount of water you drink (balancing feedback), which in turn determines your return to fluid balance (Gladding, 2014; O'Connor & McDermott, 1997).

Hierarchy, Roles, Rules, Subsystems, and Boundaries

Hierarchy refers to the structure of the family: how the members are classified according to ability or rules and role definition within their cultural perspective. *Roles* may be determined by the individual's behaviors in performing rights and obligations associated with a certain position within the family and are usually related to complementary expected roles of others with whom the person is involved. It is through these roles, and their interaction, that families act out the covert and overt family rules.

Although roles vary, some generic rules appear to define the roles of being male, female, mother, father, husband, wife, and child within a familial structure. As children grow, they will experience childhood, adolescence, and young adulthood. Additionally, throughout the individual's life cycle, a person takes on a variety of roles: child, student, worker, spouse, partner, parent, retiree, grandparent, and so on. Marital and parental roles, in particular, are often derived from the family of origin. These old roles may or may not be suitable for the present family. This situation may create unbalance and conflict as the new family endeavors to shift and change roles. Therefore, as family members move in and out of these roles and as rules change, the family becomes unbalanced and attempts to reestablish homeostasis through feedback loops to create a new structure.

Rules are the mutual assumptions of the family as to how members should behave toward each other and the outside world. Rules within families may govern:

1. what, when, and how family members can communicate their experiences about what they see, hear, feel, and think,
2. who has permission to speak to whom about what,
3. the extent and manner in which a family member can be different,
4. the manner in which sexuality can be expressed,
5. what it means to be a male or female, and
6. how family members acquire self-worth and how much self-worth a member can experience.

Culture may not change how the family is governed but may well change the consequences of breaking the family rules. For example, a Euro-American family might punish (i.e., time-out) a child who "talks back," while an Asian family might use shame to correct the child who breaks the family rule.

Subsystems are the smaller systems within each system—systems within systems. Families are composed of multiple subsystems that assist the family in carrying out its day-to-day functions. Each subsystem contributes to the entire system's maintenance. Subsystems may be established by a variety of means: along generational lines (grandparents, parents, siblings), by mutual interest (who likes to read, play ball, shop), by sex (female-female or male-male), or by task (who cleans the house, who washes the car). Within each subsystem, a family member plays a particular role that has rules and expectations accompanying it. Family members, of course, can be in more than one subsystem, requiring the person to learn the appropriate role and rules for each subsystem (Gladding, 2014; Goldenberg & Goldenberg, 2012).

The clarity of the subsystem boundaries is more important than the constitution of the subsystem (Minuchen, 1974). For example, the marital (or partner) dyad is a primary subsystem. It is a closed system in the sense that there are certain duties and primary functions that are usually performed only by this marital subsystem (e.g., earning money, managing the home). With the birth of a child, this partnership changes and expands to become a parental subsystem with added duties and functions. In effect, we now have two subsystems, the marital subsystem with responsibilities toward the relationship itself and the parental subsystem with parenting duties of caretaking, discipline, scheduling of activities, and so forth.

Boundaries, as already implied, define the subsystems. They are like fences: they keep things out and they keep things in. Boundaries exist between family members, between subsystems, and between the family and society. Boundaries can best be compared to a picket fence. It is strong enough to keep the dogs out of the garden but open enough to see the flowers across the street and to visit with friends who walk by your yard. In family systems, boundaries are on a continuum from clear and overly rigid to clear but flexible to unclear and diffuse. In families with overly rigid boundaries, communication is constricted and family members are disengaged or isolated. There is a lack of expressed love, a low sense of belonging, and a lack of family loyalty. In families with diffused boundaries, there is little if any recognition of autonomy. If one person feels, the whole family feels. There is an intense sense of family loyalty and belonging—to the exclusion of anyone outside the family.

Again, the clinician must be aware of cultural norms when evaluating families' boundaries. In Asian families, for example, the cultural expectation might be that the father is more disengaged (i.e., has more rigid boundaries). The opposite of disengagement, enmeshment, occurs when the boundaries are unclear and diffuse. Enmeshed families leave little room for difference; unity is stressed, and emotions are shared (if the mother cries, so does the child). In the Latino/Hispanic culture, what would be considered in the White culture as an "enmeshed" mother is not only expected but also highly valued (Minuchen, 1992). So, culture colors the perspective (and the pathology) of terms such as *disengagement* and *enmeshment*. It is also important to be aware of the messages about distance and closeness that are given in Western culture. For example, women are considered the nurturers of the family, but "too much" nurturing can create a "Mama's boy," which is seen as dysfunctional in White society both for the mother (enmeshed) and the son. Fathers are not given this double message about closeness and distance with their children.

The families of substance users are often disengaged, not rigidly enmeshed (Capuzzi & Stauffer, 2012). Compared with normative data from nonclinical families, the families of substance users were significantly different on cohesion but not on adaptability. The paradox of this information is that to the outside world, these families may appear enmeshed, therefore tempting the therapist to ask the family to disengage. For the adolescents in the family, this might lead to feeling even more disenfranchised from their family system.

Wholeness

Another systems concept is that of *wholeness*. Systems theorists believe that the system cannot be understood by dissecting it into its individual parts but only by observing the whole system. This concept of wholeness carries with it the idea of "emergent properties" (O'Connor & McDermott, 1997). These are the properties of the system that exist only when the system is seen in its whole and functioning form; conversely, if you take the system apart, the emergent properties no longer exist. For example, H_2O is the chemical formula for water. When you dissect water into its component parts, you have hydrogen and oxygen, but when you combine these elements, you have water. Nothing in the individual elements or even in the idea of combining the elements prepares you for the wetness of water (the emergent property). Also, the picture on a television is the emergent property of that system. Take a TV apart, and you will not find the picture anywhere in the parts.

In families, emergent properties are the behaviors that, when operating as a system, each family member exhibits but, when separated into individuals, they may not exhibit. All of us have had the experience of talking with a friend about someone with whom the friend is involved. The dynamics of the relationship are explained through the eyes of the individual (or a "part" of the system). Then, when we see our friend and the other person together, the experience may be very different than what has been explained to us. This different experience of the functioning-couple system is the emergent property of that couple system.

Further, a child's behavior within the family may be very different from the child's behavior outside of the family. Family rules apply in one situation and societal/peer rules apply in the other.

Change

We have already discussed the concept of how *change* in one part of the system (individual) changes the other parts (individuals) of the system. An important aside to this concept, especially for counseling, is *always* to expect side effects. Remember: with a family system, you can never change just one interaction or behavior because of this systemic effect (think of the mobile discussed earlier). When the user stops using (one behavior), it affects the behaviors of all the other members of the unit.

Values

The last concept in working with family systems is that of values. *Values* are the composite of the rules, roles, boundaries, and subsystems in both the nuclear family, the family of origin, and the culture. Values may be shared or more strongly valued by one partner than by another. Examples of values are receiving an education, engaging in athletics, having musical ability, becoming wealthy, being a good wife and mother, being the good male provider, or how much and when to use. Conflict occurs in families when mutually exclusive values are embraced—for example, a family that values male children has a female child. Cultural values are also superimposed on the family values, impacting the family values as well as individual members and their accomplishments and behaviors. More conflict occurs when these values are covert and not overt, which is often the case in dysfunctional families.

Not only is it important for therapists to understand the family value system, but also it is imperative for them to be aware of their own values, beliefs, and prejudices. Counselors do not leave their values at the door of the therapy room. These values are apparent in each intervention, question, or comment in therapy. The therapist's values can impact the client family system in both positive and negative ways. Therefore, it is necessary for the ethical therapist to recognize that there is no value-free therapy (Wilcoxon & Remley, 2013).

SYSTEMS AND ADDICTIVE FAMILIES

Now that we have described the major components of any system—and for our use, a family system—integrating these concepts into a description of an SUD family becomes much easier. Many addictive families share common characteristics/values. Secrecy (disengagement from the outside), for example, is extremely important. Denial of the problem is also paramount. Family members will go to extreme measures to keep the secret and to avoid dealing with the issue of alcohol/drug use. The family will readjust itself and redistribute responsibilities (change its rules and roles) to accommodate the user (new homeostasis). In fact, as early as 1983, Ackerman realized that the "key to surviving in an alcoholic home is adaptation" (p. 16).

We know that one of the developmental tasks of children is to learn to adapt to their surroundings. Therefore, the adaptation to a dysfunctional SUD system will create dysfunctional behaviors in children. Although these behaviors may serve them well in their families, they do not serve them well as they interact with outside systems and as they grow into adulthood. Taking into consideration this need to adapt, and therefore develop dysfunctional behavior, one can easily understand how growing up in a family with an alcohol or drug user can impact an individual's adult life and life choices.

Hypervigilance is also a characteristic of individuals in these families. Never knowing when or where the user will act out (no set role or rule) creates a constant state of fear for other family members. Lack of trust is a by-product of this unstable and uncertain atmosphere. Another feature of addictive families is the inability to express feelings. Because the user is the feeling carrier and the only one allowed to express feelings in the family, other family members lose the ability to identify and express appropriate feelings. This rule can especially create dysfunction in the child and in the child as an adult.

This may be an appropriate section in which to discuss *shame* as an integral part of a dysfunctional SUD family. Alcoholic and substance-using families are highly vulnerable to shame because these families construct elaborate mechanisms for denying the chemical use among themselves and with the outside world. Also, the user blames the problem on everyone else, and particularly children absorb this guilt that turns into shame. Guilt is the feeling when one knows they are responsible for doing something wrong. Shame is much more intense and is internalized as "I am bad for doing something." Shame impacts the individual in all aspects of his or her life.

Chemical use is also highly correlated with abuse, incest, and violence, as shown earlier. These behaviors feed on secrecy and blame of the victim. This in turn perpetuates the behaviors as well as the shame of the people (sometimes victims) involved in keeping the secret.

The Marital Dyad and Substance Use Disorder

Research into the dynamics of the marital dyad of substance-abusing couples provides interesting information. One study finds that marital adjustment in alcoholic couples may be driven more by the wives' use pattern than by the husbands' use (Cranford, Floyd, Schulenberg, & Zucker, 2011).

Another interesting study shows that marriage may be a protective factor for severe substance disorders but not for heavy drinking. Further, family history, antisocial behavioral tendencies and negative affect predicted the use of alcohol at the time of marriage, while changes after marriage were predicted by the drinking level of one's partner (Leonard & Hornish, 2008). The marriage may provide the individual with a drinking partner, and the two will adjust their drinking behavior until it matches. In the cases where this match does not happen, the alcohol will have a negative impact on the couple relationship.

Issues of control are central to the substance-using marriage. Both partners are endeavoring to maintain control and to decrease the chaos in the relationship, but for their own purpose. The alcohol-abusing partner does not want the other person to leave, and the non–alcohol-abusing person is also often afraid of abandonment. Conditional love becomes a daily part of their lives. Behaviors are centered on "If you love me, you will [or will not]. . . ."

Communication in these marriages is often angry, hostile, and critical. They appear to have an extensive use of projection, display poor psychological boundaries, and use blame frequently. These marriages also have a "borderline personality" involving either intense love or hate, being totally in control or totally out of control, or being enmeshed or disengaged. These relationships tend to be highly symbiotic or, in the current jargon, codependent. These partners are so interrelated that they are inseparable emotionally, psychologically, and sometimes physically from each other and their drug(s) of choice. This codependence creates a highly unhealthy dynamic for children in these relationships. Children stay in a "chronic state of stress" (Doweiko, 2015, p. 310) that can create physical illness as well as mental distress.

In the 1980s the term *codependency* became a household word. In the beginning it referred to anyone who had contact with the user. Then, it became the terminology used for "women who stayed in long term relationships with chemically dependent men and, somehow, were responsible for their partner's chemical dependency" (Johnson, 2004, p. 148). In systems terms, however, *codependency* simply refers to the adaptive function of a troubled family to endeavor to maintain homeostasis or balance. The process explains how problems flow from one role to another as a family system tries to cope with an increasingly problematic person. The codependent(s) (nonusing) individual(s) are usually the people closest to the user and the first to react dysfunctionally. As the codependent becomes more vulnerable and reactive to the dependent (user), the user increases the drinking/drugging. Therefore, the codependent must become more reactive and protective, which does not allow the user to experience the consequences of the behavior. The user's rationalizations support the misunderstanding of the problem. However, this cycle engages both partners in self-deception, which allows the problem to remain hidden and progress. This is an excellent example of the feedback loop in the system that keeps the system self-regulating and self-maintaining (Cruse & Wegscheider-Cruse, 2012).

An early definition by Gorski (1992) of *codependency* states that it is a "cluster of symptoms or maladaptive behavior changes associated with living in a committed relationship with either a chemically dependent person or a chronically dysfunctional person either as children or adults" (p. 15). Today we might say that these individuals overcompensate and try to manage the use. Common elements of this behavior include overinvolvement, obsession with attempts to control the dependent person's behavior, gaining self-worth from the approval of others (many times primarily the chemically dependent person), and making great sacrifices for others. The multigenerational transmission pattern of this behavior is readily seen. No matter how abusive or unsatisfactory children saw their parents' relationship, they will likely repeat the pattern in their own relationships by seeking out users to marry or by becoming a user (Capuzzi & Stauffer, 2012).

Codependency continues to be a controversial topic in this field. Many believe that it does not exist, that the definition itself tends to blame the victim(s). Further, there is no clear clinical definition. Doweiko (2015) views codependency as a construct, not a reality. However, many agree that there are individuals who usually focus too much on the opinions of others, not knowing what they want or like, and are drawn into relationships with needy individuals (i.e., the user).

As discussed earlier in the chapter, homeostasis is an important concept in a system. In order to maintain this balance, the non-abusing partner will shield the abusing partner as much as possible from any unpleasantness—making excuses to the boss for absenteeism, justifying lies to the children, and so forth. This pattern of preserving balance soon becomes a common coping mechanism within the marriage. This form of protection is sometimes called enabling. *Enabling* is anything done to protect people from the consequences of their behavior (Doweiko, 2015). It comes from attempts to adapt to the chemical use rather than confront it. Enabling can come not only from inside the marriage or family but also from sources outside the marriage, as it does not require a committed relationship.

Codependence and enabling can be, but are not usually, mutually exclusive. In other words, someone might enable the drinker and not be codependent—for example, a coworker or an employer. Further, enabling is a way to express control. The enabler is desperately trying to control the user, the consequences of that use, and their own inner turmoil (Doweiko, 2015).

These marriages also use alcohol and/or other drugs to triangulate their relationship. Bowen (1976) says that the smallest stable relationship is a triangle. In substance-abusing marriages, when the tension reaches an unbearable level, instead of bringing in a child or another family member as the third part of the triangle to defuse the tension, these couples bring in the drug of choice. For example, if a couple is arguing, they may decide to focus on the bad grade of their child instead of the underlying cause of their problem. For the addictive family, the drug becomes the third "person" in the relationship and one that is as loved (or more so) as the partner by the user. In both examples, the third part of the triangle and refocusing on other issues, becomes the way to take the pressure off the current situation.

In summary, boundaries for these couples are not well defined, vacillating from overly rigid to overly diffuse depending on whether there is current use. Communication is usually strained and incongruent with feelings. Subsystems may be cross generational, with each partner seeking advice, consolation, or love from the mothers, fathers, sisters, brothers, or children.

THE FAMILY AND SUBSTANCE USE

From the overview of marital dynamics, it is apparent that such a marital partnership would impact children when they enter the system. Because family homeostasis and growth are organized around the user's behavior, children rarely have the opportunity for developmentally appropriate stages of life. Further, with the arrival of children into the dynamic, other aspects of the relationship change as well.

In his seminal work on alcohol family structure, Kaufman (1985) describes four different structures of alcoholic families: functional, neurotic enmeshed, disintegrated, and absent. The *functional* family is usually one in the early stages of use, and the use is connected to social or personal problems. Family members might talk about the chemical problem but are more concerned about other issues. The *neurotic enmeshed* family is the stereotypical alcoholic family. This family encompasses all the characteristics listed earlier for the alcoholic couple. Clues to the chemical use are apparent from the parental role reversal, the history of using in the family of origin, and the protection of the abusing parent by the child. The *disintegrated* family is the family in which temporary separation occurs between the user and other family members. This is usually the neurotic enmeshed family at a later stage. These families may present for therapy after the user has completed an inpatient or intensive outpatient program. Very early Kaufman and Kaufman (1992) further separated the disintegrated family into two stages: the first stage involves the temporary separation, and the second stage is where chemicals are the focus of the family and conflict is open and apparent. The *absent* family is one with a permanent separation between the user and the other members. This situation is usually seen with chronic severe users.

Steinglass's seminal model (1980) of a family life history model evaluates the alcoholic family system using a developmental model. The author describes three developmental phases: early, middle, and late. This model echoes the early model of the individual's development of alcoholism. In the *early phase*, the family is in the process of developing a solid family identity. They may over- or underreact to problems related to the alcoholism. In the *middle phase*, the family has already established identity. This family usually presents with a nonalcoholic problem and a vague history of SUD. They will develop short-term, rigid methods for maintaining homeostasis that incorporate the chemical use behavior in the system. *Late phase* families focus on the intergenerational issues regarding chemical use. The wife might ask the husband to resolve issues about his father's alcoholism before they have children, or the wife might need to "do something" about her alcoholic mother.

It is important to understand that each member of a family with an alcoholic member is impacted by the person's using the same way that families with a mental or physical illness are impacted by those illnesses. Alcohol/drug use regulates all behaviors in the family life. Therefore, if the primary regulatory relationship in the family is with alcohol or drugs, then other relationships in the family become secondary and do not prosper as well as in a family without substance use. Because denial is an integral component of the SUD family homeostasis mechanism, the family will blame factors outside of the family for their problems (e.g., loss of job, lack of money, problems at work/school, argument with friend). This externalization of blame reflects the powerlessness felt throughout the family system. The user functions to bring the family together as they bond against these outside issues through the crises that are caused by continuing use.

Families with substance use problems use criticism, anger, blame, guilt, and judgment in the family communication process as is seen in the marital dyad. Parenting is inconsistent, and the boundaries are unclear and constantly changing. Rules and limits are also in flux depending on whether the ATOD family member is "wet" or "dry" (i.e., using or nonusing). Black (1981)—whose work has never been empirically tested but is still used in the majority of treatment programs and self-help literature and is anecdotally proven by most members of alcoholic families—states three rules that govern the alcoholic family:

- Don't talk
- Don't trust
- Don't feel

These three rules sum up the interactions seen within the substance-using family. Family members develop survival roles to cope with the increasing dysfunction in the family. These roles build a wall of defenses around the individual members that allow each person to deny feelings and to fit into the family. The continuing action/reaction to the user is self-deluding. As the protective barriers increase, family members become more out of touch with themselves and with each other. These protective barriers serve the members of the family well, but they may become destructive behaviors as the person moves out of the family and into mainstream society and relationships without alcohol or drugs involved.

In many dysfunctional families, the identified patients or symptom bearers are the children. The actual symptom bearers may be the parents, but this may not be the presenting problem.

It is the clinician's responsibility to use systemic thinking to understand the system as a whole. It is also important to remember that the adult user may have developed the problem in adolescence, thereby being the symptom bearer in his family of origin where parents were also symptom bearers.

It is important for the counselor working with these families to understand the process that the symptom (alcohol/drug use) serves in the family. It is also imperative to remember that no matter how sick it may appear to the outside observer, the established equilibrium (homeostasis) represents that family's attempt to minimize the threats and disruption in the family system. This understanding is extremely important for clinicians as they endeavor to establish rapport and trust with these families. It is imperative *never* to discount the survival skills of the members of these families.

CHILDREN IN THE SUBSTANCE USE FAMILY

Long-term parental substance use appears to create the same type of dysfunction that exists in families with sexual, physical, or emotional abuse. This makes the children in these families at high risk for the development of a variety of stress-related disorders including conduct disorders, poor academic performance, and inattentiveness. Most children in substance-using families are socially immature, lack self-esteem and self-efficacy, and have deficits in social skills. Furthermore, because these children live in chronic chaos and trauma, they might develop long-lasting emotional disturbances, antisocial personality disorders, or SUD in later life. Children may become addicted to excitement or chaos and may develop inappropriate behaviors such as fire setting or, conversely, may become the "super responsible" child in the family, taking on parental roles (Doweiko, 2015).

A number of factors affect the impact of the parental use on children. One is the sex of the using parent: the impact of a SUD mother is far different from that of a SUD father. Because mothers commonly have the primary care position in the family, this dynamic often creates a greater sense of loss and greater need for inappropriate responsibility (parentified child) than does fraternal use. The second factor is the sex of the child. Male and female children may respond differently. The sex of the parent in conjunction with the sex of the child is also a complicating factor, with mother–daughter, mother–son, father–daughter, and father–son pairings all having different dynamics. The third factor is the length of time the parent has been actively using. A fourth factor is the age of the child during the period of active use. Finally, the extent of the use of the chemical(s) influences the effects on children.

Pseudomutuality is a common dynamic in the SUD family. Children do not feel a part of the family but yet believe that they can never leave the dynamics of the family behind. This explains some of the problems experienced by these children as they move out into the world. This connectedness to the family of origin creates the highest probability for the child to re-create that family's dynamics in their present family. (For an in-depth understanding of this process, see David H. Olsen's work and the Circumplex Model of Marital and Family Systems.)

As early as 1983, Ackerman along with other, more recent researchers (SAMHSA, 2013; Zimmerman, 2014) in the field of resiliency believe that children can avoid the worst of the impact if they are able to find a parental surrogate. The impact that one stable, caring adult—whether a family member or not—can have in a child's life has since been researched and proven. The presence of such a person is one of the major factors in children who are resilient—who survive dysfunctional families and environments with healthy attitudes and behaviors.

Factors that distinguish these children from less resilient children continue to be researched but may include the child's personal characteristics. Other factors that seem to impact a child's resilience are environmental factors and the support from the larger social system, such as religious influence, peer influences, and community or educational influences (Goldstein & Brooks, 2013).

Children's Roles in SUD Families

Claudia Black (1981), in her early research on children in these families (based on the 1967 works of Satir) presents a structure for child behavior. While many find these roles to be too restrictive, others who work in the field see these roles played out in the children of these families as well as when these children reach adulthood and form relationships of their own.

Black (2010) describes the following roles taken by children in SUD families:

The Family Hero (Responsible Child)

Positives: Successful, decisive, leader, self-motivated

Negatives: Perfectionistic, inflexible, severe need to control

The Placatory (Pleaser)

Positives: Caring, good listener, smiles, sensitive to others

Negatives: Denies personal needs, anxious, false guilt, hypervigilant

The Scapegoat—(Acting Out Child)

Positives: Creative, sense of humor, leader (usually in wrong direction)

Negatives: Self-destructive, inappropriate displays of anger, social problems, underachiever

The Lost Child (Adjuster)

Positives: Independent, flexible, easy going, quiet

Negatives: Withdrawn, fearful, lack of direction, difficulty making choices

The Mascot (Clown)

Positives: Sense of humor, flexible

Negatives: Attention seeker, distractive, immature

Although these roles may serve the child well in surviving the SUD family, you can understand the difficulties that this would create in an adult relationship, either with another adult from an SUD family who has his/her own dysfunctional/rigid role to play or with an individual from a non-using family who may have healthier, more flexible role/rule models.

Black (2010) also discusses how these roles restrict an individual by how they dictate the way shame may manifest itself in adult years:

"The Responsible Child shows shame with control, perfectionism, and compulsivity.

The Adjuster Child shows shame with procrastination, and victimization.

The Placate Child shows shame with victimization, depression, and perfection.

The Acting Out Child shows shame with rage, addiction, and procrastination.

Mascot Child shows shame with depression and addiction." (p. 4)

(For more in-depth information regarding these roles and how to use this information in your therapy, see www.claudiablack.com)

TREATMENT WITH SUBSTANCE DISORDERED FAMILIES

With compelling evidence of the family's impact in the etiology and maintenance of use from moderate to severe, it seems appropriate to incorporate family systems therapy in the treatment process.

As already discussed, an underlying principle of systems theory, no matter which school of family theory one adheres to, is that systems (in this case, families) are self-regulating and self-maintaining. This one sentence speaks volumes for the inclusion of family members in treatment. The identified patient (IP) or SUD client would be unable to continue the behavior without a system (family or other significant support system) to maintain the behavior. This in no way implies that the system prefers the individual's continued use. Rather, it implies that the system accommodates and adjusts itself to the individual's use. The family may be traumatized by the consequences of the use but at the same time finds it essential that the individual continue using to maintain the system's homeostasis. Therefore, when the individual decides to stop using, the family balance is disrupted. Based on systems theory, without intervention the system will seek to return to its previous homeostasis or balance, which in this case includes a substance-using family member.

It is important to note that this author shares with many other practitioners in the field the belief that meaningful psychotherapy can begin only after an individual stops using mind-altering drugs. Therefore, detoxification is a fundamental beginning for treatment and must happen before any ongoing therapy will be effective. The family therapy approach to detoxification includes a contract with the entire family for detoxification that involves not only the abstinence of the individual but also a shift in the self-regulating patterns of behavior that have developed around the use of drugs in the family.

When an individual stops using alcohol or other drugs, the family is destabilized. Many times this new situation creates a crisis within the family. Sometimes other problems increase: an adolescent will begin to act out, a physical illness will become worse, or another family member's drug use will worsen. A systems approach recognizes the family's attempt at returning to balance and addresses these issues from that perspective. Just as the family learned to organize itself around the substance use, it must now reorganize itself when there is no substance use in the family. This reordering will require the restructuring of family rituals, roles, and rules. For many families, daily routines will be significantly altered without the presence of alcohol or other drug use. In the cases of long-term substance use, families may have no concept of ways of interacting in the world other than those that are centered around the user's behavioral shifts.

A few general considerations should be discussed before examining the treatment process of working with SUD families. Generally, systems theorists believe that a symptomology in the child or children helps stabilize or balance a dysfunctional marital partnership. Therefore, when the child's behavior becomes healthier (non-use), the marital distress level will rise greatly. Often, to maintain the homeostasis, family members will manipulate the individual's behavior back toward chemical use. This can also be true of a partner relationship, engaging the child when the using partner destabilizes the system by stopping the use.

A family member is always primarily loyal to the family, no matter how dysfunctional or "crazy" the family appears to outsiders. The counselor must be cautious of criticizing or demeaning the family in any way.

There is no ideal family structure. Each family has its own personality and structure. The level of chemical use may affect the system differently based on many factors, including the learned behaviors from the family of origin. High levels of use may not affect one family as profoundly as lower levels affect another. Remember: each family is a unique system. All of these families, to one degree or another, operate in a crisis mode. The family moves from one crisis to another as a normal part of daily functioning.

Families operate in an emotional field of past, present, and future. This three-tiered emotional field includes the family of origin, the present nuclear family, and the future generations of this family. Family therapy provides the unequaled opportunity to impact, or change, not only the present generation we have in treatment but, through changing the family patterns and structures, future generations as well.

To be effective when working with SUD families, the counselor must first develop a framework or theoretical orientation within systems theories. This approach allows the counselor to organize the assessment, diagnosis, treatment planning, and goals of therapy. The basic goal of all systems theories is for the members of the family to achieve a higher level of functioning and to experience symptom relief.

The value of including the family in assessment lies in the multiple perspectives that become available when family members are included. No longer does the clinician have to rely on the individual user's information about use; the clinician now has access to a variety of information about the individual's patterns of behavior. Additionally, the clinician has information concerning the effects on the family's problem-solving skills, daily routines, and rituals or, more specifically, how the family maintains itself in the face of the dysfunctionality.

However, many treatment programs still do no more than pay lip service to family therapy. Partially, this may be due to the politics and/or available monies through managed care for SUD treatment today. Some treatment programs tend to compartmentalize individual and family therapy, offering a time-limited family component to augment ongoing individual treatment; some offer no family therapy. One variation of family therapy that is often included in residential treatment is family week. However, this artificial compartmentalization itself denies a holistic or systems approach to treatment. Another issue is that many treatment facilities do not have clinicians trained in family systems theory. Therefore, counselors who are minimally trained in the theory and techniques of family theory are offering the "family therapy" component. In spite of these problems, family therapy can be a powerful adjunct in the treatment of SUD clients, from assessment, to detoxification, and through treatment and aftercare.

Effectively working with SUD families requires a long-term developmental treatment plan. Many treatment programs (involving either inpatient or intensive outpatient care) may only have the resources to offer a family week during the treatment period. Family week does offer an excellent beginning for family change. The week is usually structured so that the morning meetings are with the SUD client and the family and/or perhaps with a family group of three or so families. The afternoons are reserved for individual work with the SUD client and the family, and also for leisure time.

Families must be prepared in many ways for the intensity of this week. First, they must be given the ground rules, which include the way in which the therapy will be structured (who will meet with whom and when), confidentiality limits, examples of healthy communication ("I" statements), and group norms and expectations. Furthermore, families need to understand that this is time to focus on immediate stressors and concerns. This week will be used to practice communicating honestly, expressing feelings, taking appropriate responsibility, and establishing appropriate boundaries. A relapse plan will be developed and discussed with the entire family.

Family week is usually a highly volatile and emotional week for all concerned, including the counselors. Families can observe how other families are handling their problems and learn from their strengths. They also learn from the therapists' role modeling as well as many of the interactive techniques that might be used, such as family sculpting, role-playing, and reenactment. Family members are taught to interact more honestly and are allowed sufficient time to express their emotions.

It may also be important for the counselor to address the difference in the family's behavior patterns when an individual is using and when the individual is not using (wet and dry conditions). Developing a clear understanding of these behavior patterns can be essential in assisting the family in change.

Most families who have stayed together and get to family week usually survive family week together also. These families are then ready to continue therapy outside the treatment facility. This ongoing therapy will begin to explore the family-of-origin issues that assisted in the development of the ongoing chemical use.

PROGRAMS USING FAMILY THERAPY

While many treatment facilities are not using family therapy to the maximum, there are multiple evidence-based programs available today. These programs are specifically designed to engage couples, families, and communities in treatment. SAMHSA's website, the National Registry of Evidence Based Programs and Practices (SAMHSA, 2014b), provides a complete list of programs deemed to have high efficacy and low recidivism.

One such program is Multidimensional Family Therapy (MDFT), which focuses on adolescent use. MDFT uses treatment in five areas: the individual adolescent, the adolescent's family, members as individuals, the family unit, and how the unit interacts with the social environment. This particular program is solution focused and strives to provide immediate practical outcomes that affect all aspects of the family's life.

As an evidence-based program, MDFT results indicate:

✓ 93% of youth receiving treatment reported no substance-related problem at one year post intake
✓ Reduction in negative attitudes/behaviors and improvement in school functioning
✓ Parents increased their involvement in teen's lives, improved their parenting skills, and decreased their stress (Liddle, Rowe, Dakof, Henderson, & Greenbaum, 2009)

Another evidenced-based program is Alcohol Behavioral Couple Therapy (ABCT). ABCT is an outpatient treatment for individuals with alcohol use disorders and their intimate partners. It is based on two assumptions: intimate partner behaviors and couple interactions can be triggers for drinking, and a positive intimate relationship is a key source of motivation to change drinking behavior. Using cognitive–behavioral therapy, ABCT aims to identify and decrease the partner's behaviors that cue or reinforce the client's drinking; strengthen the partner's support of the client's efforts to change; increase positive couple interactions by improving interpersonal communication and problem-solving skills as a couple; and improve the client's coping skills and relapse prevention techniques to achieve and maintain abstinence. This program is based on several research studies (McCrady, Epstein, Cook, Jensen, & Hildebrandt, 2009; Powers, Vedel, & Emmelkamp, 2008).

The research indicated that in all groups over an 18-month period, there were significant increases in days of abstinence. Further, fewer days of heavy drinking were reported over a 12-month period.

How Successful Is Family Therapy in SUD Treatment?

Family therapy is successful if used in conjunction with individual and group therapy over the period of treatment and recovery. We all know that individuals get better in different ways and at different rates, so many variables play into the concept of success when working with the family system. For example, how long does the SUD person need to be clean, or clean and sober, to claim success? What is the difference? How many of the family members must be using new coping skills? For how long? By what means do we measure this: self-report or outsiders' observations?

For success to be determined, it would seem that at least three criteria must be met: the family has come to value sobriety, the family has developed and implemented new problem-solving skills, and the drug-using behavior has been accepted as the primary cause of the dysfunction. Although all of these are measureable, very little research provides a definitive description of success incorporating these concepts.

CASE DISCUSSIONS

These case discussions incorporate the use of individual and group therapy (as discussed in Chapters 7 and 8) as well as systems theory to exemplify the integration of treatment modalities. They are presented here instead of being incorporated within the chapter to illustrate an integration of multiple systemic concepts.

Case 1 (Sandy and Pam)

Neither Sandy nor Pam would be referred to residential treatment at this time. Although Pam may need detoxification, more information concerning her drug use pattern would be necessary to make this decision.

Sandy exemplifies an individual who has decided to stop drinking and now needs someone to facilitate structure and develop a plan of action to avoid a relapse. Using the biopsychosocial model of treatment, Sandy would be involved in individual therapy to address relationship issues and the possibility of posttraumatic stress disorder. Both Sandy and Pam would be invited to participate in group therapy as discussed in Chapter 8. Using a solution-focused model of therapy, the therapist would build on Sandy's strengths, emphasizing the fact that she has quit drinking on her own. The therapist would ask for other exceptions to times when Sandy was drinking and explore how she managed to stay sober during those times. A plan to continue these behaviors would be developed.

Because Pam and Sandy came in together to work on their relationship, the therapist would want to honor this request and continue to work with them from a systems perspective. Using the genogram previously developed, issues of transgenerational patterns of use would be explored. From a solution-focused model, the question would be how others in the family handled stress other than by drinking. Furthermore, communication and relational issues might be discussed both in group and in sessions including both Pam and Sandy.

Pam would be asked to contract to decrease her drinking and not to use cocaine over a negotiated period of time and also agree not to come to a session having had alcohol or cocaine. The goal would be complete abstinence as soon as possible. It would also be effective to ask Pam to contract not to see Sam for a given period of time. During this time frame, the therapist might work with Pam individually on relationship issues, transgenerational patterns of coping, and alternative behaviors to using alcohol and cocaine. It would also be appropriate to work with Pam on relaxation techniques for the anxiety attacks. Referral for medication is possible but not preferable since the goal of therapy is to learn to live productively without drugs.

The therapist would recommend that both Pam and Sandy attend AA/NA/Al-Anon meetings. The 90/90 schedule would be suggested (i.e., 90 meetings in 90 days). If an outpatient group were available, the therapist might suggest attendance for additional support and therapeutic involvement not available through a 12-step program.

Case 2 (Juanita and Jose)

As noted in Chapter 4, both Juanita and Jose meet the criteria for severe chronic substance use disorder. Their chronic use of drugs spans 23 years. If possible, the therapist might suggest short-term residential treatment for Juanita and Jose. This decision is based on the admitted inability to stop using, the environment in which Juanita works, and the admitted lack of desire to quit using completely. Placing this couple in a setting at least to detoxify might enable the therapist to begin to develop an abstinence plan. Additionally, it would allow breathing space to work with their daughters Sarita and Karen to explore what is actually happening with them.

Residential treatment may not be practical for both adults in the family; if so, intensive outpatient treatment would be recommended. A regimen of individual, family, and group sessions would be designed. Both adults need to address transgenerational substance use patterns and child abuse issues as well as parenting issues in the present. A contract to remain clean and sober should be developed and a structure constructed with the family to implement the plan.

Sarita's acting-out behavior is an indication of the imbalance in the system. Also, Jose's inappropriate behavior with Sarita when drinking must be explored thoroughly. Although Karen is the quiet one, her "disappearance" from the family is also a concern for the therapist. Boundary issues and hierarchy should be discussed. Again, transgenerational patterns of SUD can be discussed and the

implications for Karen and Sarita brought into the session.

The therapist must also be aware of the possibility that Sarita is already involved in drug use. Individual sessions with the girls would be an important asset in the treatment plan. The therapist would want to gather information about the day-to-day activities in the home, at school, and in other situations. Information about peers and activities would also be helpful. Referring Sarita to Alateen and Karen to a group for children would be beneficial if available.

Couples group therapy for Juanita and Jose would prove extremely beneficial. In this setting, couple and family issues as well as parenting can be discussed freely and with others in the same situation, as well as benefiting from the facilitation of a professional. Certainly a 12-step program would be an appropriate support for both Jose and Juanita.

Case 3 (Leigh)

In working with Leigh, several factors need to be considered. The first factor is Leigh's developmental stage. Normal adolescent growth includes rebellious and sometimes dangerous behavior. It most certainly includes behaviors that are unacceptable to the parents. Additionally, many changes have occurred in Leigh's life recently: Her brother left for college, and she has moved to a new area and a new school. Her mother's stress appears to have increased, creating increased conflict between Leigh and her mother.

The therapist might address Leigh's drug use and acting-out behavior as a symptom of her discontent with her present situation. An additional important concern, and also a symptom, would be the fact that Leigh is overly thin. The possibility of an eating disorder combined with the other issues must be carefully evaluated. If the therapist determines that an eating disorder exists, a referral to an eating disorder specialist might be appropriate. Safety issues must be addressed in regard to all of Leigh's present behaviors.

(Continued)

(*Continued*)

Addressing Leigh's drug use as a symptom, rather than the problem, requires a different approach to treatment. Normalizing some of her behavior with Mom might take pressure off the situation. A "no drug" contract would be negotiated. Sessions with Mom would be scheduled to decrease the conflict and establish boundaries as well as connections. If possible, this therapist would also include the father. How to schedule these sessions would be determined after conversations with Leigh, Mom, and Dad. Mom and Dad appear to need some assistance with their relationship because Leigh feels in the middle of this situation, so parenting skills work would be one goal of therapy. Also, developing a plan in which Leigh spends quality time with her parents would be advantageous.

Leigh does not appear to need a 12-step program at this time. If a teen group were available, however, the support of other clean and sober teenagers might be beneficial.

Conclusion

Family therapy addresses the systemic circumstances in which the individual exists. If we as clinicians believe that the etiology of substance use disorder encompasses every aspect of the individual's life (biopsychosocial), then it is only reasonable that our treatment modalities mirror this belief. Family therapy not only can resolve issues in the family currently presenting for therapy but also, by addressing long-running patterns of behavior, can help prevent dysfunctionalities from arising in future generations. No one is suggesting that family/systems therapy alone be used in treatment, but it is a *crucial part* of the collaborative framework for treating all substance use disorders.

MyCounselingLab for Addictions/Substance Use

Try the Topic 8 Assignments: *Family Treatment.*

Case Study: Amanda

Amanda is a 21-year-old single woman who lives with her mother and her 17-year-old brother. Her dad is a truck driver who is on the road for weeks at a time. Amanda reports concern about her drug use but doesn't know what to do about it. She was recently arrested for her second DUI and is court mandated to residential therapy for two weeks. The residential facility has a family therapy weekend.

Amanda reports that when her dad is home, he drinks and watches the ball games on TV. When he gets drunk he yells at her, her brother, and mom and throws things. Mom also drinks some when Dad is gone and a lot more when he is home. When they are both drunk, they fight both verbally and physically. Amanda says it is best just to get out of their way.

The cops have been out to the house several times. Amanda usually leaves when they start fighting. Many times she goes to stay at her grandmother's house.

Amanda says she started drinking and smoking when she was 13, in the eighth grade. She and her friends would raid the liquor cabinet at home. At first it was every month or so, then more and more until they were drinking every day after school. She started smoking around that same time and spent her time trying to figure out where to get money for "smokes." Amanda says, "Other kids were talking about high school and the classes they were going to take, and I was just thinking about drinking and smoking and avoiding Mom and Dad."

Amanda now smokes about a pack a day, plus a couple of joints, too. She has a cup of coffee in the morning before work, and that's it. At night she drinks three or four beers plus a few shots of vodka. On the weekends is "when I really get down to partying. I've played around with lots of stuff. You know, trying to see what's out there. I've tried pot, coke, mescaline, XTC, mushrooms, meth. I've even shot up a few times. It's no big deal. When I'm partying, I like to mix things up a bit—alcohol and something else—maybe pot, maybe coke. Depends on what's going on and who's around. If I drink too much I black out. I've even OD'd a few times. I do like meth or speed though. If any drug is my favorite, aside from cigarettes and coffee, it'd be 'speed.'"

Amanda's parents took her to a doctor when she was 10. They told the doctor that she was out of control at home. Her teacher had complained of her lack of attention in school and outbursts of frustration both with the teacher and with the other children.

The doctor diagnosed her with attention deficit disorder (see DSM-5 for criteria) and gave her Ritalin, which she took for five years and then quit. She is on no prescribed medication at this time.

Amanda describes her brother as a complete math "geek." He always got good grades, has never been in trouble; is responsible, dependable, healthy, and clean. Amanda states, "He's the prince charming and I'm the evil villain in the family."

Critical Thinking Questions

1. Based on the information Amanda gave you, what other information would you need to determine her level of drug use?
2. What dynamics in Amanda's family would you consider nature and/or nurture?
3. What would be your strategy for the family therapy weekend? Who would you want to attend? What would you specifically want to know/observe?

CHAPTER 10

Retaining Sobriety: Relapse Prevention Strategies

Robert A. Dobmeier, PhD, LMHC, CRC

Individuals in recovery as well as the individuals involved in the treatment of recovering individuals recognize that sustaining a clean and sober life is significantly more difficult than eliminating the actual use of any alcohol, tobacco, or other drugs. There is a high degree of consensus in the field that lapses usually are a common element in the recovery process (Witkiewitz, Lustyk, & Bowen, 2013b). More research is emerging on substance use relapse and its prevention (Miller & Rollnick, 2014). The process of change in the modification of substance-using behavior includes influences related to the person, provider, intervention, and environment (DiClemente, 2007).

Recovery is defined not only as abstinence from mind-altering chemicals or nonproductive compulsive behaviors but also as changes in physical, psychological, social, familial, and spiritual areas of functioning. These changes are a process and not an event in the recovering individual's life. The biological and social dynamics that enable an individual to maintain sobriety are as various as those that initiate sobriety (Witkiewitz et al., 2013b). Just as there are differences in individuals in the treatment process, there are differences in individuals in the recovery process. Unique individual differences as well as the stage of recovery affect the path that recovery takes.

Some important intrapersonal factors in the recovery process are self-efficacy, outcome expectancies, craving, motivation toward positive behavior change and toward use of the substance, and neurological substrates associated with these factors. Coping behavior skills and intense negative and positive emotional states are intrapersonal forces that affect recovery. The availability of social support, particularly from significant others who do not abuse a substance, positively impacts the recovery outcome (Witkiewitz et al., 2013b).

A recovery plan must take into account all of these factors. It would be fair to say that recovery, as with all changes in a person's life, is ultimately governed by the client's drives and motivation to change. Motivation is a key predictor of treatment success (Freyer-Adam et al., 2009). In counseling for disordered substance use, as in other areas of psychotherapy, the individual's motivation for change must be greater than that of the therapist or significant other for changes to take root (Wahab, 2010).

Many individuals are "dry" or "clean," referring to having completed withdrawal and being physically free of ATOD. However, this state should not be confused with recovery. Being physically without ATOD but making no other lifestyle changes most frequently leads to chronic lapses or relapse. And, even if individuals do not begin to use again, their behaviors mimic their active drug-using behaviors, particularly those observed in the precontemplation stage of active use. This is sometimes called "white-knuckle sobriety."

Relapse has many definitions. Marlatt (1985b), in his seminal work, defines relapse as a *breakdown or setback in a person's attempt to change or modify a target behavior.* A current use of *relapse* is a "return to any use of a substance" (Moore et al., 2014, p. 619). "[E]ssentially, when individuals attempt to change a problematic behavior, an initial setback (lapse) is highly probable. One possible outcome, following the initial setback, is a return to the previous problematic behavior pattern (relapse)" (Witkiewitz & Marlatt, 2004, p. 224). A simple definition would be the continuous return to ATOD use or to the dysfunctional patterns of compulsive behavior.

Relapse can be seen from two dimensions. The first is the "event" of resumption of use; the second is the "process" whereby attitudes and/or behaviors are exhibited that indicate a likelihood of resumption of use. It is also true that these indicators vary widely from individual to individual and, therefore, may be difficult to recognize and identify. The decision to start use may also be influenced by the person's expectations for the initial effect of use (Raylu & Kaur, 2012).

Lapse is the initial return to use after a period of abstinence or sobriety. This may be a single episode, or it may lead to relapse—as indicated in the word itself, to lapse and lapse again. A lapse is usually temporary, as opposed to a relapse, which is considered a return to uncontrolled use. Although AA defines a *lapse* as a failure in abstinence and indicates that the individuals must begin their path to sobriety again, many mental health practitioners and other self-help groups believe that a lapse may be used to assist the client (and the therapist) in learning what factors motivate the client to return to substance use or relapse. This information can be used to develop a plan to prevent further lapses. In truth, some clients gain valuable self-information from a lapse and are strengthened by this new knowledge.

As the concepts of both etiology and maintenance of dependency have changed, the view of relapse has changed. Most now view relapse as a normal part of the recovery process and as a learning experience for the recovering individual (Capuzzi & Stauffer, 2012; Thakker & Ward, 2010). In fact, after treatment many individuals still use substances on an episodic basis and consider themselves successful in their struggle with ATOD. This model of recovery is based in the theory of harm reduction (Rowland, Allen, & Toumbourou, 2012). We have progressed in our beliefs from the forced choice position of alcoholic/nonalcoholic or clean/addict to understanding that use and moderate/severe misuse is a continuum. Recovery is now considered a continuum, from total abstinence to drinking/using in moderation or socially. Watch the SAMHSA video "Recovery and Health: Echoing through the Community Webcast," available on YouTube.

Relapse is a part of treatment and recovery. Relapse models that are discussed in this chapter could also be discussed in the chapters on individual and group treatment because the process of treatment is a continuum that often includes relapse. The fact that we have chosen to discuss these models here indicates the importance that we place on relapse planning for all clients who have a substance use disorder.

DETERMINANTS OF RELAPSE

The first 90 days after the individual stops using ATOD appear to be when clients are the most vulnerable to relapse. Clients have not developed strong coping skills this early in the process (some have been in controlled settings; others are in family systems that are dysfunctional and unable to appropriately support nonuse) and, therefore, tend to be unable to make healthy decisions in regard to their life choices (Doweiko, 2012; Thakker & Ward, 2010).

Several models of relapse prevention are discussed later in this chapter. It is interesting to note that all of these models incorporate, in some manner, common elements that are precursors of renewed substance use. The counselor should be aware that these different elements are overlapping and integrated. They represent every aspect of the client's life. No matter which model is chosen by the client or the counselor, recovery means a restructuring of the client's entire life system.

Environmental

When clients are in treatment, either residential or intensive outpatient, they usually believe strongly that they can abstain from use. This belief has its basis in the comfort of the protected and supportive atmosphere of treatment. When they return to their own environment, many times this protection and support are not as available as during treatment. Feelings of self-efficacy, an important aspect of recovery (Moore et al., 2014; Senbanjo, Wolff, Marshall, & Strang, 2009), and control are replaced by anxiety, insecurity, and doubt.

High-risk situations—negative emotional states, interpersonal conflict, social pressure, environmental stimuli such as places and activities associated with former substance use life-styles, and craving—threaten the client's control and increase the likelihood of a return to use (Doan, Dich, & Evans, 2013; Noël, Bechara, Brevers, Verbanck, & Campanella, 2010).

Stressful conditions associated with substance-related environmental cues accompany increased craving, increased negative emotion, and decreased positive emotion, contributing to the risk of relapse (Nattala, Leung, Nagarajaiah, & Murthy, 2010). Interpersonal factors such as conflict with others, which may be high during recovery as the client endeavors to decide which behaviors to engage in, accounted for greater use of alcohol, number of drinking days, number of days with dysfunction in the family, and occupational and financial problems when family members did not participate in alcohol treatment.

Interpersonal conflict refers to arguments or confrontation with family, friends, or other significant individuals in the client's life that lead to negative feelings. Negative emotions such as anger, anxiety, frustration, depression, and/or boredom may occur from these conflicts. Clients who have not developed new and more productive coping may resume substance use (Capuzzi & Stauffer, 2012). As you can see, environmental, intrapersonal, and interpersonal components interact to contribute to a high-risk situation for relapse.

Urges and craving for ATOD are also a part of the relapse process. *Craving* is a subjective experience with affective and cognitive components wherein the individual relives the positive feelings of substance use through anticipation of use (Doweiko, 2012). A craving, or jonesing, is the desire for a substance—drug wanting; an urge is being drawn to fulfill the desire—drug-seeking (Wanberg & Milkman, 2008). Urge surfing refers to going with the craving, without fighting it or giving in to it. It allows recognition of craving as a time-limited, normal experience that can be managed without relapsing (Capuzzi & Stauffer, 2012). It is imperative that clients learn their own cues or triggers and that they develop practical and effective methods for dealing with these situations. Doing so may well decrease the possibility of relapse.

Behavioral

Clients who have few or no coping skills to handle high-risk situations are more likely to return to substance use. Several studies emphasize the importance of teaching clients alternative coping skills to deal with these situations (Jafari, Eskandari, Sohrabi, Delavar, & Heshmati, 2010; Senbanjo et al., 2009). It is also important for the client to develop new decision-making skills (Murphy, Taylor, & Elliott, 2012; Zois et al., 2014). A sober lifestyle requires integration into a productive family life, work, recreation, diet and exercise, stress management, and handling the desire to use ATOD again. Each of these represents stress in the client's life. Clients learn that abstinence does not mean an absence of problems in one's life; even if some of the problems were caused by use, others are a part of living. Learning to deal with stress in a healthy way is imperative to recovery.

Although many think that it is major life decisions or situations that cause one to return to use, the reason is usually much less dramatic. Dealing with daily life requires constant mini-decisions that are affected by a host of environmental, cognitive, affective, and interpersonal influences. It is the unforeseen mini-decisions (taking a shortcut to work and driving by the dealer's house, not getting enough sleep, a conflict with the boss, etc.) that often lead the individual to relapse.

Cognitive

Researchers have found a variety of cognitive variables that affect relapse. The person's attitude toward sobriety (motivation to quit or not) (Miller & Rollnick, 2009), perception of his or her coping self-efficacy (the person's belief that he or she has good coping skills; Minervini, Palandri, Bianchi, Bastiani, & Paffi, 2011; Senbanjo et al., 2009), and expectation of relapse are important factors (Raylu & Kaur, 2012). AA and Narcotics Anonymous (NA) refer to "stinking thinking" or the faulty thinking of substance users that can contribute to relapse. Irrational beliefs both about self and the present circumstances create negative emotions for the client. Rational Recovery (RR) and Save Our Selves (SOS) use cognitive–behavioral terminology and interventions that support rational thinking. It may not be the actual thought or pattern of thinking but more how the abuser interprets or manages situations that determines the outcome (Hendershot, Witkiewitz, George, & Marlatt, 2011).

Affective

Much discussion continues about dual diagnosis of coexisting mood and anxiety disorders with a substance use disorder in this field (see Chapter 5 for a full discussion on dual diagnosis).

The stress of everyday living can create negative emotions in the recovering person. Twelve-step programs use the acronym *HALT* (don't get too hungry, angry, lonely, or tired) to alert individuals to emotions that lead to reuse. AA tells members to "get off the pity pot" when they are overwhelmed by feelings of depression and hopelessness. For many clients, the purpose of using was to numb negative feelings. Anxiety, depression, and other negative emotions have been shown to be major determinants of relapse (Fox et al., 2012; Moore et al., 2014). In their 2014 study, Moore et al. (2014) concluded that mindfulness-based treatments may reduce relapse by helping individuals to better manage affect and cravings by using acceptance-based coping. Fox et al. (2012), exploring the underlying physiological changes associated with negative emotions, discovered that prazosin, an alpha-1 receptor antagonist, appeared to decrease stress and alcohol craving, thereby increasing the likelihood of individuals being able to manage stress experienced during early recovery from alcoholism.

So, among the first steps in avoiding relapse is learning to recognize, label, and be able to communicate feelings in a productive way (Sinha, 2012). Relaxation techniques, meditation, assertiveness skills, medication, and other emotion management skills will be important in reducing the risk of relapse.

Two very strong emotions that must be dealt with in recovery are shame and guilt. Guilt is a consequence of the dependency process both for the addict and for the significant others in the addict's life. When the guilt becomes tied to "who I am" and not "what I did," it is known as *shame*. Dealing with guilt and shame affects an individual's self-esteem through negative feedback. These emotions may become overwhelming in recovery and easily lead to relapse in an attempt to protect oneself from the feelings (Sinha, 2012).

Recognizing that positive emotional states also create stress is imperative when working with this population. Positive events such as a new job, a child's wedding, or a renewal of an intimate relationship may be seen as more stressful than negative events because the abuser may be familiar with negative emotions associated with negative events. In fact, success may be the most stressful event in recovery, as it often heightens expectations that the individual be even more successful in the future. Recognition that one is feeling stressed, be it from positive or negative emotions, and learning behaviors that help to calm one such as taking a walk are important skills to learn.

Interpersonal Determinants

The lack of a supportive family or social network has been highly correlated with a return to substance use (Bertrand et al., 2013; Nattala et al., 2010). The support of a partner to accomplish abstinence goals is particularly relevant to success (Hunter-Reel, Witkiewitz, & Zweben, 2012). Often the primary significant other is also an active substance user, and, as noted earlier in this book, many of these individuals come from families with disordered use of a substance that spans generations.

The family is usually the primary relationship and, therefore, the relationship that is most harmed in disordered use of a substance. Broken promises, hurts, isolation, and in many cases verbal, physical, and/or sexual abuse have been present. Taking responsibility for the behaviors and mending the relationships are a large part of recovery. Research indicates that family involvement in treatment is critical; families who are involved support rather than sabotage the process (Bertrand et al., 2013; Nattala et al., 2010; Slesnick & Prestopnik, 2009). If the family is not engaged in the recovery process along with the recovering individual, the results can be devastating (Kinney, 2009). If they fail to support the recovering individual's efforts to make changes in lifestyle, family members risk contributing to a relapse (see Chapter 9 on codependency and enabling behaviors). There has been a remarkable increase in the use of nonmedical prescription drugs among adolescents (Drazdowski, Jäggi, Borre, & Kliewer, 2015) and adults (Shepherd, 2014). Among illicit drugs, only marijuana is used more regularly by teens. In a review of studies from 2003 to 2010, Rowe (2012) discovered that teens and adults with strong bonds to family are not as likely to continue or to start abusing prescription drugs.

Work and leisure time are two other components that may create a problem in recovery. Many times the individual has lost a job or been demoted because of the substance use disorder. Finding satisfying work is an important component of avoiding relapse. Leisure time for substance users has previously meant looking for their drug of choice, using the drug, or hiding the fact that they were using. Without these activities, recovering individuals find themselves with lots of time on their hands. Boredom, because of a lack of social support or activities, is a significant factor in relapse. Work and leisure-time activities have been shown to be resources for preventing relapse (Bahr, Harris, Fisher, & Harker Armstrong, 2010).

Summary

It is easy to see that recovery, like moderate or severe disordered substance use and treatment, is a complex system. Every aspect of the individual's life has been affected by substance use.

Every aspect must now be examined and redefined. Change, positive or negative, creates stress. Stress, without appropriate coping skills, may lead to relapse. So, again, we see the convolution of so many elements of the client's life that are involved in relapse and relapse planning and management.

MODELS OF RELAPSE PLANNING AND MANAGEMENT

Several models of relapse prevention have developed through the years. The first model was Alcoholics Anonymous. This model has become the framework for a multitude of self-help/support groups including Narcotics Anonymous (NA), Cocaine Anonymous (CA), Sex Addicts Anonymous (SAA), Gamblers Anonymous (GA), and Overeaters Anonymous (OA), to name a few. Through the years, other researchers and recovering people have developed different models of relapse prevention (e.g., Rational Recovery, Women for Sobriety, Moderation Management, and Secular Organizations for Sobriety/Save Our Selves). We first discuss the overarching models of recovery that are shown to be of value in the literature for maintaining sobriety: the disease model, a developmental model, and a cognitive-behavioral/social learning model. These models are used in treatment and in aftercare programs as well as being components of some of the self-help groups that have been established throughout the world. Following this discussion, examples of the current available self-help organizations are presented.

The Disease Model

Addictionology, the study of the addiction process, began with one of the earliest models to explain alcoholism—the disease model. It was developed by Jellinek in the 1940s, and his seminal work, *The Disease Concept of Alcoholism*, was published in 1960. Jellinek concluded that individuals suffering from alcoholism had a physiological problem with alcohol. He believed that the physical, emotional, and cognitive problems were a result of this physiological disease, not because of a lack of moral fortitude (the previous belief being that one who was alcoholic lacked morals). In the 1940s, this was cutting-edge research that shifted the focus from the individual's willpower to abstain from the drug (alcohol) to the drug's effect on the body. The disease model, adopted by some as a way to understand attachment to alcohol, other substances, or activities (e.g., gambling, risky sexual behaviors), conveys that the behavior is a sickness or illness that the individual cannot control without intervention (Dunnington, 2011; Russell, Davies, & Hunter, 2011). The acceptance of alcoholism and, by association, other drug addiction, as a disease by the American Medical Association in the 1950s put treatment centers on the same level as medical and psychiatric care facilities.

The public and treatment personnel have widely and enthusiastically accepted the concept of the disease model through the years. The concept has been used to explain all addictions. Alcoholism and addiction are seen as a disease that is progressive and irreversible (see Chapter 4 for a view of Jellinek's chart of the disease process). Under this premise, the only "cure" for the disease is total abstinence. In this model of addiction and recovery all "slips" or "lapses" are viewed as a setback. Relapses constitute a return to the disease and negate all progress that the person has made in recovery before the relapse. Recovery must start again at the beginning as one has "become ill" again and the disease process has restarted. Therefore, abstinence equals a healthy lifestyle and relapse equals sickness. Alcoholics Anonymous adopted the disease model of addiction and recovery.

Developmental Models

The developmental theorists integrate concepts of the disease model with a developmental model of recovery. Gorski and Miller (1986) first developed a six-stage/nine-step model of recovery. Known as the CENAPS (Center for Applied Sciences) Model of Relapse Prevention (Gorski, 1990, 2007; Gorski & Grinstead, 2010), it is based on the belief that disordered substance use creates dysfunction at every level in an individual's life. It is, therefore, imperative in relapse prevention to focus on treatment at each of these levels. This model has been used extensively in private treatment facilities. The model addresses the need for client responsibility of behavior including triggers for relapse and coping behaviors other than ATOD use. It is based on the 12-step model of AA and is used by Minnesota Model treatment facilities. (For more information regarding the Minnesota Model, you might review the National Institute of Drug Abuse website at http://archives.drugabuse.gov/ADAC/ADAC11.html).

THE GORSKI MODEL This model takes into consideration that relapse is a progression of behaviors that allows the substance use to be reactivated if intervention does not take place. Gorski (2007; Gorski & Grinstead, 2010) views addiction as a chronic and progressive disease and advocates for change in all aspects of an individual's life for recovery to happen. Another aspect of this developmental model, which borrows from the AA model, is the belief that individuals must admit they have a problem and then abstain from substance use. Gorski and Miller (1986) believed that this model works best for patients who have been in treatment and relapsed.

The six stages of the developmental model are as follows:

1. *Transition*   The individual begins to experience more severe symptoms and dependency, recognizes the need for treatment, and seeks it.
2. *Stabilization*   This is the beginning stage of treatment and may include detoxification. The individual is stabilized, and immediate problems are solved to facilitate the termination of substance use.
3. *Early recovery*   The client is becoming aware of how the use of substances affected thinking and begins to manage feelings without use.
4. *Middle recovery*   A balanced lifestyle change begins.
5. *Late recovery*   The client has used the counseling process to understand core psychological issues that might create relapse potential.
6. *Maintenance*   Maintenance is a lifelong process of sharpening coping skills to deal with life problems (Gorski, 2007).

In their early work Gorski and Miller (1986) and later Gorski (1990, 2007) developed nine steps or principles to facilitate relapse prevention. Skills are needed at each stage of recovery, and the role of the counselor is to assist the client with each of these steps or principles.

Similar to the AA model, the developmental model is structured with the assumption that relapse problems and warning signs will change as the individual progresses through the stages of recovery. These changes will necessitate the reworking of these steps or principles with each developmental stage of recovery.

THE STAGE MODEL In their seminal article, Prochaska, DiClemente, and Norcross (1992) also suggested a developmental stage model of recovery. This model incorporates five definite stages of recovery. The model assumes that change is intentional on the part of the individual. Ten change processes were identified as operational across many psychotherapy theories. These include consciousness raising, self-reevaluation, self-liberation, stimulus control, and helping relationships (Prochaska et al.). The stages of change are precontemplation, contemplation, preparation, action, and maintenance.

Precontemplation is the stage in which the individual has no intention to change behavior. One is unaware or underaware of problems related to use or addiction. Others close to the person usually recognize that a problem exists. *Contemplation* represents the stage of awareness that a problem exists and one is thinking seriously about addressing it but has not yet committed to taking action. People can remain stuck in this stage for a long time. *Preparation* is the stage of intention along with behavioral criteria (e.g., intending to take action in the next month and beginning to try out cutting down on smoking). One is still uncertain about a criterion for effective action, such as total abstinence from alcohol. *Action* is the stage in which one modifies behavior, experiences, and the environment to allow recovery from the addiction. It requires much commitment of time and energy. Typically, one is in the action stage of change up to six months. *Maintenance* is the stage in which one strives to prevent relapse and consolidates the gains made in the action stage. Maintenance is a continuation and development of the change initiated in the action stage. Remaining free of the addictive behavior and ongoing engagement in alternative constructive behaviors for more than six months are the criteria for entry to the maintenance stage (Prochaska et al., 1992).

This transtheoretical model assumes that change is cyclical and dynamic. The individual typically has to cycle through stages multiple times to achieve abstinence (see Figure 10.1). According to Doweiko (2012), approximately 40% of the substance-abusing population falls into the precontemplative stage and another 40% in the contemplative stage. Only 20% of the substance-abusing population falls within the last three stages of this model.

Prochaska and others have applied the stages of change model to a number of addictions including nicotine, heroin, alcohol, eating, and bullying (e.g., D'Sylva, Graffam, Hardcastle, & Shinkfield, 2012; Fanton, Azzollini, Ayi, Sio, & Mora, 2013; Prochaska & Prochaska, 2011). Given its intuitive accuracy and a growing body of empirical evidence of its effectiveness, numerous researchers (e.g., Di Noia, Mauriello, Byrd-Bredbenner, & Thompson, 2012; Ferrer et al., 2009) and practitioners have applied the stages of change model to a host of addictions, compulsive habits, and behavior problems.

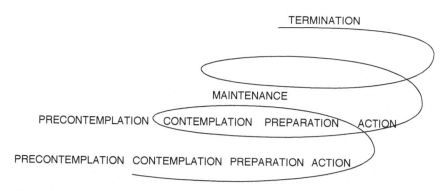

FIGURE 10.1 A spiral model of the stages of change.

A Cognitive-Behavioral/Social Learning Model

The cognitive–behavioral model (Marlatt, 1985a; Marlatt & Witkiewitz, 2011) is based on early social learning theory of Albert Bandura (1969, 1977). Social learning theory holds that substance misuse represents learned behaviors in which use has been increased in frequency, duration, and intensity for psychological benefit (Petry, Barry, Alessi, Rounsaville, & Carroll, 2012). In other words, use is associated with reinforcement, either immediate or delayed.

SOCIAL LEARNING THEORIES   The primary learning principle in social behavior is operant conditioning, in which behavior is shaped by the stimuli that follow. Social behavior is taken on through direct conditioning and through modeling of the behavior of others. Behavior is strengthened through reward (positive reinforcement) and avoidance of punishment (negative reinforcement). Influences on one's substance-using behavior come from interaction with those groups that control reinforcement and punishment, such as substance-using acquaintances, family, and work companions. Individuals learn from these significant groups' definitions (norms and attitudes) of a behavior as good or bad, for example, getting high. Substance-using behavior results when greater reinforcement of social acceptance and the other benefits of use are greater than any punishing contingencies (Akins, Smith, & Mosher, 2010).

Another social learning theory perspective examines the effect of psychological stress on substance use. This theory asserts that substance use is a mechanism, learned through reinforcement and modeling, to reduce stress. As substance use continues, the individual may use more frequently and at higher dosages to avoid withdrawal (Samek & Rueter, 2011).

The importance of self-efficacy must not be overlooked in any discussion of social learning theory. Self-efficacy reflects the individual's belief that it is within one's capacity to not use the substance that has created dependency. Research substantiates the interactive effect of self-efficacy with other treatment variables on alcohol treatment outcome—abstinence confidence, self-consciousness, and coping with stress (Rosenberg et al., 2011). However, there is a need for further studies to identify how to successfully incorporate self-efficacy into treatment of substance use disorders (Kadden & Litt, 2011). Therefore, if high self-efficacy is positively correlated with abstinence, then a crucial element in relapse prevention would be the development of a strong sense of capacity to handle situations. Self-efficacy theory provides that "hands-on" practice handling situations of ever-increasing difficulty creates a sense of ability to manage risks of using.

COGNITIVE-BEHAVIORAL MODEL   Marlatt and his colleagues have developed the most widely used cognitive–behavioral model of relapse prevention based on social learning theory. Marlatt and Gordon (1985) first proposed the premise of the relapse prevention (RP) model, that individuals attempting to stop or reduce substance use will face risks of relapse (Marlatt, Larimer, & Witkiewitz, 2012; Witkiewitz, Bowen, Douglas, & Hsu, 2013a). Although this model was initially developed to identify the challenges of maintaining abstinence for substance abusers, it has been used with other compulsive or addictive behavior patterns, including gambling, sexual addiction, and eating disorders. When individuals attempt to change a problematic behavior, an initial return to the behavior, lapse, is common. A return to the addictive behavior pattern is relapse. An alternative outcome to the lapse, prolapse, is getting back on track with the positive change.

In this model, relapse may be viewed as an opportunity for transition to a new level. In contrast to the AA model, relapse is not seen as a failure but as a learning tool for the individual.

The lapse is used as a means to assess the antecedents to the lapse and to formulate a more successful coping strategy for the future. One of the most important factors in determining whether the individual will return to substance use is the individual's perception of the lapse. The client may see this as a failure or as a way to learn and develop stronger skills. There is the need to be mindful, in a nonjudgmental way, of one's cravings and how one responds to those cravings (Witkiewitz et al., 2013a).

The RP model is useful with any behaviors that are part of a compulsive habit pattern and makes the following assumptions about attempts to change the problem behavior:

1. The individual's addictive behavior emerges from one's thought processes.
2. There are multiple cognitive, affective, social, environmental, spiritual, and neurological influences that bear on the outcome of attempts at abstinence.
3. There is often ambivalence about giving up the substance or habit.
4. Multiple treatment episodes are usually required before one is able to discontinue or control the addictive behavior.
5. Successful attempts at abstinence and other kinds of behavioral change need to be generalizable to multiple settings.
6. Individuals who have been addicted need to discover positive experiences in their lives without use (Thakker & Ward, 2010).

Thakker and Ward (2010) recommend that in addition to abstinence or moderation of use or habit, individuals in recovery have a need to experience good things in themselves and in the world. Lack of hope, inspiration, and joy can contribute to negative emotions that increase the risk of returning to old behaviors. In the Good Lives model (GLM) every individual needs to pursue 10 primary goods: healthy living, knowledge, excellence in play and work (mastery experiences), excellence in agency (autonomy and self-directedness), inner peace (freedom from emotional turmoil and stress), friendship (intimate, romantic, and family relationships), community, spirituality (meaning and purpose in life), happiness, and creativity (Ward & Fortune, 2013; Willis, Ward, & Levenson, 2014). Relapse prevention underscores the need for lifestyle or systemic change for the client. Exercise, biofeedback, meditation, stress management techniques, assertiveness training, and relaxation skills are a few examples of participatory changes. Cognitive restructuring, imagery, and self-talk might also be implemented. A balanced lifestyle is emphasized throughout this model.

Abstinence violation effect (AVE) is an important cognitive concept in cognitive–behavioral/social learning theory of relapse proposed in the early work of Curry, Marlatt, and Gordon (1987; Hendershot et al., 2011). AVE occurs when an individual, having made a personal commitment to abstain from using a substance or to cease engaging in some other unwanted behavior, has an initial lapse whereby the substance or behavior is engaged in at least once. Some individuals may then proceed to uncontrolled use. The AVE occurs when the person attributes the cause of the initial lapse (the first violation of abstinence/lapse) to internal, stable, and global factors within (e.g., lack of willpower or the underlying addiction or disease).

AVE creates cognitive dissonance (the contrast between what people believe about themselves and how they behave). AVE also involves self-attribution effect. In other words, how does the person explain the lapse? Is it a personal weakness, a unique response, a lack of discipline, or a mistake that can be corrected? The explanation of the event may create either more or less guilt, conflict, or a sense of personal failure. The higher the AVE, the more likely the person is to continue the relapse. Conversely, a weaker AVE creates a situation where the client may be able to choose an explanation for the behavior that will result in more sense of control with regard to changing the behavior. For example, if the explanation of the lapse is "I drank because of an unusually high level of stress about my marriage and my legal status that does not happen often in my life," the individual may well be able to use learned coping mechanisms to avoid a lapse when future high stress appears.

The aim of relapse prevention is to teach people how to minimize the size of the relapse (i.e., to weaken the AVE) by directing attention to the more controllable external or situational factors that triggered the lapse (e.g., high-risk situations, coping skills, and outcome expectancies), so that the person can quickly return to the goal of abstinence and not "lose control" of the behavior.

Although all the aforementioned concepts and steps are part of the Marlatt model, his most recent reconceptualization of the model is multidimensional and complex, recognizing the systemic nature of treatment and recovery (see Figure 10.2). The model is dynamic in nature rather than the linear model proposed in the 1980s. It recognizes the integration of a variety of factors as well as timeliness in these factors. Tonic, or ongoing, processes (Hendershot et al., 2011) frequently accumulate over time, thereby increasing the risk for relapse. They might include distal risks such as family history and social support, cognitive processes such as self-efficacy, and physical withdrawal. Phasic response (Hendershot et al.) comprises immediate, situational behavioral/cognitive coping, affective states, and perceived effects of substance use. It is the core of the system where behavioral responding will result in a sudden change in substance use behavior. Witkiewitz and Marlatt (2004) state that the "clinical utility of the proposed model depends on clinicians' ability to gather detailed information about an individual's background, substance use history, personality, coping skills, self-efficacy, and affective state" (p. 231).

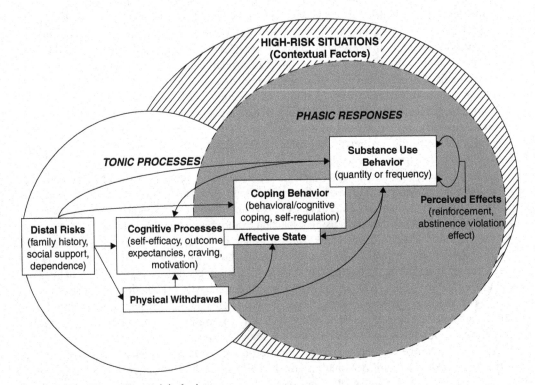

FIGURE 10.2 Dynamic model of relapse.

Source: Witkiewitz, K., & Marlatt, G. A. (2004). That was Zen, this is Tao. *American Psychologist, V 59*(4), 224–235.

How the individual and one's supports understand the causes and implications of relapse as represented by these cognitive behavioral models will heavily influence their response to relapse and how they go about attempting to manage it.

HARM REDUCTION

The harm reduction model represents a view that some learn to control but may not completely eliminate use of a substance in one's life. The harm reduction model had its roots in Great Britain and has been receiving increased attention in the United States (Collins et al., 2012; Marlatt et al., 2012). A distinction is made between use reduction and harm reduction. The latter focuses on shifting or abandoning use behaviors that cause harm to the individual. The impetus is empathy toward the individual who suffers the consequences of high-risk behavior and who seeks to enhance one's quality of life. A harm reduction approach is compatible with abstinence models of prevention but views abstinence as a possible rather than a necessary outcome of use management (Collins et al., 2012). An individual seeking to reduce harm related to substance use today may decide to discontinue use altogether later on. Harm reduction models recognize the importance of the individual making a choice to manage substance use.

Evidence-Based Practices toward Relapse

In the field of alcohol and drug use treatment, along with mental health and health care treatment, there has been a growing demand for use of empirically validated interventions that prevent relapse or lead to controlled use. Evidence-based practice refer to those treatments proven through empirical studies to result in abstinence or controlled use. Clinical trials, consensus reviews, and expert opinion are sources of evidence used to substantiate an intervention (Capuzzi & Stauffer, 2012). Given that relapse rates are estimated at 50 to 90 percent, there appears to be a professional ethical responsibility to recognize and use interventions proven to lower relapse rates (Capuzzi & Stauffer).

Follow-through on implementation of evidence-based practices among practitioners has been studied with mixed results, leading to new calls for verification of the reliability with which empirically validated practices are implemented as designed (Gifford et al., 2012). A severe substance use disorder is a chronic condition, characterized by relapse, which can often be managed but not cured. Yet, it is often treated like an acute disorder with short-term intervention wherein relapse is viewed as a failure of treatment and abstinence is necessary to achieve success (Vanderplasschen, Bloor, & McKeganey, 2010). Most patients require multiple treatment episodes before achieving abstinence (Klingemann, Schläfli, Eggli, & Stutz, 2013). Longer periods of treatment are associated with better outcomes (Vanderplasschen et al., 2010). An aftercare program that supports abstinence or controlled use is often required.

Furthermore, there is a need to keep in touch with clients following treatment and incarceration to monitor onset of symptoms of relapse and to offer support. In the Community Relapse Prevention and Maintenance program, women offenders were more often able to achieve a drug-free lifestyle (Matheson, Doherty, & Grant, 2011).

Bahr, Masters, and Taylor (2012) reviewed current research on effectiveness of drug treatment programs for prisoners, parolees, and probationers. Cognitive–behavioral treatment, contingency management, and pharmacological treatment offered to those participating in drug courts or therapeutic communities helped them to decrease drug use. The most effective treatment focused on high-risk offenders, strong reinforcement for receiving treatment such as freedom in the community, offering several different interventions simultaneously, offering interventions for long time periods, and aftercare.

Cognitive–behavioral therapy (CBT), motivational interviewing, and relapse prevention were effective to prevent relapse on many different drugs. Abstinence rates can be improved when psychosocial treatments such as RP, CBT, and motivational enhancement therapy (MET) are combined with acamprosate and naltrexone (Jhanjee, 2014). Furthermore, there is strong evidence that contingency management, encouraging positive behavior with positive reinforcement, is effective in preventing relapse on opioids, tobacco, and polysubstance use. Clarke and Myers (2012) call for clinical trials and outcome studies, with large samples to evaluate the effectiveness of Developmental Counseling and Therapy, an assessment model that identifies cognitive emotional style as a predictor of relapse, and to strengthen cognitive developmental needs among recovering persons.

Capuzzi and Stauffer (2012) reported empirical evidence for the effectiveness of cognitive–behavioral intervention, community reinforcement, motivational enhancement, 12-step interventions, and contingency management. Also, there is evidence for prevention of relapse with pharmacological treatment and a systems approach that recognizes the interaction of family, community, work, government, religion, and other systems. Effective prevention of substance use for teens included interventions that are interactive in nature; are smaller and more personal programs; involve engagement of multiple family, community, criminal justice, education, and other systems; include a minimum of 10 hours of care; and offered comprehensive behavioral life skills and social relationships. Watch the SAMHSA video on "The Power of Youth Development and Recovery Supports: A 'Girls Matter!' Webinar," available on YouTube.

Despite some positive trends that support the effectiveness of interventions that prevent substance use relapse, there often is insufficient evidence to support their validity and further research is needed. In addition, the effectiveness of programs often seem to be reflective of the unique circumstances of particular programs that cannot be readily replicated in other settings where client contextual variables may be quite different (Capuzzi & Stauffer, 2012).

SELF-HELP RECOVERY ORGANIZATIONS: ADJUNCTS TO PROFESSIONAL INTERVENTION

This text focuses on the moderate and severe use of substances. Many self-help groups exist that focus on other addictions (gambling, eating, sex, etc.), but this chapter reviews only those that specifically focus on disordered use of substances. Although we may mention the other groups as examples of available 12-step programs, the focus here remains on ATOD.

Alcoholics Anonymous Model

Alcoholics Anonymous (AA), as mentioned earlier, was the first self-help organization founded to assist alcoholics in recovery. It continues to be the model of recovery most widely used in treatment facilities and for individuals who may choose to start recovery on their own. Even if individuals are in long-term outpatient care, it is unusual not to include AA as an adjunct to the therapeutic process. AA's concepts are also the basis for many other self-help programs.

AA was officially founded on June 10, 1935. The groundwork for the organization was laid earlier, however, when Carl Jung, the famous psychologist, sent Ronald H. to the Oxford

Group, a popular nondenominational religious group of the time, to find a spiritual awakening that therapy could not provide. Ronald H. was able to maintain his sobriety and to assist his friend, Edwin T., to do the same. Edwin T. was a friend of Bill W. At this time, Bill W. was still drinking but later was hospitalized for detoxification. After his release, he read *The Varieties of Religious Experience* by William James, which became the foundation for the Twelve Steps of AA. During a business trip at a later date, Bill W. was fighting to keep his sobriety and, being in Akron, Ohio, was referred to Dr. Robert H. Smith (Dr. Bob). Reluctantly, Dr. Bob agreed to see him. Dr. Bob was still drinking at this time, but Bill W. found himself reaching out to him with the message of his own sobriety. Through their subsequent conversations and friendship, both remained sober and founded what we know today as Alcoholics Anonymous (White & Kurtz, 2008). Although Jellinek's model of the disease concept was not well known until the 1950s, most of the concepts of AA are based in this belief.

In 1937 the fellowship had 40 members and by 1941 membership had grown to 8,000 (White & Kurtz, 2008). The early members wrote about their struggle to maintain sobriety, publishing the first edition of the book *Alcoholics Anonymous* in 1939. Included in this first edition of the "Big Book" were the Twelve Steps and Twelve Traditions of the organization. AA has developed into a fellowship of more than 2.1 million individuals all over the globe (Alcoholics Anonymous, 2015). AA members often say, "Wherever you can find a liquor store, you can find an AA group."

The cornerstone of the AA model is the paradoxical belief that to gain control of one's life, one must give up control to a Higher Power. Although God is mentioned in AA, members believe that one's Higher Power can be many things or beings. Distinguishing between spirituality and religion, AA believes that addiction is a spiritual disease as well as a physical one. By embracing spirituality, not a specific religious dogma, AA allows all individuals to embrace a Higher Power of their own choosing. AA is a spiritual program of living.

Fundamental in the 12-step philosophy is the belief that abstinence from substance use is not enough. Individuals must be willing to make attitudinal and behavioral changes in their lifestyle. The AA model is designed to enable individuals to address every aspect of their lives—physical, emotional, social, and spiritual—and to make positive changes in each of these areas. The twelve steps of recovery are the foundation for these changes (see Table 10.1). Having made these changes, the individual will then reach out to others in an effort to offer assistance in recovering from a substance-using lifestyle. The Twelve Traditions are also an important component of AA. These traditions govern the operation of AA.

AA OUTCOME STUDIES Many recovering individuals and professionals in the field view AA as the single most important component of recovery. A number of longitudinal and well-designed studies conducted between 1989 and 2001 with focused measures of AA exposure, drinking behavior, and secondary outcomes concluded that the AA experience is multidimensional and that the latent construct representing AA participation was a strong predictor of positive outcome (Tonigan, 2008). In a meta-analysis (Forcehimes & Tonigan, 2008) of 11 studies that looked at the degree of change in self-efficacy in predicting drinking reductions among attendees, changes in self-efficacy were not uniform across AA settings, and the magnitude of benefit associated with self-efficacy was heterogeneous across studies. A study by Gossop, Stewart, and Marsden (2008) involved follow-up interviews at 1 year, 2 years, and 4 to 5 years with 142 alcohol- and drug-dependent clients following residential treatment. Those who attended NA or AA more frequently were more likely to be abstinent from opiates and alcohol when compared both to those who did not attend and those who attended infrequently (less than weekly). A 10-year

TABLE 10.1 The Twelve Steps of Alcoholics Anonymous

1. We admitted we were powerless over alcohol—that our lives had become unmanageable.

2. Came to believe that a Power greater than ourselves could restore us to sanity.

3. Made a decision to turn our will and our lives over to the care of *God as we understood Him.*

4. Made a searching and fearless moral inventory of ourselves.

5. Admitted to God, to ourselves, and to another human being the exact nature of our wrongs.

6. Were entirely ready to have God remove all these defects of character.

7. Humbly asked Him to remove our shortcomings.

8. Made a list of all persons we had harmed, and became willing to make amends to them all.

9. Made direct amends to such people wherever possible, except when to do so would injure them or others.

10. Continued to take personal inventory and when we were wrong promptly admitted it.

11. Sought through prayer and meditation to improve our conscious contact with God as we understood Him, praying only for knowledge of His will for us and the power to carry that out.

12. Having had a spiritual awakening as the result of these steps, we tried to carry this message to alcoholics, and to practice these principles in all our affairs.

Source: The Twelve Steps are reprinted with permission of Alcoholics Anonymous World Services, Inc. (A.A.W.S.). Permission to reprint the Twelve Steps does not mean that A.A.W.S. has reviewed or approved the contents of this publication, or that A.A.W.S. necessarily agrees with the views expressed herein. A.A. is a program of recovery from alcoholism *only*—use of the Twelve Steps in connection with programs and activities which are patterned after A.A., but which address other problems, or in any other non-A.A. context, does not imply otherwise.

study with 226 treatment-seeking alcoholics investigated the course and impact of AA-related helping (AAH), step-work, and meeting attendance on long-term outcomes. Significant direct effects of AAH and meeting attendance on reduced alcohol use and a direct effect of AAH on improved interest in the well-being of others were discovered (Pagano, White, Kelly, Stout, & Tonigan, 2013).

Women's groups and minority groups who feel disenfranchised have leveled criticism about the AA program. Many women believe AA perpetuates the powerlessness of women in steps 1 through 3 (Doweiko, 2012). However, approximately one third of AA members are now female, and some studies have discovered that women participate equally or more than men and benefit as much as men from AA (Kelly & Hoeppner, 2013). In a Project Match cohort study of 1,726 adults, 24% of whom were female, percentage of days abstinent were similar for women (49%) and men (53%). Both women and men improved in social factors related to addiction as a result of attending AA, with men deriving greater benefit. Number of drinks per days drinking, self-efficacy, depression, social networks, and spirituality/religiosity explained 70% of the effect of AA for men and 41% for women. Apart from AA attendance, negative emotions from low self-efficacy had a strong association to outcome for women but not for men (Kelly & Hoeppner). In a study conducted by Moos, Moos, and Timko (2006) of 461 individuals with alcohol use disorders (50% women), women were more likely than men to participate in treatment and in AA, and to achieve better alcohol-related and lifestyle outcomes. Women benefited more than men from extended participation in AA. Women and men who participated in treatment and/or AA for a longer period were more likely to have a successful recovery.

The language of the Big Book has not been significantly revised since it was written in the 1930s, retaining its paternalistic and heterosexist tendencies. Sexual minorities as well as women sometimes feel disconnected and alienated by its message. "It is vitally important that any clients who are not White, heterosexual, male, or Judeo-Christians are aware of the limitations of the 12-Step literature, which is often neither inclusive nor sensitive" (Osten & Switzer, 2014, p. 33). Twelve-step programs are effective for many individuals from diverse populations, but it is important to recognize social barriers that may make it difficult for some diverse individuals to benefit from the programs (Osten & Switzer).

Kelly, Kahler, and Humphreys (2010) conducted a study of why male veterans who are patients for a substance use disorder drop out of or never attend 12-step mutual-help groups such as AA. Comorbid psychiatric problems and, to a lesser extent, spiritual concerns were found to be obstacles. The needs of individuals striving to recover from an addiction are complex, and the varied contextual influences that play a role in abstinence and relapse make it impossible to arrive at simple prescriptions for referral to self-help and treatment sources. Some clients may be better served through different approaches, but it behooves the mental health practitioner to be aware that many individuals are served well by AA.

Spirituality as a Resource

Many authors, leaders, and individuals associated with recovery from addictions advocate the valuable contribution of spirituality in one's striving to maintain abstinence or moderation in use. Many others have reacted to the spiritual emphasis in AA and have sought alternative self-help groups in an effort to approach sobriety outside of a context of spirituality. This suggests the importance of raising the question of the nature of spirituality. Post (2014) referred to spirituality as the community of self, higher power, and neighbor wherein ties of love and service support recovery from addiction. Spirituality is the search for meaning; those undergoing recovery usually are faced with essential questions about purpose, identity, and responsibility. Spirituality can be a helpful resource for understanding a past lifestyle of a substance use disorder and for making decisions about a future free from severe substance use (Post). The Association for Spiritual, Ethical, and Religious Values in Counseling (ASERVIC, n.d.) states in a white paper that "spirituality is innate and unique to all persons . . . moving the individual toward knowledge, love, meaning, peace, hope" (p. 1). Religion is the "organization of belief which is common to a culture or subculture," which includes lifestyle, ritual activities, and institutions (p. 1). While spirituality is usually expressed through culture, it both precedes and transcends culture. A person can be spiritual, religious, or both.

Hagedorn and Moorhead (2010) offer that addictions frequently develop as a result of emotional pain from one's past, such as abuse or demeaning criticism, which may result in perfectionism. Spirituality can be a resource to fill the hole created by the hurt. Mindfulness, paying close attention to the present, can help the individual seeking to recover and avoid relapse. Getting in touch with one's feelings, recognizing cravings and urgings, and seeking positive thoughts can empower the individual in one's goal of abstinence. Horton-Parker and Fawcett (2010) recommend the following mindfulness exercises that facilitate control and balance through spirituality: focus on breathing, body scan, observing thoughts and feelings, and walking meditation. Women for Sobriety emphasize spiritual growth through meditation, discovery of self, caring and love toward self and each other, establishing life priorities, and treasuring each moment.

AA-Associated 12-Step Programs

Using the AA model of recovery as a basis, several 12-step programs have been developed, such as Narcotics Anonymous (NA), Cocaine Anonymous (CA), Gamblers Anonymous (GA), Sex Addicts Anonymous (SAA), and Overeaters Anonymous (OA). All are based on the AA philosophy and use a variation of the Twelve Steps of AA. The difference in these groups is their scope. NA, for example, is all-inclusive with its definition of addiction. It includes any mood-changing, mind-altering substance. CA limits its membership to individuals who identify cocaine as their primary drug or drug of choice, GA focuses on gambling as an addiction, and SAA focuses on sexual addictions. OA is directed toward individuals who have compulsive eating habits. Al-Anon, Alateen, and Nar-Anon are examples of support groups for partners and families of substance users. Al-Anon was founded by Lois W. (Bill W.'s wife) in 1954. While the substance abuser is in AA or NA, families often meet to share experiences and discuss problems. These groups use the same 12 steps as they work toward their own recovery process. Alateen, which began in 1957, is for teenagers who live in alcoholic or drug-abusing families and for substance-using teenagers. It also uses the 12-step model and has its own Big Book. It was started to create an opportunity for youth to come together for support and to share experiences, learn about dependency, and develop problem-solving skills. The model has been used to develop 12 steps for even very young children.

Moderation Management (MM)

Moderation Management (MM) groups were started in 1994. As you read further about MM, you will discover that it is clearly based in the cognitive–behavioral theory. Furthermore, unlike AA, this group does not rely on abstinence for success but sees moderate use as success. They are clear, however, that MM is not for individuals who are chemically addicted (Moderation Management, 2014a). The earlier DSM-IV discrete diagnostic categories of alcohol abuse and alcohol dependence, which often provided a convenient distinction between early-stage alcohol problems and addiction, have been replaced with recognition of a continuum of alcohol use. In the DSM-5 problem drinking is viewed as a continuum of alcohol use disorders (American Psychiatric Association, 2013), and members of MM are likely to fall in the less severe part of the continuum. MM recognizes the value of moderation in one's use of a substance and acknowledges that 30% of its members go on to become members of an abstinence-based group (Moderation Management, 2014a).

MM is focused on providing members with a safe supportive environment where members can share their experiences and challenges in managing moderate drinking. Like other substance use organizations, MM provides a framework for the program, which includes guidelines for members to follow in meetings, a set of steps for members to follow to achieve moderation and positive lifestyle changes, and specific criteria on what constitutes moderate drinking. The full program is available on the Moderation Management website (moderation.org). Specific guidelines and tools can be found by conducting an Internet search on "Moderation Management Readings Suggested Readings at MM Meetings."

MM has specific guidelines for participation in the program, The guidelines define what constitutes "moderate drinking" and provide specific parameters that members must fall into to be in the program. For example, the guidelines state that the moderate drinker is a person who only has an occasional drink, has friends who are either non-drinking or are also moderate drinkers, and enjoys leisure activities that do not involve drinking. The suggested guidelines allow for a degree of individual interpretation because moderation is a flexible principle and is not the same for everyone. Counselors need to work closely with clients who are involved in MM and be aware of possible limitations to the program. Contracting with the client about consequences of not following the MM guidelines, what will be considered evidence that they are in compliance, and how much failure will be tolerated are important pieces of working with clients in MM.

Moderation Management is premised on the belief that if one makes a healthy decision to drink less and to stay within moderate limits, one should not experience any health, personal, family, social, job-related, financial, or legal problems due to alcohol. MM suggests specific limits for people seeking to maintain a moderate drinking level. These limits require that a person: obey laws, including no drinking and driving; avoid drinking when in potentially dangerous situations; limit drinking to at most 3 or 4 days a week; avoid drinking at harmful levels, which MM sets at more than 3 drinks a day/9 drinks per week for women and 4 drinks a day/14 drinks per week for men (Moderation Management, 2014b).

MM also provides a "Nine Steps Toward Moderation and Positive Lifestyle Changes" list, which provides nine suggestions for its members to use to actively make the most of the program and to work to make positive changes in their lives.

Rational Recovery

Rational Recovery (RR) developed as an alternative for individuals who had difficulty with the spiritual aspect of AA. Also based in cognitive–behavioral theory, it is a secular program that deemphasizes the need for any higher power in the recovery process. This program was developed beginning in 1988 by Jack Trimpey (1996; Rational Recovery, 2013) and is based on the work of Albert Ellis. RR uses the framework of rational emotive therapy to combat the irrational thoughts and beliefs of recovering individuals. Trimpey takes the irrational beliefs about alcoholism and drug use and reframes them into rational beliefs and ideas. These irrational thoughts are labeled as "the Beast," and individuals use a "Sobriety Spreadsheet" to combat the Beast. RR has a "Little Book" that emphasizes the individual's ability to make good life choices. In 1994, RR changed its name to Self-Management and Recovery Training (SMART).

Among individuals dually diagnosed with serious mental illness and substance use disorder, SMART was more effective than a 12-step program in improving health and employment, but was less effective in decreasing alcohol use and increasing social interactions, and was associated with more marijuana use. Improvement in alcohol use and life satisfaction were observed in both the SMART and 12-step interventions (Brooks & Penn, 2003). Additional research on the effectiveness of SMART/RR is needed to assess its role among current treatment and self-help strategies.

Secular Organizations for Sobriety/Save Our Selves (SOS)

James Christopher, the sober son of an alcoholic, founded SOS in 1985. Christopher wrote an article entitled "Sobriety without Superstition" in *Free Inquiry* (The SOS Story, 2014). He received an overwhelming amount of response from the article and decided to found SOS. The response has continued to be great from the public, and SOS has also received recognition in the treatment field. In November 1987, the California courts recognized SOS as an alternative to AA in sentencing offenders to mandatory participation in a rehabilitation program. SOS now has chapters in 21 foreign countries and in all states in the United States (SOS Fast Index, 2015).

SOS does not consider itself a spin-off of any religious group, and is concerned with sobriety without religiosity. SOS claims to be a self-empowerment approach that is based on the belief that sobriety is an issue apart from any other issues in the person's life. Sobriety is

"Priority One, no matter what." Anyone who is interested in sobriety is welcome at a meeting. All meetings are self-supporting and separate from other meetings. SOS avoids outside involvement. The organization provides online real-time chats to assist individuals in their time of need.

As with other sobriety organizations, members meet to provide one another with a safe supportive environment in which to share their challenges and successes in maintaining their sobriety. And, like other sobriety organizations, SOS provides a set of guidelines for members to use for maintaining sobriety. While not a rigid requirement, SSO also provides a suggested structure for meetings. Details about the program can be found by doing an Internet search on "SOS Guidebook for Group Leaders".

As a young organization, SOS has not been empirically studied to ascertain effectiveness of its methodology. However, it holds appeal to those who fault AA for its religious (not spiritual) leanings. It also would be considered a cognitive–behavioral type of self-help group with a good dose of willpower added to the mix (Secular Organizations for Sobriety, 2015).

SOS is a harm reduction model and has received much interest in the treatment and recovery field. In their work, Marlatt et al. (2012) have shown the effectiveness of harm reduction to support anyone with an alcohol use problem to take the next step in managing their use. Other researchers (Collins et al., 2006; Rosenberg et al., 2011; Rowland et al., 2012; Witkiewitz & Marlatt, 2006) have come to the same conclusion.

Women for Sobriety (WFS)

Jean Kirkpatrick, one woman on her journey toward sobriety, founded WFS in July 1976. It is a group founded by women for women. WFS recognizes the unique issues related to women striving to reach sobriety and uses behavioral methodology to assist with those issues. WFS's philosophy is: "Forget the past, plan for tomorrow, and live for today." Its philosophy seeks to empower women to seek their own wellness and prosperity. This women's group grew out of the belief that the traditional AA 12-step program was disempowering to a group that was already disempowered in many ways by societal norms. Therefore, empowerment and self-reliance are cornerstones of this movement.

WFS promotes behavioral changes through positive reinforcement, cognitive strategies, and use of the body's healing powers through meditation, diet, and relations techniques. The goal of the program is to help women gain sobriety through self-discovery and by being part of a community of other women who face similar challenges. The Women for Sobriety website provides details about this program, including information about its "New Life" Acceptance Program. The "New Life" Acceptance program is comprised of a set of 13 acceptance statements that women are encouraged to use daily to help them change self-defeating negative thoughts with those that are self-empowering.

Self-Help for Dually Diagnosed Persons

It is estimated that 8.4 million (40.6%) of the 20.7 million U.S. adults diagnosed with a substance use disorder have also been diagnosed with a mental health disorder (Substance Abuse and Mental Health Services Administration, 2014).

Self-help groups for individuals with a substance use disorder have often not been accepting of those who have a co-occurring mental disorder due to perceived transference of reliance from alcohol or another substance of choice to psychotropic medication. Double

Trouble in Recovery, Dual Recovery Anonymous, special AA meetings for alcohol-dependent individuals with a mental disorder, and Self-Management and Recovery Training (SMART) are self-help groups that have been started to help dually diagnosed individuals. Double Trouble in Recovery (DTR) was started in 1989 to offer peer support for individuals with co-occurring disorders of mental illness and substance use (Double Trouble in Recovery, 2014). The program entails 12 traditions and 12 steps that empower members to manage or recover from mental illness and substance use disorders. As stated earlier in this chapter, although there are a multitude of other self-help groups in the world, we have tried to provide an over-view of the most well known in the disordered substance use field. As the reader can readily recognize, the majority of these groups recognize that abstinence is an essential component of a clean and sober lifestyle.

I would be remiss if I did not close this chapter with a concept that is so often ignored in both treatment and recovery—yet it may well be the basis for long-term sobriety and content-ment in each of our lives.

A Well-Rounded Life with Hope

In our diligent and caring quest to teach the individual all the cognitive and behavioral skills necessary to stay clean and sober, we may be overlooking an intrinsically important aspect of recovery. Becoming clean and sober requires the substance abuser to give up a lifestyle that is "psychologically comfortable" and to enter unfamiliar territory. Those who have misused a substance must leave friends who shared a value system and created a sense of community for them. The recovering individual many times does not know how to experience hope in everyday living. Many common social situations are uncomfortable. Friends are few, if they exist at all. Typically, addicts must learn to manage their "pleasure threshold"—in other words, learn to enjoy more moderate stimulation than that commonly accompanying substance-abusing lifestyles.

Also, early recovery means detoxification and withdrawal symptoms that may linger. It also entails facing the pain of one's life before, during, and now after the drug use. Destroyed relationships, financial and legal problems, expectations from everyone, physical pain, and the consistent—and sometimes strong—drug cravings create a heavy burden of unhappiness that drains energy and prolongs lack of hope in the individual's life. So it becomes incumbent on the counselor not to overlook the relearning of hope in the recovery process. Relearning takes time, and counselors need to remember that this relearning can be blocked by guilt and shame or sim-ply by lack of money to participate in activities.

Best and Lubman (2012) suggest that there is a growing awareness of the power of recov-ery from alcohol and other substance use disorders. More than 50 percent of addicted individuals eventually recover from severe substance use through role modeling and support from those formerly addicted, family, and professionals. Recovery has been understood in the mental health field as a process represented by the acronym CHIME: Connectedness, Hope and optimism about the future, Identity, Meaning in life, and Empowerment (Leamy, Bird, Le Boutillier, Williams, & Slade, 2011). In relapse prevention models and programs, counselors should empha-size and systematically support their clients' readiness for change, positive self-esteem, mutually supportive relationships, use of one's talents and interests, and hope for the future. Aftercare groups, AA, NA, and other social support groups can provide much-needed engagement and participation for recovering individuals.

CASE DISCUSSIONS

Case 1: Sandy and Pam

In their desire to manage their alcohol and drug use, Sandy and Pam have considered limiting their use of substances. Sandy is disposed to using in moderation rather than seeking total abstinence. She will have to be realistic about her capacity to use in a way that keeps her from falling into old habits of drinking and abusing pills when she is experiencing stress. Sandy may want to consider participating in Moderation Management. A counselor working closely with Sandy might assist her to develop alternative coping skills such as hobbies, interests, and other ways to relax. Given her prior association with AA and her desire to be abstinent from alcohol and other substances, Pam may want to pursue her association with AA. Given Sandy's and Pam's desire to build their relationship, to learn to relate with men in less destructive ways, and to learn to deal with stress without turning to substances, they will need to be honest with each other about their differing values of abstinence versus use in moderation.

Case 2: Juanita and Jose

Working with Juanita and Jose in a recovery planning process would require specific attention to the environmental factors in their lives. Juanita is still working in a bar, and this situation will create social pressure and therefore will be a significant "trigger" for use. If Jose continues to associate with drug-using acquaintances, he may become vulnerable to cravings. They both admit that using is a mechanism for handling stressful events. Jose and Juanita will need to learn and practice new coping skills that will empower them to recognize environmental and related intrapersonal and interpersonal influences. It may be beneficial for a counselor to help Juanita and Jose to develop communication skills that allow them to talk with each other about the risks for relapse associated with Juanita's working at the bar and Jose's spending time with his drug-using associates. This could involve sharing with each other the dangers to their peace of mind, relationship with each other, family, and job stability that these environments represent.

Case 3: Leigh

Leigh is an excellent example of a client who needs to develop new coping skills. Leigh is responding to the stressful events in her life by using drugs and perhaps with the development of an eating disorder. Assisting her in learning how to make day-to-day decisions that decrease her anxiety would be essential to a sober lifestyle. The therapist might want to help her to increase awareness of her life choices, assist her in developing new skills, and then facilitate the practice of these skills in individual, group, and family therapy. When Leigh becomes anxious about her belief that she is overweight, she can practice initiating a phone conversation with a friend or family member rather than exercising excessively. She might choose to listen to music, which she says has a calming effect on her.

Leigh does not recognize the harmful effects of her using alcohol, pot, and other drugs. She is not interested in looking at her substance use and its impact on her life. As for the counseling, she simply wants to "get this done." This lack of recognition and interest would best be described as Prochaska and colleagues' precontemplative stage. A counselor working with Leigh might use psychoeducational methods to help her to realize the association of family losses with her disordered use of a substance and subsequent falling grades, deteriorating hygiene, and emotional turmoil. The counselor could also work with Leigh's mother to strengthen parenting skills and ways to engage Leigh in discussion about constructive ways to meet her needs other than substance use.

Conclusion

The determinants of substance use relapse and prevention models share commonalities. Relapse prevention skills, cognitive and behavioral, are important in creating a clean and sober lifestyle. However, simply put, the intentionality and hope with which the individual is living life may be the necessary component that creates the inspiration and motivation needed to stay focused and flexible in one's recovery goals.

MyCounselingLab for Addictions/Substance Use

Try the Topic 9 Assignments: *Relapse Prevention Strategies.*

Case Study: Robert

Robert is a 34-year-old African American male who identifies himself as gay. He has been in a number of gay relationships since his early 20s, none of them lasting longer than six months. He currently lives with Larry, a 41-year-old man, whom he has known for four months. Robert is the father of two children, a son born to his girlfriend whom he hung around with in high school and a daughter conceived during a brief affair when Robert was 20 years old. Robert reports that he can remember being attracted to and associating with men during his teen years, when he was also dating women. Robert is the third son and fifth of eight children born to his mother. Robert had occasional contact with his father as a child, but has not seen him in more than 10 years. Robert's father had a drinking problem and was diagnosed with cirrhosis of the liver the last time Robert heard about him. Robert has not seen his children in many years and has had no contact with his mother or siblings for over two years.

Robert reports that he started smoking marijuana when he was around 11 years old. During his teens he would drink wine and liquor with friends and often by himself. Robert also used heroin and cocaine. He has undergone detox for alcohol, heroin, and cocaine "enough" times since his early 20s. Robert participated in chemical dependency rehabilitation for almost two months in 2004. A history of unemployment has been interrupted occasionally with short-term employment as a cook and as a maintenance worker. Robert has had bouts of depression on and off. He was hospitalized for suicidal behavior when he was 27 years old following his being diagnosed with HIV. Subsequent testing has failed to detect a presence of the virus.

The longest period of abstinence from substances that Robert has achieved is one year. He had been attending AA meetings and was feeling supported by his sponsor, to whom he was introduced during one of his detox treatments. Robert relapsed on alcohol when his sponsor moved to another city and Robert did not feel that he could connect with his new sponsor. Robert states that he believes in a higher power, but has mixed feelings about God and religion. He was raised in the Baptist Church and accepted their teachings about God and Jesus Christ. However, the alienation that he experienced in two churches when the congregations learned that he was gay created doubt about God's love for him. The teaching that homosexuality is a sin has made Robert feel that he is not wanted by God or by Christian churches. Robert was recently referred to a drug court following his arrest for possession of barbiturates. He was mandated by the judge to either attend intensive outpatient treatment and participate in a self-help group or be sentenced to jail. In assessing Robert, a substance use counselor viewed Robert as being somewhere in between a precontemplative and contemplative stage of recovery. Robert states that he recognizes that he has a number of relationship, career, and health problems that are related to his use of substances. He is losing hope that he will be able to change his life. He wonders if going to jail would be any worse than what he is currently facing. When he told the drug court coordinator about his ambivalence toward AA, he was informed about Double Trouble in Recovery, a self-help group for individuals facing severe substance use and mental illness. Robert wonders how he would be accepted in the Double Trouble group. He feels that he has failed each time that he has attempted to achieve sobriety. He would like to find a self-help group where he does not have to hide his being gay.

Critical Thinking Questions

1. Robert is facing a number of difficulties—a substance use disorder, depression, hopelessness, alienation from the church, a previous diagnosis of HIV, unemployment, and estrangement from his family. What problem does he need to address first? Provide a rationale for your choice.

2. What model/s of relapse planning and management is most relevant to Robert's situation? What, if any, self-help recovery program/s would you recommend?

3. In your view, what role, if any, should spirituality have in recovery from an addiction?

4. What should Robert do about his alienation from the church? He states that faith in God is important to him, but he has been told that homosexuality is an abomination.

5. How could a well-rounded life with hope become part of Robert's recovery from addiction? What could a counselor do to assist Robert to discover hope in recovery?

CHAPTER **11**

Working with Special Populations: Treatment Issues and Characteristics

Genevieve Weber, PhD, LMHC, & Ashby Dodge, LCSW

This chapter addresses treatment issues and characteristics of nine groups of individuals. The underlying criteria for selecting the groups was the power differential among these groups and the influence of societal perceptions and actions that have limited the full participation of these groups in mainstream society. Obviously, other groups could be included in this selection, but because of space constraints, the discussion will include children and adolescents, women, gay/lesbian/bisexual/transgender individuals, people with disabilities, elders, immigrants, the homeless, and the military.

CHILDREN AND ADOLESCENTS

For most children, the crucial risk periods for substance use occur during major transitions in their lives (National Institute on Drug Abuse [NIDA], 2007b). Research from NIDA has shown that vulnerable life periods are transitions, such as moving from one developmental stage to another (e.g., changes in physical development) or when children experience difficult life changes (e.g., moving or parents divorcing). Exposure to risks can start even before a child is born if the mother is using drugs during pregnancy, or in infancy and early childhood when mutual attachment and parental bonding are crucial.

The first main transition for children is when they leave the security of the family and enter school. When they advance from elementary school to middle school or junior high, they often face academic and social challenges, such as increased expectations for academic success and needing to get along with a wider group of peers. It is during this period of early adolescence that children are likely to encounter substance use for the first time. When they enter high school, adolescents again face more social, emotional, and educational challenges. Because of a greater exposure to available drugs, drug users, and social activities involving drugs, there is an increased risk for adolescents to become involved with substances.

Substance use in children is rarely studied because use is infrequent at these ages (Dunn & Mezzich, 2007). The Monitoring the Future Study (Johnston, O'Malley, Miech, Bachman, & Shulenberg, 2015), an annual and long-term study of American adolescents, college students, and adult high school graduates through age 55, estimates drug use among 12- to 17-year-olds but not among younger children. However, Ewing and colleagues (2015) emphasize that early initiation of substance use and regular use is often associated with negative consequences, including future substance use and concurrent physical and mental health problems.

Research conducted in The Partnership Attitude Tracking Study (Partnership for Drug-Free Kids, 2013) tracked substance use attitudes and behaviors of a teen sample of students in grades 9 through 12. The study showed overall prevalence of teens' marijuana use as remaining stable at a high level (44%) since at least 2010. Significant levels of daily use of marijuana, increases in perceived use by friends, and findings showing that one-third of teens would be more likely to use marijuana if it were legal demonstrate movement toward normalizing marijuana use among a large group of adolescents. Although there was a 33% increase in teen prescription drug use in 2012, prevalence rates have remained stable at 23% lifetime use for all teens in this study in 2013. Over the past five years, 5 to 6% of teens reported having used either synthetic human growth hormone (hGH) or steroids with a prescription at least once in their lifetime. In 2013, however, 11% of teens reported using synthetic hGH. Surprisingly, past-year (51%) and past-month (35%) alcohol use has declined to the lowest level seen in the past 5 years. Teens also reported using synthetic marijuana (17%), inhalants (16%), Ecstasy (13%), cocaine/crack (11%), salvia (10%), methamphetamine (8%), bath salts (7%), and heroin (6%) in their lifetime.

Research from the National Institute on Drug Abuse (2007b) indicates that some signs of risk can be seen as early as infancy or early childhood, such as aggressive behavior, lack of self-control, or difficult temperament. Negative behaviors can lead to additional risks, such as academic failure and social difficulties (e.g., early peer rejection, association with deviant peers), which can put children at greater risk for later drug use. Sometimes family situations increase a child's risk level for later drug use—for example, when there is:

- a lack of attachment and nurturing by parents and caregivers
- ineffective parenting
- a chaotic home environment
- lack of a significant relationship with a caring adult
- a caregiver who uses substances, lives with mental illness, or engages in criminal behavior

These problem behaviors tend to cluster in children raised in dysfunctional families by parents who were likewise raised in dysfunctional or overstressed families. In addition, studies have shown that children with poor academic success and problematic social behaviors at ages 7 to 9 are more likely to be involved with substance use by age 14 or 15 (NIDA, 2007b).

Adolescence is defined by a series of age-related transitions in social, psychological, biological, and environmental contexts (Trenz, Dunne, Zur, & Latimer, 2015). External changes substantially influence adolescents that increase their vulnerability to social pressures and overall risk, including but not limited to substance use, sexual risk-taking, violence, pregnancy, trouble with the law, school attrition, and sometimes death (Brooks-Russell et al., 2015; Obando, Trujillo, & Trujillo, 2014). The likelihood that negative health behaviors and outcomes will occur depends on the adolescent's exposure to risk and protective factors (Obando et al., 2014). Although most adolescents experience transitory problems that they can resolve, others with poor coping skills experience intense emotional pain, and substance use can become a way to cope with both internal problems (stress, depression, low self-esteem) and external problems (school, family, workplace). Youth involved with substances pose a major problem not only to themselves but also to the community as a whole.

Since 1975, the Monitoring the Future (MTF) survey has measured drug, alcohol, and cigarette use and related attitudes among adolescents. Initially, the survey included 12th graders only, but in 1991 that was expanded to include 8th and 10th graders. The 2014 MTF

(Johnston et al., 2015) survey encompassed about 41,600 8th-, 10th-, and 12th-grade students in more than 377 public and private schools nationwide. Clearly the problems of substance use remain widespread among American youth. The positive findings show that there is a decline in the use of a number of licit and illicit substances in 2014. Although marijuana use declined in 2014, attitudes toward marijuana for youth moved toward greater acceptance, supporting the findings from The Partnership Attitude Tracking Study discussed earlier. Synthetic marijuana, bath salts, narcotics other than heroin (e.g., Vicodin, OxyContin), Ecstasy (MDMA), hallucinogens other LSD, salvia, over-the-counter cough and cold medicines, amphetamine use without a doctor's orders, Ritalin, Adderall, "crack" cocaine, and any prescription drug also show declining prevalence. Substances such as inhalants, tranquilizers, GHB, LSD, cocaine, heroin, methamphetamine and crystal methamphetamine, sedatives, Rohypnol, ketamine, and anabolic steroids showed little or no change from 2013 to 2014. Cigarette smoking and alcohol use both continue to show long declines and are now at the lowest levels recorded in the history of this survey. However, the use of the new product e-cigarettes has increased rapidly among adolescents and is currently used more often than tobacco cigarette smoking (Johnston et al., 2015).

According to MTF (Johnston et al., 2015), alcohol remains the most commonly used substance by adolescents. Although its use overall is on the decline, 2 of every 3 students (66%) have consumed alcohol by the end of high school and more than 1 in 4 (27%) have done so by 8th grade. There were notable differences by race/ethnicity, with African American students having lower rates of use for most licit and illicit drugs, alcohol, and cigarettes than White students. Hispanic students over the past few years have showed the highest rates of use of any illicit drug, particularly in 8th grade and 12th grade based on their use of marijuana, inhalants, cocaine, crack, methamphetamine, and crystal methamphetamine. Table 11.1 presents lifetime prevalence of use of various drugs for grades 8, 10, and 12 combined. Adolescence is often

TABLE 11.1 Monitoring the Future: Overview of key findings. "Trends in Lifetime Prevalence of Use of Various Drugs for Grades 8, 10, 12 Combined"

Any illicit drug	34.9%
Any illicit drug other than marijuana	15.8%
Any illicit drug including inhalants	37.9%
Marijuana/hashish	30.5%
Inhalants	8.8%
Hallucinogens	4.3%
Cocaine	2.9%
Heroin	0.9%
Amphetamines	9.7%
Tranquilizers	5.3%
Alcohol	46.4%
Cigarettes	22.9%
Smokeless tobacco	12.1%
Steroids	1.4%

Source: *Monitoring the Future: 2014 overview of key findings on adolescent drug use*, by L. D. Johnston, P. M. O'Malley, R. A. Miech, J. G. Bachman, & J. E. Schulenberg. Ann Arbor: Institute for Social Research, The University of Michigan.

punctuated with "heightened propensity for sensation seeking and risk taking that can result in negative consequences" (Brown et al., 2015, p. 895). Because substance use dramatically increases during the adolescent years, this period is crucial to emphasize. Some of these youth may be experimenting with substances, others attempting to ease the stress of adolescence, and still others modeling the behavior of family members and peers. Regardless of the reasons, the consequences of substance use are serious. Researchers propose that early initiation and regular use of substances are often associated with problems in school, early initiation of sexual intercourse, sexual risk-taking, delinquent behavior, assault, unsafe driving behaviors, and future substance use and concurrent physical and mental health problems (Brooks-Russell et al., 2015; Obando et al., 2014). These adolescents enter into adult roles before they are ready and without critical life skills.

Risk Factors

No single profile identifies who will or will not engage in substance use. Adolescent substance users have different personality types, family histories, socioeconomic levels, and life experiences. Risk factors can increase a youth's probability of a substance use problem occurring, while protective factors can reduce the likelihood of substance use or deviant behaviors (Obando et al., 2014). A risk factor for one person may not be a risk factor for another person. Although most youth do not progress beyond initial use, a small percentage rapidly escalate their substance use and face challenges in multiple areas of their lives. In general, risk factors can be seen as operating along five domains: (a) personal, (b) family, (c) school, (d) community, and (e) peer (Brooks-Russell et al., 2015; Obando et al., 2014). Conclusions from research indicate that the more risks a child or adolescent is exposed to, the more likely it is that the child will use substances.

Brooks-Russell (2015), Obando (2014), Trenz (2015), and their colleagues identified risk factors from the various domains:

- Depressive symptoms
- Sensation-seeking tendencies
- Peer pressure
- Low risk perception
- Drug use at an early age
- Favorable attitude toward substance use
- Violent and delinquent behavior
- Associating with peers who use
- Low commitment to school/lack of school bonding
- School failure/dropout
- Lack of social competence
- Low parental involvement and parental monitoring
- Family history of alcohol or drug use
- Low self-esteem
- Poverty
- Community and interpersonal violence

Because many risk factors are difficult or impossible to change, an important goal of prevention is to concentrate on protective factors. Having protective factors in the multiple domains is what is particularly effective in buffering adolescents from the effects of earlier circumstances that place them at risk, and in fostering competence and promoting successful development (Piko & Kovacs, 2010).

Family members are a significant factor in adolescent development because they are role models and major sources of support. Among the most frequently identified protective processes against child and adolescent substance use are family protective factors (Blustein et al., 2015; Ewing et al., 2015; Piko & Kovacs, 2010; Stone, Becker, Huber, & Catalano, 2012):

- family management (e.g., parental monitoring, discipline, and behavioral control)
- family bonding and support (e.g., talking about problems with parents)
- encouragement to make healthy choices
- family structure (e.g., intact nuclear family or two-parent household)
- familism (i.e., placing familial needs over individual needs)
- filial piety (i.e., respect for parents)

Family structure that decreases family conflict, facilitates positive interactions across family members, establishes clear rules about substance use, and fosters parental respect should reduce later youth problem behaviors, most importantly substance use.

The second most important socializing agent for children and adolescents, after the family, is the school. Peers influence adolescent substance use, and that peer influence often increases during middle school and high school (Ewing et al., 2105). Therefore, school-related protection should be considered. School climate and attachment to school and teachers can serve as a type of protection for adolescents, particularly because they spend a great deal of time at school (Piko & Kovacs, 2010; Trenz et al., 2015). School bonding contributes protection for youth and includes factors such as liking school, striving to succeed academically/school effort, and having high expectations for educational achievement (Stone et al., 2012).

In addition to protective influences, factors related to resiliency also need to be explored. Reivich (2010) defined resilience as the ability to persist in the face of challenges and bounce back from adversity. The following factors were found to increase resiliency:

- Optimism and hope
- Self-efficacy
- Strong self-regulation skills
- Problem-solving skills
- Adaptability
- Self-regulation
- Sense of humor
- Easy temperament
- Close relationships among family members
- Low discord between parents
- Warm and structured parenting style

The research on resilience shows that youth with strong resilience skills do better in a variety of domains compared to those with less resilience. A number of programs are attempting to incorporate resiliency training into adolescent substance use prevention programs.

Prevention and Intervention

Over the last 20-plus years, the field of childhood and adolescent substance use has changed dramatically. Prevention and treatment efforts have improved through the identification of risk and protective factors (Stone et al., 2012). Consequently, there is now a growing body of evidence-based practices to address risk and protection across childhood and adolescence. According to Stone and colleagues (2012), many of the risk and protective factors at play during childhood and adolescence remained relevant in young adulthood. Effective identification and assessment of substance use is therefore a crucial early step in both treatment and prevention programs.

Prevention efforts should be interrelated activities that include the home, school, and community. Researchers have described contemporary evidence-based prevention programs at the school, family, and community levels.

Schools are a crucial element in the prevention of substance use by youth and are efficient in that they offer access to large numbers of students (Griffin & Botvin, 2010; Tze, Li, & Pei, 2012). Prevention programs in schools educate youth about the effects and consequences of substance use; develop their refusal skills to protect themselves in problematic situations; and train them in necessary social and self-management skills, which empowers them to make informed decisions and to pursue a healthy lifestyle (Tze et al., 2012). Further, effective school-based prevention addresses cognition (e.g., anti-drug knowledge); unique psychosocial factors (e.g., peer relationships, identity issues, self-efficacy and assertiveness, and social learning/skills); attachment issues (i.e., connection to the school environment and personnel); and the decision-making process (i.e., decisions based on social norms, values, and morality) that underlies youth substance use. A comprehensive drug prevention curriculum for kindergarten through grade 12 is essential to teach students that drug use is wrong and harmful and to support and strengthen resistance to drugs.

There are a number of effective family-based prevention programs for youth substance use (Griffin & Botvin, 2010). Family support programs that encourage involvement of parents in their children's lives are a major key to making adolescents less vulnerable to alcohol and drugs. Regardless of the parents' relationship to their child, they need to be involved in the solution. NIDA (2007b) stated that family-based prevention programs should enhance family bonding and relationships and include parenting skills; practice in developing, discussing, and enforcing family policies on substance use; and training in drug education and information.

Further, community-based prevention programs that deliver a coordinated, comprehensive, and clear message about prevention can have a positive impact on youth substance use (Griffin & Botvin, 2010). Empirically supported community-based prevention programs delivered to entire communities usually are multifaceted, including school-based and family or parenting components. Concurrent with these components, it is common to include mass media campaigns, public policy initiatives, and other kinds of community organization and activities. Such initiatives demand a substantial amount of resources and coordination given the wide range of activities involved, and often are facilitated by stakeholders such as educators, parents, and community leaders.

In combination with prevention efforts, effective treatment approaches need to be designed to meet adolescents' specific needs. Gans, Falco, Schackman, and Winters (2010) noted that teenagers have different patterns of substance use, unique developmental and social issues, and a higher prevalence of co-occurring disorders. Adolescent treatment programs need to address the various factors that affect the adolescent's life, including education, family, recreation, peers, juvenile court, probation, and mental and physical health. The recommended first step in finding appropriate help is an initial screening followed by an in-depth assessment of the presenting symptoms and needs. Assessments should cover psychological and medical problems, learning disabilities, family functioning, and other aspects of youths' lives. (See Chapter 5 for more details on assessment.)

It is recommended that treatment programs contain the following elements (U.S. Department of Health and Human Services, 2005b):

- Services should address all of aspects of youths' lives: school, home, public activities
- Parents should be involved in the youths' drug use treatment
- Programming should reflect developmental differences between adolescents and adults
- Treatment programs should build a climate of trust
- Staff should be well trained in adolescent development, comorbidity issues, and substance use
- Programs should address the distinct needs of youths based on gender and ethnicity
- Information should be provided on continuing care (relapse prevention, aftercare plans, and follow-up)
- Rigorous evaluations to measure success and improve treatment services should be included

Substance use among children and adolescents has long been an important concern in society. Given the vulnerability of youth to substance use disorders, effective prevention and intervention strategies are hot discussion topics in the field of education and mental health (Tze et al., 2012). More work is needed to advance knowledge in this area.

WOMEN

It is well known that substance use problems are more common in men than in women, yet women who do use substances experience a serious toll on their health and the health of their families (Greenfield, Back, Lawson, & Brady, 2010; Martin & Aston, 2014; Sharma, 2014). Women are usually late to initiate substance use and are often influenced by men in their lives such as a partner/spouse. Comorbid psychiatric problems such as depression, anxiety, or bipolar disorder are common, which might contribute to women seeking treatment earlier in the course of their substance use disorder. Problems related to substance use also cause more impairment for women in all areas of their lives as compared to their male counterparts (Sharma, 2014).

In 2013, 11.9% of young women aged 12 to 17; 56.9% of women aged 18 to 25; and 50.1% of women aged 26 or older were current drinkers of alcohol (Substance Abuse and Mental Health Services Administration [SAMHSA], 2014a). Among the women aged 18 to 25, 31.4% reported binge drinking. Among the women aged 26 or older, 14.7% reported binge drinking. Nine percent of pregnant women aged 15 to 44 reported current alcohol use, and 2.3% reported binge drinking. With regard to illicit drug use, 8.0% of young women aged 12 to 17 reported using illicit drugs, with 6.2% using marijuana. Further, 5.3% of young women aged 12 to 17 and 5.8% of women aged 18 or older reported moderate to severe substance use (SAMHSA, 2014a).

The history of substance use among women suggests that severe substance use disorder among women is closely connected to negative and sanctioned socialization and with experiences of disempowerment (White & Kilbourne, 2006). Throughout history, women have experienced varied forms of oppression from economic to personal that injure women in unique ways (Lanzetta, 2005). Oppression invades women in such a way that it is difficult to identify the source of their pain. Women may react in unhealthy ways by numbing the feelings through the use of prescribed, legal, or illicit substances (Stevens, 2006). Regardless of this history, women were entirely "hidden from view" in substance use research until the late 1970s (Martin & Aston, 2014, p. 336).

Women frequently initiate substance use as a result of traumatic life events such as physical or sexual violence, sudden physical illness, an accident, or disruption in family life

(Martin & Aston, 2014; Stevens, Andrade, & Ruiz, 2009). Those women reported that the traumatic experiences occurred before substance use. In one study (Stevens et al., 2009), of the 80 women enrolled in a treatment program, 74% reported having been raped and 80% reported having been physically assaulted.

Social stigma, shame, and embarrassment continue to be a part of women's substance use (Sharma, 2014; Stevens et al., 2009). Society's expectation for women is to provide the moral foundation for the family, and to be the caretakers and nurturers. Such expectations discourage women from admitting their substance use problems and seeking professional help.

Risk Factors

A history of marital discord, divorce, and interpersonal conflict is positively associated with substance use (Greenfield et al., 2010). Some women may drink larger quantities of alcohol and use other substances to have an activity in common with their partners or to facilitate and maintain the relationship (Kaya, Iwamoto, Grivel, Clinton, & Brady, 2015). In addition, having a partner who uses substances places women at higher risk for relapse than for their male counterparts (Greenfield et al., 2010).

Gender difference in the mental health of adult substance users indicate that women are more likely than men to have co-occurring mental and substance use disorders (Greenfield et al., 2010; Sharma, 2014). For women, anxiety disorders, major depression, eating disorders, and posttraumatic stress disorder (e.g., physical and sexual abuse) are positively associated with substance use.

Women who become pregnant during their 30s and 40s might be more likely to drink alcohol during pregnancy than their younger counterparts (Wilsnack, Wilsnack, & Wolfgang Kantor, 2014). The use of substances can affect a pregnant woman in a variety of ways, from an increased risk of miscarriage to preterm birth, low birth weight, and significant disorders in children (Stade et al., 2009). Above all other drugs, alcohol is the most common cause of malformation to the embryo or fetus in pregnancy. Maternal alcohol use contributes to a range of effects such as fetal alcohol spectrum disorders (FASDs) and fetal alcohol syndrome (FAS), which include deficits such as poor impulse control; problems in social perception and receptive and expressive language; limited abstraction; and problems in memory, attention and judgment.

According to Kaya and colleagues (2015), women are more sensitive to the consumption and long-term effects of alcohol and other substances than men, therefore presenting a significant public health concern. From absorption to metabolic processes, women display more difficulty in physically managing the consequences of use (e.g., women tend to be physically smaller than men, store less body water, and have lower levels of alcohol-metabolizing enzymes). With higher levels of substances in the system for longer periods of time, women are more susceptible to substance-related diseases (e.g., liver cancer, breast cancer, accelerated brain atrophy, and cognitive deficits) and organ damage.

Women have a greater reluctance than men to admit they have a problem with substances. They often encounter barriers to finding, entering, and completing treatment programs. Society imposes some of the barriers, while others are internal within the woman herself. Examples of factors that impede access to treatment include childcare responsibilities, transportation, financial concerns, social stigma, lack of awareness of treatment options, homelessness, and concerns about confrontational approaches that were common in male-dominated traditional treatment (Greenfield et al., 2010). Those who have been most successful have had the help and support of significant others, family members, friends, treatment providers, and the community.

Prevention and Intervention

Gender is an important variable when considering substance use prevention and treatment. As a result of the impairment caused by substance use disorders often comorbid with other psychiatric disorders, women seek treatment earlier than men (Sharma, 2014). Reports concerning treatment of women have shown the following: (1) Women experience a number of barriers to receiving treatment; (2) women are more vulnerable than men to some of the physiological effects of substance use; and (3) substance use among women is more often rooted in psychosocial problems and traumatic life events. These important gender differences suggest the need for specialized treatment programs for women (Greenfield et al., 2010; Sharma, 2014).

Diverse services that aim to reduce the barriers women face entering and staying in treatment and address the specific substance use–related problems of women should be incorporated into treatment programs (Greenfield et al, 2010; Sharma, 2014). Specific program aspects can include child care, prenatal care, women-only treatment, financial support, and services tailored to women's issues. Retention in treatment is positively influenced by many factors, such as better overall functioning, higher levels of personal stability and social support (e.g., housing, transportation, education, and income), lower anger levels, beliefs about treatment, and referral source.

Gender-sensitive treatment (Greenfield et al., 2010; Martin & Aston, 2014; Sharma, 2014; Stevens et al., 2009) should emphasize women's issues such as:

- Childcare
- Pregnancy
- Parenting
- Domestic violence and victimization
- Grief and loss
- Stigma/not wanting others to know
- Sexual trauma and victimization
- Psychiatric comorbidity
- Housing income/financial support
- Social services
- Medical health education
- Family/partner characteristics

Stevens and colleagues (2009) encourage a focus on empowerment, with service providers thinking in terms of wellness versus illness, competence instead of deficits, and strengths versus weaknesses. Programs should provide opportunities for women to establish a sense of self-empowerment, self-efficacy, and self-control to assist them in gaining the skills and resources that they need to take control of their lives. During the recovery process, women need the support of the community and encouragement of those closest to them to assist with possible relapses. After completing treatment, women also need the services to assist them in sustaining their recovery and in rejoining the community.

In addition to entering a treatment program, a number of protective factors have been identified that are associated with a reduced risk for substance use (Agrawal, 2005):

- Parental warmth: If a woman comes from a family of origin where high warmth and caring are present, she is less likely to initiate the use of substances.

- Partner support: Good relationships can reduce the likelihood of alcohol abuse in women with a familial history of abuse. Partners can be key motivators to bring women into treatment.
- Spiritual practices: Higher levels of personal devotion and faith-based affiliation can reduce the risk for substance use and dependence.
- Coping skills: Using problem-solving skills, accepting support from others, and coping effectively with one's feelings can be key protective factors.

In summary, NIDA (2007b) states that the best substance use and treatment message is that "one size fits all" approaches do not always work. Treatment approaches and programs for women need to be more tailored and effective in recognizing gender implications (Martin & Aston, 2014; Sharma, 2014).

THE LGBTQ COMMUNITY

According to Brown (2010), "I define connection as the energy that exists between people when they feel seen, heard, and valued; when they can give and receive without judgement; and when they derive sustenance and strength from the relationship" (p. 19).

Connecting with the individuals with whom we work is imperative to provide the help and support they need. Culturally competent treatment most often results in effective outcomes. Understanding the appropriate terminology is essential to working with lesbian, gay, bisexual, transgender, questioning, and/or queer (hereafter also referred to as LGBTQ) clients. LGBTQ people are from all cultural backgrounds, ethnicities, and racial groups; can be any age; can have attained any educational or income level; and live in all geographic areas in the United States. The LGBTQ minority group differs from other minority groups in that LGBTQ people do not come from a common geographic area or have certain physical characteristics in common (Center for Substance Abuse Treatment [CSAT], 2012a). Sexual orientation and gender identity are independent variables in an individual's definition of self. How a person learns to acknowledge and accept one's sexual orientation is largely shaped by cultural, religious, societal, and familial factors. Transgender people face a similar yet unique challenge in trying to come to terms with a gender identity that differs from their assigned birth sex.

The psychosocial stress of being an LGBTQ person in a society largely dominated by a heterosexual orientation places LGBTQ individuals at a higher risk for substance use disorder (SUD). According to McCabe, Bostwick, Hughes, West, and Boyd (2010), a minority stress model indicates that discrimination, internalized homophobia, and social stigma can create a hostile and stressful social environment for LGBT individuals, which contributes to mental health problems, including substance use disorders.

It is important to have a general understanding of heterosexism and homophobia as SUD treatment providers working with the LGBTQ population. Heterosexism and homophobia are forms of bigotry against LGBTQ people. Heterosexism denies, ignores, denigrates, or stigmatizes nonheterosexual forms of emotional and affectional expression, sexual behavior, or community. Homophobia is defined as the irrational fear of, aversion to, or discrimination against LGBTQ behavior or persons. Internalized homophobia describes the self-loathing or resistance to accepting an LGBTQ sexual orientation and is an important concept in understanding and connecting with LGBTQ clients (CSAT, 2012a).

The negative effects of these attitudes include:

- Self-blame for the victimization one has suffered
- Poor self-concept as a result of negative messages about homosexuality

- Anger directed inward resulting in destructive patterns such as substance use
- Victim mentality or feelings of inadequacy, hopelessness, and despair that interfere with leading a fulfilling life
- Self-victimization that may hinder emotional growth and development

Heterosexism can cause internalized homophobia, shame, and a poor self-concept in some LGBTQ people. Further, as one of the several marginalized communities in our society, the LGBTQ community often reports feelings of isolation, fear, depression, distrust, and anger. Such negative experiences and perceptions place LGBTQ individuals at a higher risk of using substances as a means of coping. It is important to recognize that these possible effects result from prejudice and discrimination in society and are not a direct consequence of one's sexual identity.

According to *Healthy People 2010* (U.S. Department of Health and Human Services, 2000), there is evidence to suggest that LGBTQ individuals perceive themselves to be at increased risk for SUD. It was also indicated that when compared to the heterosexual population, LGBTQ individuals are more likely to use substances, have higher rates of moderate to severe substance use, and are more likely to continue this into later life (CSAT, 2012a). Although members of the LGBTQ community have been shown to use all types of drugs, certain drugs appear to be more popular. For example, Cabaj and Smith (2012) reported that gay men are significantly more likely to have used marijuana, stimulants, sedatives, cocaine, and party drugs than men in the general population. Methamphetamine use is nearly epidemic in gay men in some parts of the United States (Cabaj & Smith, 2012).) Use of this drug often results in strong cravings and frequent relapses and may require extensive and highly focused treatment. Conversely, Finnegan (2012) pointed out that lesbians exhibit great diversity in their substance use. There is no single pattern of use behavior among lesbians who are substance users. According to the Center for Substance Abuse Treatment (CSAT, 2012a), gay men and lesbians have a higher rate of substance use disorders than their heterosexual counterparts. It was also found that 30% of all lesbians reported having an alcohol use problem. Other studies listed found that gay men and lesbians were heavier substance users than the general or heterosexual population. It should be noted that precise incidence and prevalence rates of substance use in the LGBTQ community has been difficult to determine, because of a lack of reliable information on the size of the LGBTQ population (CSAT, 2012a).

LGBTQ clients in recovery have similar health concerns and face many of the same physical and mental health crises as other clients. As with every client, it is important to screen for other health problems, including possible co-occurring mental health disorders, liver disease, sexually transmitted infections (STIs), HIV/AIDS, poor nutrition, and sexual abuse. All clients should be screened for hepatitis B and hepatitis C and referred for hepatitis A and hepatitis B vaccinations (CSAT, 2012a). LGBTQ people have likely been marginalized and treated poorly by medical practitioners in the past who have perceived their identity as deviant or pathological. Based on these experiences, LGBTQ individuals may be more hesitant to disclose their true gender identity and/or sexual orientation, creating a barrier to adequate health care. It is important to be mindful to help these clients overcome their anxiety or discomfort and maintain sensitivity to their specific needs.

LGBTQ Identity Development

According to Cass (1979), coming out is a lifelong process toward self-acceptance where an individual explores one's sexual and/or gender identity. People forge a lesbian, gay, bisexual or transgender identity first to themselves. They then may share that identity with others. Publicly revealing one's orientation may or may not be part of coming out.

"Coming out" refers to the experiences of some LGBTQ people as they explore their sexual and/or gender identity. There is no concrete or correct process of coming out, and some LGBTQ people do not come out at all. It is important to remember that coming out is different for every person. It is both an internal and external process. Every person has multiple identities that intersect and subsequently impact the coming out process. Sometimes, coming to terms with one's identity can be a crisis issue. There is elevated risk of suicide attempts among lesbian, gay, and bisexual adolescents, which is a consequence of the psychosocial stressors associated with being LGBTQ, including gender nonconformity, victimization, lack of support, family problems, suicide attempts by acquaintances, homelessness, substance use, and psychiatric disorders (Suicide Prevention Resource Center, 2008). When treating LGBTQ clients, the clinician should consider which part of the coming out process the clients are currently in and should be aware of clients' comfort level with their identity and treat them accordingly. As always, it is best to not make assumptions and to find out from the clients their own feelings and possible anxieties about their sexual identity.

The coming-out journey begins with an early awareness of feelings of difference to the development of an integrated identity. The reasons that people move from stage to stage, or fail to move, are very complex. Stage models can provide a useful description of the process and suggest a way of looking at how substance use and recovery interact with being LGBTQ (McNally, 2012).

Cass (1979, 1984) proposed a theoretical model of homosexual identity formation comprising six stages of development through which an individual moves to achieve an LGBTQ identity. The model is based on two broad assumptions: (a) identity is acquired through a developmental process, and (b) change in behavior stems from the interaction between individuals and their environment.

The first stage of identity confusion is characterized by confusion, turmoil, and doubt as individuals begin to question their sexual orientation. Identity comparison, the second stage, occurs when they have accepted the possibility of being homosexual. In the third stage of identity tolerance, individuals increase their commitment to a homosexual identity but keep public and private identities separate. The fourth stage of identity acceptance is characterized by acceptance of a homosexual identity rather than tolerating this identity. Disclosure of homosexual identity remains selective. Identity pride is the fifth stage, characterized by anger, pride, and activism, which lead to immersion in the homosexual culture and rejection of the values of the heterosexual community. Finally, identity synthesis occurs with a fusion of the homosexual identity with all other aspects of self, as individuals no longer dichotomize the heterosexual and homosexual world.

Models such as this (Cass, 1979, 1984) can help both clients and professionals reach a better understanding of the challenges of each developmental stage and the particular supports that might be necessary to attain an integrated identity. McNally (2012) states that stage models are general guides to help counselors understand the coming-out process. The models are not linear, and people do not necessarily move through them in order. One stage is not better than another, and people should not be seen as more advanced and mature if they are in a later stage. In fact, Cass (1984) has revised her model based on a lack of empirical evidence for some of the stages. Although the model has been criticized, it is useful in approaching the complexity of sexual orientation and identity formation.

Risk Factors

There are numerous factors that place LGBTQ individuals at higher risk for SUD. CSAT (2012a) discusses several factors that may explain the etiology of problem substance use in the LGBTQ population:

- Prejudice and discrimination: The effects can result in feelings of isolation, fear, depression, anxiety, and anger. LGBTQ people may be victims of antigay violence and hate crimes such as verbal and physical attacks.
- Cultural issues: For LGBTQ individuals, coming from an ethnic or racial minority makes coping with one's sexual orientation even more complex and difficult due to cultural traditions, values, and norms.
- Legal issues: Disclosure of one's sexual orientation can lead to employment problems, denial of housing, and loss of custody of one's children.
- Accessibility: Because of homophobia and discrimination, some LGBTQ individuals may find it difficult or uncomfortable to access treatment services.
- Families of origin: The family of origin's response to one's disclosure of an LGBT identity can have a long-lasting and sometimes devastating effect on an individual. Unresolved issues with the family of origin can act as emotional triggers to a relapse.
- Health issues: LGBTQ individuals may face a variety of additional health problems such as co-occurring mental health disorders, posttraumatic stress disorder (PTSD), human immunodeficiency virus/acquired immunodeficiency syndrome (HIV/AIDS), sexually transmitted diseases, hepatitis, and other injuries.
- Gay bars: Discrimination has often in the past limited LGBTQ people's social outlets to bars, private homes, or clubs where alcohol and drugs often play a prominent role.

Health care providers need to be aware of the myriad issues specific to the LGBTQ population. Providers can enhance treatment and recovery by being knowledgeable about the client's unique needs and being sensitive to issues surrounding identity, homophobia, and heterosexism.

Prevention and Intervention

SUD treatment for an LGBTQ client is the same as that for other individuals and primarily focuses on stopping the substance use disorder that interferes with the well-being of the client. The way that it differs in this community is the need for the treatment to address the clients' feelings about their sexual identity, as well as the potential impact that homophobia and heterosexism has had on their lives and might have on their recovery. The client may be harboring the effects of society's negative attitudes—which often result in painful and uncomfortable feelings that the client may want to medicate. SUD treatment providers should develop a basic understanding of the population so they can provide productive, culturally sensitive, and effective services with an understanding of the homosexual identity formation issues and their possible correlation with SUD (CSAT, 2012a).

Using preferred language is critical to an effective helping relationship with an LGBTQ client. It is important to call the client by his or her preferred name and always use the pronoun that the client has specified. Counselors should ask a self-identified LGBTQ client by which name they prefer to be called. Using gender-neutral language until the client says otherwise is a great way to avoid making assumptions. This sensitive use of language can be an important sign of respect and acknowledgement and help to create a connective and healing environment for LGBTQ clients.

LGBTQ clients may have additional concerns with which they are dealing, such as coping with coming out, societal stigmas, HIV/AIDS, discrimination, death and dying, and people close to them struggling with homophobia. At times, these concerns create intense challenges, especially when LGBTQ individuals are attempting to change their substance use patterns and coping mechanisms that may have worked for them in the past. It is important for treatment providers to understand that part of the recovery process for some LGBTQ people is accepting themselves as gay, lesbian, bisexual, or transgender and finding their desired fit in society.

LGBTQ individuals may experience barriers to accessing treatment services, as SUD treatment programs are often not equipped to meet the needs of this population. Heterosexual treatment staff may be uninformed about LGBTQ issues, may be insensitive to or antagonistic toward LGBTQ clients, or may falsely believe that sexual orientation/gender identity causes substance use disorders or can be changed by therapy. These attitudes may be based on misinformation or personal beliefs. However, someone's sexual orientation and/or gender identity should never be viewed as in need of changing. These beliefs by treatment staff become major barriers to treating LGBTQ clients and demonstrate the staff's need for cultural training.

It is important to offer SUD treatment that is in line with and supportive to the needs of the LGBTQ population. In order to do this, some changes may need to be made. For example, some programs that use observers when administering their urine drug screens need to consider the client's concerns and ask which gender of observer they prefer. Another change for residential treatment facilities would be to designate a non–gender-specific toilet and shower to meet the needs of some LGBTQ individuals. Intake forms are great opportunities to convey recognition by using gender/sex-neutral language and assessing all domains of sexuality (Levounis, Drescher, & Barber, 2012). Documentation of gender identity and sexual orientation should encourage truthful disclosure by providing many different options to choose from and, when appropriate, a fill-in section where an individual can provide information that might not be listed. This attention to language and difference shows support and validation for the client's identity.

Because of the unique needs of transgender and gender non-conforming clients and necessary sensitivity/skill set of clinicians, CSAT (2012a, p. 99) offered the do's and don'ts of working with transgender and gender nonconforming clients.

Do ...

- Use the proper pronouns based on their self-identity
- Receive clinical supervision if you have issues or feelings about working with trans individuals
- Require training on transgender issues for all staff
- Allow transgender clients to continue the use of hormones when they are prescribed.
- Advocate that the transgender client using "street" hormones get immediate medical care and legally prescribed hormones
- Allow transgender/gender-nonconforming clients to use bathrooms and showers based on their gender self-identity and gender role
- Require that all clients and staff maintain a safe environment for all transgender clients
- Post a nondiscrimination policy in the waiting room that explicitly includes sexual orientation and gender identity

Don't ...

- Don't call clients who identify themselves as females "he" or "him," or call clients who identify themselves as male "she" or "her"
- Don't project your transphobia onto the transgender client or share transphobic comments with other staff or clients
- Never make the transgender client choose between hormones and treatment/recovery
- Don't make the transgender client educate the staff
- Don't assume transgender women or men are gay
- Don't make transgender individuals living as females use male facilities or transgender individuals living as males use female facilities
- Never allow staff or clients to make transphobic comments or put transgender clients at risk for physical or sexual abuse or harassment

Brooks (2012) and Cabaj and Smith (2012) suggested that programs incorporate the following culturally sensitive strategies and considerations:

- Programs should screen and train staff to ensure they are LGBTQ competent.
- Educate and train treatment staff on LGBTQ issues, appropriate services, and about state and local laws and regulations regarding their LGBTQ clients.
- Refer clients to LGBTQ-appropriate centers and organizations and self-help groups.
- Establish and enforce written policies that ensure confidentiality.
- LGBTQ clients should be encouraged to consider the pros and cons of disclosing their sexual orientation/gender identity and substance use histories to others unless they are fairly sure how the information will be received. Safety planning with treatment staff is strongly encouraged.
- Programs should create a safe place for healing. This safety should include respect, understanding, and support for the life partners, significant others, and spouses of the LGBTQ clients. These individuals must be included in services similar to those offered to the spouses/partners of heterosexual clients.
- The impact of heterosexism and homophobia should be considered when creating treatment plans.
- Promote self-respect and personal dignity through intentional and inclusive service delivery.
- Promote healthier safer sex behaviors, stronger supportive relationships, and compliance with medication regimes.

McCabe (2012) stressed providing support for LGBTQ clients and their families as a significant and important element of treatment. However, an LGBTQ client may have unresolved issues with their family of origin stemming from the family's reaction to the disclosure of their sexual orientation/gender identity. There could be a wide range of responses—from abusive, rejecting, or avoidant to tolerant, supportive, and inclusive. As with all clients, counselors need to review the client's role in their family of origin, because unresolved issues can act as emotional triggers to a relapse. Questions regarding families should be asked with sensitivity. Something that makes the LGBTQ experience different from other cultural minorities is that LGBTQ individuals experience prejudice and oftentimes a disconnection from other members within their minority group. Even in a multicultural family, a youth is usually able to look beyond their immediate family to the cultural community and find someone with whom they identify.

This is typically not the case for LGBTQ people, who often grow up with a lack of role models, information, or connection with other LGBTQ individuals. A support group that works with families of origin is known as PFLAG (Parents, Families, and Friends of Lesbians and Gays). PFLAG may be a helpful place to start and provide a supportive environment for the client to explore family issues.

Most major metropolitan communities have both inpatient and outpatient treatment centers that provide SUD services for LGBTQ clients. Recovery.org is a great resource for finding appropriate support groups and treatment centers for the LGBTQ community. The mission at recovery.org is to connect people and their families with the information and resources to help them recover from substance use and behavioral disorders. The National Association of Lesbian and Gay Addictions Professionals (NALGAP) operates to create a network for support and communications among addiction professionals to educate agencies and organizations about LGBTQ people and addictions; acts as a clearinghouse for resources; raises the queer community's consciousness and combats its denial of the problem of addictions; and strives to improve substance use treatment for LGBTQ individuals (CSAT, 2012a). Counselors can encourage clients to establish an LGBTQ support system, can be familiar with community resources, and can make the information available to all clients within the treatment center. The Center for Substance Abuse Treatment (CSAT) of the Substance Abuse and Mental Health Services Administration (SAMHSA) is an important resource to look into when embarking on substance use treatment work and seeking out best practices.

Substance use treatment providers, counselors, and administrators need to be culturally competent and aware of the issues facing LGBTQ clients. With this knowledge, they can design quality treatment programs that provide effective, ethical, and informed care. With these care provisions in place, outcomes will improve and providers will reach a previously underserved population (CSAT, 2012a). The most important thing to remember when treating any client, especially clients belonging to marginalized communities, is to not make assumptions. The client is the expert on his or her own experience. It is important to listen to each client and hear his or her experiences as new and unique. Providing this level of care will ensure that LGBTQ clients will feel safe in engaging in the treatment and care they need.

PEOPLE WITH DISABILITIES

It is estimated that about 56.7 million people in the United States (19% of the population) had a disability in 2010 (U.S. Bureau of the Census, 2010). More than half of these reporting individuals (38.3 million) indicated that the disability was severe. Based on this report, the number of people with disabilities increased by 2.2 million and the number and percentage needing assistance also increased when compared with a similar 2005 report. About 12.3 million people aged 6 years or older (4.4%) needed assistance with one or more activities of daily living (ADLs) or instrumental activities of daily living (IADLs). Disability prevalence rates increase with age (U.S. Bureau of the Census, 2010):

- 8% of children under 15 years of age
- 10% of people ages 15 to 24 years
- 11% of people ages 25 to 44 years
- 20% of people ages 45 to 54 years
- 29% of people ages 55 to 64 years

- 35% of people ages 65 to 69 years
- 43% of people ages 70 to 74 years
- 54% of people ages 75 to 79 years
- 71% of people ages 80 and over

In 1990 the Americans with Disabilities Act (ADA) was enacted. The act guarantees equal opportunity for people with disabilities in public accommodations, commercial facilities, employment, transportation, state and local government services, and telecommunications. Although estimates of people with disabilities vary, depending on how *disability* is operationally defined, ADA's definition for people with disabilities is those who have a "physical or mental impairment that substantially limits one or more major life activities, or a person who is perceived by others as having such an impairment."

Brault (2012) describes three domains of disability (p. 2):

1. Communicative

   - Blind or had difficulty seeing
   - Deaf or had difficult hearing
   - Difficulty having their speech understood

2. Mental

   - Learning disability, an intellectual disability, developmental disability or Alzheimer's disease, senility, or dementia
   - Other mental or emotional condition that seriously interfered with everyday activities

3. Physical

   - Used a wheelchair, cane, crutches, or walker
   - Difficulty walking a quarter of a mile, climbing a flight of stairs, lifting something as heavy as a 10-pound bag of groceries, grasping objects, or getting in or out of bed
   - Listed medical conditions such as arthritis, back or spine problem, broken bone or fracture, cancer, cerebral palsy, diabetes, epilepsy, head or spinal cord injury, heart trouble or atherosclerosis, high blood pressure, kidney problems, lung or respiratory problem, missing limbs, paralysis, stomach/digestive problems, stroke, thyroid problem

The Office of Disability suggests that people with a disability are two to four times more likely than their nondisabled peers to experience SUD. Rates of use vary considerably depending on the nature of the disability, and whether it was acquired or a lifelong disability (O'Sullivan, Blum, Watts, & Bates, 2015). Individuals with acquired disabilities use substances at higher rates than those who have a disability from birth. Approximately half of people with spinal cord injury, traumatic brain injury (TBI), and psychiatric disability experience substance use disorders. Among those with an acquired TBI, almost half were found to be under the influence of alcohol at the time of the injury, and up to one-third continued to use substances after their injury. Among persons with physical disabilities and limited activity levels, risk of substance use disorders is higher (O'Sullivan et al., 2015).

Prevalence indicators note the rates of substance use disorders in this group to be greater than among nondisabled persons, yet the participation of people with disabilities in treatment is thought to be minimal. There is continual concern about the ability of people with disabilities to access SUD treatment services (O'Sullivan et al., 2015).

Risk Factors

According to Capuzzi and Gross (2012), people with disabilities face numerous problems that can be seen to arise as a result of (a) the disability itself, (b) the environment in which the disability is experienced, (c) the individual's response to the disability, or (d) the response of family members and others in the social environment. It must be established whether substance use behaviors are a consequence of or a response to the disabling event, or whether individuals participated in the same behaviors prior to the disability. Other contributing factors appear to be frustration, oppression, limited financial resources, or social isolation that some individuals with disabilities experience and seek to escape through substance use (Capuzzi & Gross, 2012; O'Sullivan et al, 2015).

Livneh and Antonak (2007) examined the psychological adaptation to having a disability. Many factors, some disability-related and some not, interact to create a profound effect on the lives of those with disabilities, which may lead to SUD:

> *Stress:* Persons with disabilities normally face an increase in both the frequency and severity of stressful situations. Stress may increase because of the need to cope with daily threats to independence, fulfillment of life roles, and economic stability.

> *Crisis:* The sudden onset of many disabilities, loss of valued functions, or a life-threatening diagnosis can be highly traumatic. The psychological consequences of crisis may be long lasting and evolve into pathological conditions.

> *Loss and Grief:* The crisis experienced following the onset of a traumatic or progressive disability triggers mourning for the loss of function. The individual expresses feelings of grief and despair.

> *Body Image:* The onset of a disability may alter or distort one's body image, self-perception, and self-concept, leading to feelings of anxiety and depression, as well as cognitive distortions.

> *Stigma:* Stereotypes and prejudice can increase the stigma associated with having a disability. *Handicapism* is defined as a set of assumptions and practices that promote the differential and unequal treatment of people because of apparent or assumed physical, mental, or behavioral differences (Smart, 2009).

Livneh and Antonak (2007) identified the most frequently experienced psychosocial reactions to a disability that affect one's ability to cope:

- Shock
- Anxiety
- Denial
- Depression
- Anger/hostility

Understanding how people navigate the process of adapting to an acquired disability and applying this understanding in the form of effective clinical interventions is critical to successful treatment outcomes (O'Sullivan et al., 2015).

Prevention and Intervention

The U.S. Department of Health and Human Services (2005b) reported that existing SUD prevention, intervention, and treatment services are not sufficiently responsive to the needs of people with disabilities. As a result, access to education, prevention, and treatment services for SUDs can be limited, incomplete, or misdirected. It was also noted that treatment centers and meeting spaces for peer support groups are often inaccessible to those with physical disabilities (Office of Disability, 2010; O'Sullivan et al, 2015):

- Transportation and sheer distance can complicate access to specialized treatment centers.
- Cultural insensitivity by health care providers may prevent persons with disabilities from seeking education, risk management, and treatment for SUD. According to the Bureau of Labor Statistics in 2014, SUD and behavioral disorder counselors are not required to have any knowledge or training about disabilities (O'Sullivan et al., 2015).
- Effective communication may be frustrating because of the limited availability of assistive supports, such as interpreters for persons who are deaf or have hearing problems.
- Often health care providers focus solely on a person's disability and may fail to discuss substance use prevention/intervention.
- Physical barriers can prevent access by many people with disabilities. Barriers that might affect accessibility include inaccessible parking, wheelchair-inaccessible bathroom stalls, doors with inaccessible handles, inaccessible bathing facilities (in residential facilities), and inaccessible hallways/stairs (West, Graham, & Cifu, 2009).

Interventions need to be designed that are sensitive to the particular disability and life circumstance of the individual. The psychological challenges of adjusting to a disability and working toward recovery from a substance use disorder; taking medications for symptoms; and coping with the dual stigma of disability and substance use can present a challenge to the treatment process (O'Sullivan et al., 2015). *The Counselor* magazine (2006) stressed the need for counselors who have specific training for working with people who are mentally or physically disabled, with some cross training in substance use services, to satisfy the demand for more specialized programs. It is recommended that SUD treatment for people with disabilities include the following:

- Family psychoeducation
- Disability and medication management and education
- Independent living skills education
- Anger and stress management
- HIV risk reduction, counseling, and testing
- STI and infectious disease education
- Interpreted self-help meetings for the deaf and hard of hearing
- Health and wellness education
- Case management and crisis intervention
- Educational, vocational, and residential referrals
- Medical and psychiatric services
- Domestic violence and victim assistance counseling
- Development of social support networks
- Self-esteem and body image

For the general population, inability to afford treatment, lack of health insurance, multi-leveled stigma, lack of knowledge of treatment options, and lack of time for treatment are primary reasons why people in need of substance use services do not access treatment. For people with disabilities, the added challenges of adapting to a disability and coping with the unique risk factors for this group may result in even more barriers to treatment (O'Sullivan et al., 2015).

There are few SUD treatment options for people with disabilities, and a lack of cross-training and guides to best practices for staff who serve this population. Changes in policy, advocacy, and attitudes are necessary for specialized programs to catch up with traditional treatment programs. Treatment for special populations is more expensive because of the need for smaller group sizes, modified materials, and additional staff. If more programming options were available, treatment services could be better customized. As people with disabilities leave treatment programs, they face the same challenges that other people with SUDs face, except to a greater degree. They face a shortage of sober living arrangements, employment opportunities (e.g., lower employment rates therefore lack of health insurance with coverage), leisure activities, and support systems, and many must use prescribed medications to alleviate symptoms (e.g., for chronic pain or psychiatric symptoms with high potential for abuse and dependence). All programs should be fully accessible—physically, attitudinally, and programmatically (Counselor, 2006; O'Sullivan et al., 2015).

IMMIGRANTS

The U.S. immigrant population (legal and illegal) hit a record high of 42.1 million in the second quarter of 2015—an increase of 1.7 million since the same quarter in 2014 (Camarota & Zeigler, 2015b). Growth over that year was led by an influx of Mexican immigrants, which increased by 740,000 from 2014 to 2015.

After growing little from 2007 to 2011, the nation's immigrant population has increased by 4.1 million from 2011 to 2015. In 2015, immigrants accounted for 13.3% of the total U.S. population—the largest share in 105 years (Camarota & Zeigler, 2015b). It is predicted that the total net immigration (e.g., the difference between those coming in and going out) will increase steadily to 64 million over the next 45 years (Camarota & Zeigler, 2015a).

The U.S. Census Bureau refers to the immigrant population as those who were "foreign born" and those residing in the United States who were not American citizens at birth. This definition also includes those in the country illegally. According to Camarota & Zeigler (2015a), legal immigration includes individuals who are permanent residents or those who have been granted authorization to live and work in the United States on a permanent basis. Illegal immigration includes unauthorized residents, defined as all foreign-born noncitizens who are not legal residents. Most unauthorized residents either entered the United States without inspection or were admitted on a temporary basis yet stayed past the date that they were required to leave.

There are a few reasons why immigration to the United States is on the rise (Camarota & Zeigler, 2015b). First, significant cutbacks in enforcement in recent years have led to easier access to the borders. Second, the permissive nature of the legal immigration system has made the move more attractive for those who are foreign born. Third, improvements in the economy have acted as an incentive for a geographical shift.

Although Latinos make up approximately half of all foreign-born individuals in the United States, in more recent decades, a growing number of immigrants from other regions in the world such as Asia and Africa have entered the United States (Li & Wen, 2015). As a result of the projected immigration population growth and its impact on the population health of the United States, immigrant health has become an essential focus of the public health domain. It is well documented that immigrants are healthier than those born in the United States with same ethnicity (Salas-Wright, Vaughn, Clark, Terzis, & Cordova, 2014; Salas-Wright & Vaughn, 2014), but are at risk for compromised health over time as their length of stay in the United States increases (Li & Wen, 2015; Szaflarski, Cubbins, & Ying, 2011).

This pattern has been observed in many health outcomes and referred to as the *immigrant paradox*: that is, despite their lower income and educational levels, and barriers to health care, immigrants tend to show better health at their arrival than native individuals of the same ethnicity. However, these initial health advantages disappear and their health begins to resemble that of the native population as they stay and assimilate into the dominant culture (Li & Wen, 2015; Salas-Wright et al., 2014; Salas-Wright & Vaughn, 2014). It has been suggested that second-generation (U.S.-born) children of Latino and Asian immigrants have a higher prevalence of substance use disorders than first-generation immigrants (Mancini, Salas-Wright, & Vaughn, 2015; Savage & Mezuk, 2014). Even among first-generation immigrants, those who have resided in the United States longer have greater development of substance use disorders, which suggests that environment and exposures in the United States may directly affect initiation of substance use.

There are a number of theories as to what contributes to this healthy immigrant effect, and some explanations of what might lead to an increase in deleterious health of immigrants, particularly substance use, once they have been in the United States for long periods of time (Salas-Wright et al., 2014). It is possible that individuals who are willing and able to uproot their lives and move to a foreign land are highly capable, self-disciplined, more motivated, and have good physical and mental health. Based on this paradigm, immigrants are less likely to participate in high-risk behaviors such as substance use. Further, immigrants bring with them cultural norms and practices that may provide a form of "herd immunity," which can protect from involvement in health-risk behaviors (Salas-Wright et al., 2014, p. 958). Congregating with other immigrants who adhere to anti–substance use norms can limit the exposure to substance use. A third possibility is that immigrants fear deportation or foreign criminal justice involvement and therefore abstain from high-risk or illegal activities involved with substance use.

One explanation of what leads to the decrease in overall health is that many immigrants begin to make the unhealthy behavioral choices prominent in the American lifestyle while losing touch with their protective habits and traditions (Li & Wen, 2015; Salas-Wright et al., 2014; Salas-Wright & Vaughn, 2014).

Consistent with the immigrant paradox, immigrants tend to have lower prevalence of substance use upon or shortly after arrival in the United States, and longer residence in the United States is linked to higher substance use for some but not all groups. In other words, the paradox might not apply to all immigrant groups such as Latinos, Asians, or Middle Easterners because of different societal and cultural norms toward such behaviors in their cultures of origin (Li & Wen, 2015). Szaflarski and colleagues (2011) posit that migrants take their drinking habits with them, and although alcohol use occurs worldwide, it is not uniform throughout the world. In particular, alcohol consumption is generally higher in Europe and North America than in Africa and Asia.

Risk and Protective Factors

According to Li and Wen (2015), there are a number of factors that might predict health risks such as substance use. Age at migration, for example, shapes the level of acculturation of immigrants in how they perceive and interact with the host culture. Immigrants who enter the United States before adulthood usually have greater proficiency in English and experience greater levels of assimilation, and thus are more easily influenced by American norms on substance use. For example, a young individual in a life stage that is more easily influenced by peer environment might be more likely to initiate substance use once in the United States than an adult immigrant who feels connected to a strong immigrant network (Mancini et al., 2015). When protective factors of the original culture (e.g., families, elders, sense of community) are absent in the new country, substance use might result.

Also, acculturative stress related to feelings of being "dislocated," language barriers, feelings of grief and loss of one's homeland, loneliness, family separation, social isolation, unemployment, economic worries, and experiences with discrimination and harassment based on one's ethnicity might all contribute to the onset of substance use for an immigrant, particularly an individual who arrived at a young age (Li & Wen, 2015; Szaflarski et al., 2011).

Discrimination contributes to the unique stress experienced by immigrants (Tran, Lee, & Burgess, 2010). Despite historical and current efforts to reduce or eliminate discrimination against immigrants, there is evidence that discrimination persists in a number of social domains, including housing; hiring, promotion, and job termination; law enforcement; financial services and support; and medical care. Tran and colleagues (2010) state that discrimination is most often based on race/ethnicity, and major lifetime discrimination is more common among people of color compared to White people. Discrimination can have a negative impact on immigrants' socioeconomic mobility, their stress level and subsequent functioning, and their mental and behavioral well-being, because discrimination often causes them to internalize a sense of inferiority and have low self-esteem. In a study of the relationship between perceived discrimination and substance use, Tran and colleagues (2010) found that nearly 30% of immigrants in their sample experienced discrimination and that this discrimination was related to cigarette smoking, number of days they drank in the previous month, and engagement in recent binge drinking.

Protective factors identified in the professional literature include a strong ethnic identity, relatively safe neighborhoods, family cohesion/involvement, and a risk-reducing familial context. This context includes negative attitudes toward substance use and abstention from substance use by parents and siblings (Mancini et al., 2015; Ojeda, Patterson & Strathdee, 2008; Savage & Mezuk, 2014).

Barriers to Treatment

It is well documented that use of services for mental health disorders is low for minorities in the United States (Mancini et al., 2015). Immigrants use SUD services even less than their native-born counterparts because of financial, cultural, and sociopolitical barriers (Moya & Shedlin, 2008). The most common reasons for not accessing services include lack of medical care/insurance, structural barriers such as lack of transportation or lack of knowledge of available services, and perceived prejudice and discrimination. Latino individuals are the group that most often discontinues treatment and reports less satisfaction with services, longer wait times, poorer quality of services, and unmet treatment needs. Further, Latino immigrants who are less acculturated to the United States have lower rates of mental health treatment service utilization (Mancini et al., 2015).

Language barriers can limit immigrants' ability to navigate the health care system and understand treatment options; they can also lead to miscommunication and a disconnect between patient and clinician (Carlini, Safioti, Rue, & Miles, 2015). Immigrants who entered the United States illegally might fear deportation by immigrant officials and therefore not access public health prevention or treatment services.

Because immigrants often use family/social service supports before treatment services from health care providers, Mancini and colleagues (2015) recommended a number of considerations when providing outreach and working with immigrants. First, integrate services to provide health, mental health, and family/social services that are located within easy access to foreign-born residents. Second, train practitioners in family/social service agencies and other informal service providers (community-based groups, religious organizations) to recognize and respond to substance use issues. Third, link and help coordinate community organizations with treatment providers. Fourth, offer prevention/education efforts at family/social service sites and religious or community-based programs. Finally, help family members recognize and respond to persons suspected of substance use problems.

There is a strong need for the development and evaluation of substance use treatment programs that respond to the multiple life domains of immigrants, including their familial, social, cultural, and linguistic needs. Treatment programs that extend support in the areas of child care, language, transportation, medical and social services, familial conflict resolution, and vocational and educational services find their outcomes to be more positive than programs that do not offer these components (Mancini et al., 2015).

OLDER PEOPLE

According to the 2010 U.S. Bureau of the Census, there were 40.3 million people who were 65 years and over on April 1, 2010. This population had increased by 5.3 million since Census 2000. In 2010, older or aged people represented 13% of the total population, an increase from 12.4% in 2000. Older people are the fastest-growing section of the U.S. population. A majority of the baby boomer cohort, people born from 1946 to 1964, has used illicit drugs at some time in their lives (U.S. Bureau of the Census, 2010). As a result, an increase in substance use and its related physical and mental challenges among older adults is expected.

According to CSAT (2012b), 2.5 million older Americans struggle with alcohol use and its associated medical and social consequences. This number is predicted to double to 5 million by 2020. Comorbidity of alcohol and other substance use, particularly prescription drug use, is of particular concern with this population. Comorbid depression and anxiety, as well as other psychiatric disorders, are also common among elders. Consequently, it is estimated that the number of older adults in need of SUD treatment will more than double from 1.7 million in 2000–2001 to 4.4 million in 2020 (Blank, 2009; Kinney, 2009).

Although the use of alcohol generally declines in old age, it still remains a major problem for some elders and is often an underreported and/or hidden problem. The use of alcohol among older adults, including drinking above age-recommended limits, binge drinking, or combining alcohol with other medications, is a growing concern. Accurate identification of alcohol use and risky drinking behaviors is important in the prevention and early intervention of elderly alcohol use disorder (SAMHSA, 2006).

Severe nicotine disorder often co-occurs with other substance use or can be an indicator of other substance use. Smoking in older adult mild to moderate drinkers is more prevalent than in the general older adult population. Some studies indicate the smoking among severe-alcohol-use older individuals generally is above 80%. Approximately 60% to 70% of older male alcohol users smoke a pack or more a day of cigarettes (SAMHSA, 2006).

Risk Factors

Various biological, psychological, and social changes that accompany aging make elders uniquely vulnerable to problems associated with SUDs. Some of these include changes in how the body metabolizes alcohol and drugs; commonly used medications that may worsen physical or mental health problems; increased risk of medication overdose; loss (death of a spouse); cognitive, functional, and sensory impairments associated with aging; limited financial resources; and lack of social support (Institute of Medicine, 2012). Additionally, the societal stigma about growing old can foster low self-esteem and self-doubt. There is a myth that for elders there is no play or fun, no money, no usefulness, and no attractiveness (Kinney, 2009).

Physical changes take place in the body as it ages. Some of these changes directly relate to the body's ability to metabolize drugs. Kinney (2009) states that with normal aging, there is a decrease in total body water content and an increase in the proportion of body fat. Alcohol is rapidly distributed in body water after ingestion. With the decrease in body water as we age, the volume for distribution decreases, and therefore the amount of alcohol that reaches the central nervous system increases.

In addition to the increased acute effects of alcohol, a variety of other physical changes make elders more vulnerable to the medical consequences of use (Kinney, 2009). By age 75, there is a 50% reduction in lung capacity, the kidneys work at only 45% of their previous capacity, and heart function is reduced by 35%.

Another major risk factor is the change in social support and work-related activities for elders. Older adults have fewer family responsibilities and work-related duties. Many families live far apart, and when older friends begin to die, the person is left with a small or no social support network. Also, many older adults are retired, leaving the days empty of structured activity and creating the need for a substitute activity. Sometimes the substitute activity is substance consumption.

Kinney (2009) states that one of the greatest psychological stressors faced by elders is loss. There is loss that comes from the illnesses and deaths of family and friends, loss of money through earned income, loss of status due to retirement, and loss of body functions and skills. The result of these losses is that self-respect, dignity, and self-esteem are threatened.

According to the Institute of Medicine (2012), at least 5.6 million to 8 million (one in five) older adults in the United States have one or more mental health or substance use conditions. The most common mental health problems are depression, anxiety disorders, and dementia-related behavioral and psychiatric symptoms. The elderly also have the highest suicide rate of any age group, with the greatest risk among men with the presence of alcohol use and depressive symptoms. Although medical offices often frequented by older adults are strategic places to screen for substance use, health care providers tend to overlook substance use among older patients. Further, older adults and their families tend to hide their substance use and are less likely to seek help. The increase in substance use among the older adult population, the high comorbidity of substance use with mental health disorders, the stigma associated with help-seeking, and the common failure to diagnose older adults with substance use disorders complicate prevention, intervention, and treatment efforts (Cooper, 2012).

Prevention and Intervention

In order to provide the best services to older adults with substance use disorders, greater attention needs to be given to prevention, detection, early intervention, and treatment (Rosen, Heberlein, & Engel, 2013). Many elderly people are unaware of the effects of aging in combination with the use of substances. Therefore, beginning with an educational discussion may be extremely helpful. Counselors should ask specifically about the frequency and quantity of all substance use, including over-the-counter medications, herbal supplements, and prescriptions. If possible, external verification of these facts should be sought. Possible symptoms of use should not be ignored. Hesitancy to confront an older adult and not wanting to take away "their last pleasure" sets the stage for denial and enabling behavior on the part of the clinician or family member (Rosen et al., 2013).

Older people need the same type of rehabilitation services as younger people: education, counseling, and involvement in self-help groups (Kinney, 2009). Some recent studies have shown that programs designed for elders enhance outcomes by reducing treatment dropout, increasing rates of aftercare, and dealing with relapses if they occur. Cooper (2012) developed a program called "HeLP" to address barriers to appropriate assessment and effective treatment of substance use among older adults. Elements of HeLP intervention include:

- In-home screen and assessment
- Assessment of illicit and prescription drug use as well as alcohol use
- Personalized age-appropriate feedback on alcohol and drug use
- Focus on the interactions of prescription drug use with alcohol and other drug use
- Flexible cognitive–behavioral therapy (CBT) intervention addressing alcohol and drug use as well as mental health symptoms
- Referral to mental health and physical care providers
- Enhancement of social support through CBT intervention

Korper and Raskin (2008) indicate that there is evidence supporting a variety of pharmacological and psychotherapeutic interventions for substance use problems and psychiatric disorders in older persons. Echoing the voice of Cooper (2012), Korper and Raskin proposed promising treatment practices that include brief alcohol interventions; home- and community-based mental health outreach; integration of substance use, mental health, and primary care services; geriatric mental health consultation and treatment teams in nursing homes; support interventions for family and caregivers; and a variety of pharmacological interventions.

SUD treatment for elders should include the following (Choi, DiNitto, & Marti, 2014; Korper & Raskin, 2008):

- Age-specific group treatment that is supportive and non-confrontational
- Treatment that focuses on self-esteem building, the health benefits of treatment, and the deleterious effects that can occur from substance use
- Coping with depression, loneliness, and loss
- Emphasis on comorbidity of physical and mental health disorders
- Rebuilding the client's social support network
- Staff members who are interested and experienced in working with older adults
- Linkages with medical services, services for the aging, institutions for treatment, and case management (consider no-cost resources for those with affordability issues)

Kinney (2009) stresses the importance of groups in substance use treatment for older people. Groups can reduce the sense of isolation, enhance communication skills, provide a setting for problem solving, and address issues of denial. Small-group sessions or individual therapy within a treatment program can help develop skills for coping with loss, enjoying leisure time, and developing new relationships.

The growth in the aging population will have a significant impact on health services for treatment of substance use and mental health. Mental health practitioners will likely see more aging adults in their clinical practices. It is therefore essential that improved tools and programs specific to the needs of elders be developed, evaluated, and reported in the professional literature to inform best practices.

HOMELESSNESS

Homelessness is one of our most pressing and complex social problems. It is estimated that each year at least 2.5 to 3.5 million Americans sleep in shelters, transitional housing, and public places not meant for human living (National Law Center on Homelessness and Poverty, 2015). The housing crisis has deepened since the 2008 recession, with 7.4 million people in 2012 who had lost their homes or were living doubled-up with family or friends as a result of economic necessity. According to the National Alliance to End Homelessness (2016a), the largest sub-group of individuals experiencing homelessness was individuals, comprising almost 63% of all homeless people. Approximately 37% of homeless people were families. Although a majority of homeless individuals lived in some type of shelter or transitional housing, 31% lived in habitats not meant for human occupancy (e.g., street or an abandoned building). Furthermore, at least one-third of the single adult homeless population lives with a severe or persistent mental disorder (Coalition for the Homeless, 2016). Substance use is more common among the homeless population than in the general population.

The definition of *homeless* is provided by the Stewart B. McKinney Homeless Assistance Act (PL 106-400). A homeless person is one whose nighttime residence is

- A supervised publicly or privately operated shelter designed to provide temporary living accommodations (including welfare hotels, congregate shelters, and transitional housing for the mentally ill)
- A public or private place not designed for, or ordinarily used as, a regular sleeping accommodation for human beings (for example, cars, campgrounds, motels, and other temporary places)
- A doubled-up accommodation (i.e., sharing housing with other families or individuals due to loss of housing or other similar situations)

The stereotype of homelessness is often the bag lady or single man living on the street. However, since the early 1980s, there has been an alarming rise in family homelessness with approximately one of 30 children or about 2.5 million children homeless annually (National Center on Family Homelessness, 2016). Being homeless can range from transitional (e.g., persons enter the shelter system for one short-term period), to episodic (e.g., persons who shuttle in and out of homelessness), to chronic homelessness (e.g., without a home for six months or more) with extreme poverty (Ibabe, Stein, Nyamathi, & Bentler, 2014). Families experiencing homelessness are exposed to extraordinary stress that significantly affects the health and well-being of its members.

Risk Factors

The National Alliance to End Homelessness (2016b) points out that although circumstances vary, homelessness occurs when people or households are unable to acquire or maintain housing they can afford. The Alliance has focused on four main groups that often suffer from homelessness and its effects (2016):

- *Families:* Homeless families are similar to other poor families. Often, families become homeless as a result of some unforeseen financial crisis—medical emergency, car accident, or death in the family—that prevents them from being able to keep their housing. Most homeless families are able to bounce back fairly quickly with community assistance.
- *Youth:* Young people often become homeless because of some familial disruption, including divorce, neglect, or abuse. A large majority experience short-term homelessness

and return home or to family/friends. Homeless youth are particularly at risk because of their exposure to crime, violence, sexual victimization, and criminal involvement while on the streets.

• *Veterans:* 20% of the homeless population is made up of veterans. On any given night, 200,000 veterans are homeless. Veterans often become homeless due to war-related disability. For various reasons—physical disability, mental anguish, posttraumatic stress disorder, stress, substance use—many veterans find it difficult to readjust to civilian life. These difficulties can lead to homelessness.

• *Chronic Homelessness:* Chronic homelessness involves long-term and/or repeated periods of homelessness coupled with some sort of physical or mental disability. These individuals often end up living in shelters. It is a common misconception that this group represents the majority of homeless persons; rather, they account for about 20% of the entire homeless population.

These four groups do not represent the entire homeless population. Other groups experiencing homelessness are non-chronic single adults, survivors of domestic violence, and former prisoners reentering society.

People with intermittent periods of homelessness report significant levels of substance use problems, but among those who are chronically homeless, lifetime rates of SUD have been reported to be as high as 80% (Ibabe et al., 2014). Further, chronic and severe homelessness was related to severe substance use. SUD and homelessness are mutual risk factors (Ibabe et al., 2014). The National Coalition for the Homeless (2009) suggests that SUD is often a *cause* of homelessness, but, in many other situations, SUD is a *result* of homelessness. Substance use disorders often cause family discord and job loss, two factors that place individuals at higher risk for homelessness. On the other hand, newly homeless people encounter an environment where substance use is accepted as the norm. For some, substance use stems from their socialization into the homeless culture. For others, substance use emerges as a means of coping with the uncertainty, instability, and chaotic conditions of their daily lives. SUD and homelessness is a complex issue because there is considerable variation between individual cases, and homelessness is usually caused by more than one factor.

A survey conducted by the United States Conference of Mayors (2014) asked cities for their top causes of homelessness. For unaccompanied individuals, substance use and the lack of needed services placed among the top five causes, along with lack of affordable housing, unemployment, poverty, mental illness, and the lack of needed services. Further, on average, 28% of homeless adults had severe mental disorders, 22% were physically disabled, 15% were survivors of domestic violence, and 3% had HIV/AIDS. In addition, half of the homeless population with mental disorders also suffers from SUD (National Coalition for the Homeless, 2009). Some people with mental disorders self-medicate using "street drugs." This may lead to severe SUD as well as disease from using needles. For the homeless, poor mental health is more likely to affect physical health. The combination of mental illness, substance use, and poor physical health makes it difficult for people to obtain employment and residential stability.

The National Coalition for the Homeless (2009) noted that homeless persons with substance use problems are at higher risk for HIV infection and are more likely to have serious health problems and severe mental illness, to be arrested, to be victimized on the streets, and to suffer an early death. Alcohol and drug use are frequently cited as a major obstacle to ending an individual's homelessness. Many homeless people have become estranged from their families and friends. Without a support network, recovering from SUD is very difficult.

Between 1999 and 2010, there were 1,184 acts of violence (e.g., men, women, and children being harassed, kicked, set on fire, or beaten to death) against homeless individuals with 312 known deaths (National Coalition for the Homeless, 2012). These crimes are believed to be hate crimes. The Coalition noted that because the homeless community is treated so poorly in our society, many more attacks go unreported.

There are numerous barriers to treatment and recovery opportunities (e.g., general lack of social support system, distrust, difficulty in engaging in a long-term treatment plan, and multiplicity of needs); consequently, engagement and retention in outpatient treatment are typically low (Ibabe et al., 2014). Seeking physical or mental health care is usually not a main priority for homeless individuals because of more immediate needs such as finding food and shelter. Also, homeless people usually do not have health insurance, including Medicaid. This means that few homeless people with substance use disorders are able to find the resources necessary to access or pay for their own treatment or health care. In addition, there are often extensive waiting lists for substance use treatment in most states.

Treatment

According to the United States Conference of Mayors (2014), additional SUD services are indicated as a necessary resource to combat homelessness. Substance users who are homeless, particularly veterans, have different needs than those who are housed, and programs need to be created that address these needs. Few federal substance-use treatment and prevention programs target funds specifically to the homeless population. Much of public policy has favored a punitive approach to substance use, even though health experts agree that treatment and prevention are effective.

Lee and Petersen (2009) noted that homeless substance users often report feeling dehumanized, disrespected, and treated as second-class citizens. Added to their sense of isolation and disadvantage, the replication of this in social service agencies can further alienate individuals who may need the services the most. It is argued that when homeless individuals feel humanized and treated with respect, they are more receptive to treatment services.

Because of the variety of risk factors and barriers to treatment that complicate homeless individuals' engagement in substance use services, a holistic approach is necessary where meaningful change is possible (Ibabe et al., 2014). Service integration, including meaningful collaborations between housing and mental health professionals, as well as interventions tailored to the unique characteristics of this population, may lead to more successful outcomes. Supportive housing programs offer services such as mental health treatment, physical health care, education and employment opportunities, peer support, and daily living and money management skills. In addition, supportive housing programs include services to help people reintegrate into their communities. The training of counselors, social workers, nurses, psychologists, physicians and other helping professionals who engage with the homeless population is key to breaking these barriers to treatment (Ibabe et al., 2014).

THE MILITARY

Drugs and alcohol are commonly used in combat settings to deal with the challenges of war and being away from family (SAMHSA, 2014b). For many military personnel, this results in the development of substance use disorders, yet barriers to mental health treatment are considerable among this population. In a U.S. Department of Defense (DOD) (2013) report, one third (37.7%) of military personnel surveyed reported that seeking treatment for mental health problems would damage their careers. In fact, 21.3% who sought mental health treatment in the previous year reported that it had a negative effect on their careers. In addition to stigma and military culture, zero-tolerance policies create barriers to identifying and treating addictive disorders (McFarling, D'Angelo, Drain, Gibbs, & Rae Olmsted, 2011).

Because of the stigma associated with seeking mental health treatment in the military and the profound negative impact it can have on a service member's career, many do not seek treatment for peritraumatic symptoms, including PTSD, suicidality, and aggression (Hazle, Wilcox, & Hassan, 2012). SAMHSA (2014b) reports that PTSD among Iraq and Afghanistan veterans occurs at a rate of 18.5% and TBI at 19.5%. Additionally, 7.1% of veterans met the criteria for substance use disorder between 2004 and 2006. The DOD (2013) acknowledged that combat deployment increased posttraumatic, depressive, and anxiety symptoms as well as suicidality among military personnel and that these often co-occur with substance use problems. However, only half of returning service members sought out mental health care, according to the SAMHSA report (2014b). As a result, this population may use substances to self-medicate the symptoms associated with these issues, leading to co-occurring substance use disorders.

Additionally, of active-duty Army suicides between 2005 and 2009, 29% were reported to involve substance, use with one-third involving prescription drug use in 2009 (U.S. Department of Defense, 2010). This was before the Army suicide rate reached an all-time high in 2012 (SAMHSA, 2014b). The average rate of completed suicides among all military personnel was one every 36 hours from 2005 to 2009. It is unknown whether substance use disorders preceded suicidality or if substances were used in the absence of a diagnosable behavior.

The Institute of Medicine (IOM, 2012) identified a number of barriers military personnel have to overcome to get treatment for substance use disorders. There are issues with lack of screening and treatment services available. Gaps in insurance coverage were indicated as an impediment to getting treatment. Additionally, stigma and fear of negative consequences due to lack of confidentiality in treatment were considerable barriers to SUD treatment.

Although reported rates of illicit substance use are lower among military personnel than in the general population, such use is still prevalent (NIDA, 2013). When the Department of Defense Survey of Health Related Behaviors among Active Duty Military Personnel (DOD, 2013) asked about substance use in the previous month, 33% reported binge drinking, which was higher than the rate in civilian populations. Rates of binge drinking ranged from 28.1% among Air Force personnel to 56.7% among Marines surveyed. However, only 11.3% of active duty personnel were classified as problem drinkers, with only 58.4% of self-identified heavy drinkers considered problem drinkers. Only 1.3% of all military personnel reported use of prescription drugs (other than for the condition prescribed) in the previous year, including 5.7% reporting this use most commonly with steroids (16.6%) and stimulants (11.6%), with Army personnel most likely to use prescription drugs (31.4%).

Only 1.5% of the military personnel self-identifying as binge drinkers reported they were either in treatment or likely to seek treatment in the near future (DOD, 2013). Most reported they would seek help from church (30%) or a military chaplain (29.7%), and only a small number reported going to military (13.2%) or civilian (12.7%) residential treatment facilities (DOD, 2013). According to SAMHSA (2014b), mental health and substance use disorders resulted in more hospitalizations among U.S. troops in 2009 than any other cause.

Risk Factors

The DOD (2013) reported that military personnel who experienced high levels of combat were more likely to be heavy drinkers (10.3%) and use prescription drugs (34.2%) than those exposed to low levels or no combat. Also, those who were combat deployed after September 11, 2001, were more likely to be heavy cigarette smokers than those who were not combat deployed. The Coast Guard (15.2%) and Navy (12.7%) reported more alcohol use when deployed. Army personnel reported more cigarette (20.7%) and cigar use (12.4%), and Marine Corps personnel reported more cigarette (23.5%), cigar (10.7%), and smokeless tobacco use (15.9%) when deployed.

Military personnel report experiencing stress related to money (30.2%), family members' health problems (28.9%), changes in work load (41.5%), and, predictably, being away from social support of family and friends (42.3%) (DOD, 2013). In order to cope with stressors, military personnel most often reported having a cigarette (21.5% male, 17.7% female), drinking alcohol (23.8% male, 21% female), eating (42.8% male, 52.8% female), and sleeping (48.6% male, 65.5% female). Those self-identifying as heavy drinkers most often reported high overall stress (63.4%), anxiety symptoms (32.9%), depressive symptoms (20.8%), posttraumatic stress symptoms (13.2%), and suicidal ideation (33.2%). Additionally, this population reported high risk-taking (23.3%) and high anger (18%) compared to individuals identifying as having low alcohol use.

Prevention and Treatment

Because of the heightened stress issues of combat and the now-common occurrence of multiple deployments, SUDs during and after military service are a growing issue. Consequently, all branches of the military have developed SUD programs. These programs resemble civilian treatment for substance use. Most include medical management, individual counseling, group therapy, psychoeducation, and 12-step group participation. They provide drug information, prevention activities, screening, testing, and full treatment (DOD, 2013). Soldiers who fail to participate as directed by their commander or who do not successfully complete treatment are subject to administrative separation, a type of military discharge.

According to the DOD (2013), service members most commonly seek mental health treatment for depression (11.6%), anxiety (10.4%), stress management (10.3%), and family problems (10.2%). This may indicate that they are more likely to seek help for a non–substance use problem. Therefore, in light of the statistics regarding use of substances and other behaviors as coping sources, regular screening for these behaviors with military clients may help improve identification of individuals who need intervention.

Little peer-reviewed research exists that evaluates outcomes of mental health or SUD programs in the military. However, following a whistle-blowing incident at a Midwestern Army base, the DOD commissioned the Institute of Medicine (IOM, 2012) to evaluate their prevention, screening, diagnosis and treatment services for substance use disorders. Their findings indicate that military leadership has not acknowledged the public health crisis of SUDs in the military (IOM, 2012).

The report called for limiting access to substances, training prescribers to identify medication-seeking behaviors, and implementing routine screening and brief interventions for SUDs within a primary care context. The Army's implementation of the Confidential Alcohol Treatment and Education Pilot is an example of one effort to reduce barriers to treatment. This program demonstrated that when service members were allowed to use confidential treatment services, they were more likely to seek treatment for substance use disorders. Additionally, the opportunity to get treatment without the threat of disciplinary action resulted in better care and increased troop resilience

CASE DISCUSSION

Case 1: Sandy and Pam

Sandy and Pam experienced major disruptions in their family life. Sandy's parents both had alcohol use disorders and divorced when Sandy was 10 years old. Sandy's father never returned, and her mother remarried a man who was also a heavy drinker when Sandy was 17. As the caretaker of her siblings due to her mother's alcohol use, Sandy was forced to mature quickly and as a result became a rebellious child. Sandy's mother passed away tragically in a car accident when Sandy was 30 years old. A similar pattern of disrupted family life occurred after Sandy married Jim and gave birth to Pam and Albert. Sandy and Jim separated when Pam was 7 years old, and Pam had an unsatisfying and inconsistent relationship with her dad. Sandy continued to drink during Pam's childhood, often leaving her alone to fend for herself and care for her younger brother. It was not long before Pam started using substances on her own and was "following in her mother's footsteps." Pam also entered an abusive relationship with a man who abused alcohol. There are significant parallels between Sandy and Pam's family dynamics and experiences with trauma, both major risk factors for substance use disorders.

Conclusion

Among children and adolescents, women, gay/lesbian/bisexual/transgender individuals, people with disabilities, immigrants, elders, the homeless, and the military, we are witnessing a growth in substance use. A common need among these groups is identification and early intervention. All these groups share the experience of being marginalized within our society, which in turn influences self-esteem as well as self-efficacy skills. These issues, then, are not only individual issues but issues of social importance. Interventions need to be designed to meet individual and group needs, and professionals must act as change agents within their communities and society. As change agents, helping professionals can assist in challenging myths and educating the community of particular individual and group needs revolving around substance use behaviors and risk and protective factors for the groups presented in this chapter.

MyCounselingLab for Addictions/Substance Use

Try the Topic 10 Assignments: *Working with Specific Populations and Cultural Groups.*

Case Study: Loren

A 22-year-old transgender person named Loren presents for an intake interview at your residential substance use treatment program. She is dressed in feminine attire and tells you she has been living full-time as a woman for more than three years. Loren has had a legal name change and has identification that states she is female. She tells you she has been in treatment before and described a very bad experience. For example, the staff at her previous treatment refused to address her as a woman. Further, other clients sexually and verbally harassed her based on gender identity and gender expression. She felt very unsafe during her first treatment experience and has carried over some of those fears and overall discomfort to your counseling relationship. Loren shared that she has a long history of abusing crystal methamphetamine with serious consequences including but not limited to unemployment, unstable family relationships, and mental health problems such as depression, low self-esteem, and difficulty sleeping. Although Loren indicated that she has family discord as a result of her substance use, she described her family as supportive of her transition and positive supports in her recovery. Loren demonstrated a willingness and readiness to change and wants to begin treatment immediately in your residential treatment program.

Critical Thinking Questions

1. Describe how you would protect Loren and ensure that her negative experiences in her first treatment episode are not repeated. Keep in mind that this is a residential treatment center where Loren will be staying for a minimum of 28 days.

2. Social support is very important as an individual enters into and maintains recovery from substance use. Based on the vignette, how would you as Loren's counselor help her use and strengthen her support network?

Working with Diverse Cultures: Exploring Sociocultural Influences and Realities in Substance Use Disorder Treatment and Prevention

Daniel Sciarra, PhD, LMHC, NCC & Genevieve Weber, PhD, LMHC

T his chapter presents a background for viewing factors that affect diverse cultural groups related to disordered substance use, prevalence, and effective prevention and intervention strategies. The groups discussed in this chapter are limited to nondominant racial cultures that have historical roots, are prevalent in the United States, and share a history of oppression.

The assumption at the foundation of this chapter is simple yet often overlooked in the implementation of individual and community substance use disorder interventions: Programs designed for particular groups *need* to be developed within the sociocultural worldview in which they are applied. Substance use cannot be addressed without examining the dynamics that influence the context and systems in ethnic communities, which include issues of poverty, the lack of health and child care, education, unemployment, covert and overt racism, within-group diversity, and the role and level of acculturation. Our individual identity (genetic endowment and unique experiences), group identity (gender, race age, ethnicity, sexual orientation, socioeconomic status, geographic location, disability/ability), and universal identity (part of the human condition with needs of love and belonging) all influence how the individual creates and makes sense of his or her world (Sue & Sue, 2013) and, consequently, the role substance use plays in one's life. The Substance Abuse and Mental Health Services Administration (SAMHSA), a federal program, and other funding and research organizations have adopted similar assumptions regarding treatment and research (Bernal, Cumba-Avilés, & Rodriguez-Quintana, 2014; SAMHSA, 2013).

Substance use is universal and, therefore, regarded as *etic* (culturally universal). We believe, however, that effective treatment of substance use needs to be at least in part *emic* (culturally specific). The vast majority of treatment facilities are not linguistically or culturally skilled, and practitioners with multicultural skills are limited. Efforts to train practitioners are ongoing. Training programs need to go beyond the etic perspective (good counseling is good counseling regardless of culture) and sensitize trainees to the emic perspective (good counseling is culture specific) (Sue & Sue, 2013).

Cultural/ethnic group divides the chapter into sections. Each section has subsections that provide a demographic overview, which may include cultural values and sociocultural perspectives, risk factors affecting each group, barriers to treatment, and considerations in prevention and intervention with each group.

AMERICAN INDIANS AND ALASKAN NATIVES

American Indians and Alaskan Natives are a heterogeneous group made up of 569 federally recognized tribes and a number of tribes that are not federally recognized (Peregoy & Gloria, 2007). The most recent census data indicate that there are 4.9 million (1.6% of the U.S. population) American Indians and Alaskan Natives (U.S. Census Bureau, 2010). About 41% of American Indians and Alaskan Natives were younger than 29 years of age compared with 29% of the total U.S. population. Of this population, 57% can be considered in the childbearing years (ages 10 to 44). This group is growing and exceeding demographic projections. If the current rate of population growth continues, it is projected that by 2050, the Indian/Native population will increase about 75% and reach 8.6 million (U.S. Census Bureau, 2010). High school graduation rates are low, about 50% versus nearly 70% for the general U.S. population (Pamber, 2010). In addition, income for Indians/Natives is about 62% of the national average, with their poverty rate being about two times the national average (U.S. Census Bureau, 2010).

Each tribe has unique customs, values, and religious/spiritual practices. A tribe's commitment to traditionalism ranges from very traditional, in which members speak their tribal language at home, to tribes that use English as their first language. Some historians have said that the intent of Indian education in the 1800s and early 1900s was to kill the Indian and save the child (Morning Edition, 2008). This has resulted in varying degrees of loss of custom and language among tribal peoples. About 67% of all American Indians and Alaskan Natives live outside a reservation, and since the late 1950s, more Indians/Natives have been moving to urban settings. With this shift to the cities, an increase in interethnic and intertribal marriages has occurred. This diversity is also compounded by the fact that more than 60% of all Indians are of mixed background, the result of intermarriages among African American, White, Hispanic/Latino, and Asian and Native Hawaiian and Pacific Islander populations (Kochanek, Xu, Murphy, Miniño, & Kung, 2011). Nonetheless, a person who meets tribal enrollment criteria and is registered on the rolls, or tribal records, is entitled to services from the tribe, has voting rights within tribal elections, and has eligibility for government services provided by treaty agreements.

With the arrival of Columbus and the principle of Manifest Destiny, alcohol has eroded the bedrock of individuals, families, communities, and tribes, yesterday and today. Reliable data on the extent and pattern of substance use (including alcohol) among American Indians has been scarce and compounded by questions about the generalizability of findings (Novins et al., 2012). The greatest proportion of adults who drink is between the ages of 15 and 29, and drinking behaviors appear to decline after age 40. Binge drinking among American Indians is high, and they reportedly have the highest weekly alcohol consumption of any ethnic group (Chartier & Caetano, 2010). Substance use behaviors may taper off with age, and the data indicate that there is a slight decrease in lifetime prevalence. Yet, for those who drink heavily, the behavior is killing.

Substance use in the Indian/Native communities takes a drastic toll. Many Indian/Native deaths—including accidental deaths, homicides, suicides, and terminal health status, such as cirrhosis and other liver diseases—can be attributed to alcohol and substance use. Alcoholism death rates for Indians/Natives range to about six times the national average (Landen, Roeber, Naimi, Nielsen, & Sewell, 2014). In reviewing the 10 leading causes of death in the

Indian/Native communities, researchers found that alcohol use was directly implicated in four causes: accidents, cirrhosis of the liver, homicides, and suicides. Nearly one-third of all outpatient visits to Indian Public Health Services were related to substance disorders (Indian Health Service, 2014). For those over 18 years of age, this population experiences nearly three times more average distress (e.g., alcoholism, depression, suicide) than Whites in their everyday life (Barnes, Adams, & Powell-Griner, 2010).

Indian Health Service has identified that age-adjusted mortality rates were considerably higher for Indians/Natives than for all other races. For example, the following rates were identified but are by no means exhaustive: alcoholism was nearly 600 times greater, accidents over 200% greater, suicide within specific age groups is up to 10 times greater (U.S. Department of Health and Human Services, 2006), and homicide was 41% greater than the national average (U.S. Department of Justice, 2011).

Nationally, across all crime categories, victims report that perpetrators were perceived to have been under the influence of alcohol or substances, regardless of the race of the perpetrator. The average annual number of victimizations for Indians/Natives aged 12 and older is nearly 2.5 times higher than that for the rest of the nation. A report by the Bureau of Justice Statistics (U.S. Department of Justice, 2011) observed that intimate partner and family violence involves a comparatively high level of alcohol and substance abuse by offenders as perceived by the victims. Indian/Native victims of intimate and family violence, however, are more likely than others to be injured and need hospital care.

The rate of victimization among Indian/Native women was more than double that among women in the general population. This group was more likely to be victims of assault, including rape/sexual assault committed by a stranger, not a family member or person known to the victim. Sixty percent of the time the perpetrator was reported to be White. Acts of violence toward Indian/Native people, regardless of assailant, were implicated with alcohol (U.S. Department of Justice, 2011).

Another issue related to substance use concerns the effect on maternal and infant health. In 2010, the infant mortality rate in Indian country was 8.28 per 1000 live births, the second highest among racial groups in the United States (Matthews & MacDorman, 2013). Fetal alcohol syndrome (FAS) and fetal alcohol effects (FAEs) continue as consequences of women consuming alcohol during pregnancy. The child can then suffer from neurosensory and developmental disabilities. Although FAS and FAEs occur in every cultural community and socioeconomic group, the occurrences vary by subpopulation. FAS is estimated to occur in the general population at about 1 in 750 live births. FAS and FAEs vary by tribe, yet the American Indians/Alaskan Natives populations are hit hardest. Studies show that the fetal alcohol rate among Indians is 30 times greater than that among Whites (Denny, Floyd, Green, & Hayes, 2012). It appears that the impacts vary. Speculation regarding the influence of the male donors' influence on the constellation of FAE effects during conception has not found strong support in research.

Cultural Values

Keeping in mind the heterogeneity that exists in Indian country, values shared across different tribes will be presented. This information is presented here not to perpetuate stereotypes but rather to explore your clients' worldview and sociocultural orientation. As discussed elsewhere, Indians/Natives differ in their level of acculturation and Indian/Native identity.

Hall, in his seminal work (1984), identified Indians/Natives as living in high-context cultures. For the traditional Native, this means that they implicitly embed meanings at different levels of the sociocultural context, value a group sense, tend to take time to cultivate and establish a permanent personal relationship, emphasize spiral logic, value indirect verbal interaction, and are more able to read nonverbal expressions. Values most cited in the literature for American Indians and Alaskan Natives include sharing and generosity, cooperation, noninterference, time orientation, spirituality, humor, and humility (Sue & Sue, 2013).

Sharing is a mechanism to gain both honor and respect. It is a value embedded across tribes. Generosity is tightly intertwined with sharing. Accumulation of wealth is a hollow activity if it cannot be shared with others. At the same time, sharing and generosity play a role in substance use. Strategies to deal with substance use need to consider this value in using behaviors and group interaction (Sue & Sue, 2013).

Cooperation is grounded in the value of group and others. Group includes the tribe, clan, and family system. The extended family and tribal group take precedence over outside influences. The tribe is not perceived as made up of separate individuals, but rather as a whole entity in and of itself. As such, actions reflect upon the tribe and family. One considers one's self in relation to the tribe and family. Accusing someone of acting as if he or she has no family is an insult in the Indian community. This insult highlights the importance of cooperation and the value of family and infers the extended family, clan, and tribe.

Noninterference is a value based in a sociospiritual orientation. It is grounded in the belief that as human beings we intrinsically know the right way to act or are at least capable of learning to act in a good way on our own. This value highlights the importance of learning by observation, and observing rather than acting impulsively. As a result, rights of others are respected, which then influences parenting style. This parenting style values children making their own decisions, to the extent that our social services systems (based on Euro-American values) sometimes view this behavior as child neglect or, at the very least, as "permissive." In part, the Indian Child Welfare Act was passed in 1974 to support Indian/Native parenting practices and protect families from being separated due to cultural misinterpretation by social service agencies.

Time orientation is an often-misunderstood construct. The myth surrounding the concept of time in Indian country is that Indians/Natives do not care about time or, in the therapeutic relationship, are resistant to therapy. This is due to the imposition of a linear concept of time, which is largely Euro-American (i.e., If I miss an appointment, that moment will never be available in the same way or have the same meaning as if I had been "on time"). To begin to understand the concept of Indian time, one needs to understand the Indian/Native as being and becoming, a construct borrowed from the social work literature. The individual operates actively on two levels: one is the here and now, and the other is a spiritual plane. Both are active simultaneously, the spiritual world consciously or unconsciously. Time is seen as a spiral, with no value on up or down or sideways. The spiral overlaps, so if an appointment is missed "in the here and now," the opportunity for the same life experience will return. This concept makes sense within the concept of being and becoming.

Spirituality in Indian country is a belief that spirit, mind, and body are all interconnected. The belief is that there is a Higher Being, or Creator, and that all things have spirit.

Humor is seen as a value. Humor serves many purposes in the Indian/Native world. It can be used as a form of social control through storytelling, a path to relieve stress, and to create an atmosphere of sharing and connectedness.

Humility, the last value to be mentioned, is central to recognizing one's place in the circle of life. Modesty and humility are essential to a harmonious way of life, reflecting a balanced perspective of oneself in relation to others and the spirit world.

Risk Factors

The elements underlying Indian/Native substance use are complex and fall into three primary categories: biological, psychological, and sociocultural. Biological factors include physiology, or the body's response to substances that influence substance use disorders. Psychological factors include an individual and community's response to the stresses of oppression and other stressors that affect sobriety or use. Sociocultural factors include a community's values surrounding substance use, and the acceptance or sanctions used in the cultural milieu to manage use and/or use.

Sociocultural factors encompass culturally influenced perceptions in response to larger social pressures as they relate to substance use. Education levels are low—the average education is completion of the ninth grade, and only 50% obtain a high school diploma. Unemployment rates exceed 90% on some reservations, and family income is about one-third of the national average. The comparison of family income is faulty in that it does not take into consideration cultural obligations to extended family members and is therefore an overestimate of available resources in many instances.

The literature on Indian/Native substance use often cites stress as a precipitating or causal factor in alcohol and substance abuse (Whitesell et al., 2014). This stress has been referred to as *acculturative stress*, defined as the demands to integrate into and identify with a more dominant culture. Simultaneously, *deculturative stress* also takes place, defined as stress resulting from the loss or devaluation of historical tradition (Sue & Sue, 2013). Suicide, where rates in the Indian/Native community can be 5 to 10 times higher than the national average, is thought to be partly due to acculturative and deculturative stress. This phenomenon can be seen in two disparate examples: the first at the Standing Rock Sioux Reservation and the second on the Red Lakes Reservation. Between January and July of 2010 there were 10 recorded suicides, primarily among young people on the Standing Rock Sioux Reservation (Hummingbird, 2011). An earlier incident occurred on March 21, 2005, at Red Lakes; this was the homicide of eight youth and the suicide of the young gunman. Acculturation and deculturative stress contributed to these horrific events, making suicide and cluster suicide daily concerns for many tribes and their people.

Acculturation can be viewed as the outcome of processes that occur at multiple levels in a society, starting with the acquisition of foreign (mainstream) beliefs and values, producing stress that may be alleviated by substance use and abuse. High rates of substance disorders, family disruption, criminal behavior, and mental illness can be attributed to deculturative stress (Sue & Sue, 2013).

Researchers have proposed using a social integration model for understanding how communities influence substance use (Cleveland, Feinberg, & Greenberg, 2010). The assumption underlying this approach is the belief that cohesive, well-integrated communities provide mitigating influences on stress, whereas poorly integrated communities tend to demonstrate high levels of stress and concomitant substance use. Alcohol may become a primary coping response for some individuals living in less integrated communities where peer groups may also wield a more powerful influence.

The costs of substance disorders go beyond the emotional and physical dangers and include the use of scarce economic resources. Money that is spent on substances and alcohol becomes unavailable for individual or family purchases. Also, reservation economies are affected by economic leakage, the drain of reservation resources being spent outside the reservation economy.

Barriers to Treatment

Barriers exist in the provision of services offered in the non-Indian community. These include historical distrust; difficulties in cross-cultural communication stemming from a lack of shared meaning; the use of extended family systems, which can be misunderstood as child neglect or social instability within the family unit; and unfamiliarity of non-Indian counselors with Indian/Native conversational styles among traditional and transitional family groups (Garrett & Portman, 2011; Sue & Sue, 2013). These groups do not emphasize personal issues and may refer only peripherally to matters of great importance to the family.

Non-Indian agencies have not demonstrated the ability to cross-culturalize their services to benefit Indian/Native families (Garrett & Portman, 2011; Trimble, 2010). There is some resistance to providing home-based services, which is interpreted by the Indian community as a fear of cultural differences on the part of non-Indian providers. This matter speaks to the need for cultural sensitivity on the part of the non-Indian service provider.

Prevention and Intervention

In order for programming to be effective, from prevention to rehabilitation, it needs to be developed within the context of the community and the individual. Traditional healing practices, such as the sweat lodge, the talking circle, and other traditional ceremonial or religious activities, have been found to aid American Indian clients (Blume & Escobedo, 2005; Carvajal & Young, 2009). These programs appear to be successful for clients who have a strong attachment to traditional Indian/Native cultures. These approaches would not be applicable to clients who do not have a strong attachment to Indian/Native culture and religion. Before implementing services for any client, it is important to understand his or her level of acculturation and commitment to traditional Indian/Native religions.

Prevention programming could take several other paths to be effective, including offering alternatives to substance use by strengthening community projects such as recreational opportunities, cultural heritage programs, and employment opportunities and training (Cleveland et al., 2010) and incorporating tribal centric treatment programs (Blume & Escobedo, 2005).

Elements that run consistently through the literature for prevention and intervention programs divide programming into two areas: on-reservation and off-reservation programming. Intervention specialists and providers need to have:

- knowledge of Indian/Native characteristics, such as tribalism (an attitude toward other tribes), identity issues, level of acculturation of the client and the community they come from, and issues surrounding biculturalism, which is essential for integrating mainstream and traditional healing techniques;
- an understanding that there is no single explanation for Indian/Native substance use; and
- awareness that a treatment orientation based on the notion that alcoholism is a disease excludes the social and cultural aspects of drinking (Thomas, 2005).

Counselors also have a better chance of reducing the frequency of disordered substance use if they acknowledge that it is learned in a cultural context (Spillane & Smith, 2010).

Communities need to respond to substance use issues in a comprehensive fashion. Communities, both urban and rural/reservation, can begin to develop a comprehensive substance use plan by (a) forming a consensus of the problem, (b) defining safe drinking practices, (c) determining and promoting specific safety provisions, and (d) building support for a comprehensive prevention plan.

Many people who have a thorough understanding of these issues argue that strong community policies need to be developed that are comprehensive, consistent, and clearly defined in relationship to alcohol. This argument describes the necessity to use a public health approach integrating all major institutions, such as the family, school, religion, law enforcement, courts, health services, and the media. The communities, through culturally appropriate facilitation, need to incorporate activities to identify both protective and risk factors in the community (Cleveland et al., 2010; Spillane & Smith, 2010).

ASIAN AMERICANS

The Asian, Native Hawaiians, and Pacific Islanders (ANHAPI) population is growing rapidly in the United States and is estimated at 18.9 million (these population figures represent individuals who identified as Asian or in combination with one or more races) (U.S. Census Bureau, 2012a). The ANHAPI population increase is due to changes in immigration laws that occurred in 1965 and the entry of Southeast Asian refugees since 1975. The ANHAPI population grew 46% between the 2000 and 2010 censuses. This was more than any other racial group (U.S. Census Bureau, 2010). By the year 2050, the ANHAPI population is projected to reach 38 million, meaning that 1 of every 10 Americans will be of Asian or Pacific Islander descent.

This is a diverse population, consisting of at least 40 distinct subgroups that differ in language, religion, and values (Sue & Sue, 2013). The larger ANHAPI groups, in numbers, in the United States are Chinese, Filipinos, Koreans, Asian Indians, and Japanese; refugees and immigrants from Southeast Asia including Vietnamese, Laotians, Cambodians, and Hmongs; and Pacific Islanders including Native Hawaiians, Guamanians, and Samoans. Between-group differences within the ANHAPI populations may be great, but within-group differences also compound the difficulty of making any generalizations about this population. Individuals differ on variables such as migration or relocation experiences, degree of assimilation or acculturation, identification with the home country, use of their native language and English, composition and intactness of the family system, amount of education, and adherence to religious beliefs (Sue & Sue, 2013). This diversity has made the challenge of culturally competent substance use treatment services a complex one for providers.

Educational attainment for the percentage of single race Asians 25 years of age or older who hold a bachelor's degree or higher is 50%. At least 85% of single race ANHAPI 25 years of age or older hold at least a high school diploma. Twenty percent of ANHAPI 25 years of age or older hold a graduate or professional degree (Le, 2011). These percentages attest to the value ANHAPI cultures place on education in the United States. This educational status has fueled the "model minority" myth promulgated during the 1980s (Chou & Feagin, 2008), suggesting that the model minority myth has infiltrated the arena of research as a bias (Mahalingam, 2013).

The health statistics across cultures for Asian, Native Hawaiians, and Pacific Islanders reveal coronary heart disease at 2.9%, diabetes at 8%, and hypertension at 21% of the population. Research and information on substance use among ANHAPI is relatively small but suggests that these populations use and abuse substances less frequently than do members of other racial/ethnic groups (Wu, Blazer, Swartz, Burchett, & Brady, 2013). This observation can be partially attributed to the "model minority" stereotype held by SUD researchers and mental health professionals that Asians do not have SUD problems and therefore are in little need of study (Chang & Subramaniam, 2008).

The "model minority" belief only adds pressure on Asian Americans. Some ANHAPI immigrants have found success in society, while 12.5% live at or below the poverty level, struggling to survive. Households are not necessarily the average U.S. nuclear family size of 3.2 (U.S. Census Bureau, 2012a); many more persons can live under one roof, contributing to the total income for the household. This fact confounds income levels, as a household reporting

$85,000 per year may represent four or five fully employed persons under one roof. The model minority concept can lead to stress, as we find many persons of ANHAPI origin feeling nervous, tense, and depressed as they compete with everyone around them. Help-seeking is not culturally central to many of the ANHAPI cultures (Kim & Lee, 2014; Sue & Sue, 2013).

Suicide can be a response to the constellation of stressors experienced by any acculturating group. Suicide ranked as the eighth leading cause of death for ANHAPI groups, compared to the overall population as the 11th-greatest cause of death. The highest rate of suicide is found among men 85 years of age and older, followed by women 75 years of age and older (American Foundation for Suicide Prevention, 2014). One question that emerges is about the cause of elder suicide within these populations. Culture of origin stressors competing with the stressors of acculturation can certainly be a factor.

A report by SAMHSA (2013) using the National Household Survey on Substance Use and Health revealed that in 2012, an estimated 23.9 million Americans aged 12 or older were current (past month) illicit substance users, meaning they had used an illicit substance during the month prior to the survey interview. This estimate represents 9.2% of the population aged 12 or older. In contrast, the rate of current illicit substance use was 3.7% among Asians, and 7.8% among Native Hawaiians or Other Pacific Islanders aged 12 or older. Among persons aged 12 or older, 36.9% of Asians reported current alcohol use. The rate of binge alcohol use was lowest among Asians (12.7%). The SAMHSA report supports previous research in showing that Asian, Native Hawaiians, and Pacific Islanders' prevalence of substance use, severe alcohol disorder, and need for illicit substance use treatment, while clearly high enough to warrant attention, are low relative to those of the total U.S. population.

Cultural backgrounds and norms governing substance-using styles in various cultures differ. Mosher and Akins (2007) noted that Asian drinking is thought to be more social than solitary, occurring in prescribed settings (usually with food) to enhance social interaction rather than as a method of escapism and within the context of moderate drinking norms. Asian women are expected to drink little or no alcohol. It is true that drinking attitudes and customs of the various Asian American cultures are similar in their encouragement of moderation and that no Asian American culture advocates or encourages excessive alcohol use. These views may account for a significantly lower prevalence rate of alcohol use among Asian American groups than among Whites. When disaggregating data, we see differences in Native Hawaiian and Pacific Islander (NHPI) patterns of substance use. NHPI use of alcohol, tobacco, and other substances appears to parallel that of American Indians and Alaskan Natives (AI/ANs). When looking at binge drinking and alcohol consumption, NHPI is very similar to that of AI/ANs (SAMSHA, 2013)

Cultural Values

To fully understand the ANHAPI client, a mental health professional absolutely must consider culture in the counseling process. Although ANHAPI immigrants and refugees form diverse groups, certain commonalities can be generalized to the Asian, Native Hawaiian, and Pacific Islander populations. Sue and Sue (2013) and Chang and Subramaniam (2008) have discussed the following salient cultural values operating among these groups:

- *Filial piety* Filial piety is the respectful love, obligation, and duty to one's parents. Asian children are expected to comply with familial and social authority even if they must sacrifice their personal desires and ambitions. As children become acculturated into the dominant U.S. culture, pressure to meet parental obligations and expectations can lead to stress and conflict.

- *Shame as a behavioral control*   Traditionally, shaming is used to help reinforce familial expectations and proper behavior within and outside the family. Individuals who behave inappropriately will "lose face" and may cause the family to withdraw support. With the importance of interdependence, the withdrawal of support can cause considerable anxiety in having to face life alone.
- *Self-control*   The Confucian and Taoist philosophies emphasize the need for moderation—to maintain modesty in behavior, be humble in expectations, and restrain emotional expression. Love, respect, and affection are shown through behaviors that benefit the family and its members. Hence, the ANHAPI client may lack experience in identifying and communicating emotional states.
- *Awareness of social milieu*   Individuals tend to be very sensitive to the opinions of peers, allowing the social norms to define their thoughts, feelings, and actions. One subordinates to the group to maintain solidarity. Social esteem and self-respect are maintained by complying with social norms.
- *Fatalism*   Asians, Native Hawaiians, and Pacific Islanders may accept their fate and maintain a philosophical detachment. This silent acceptance contributes to their unwillingness to seek professional help. Mental health professionals often misconstrue a fatalist view of life, "what will happen, will happen," as resistance to treatment.
- *Role and status*   The hierarchy of the Asian, Native Hawaiian, and Pacific Islander family and community is based on a cultural tradition of male dominance. Men and elders are afforded greater importance than women and youths. The father makes the major decisions, and the mother is responsible for the children. The greatest responsibility is placed on the eldest son, who is expected to be a role model for younger siblings and help raise them. Upon the death of the father, the eldest son takes on the family leadership. Fewer demands are placed on daughters, because they leave their family of origin upon marriage. Therapy with Asian Americans must take into account family hierarchy and the demands placed on each member.
- *Somatization*   Asians, Native Hawaiians, and Pacific Islanders perceive problems as difficulties with physical health. Physical illness is believed to cause psychological problems. Complaints such as headaches, stomachaches, and muscle aches are often expressed in response to stressors. Mental health professionals need to take into account physical complaints as real problems to improve other aspects of the client's life.
- *Interdependence*   The culture has a relational orientation and a cultural frame in which one is defined by his or her continued interdependence with the group and where the group needs are held above those of the individual.

Risk Factors

Substance-using behavior is influenced by many cultural and situational variables pertinent to ANHAPI groups. Such variables identified in the literature include cultural values, traditions, attitudes, and beliefs (Beauvais, 2014); the degree to which one is socialized to the native culture and the degree of acculturation to the dominant values of the host culture (acculturation can lead to conflicts, including conflict across generations) (Schwartz et al., 2011); family conflicts; role conflicts; alienation and identity conflict; racism (Chou, Asnaani, & Hofmann, 2012); and other factors related to immigration and refugee status combined with economic stressors. In addition to these risk factors, Asians', Native Hawaiians', and Pacific Islanders' personal and social problems may be caused by their immigration/refugee status (Abe-Kim et al., 2007). According to Mui and Kang (2006), these risk factors may include:

- *Feelings of personal failure* For many immigrants there is great stress placed on basic survival needs and adjustment. This detracts from individual and family life just when the family member is needed most. Often immigrants are underemployed, reducing the social status that they held in the home country.
- *Family role reversals* In families in which the parents do not speak English, children may be forced to accept adult responsibilities, such as being the spokesperson for the family. This is a role reversal for the father, who is traditionally the family authority. Youth may lose respect for their elders because they are unable to assume the traditional roles or provide financial support. The impact on the family can be depression, alienation, family conflicts, and disordered substance use.
- *Economic stress* Many immigrant Asian families are unable to support themselves financially owing to a lack of job skills, low English proficiency, and large family sizes. Several of these families are also supporting their extended family in their native countries, contributing to additional economic pressures and subsequently the risk of substance use.

Asian American mental health experts generally agree that Southeast Asian refugees are at the highest risk of these and other even more severe stressors (Abe-Kim et al., 2007). These authors and others have discussed the impact of refugees who experienced traumatization from political violence: witnessing family members or friends tortured and/or murdered; and uprooting. They have encountered repression, torture, violence, separation and loss, hardships, and exile. These experiences are so painful that the refugee is likely to suffer psychological dysfunction in both the short and long term. Symptoms of mental and emotional distress common among refugees include insomnia, eating disorders, moderate to severe depression, culture shock, and homesickness. These symptoms are characteristic of posttraumatic stress disorder (PTSD). Upon arrival in the United States, refugees experience what can be a new constellation of stressors. The sources of stress that emerge can include unemployment, underemployment, poverty, shifting family roles related to employment, loss of status from their community of origin, and a host of other issues common to refugees (Le, Goebert, & Wallen, 2009; Rosario-Sim & O'Connell, 2009). The use of alcohol and substances can be seen as helpful for dealing with sadness and forgetting painful memories (Juthani & Mishra, 2009).

Relying on Huang (1994), Sue and Sue (2013) articulated four possible responses of ANHAPI facing acculturation conflicts:

1. *Assimilation:* Seeking to become part of the dominant society to the exclusion of one's own cultural group
2. *Separation of enculturation:* Identifying exclusively with the Asian culture
3. *Integration/biculturalism:* Retaining many Asian values while simultaneously learning the necessary skills and values for adaptation to the dominant culture
4. *Marginalization:* Perceiving one's own culture as negative but feeling inept at adapting to the majority culture

Source: Sue and Sue (2013), p. 402

Accurate assessment of an individual's acculturation level assists the therapist in data collection, analysis, interpretation, and determination of whether the client will return for future therapy (Sue & Sue, 2013). Awareness of the influence of generational status in the United States will aid the therapist in understanding individual struggles and perhaps family issues as well.

Understanding the culture of Asian Americans and potential adjustment problems is a necessary first step in providing sensitive interventions to facilitate a positive therapeutic experience (Juthani & Mishra, 2009).

Prevention and Intervention

The use of mental health services by Asian Americans remains quite low because of the stigma and shame of talking about one's problems (Uhm, 2014). Prevention and treatment programs for this population will be most effective if they reflect the values and norms of the population being served. To be successful, recovery programs for Asians, Native Hawaiians, and Pacific Islanders should address a variety of important issues: language, socioeconomic, cultural, and geographic barriers to treatment; status and length of time in the United States; refugee or immigrant status and history; and level of acculturation or assimilation into mainstream American culture. Addressing the following areas would lead to an increased possibility of successful treatment:

- Acknowledge the diversity, including the conflicts, shared values, and attitudes, of the many cultures within the Asian, Native Hawaiian, and Pacific Islander populations.
- Involve community members in treatment efforts whose voices command the respect of both parents and youth, such as elders, teachers, doctors, business leaders, community leaders, and youth role models.
- Help recent immigrants adapt to the English language and American culture.
- Acknowledge and respect prevention/healing practices of traditional cultures. Treatment should incorporate culturally based support systems in families and communities, as well as Eastern and Western wellness models.
- Conduct outreach about important substance use treatment issues in newspapers, magazines, and media that provide information in Asian/Pacific Islander languages.
- Provide education to young people on ethnic heritage and customs to promote positive cultural identity, self-esteem, and family communications. Education for parents on U.S. life and substance use issues will help them understand their children's acculturation and the stressors related to that process.

Sue and Sue (2013) recommended giving Asian/Pacific Islander clients an overview of the counseling process to familiarize them with roles and expectations. The following guidelines, drawn from the literature, suggest how mental health professionals could proceed with clients:

- Use restraint when gathering information. Because of the stigma associated with mental illness, the therapist should limit the number of personal questions they ask during the initial session.
- Do a thorough analysis of current environmental concerns, including but not limited to the need for food and shelter. Clients may need information on services that are available to them. Assess financial and social needs.
- Assess clients' worldviews, the way they view the problem, and determine appropriate solutions.
- Focus on the specific problem brought in by clients, and facilitate the development of goals for treatment.
- Take an active and directive role. Because of cultural expectations, clients will rely on the therapist to provide direction.
- In working with families, consider the intergenerational conflicts. Be willing to accept and support the hierarchical structure of the family.

- Focus on concrete resolution of problems, and deal with the present or immediate future.
- In the case of refugees, conduct a careful assessment of their history and gather information on their family life in their home country, their escape, and how this was experienced. Also important to refugees are the adjustment to the new culture, their methods of coping, and any marital or family problems that have resulted.

Undoubtedly, more research is needed to increase our understanding of the causes of substance use among various Asian, Native Hawaiian, and Pacific Islander groups and effective prevention and treatment approaches. Mental health professionals must educate themselves about cultural differences if they are to provide services to address the unique needs of this population. SAMHSA has recognized the need for developing culturally appropriate services to ANHAPI populations and has funded community-developed programs for building resiliency in youth and families. This is a beginning; it will take time to develop programming and services to effectively meet the needs of both immigrants and refugees.

AFRICAN AMERICANS

African Americans constitute about 15% of the total U.S. population. This percentage translates into approximately 44.5 million people of African descent and identity in the United States today (U.S. Census Bureau, 2014a). Wide gaps exist between African Americans and the general population in the arenas of education, employment, and income.

In 2012, about 83.2% of Blacks 25 years of age or older held at least a high school diploma. Of all individuals identifying as Black and identifying with more than one other racial identifier, 18.7% held bachelor's degrees in 2009, and 1.6 million had advanced degrees. Ten years earlier only about 900,000 Blacks held advanced degrees. In 2012, 3.7 million Black students enrolled in college compared with 2.9 million in 2007, a 28% increase. This is roughly twice the number who attended college 25 years earlier (U.S. Census Bureau, 2014a).

In 2013, among Black households (a household can include both related and unrelated persons including children), 61.8% contained families. There were 9.8 million Black family households. Of these, 45.7% were married couples. This does not include households of unmarried parents. This statistic challenges one of the mainstream misconceptions of the Black family: that the Black family is made up of a single-parent household. About 1.3 million single-race Black grandparents lived with their own grandchildren who were 18 years of age or younger. Of this number, 47.6% were also responsible for their grandchildren's care (U.S. Census Bureau, 2014a). In 2012, the annual median income for Black households was $33,321 compared with the nation at $51,017. The poverty rate in 2012 for Blacks was 27.2%, whereas nationally it was 15.0%. (U.S. Census Bureau, 2014a).

As a minority group, African Americans' disadvantaged status and poverty, as well as racism, contribute to the following statistics. Incarceration for young African American men in their 20s who were high school dropouts is about 37%. A full 33% of all Black men will spend time in jail or prison in their lifetime, compared with 1 in 87 of all White males. African American women represent 12% of the general female population but represent a little over 30% of females in prison (Mauer, 2013). The life span of African Americans is on average 5.6 years shorter than the average White person (combined male and female average is 77.8 years of age) (Edlin & Golanty, 2010).

Educationally, the opportunities for African American youths have yet to improve significantly, especially in urban areas (Banks & McGee Banks, 2010). Only about 52% of Black males graduate high school in four years compared to 73% for White children (Schott Foundation, 2012). A variety of theories exist for this education/learning gap: teachers are not sensitive to cultural differences; the curriculum may also not be meaningful to the experiences of minority group children; teaching/working conditions in lower income schools are not conducive to learning; lack of appropriate supplies; and so on (Banks & McGee Banks, 2010). Substance use may also contribute to the lack of achievement for some African American children.

For many urban African American adolescents, life is complicated by problems of poverty, illiteracy, and racism (Palmer, Davis, Moore, & Hilton, 2010). For Black youth, unemployment is three times as likely than for White youth, and for Black men it is twice as likely as for White men (Pollard, 2011). In 2010, for African American males aged 15 to 19, homicide was the cause of death in over 50% of cases (Centers for Disease Control and Prevention [CDC], 2010). Although many of these statistics are bleak, it appears that much of our literature is based on individuals of the lower class, those on public assistance, or unemployed, while failing to examine other segments of the African American population. More than a third of all Blacks are now middle-class or higher. They tend to be well educated, professionals, homeowners, and married (Hardaway & McLoyd, 2009). The success of this portion of the population is not without frustrations; many may feel bicultural stress. Middle-class African Americans can experience feelings of guilt for having made it, as well as frustrations from surpassing the present effects of past discrimination accompanied by feelings of isolation.

Risk Factors

African Americans have been particularly vulnerable to the negative social and health consequences of disordered substance use. Research (see, for example, Maslowsky et al., 2015) suggests that Black youth experience an earlier onset of substance use problems, a greater likelihood of being routed to the criminal justice system than to treatment for problems caused by substance use, and higher rates of illnesses, such as liver cirrhosis and esophageal cancer.

There is increasing concern that African Americans who are concentrated in urban environments may be at greater risk for the transmission of HIV due in part to the high level of intravenous heroin and cocaine use and the exchange of sexual favors for crack cocaine. The number of crack cocaine users among Blacks has risen in the past decade (Bowser, Word, Fulliove, & Fulliove, 2014). In 2010, African American women made up 64% of the estimated 9,500 new HIV infections in women (Ivy, Miles, Le, & Paz-Bailey, 2014).

African Americans have historically been underserved by traditional counseling services (Fortuna, Alegria, & Gao, 2010; Lester, Artz, Resick, & Young-Xu, 2010). The reasons suggested for this gap in service are poverty, lack of accessible facilities, lack of awareness of service facilities or their purpose, and the absence of culturally acceptable treatment models.

According to Sue and Sue (2013), other problems that African Americans face include:

- Adverse effects of myths and stereotypes regarding the African American culture
- Historical and contemporary racism and discrimination
- Decreased levels of self-esteem and life satisfaction
- Increased depressive symptoms
- Negative educational environment/lack of education
- Communication problems
- Intersection between sexism and racism
- Unequal employment and housing opportunities
- Low socioeconomic status

- Increasing number of one-parent or female-headed households
- Living in high-stress environments, such as those with low income, high rates of crime, and high unemployment

Cultural Values

The African American family has been identified as having strengths that help overcome oppressive societal conditions and contribute to both family/community cohesiveness and resilience. These seminal findings were identified as strengths in the early 1970s and they have continued to be supported by other investigators (Marsh, Chaney, & Jones, 2012). These strengths include (a) collectivism that can be seen as strong kinship bonds across a variety of households; (b) strong work, education, and achievement orientation; (c) a high level of flexibility in family roles, and developing family-like relationships with people outside of the biological family; (d) a commitment to spiritualism reflected through a strong commitment to religious values and church participation; and (e) "diunital" views of the world, where it is important to integrate all elements in life, striving for balance.

As a group, African Americans tend to be more group centered and sensitive to interpersonal matters and to emphasize community, cooperation, interdependence, and being one with nature. In contrast, White middle-class values stress individuality, uniqueness, competition, and control over nature (Sue & Sue, 2013).

Many African Americans have an extended family network that provides emotional and economic support. Among families headed by females, the care of children is often undertaken by a large number of relatives, older children, and close friends (Simpson & Lawrence-Webb, 2009). African American men and women value behaviors such as assertiveness, and within the family, men are more accepting of women's work and willing to share in the responsibilities traditionally assigned to women. Many African American families have instilled positive self-esteem in their children despite the problems with racism and prejudice (Hardaway & McLoyd, 2009; Taylor, 2010).

As in many ethnic minority cultures, older adults in the Black culture in America play vital roles in the family beyond caregiving and community leadership and are respected for their knowledge and experience. Younger family members experiencing difficulties are often referred to their grandparents for counsel. Many grandparents accept the responsibility for rearing their grandchildren while the parents work or acquire education. In addition, older African American family members play a significant role in passing on cultural values, customs, and traditions to their children (Hardaway & McLoyd, 2009; Taylor, 2010).

Spirituality and religion are essential elements of the African American way of life. African American churches have always been more than houses of worship, and the African American minister has been more than a preacher. The church has historically served as a spiritual, intellectual, and political arena for the African American community, and the ministers have traditionally served as teachers, counselors, and political activists. The churches are agents for transmitting traditional values, strengthening family ties, and providing opportunities to learn about their ancestry. Spirituality differs from religion and is a personal commitment to a higher being. This, too, is a strong value among African Americans (Bell-Tolliver, Burgess, & Brock, 2009; Watkins, LaBarrie, & Appio, 2010).

Barriers to Treatment

African Americans who seek treatment are often thought to have a negative view of mental health services. Some potential Black clients may have distrust for the therapeutic relationship and service delivery organizations due to a prolonged history of systematic mistreatment and racial oppression that has treated the Black American as a marginal person. African Americans underuse counseling services because they perceive counselors as insensitive to their needs, believe that counselors fail to provide equal energy and time working with underrepresented groups, and feel that counselors do not accept, understand, or respect cultural differences (Ojelade, McCray, Ashby, & Meyers, 2011).

Counselors also need to understand that African Americans often rely heavily on their church for help. Mental health professionals are becoming increasingly open to the advantages of religious involvement and how a strong spiritual base can support resilience to life's problems (Hardy, 2012).

Other barriers that contribute to underusing mental health services for the African American community include (a) the lack of a historical perspective on the development of the family and support systems within the African American community, (b) a lack of awareness and understanding of the unique characteristics of the value systems of African American families, and (c) communication barriers that hinder the development of trust between the African American client and the non-African American therapist (Bell-Tolliver et al., 2009).

Prevention and Intervention

Prevention and intervention strategies for Black Americans that meet the needs of the individual, family, and community will prove successful over those strategies that focus on the individual alone. Mental health professionals must be capable of analyzing adaptive behavior patterns, the cultural rituals of alcohol and substance use, and the specific sociopolitical influences of disordered substance use with African Americans. The counselor's process, goals, and expectations need to fit the worldview of the African American client.

Because of past experiences with racism and prejudice, African American clients are often distrustful of White counselors. Sue and Sue (2013) noted that to make headway, the therapist must establish a trusting relationship. African American clients are especially sensitive to interpersonal processes and will test the relationship. They may directly challenge the therapist's values and qualifications or act in a very guarded and aloof manner. These behaviors are part of a protective mechanism. A relationship may develop if the counselor can respond in a straightforward manner. Self-disclosure is very difficult for many African American clients because it leaves them vulnerable to racism (Bell-Tolliver et al., 2009; Choudhuri, Santiago-Rivera, & Garrett, 2012).

African Americans have traditionally relied on the support of the family, the church, and the community (SAMHSA, 2013). Culturally sensitive and relevant treatment programs and materials specifically targeting African Americans are essential to successful programs. Inclusion of the family system in the treatment process to explore sources of strength is an important first step. Spirituality is also recognized as a tool in the treatment of African Americans. A strong spiritual leader may be included as reflective of the community culture and as an extended family member.

In working with African American youth and adults, Sue and Sue (2013) suggested the following:

- It is often beneficial to bring up the client's reaction to a counselor of a different ethnic background.
- If the client was referred, determine the feelings about counseling and how it can be made useful.

- Identify the expectations and worldview of the African American client. Determine how the individual views the problem and the possible solutions.
- Establish an egalitarian relationship. Most African Americans tend to establish a personal commonality with the counselor.
- Determine how the client has responded to discrimination and racism in both unhealthy and healthy ways. Also examine issues around racial identity.
- Assess the positive assets of the client, such as family, community resources, and church.
- Determine the external factors that might be related to the presenting problem. This may involve contact with outside agencies for assistance.
- Help the client define goals and appropriate means of attaining them. Assess ways in which the client, family members, and friends handled their problems successfully.

HISPANICS

The term *Hispanic* was generated as a U.S. government catch phrase to conveniently classify different subgroups and subcultures of people who are of Cuban, Mexican, Puerto Rican, and South or Central American descent. Although Hispanics do have much in common (language; religion; customs; and attitudes toward self, family, and community), the subgroups have considerable variation in ethnic origins, socioeconomic groups, dialects, immigration status, and histories. Between 2000 and 2010, Hispanics accounted for one-half of the nation's growth. In particular, the Hispanic population increased by 15.2 million between 2000 and 2010, accounting for over half of the 27.3 million increase in the total population of the United States (U.S. Census Bureau, 2011).

New census data estimate that the U.S. Hispanic population topped 54 million as of July 1, 2013, an increase of 2.1% over 2012, and make up 17% of the nation's population (U.S. Census Bureau, 2014b). Nearly two-thirds of the population (64%) are of Mexican descent, 9% from Puerto Rico, 3.4% Cuban, and about 7.6% from Central American countries (U.S. Census Bureau, 2014b). These numbers reflect a population increase of 46.3% since the 2000 census (Pew Hispanic Center, 2011). This increase has been attributed to both immigration and high fertility rates. The census data do not reflect undocumented Hispanics who choose to "pass" because of fear of deportation or for economic, political, or personal reasons; they represent an estimated 13 million undocumented immigrants (Pew Hispanic Center, 2011). The average age for Hispanic males is 27 and the average age for females is 27.6 years. Sixty percent of all Latinos were native born; a full 40% were foreign born. There is little age difference at age of first marriage from the U.S. population in general. Seventeen million Latinos were under the age of 17, representing 23% of this age group (Pew Hispanic Center, 2011).

About 25% of the population 25 years of age or older do not have a high school diploma or GED. The median earnings for males is $27,490 and for females it is $24,738 (U.S. Census Bureau, 2011). Health status and disparities are large among this population. Hispanic and Black youth under 18 experience poverty at a greater rate than their peers (CDC, 2011).

The eight top leading causes of death for Hispanics are heart disease, cancer, unintentional accidents and injuries, stroke, diabetes, chronic liver disease, and homicide (CDC, 2011). Mexican Americans suffer more from diabetes than do those with origins in Puerto Rico. Puerto Ricans suffer disproportionately compared with others, with a greater incidence of asthma, HIV/AIDS, and infant mortality (CDC, 2009).

Hispanic substance use increased from 7.9% in 2009 to 8.3% in 2012 (SAMHSA, 2013). Early research failed to delineate between Hispanic subgroups. Current research overcomes some of the methodological weakness that prior research included across subgroups. Earlier, generalizations emerged that Hispanics were more likely to use substances than other groups. The most recent information, however, indicates that although portions of the Hispanic community have been affected by serious substance problems, the Hispanic population as a whole (use rate of 8.3%) is not more likely to use substances than other groups (the White use rate is 9.2%) (SAMHSA, 2013). Variability among the seven Hispanic American subgroups was significant for substance use and the need for substance disorder treatment. Mexican Americans and Puerto Ricans exhibited higher prevalence of illicit substance use (including marijuana and cocaine), heavy alcohol use, and the need for illicit substance use treatment. Caribbean Americans, Central Americans, and Cuban Americans, however, showed lower prevalence. South Americans and other Hispanics reported prevalence close to the total population (SAMHSA, 2013). Many of the factors associated with disordered substance use among other oppressed minority groups in the United States appear to operate for Hispanics as well.

Research has shown that Hispanics suffer the full impact of poverty that includes low income, unemployment, underemployment, undereducation, poor housing, prejudice, discrimination, and cultural/linguistic barriers (Pew Hispanic Center, 2011). In addition to the stress of the culture of poverty, many Hispanics also experience acculturation stress. The intergenerational transition from one's culture of origin to the development of bicultural abilities places stress and strain on the individual and the family system (Perez-Rodriguez et al., 2014).

One pattern of second culture acquisition is known as *cultural shift,* whereby an individual substitutes one set of practices with alternative cultural characteristics. Generally, this shift occurs out of the necessity to adapt to the dominant society and is sometimes an act of survival rather than choice. In the case of Hispanics, a dramatic point of stress in this process is a shift from a culture that values family unity and subordination of the individual to the welfare of the group, to the highly individualistic culture predominant in U.S. society. If substances are used to cope with stress, then levels of use will vary depending on how well an individual is able to integrate characteristics and demands of the dominant culture (Unger, Schwartz, Huh, Soto, & Baezconde-Garbanati, 2014).

Cultural Values

Discord and family disruption have been identified as an antecedent of disordered substance use among Hispanic adolescents and young adults (Rojas, Hallford, Brand, & Tivis, 2012). To gain insight into the Hispanic individual, investigation of *la familia* is paramount, because the family is the basis of Hispanic cultures. Often divided by generation, the immigrant's status tends to guide the adherence to the values and mores of one's culture of origin. The difference between the cultural orientation of the family and the cultural identity of the child may cause intergenerational conflicts. For example, immigrant families tend to develop a family struggle in which younger members struggle for autonomy (i.e., an American value) and the older family members struggle for connectedness (i.e., a Hispanic value) (Baumann, Kuhlberg, & Zayas, 2010).

The acculturation process can produce tremendous amounts of stress for the individual and place dramatic strains on the family system. Those who have immigrated alone, leaving behind their extended family support system, face the potential of adjustment problems (Falconier, Nussbeck, & Bodenmann, 2013).

Hispanics tend to underuse mental health services and terminate prematurely when they do access such services (Bridges, Andrews, & Deen, 2012). Sue and Sue (2013) suggest that ineffective and inappropriate counseling approaches to the values held by this group are often reasons for early termination. Certain unifying cultural values distinguish Hispanics from the dominant culture. An increased awareness of the cultural concepts can foster a positive therapeutic experience for the Hispanic client.

The Hispanic family provides support, identity, and security for its members. The strong sense of obligation ensures that the family's needs as a unit supersede individual needs. Garza and Watts (2010) noted that children are expected to be obedient and are not generally consulted on family decisions, and adolescents are expected to take responsibility for younger siblings at an early age.

The Hispanic nuclear family is embedded in the extended family consisting of aunts, uncles, grandparents, cousins, godparents, and lifelong friends. During times of crisis, the family is the first resource for advice before help is sought from others. The downside, however, is that the extended family system can serve as a stressor due to the emotional involvement and obligations with a large number of family and friends. Nonetheless, this strong tie highlights the importance of enlisting the family in therapy.

The cultural value of personalism defines an individual's self-worth and dignity from inner qualities that give self-respect. The Hispanic culture values the uniqueness of inner qualities that constitute personal dignity. This sense of self-respect, self-worth, and dignity in oneself and others demands showing and receiving proper respect. A therapist who conveys personalism develops trust and obligation with the Hispanic client (Garza & Watts, 2010). Gender-role norms and hierarchy within the family unit continue to influence both Hispanic men and women; however, acculturation and urbanization appear to be affecting both of these standards. Traditionally, males are expected to be strong and dominant providers, whereas females are more nurturant, self-sacrificing, and submissive to males. Some Hispanic women are more modern in their views of education and work but remain traditional in their personal relationships (Garza & Watts, 2010; Sue & Sue, 2013).

In addition to gender roles, a hierarchy of leadership and authority is related to sex and generation. The father's role is one of superior authority, and the mother's role can be viewed as the center of the family and purveyor of culture. Roles appear to include egalitarian decision making and indirect assertion by women, which may serve to preserve the appearance of male control. Children are expected to obey their parents, and younger children are expected to obey older siblings who are role models. Understanding the roles and hierarchy of each Hispanic family is vital in assisting with problem solving, renegotiation, and redefinition of power relationships (Garza & Watts, 2010).

Spiritual values and the importance of religion can be a strong influence on the behavior of Hispanics. Spiritualism assumes an invisible world of good and evil spirits who influence behavior. The spirits can protect or cause illness, so an individual is expected to do charitable deeds to be protected by the good spirits (Chavez, 2005; Furman et al., 2009).

Catholicism is the primary religion for Hispanics, although evangelical Christianity is on the rise in many parts of Latin America. Traditional adherence to the religious values of enduring suffering and self-denial may prevent some Hispanics from seeking mental health treatment. Catholicism, like many other religions, has powerful moral and social influences on day-to-day living. Religion and shared spiritual beliefs and practices are built on the idea of natural and supernatural forces that link an individual to a greater power. The three main healing/spiritual systems among Hispanics in the United States include *curanderismo* (Mexican American indigenous healers), *espiritismo* (Puerto Rican), and *santeria* (Cuban). Under each of these systems, life is governed by thoughts, intentions, and behaviors. Harmony is a unifying balance; failure to follow prescribed rules of belief can lead to imbalance and stress, including suffering, sickness, and bad fortune. Therapy can be augmented by enlisting other support systems, such as the church or folk healers (*curanderos/-as*). The reader is cautioned that when working with indigenous healers, traditional healing practices need to be understood. For example, *curanderas* on the California–Mexico border were prescribing dried rattlesnake meat for HIV-positive clients. Many of these clients contracted salmonella poisoning as a result (Alarcon & Ruiz, 2010).

Barriers to Treatment

Barriers to treatment for Hispanic groups include the disproportionate number of Hispanics enrolled in programs that emphasize pharmacological treatment rather than psychological treatment (Alarcon & Ruiz, 2010). This barrier may be due to the economics of treatment costs or the failure of treatment programs to operate effectively across cultural milieus. Several factors influence the inability of service agencies to respond to the needs of Hispanics.

First, cross-cultural counseling has been recognized as a viable force in the mental health field. The responsibility of this approach requires that mental health professionals be familiar with standard models of treatment in the field and that these models be analyzed as to how they may complement or belittle cultural beliefs and perspectives. These perspectives would include, for example, the view of alcoholism as a disease as well as the belief that an individual who uses it is morally weak. The latter view is not consistent with the disease model of alcoholism but is a common perspective among Hispanics. Moreover, cultural perspectives, across and within groups, and gender-role expectations need to be understood. The perspective in some Hispanic cultures that alcohol use/abuse in men maintains a romantic element puts abuse in a different light within a cultural lens (Alarcon & Ruiz, 2010; Furman et al., 2009).

Cultural perspectives such as this one have implications for service delivery at all levels. As an example, working with a self-referred Hispanic male who believes these cultural values, the mental health worker may need to help him work through the shame of being morally weak within a traditional concept of machismo. In addition, an understanding of the meaning of substance use disorder behaviors and their social contexts may produce an awareness of how competing values cause stress and influence substance disorder coping responses. Bilingual language ability and bicultural skills have been identified as essential elements in the provision of services to Hispanic groups, which, until the early 1980s, were vastly underrepresented in service delivery (Furman et al., 2009; Sue & Sue, 2013). This problem speaks to the need for training programs to actively recruit and train Hispanics or bilingual individuals into the human services professions.

Immigrant legal status can also be a barrier if individuals have entered the country illegally. These individuals may not seek assistance owing to fear of deportation. This group may be at particular risk for substance use disorders, especially if they do not have well-developed support systems in place (Sue & Sue, 2013).

When considering Hispanic SUD behaviors together with the effect of ethnic minority status and stresses of recent immigration or refugee status to the United States, earlier models of substance use are not sufficient to explain SUD behaviors of Hispanics. Acculturational stress, socioeconomic status (SES) and poverty, role strain and conflict, unemployment, and discrimination are all factors that play into disordered substance use (Furman et al., 2009).

Current research findings provide a better perspective on SUD patterns based on gender and age among Hispanic populations. Data also reveal sex differences in use and experimentation up to age 35 with substance use among Hispanic populations, with males more likely to use and experiment with substances than females. One hypothesis that may contribute to this difference of use in age and sex is that older cohorts were probably raised with stronger traditional norms discouraging substance use among women, whereas those in younger cohorts appear to be experimenting and using at higher rates (SAMHSA, 2013). Other possible explanations may be the level of acculturation or the belief in machismo and risk taking, and for younger Hispanics, the influence of peer pressure combined with stages of development.

Contrary to popular myth about minority substance use disorders, data on national substance use patterns indicate that Whites have the highest lifetime use of cigarettes, alcohol, hallucinogens, and stimulants, regardless of age (SAMHSA, 2013). Another study also revealed differences among subgroups of Hispanics. For example, Puerto Ricans between the ages of 18 and 34 had the highest rates of lifetime substance use (SAMHSA, 2013). Puerto Ricans reported greater use of cocaine than Whites, African Americans, or any other Hispanic subgroup. It has been documented that inhalant use is much lower among Hispanic populations than current stereotypes would suggest (SAMHSA, 2013). From these differences it is hypothesized that subcultural experiences may be critical to substance use and that socioeconomic status and level of urbanization may be causal factors related to abuse and lifetime prevalence. Acculturation, too, is important in assessing abuse patterns. Acculturation levels have been associated with greater lifetime rates of substance use.

Prevention and Intervention

Although research on treatment for Hispanics in general and respective subgroups has increased over the past 20 years, less is known about long-term effects of intervention. The following recommendations are drawn from the literature and presented as a guide. Prevention and intervention with Hispanic groups need to be culturally sensitive to the individual client's life circumstances, including the level of acculturation, availability of natural support systems, and environmental conditions. In addition, mental health professionals working with Hispanic populations need to incorporate into the counseling process such cultural concepts as *confianza* (trust), *dignidad* (dignity), and *respeto* (respect); current time orientation; preference for action-oriented advice; and the belief that human beings are at the mercy of supernatural forces (Espirito Santo, 2010; Furman et al., 2009).

Primary prevention programming can use characteristics of Hispanic communities such as strong family units and extended family ties to support efforts aimed at adolescents and adults. Programming that addresses anticipated stressors or themes of conflict and that focus on strengths and skills for optimum functioning will enable individuals to combat potential negative effects of acculturational stressors. Peer pressure has been cited as a strong factor in substance use (Lewis-Fernandez, Das, Alfonso, Weisman, & Olfson, 2005). Community and school programming that focuses on leadership skills and problem solving can be helpful if it is continuous and provides consistent opportunities for youth to explore their own creativity. In rural areas it has been suggested that community-based approaches should focus on educational systems (SAMHSA, 2013).

SOCIOECONOMIC STATUS (SES) AND SUBSTANCE USE DISORDERS

It is a well-known fact that SUD crosses socioeconomic lines and there is no direct link between poverty and substance disorders. Poverty, however, is considered a risk factor along the path to disordered substance use since it is correlated with other factors that contribute significantly to substance use. For example, there is a higher incidence of child maltreatment (especially neglect and physical abuse) among low-income families, and early child maltreatment is a significant predictor of later disordered substance use. The same is true for school failure (Appleyard, Berlin, Rosanbalm, & Dodge, 2011). Children from poor families tend to go to lower-quality, lower-achieving schools and are at greater risk for school failure, another significant predictor of substance disorders (Trenz, Harrell, Scherer, Mancha, & Latimer, 2012). Three of the four racial groups examined in the previous pages all have higher percentages of individuals living in poverty than the national average: American Indian (29.1%), African-American (27.4%), Hispanic (26.6%), and Asian-American (12.1%) compared to the national average (15.1%). It would therefore seem important to examine closely the relationships between low SES and disordered substance use.

SES and Substance Use Disorder Outcomes

This section summarizes the research in regard to neighborhood SES and it relationship to tobacco, alcohol, illegal substance, and general substance use between adolescent and adults as outlined in a chapter written by Gardner, Barajas, and Brooks-Gunn (2010).

TOBACCO   Among adolescents, there does not seem to be a strong or direct correlation between SES and tobacco use. Several studies have generated mixed results (see, for example, Kling, Leibman, & Katz, 2007; Kulis, Marsiglia, Sicotte, & Nieri, 2007). One study found that low SES was associated with less adolescent tobacco use but this was mediated through parental monitoring (Tobler & Komro, 2010). Among adults, on the other hand, studies have shown more consistently that those from low SES backgrounds are at greater risk for smoking tobacco (Carpiano, 2007; Datta et al., 2006; Stimpson, Ju, Raji, & Eschbach, 2007).

ALCOHOL   Among adolescents, the results are again mixed, with two studies (Kling et al., 2007; Kulis et al., 2007) finding no relationship between neighborhood SES and alcohol consumption. One study did find greater alcohol use among low SES adolescents; however, this was mediated by greater peer alcohol use (Chuang, Ennett, Bauman, & Foshee, 2005). For adults, the results are also somewhat mixed. Two studies (Carpiano, 2007; Stimpson et al., 2007) found significant associations between low SES and excessive/binge drinking, whereas another study (Pollack, Cubbin, Ahn, & Winkleby, 2005) found that neighborhood deprivation was inversely related to the odds of heavy alcohol consumption. On the other hand, several studies have shown the frequency of alcohol use to be positively associated with educational attainment and income (Galea, Ahern, Tracy, Rudenstine, & Vlahov, 2007a; Galea, Ahern, Tracy, & Vlahov, 2007b).

ILLEGAL SUBSTANCE USE   Few studies exist that investigated a link between SES and adolescent illicit substance use as an outcome variable. Research has tended more to examine adolescents' attitudes toward illegal substances. Kulis et al. (2007) found no relationship between poverty and recent marijuana use among adolescents. For adults, research results are also mixed. Some studies have shown a positive correlation between SES and marijuana use (Galea et al., 2007a, 2007b), whereas another study (Williams & Latkin, 2007) found a greater risk of use for heroin and cocaine and/or crack among those living in poverty and who were part of an HIV intervention study. Other studies have found a similar correlation between poverty and illicit substance use (Boardman, Finch, Ellison, Williams, & Jackson, 2001; Saxe et al., 2001).

GENERAL SUBSTANCE USE   Research has also investigated SES and general substance use rather than examine a particular substance. Fauth, Leventhal, and Brooks-Gunn (2007) found that adolescents who moved to high-SES neighborhoods reported more substance use on measures of marijuana, tobacco, and alcohol. Another study with an adult sample found a positive association between neighborhood poverty and the odds of substance use (Chaix, Merlo, Subramanian, Lynch, & Chauvin, 2005).

Research shows quite convincingly that substance use and abuse cross SES barriers. There is insufficient evidence to draw conclusions about the relationship between SES and illegal substances use, at least in regard to the adolescent population. In regard to alcohol and tobacco, adolescents who are at either at the low or high end of the SES curve seem to be more at risk for using these substances. Adults at the higher end of the SES curve are more at risk for alcohol use while those at the lower end are more at risk for illegal substance and tobacco use.

The Indirect Effects of SES

Although it is clear that a direct link between poverty and substance use disorders is weak at best, the indirect effect may be stronger when poverty can influence the shape of family and neighborhood. Following Gardner et al. (2010), we divide our discussion into three dimensions: institutions, relationships, and neighborhood disorder.

INSTITUTIONS As mentioned at the beginning of the section on SES and SUD, school failure is a risk factor for substance use, so children who attend poorly performing schools are at greater risk, and such schools are often located in low-SES neighborhoods. On the other hand, one might argue that those who come from high-SES backgrounds and attend high-performing schools suffer greater pressure and stress to perform and therefore are also at greater risk for substance use.

Organized prosocial neighborhood activities provide a buffer against substance use. Therefore, one could argue that neighborhoods with a strong youth organization network provide a protective factor. Since low-SES neighborhoods generally have fewer organized youth activities, one could argue that children living in such neighborhoods are at greater risk.

Unemployment among adults and SUD are correlated. Poor neighborhoods offer less employment opportunities, and it is a well-known fact that the Great Recession hurt the poor in disproportionate fashion (Seefeldt & Graham, 2013). Although unemployment can increase the risk for substance use disorder, the opposite is also true—that SUD increases the risk of becoming unemployed. In addition, the poor are concentrated in very demanding service jobs that could also increase the risk of SUD. In regard to adolescents, the question of employment is a bit more confusing. Some studies have shown that among youth from diverse SES backgrounds, employment can actually increase the risk of substance use due to the availability of disposable income (Bachman, Staff, O'Malley, & Freedman-Doan, 2013). On the other hand, adolescents who do not work get bored (especially in the summers), and boredom can often lead to increased substance use (Henkel, 2011). Because there are fewer job opportunities in low SES neighborhoods, those who live there can be at greater risk.

RELATIONSHIPS Living in poverty is stressful, and it can lead to increased family conflict, a commonly recognized risk factor for substance disorders. Parents often have to work long hours that can decrease the amount of involvement, quality time, and supervision available for their children. On the other hand, there is some evidence to support that parents from higher SES strata monitor their children less closely than those from lower SES environments (Chuang et al., 2005), which might also increase the risk of substance use. Social support has been known to decrease the risk of substance use. Being able to count on others (e.g., extended family, neighbors, church members) decreases the risk among both adolescents and adults as it most likely reduces the amount of stress a parent(s) might experience. High-SES parents might pay for extra child care when needed, which is not the case for low-SES parents. If they can count on others to help out when needed, it is a huge asset, but if they cannot, it will only increase the stress and family conflict.

NEIGHBORHOOD DISORDER   Studies have shown a positive association between neighborhood disorder and both adolescent and adult SUD (Choi, Harachi, & Catalano, 2006; Latkin, Curry, Hua, & Davey, 2007; Latkin, German, Hua, & Curry, 2009). Neighborhood disorder is understood as either physical (signs of property decay and abandonment) or social (signs of substance trafficking, violence, etc.). Low-SES neighborhoods often suffer from what sociologists refer to as "low collective efficacy," meaning that there is a lack of social cohesion that makes it difficult to mobilize any sustained intervention against the disorder. There is a generalized feeling that nothing can be done about it. Widespread disordered substance use in a neighborhood can result in disorder, but the reverse is also true. Low collective efficacy can result in use, which can then result in the widespread dealing and selling of both legal and illegal substances. It should also be mentioned, however, that affluent neighborhoods also suffer from a lack of social cohesion in that families can often live in isolation and in a very private manner (Gardner et al., 2010). The consequence is that SUD use can easily go undetected or unrecognized.

This section on SES has reviewed numerous factors that can put those living in poverty at greater risk for substance disorders. It has also highlighted how those from high-SES environments also have a different set of risk factors. In the end, the simple truth is that protective factors must outweigh risk factors to prevent the occurrence of substance disorders, regardless of an individual's SES status. People of color in the United States are more likely to be poor than their White counterparts, and being both poor and a racial minority can result in a set of psychological stressors that elevate the risk of disordered substance use.

CASE DISCUSSION

Case 1: Sandy and Pam

Both Sandy and Pam have a sporadic job history. Sandy has not worked in five years and is on welfare, while Pam demonstrates an inability to maintain employment. Without steady employment, Sandy might drink out of boredom and a lack of vocational motivation in her life. Pam, on the other hand, usually drinks and drugs heavily after quitting her job, only to accept another job she dislikes once she is "getting it together." Sandy's lack of structure and limited funds due to her low welfare income, and Pam's cyclical drinking patterns in response to unfulfilling employment, are risk factors for substance use and abuse.

Case 2: Juanita and Jose

There are differences between the cultural orientation of Sarita's and Karen's mother, stepfather, and biological father. Sarita, in particular, was raised with the conflicting values and messages from the Spanish culture that her mother knows and her birth father supports, and the American culture to which her stepfather acclimated. This has led the family to a struggle for connectedness to Hispanic values, and it might be contributing to Sarita's acting out both at home and in the classroom.

In order to meet Juanita's goal for her girls of learning more about their culture, thus helping Sarita understand herself in a deeper way, counseling can

(Continued)

(Continued)

take a bicultural effectiveness approach where the Identified Patient (IP) is not any one individual, but culture—or the various "cultures" existing within the family system. Culture becomes the repository of the family's dysfunction. Each member has a point of view that is culturally determined and demands a reframing of the problem. For example, the counselor could say to Jose: *I do not believe that Sarita disrespects you. What I believe is that she is trying to give you something of value and at the same time asking you to give her something of value. I believe this something of value to be your different cultural understandings and appreciations.*

In this approach, the various forms and levels of second culture acquisition convert the IP (culture) into an asset. The goal is to achieve a biculturalism within the family that enriches family members who are given the opportunity to hear, understand, and value aspects of each other's culture that, in the case of the Martinez family, include more traditional Mexican culture and the more dominant "American" culture. Ideally, Sarita's natural father, Hector, could be included in these sessions, as he seems to be the main representative of more traditional Mexican culture. If he and Jose had an amiable relationship, they could enrich each other with their distinctive cultural representations, and the effect on Sarita might be that she would not feel forced to choose. It is never a question of choosing one culture over the other, but of promoting a biculturalism or even a multiculturalism within the family. If this were achieved, the conflict between Sarita and Jose ought to be severely reduced.

Conclusion

Four themes emerge from the selected groups presented in this chapter. The first is the broad effect of stressors—environmental, social, and cultural—on, among, and within group interactions. This theme challenges us as mental health workers to expand our understanding of the interplay of populations outside the mainstream with those who have full participation within the mainstream.

The second theme can be summed up as perception, which is influenced by culture. This theme requires investigation into cultural and environmental conditions as they relate to community perceptions of SUD behaviors. The question that arises from this theme is how to mobilize a community against the detrimental effects of substance use within a culturally relevant and meaningful approach.

The third theme speaks to acculturation and identity development. All the groups presented in this chapter, at some level, need to learn to cope with the development of bicultural skills. We believe that the learning of bicultural skills and the appreciation of diversity are not only the responsibility of selected populations but also the necessary responsibility of us all.

Finally, the fourth theme to emerge is the multiplicity in ways of knowing, which are influenced by society, culture, socioeconomic status, age, and cultural, social, religion/spirituality, and gender identity development.

All these themes speak to the need of mental health workers to challenge their perspective of the world and develop an awareness of how one perceives culturally different clients. In developing this awareness, counselors need to gain an understanding of the history and background of their clients to address their issues within the context in which they are presented. By doing so, they will not only serve their clients' needs more fully but also empower them within the process.

MyCounselingLab for Addictions/Substance Use

Start with the Topic 11 Assignments: *Working with Diverse Cultures* and then try the Topic 10 Assignments: *Working with Specific Populations and Cultural Groups.*

Case Study: The Gutierrez Family

Angela and Miguel Gutierrez married in their late teens in Guatemala and shortly thereafter came illegally to the United States. Miguel had many of his family living here already, whereas Angela had no one from her family. Soon after arriving to the United States, they had their first child, Joaquin, who is now 13, and six years later had their second child, Daisy. The school encouraged the mother to seek counseling services for Joaquin because he appeared depressed and was not achieving academically in spite of having the ability to do so.

During the intake, Angela disclosed severe marital problems that she believed were based on her husband's drinking. He would drink heavily with his co-workers and family members, and subsequently become verbally abusive at home to her and Joaquin, but less so to Daisy. In response, Angela would start yelling, which lead to loud fighting; this discord, according to Angela, contributed to Joaquin's depressed mood. The father would often call Joaquin "stupid" and order him to go to bed at 5 in the afternoon. More recently, Joaquin greeted his father (reportedly drunk) at a family event with "Hi, Daddy," to which Miguel responded: "Shut up."

During the last three years, there have been two instances of physical abuse. Both times the police were called, and Miguel was arrested and sent to anger management classes. After the second incident, Angela insisted that Miguel find his own place to stay, which he did reluctantly. Angela also took out an order of protection against Miguel, who repeatedly violated the order by coming to the house, banging on the door, and demanding that he be let in. Angela would comply and said she could not report Miguel for violating the order of protection because if she did he would be deported, and she could not do that to the father of her children. When Miguel continued his verbal assaults on Angela, she felt confident that she could at least get him out of the house since he had another place to stay. Other times, Miguel would pass out on the couch.

All three family members admit that not having father living in the house has led to a more peaceful living situation, but they never know what to expect when father shows up. Angela has refrained from

getting into arguments with Miguel, but at times she finds it impossible. For example, one Friday evening Miguel showed up and demanded that they all go for ice cream. Angela went but said she did not want ice cream, yet Miguel demanded that she eat ice cream. She refused and at one point he told her to "Shut up." Angela admits to losing it and yelled back at Miguel that he was never to tell her to shut up again.

Angela feels this was a significant moment for her because when she first came to the United States she lived totally dependent on Miguel. She rarely ventured out of the house and lived by Miguel's rules. As time went on, Angela became more independent by working as a housekeeper and babysitter. Through working in the houses of wealthy people, Angela learned a great deal about the dominant culture in the United States and the blurry lines between the roles of men and women. In response to her newfound freedom, Miguel would accuse her of having lovers and living like a prostitute. He was quick to remind her that her role was to live by his rules. At other times, Miguel would admit that his wife was too "far gone," and there was nothing he could do about it. For her part, Angela says there is "no going back," but she still loves Miguel, and even though he has another place to live, she cannot separate from him both psychologically and physically. They continue to have sporadic intimacy when Miguel sleeps over and does not pass out on the couch. Angela feels that all would be well if Miguel stopped drinking, but any attempts toward this end or even to decrease his drinking have proven fruitless.

Critical Thinking Questions

1. Given your reading of this chapter, identify and describe three assumptions related to Hispanic cultural values that you would make about this case.
2. Identify all of the possible people who are directly and indirectly involved in this case. Briefly describe how they are—or should be—involved, and why.
3. Describe how the acculturation process produced stress for Angela and strain on the Gutierrez family.

CHAPTER 13

Prevention

Leigh Falls Holman, PhD, LPC-MHSP-S, RPTS, LSC, NCC

In public health, it is generally accepted that prevention and early intervention are the most effective ways to keep potential mental health issues from developing into chronic complex conditions. This is true of substance use disorders (SUDs) as well. Consistent with the strengths-based developmental approach that is a hallmark of the counseling profession, prevention is considered an important part of working with individuals and communities impacted by SUDs. Additionally, with the focus on prevention and integrated health care under the Affordable Care Act (42 U. S. C. § 18001, 2010), mental health professionals will increasingly find opportunities to work in medical settings screening individuals at risk of developing a substance use disorder and to provide prevention and early intervention for them.

When a need for prevention is identified, the initial questions should be *who* the target audience is and *what goals* should be set. The target audience and goals inform the category the prevention strategy will fall within. The World Health Organization (WHO) uses three categories to classify types of prevention strategies, which have traditionally been used to organize prevention campaigns: primary, secondary, and tertiary. This chapter focuses on primary and secondary prevention. *Primary* prevention (Cooper, Eisenberg, Sell, & Bertolote, n.d.) is anything targeted at completely avoiding a disorder, such as implementing legislation and enforcing existing laws and ordinances in order to control access. Another common example is a strategy providing education to raise awareness of risks and promote healthy attitudes and behaviors. Primary prevention efforts tend to focus on younger people, particularly those who are considered at high risk for developing substance use disorders.

Once a disorder has occurred, we move into *secondary* prevention. Secondary prevention is targeted at people who demonstrate problems with substance use, such as individuals who are arrested for driving under the influence (DUI) of substances. We attempt to assess and provide early intervention to prevent development of moderate or severe substance use disorders and to change attitudes, beliefs, and behaviors early in the SUD's development. Finally, *tertiary* prevention involves management of complex chronic health issues in order to improve functioning and quality of life. These strategies are more consistent with traditional counseling interventions discussed in other parts of this text. In the 1980s there was criticism of this classification system because it assumed that the development and etiology of disorders were clearly understood, and therefore that primary, secondary, and tertiary interventions could be easily identified (O'Connell, Boat, & Warner, 2009).

As a result, in 1997 the Institute of Medicine (IOM) developed a different categorical classification for prevention strategies (IOM, 1997, 2009, 2013). These include universal, selective, and indicated. *Universal* prevention strategies target an entire population, such as adolescents. *Selective* prevention strategies target a subpopulation known to be at higher risk, such as minority youth in impoverished, high-crime neighborhoods. Finally, for individuals who have been identified as having a risk factor that further increases the probability that they will develop a substance use disorder (e.g., having a parent with a substance use disorder), *indicated* prevention strategies are used. IOM recommends that prevention campaigns work simultaneously to target all of these. Today, most organizations in the United States use the IOM categories when developing prevention campaigns.

In constructing or evaluating substance use prevention programs, particularly those aimed at youth and young adults, it is important to consider *risk* factors that may predispose vulnerable individuals or groups to use, and *protective* factors that may inoculate individuals or groups against developing substance use disorders (OASAS, n.d.). A brief summary of such factors is provided in Table 13.1. Risk factors are considered to be characteristics that occur statistically more often for individuals who develop substance use disorder.

A prevention model using risk and protective factors ought to encompass the *agent* (e.g., alcohol or marijuana) involved, the *host* (individual) who uses the agent, and the *environment*

TABLE 13.1 Risk and Protective Factors*

Levels	Risk Factors	Protective Factors
I. Agent	Early onset of use	Delayed onset of use
	Choice of drug	
	Experimentation	
	"Gateway" effect	
II. Host		
1. Biomedical	Genetic vulnerability	
	Physiological vulnerability	
	Age	
	Sex	
	Race/ethnicity	
2. Personality/ character	Novelty and thrill seeking/risk taking	Self-esteem and internal locus of control
	Alienation and rebelliousness	Self-discipline
	Poor impulse control	Problem-solving and critical thinking skills
	Poor coping skills	Sense of humor
	Co-occurrence of psychiatric disorders	
	High stress (inter- or intrapersonal, life transitions)	
	Misperceptions of peer use	
	Particular life challenges (e.g., homosexuality, disability, oppression)	

(continued)

TABLE 13.1 *(Continued)*

Levels	Risk Factors	Protective Factors
3. Behavioral/ attitudinal	Social marginalization ("failure to fit in")	Positive peer influence
	Early antisocial behavior	Effectiveness in work, play, and relationships
	Perceived "invulnerability"	Perceived dangers of ATOD use and consequences
	Favorable attitudes toward ATOD use	Healthy expectations and positive assessment of future
	Susceptibility to peer influence	
	Friends who use ATOD	Relationship with caring adult
	Perceived benefits (e.g., social acceptance, anxiety reduction, performance enhancement)	Positive moral values
		Opportunities to contribute positively
	Other risky behaviors (e.g., risky driving, violence)	Religious involvement
III. Environment		
1. Family	Family dysfunction/trauma/major loss	Family bonding ("nurturing attachments")
	Lack of caring	Clear and high expectations
	Lack of clear behavioral expectations	Parent communication and involvement
	Poor supervision	Consistent praise/low criticism
	Inconsistent or excessive discipline	"Quality" time
	Low expectations for individual success	"Responsible decisions" message
	Permissive parental attitudes re ATOD use	Influence of older siblings
	Influence of older siblings	Healthy stress management
	History of ATOD use	Sharing responsibilities
2. School	Alienation	Involvement (e.g., athletics, extracurricular activities)
	Poor performance	School performance
	Learning problems (e.g., ADHD)	Positive school climate
	School dropout	
3. Community	Availability	Access barriers (e.g., pricing, age restrictions)
	Unhealthy/ambivalent social norms	Clear messages re use
		Drug-free alternatives

Levels	Risk Factors	Protective Factors
		Opportunities for prosocial action (e.g., mentoring, peer support, community service)
4. Other	Media/advertising portrayals of ATOD	Healthy norms in larger community (e.g., media)
	Societal institutions disintegrating, ignoring youth needs, or having lack of appeal	Cultural focus on healthy decisions
		Honest and comprehensive ATOD education
		Religious involvement

*No single risk factor is determinative; multiple factors interact in an additive manner. ATOD, Alcohol, tobacco, and other drugs.

(social context, immediate surroundings, local community, society) in which an individual obtains or uses substances. These elements are interactive in nature, which suggests interventions at any level that may address or reduce risk.

THE NEED FOR PREVENTION

According to the National Survey on Drug Use and Health (Substance Abuse and Mental Health Services Administration [SAMHSA], 2013), 1 in 10 people 12 years and older who were surveyed reported using an addictive drug in the previous 30 days. This was an increase from previous years, primarily attributed to an increase in marijuana use. Although misused pain medication was the second most used drug after marijuana, there was a decrease in use of pain medication from previous years for 12- to 25-year-olds. Cigarette smoking was also reduced from 13% to 4.9% among 12- to 17-year-olds. Similarly, alcohol use by 12- to 20-year-olds and binge drinking and heavy drinking have declined but still remain a significant issue. "In 2014, 22.8% of underage people were current alcohol users, 13.8% were binge alcohol users, and 3.4% were heavy alcohol users" (SAMHSA, 2015, p. 5). This indicates that more than one third of 12- to 20-year-olds were binge drinkers (drinking five or more drinks in one day) and 1 in 10 were heavy alcohol users (drinking five or more drinks on the same occasion on five or more days during the previous month). However, the number of adolescents and young adults who had an alcohol use disorder or marijuana use disorder or abused pain medications decreased from previous years. The Office of National Drug Control Policy (1999) stated that "successful substance-abuse prevention leads to reductions in traffic fatalities, violence, unwanted pregnancy, child abuse, sexually transmitted diseases, HIV/AIDS, injuries, cancer, heart disease, and lost productivity."

Emotional Impact

The emotional impact is evident both as a cause and as a consequence to other mental health issues. People with mental health issues are more likely to use alcohol or drugs (SAMHSA, 2016). When someone has both a mental health disorder and a substance use disorder or addictive behavior (e.g., gambling use disorder), they are said to have co-occurring disorders. Of the 20 million adults with a substance use disorder, 39.1% had a co-occurring mental illness, contrasted with only 16.2% of people without substance use disorders who suffered from mental illness in the previous year (SAMHSA, 2015). Among individuals with a reported mental illness, substance use disorders co-occurred in 18.2%, whereas for those with no mental illness, only 6.3% reported a substance use disorder (SAMHSA, 2016). Therefore, targeting individuals with non-substance mental health issues may be a consideration in prevention planning. Mental health disorders impact a person's ability to function in relationships, complete necessary work/school tasks, and fulfill other life roles. Serious mental illness includes any "mental, behavioral, or emotional disorder that substantially interfered with or limited one or more major life activities" (SAMHSA, 2013, p. 32). However, data indicate that early intervention following an initial episode of mental illness can improve outcomes (SAMHSA, 2016).

More than 20 million people 12 and older surveyed by the National Survey on Drug Use and Health reported having substance use disorders in the previous year, and adolescents who reported having a major depressive episode in the previous year were more likely to have misused drugs. Of the 11.4% of 12- to 17-year-olds who reported an episode of major depression in the previous year, 8.2% had major impairment in at least one role domain (e.g., ability to do chores, complete school work, get along with family and friends). Adults with co-occurring mental health disorders and substance use disorders in the previous years were most frequently occurring among 26- to 49-year-olds (42.7%), followed by those 18 to 25 (36%) and 50 or older (35.6%). However, those with a serious mental illness with significant role impairment was highest among 18- to 25-year-olds (35.3%), followed by 26 to 49 (24.9%) and 50 or older (15.1%).

Social Impact

Beginning at conception, people are at risk of being socially impacted by substance use disorders. In fact, 10% of all births demonstrate prenatal exposure to substances, with 5.9% of pregnant women 15 to 44 reporting current illegal drug use (SAMHSA, 2013). These infants are at risk for being born prematurely and at low birth weight, which can lead to lifelong learning disabilities, emotional and behavioral problems, and health problems. The National Institute on Drug Abuse (NIDA, 2015a) indicates that up to 45,000 cocaine-exposed babies are born annually. Infants exposed to cocaine in utero are 1.5 times more likely to need special education services in schools, at an estimated $23 million price tag annually (in 2015).

Approximately 12% of children in the United States are living with a parent who has a substance use issue (Child Welfare Information Gateway [CWIG], 2014). When parents have SUDs, there is an increased risk for children to be abused or neglected, thus becoming involved in the foster care system (IOM, 2013). Fifty-eighty percent of all child abuse and neglect cases involve substance use, according to NIDA (2015b). In fact, it is estimated that 61% of infants and 41% of older children in foster care come from families with active substance use disorders (Wulczyn, Ernst, & Fisher, 2011). Perhaps more significant, parental alcohol or drug use was the documented reason for removal for 31% to 60% of children in foster care throughout the United States (Correia, 2013; National Data Archive on Child Abuse and Neglect, 2012).

There is also an increased risk that children who grow up in families impacted by SUDs will be involved in crime. Parents with a SUD are three times more likely to physically or sexually abuse a child (Lander, Howsare, & Byrne, 2013). Subsequently these kids are at a significantly increased risk of being involved with the law, including being 40% more likely to become a violent juvenile offender. According to NIDA (2015b), at least 50% of people arrested for crimes such as homicide, theft, and assault are under the influence of substances. In addition to criminal involvement, people challenged with substance use disorders are more likely to have multiple job disruptions and to miss more work than non-substance users (NIDA, 2015b).

Medical Impact

Drug and alcohol use can lead to chronic medical issues such as diabetes and heart disease (SAMHSA, 2016). NIDA reports that substance use disorders can negatively impact outcomes for cardiovascular disease, stroke, cancer, human immunodeficiency virus/acquires immunodeficiency syndrome (HIV/AIDS), hepatitis, and lung disease (NIDA, 2012). In fact, every major organ system could potentially be impacted by drug and alcohol use. It is estimated that 40 million serious illnesses, injuries, and deaths annually can be attributed to substance use disorders (NIDA, 2015b).

In addition to medical consequences resulting in disease, the Centers for Disease Control and Prevention (CDC, 2016) indicate that every day 30 people in the United States die in car crashes involving alcohol. This amounts to one third of all traffic-related deaths in the United States. In 2014 more than 1 million drivers were arrested for driving while using alcohol or drugs. Substance use is involved in 16% of motor vehicle crashes annually (CDC, 2016).

Accidental deaths are also of medical concern. From 2001 to 2014, the total number of deaths due to overdose of prescription drugs almost tripled (NIDA, 2015b). Deaths attributed to overdose of prescription opioids alone increased 3.4-fold during the same time period, with males consistently having higher death rates. Deaths from benzodiazepines were 5 times greater, and deaths were 6 times greater for heroin overdoses from 2001 to 2014. During the same period, cocaine deaths rose 42%.

Financial Impact

Emotional, social, and medical consequences of substance use disorders all have financial impacts. To consider the full economic impact, the International Guidelines for Estimating the Costs of Substance Abuse (Single et al., 2001) suggest including health care and health services, including treatment and comorbidity and trauma related to substance use; productivity costs including premature mortality, morbidity/lost employment or productivity, treatment of non-workforce mortality and morbidity; crime and law enforcement costs including criminal justice expenditures, crime victim's time losses, incarceration, and crime career costs; and other costs such as research, education and law enforcement, prevention efforts, property destruction for crime or accidents, and welfare costs.

NIDA reports that the cost of substance use disorders and their impact on health care, productivity loss, crime, incarceration, and drug enforcement is estimated at $524 billion annually (NIDA, 2015a), whereas SAMHSA estimates cost to Americans of over $600 billion annually (http://www.samhsa.gov/prevention). Just the annual cost of alcohol-related crashes is over $44 billion (CDC, 2016). According to the Institute of Medicine and National Research Council's report on Preventing Mental, Emotional, and Behavioral Disorders among Young People (IOM, 2009), for every dollar invested there is a savings of $2 to $10 in spending for health, criminal and juvenile justice, education, and lost productivity. With estimates like these, prevention is the most sensible investment for communities with limited resources.

HISTORY OF SUBSTANCE USE PREVENTION

Although initial prevention efforts were harsh, such as sterilization of alcoholics and addicts in the 1900s (White, 2014), they evolved to include legislation to control access, funding research, and education campaigns to increase awareness of the problem. An early example is the 1914 Harrison Narcotics Tax Act (Public Law Ch. 1, 38 Stat. 784), which was passed as a measure to prevent access to opiates and cocaine. This legislation resulted in a federal requirement for a prescription to access these drugs. As a result, the first morphine maintenance clinics were established in 44 communities. However, the Supreme Court decided in *Webb v. United States* that a doctor prescribing regular doses of narcotic medication to an addict was not a "good faith" medical practice under the Harrison Act. Thus, doing so became a criminal offense, resulting in subsequent closure of these morphine maintenance clinics (White, 2014).

Prevention efforts were aided in the 1930s and '40s by an increase in the scientific study of alcohol and drug use, which correlated with the publishing of *Alcoholics Anonymous* (Wilson, 1939, 1955, 1976, 2001) and the spread of AA as a method for intervention. In 1942, the Research Council on Problems of Alcohol developed a primary prevention education campaign to impact public perception of individuals with alcohol use disorders. Around the same time, the National Committee for Education on Alcoholism (1950), now the National Council on Alcoholism and Drug Dependence (NCADD), promoted the following positions: (a) alcoholism is a disease; (b) the alcoholic, therefore, is a sick person; (c) the alcoholic can be helped; (d) the alcoholic is worth helping; and (e) alcoholism is the fourth largest public health problem and therefore our public responsibility (White, 2014). A five-pronged comprehensive prevention campaign developed by Marty Mann was used to promote these positions, including:

1. Launching local public education campaigns on alcoholism
2. Encouraging hospitals to admit alcoholics for acute detoxification
3. Establishing local alcohol information centers
4. Establishing local clinics for the diagnosis and treatment of alcoholism
5. Establishing "rest centers" for the long-term care of alcoholics

During this time, the first state alcohol commissions were founded to support local community education and treatment efforts. Public awareness was further enhanced by the inclusion of alcoholism in several novels published between 1944 and 1947 and popular movies produced in the early 1950s.

In 1950, the National Institute of Mental Health (NIMH) established a special division to address alcoholism. In the same year, the American Medical Association (AMA) created a special work committee that developed the first definition of alcoholism. Al-Anon Family Groups was formally organized shortly thereafter (Al-Anon, n.d.). In 1952 the Christopher D. Smithers Foundation (n.d.) was established with the mission of improving education and treatment for alcoholism. By the mid-1990s the foundation had funded more than $37 million in educational projects. What we now know as the American Society of Addiction Medicine (ASAM) was established as the New York City Medical Society on Alcoholism in 1954 (ASAM, n.d.).

During the 1960s there was an increased awareness of the need for intervention, partially due to the publication of *The Disease Concept of Alcoholism* (Jellinek, 1960), prompting passage of federal legislation that funded community mental health treatment (White, 2014). The American Psychiatric Association (APA) began to encourage members to learn about alcoholism and advocated for reimbursement from insurance plans for treatment of the disorder beginning in 1965. The following year, two federal appeals court decisions included language supporting the disease concept of alcoholism. This contributed to President Johnson's appointment of the first National Advisory Committee on Alcoholism. The same year, the National Center for the Prevention and Control of Alcoholism (NCPCA) was created within the NIMH, and a report calling for a national action plan addressing research, education, and treatment for alcoholism was released by the Cooperative Commission on the Study of Alcoholism.

Early prevention efforts in the 1960s and 1970s focused on classroom education, dissemination of information to potential users, and scare tactics. The rationale for these efforts was a basic belief: If potential or experimenting users received accurate information about the negative consequences of use, their attitudes would change, and they would modify their behavior. Lectures by doctors, law enforcement, pharmacists, and people in recovery offered warnings of dire consequences, including overstatements about experimentation almost certainly leading to severe SUDs and moralizing about the destructive lifestyles of people with SUDs, resulting in stereotyping. These descriptions often resulted in a misunderstanding that someone could have a SUD and still work, have a nice home, and be involved with family and friends.

Between 1967 and 1971, all major branches of the U.S. Armed Forces began special alcohol counseling initiatives (White, 2014). In 1970 the Comprehensive Alcohol Abuse and Alcoholism Prevention Treatment and Rehabilitation Act (Public Law 93 STAT. 1301), popularly called the Hughes Act, was passed, establishing the National Institute on Alcohol Abuse and Alcoholism (NIAAA), and the Drug Abuse Treatment Act of 1972 (Public Law 92-255) created a special office for drug abuse prevention that later became the National Institute on Drug Abuse. Both government organizations provided funding and dissemination of research and educational materials addressing substance use disorders. During this time, the National Clearinghouse for Alcohol Information implemented a mass media campaign to reduce stigma associated with substance use disorders and to use education as a major primary prevention strategy. Credentialing through certification and licensure of alcohol and drug counselors followed. Interestingly, during the 1970s there were intense arguments over whether alcoholism and drug abuse prevention, diagnosis, and treatment should be merged into one clinical category (White, 2014). This is similar to the recent debates about the inclusion of addictive behaviors such as gambling use disorder into the DSM-5 chapter on Substance Related and Addictive Behaviors (Potenza, 2014).

During this time, the Federal Advisory Committee on Traffic Safety also began efforts to prevent people from driving under the influence of alcohol through promotion of legislation to prohibit DUI, preventative education, and diversion programs requiring assessment, referral, and treatment for individuals with DUI arrests (White, 2014). In the late 1970s, public awareness and acceptance of people with alcohol and drug problems was aided by a media campaign including Operation Understanding, a news conference where 52 prominent members of society publically acknowledged their issues with alcoholism. First Lady Betty Ford also made a significant impact on destigmatizing substance use issues when she publicly acknowledged her own recovery from addictive substances (White, 2014).

The 1980s saw the development of a variety of newer approaches to drug prevention and education. Moving beyond the traditional information-based approaches, these newer methods included *affective education* (helping students identify and express their feelings; helping them feel valued and accepted; building self-esteem), *values clarification* (assisting students in deciding what was important to reaching their goals), teaching *alternatives* to drug use (e.g., relaxation, meditation, exercise, involvement with the arts), and development of personal and social *skills* (e.g., problem solving, self-management, and leadership skills; recognition of peer pressure and methods of resistance). The basic belief undergirding these programs was that adolescents and others would be deterred from using drugs if their self-esteem, social and communication skills, and decision-making, problem-solving, and resistance tools were improved. Many of these approaches showed some initial promise, but rigorous evaluation was still spotty or gave ambiguous results. As early as 1984, a review of prevention programs suggested the need for more adequate evaluation, again debunked the supposed benefits of solely educational-based models, and criticized existing approaches for lack of success in actually preventing substance use (National Institute on Drug Abuse [NIDA], 1984).

In 1980 Mothers Against Drunk Driving (MADD, n.d.) was formed, and President Carter appointed the National Commission on Alcoholism and Other Alcohol Related Problems to study the issue (Gerhard & Woolley, 1980). This was followed by an effort to prevent young people from drinking, with the passage of the National Minimum Drinking Age Act (1984) requiring all states to change the drinking age to 21 or lose federal funding for highways (Public Law 23 U.S. Code § 158, 1984). When Ronald Reagan became president, First Lady Nancy Reagan promoted an anti-drug campaign called "Just Say No" (Ronald Reagan Presidential Foundation & Library, 2010). Unfortunately, this platform was part of a larger "zero tolerance" policy campaign that resulted in a dramatic reduction in federal support for treatment and a corresponding rise in incarcerated drug users (Coulson, 2012). Subsequently, prisons became the largest provider of substance use treatment.

During the mid-1980s President Reagan signed an executive order mandating federal Drug-Free Workplace programs, rather than referring drug-impaired workers to treatment resources in the community (Anti-Drug Abuse Act of 1986, H.R. 5484). Similarly, he signed the Anti-Drug Abuse Act providing $4 billion to fight drugs by focusing on law enforcement efforts instead of preventative education and early intervention. He formally announced the "War on Drugs" in 1987, further shifting focus from treatment to punishment and incarceration of drug offenders.

Under the War on Drugs, the Drug Abuse Resistance Education (D.A.R.E.) program was first developed in 1983 as a joint initiative of the Los Angeles Police Department and the L.A. Unified School District (Cima, 2015). D.A.R.E. featured uniformed police officers presenting a multisession program of information and affective prevention with the delivery focused on fifth and sixth graders (Rosenbaum, 2007). It included multiple prevention components such as building self-esteem, helping students to recognize and resist peer pressure, practicing specific strategies for resistance, using alternative ways of coping, and emphasizing information about the consequences of substance use. The program spread rapidly across the country during the 1980s and 1990s. However, a vigorous debate arose about the effectiveness of primarily didactic approaches. Pressure increased as studies showed a lack of effectiveness (Rosenbaum, 2007). The U.S. Surgeon General and the National Academy of Sciences even offered criticism. Between 2001 and 2008, multiple iterations were developed, but each proved ineffective. A meta-analysis of studies conducted between 1983 and 2005 concluded that the program was ineffective in preventing drug use or promoting prosocial behaviors (Pan & Bai, 2009). This resulted in a revision to the curriculum in 2010.

Also in the 1980s, the Supreme Court upheld the Veterans Administration regulation classifying alcoholism as "willful misconduct;" under *Traynor v. Turnage* and *McKelvey v. Walters* U.S., 56 U.S.L.W. 4319; however, this was later overturned by Congress. Currently, Veterans Treatment Courts provide early intervention for veterans who become involved with the justice system as a result of substance use disorders. These are modeled on Drug Courts, which were first established by Miami Judge Stanley Goldstein. This model led to a national movement that diverts nonviolent drug offenders to treatment rather than incarceration (National Association of Drug Court Professionals, n.d.). By 2012, every state and territory in the United States had drug courts that focused on early intervention.

Collaboration between systems and integration of services have been preferred prevention strategies since the 1990s (CWIG, 2014). The Federal Block Grant Program was established in 1993 delineating six forms of prevention including:

1. Information dissemination
2. Education

3. Alternatives to substance use
4. Problem identification and referral
5. Community-based process
6. Policy and other environmental change processes

In both 1994 and 1996, the RAND Corporation released reports demonstrating that preventative education and early intervention is seven times more cost-effective than criminalizing drug use or prohibiting access to drugs. In the late 1990s innovative prevention and treatment programs were developed, which have improved efficacy including promotion of protective factors, early identification of at-risk families, culturally competent prevention efforts, mentoring, and wrap-around services for additional community-based support (CWIG, 2014).

The 21st century ushered in the age of harm reduction, which asserted that people are going to engage in risky behaviors, so it is better to mitigate the potential harm associated with risky behaviors than to try to stop something that will happen anyway. This indicated a shift to increasing resources for secondary prevention. Prevention efforts also began to shift from focusing on the at-risk individual or population to intervention into the *environment* of (potential) users, focusing on the social environment in which students and potential users live and the temptations that they face (Van Wormer & Davis, 2013). Programs that were undertaken using this view included sensitivity to the social and interpersonal environment of students (e.g., family, school, neighborhood, peers), exploration of risk and protective factors that are important in these environments and are related to individual development and life transitions, training in "refusal" skills, and "normative education" (or social marketing) that was intended to correct misperceptions about the social norms governing use within peer and social groups.

A variety of social influences affect substance use. All communities or groupings of people have social norms about a variety of things from acceptable language and dress to rules of proper conduct, values, and beliefs about use. *Norms* are perceived rules of behavior or values that influence a person's attitudes and actions. In prevention terms, norms set limits or establish guidelines that are the background or framework for substance use. Another aspect of the environmental or ecological perspective of prevention work is that there are embedded systems that have reciprocal causality in the development of SUDs. Individuals are influenced by families, which in turn are influenced by social networks, and vice versa. An environmental intervention at one level may also produce bidirectional change at another level. Accordingly, social norms are properties of large communities as well as of small subgroups, and the norms may conflict between groups. Although norms can influence a person's behavior and attitudes directly, they can also be *misperceived* and still exert influence. For example, teens may overestimate the number of their peers who smoke, drink, use drugs, or engage in sex, and this can powerfully influence an individual's attitudes toward substance use. Normative education attempted to present factual information about students' social environments, creating a more realistic picture of social norms as they actually exist and reducing the "everybody does it" belief and pro-drug attitude.

When the Affordable Care Act was passed (42 U. S. C. § 18001, 2010), the Prevention and Public Health fund was established to provide sustained investment in prevention efforts in order to improve quality and outcomes of health care. The fund supports community and clinical prevention activities, including those for mental health and substance use disorders. Because of this legislation, SAMHSA began focusing on local communities as the foundation for its prevention efforts, identifying 12 stakeholder groups necessary for success, including youth, parents, businesses, media, schools, youth-serving organizations, law enforcement, religious or fraternal organizations, civic or volunteer groups, health care professionals, governmental agencies with substance use expertise, and other organizations involved in reducing use, such as treatment providers. SAMHSA also established the Center for the Application of Prevention Technologies (CAPT). CAPT provides information and resources to communities interested in developing strategic prevention frameworks and effective prevention strategies (CAPT, 2016).

The national prevention and drug control strategy under President Obama, as outlined by the White House (Office of National Drug Control Policy, n.d.), includes 18 drug prevention actions under five principles:

1. A national prevention system must be grounded at the community level.
   a. Develop prevention-prepared communities.
   b. Collaborate with states to support communities.
   c. Spread prevention to workplaces.

2. Prevention efforts must encompass the range of settings in which young people live.
   a. Strengthen the Drug Free Communities Program.
   b. Revamp and reenergize the National Youth Anti-Drug Media Campaign.
   c. Support mentoring initiatives, especially among at-risk youth.
   d. Mobilize parents to educate youth to reject drug use.

3. Develop and disseminate information on youth drug, alcohol, and tobacco use.
   a. Support substance use prevention on college campuses.
   b. Expand research on understudied substances.
   c. Prepare a report on health risks of youth substance use.

4. Criminal justice agencies and prevention organizations must collaborate.
   a. Provide information on effective prevention strategies to law enforcement.
   b. Enable law enforcement to participate in community prevention programs in schools, community coalitions, civic organizations, and faith-based organizations.
   c. Strengthen prevention efforts along the southwest border.

5. Preventing drugged driving must become a national priority on par with preventing drunk driving.
   a. Encourage states to adopt per se drug impairment laws.
   b. Collect further data on drugged driving.
   c. Enhance prevention of drugged driving by educating communities and professionals.
   d. Provide increased training to law enforcement on identifying drugged drivers.
   e. Develop standard screening methodologies.

As part of this effort in 2011, President Obama issued the first Presidential Proclamation designating October as National Substance Abuse Prevention Month, which continued annually throughout his presidency (Obama, 2015). According to the White House (https://www.whitehouse.gov/prevention-intro), the President's Drug Control Strategy promotes the expansion of national and community-based prevention and early intervention programs aimed at encouraging healthy decision making. They cited research indicating that $18 is saved for every prevention dollar spent on substance use disorders.

CONCEPTUALIZING PREVENTION

Substance use disorders occur within complex systems involving individual, family, community, genetic, psychological, and sociocultural factors that interact with one another. Therefore, comprehensive prevention campaigns should involve multiple targets. The World Health Organization suggests that a public health focus will have more impact than focusing on the at-risk individual (Cooper et al., n.d.). Within public health, there are a variety of models and theories that are used to conceptualize prevention efforts. Sometimes these theories are also combined to develop prevention strategies that maximize effects (Johnson, Amatetti, Funkhouser, & Johnson, 1988). We focus first on discussing the overarching concept of public health, and then we briefly discuss some major theoretical approaches to prevention of substance use disorders.

Public Health

The concept of public health developed out of epidemiology and emphasizes the health of the public as a whole over that of one individual. There are five principles important to public health: (1) levels of prevention; (2) the epidemiology triangle; (3) passive and active approaches; (4) multiple program targets; and (5) effective strategies (Portland Injury Prevention, n.d.). We discuss each principle here, with examples to illustrate the principle in a substance use prevention context. At the beginning of this chapter, we described the WHO and the IOM levels of prevention, so we will not reiterate that here.

The *epidemiological triangle* is used to identify major risk factor categories to target with prevention efforts. The first side is the *host* (community or individual at risk), next is the *agent* (substance or behavior targeted), and finally the *environmental context* (Horvath, Misra, Epner, & Cooper, 2016). Prevention strategies under this model may be directed at any one of the three sides of the triangle. For instance, an individual who is at risk of developing a substance use disorder (host) may be taught refusal skills in order to decrease his or her susceptibility. Controlling access to drugs or alcohol, often through laws regulating use, is an example of targeting the agent. Finally, an educational media campaign aimed at changing attitudes toward substance use or gambling use disorders is an example of targeting the environmental context. All of these are considered primary prevention measures. One type of public health strategy that is a secondary prevention method is harm reduction, which accepts that eliminating risk is impossible. So the goal is to reduce or minimize the harmful impact of substance use in communities. An example of this is a public health campaign that encourages people to have "designated drivers" who do not drink and can drive the other members of a group who are drinking, thus reducing the likelihood of substance-related auto accidents.

Strategies can be considered passive or active approaches to prevention. *Passive approaches*, such as requiring air bags in cars to reduce the number of injuries and deaths from auto accidents, automatically protect everyone and do not require the individual to act. Therefore, passive approaches are preferred over active approaches. Alternatively, *active approaches* require individual action for the intervention to work. An example would be DUI checkpoints. It is important to note that passive strategies may not be practical because of social and political will and/or because resources are lacking.

Program targets can be individual, societal, and environmental/engineering. Prevention campaigns often focus on more than one of these targets. Education and raising public awareness about substance use risks and consequences is considered to be a strategy targeting the *individual*. A *societal* targeting strategy would be legislation passed to increase the drinking age to 21. Finally, the development and implementation of an alcohol interlock device that requires drivers to use a breathalyzer to demonstrate they have not been drinking alcohol in order to unlock the car's ignition is an example of a strategy focused on an *environmental/engineering* program target.

The final public health principle involves developing and implementing prevention strategies that are effective. To determine whether a strategy is effective, outcome studies should be conducted to evaluate the impact. It is challenging to determine the impact of some strategies because of confounding variables that may be affecting outcomes. Ideally, these variables are considered in the methodology used to evaluate the strategy, and controls are put into place to minimize the impact on data analysis. Through outcome studies, evidence-based practices can be established. However, it is crucial that methodology be critically evaluated when accepting a strategy as effective. Additionally, it is important to consider sociocultural context and individual factors that may result in less impactful strategies, even if they were proven effective within different contexts. For instance, an educational social media campaign to raise awareness about gambling use disorder targeting suburban males from middle-class neighborhoods may not work at the same level of effectiveness if the target were elderly, depressed widowed women.

Models and Theories of Public Health

Within the public health model, there are different approaches that may be used to assess a community's needs and to develop innovative prevention strategies that would theoretically be effective within the community. It is helpful to have a conceptual framework to structure a comprehensive prevention campaign. These include psychosocial models, communication models, and public policy models. We now describe and discuss some examples of each model.

PSYCHOSOCIAL MODELS Psychosocial factors attempt to identify individuals or communities that are at risk of having substance use issues so they can be targeted for prevention and early intervention. To determine this, assessment of both *risk and protective factors* needs to occur within each of the following domains: individual/peer, family, school, and community (OASAS, n.d.). In the *individual/peer domain*, risk factors include high levels of rebelliousness, difficult temperament, having friends who use substances and who reward use as "cool," exposure to illegal behavior and/or alcohol or drug use before the age of 15, perception that alcohol or drug use is not harmful, and preexisting depression before the age of 11 (OASAS). Individual/peer domain protective factors include regular involvement in a religious group, having strong moral beliefs, and possessing the social skills to engage in positive interpersonal relationships.

Family domain risk factors include a positive family history of SUDs, indicating a genetic predisposition and potentially for negative role modeling that combine to increase the probability of developing a SUD (OASAS, n.d.). Living in a family where there is violence or family members engage in criminal behaviors is also a risk factor. Either inconsistent parenting or severely rigid parenting can be risk factors. Parents who do not provide clear expectations that the child should not use substances are further placing their child(ren) at risk. Finally, if a parent's attitudes toward drug and alcohol use are favorable, their children are more likely to use. However, families can also provide protection from developing substance use disorders as well. When kids have meaningful relationships with family members and developmentally appropriate responsibilities at home, they are less likely to use alcohol or drugs. Additionally, parents and other family members can protect kids from developing substance use disorders by encouraging them and demonstrating the child's value in the family.

Risk factors in the *school domain* include academic failure, particularly if this is experienced between fourth and sixth grade, and low commitment to school, which results in truancy and failure (OASAS, n.d.). However, when schools provide opportunities for kids to become meaningfully involved in both academic and non-academic activities, and that involvement is recognized, kids are less likely to engage in problematic substance use behaviors (OASAS).

Finally, community-level risk factors include availability of addictive substances; favorable community attitudes toward substance use; few legal restrictions against access or use of substances or lack of enforcement of existing laws; high rates of mobility of residents resulting in low levels of attachment to the community; community disorganization; and poverty (OASAS, n.d.). When communities offer opportunities for kids to be involved in the community in prosocial ways, particularly if activities are structured and supervised by positive role models who recognize their kids' involvement, this offers protection from developing SUDs.

SOCIAL LEARNING   Albert Bandura's social learning theory suggests that learning behavior is a process that takes place in a social setting, and therefore contextual factors such as observation, instruction, and reinforcement strategies are likely to increase desired behavior (Johnson et al., 1988). Examples of strategies that use social learning include instruction in refusal skills, acting out role-playing exercises to practice refusal skills, gaining reinforcement for demonstrating refusal skills, and having role models that demonstrate desired prosocial behaviors.

COGNITIVE DISSONANCE   Cognitive dissonance is experienced when someone's behavior is inconsistent with the person's stated beliefs and attitudes. Cognitive inoculation is one strategy that uses this concept to identify and encourage desired beliefs and attitudes (e.g., I value my athletic ability, and I believe alcohol and drugs will hurt my performance) to impact their behavior (e.g., refusing alcohol or drugs because it will hurt my athletic performance). Another example is the use of social contracts, like the Contract for Life from Students Against Destructive Decisions (SADD, n.d.). The prevention strategy asks students to sign a contract that they will not use alcohol or drugs, with the hope that they will experience cognitive dissonance if they are in a situation where they are offered such substances and are tempted to use, thus resulting in their refusal.

SOCIAL INOCULATION   This theory builds on the cognitive dissonance theory to influence kids' attitudes and beliefs through social influences. A well-known example of this strategy was Nancy Reagan's "Just Say No" campaign. Students were taught about peer pressure and then taught refusal skills and alternative responses (e.g., I'm not interested in drugs). Although inoculating students against peer pressure may be helpful, results on this program were mixed (Johnson et al., n.d.).

PSYCHOSOCIAL DEVELOPMENT   Erik Erikson wrote about his theory of psychosocial development in his book *Childhood and Society*. He identified psychosocial tasks that correlated to different developmental stages that all people go through. If the individual does not resolve the task, then he experiences a psychosocial crisis (Hefner, 2016). The task for adolescence is identity versus role confusion. During this stage, adolescents are developing their individual identities. They often engage in experimentation with behaviors they have observed in others (in person or through media) to determine if these behaviors "fit" the adolescent's self-image. Therefore, experimentation with alcohol and drugs is potentially a pitfall for some kids during this stage of development. Prevention efforts using this theory focus on helping kids develop prosocial identities through involvement in activities such as volunteering, athletics, and groups like SADD (n.d.).

SOCIAL DEVELOPMENT This theory builds on social and emotional attachments people have to friends, family members, and their community (Johnson et al., n.d.). The theory indicates that prevention should target developmentally appropriate social bonds to impact the child's behavior. So in elementary school, prevention messages should come from parents and teachers (e.g., Red Ribbon Week classroom lessons and parent communication). In middle and high school, prevention should be tied to peer relationships (involvement in SADD groups, Red Ribbon Week decorating contests).

BEHAVIORAL INTENTION This theory posits that a person's beliefs about the outcome of her behavior result in her forming an attitude toward that behavior (Bock, Zmud, Kim, & Lee, 2005). For instance, if a good student believes her use of marijuana will result in academic failure and possible school suspension, she is more likely to form an attitude that marijuana use is bad. This attitude will then inform her decision about whether to engage in the behavior. She will likely avoid peers, activities, and environments where marijuana is used, and if offered the drug, she will likely refuse it. This theory is the basis for education campaigns that provide information about harmful consequences of alcohol and drugs.

STAGES OF CHANGE This model targets the individual who is at risk of developing a substance use disorder. The level of the person's motivation to change his or her current beliefs or behaviors is assessed through motivational interviewing (MI) techniques (Prochaska & Di Clemente, 1982). There are five stages of change that someone can move through in stepwise fashion (although this is not always how someone progresses), including:

- *Precontemplation:* The target lacks awareness of danger or does not acknowledge risks. They are not even considering changing behavior (e.g., does not understand there is a risk to skipping school occasionally to drink with friends).
- *Contemplation:* The target recognizes the problems with the behavior and is considering behavior change by analyzing the pros and cons of engaging in the behavior (e.g., gets suspended for skipping school and grounded at home and begins weighing whether the rewards for the behavior are worth the risks).
- *Preparation:* At this point the person has decided to change a behavior and begins to plan when and how the change will occur (e.g., identifies high-risk friends and environments, begins learning and practicing refusal skills).
- *Action:* The change plan is being implemented (e.g., using refusal skills and avoiding high-risk environments and friends).
- *Maintenance:* The behavior becomes a new habit.

For each stage there are corresponding prescribed MI techniques used to help the person move to the next level.

COMMUNICATION MODELS These models attend to communication processes and methods. Processes for communication inform how prevention strategies will be developed and disseminated across the whole process, not only a single point in the process. Multiple methods are used to communicate the message to the target population through media campaigns.

HEALTH PROMOTION This model expands on the behavioral intention model; however, instead of targeting general attitudes, this model targets behavioral intention through a comprehensive campaign using multiple strategies (Galloway, 2003). Elements that need to be addressed by prevention efforts include countermeasures (e.g., anti–substance use advertising that competes with alcohol commercials); level of difficulty (e.g., identifying targets that can be realistically accomplished); addictive properties of substances; and social pressures to use. Additionally, the model takes into account communication skills such as attending to the source of the message, the message itself, the channel or medium through which the message is communicated, the receiver of the message, and finally the destination of the message. An example of a health promotion prevention strategy would be a targeted media campaign about the dangers of smoking using a popular teen actress as a spokesperson who conveys the message through social media, print ads in teen magazines, and electronic media with an adolescent demographic target.

COMMUNICATION AND BEHAVIOR CHANGE This model involves media campaigns that identify the steps necessary to move a targeted population from awareness to interest to action regarding adopting a promoted attitude (e.g., drugs are destructive to relationships) and maintaining that attitude and associated behaviors (e.g., refusal to use). Media is used to target not only the intended population but also a secondary audience, like parents or communities. Contemporary interventions use not only print and electronic media but also social media such as Facebook, Twitter, and SnapChat.

PERSUASION-COMMUNICATION Traditional media campaigns focus on communicating information about the negative consequences of using alcohol or drugs. Because these have not been very successful, the model focuses on communicating about alternative solutions for the problem. A multistep process is used to help the targeted population move from awareness to behavior change (Johnson et al., n.d.).

PUBLIC POLICY MODELS Public policy models tend to be developed by government organizations and, to a lesser extent, nonprofit organizations responsible for addressing public health issues in a particular community, state, or nation (e.g., SAMHSA). Visual representations of the problem, the etiology, and the consequences are usually developed based on data gathered about the targeted population.

CAUSAL MODEL Proponents of the causal model believe that targeting the problem directly (e.g., the D.A.R.E. program for urban minority youth) rarely works, so it is crucial to identify and work with key variables that impact the targeted behavior (e.g., not using drugs; Brickmayer, Holder, Yacoubian, & Friend, 2004). The first step is to identify, through the use of methodologically sound studies, empirically identified variables that contribute to the target behavior (e.g., lack of after-school programs). Also, consequences of the target behavior are identified through reviewing research (e.g., use drugs and get approached by a gang to sell for them). The identified variables are visually diagrammed and then used to inform decisions about intervention strategies.

SOCIAL-ECOLOGICAL MODEL Used by the Centers for Disease Control and Prevention, this model values the complexity between multiple systems that interact to create a potentially problematic situation (CDC, 2016). Factors at each of the following levels are identified, and strategies are chosen to maximize impact across multiple domains:

- *Individual Level:* Factors that distinguish at-risk individuals include gender, ethnicity, age, academic success, and trauma history. Prevention strategies target changing beliefs, attitudes, and behaviors such as skills training.

- *Interpersonal Level:* Close relationships with family and friends are analyzed to identify how they impact the individual. Some prevention strategies include mentoring relationships such as Big Brothers/Big Sisters.
- *Organizational Level:* This includes professional organizations and associations, health departments, clinics, and institutions. Prevention strategies may include psychoeducation about the risks of drug use provided by a nurse at a primary care clinic.
- *Community Level:* At this level school, work, and neighborhood contexts are considered, including characteristics such as safety, criminal behavior, socioeconomic status, and social isolation. Community prevention might include things like community policing efforts that target increasing the police presence in a neighborhood by assigning police who look like the people in the neighborhood to become engaged by patrolling on foot, getting to know the residents, and building relationships with them.
- *Societal Level:* Broad sociocultural contexts need to be analyzed to determine factors that increase or decrease risk. Policy decisions and legislation are often the focus at this level. For instance, some states have legalized recreational use of marijuana, which may have a society-level impact on risk. Factors include trends in health, education, economics, and social policies. An example of a societal level prevention measure was the "zero tolerance" campaign under Ronald Reagan, which had unintended consequences resulting in mass incarceration of black males disproportionately arrested, charged, and convicted for drug-related offenses.

LOGIC MODEL   The logic model builds on the causal model by also diagramming dynamics between variables. Specific relationships between variables are diagrammed (Holder & Carina, 2012). Here is a simple example:

Variable 1: Living in an impoverished neighborhood in an urban environment

Relationship: is more like to result in

Variable 2: lack of community resources like after-school activities.

Specific relationships between the variables and the problem are also diagrammed.

Variable 1: Living in an impoverished neighborhood in an urban environment, and

Variable 2: lack of community resources like after-school activities, and

Variable 3: high levels of crime and low parental supervision

Relationship: correlate with

Problem/Outcome: drug use.

Like the causal model, the logic model is used to inform selection of prevention strategies. Prevention is focused on community-wide evidence-based environmental strategies. The model may also further specify the specific prevention activities chosen to impact outcomes.

INSTITUTE OF MEDICINE (IOM)   This model was developed after the health model came under criticism in the 1980s because it assumed the development and etiology of SUDs were clearly understood, and therefore that primary, secondary, and tertiary interventions could be clearly identified (O'Connell et al., 2009). The model uses the categories of universal, selected, and indicated to define levels of prevention. These were previously described in this chapter. The IOM model takes into account the complex interactions between multiple individual and environmental risk and protective factors that contribute to substance use disorders.

Universal prevention strategies include schoolwide campaigns, media campaigns, legislative and administrative policies impacting communities, and prevention outreach through health departments. Selected prevention includes identification high risk or "vulnerable" populations and creating targeted prevention for the group's unique risk factors. Finally, indicated prevention includes things like individual counseling targeted at people who have early stages of substance use issues.

SPECTRUM OF PREVENTION MODEL Intended to be comprehensive, the model encourages people to expand their prevention planning beyond raising awareness and skills training (Prevention Institute, 1999). It promotes the importance of including advocacy for the broader policy issues impacting the problem. According to the model, there are six levels where prevention strategies should be targeted:

- Influencing policy and legislation
- Changing organizational practices
- Fostering coalitions and networks
- Educating providers
- Promoting community education
- Strengthening individual knowledge and skills

By implementing prevention strategies using each of these, the levels can work together in a complementary fashion to improve efficacy and create improved outcomes.

DEVELOPING PREVENTION STRATEGIES

Once a model or a combination of models for conceptualizing a public health issue is decided on, the process for developing prevention strategies or campaigns can begin. For the purposes of this section, we assume that a logic model is being used for prevention planning. Effective prevention planning begins with needs clarification, assessment, and development of goals and "measurable" objectives buttressed by consistent evaluation procedures. These early steps are essential, and prevention planners must be willing to expend the time and effort to pursue them thoroughly (Holder & Carina, 2012). Affirmation and acceptance by community leaders ("gatekeepers," such as school administrators and parents) of the needs, goals, and objectives that are developed in these steps are essential for program success. Notice, too, that these steps are tied to ongoing evaluation and program modification. Without clear and measurable objectives, effective evaluation will falter.

Prevention planners should have no illusions, however, about the ease or time frame required to achieve these first three steps. School personnel, and even parents, can be hesitant about conducting a thorough needs assessment. Although it may seem obvious that prevention initiatives require a sound understanding of the extent and scope of the problem in a particular setting, this information can also be disquieting and may be perceived as damaging in the short term from a public relations point of view.

In addition, gatekeepers themselves may need to be educated about the approaches and underlying assumptions that guide selection of specific goals and objectives. Here, prevention planners may have to confront misperceptions about the effectiveness of some "commonsense" strategies on a long-standing structure (e.g., information dissemination and scare tactics) and will have to address potential strongly held value positions among gatekeepers to win their assent and support (Rosenbaum, 2007). Discussions of issues such as the (potential) objective of "zero tolerance" versus "responsible decisions," or "abstinence" versus "harm reduction," will inevitably have to occur. Winning the support of gatekeepers will take time in such cases but is critical for long-term program support, resource collection, implementation, and effectiveness.

A needs assessment includes careful collection of information about the target population, current environmental context, and trends. A well-designed needs assessment will include multiple methods and gather information and input from a variety of stakeholder groups. Stakeholders include public officials, agencies that serve the target population (schools, Boys & Girls Club, churches, etc.), parents, law enforcement, businesses in the community, and members of the target population. You may begin to identify community partners who might also want to work with your organization on prevention efforts, as you go through the process. According to SAMHSA (2010), there are six levels of partner engagement that may be considered for these relationships:

1. *Networking:* Partners are minimally involved, primarily to share information.
2. *Publicity:* Partners serve as channels for spreading information.
3. *Endorsement:* Partners publicly endorse prevention strategies or programs to broaden appeal or lend credibility.
4. *Coordination:* Partners remain self-directed but conduct mutually beneficial activities and work together with a common purpose.
5. *Co-sponsorship:* Partners share resources.
6. *Collaboration:* Partners work together from beginning to end to create a vision and to carry out a program.

Needs assessments should examine attitudes, beliefs, behaviors, and community conditions that condone or promote substance use (SAMHSA, 2010). This process may also help you identify community leaders who may be important to include in advocacy efforts. Additionally, professional literature from peer-reviewed sources should be reviewed as well as relevant public records and reports.

The next step is analyzing the data collected identifying at-risk populations or individuals and analyzing the risk and protective factors for the target population. This process can be aided by examining "webs of influence" in each of the following domains: individual, peer, family, school, community, and society. As you discover important elements of the problem, you can begin to diagram them into the logic model. As you discover variables contributing to the problem and the consequences of the problem, you can add these to the logic model.

As you go through this process, ask how substance use problems arise. This will help you define the agents, hosts, and environment that will ultimately be targeted by prevention strategies. In comprehensive prevention programs, multiple strategies may be developed to impact different levels of the problem. Next, you should examine any relationships between variables and add those relationships to the logic model. Once all of these elements are diagrammed into the logic model, clear goals and objectives should be established based on data analysis from the needs assessment. Once data is evaluated and conclusions drawn, you should have the evidence necessary to present to stakeholders that will prove there is a public health concern that needs intervention.

Planning then changes focus to identifying and developing specific prevention strategies. SAMHSA (2010) identifies three essential qualities of a prevention strategy: accountability, capacity, and effectiveness. *Accountability* means that you need to have measures in place to evaluate the strategy and that you report program results to stakeholders. *Capacity* means that you are building new resources for the community or target population. And *effectiveness* indicates that you demonstrate evidence that you are actually positively impacting the targeted outcomes.

When designing a comprehensive prevention campaign, there are several principles that can guide planning to help ensure that strategies chosen address multiple variables, at different levels, with diverse targets. The first principle is that prevention is a continuum involving multiple levels including primary, secondary, and tertiary prevention strategies and universal, selected, and indicated. The next principle identified by SAMHSA's Focus on Prevention (2010) is that prevention is prevention is prevention, meaning that it targets attitudes, feelings, beliefs, and behaviors by focusing both the message and specific activities on areas of influence in multiple domains. The third principle is that successful prevention should both decrease risk and increase protection against risk factors for the targeted population. Fourth, systems of prevention work better together than they do when isolated from one another. Partnerships improve influence and impact. Fifth, it is important that information and resources be shared across multiple service systems, including national, state, and local. The final principle outlined by SAMHSA is that substance use prevention should use multiple strategies that impact a variety of targets that contribute to the desired outcome.

Once prevention strategies and activities are developed, then the next step is putting them into action. Initially, any training or technical support that may be needed to support successful strategy implementation should be put into place. This includes ensuring that the message conveyed and the strategies developed are culturally competent. For each strategy, it is important to identify and include engaged partners; undertake activities that increase support for the strategy; maximize participation by offering incentives (fun, food, prizes, etc.) and by reducing barriers to participation (offer transportation, choose convenient times); and look for ways to maximize the likelihood that the strategy will be implemented as intended (monitor activities at each stage, implement comprehensive evaluation process).

SAMHSA advocates for evidence-based strategies that have been proven through empirical analysis to be effective. The Center for Substance Abuse Prevention (SAMHSA, 2010) identifies six recommended strategies:

1. *Information dissemination* increases awareness and attitudes. Examples are media campaigns or inviting special speakers to a meeting or class.
2. *Prevention education* moves from the one-way communication of information dissemination to a two-way process where participants are taught important skills such as peer resistance, critically evaluating advertising, healthy decision making, or refusal skills.
3. *Positive alternative activities* can be structured that will motivate people to engage in healthy constructive interactions rather than activities that will increase risk of substance use. Examples may be after-school community center ball games, or involvement in a community garden.
4. *Environmental strategies* that focus on the contexts and larger policy issues to reduce risk and increase protective factors. Examples include implementing legislation and community policing efforts.
5. *Community-based processes* are strategies that focus on building community coalitions to maximize resources in order to improve the community's ability to implement effective prevention and early intervention services.
6. *Identification of problems and referral to services at the first signs of problems.* Examples include screening for substance use issues in primary care settings and implementing drug court diversion programs for first-time DUI offenders.

With any strategy it is important to remember that they need to fit the sociocultural environment and unique population that is being targeted. Prevention activities need to be intensive to improve results (SAMHSA, 2010). Remember to be flexible and provide feedback about progress and service delivery issues on an ongoing basis to stakeholders. Initially activities should be implemented as planned in their complete form; however, if necessary following

TABLE 13.2 Considerations in Comprehensive Prevention Planning

Procedures	Questions for the Planning Process
Needs clarification	What salient patterns of ATOD problems and co-occurring disorders appear in our community? What specific factors (e.g., socioeconomic and multicultural influence) affect these patterns?
Assessment	Are recent statistics and other sources of reliable information available, or is funding/planning needed for additional investigation (e.g., surveys)?
Goals	In concrete terms, what needs to be accomplished? What can realistically be achieved in the short term, and what is designated as long term?
Objectives	With further clarification and evaluation of desired results, what is specifically measureable and in what workable timeframe?
Resources	Stakeholders investigate which resources are attainable from which parties (e.g., facilities, finances, staff). What additional resources are needed to meet stated objectives?
Funding sources	Stakeholders analyze financial existing resources and consider options for expanding funding as needed.
Leadership and organization	Which stakeholder offers the most productive resources for each task? Is there an equitable distribution of responsibilities among participants?
Action	Are program components evidence-based? How to maintain consistent forward movement in program implementation? Is the timetable being followed?
Monitoring and evaluation	Are the prevention strategies adhering to stated goals? Are objectives being met? How is progress being measured? Are stakeholders able to evaluate progress, or will additional parties be needed?
Modification	Are goals/objectives being met? (Is it working?) What changes are needed, and how/by whom will they be implemented?

evaluation, try different versions of the strategy to improve outcomes. Finally, consider using long-term approaches to prevention, because reinforcement over time is more likely to have a sustained impact than a single activity done once.

Before implanting implementing any strategy, evaluative assessment methods need to be planned, and all elements of the program evaluation need to be in place before implementation. As implementation begins, evaluative assessments need to be monitored to ensure they are being properly implemented, because flaws in methodology of program evaluation may invalidate results. Evaluative assessments should address effectiveness of the strategy on the desired outcome, the quality of service delivery, and identification of necessary changes to improve the desired impact. A well-thought-out plan of evaluation can help in assessing program successes, in addressing program failures, and in revising program delivery to increase positive outcomes. This, too, will take time and energy but is essential in achieving prevention goals. A sound planning process is only the first step, however, in constructing an effective and comprehensive prevention program. Planning, implementation, evaluation, and ongoing program revision are the hallmarks of the best programs. Prevention providers will benefit from a careful review of these important attributes. To learn more about current evidence-based prevention strategies, visit the SAMHSA website for substance abuse prevention evidence-based practice (EBP) (SAMHSA, 2014) web guide (http://www.samhsa.gov/ebp-web-guide/substance-abuse-prevention). This site is continually updated by SAMSHA to include the most recent information on EBPs. The strategies on this site are evaluated based on these criteria: (a) There is information about the effectiveness of specific interventions; (b) each program site identifies multiple EBPs; (c) all primary links are functional; (d) information about interventions is not exclusively provided in PDF format; and (e) they do not charge fees for using the strategies or programs.

CASE DISCUSSION

Case 3: Leigh

Imagine that you are Leigh's counselor at the new school she is attending. You are called to a "special" evening meeting at the invitation of the principal; a number of concerned parents and community representatives are also attending. The topic is a perceived rise in drug use among students at the school. The goal is to formulate some way to address the problem.

You have gotten to know Leigh only recently. Her acknowledgment of "smoking some dope" every so often and drinking with friends rings true to you; you know that she is hanging out with other students about whom you are increasingly concerned. You are also aware of too many students in the school who live with ongoing parental conflict or are struggling with parents' marital separation or divorce. You know other students who seem withdrawn and isolated or who are experiencing academic difficulty for no apparent reason. You have come to think of Leigh, her new friends, and these other students as at risk for a whole variety of problems. Your hope is that the meeting will shed some light on these concerns.

The meeting begins with the principal and several community leaders presenting anecdotal evidence of drug use among students at several other schools in the region. The local police chief and a juvenile officer speak about increased incidences of drug sales and arrests within the community. Several teachers address their concerns about students in academic difficulty and a growing sense that some of the students are distracted and uninvolved in the classroom. Several parents speak to their worries about peer pressure and their children's "friends." They demand that something be done.

As the meeting progresses, there are calls for more drug information for students, for student assemblies at which the police warn of impending trouble for students caught using or selling drugs, and for classroom presentations by recovering addicts who can portray the perils of drug addiction. There are calls for action by law enforcement against street dealers and even against bar owners and alcohol distributors who are suspected of providing alcohol to underage persons. Although many of the parents seem unwilling to acknowledge a potential problem with their own daughters or sons, they do insist that the school and community agencies do "something" about the problem.

The principal turns to you as the school counselor to help provide a "way forward." He asks you to chair a working group of teachers and parents, charged with constructing a prevention program to be implemented in the fall. What resources are available to you and the working group? What approaches make the most sense? What students would you target for intervention? How can you find out what is most likely to work? What would be the first step to take in this process?

Conclusion

This chapter was designed to provide the foundational concepts and knowledge that will enable mental health providers to understand the need for prevention, the history of prevention in the United States, and current trends in prevention of substance use disorders. With this foundational knowledge, counselors can begin to engage in planning and evaluating evidence-based prevention strategies for substance use disorders. This work is both exciting and challenging. Building on lessons learned from the past, today's prevention efforts need to be comprehensive and collaborative. The most effective prevention programs are integrated and include a coordinated set of strategies that enhance the health and total well-being of persons to reduce the risk of destructive behavior and its consequences.

MyCounselingLab for Addictions/Substance Use

Try the Topic 12 Assignments: *Prevention.*

Case Study: Marci and Joey

Marciela, a 19-year-old woman of bicultural background (Latina and Anglo), is struggling socially and academically during her senior year of high school, and lives with her siblings in her parents' suburban home in a small Southern city. Mr. and Mrs. Soliz are small-business owners, operating a retail store featuring the sale and installation of home water and air filtering systems. Mrs. Soliz works part-time as an administrator and bookkeeper for the business, and considers her "main job" to be caring for their four children, which includes Marci's siblings, 16-year-old Joey and "the twins," Suzi and Marcos at 12 years of age. With the faltering economy, Mr. and Mrs. Soliz have been logging long hours at the store and rely on Marci and Joey to help with the store on a part-time basis as well as supervising the twins while their parents are at work. Typically, the parents are known to drink alcohol minimally, only a few times each year, usually on holidays or during celebrations with extended family.

Marci failed the 10th grade because of absences and poor grades that coincided with her initiating use of alcohol and marijuana. She explained to her counselor that it was "boring at home" because of her parents' extended hours at the store. Marci expanded that she and her friends were able to effectively "watch the younger kids okay and still smoke a little [marijuana]." Marci has gone through periods of sobriety during the last 3 years, sometimes lasting as long as 6 months. She vacillates between recognizing the detrimental effects of alcohol and marijuana on her academic and social life, and minimizing her use as "no big deal." Marci reported that she feels "invisible" at school except to her small circle of close friends.

Joey, known for his outgoing personality, has been a class leader in student government and athletics; he is part of the "popular crowd" at the high school. Joey received scholastic and athletic notice at the yearly awards banquets. However, during the recent semester, Joey's grades in some of his classes have begun to fluctuate. Mr. and Mrs. Soliz have talked to their son about "partying" with his friends repeatedly. Additionally, Mrs. Soliz is often frustrated by her inability to personally supervise her children at home because she is needed at the family business. When she is on "home duty" Mrs. Soliz is frequently out of the house, driving the twins to their extracurricular activities of soccer and piano lessons.

Marci has been feeling much self-recrimination, blaming herself for the negative consequences of her brother's experimentation with alcohol and tobacco. Joey recently got a warning ticket from a police officer for approaching a man at a convenience store, asking that beer and cigarettes be purchased for his friends. Mr. and Mrs. Soliz grounded Joey for 6 weeks, not allowing him to drive anywhere except to school and work. About the same time, they noticed that Marci seemed more reticent and withdrawn. Mr. and Mrs. Soliz have discussed starting family counseling in addition to Marci's individual therapy.

Mr. and Mrs. Soliz talked to the parents of Joey's friends who were involved in the incident, alerting them to their children's use of alcohol. Though hesitant at first, they further expressed concerns about the effects of using substances on Marci and their desire to avoid a similar outcome with her siblings. Several adults agreed that a more formal prevention effort would be helpful to support each family. An informal meeting at the high school was scheduled with concerned parents, teachers, and administrators to outline a program strategy.

Critical Thinking Questions

1. Joey and Marci are from the same family; however, their situations are different. Considering each of them, compare and contrast the risk factors and protective factors, including all levels and domains discussed in the chapter that should be considered when determining the appropriate strategies to prevent them from developing a moderate or severe substance use disorder.

2. Identify the levels of prevention (primary, secondary, tertiary and universal, selective, and indicated) that are most appropriate for this problem, and give examples that the PTA could develop to deal with the presenting problem.

3. List and describe the five public health principles that should be considered by the prevention planning workgroup and give relevant examples.

CHAPTER | **14**

Behavioral Addictions/ Non–Substance-Related Disorders: An Overview

Patricia W. Stevens, PhD, Karisse A. Callender, MS, LPC, SAC, Robert L. Smith, PhD, NCC, CFT, FPPR

N on–substance-related disorders have recently been added to the DSM-5 under the category of Substance-Related Addictive Disorders. The only non–substance-related disorder included in the diagnostic section of the DSM-5 is gambling. However, in Section III, Conditions for Future Study, Internet gambling disorder is proposed as a diagnosis for future research and inclusion. History is filled with individuals who engaged in excessive behaviors (gambling, sex, eating, work) from early Rome to present day, but the criteria for a non–substance-related addictive disorder has not been included until now in the DSM-5 (American Psychiatric Association [APA], 2013). Previously pathological gambling was considered an impulsive control disorder. These new criteria and this new category lead us to new research and clinical decisions.

Many behavioral disorders/addictions have been explained through the terms *compulsivity* and *impulsivity*. Key aspects of impulsivity include "a maladaptive predisposition toward rapid reactions, reduced motor or response inhibition, automatic response to urges and impulses, delay aversion, insensitivity to delayed rewards, and lack of reflection when making decisions" (Rosenberg & Feder, 2014, p. 19). Excessive impulsivity is usually non-productive and an element in many psychological diagnoses. Compulsivity refers to "persistent or perseverative behavior that is inappropriate to the situation and has no obvious relationship to the overall goal" (p. 20).

Although these two constructs have been seen as opposites, recent research changes that view. Studies have shown that primary impulsive psychopathology (gambling disorder/ pathological gambling) may also show traits of compulsivity (Cuzen & Stein, 2014). Further, an argument can be made that impulsivity is the key to initiation of behavior and compulsivity develops. As an example of the complexity of this distinction, remember that previously in the DSM-IV, gambling was included under Impulse Control Disorders. The interrelatedness of these two constructs forms an important part in defining a behavioral addiction.

There are neurobiological models for the addictive cycle that may explain the brain alteration of the addict (O'Brien, Volkow, & Li, 2006; Saktor, 2011), which may influence impulsivity and/or compulsivity. These theories address brain chemistry changes, cellular memory, and optimal flow as possible explanations for the addictive behavior.

This chapter provides an overview of the general criteria for assessment, diagnosis, and treatment of behavioral disorders. It provides the specific DSM-5 criteria for gambling disorder with specific assessment tools and treatment plans. The chapter also provides an overview of other behavioral disorders that are identified in the mental health field but have no formal diagnostic criteria in the DSM-5. These include sex addiction, Internet addiction, exercise addiction, and compulsive buying. We do not discuss disordered eating in this chapter, as it is categorized in the DSM-5 as a Feeding and Eating Disorder.

Currently there are more research studies addressing substance use than behavioral addictions. The continued increase in the use of substances produces many funded research investigations attempting to understand, prevent, and treat substance use. Attention given to behavioral addictions, particularly the funding of research, has evolved at a slower pace, possibly owing to several factors: (1) Substance use is transparent, recognizable; (2) substance use is still often viewed as a moral issue; (3) consequences of long-term substance use are explicit and physical; (4) severe substance use has a lethal nature; (5) substance use has a history of research; (6) symptoms related to substance use have been included in the Diagnostic and Statistical Manual for several editions, whereas behavioral addictions are new to this edition; (7) behavioral addictions are minimized and often referred to as just a habit; and (8) behavioral addictions involved "normal" human activities.

The American Society of Addiction Medicine (ASAM) (2011) and the American Psychiatric Association (2013) have acknowledged the existence of behavioral addictions to varying degrees, but with similarity of clinical criteria. They acknowledge that there are recognized similarities between behavioral addictions and SUDs, specifically as related to mechanisms of the brain.

A DEFINITION OF BEHAVIORAL ADDICTION

Defining behavioral addiction is a complicated effort. One reason is that behaviors in this group involve "normal" drives: sex, love, and/or money. These behaviors become "addiction" only when they begin to detrimentally affect other aspects of the individual's life.

Behavioral addiction in general is defined as a relentless pursuit of a sensation or activity such as gambling, despite consequences to one's health or well-being (Miller, Forcehimes, & Zweben, 2011). A significant indicator of behavioral addiction is when an individual persistently practices a behavior despite the consequences. Consequences might affect the individual's health and well-being, including one's personal, social, and emotional life. Furthermore, consequences often involve finances and legal matters. When diagnosing a substance use disorder, consideration is given to the pathological behavioral patterns related to the use of the substance. Symptoms of behavioral addiction are similar to those of substance use disorders and can be classified into cognitive, behavioral, and physiological clusters. Although the diagnosis is often based on a pathological pattern, criteria can be organized into impaired control, social impairment, risky use, and pharmacological criteria groupings (APA, 2013).

The foregoing definition of behavioral addiction includes several important elements. Using gambling as our example: First, a behavioral addiction involves a behavior that includes relentless pursuit, perhaps similar to that of craving, a characteristic of individuals with a substance use disorder (SUD). Second, it involves the pursuit of a sensation or activity. Sensation means feeling good, aroused, excited, numb, or relaxed. These sensations take place during the pursuit of something, as well as when the activity is being performed, such as pulling the handle of a slot machine in anticipation of winning the jackpot. A third element that defines behavioral addiction involves consequences. The presence of consequences, similar to that of SUD, is a significant factor to consider when assessing whether an individual is addicted. As an example, there can be severe consequences of a gambling addiction including bankruptcy, family break up, loss of a home, job loss, legal issues, and marital discord.

A WORD OF CAUTION

Although many mental health professionals believe in behavioral addictions, others worry that making these behaviors a legitimized disorder will result in pardoning or excusing criminal behavior. Others worry that this will create new disorders that simply excuse bad behavior. Will irresponsible accumulation of debt be considered compulsive buying disorder? Will stealing be kleptomania? Will a "wandering" spouse call him/herself a sex addict? The social implications are profound, and the authors support rigorous research and clinical definitions to define true disorders (Rosenberg & Feder, 2014).

General Criteria for Behavioral Addictions

Trained health care and mental health care professionals make crucial assessments for diagnoses of disorders. The purpose of these assessments is to determine whether an individual shows signs of a behavioral addiction and what the treatment plan should be to assist the individual into recovery. Diagnostic criteria for behavioral disorders are limited.

The DSM-5 (APA, 2013) identifies gambling as the only behavioral addiction under the category of "Non Substance-Related Disorders." There are nine indicators used to identify a gambling addiction, with severity levels ranging from mild to severe, depending on the identified criteria (APA, 2013). For the other addictions that we discuss in this chapter, there are no DSM-5 criteria. There are, however, general criteria for identifying addictive behavior.

The ASAM (2011) has identified addiction in terms of impaired control, including the following:

- A higher frequency and/or quantity of engagement in addictive behaviors than the person first intended, often associated with unsuccessful attempts at behavioral control despite persistent desire for change.
- An excessive amount of time lost when using substances or recovering from the effects of drug use and/or engagement in addictive behaviors. As a result, there is significant adverse impact on functioning in both social and occupational dimensions of the individual's life.
- Despite the presence of physical or psychological problems that may have been caused by substance misuse or an addictive behavior, the individual continues to engage in using the substance, or continues the behavior.
- One's behavior is focused on the addictive reward.
- The individual is either unable, or not ready, to take action to change despite an awareness and recognition of problems.

ASAM (2011) identified the following changes occurring during the process of becoming addicted.

Cognitive Changes

- Preoccupation with the use of a substance or behavior.
- An altered evaluation of benefits and affliction associated with substance use or rewarding behaviors.
- Believing that problems are attributed to other causes rather than being a consequence of addictive behavior.

EMOTIONAL CHANGES

- An increase in anxiety, emotional pain, and dysphonia.
- Increased sensitivity to stressors associated with the brain and body.
- Difficulty identifying and making a distinction between emotions and body sensations such as emotional arousal. In addition, the individual experiences *alexithymia,* which refers to difficulty describing feelings to others.

Hartney (2011) identified the following signs and symptoms that seem to be associated with behavioral addictions: mood changes, change in sleep patterns, fluctuation in energy, weight change, not feeling well most of the time, clandestine behavior, lying, stealing, financial unpredictability, and changes in friends. Engs (2012) also identified the following characteristics common among individuals with behavioral addictions: obsession with an object, substance, or behavior; engaging in high-risk behavior; practicing compulsive behaviors that are difficult to stop; withdrawal; lack of control over a behavior; denial; attempts to hide the behavior; depression; low self-esteem; and anxiety.

Clinicians who work with SUD recognize many of these symptoms. They are the same or highly similar to ones that would define an SUD. This is no surprise as we are discussing dysfunctional behaviors that have multiple consequences, as does an SUD. Additionally, many behavioral addiction clients also have substance use disorders as well as other disorders.

Gambling Disorder (GD)

Gambling in the United States is a very profitable business, with the American Gaming Association (2012) reporting annual gross income for casinos at over $34 billion. About 86% of Americans have gambled in their lifetime, and 60% have gambled within the past year (Jazaeri & Bin Habil, 2012). Estimates from large national surveys show that about 0.5 percent of Americans had a severe gambling disorder at some time in their lives. Extrapolating from the survey estimates suggests that roughly 1.5 million Americans have experienced severe gambling disorder. The less crucial conditions, mild to moderate gambling disorder, is more common and may affect two to four times as many Americans (Kessler et al., 2008).

Prevalence in women is lower (0.2%) than in men (0.6%), with greater prevalence among African Americans (0.9%) when compared to Whites (0.4%) or Hispanics (0.3%) (APA, 2013). A gambling disorder is likely to develop in childhood or adolescence, with higher rates reported in men. Men are more likely to start at an earlier age than women, whereas women initiate gambling behavior later in life and become addicted over a shorter period of time than men (Grant, Odlaug, & Mooney, 2012). Younger individuals are less likely to seek treatment. Women are more likely to have symptoms of depression, bipolar disorder, and anxiety disorders and may seek treatment sooner than males (APA, 2013).

According to Hardoon and Derevensky (2002), the onset of a gambling disorder appears in adolescence or young adulthood with an estimated 10% to 15% of children at risk of developing this trait. The progression of consequences is gradual and characterized by loss, impairment, and concealment. Although individuals may report problems with one or two types of gambling, the frequency, number of incidents, and duration of gambling may increase as access to varied types of gambling increases (e.g., Internet gambling). Older gamblers engage in games that require chance such as bingo or slot machines, whereas younger male gamblers engage in betting, horse racing, and card playing.

Internet gambling has increased in popularity, with online poker being the fastest-growing form. When compared to non-Internet gamblers, Internet gamblers are more likely to be problematic gamblers who also engage in offline gambling. The Internet provides both convenience and accessibility for vulnerable individuals. According to a study of Internet gambling in the United Kingdom, poker was reported to have the highest rate of participation (54.1%) with Internet gamblers engaging in 4.1 types of gambling and non-Internet gamblers engaged in 2.6 types. Online gamblers are more likely to be younger, single, and males with full-time employment (Wood & Williams, 2011).

Pathological gambling was first recognized in the DSM-III as an impulse control disorder (Black & Grant, 2015). There has not been a substantial amount of research on pathological gambling alone; most of the studies occurred in the 1990s. There are, however, studies investigating gambling disorder with co-occurring disorders of substance use, depression, anxiety, PTSD, antisocial personality disorder, and schizophrenia. The DSM-5 lists multiple disorders throughout that are co-occurring with substance use and gambling disorder (APA, 2013). In fact, psychiatric comorbidity may be the rule, not the exception, and needs to be addressed simultaneously (Chou & Afifi, 2011). Further, gambling disorder has been shown to be associated with high rates of suicidal ideation and attempts (Wong, Chan, Conwell, Conner, & Yip, 2010). The question of which disorder is secondary to the other is not determined within these studies. This leaves clinicians with complex assessment and treatment options.

Diagnosis and Assessment

Although the section of the DSM-5 that includes gambling is titled Substance-Related and Addictive Disorders, the criteria set forth are for gambling disorder. The criteria include:

A. Persistent and recurrent problematic gambling behavior leading to clinically significant impairment or distress, as indicated by the individual exhibiting four (or more) of the following in a 12-month period:

1. Needs to gamble with increasing amounts of money in order to achieve the desired excitement.
2. Is restless or irritable when attempting to cut down or stop gambling.
3. Has made repeated unsuccessful efforts to control, cut back, or stop gambling.
4. Is often preoccupied with gambling (e.g., having persistent thoughts of reliving past gambling experiences, handicapping or planning the next venture, thinking of ways to get money with which to gamble).
5. Often gambles when feeling distressed (e.g., helpless, guilty, anxious, depressed).
6. After losing money gambling, often returns another day to get even ("chasing" one's losses).
7. Lies to conceal the extent of involvement with gambling.
8. Has jeopardized or lost a significant relationship, job, or educational or career opportunity because of gambling.
9. Relies on others to provide money to relieve desperate financial situations caused by gambling.

B. The gambling behavior is not better explained by a manic episode.

Specify current severity:

Mild: 4–5 criteria met.

Moderate: 6–7 criteria met.

Severe: 8–9 criteria met.

There are numerous assessments available for the evaluation of clients who might be at risk for a behavioral addiction. With gambling being included in the DSM-5, these assessments are the most available (e.g. Gamblers Anonymous 20 Questions, Early Intervention Gambling Health Test) (Toneatto, 2008). Add online to the pathological gambling assessments and the variety expands (e.g., Problematic Online Gambling Questionnaire [POGQ], POGQ Short Form, Pathological Gambling Scale) (Demetrovics et al., 2012; Gentile, 2009; Pápay et al., 2013).

Each of these assessments has its own criteria for diagnosis that were established based on the DSM-IV. Therefore, they will need to be revised to fit the new DSM-5 criteria. This leaves the clinician with the DSM-5 criteria and evaluative interviews as the best method of assessment.

Treatment Options

Treatment of gambling disorder involves many of the evidence-based practices used to treat SUD. Motivational interviewing (MI), cognitive/cognitive–behavioral Therapy (CBT), and 12-step programs appear to be effective modes of therapy for gambling disorder, with CBT considered as the only widely recognized evidence-based treatment (Gooding & Tarrier, 2009). A meta-analysis by Gooding and Tarrier found that various CBTs were effective in reducing pathological gambling. Topf, Yip, and Potenza (2009) reviewed CBT studies, several of which included relapse prevention interventions, and also found that CBT was beneficial in the treatment of pathological gambling.

Psychosocial interventions are often used, depending on the relapse prevention approach. In most treatment approaches, individuals are encouraged to identify use patterns, learn how to avoid or cope with triggers and high-risk situations, and identify lifestyle changes to reinforce healthy behavior (Grant, Potenza, Weinstein, & Gorelick, 2010). Self-help groups such as Gamblers Anonymous (GA) often help gamblers achieve abstinence in the early months of recovery. Participation in self-help groups encourages gamblers to continue seeking professional treatment and support. Motivational enhancement is a crucial treatment component during the early stages of abstinence. In addition, individuals can seek support from gambling help lines, by self-monitoring, and by completing at-home exercises.

There are no FDA-approved medications for specifically treating gambling disorder. However, some medications show promise. Naltrexone, an opioid receptor antagonist, has shown good efficacy in the treatment of gambling disorder. In one study, 40% of the naltrexone group reported abstinence for a 1-month period after the study as compared to 10.5% of the placebo subjects (Grant et al., 2010; Grant, Kim & Hartman, 2008). Nalmefene has also been showed to be effective with gambling disorder. Other medications that have shown efficacy with gambling disorder include N-acetylcysteine (NAC) and antidepressants.

Family needs as well as those of the individual should be considered when seeking effective treatment for gambling disorder. Families feel distrust over the deceptions of the gambler. Further, there may be multiple issues associated with the gambling, such as financial problems, legal problems, and employment issues. These all contribute to the stress on the family system. Engaging the family in treatment is invaluable as a part of recovery. Many of the same roles and rules that we see in SUD families will apply to gambling-disordered families. In addition to treatment involvement, Gamblers Anonymous for families (GAM-ANON) provides support and education for family members.

Summary

Gambling disorder is a new diagnosis in the Substance-Related and Addictive Disorders section of the DSM-5. Although there is 1.0% or less prevalence for severe gambling disorder, the consequences for individuals and families remain significant. The development of pathological gambling can begin as early as childhood, with younger and male gamblers presenting with more risk factors predisposing them to SUD and other co-occurring disorders. Although it is true that most gamblers are not diagnosable, others have a difficult time abstaining and continue to engage in risky behaviors despite the consequences. Treatment can vary from motivational interviewing to 12-step based programs, with CBT viewed as the major evidence-based program for gambling disorder. There is a continued need for further studies investigating the process of and treatment efficacy for gambling disorder.

SEX ADDICTION

A significant barrier to understanding sex addiction has been the lack of clear definitions of what constitutes addictive sexual behavior. Because sex is a normal human activity with a wide range of differences engaged in by individuals across cultures, ethnicities and sexual orientation, defining an abnormal or addictive behavior has many complexities.

Sexuality in the United States has never been more socially acceptable; it is part of mainstream culture. One only needs to look at the explicit coverage of sexual behaviors in the media, movies, newspapers, and magazines. Internet pornography has become a billion-dollar industry. Digital media offers access to visually explicit depictions of sexual acts. The adult entertainment industry generates close to $4 billion per year, and its acceptability in society is reflected in the mainstreaming of its products into traditional retail stores and the portrayal of its actors and actresses as role models and celebrities.

Strip clubs, present in almost every U.S. city, are now large multimillion-dollar nightclubs, and the degree of physical contact in these clubs has increased to the point that what constitutes sexual intercourse is blurred. Escort services, massage parlors, and street prostitution all use the Internet as an information portal for online dating services, classified ads, and discussion boards for those in pursuit of sexual gratification (Fong, 2006).

Given these cultural standards of behavior, the boundaries among what is considered "normal," "excessive," "pathological," or "addictive" become confused. It is, however, possible to look at the consequences of these behaviors to perhaps provide criteria for diagnosis and treatment for those in need.

As early as 1812, Benjamin Rush noted a case where a man's excessive sexual behavior caused him psychological distress (Rush, 1812). In Britain, well over a century later, Dr. Jim Orford (1978) argued for the inclusion of hypersexuality in the spectrum of addictive disorders, but also noted problems with this determination of a diagnosis. Carnes (1983) was one of the first to write about sexual addiction in his book *Out of the Shadows*.

The *Diagnostic and Statistical Manual of Mental Health Disorders* (DSM) included "sexual addiction" in the DSM-III-R, but deleted it from the DSM-IV and has not included the diagnosis in the DSM-5. In fact, sex addiction is not even included in diagnoses for future research in the DSM-5 (APA, 2013). Additionally, the ICD-10 was not able to come to an agreement about "excessive sexual drive" and did not include it in their categories (World Health Organization, 1992). Reasons for exclusion include the lack of consensus-based diagnostic criteria, lack of empirical research, and lack of consensus on the basic tenets of normal sexual behavior.

Inconsistency in the way sex addiction is diagnosed makes it hard to determine prevalence. The private nature of sexual behavior and the lack of consistent criteria make it difficult to determine the extent of this disorder. Best estimates indicate that between 3 percent and 6 percent of Americans suffer from some form of sex addiction (Kuzma & Black, 2008). Sex addiction does appear to be more common among people who have a variety of other disorders, such as substance use, depression and anxiety, affect dysregulation, insecure attachment styles, personal distress, and self-hatred and shame (Rosenberg & Feder, 2014).

Kuzma and Black (2008) surveyed 290 persons who self-identified as having a sexual disorder. Of those who self-identified, 80% were male. Kaplan and Krueger (2010) found that approximately 8% to 20% of women reported hypersexuality. Another study reported that 59% of gay or bisexual men reported lifetime compulsive sexual behavior (Grant & Potenza, 2006).

Hypersexual or compulsive behaviors vary depending on gender. Use of pornography, paying for sexual favors, anonymous one-night stands, and using pornography are more likely to be reported by men (Kuzma & Black, 2008). Gordon-Lamoureux (2007) stated that out of a study of 42 men arrested for solicitation and recruited from "John schools," one third reported characteristics of sexual addiction. Kuzma and Black (2008) reported that women are more likely to use sex as a business transaction, engage in fantasy sex, and refer to themselves as love addicts.

Carnes (2004) infers that sex addiction is initiated in adolescence with paraphilia-type behaviors having an earlier onset. Research suggests that the majority of individuals with CSB come from dysfunctional families (86.8% and 77% were from disengaged and rigid families, respectively; Augustine Fellowship, 1986).

A number of factors need to be considered when understanding sex addiction, including trauma, shame, attachment style, and culture. Childhood trauma is a major factor, with women reporting more trauma than men. Attachment styles in childhood can contribute to the dysfunctional perception of relationships, which could develop into a sex addiction. Men and women appear to display a similar set of dysfunctions based on family of origin. Men and women also learn how to identify with their own gender based on interactions with parents. Men with disrupted relationships with their father and women with broken relationships with their mother often develop a sex addiction Rosenberg & Feder, 2014).

Shame is considered to be one of the most damaging consequences of trauma, and as a result can manifest in many ways, including sex addiction. Cultural messages also contribute to the development of sex addictions. Messages that suggest that sex is synonymous with love can be damaging and foster unhealthy relationships (McKeague, 2014).

Diagnosis and Assessment

A variety of labels have been used through the years when discussing disordered sexual behavior. Terms such as *satyriasis, nymphomania, Don Juanism, perversion, paraphilia, compulsive sexual behavior, sexual addiction, impulse control disorder,* and *sin* are words often used to classify or describe "abnormal" sexual behavior (Garcia & Thibaut, 2010). Like other behavioral addictions, sexual behavior becomes problematic when it creates impairment in social functioning, relationships, one's work environment, and possible involvement in ethical and legal issues. Sexual behaviors that include the criteria for general addictive behavior may be a serious condition for the client and the family.

Carnes (1983, 2004) suggested that sex addiction could be defined when the problems identified in the Twelve-Step philosophy are apparent: experiencing a loss of control, powerlessness, tolerance changes, an inability to manage life, and a progression of the behavior. Carnes further suggested levels of progression that range from mild to severe behaviors, mimicking the new DSM-5 criteria for gambling disorder. Examples of mild behaviors included having affairs, use of pornography, and masturbation. More intense behaviors included voyeurism, exhibitionism, and the use of paraphernalia. Severe behaviors included incest, pedophilia, and rape.

Kafka (2010) proposed diagnostic criteria for hypersexual disorder while participating with the Sexual and Gender Identity Disorder Working Group for the DSM-5 revision. His criteria included:

A. Over a period of at least 6 months, recurrent and intense sexual fantasies, sexual urges, or sexual behaviors in association with 3 or more of the following 5 criteria:

A1. Time consumed by sexual fantasies, urges or behaviors repetitively interferes with other important (non-sexual) goals, activities and obligations.

A2. Repetitively engaging in sexual fantasies, urges or behaviors in response to dysphonic mood states (e.g., anxiety, depression, boredom, irritability).

A3. Repetitively engaging in sexual fantasies, urges or behaviors in response to stressful life events.

A4. Repetitive but unsuccessful efforts to control or significantly reduce these sexual fantasies, urges or behaviors.

A5. Repetitively engaging in sexual behaviors while disregarding the risk for physical or emotional harm to self or others.

B. There is clinically significant personal distress or impairment in social, occupational or other important areas of functioning associated with the frequency and intensity of these sexual fantasies, urges or behaviors.

C. These sexual fantasies, urges or behaviors are not due to the direct physiological effect of an exogenous substance (e.g., a drug of abuse or a medication).

D. The person is at least 18 years of age.

Specify if: Masturbation, Pornography, Sexual Behavior with Consenting Adults, Cybersex, Telephone Sex, Strip Clubs.

Although not included in the DSM-5, this criterion gives us guidelines to assess and diagnose individual clients. Withdrawal and tolerance are not included in the criteria; however, many of the same behaviors symptomatic of substance use are included.

There are a variety of assessment instruments to evaluate clients. The Sexual Addiction Screening Test (Carnes, Green, & Carnes, 2010), PATHOS (Carnes et al., 2011), the MMPI-2 (Hathaway & McKinley, 1989), and the Sexual Dependency Inventory (Hook, Hook, Davis, Worthington, & Penberthy, 2010) are a few with validity and reliability.

Treatment

Treatment for sex addiction follows the guidelines for the treatment of SUD. Treatment programs use the same methods: motivational interviewing, cognitive–behavioral therapy, group therapy, individual therapy, eye movement desensitization and reprocessing therapy (EMDR), dialectic behavioral techniques, and family therapy.

Group therapy has been identified as a primary treatment modality for sex addiction (Hook, Hook, & Hines, 2008). Through group therapy, focus can be placed on shame reduction, impulse control, relapse cycle, and ways to develop healthy intimacy. Psychoeducational groups may also help family members to understand sex addiction and the process of healing and recovery. Multifamily groups will also assist couples affected by sex addiction. Their experience with communication difficulties, intimacy, finances, and recreational activities can be addressed. Many partners of sexual addicts came from a history of addiction, intimacy dysfunction, or abuse in their family of origin. Without appropriate therapy, sex addicts and their partners have an increased chance of repeating dysfunctional patterns experienced in childhood (Rosenberg & Feder, 2014).

Additional 12-step groups are highly integrated into the treatment program, including Sex Anonymous, Sexaholics Anonymous, Sex Addicts Anonymous, and Sex and Love Anonymous.

Partners and families have access to S-Anon family groups. In addition to therapies and self-help groups, medications may also be used in the treatment protocol.

Again, there are no FDA-approved medications for sex addiction. However, some of the same drugs mentioned for gambling disorder seem to assist those with disordered sexual behaviors. Naltrexone, selective serotonin uptake inhibitors (SSRIs, particularly citalopram), and SSNIs all show the possibility of positive results. Citalopram has demonstrated a moderate to significant reduction in masturbation and use of pornography (Tosto, Talarico, Lenzi, & Bruno, 2008).

As stated previously, sex addiction clients have a high comorbidity with other mental disorders. It is imperative that clinicians assess and diagnose these disorders and treat them either simultaneously or sequentially. Without dual diagnosis treatment, recovery will be compromised.

Summary

Patrick Carnes and colleagues, beginning in 1983, have been instrumental in shaping the treatment of sex addiction. Although still not a formal diagnosis in the DSM-5, many individuals suffer from disordered sexual behavior both with and without co-occurring mental disorders.

There is a need for continued research on treatment interventions with an evidence-based philosophy specific to sex addiction. Clinicians should be aware and assess for this behavior in clients if appropriate. Additionally, clinicians should continue to work not only with the addict, but also with their partners, families, and other loved ones to promote a balanced life of recovery and support.

EXERCISE ADDICTION

Exercise is considered an integral part of a healthy lifestyle, and research confirms that regular exercise contributes to the maintenance of good health (Department of Health and Human Services, 2015). Western society is inundated with documentaries, television shows, advertisements, and personal stories about the value of exercise leading to a healthier physical and psychological lifestyle. The questions arise when we consider what happens when exercise turns into excessive behavior. Or, how do we know when we stop engaging in healthy exercise? At what point do we determine whether excessive exercise turns into an addiction? (Berczik et al., 2012).

Rewards of a personal nature can facilitate excessive exercise. Rewards include getting in top physical condition, feeling better, looking better, weight reduction, or enhancing one's muscles. These rewards are motivators and strengthen a need to exercise. It is believed that individuals addicted to exercise are motivated by negative (gaining weight) as well as positive reinforcements (Berczik et al, 2012).

Another explanation of excessive exercise has been that individuals who exercise seek out the reward or euphoria feeling, sometimes known as the *runner's high* hypothesis. This sensation involves the beta-endorphin brain activity. However, research has shown that because of its chemical structure, beta-endorphins cannot cross the blood–brain barrier. This means that the changes seen in runners' blood plasma may not be accompanied by brain changes. Another physiological theory is that endogenous opiates in the plasma can act systemically (cross the blood–brain barrier), creating the feeling described (Biddle & Mutrie, 1991). Landolfi (2013) suggests that individuals who are addicted to exercise do seek the experience of a psychological "high" regardless of any pain that results from the exercise.

A third theory is that aerobic exercise, such as running, if engaged in for a significant period of time, can lower heart rate and adaptation to the exercise. When the individual experiences lower sympathetic activity at rest, they take action in the form of more exercise to increase arousal levels. However, because the effect of exercise is temporary, individuals may seek to increase the behavior by increasing frequency and intensity of the exercise (Rosenberg & Feder, 2014).

As with all the behavioral addictions except gambling, it is difficult to define exercise addiction with no formal diagnostic criteria present. Further, it is difficult to interpret the research for the same reason. Using the criteria for substance use disorder, if exercise is taken to the extreme with the result being consequences to one's health, body functioning, disruption of work, family, and social life, one might identify as having an exercise addiction.

Glasser (1976) introduced the concept of "positive addiction" into the literature in an endeavor to propose the positive benefits of all exercise. Morgan (1979) disagreed, asserting that the typical symptoms of addiction could be applied to excessive exercise. Various terms have been used to describe these behaviors, including obligatory exercise, exercise abuse, and compulsive exercise. At this point, the most commonly used term is "exercise addiction" (Berczik et al., 2012).

Exercise addiction includes the involvement of an inadequate pattern of exercise that leads to significant negative results. There appears to be six common components of addiction that apply to exercise addiction: salience, mood modification, tolerance, withdrawal, personal conflict, and relapse (Griffiths, 2005).

Exercise addiction has been classified as either primary or secondary (Blaydon, Lindner, & Kerr, 2004). Primary exercise addiction includes behavior that is isolated from other activities and does not have a co-occurring disorder. Secondary exercise addiction involves an attempt to control various aspects of the individual's life in addition to altering body composition (Hausenblas & Symons Downs, 2002). Among all factors, only an eating disorder differentiates primary from secondary exercise addiction (Bamber, Cockerill, Rodgers, & Carroll, 2003).

With the foregoing comments in regard to the lack of consistency in terminology and diagnostic criteria, the prevalence rate must be discussed. Blaydon and Linder (2002) suggested that prevalence rate among triathletes was 30.4% with primary exercise addiction and another 21.6% with secondary exercise addiction. Prevalence rates for ultra-marathoners was reported at 3.2%. The only national study that did not use convenience sampling was conducted in Hungary by Monok et al. (2012). The results showed only 0.3% to 0.5% to be at risk for exercise addiction.

Diagnosis and Assessment

There are a variety of instruments available to assess exercise addiction. The three most psychometrically valid and reliable are the Obligatory Exercise Questionnaire (Ackard, Brehm, & Stefen, 2002), the Exercise Dependence Scale (Symons Downs, Hausenblas, & Nigg, 2004), and the Exercise Dependence Questionnaire (Ogden, Veale, & Summers, 1997). Although there are other scales, they tend to evaluate and assess specific subsections within exercise (e.g., bodybuilding or marathon runners). Another scale, the Exercise Dependence Scale, assesses not only exercise addiction but also eating disorders (Bamber et al., 2003).

The diagnostic criteria that must be used are the general criteria for addiction and the criteria for substance use disorder. As stated, this includes behaviors that negatively impact any aspect of the individual's life.

Treatment

Therapeutic guidelines for treatment of an exercise addiction have not been developed. This is due to the lack of diagnostic criteria, the lack of empirical research, and the fact that the incidence is low and that even individuals with the "addiction" rarely seek treatment. With that said, motivational interviewing and cognitive-behavioral therapy have proven to be effective (Miller & Rollnick, 2002). As with all of these behavioral addictions, it is imperative to evaluate co-occurring disorders. Common dual diagnoses are eating disorders, depression, anxiety, and body image disorders.

Treatment programs are available to work with exercise addiction on both an outpatient and inpatient basis. The majority of these programs operate on the 12-step principles, which function well with all addictions. Insurance companies may not fund treatment for exercise addiction unless there is a co-occurring disorder. Self-help groups such as Exercise Addiction Support Group and SmartRecovery are available outside the treatment arena.

Summary

Exercise has many health benefits. It is viewed as an activity for maintaining a healthy lifestyle. However, when it is taken to the extreme, it can become an addiction. Research supports exercise addiction as having similar characteristics to a substance use disorder and other behavioral addictions such as gambling or sex. Consequences of exercise addiction can be physical and psychological. Time spent engaging in an exercise takes away from family, friends, work, and other social activities. Individuals often experience the physical effects of injuries and the time it takes to heal. Further research is needed that examines evidence-based diagnostic criteria and effective treatment for individuals with an exercise addiction.

COMPULSIVE BUYING DISORDER (CBD)

CBD, like all the behavior disorders, is difficult to define and diagnose. CBD is most frequently seen in developed Western countries, although socioeconomic status does not seem to be correlated with CBD; indeed, individuals with less than $50,000 income have a disproportionate rate of CBD tendencies (Dell'Osso, Allen, Altamura, Buoli, & Hollander, 2008b). The increase in availability of goods, attainable credit, and free time appear to have led to the increase in CBD (Black, 2011). Add to those factors a value of materialism prevalent in Western culture and the rise in the advertising profession. Advertising promotes the *need* for goods that are truly *not needed*. This translates into a desire for a product that will make one feel better (Benson, Dittmar, & Wolfsohn, 2010).

This is another behavioral disorder not included in the DSM-5. The characteristics of this order mimic substance use disorder and the other behavioral disorders that we have discussed. In some cases, individuals who meet criteria for CBD may be diagnosed under other specified disruptive, impulse-control, or conduct disorder.

Some researchers (Potenza, Koran, & Pallanti, 2010) consider this disorder on the impulsivity/compulsivity spectrum. The urges to purchase (impulsive) continue to arise even after the behavior has been acted upon, and there is an inability to defy the urge to purchase (compulsive). Further, like OCD, individuals engage in the activity more to reduce anxiety than for pleasure (Potenza et al., 2001). This being said, the reader can observe that this process is also present in a substance use disorder.

Like SUD, when buying becomes unrestrained and includes an adverse effect for the individuals and their family, individuals need to examine the behavior. Compulsive buying is dysfunctional, particularly when it creates havoc with finances. The aftereffect of a CBD spree may include feelings of anxiety and guilt due to an inability to control finances and what this means to others in the family system. A prime characteristic of compulsive buying is persistent and uncontrolled purchasing despite negative feedback from others (Sohn & Choi, 2014).

Individuals often engage in buying as a way to relieve stress or produce good feelings about themselves. However, CBD becomes more than just a leisure activity; it becomes part of a lifestyle and usually involves excessive purchasing with negative consequences. Through the years, compulsive buying disorder has been referred to as *addictive buying, compulsive buying, excessive buying, uncontrolled buying,* and *spendaholism* (Dell'Osso, Allen, Altamura, Buoli, & Hollander, 2008a).

CBD is estimated to impact between 1% and 10% of the U.S. population (Benson & Eisenach, 2013; Hartston, 2012). Results from studies investigating consequences of compulsive shopping indicate that 53% of shoppers had significant debt, with 41% unable to pay off their debt. Some individuals suffered legal consequences (8%), while others had criminal issues connected with their use (8%). Feelings of guilt had a prevalence rate of 45% (Dell'Osso et al., 2008b).

Most compulsive buyers are younger individuals, under 30 years of age and 8 to 11 years younger than ordinary buyers (Benson et al., 2010). General age of onset is late teens to early 20s (Black, 2011). Recent findings in the pattern of sex differential seems to indicate that men and women are fairly equally affected, with 5.5% of women and 6% of men reporting (Koran, Faber, Aboujaoude, Large, & Serpe, 2006). Specifics of what one buys does vary by sex, with men purchasing more functional, utilitarian items and women purchasing more items that are associated with identity or appearance and may be rooted in mood control (Muller et al., 2011).

Diagnosis and Assessment

With no clear DSM-5 diagnostic criteria, we look to the research to provide criteria. In 2005 Dittmar (as cited in Rosenberg & Feder, 2014, p. 288) provided three core criteria: "1) the act of buying is irrepressible (the urge); 2) one's buying tendencies are uncontrollable (the behavior), and 3) one's behavior continues regardless of the negative consequences." Mirroring SUD and OCD, these criteria allow us to assess the behavior involved.

There are multiple instruments for assessing CBD. Three major ones are discussed here. The Compulsive Buying Scale (Faber & O'Guinn, 1992) is the most commonly used in the United States. It is composed of seven items that have been shown to successfully identify 88% of individuals with CBD.

The Compulsive Buying Measurement Scale (Dittmar, 2005) is mostly used in the UK, Europe, and Canada. The revised edition has 16 items rated on a four-point scale and has high reliability and validity.

The Yale-Brown Obsessive Compulsive Scale (YBOCS) was modified to develop the YBOSC-SV (shopping version). The YBOSC-SV is composed of 10 items, 5 that measure obsession and 5 that address compulsions. This instrument also has high validity and reliability and is excellent at measuring improvement during clinical trials (Black, 2011).

As with other behavioral addictions, individuals with CBD often present with multiple comorbid diagnoses—mood disorders, anxiety disorders, low self-esteem, and substance use disorders. Mueller et al., in a 2010 study reported in 2011, found that 57% of the CBD sample had a lifetime comorbid anxiety disorder and 21% had a comorbid impulse control disorder. Further, 22% suffered from obsessive-compulsive disorder, 15% from borderline disorder, and 15% from avoidant disorder (Sharma, Narang, Rajender, & Bhatia, 2009).

A very interesting finding was that first-degree relatives of those with CBD also had multiple mood and personality disorders. Eighteen percent of CBD relatives suffered from depression and 20% from a severe alcohol disorder (Black, 2011).

Treatment

Treatment for CBD follows the pattern of treatment for both substance use and other behavioral disorders. Although no one treatment model has proved significantly effective, suggested treatment protocols include cognitive–behavioral therapy and dialectical behavioral therapy. Group therapy also seems effective with CBD individuals. It allows for a support system, feedback from more than the counselor, and opportunities to try new behaviors. Stages of recovery, including 12-step support groups, are often used (Benson & Eisenach, 2013).

Pharmacological treatment including antidepressants and other mood stabilizers is suggested to help in managing emotions associated with compulsive buying (Rosenberg & Feder, 2014). With the high prevalence of comorbid disorders, careful attention needs to be given to any pharmacological treatments, with management of the comorbid diagnosis always in mind.

Summary

CBD remains difficult to diagnose. Both men and women experience CBD, with the major difference being the actual items purchased. A co-occurring mental health disorder is often present, requiring careful pharmacological treatment. As with other behavioral addictions and substance use disorders, there appears to be a cycle of symptoms that increases tolerance, creates a dependence on the behavior no matter the consequences, and produces withdrawal when the individual is not able to engage in the addictive behavior.

Internet Addiction Disorder (IAD)

As of November 2015, there are an estimated 3.4 billion people who use the Internet (Internet World Stats, 2016). The Internet is accessed for a variety of reasons, including but not limited to entertainment, banking, social connections, work-related issues, leisure, and education. Because of the Internet's multiple uses, it can be an amazing resource and educational tool or a resource that leads to problematic behavior.

Individuals who may have a predisposition to impulse control disorders find themselves in a position where the use of the Internet has become a problem for them, their families, work, and finances. These individuals isolate themselves from others and spend most or all of their time on the Internet. The "need to escape oneself" and "create an ideal online self" seems to be a continuing theme heard from IAD clients (Achab et al., 2011).

Addiction to use of the Internet is discussed in this section of the chapter so that the reader will have an overview of various problematic Internet behaviors. Internet gaming disorder, a specific form of the disorder, has been included in Section III of the DSM-5 for future research. Possible criteria for diagnosis of this disorder are included in this section of the DSM-5.

As one might assume, Internet addiction has grown with the growth of computer use and Internet access. With an 833% increase in rate of users between 2000 and 2015, the possibility of misuse has also grown exponentially. In researching this issue, there appear to be three subtypes of the disorder: excessive gaming/gambling, sexual preoccupations (cybersex), and social networking (Shaw & Black, 2008; Wood & Williams, 2009; Young, 2012).

As with all behavioral addictions, Internet addiction often includes impulse control, substance use, and obsessive-compulsive behaviors. Anxiety and pleasure seeking are common. IAD individuals experience increase in tolerance, dependence on the activity, and withdrawal symptoms if they cease the activity. Insistent checking of one's email, phone messages, preferred websites, or other electronic services can become obsessive, induced by a fear of missing out on something (Aboujaoude, Koran, Gamel, Large, & Serpe, 2006).

Internet use, as characterized by an inability to control one's use of the Internet, creates an Internet addiction (Young, 2012). Eventually consequences are psychological, social, and physical. Factors that contribute to this addiction include preexisting pathology such as depression, social anxiety, and substance dependence. Maladaptive cognitions such as obsessive thoughts, lack of impulse control, and low self-esteem can create a dependency on the Internet. Other factors influencing the development of an Internet addiction include poor emotional well-being, loneliness, low levels of motivation, lacking satisfaction with life, and neurological deficiencies (Rosenberg & Feder, 2014). One's inability to manage and regulate emotions is a risk factor for developing an Internet addiction.

Research involving 1,618 students, 13 to 18 years of age, examined the effect of the Internet on the mental health of adolescents. Findings were that 6.4% reported being at moderate to high risk for an addiction. Subjects developing this pathology were 2.5 times more likely to experience symptoms of depression (Lam, Peng, Mai, & Jing, 2009). Prevalence rates are believed to be higher among college-level students when compared to the general population.

In a survey of 2,513 adults, it was estimated that one in eight Americans suffer from signs of an Internet addiction (Aboujaoude et al., 2006). Findings have indicated that 4% are preoccupied with the Internet even when offline, with 9% believing they need to hide their Internet use from family and friends, and 14% experiencing difficulty in disconnecting for more than 4 consecutive days. Young (2012) has estimated that of the general population, 6% to 15% demonstrate signs of addiction requiring clinical intervention. Other researchers quote a much lower U.S. percentage of 0.3% to 4% (Christakis, Moreno, Jelenchick, Myaing, & Zhou, 2011; Shaw & Black, 2008).

An interesting fact is that IAD is highest in Asian countries. Researchers quote 0.6% to 10.2% in various regions of China; Taiwan shows 17.9% among students; South Korean middle schoolers were reported at 16% (Rosenberg & Feder, 2014). This might impact clients from these countries who migrate to the United States.

ASSESSMENT AND DIAGNOSIS

IAD individuals exhibit poor coping skills for stress, developmental challenges, and social anxiety (Isrealashvili, Kim, & Bukobza, 2012; Lee & Stapinski, 2012). Personality factors including lack of perseverance, neuroticism, sensation seeking, and aggressiveness have been correlated with IAD. Additionally, low self-esteem, family dissatisfaction, and poor relations with parents, teachers, and peers are seen (Rosenberg & Feder, 2014).

Comorbidity with affective disorders, anxiety disorders, obsessive–compulsive disorder, and attention deficit disorders are common. Substance use disorders were prevalent co-occurring disorders (Dong, Lu, Zhou, & Zhao, 2011).

Assessment instruments frequently use items from substance use disorder questionnaires. The most commonly used questionnaire is Young's Internet Addiction Test (IAT) (Young, 1998). This instrument has high reliability and validity.

Treatment

Limited effective treatment options are available for IAD. One specifically designed treatment for Internet addiction is Cognitive Behavioral Therapy—Internet Addiction (CBT-IA) (Young, 2012). This approach combines components of CBT and harm reduction therapy. As with other addictions, individuals are encouraged to identify thoughts that trigger maladaptive behavior. The three phases to this approach are behavioral modification, cognitive restructuring, and harm reduction.

Pharmacological interventions include extended-release methylphenidate, a drug previously used for ADHD and OCD treatment, as well as SSRIs (Dell'Osso et al., 2008b). Bupropion, a dopamine and norepinephrine inhibitor used for substance use disorders, showed excellent results with decrease of Internet use and lowering depression scores (Han & Renshaw, 2012). Electro-acupuncture is an alternative treatment that has had high success rates. Not only were IAD scores lowered, but also short-term memory capacity and short-term memory span increased significantly.

Summary

IAD is one of the fastest growing behavioral addictions. Because of the Internet's growth and popularity, IAD has caught the eye of researchers and programs funding treatment for these disorders. Research taking place today will more clearly define Internet addictions, identify symptoms, assist in diagnosing, and suggest models of treatment. As with all the behavioral addictions, findings from neuroscience research have discovered that Internet addictions include a similar behavioral pattern as other addictions involving the brain's pleasure-seeking reward system.

Conclusion

This chapter has provided an overview of several behavioral addictions. From the literature, it is apparent that there is much overlap between and among substance use disorders, behavioral disorders, mood disorders, anxiety disorders, and personality disorders. This means that the assessment, diagnosis, and treatment of behavioral disorders are extremely complex.

Clinicians need to be aware of behavioral addiction markers: an excessive or repeated use of a behavior, loss of time due to the use of a behavior, continuing a behavior despite persistent or recurrent consequences, lack of ability to take responsibility for change, and preoccupation with the behavior. Clinicians also must assess for the variety of other disorders mentioned earlier and determine which is the primary diagnosis.

Treatment for behavioral addictions range from evidence-based programs such as cognitive–behavioral therapy (CBT) and dialectical behavior therapy (DBT) to 12-step self-help groups, family therapy, inpatient and outpatient treatment, and, when necessary, partial hospitalization for stabilizing clients. Some pharmacological interventions seem to provide treatment possibilities for behavioral addictions, such as naltrexone, bupropion, and SSRIs.

With the inclusion of gambling addiction in the DSM-5 and Internet gaming disorder in Section III (APA, 2013) comes a call for research into these behavioral disorders and their effect on individuals, families, and society. It is imperative that we research these issues in a timely manner so that effective treatment modalities can be developed.

Case Study: Helen

Helen is a 38-year-old woman who lives alone in an exquisite apartment complex. She is surrounded by singles who like to party and socialize. Helen enjoys going to these parties and enjoys the people. This gives her the opportunity to show off her new outfits and jewelry at social events held within the complex. Receiving compliments on her wardrobe makes her feel worthwhile and liked.

Helen feels she has earned the right to "take care of herself" by purchasing what is attractive to her and what makes her feel good. When she is not shopping or buying something, she experiences episodes of anxiety and depression. She does not eat well, and sleeping can be a problem. Helen has few interests except for shopping both on site and online. She does experience anxiety over her credit card balances, her recent divorce, lack of employment, and lack of an "intimate relationship." Helen says her drinking is only when she can't go shopping because the credit cards are "maxed out."

Helen has a history of excessive shopping and spending that led to her husband's bankruptcy and their eventual divorce. Helen denies she is a "shopaholic" and claims the problems with her ex-husband drove her to shopping binges, as well as drinking and experimenting with drugs.

Helen enjoys the freedom to shop without "having to face an angry husband who would scold her" for spending thousands of dollars on clothes and jewelry. Helen says that he "never understood how important it was to her to look good."

Helen is angry at her few close friends who stated she needs professional help for shopping and substance use. Although she is worried, she believes that she "has it under control" and will "stop as soon as she feels better about herself after the divorce.

Critical Thinking Questions

1. Even before evaluations, what are the physical/mental characteristics observed in the case study that are relevant to substance use disorder and compulsive buying disorder?

2. What instruments or evaluations would you use to determine what level of substance use disorder Helen has? Her mood disorder? What would you use to screen for compulsive buying disorder?

3. What type(s) of treatment would you recommend for Helen?

APPENDIX

Case Study Possible Answers to Critical Thinking Questions

Chapter 2   Case Study: Jamal

1. **What are the possible legal issues in this situation?**

   Performance enhancement drugs, depending on the substance (e.g., steroids), may be illegal and may involve imprisonment and fines for Jamal. Assuming that the substances in question are illegal, the coach is likely distributing the drugs illegally. If the coach is selling the substances, rather than just supplying the athletes, he is also likely violating several federal and state laws. If caught, the coach could be sentenced to imprisonment and fines as well. In some states, the coach may also be violating bullying, intimidation, and harassment laws. Finally, Jamal likely signed a binding National Collegiate Athletic Association (NCAA) agreement indicating that he would not use illegal or performance-enhancing substances. Thus, both Jamal and the coach could face significant legal consequences. Other coaches and players who are also involved with the knowledge, distribution, or use of the substances could also face serious consequences.

2. **What are the possible ethical issues in this situation?**

   The SUD mental health professional may be concerned that widespread intimidation is occurring on the football team. If the counselor works at the same university as the coach, the counselor may feel compelled to report the coach with the intention of protecting current and future players. Furthermore, some institutions may have regulations that require employees to report fellow employees who are engaging in illegal behavior. The counselor may also be concerned about the health and safety of Jamal, as he may be using substances that are "causing harm." Finally, the counselor may be concerned that Jamal has a substance use disorder for which he needs treatment.

3. **What impact does CFR 42 have on the counselor's obligations to the client?**

   If the client seeks treatment for substances, the client would be protected under CFR 42.

4. **What are the personal implications that the counselor may face in this situation?**

   The counselor may experience conflict knowing that Jamal believes that he is being coerced to use performance-enhancing drugs. If the counselor reports the coach to the university, the investigation of the coach may lead to the counselor being court ordered to break confidentiality and reveal Jamal's name, thus leading to potential legal action against the client. Furthermore, once Jamal's privacy is violated, he will likely be denied the opportunity to play professional sports. Jamal may lose the trust of the counselor and feel like the counselor engaged in several ethical violations by causing harm and denying Jamal's autonomy.

5. **Using the ethical decision-making model, how could this case be resolved?**

   1. **Identify the problem.** The client is feeling coerced to engage in illegal and unethical behavior in his football career. The client is experiencing anxiety over his desire to stop using the performance-enhancing drugs, but also feeling dependent on them for his performance. He is afraid to tell his coach that he will no longer use the drugs, as the coach has threatened consequences.

   2. **Identify the potential issues involved.** Jamal may have an addiction to the performance-enhancing drugs, may be in physical danger as a result of using the substances, may face legal issues as a result of using the substances, and may face career-ending consequences if found using the substances. He believes that his coach is coercing him to use the substances, as the coach threatened reduced field time if he refuses to continue to use the substances. The coach may be intimidating and coercing other players, which may present as a social justice issue. The coach, if discovered, could face legal issues. Jamal and the other players and coaches could also face legal issues.

3. **Review relevant ethical guidelines.** The counselor is faced with maintaining Jamal's privacy, while also considering the safety of Jamal and the other players.

4. **Know relevant laws and regulations.** The coach and Jamal may be violating several federal and state laws. They are likely violating NCAA rules and agreements. The counselor may be violating university regulations by not reporting the coach.

5. **Obtain consultation.** The counselor would need to seek consultation with peer counselors about what would be the best course of action.

6. **Consider possible and probable courses of action.**
   - Report the coach.
   - Do not report the coach.
   - Encourage Jamal to report the coach and to seek legal assistance to minimize the consequences that he may face as a user of performance enhancers.
   - Seek permission from Jamal to report the coach, and encourage Jamal to seek legal assistance to minimize the consequences that he may face as a user of performance enhancers.

7. **List the consequences of the probable courses of action.**
   - Report the coach: The university and NCAA each launch investigations into the allegation. The counselor is court ordered to reveal Jamal's identity and other private information that he shared in confidence with the counselor. The coach is fired and faces legal consequences. Jamal and several other players face legal and career-ending consequences. Jamal is harassed by his former teammates. Jamal returns home and faces, what he considers, a bleak future. Jamal sues the counselor for violating his client rights, causing emotional harm, and for financial damages. Future players on the team are protected from the coercive coach.
   - Do not report the coach: Jamal works with the counselor to arrive at a decision to either keep using the performance-enhancing drugs or to stop using them. The counselor helps Jamal to sort through the possible long- and short-term consequences of his decision. Jamal receives the support he needs to work through his potential substance use disorder, when he decides he is ready. The counselor, however, has not adhered to university policy and is at legal risk if the performance enhancement story is ever revealed.
   - Jamal and the counselor explore the possibility of Jamal reporting the coach or allowing the counselor to report the coach: The counselor adheres to university policy and reveals only the information that Jamal has approved to be shared.

8. **Decide on what appears to be the best course of action.** Given that Jamal is an adult, he is in a position to make informed decisions about using substances. He also has the right to decide if he wants to remain in an abusive and/or coercive relationship with his coach. While Jamal is at risk for harm, he is aware of the potential harm. In this case, his right to autonomy likely outweighs the other potential issues, which could result in greater harm to the client. The counselor should help Jamal to make some informed decisions about what do about the coach, his own use of substances to increase his performance, and his potential substance use disorder. The counselor, while possibly violating university regulations, has a reasonable case for not reporting the coach. The counselor: placed greater value on the risk to the client over that of the counselor, followed an ethical decision-making model, and sought peer consultation on the issue.

Chapter 3   Case Study

1. **What additional information would you need from this client in order to properly assess damage potentially caused by the long-term use of substances?**
   His use of cocaine, use of narcotics, the ethics of misusing substances prescribed for pain management, withdrawal issues, brain damage, and treatment strategies. Other pertinent information includes level of responsibility, degree of denial, attitude toward treatment, family support, methods of treatment, and severity of brain damage.

2. **What would you expect to find through neuroscience brain imaging considering cocaine and prescription substance use?**

Because of the high levels of cocaine and prescription drug abuse, one would expect alternations to brain chemistry that affect physical movements. Further, we would anticipate seeing *long-term potentiation* (LTP). N-methyl-d-aspartate (NMDA) receptors are thought to be pivotal in LTP, plasticity, and long-term depression. Repeated exposure to substances creates a condition called *excitotoxicity,* which damages and eventually kills NMDA neurons, thus altering plasticity. We would also anticipate seeing premature brain aging, as a result of the loss of gray brain matter and cognitive deficits. Specifically, we might see deficits in the prefrontal cortex.

3. **Is it possible for the brain to repair itself under the above circumstances of long-term polysubstance use?**

Due to brain plasticity, the brain has the ability to relearn. Although some damage of substance use cannot be undone, the brain has an amazing ability to adapt. Therefore, with treatment and time, the brain can relearn and rewire itself to function in similar ways to before substance use.

Chapter 4   Case Study: Tom

1. **How would you apply the moral theory to Tom's case?**

For each case, moral theory would explain that the disorder was a result of a lack of willpower and moral integrity.

2. **How would you apply both the behavioral theory and sociocultural theory to Tom's case?**

The positive reinforcement (behavioral theory) that Tom receives from his peers for using substances causes continued use. He says that he does not really like using substances but uses them to fit in with his peer group (sociocultural theory). Although Tom may not be addicted yet, his continued use has caused negative reinforcement (being arrested). This is an ideal time for intervention with Tom in order to try to motivate Tom to engage in other positively reinforced behaviors (behavioral theory) and to encourage him to seek out new social environments (sociocultural theory).

Chapter 5   Case Study: Tania

1. **Identify the primary problem areas and issues that need to be assessed and which assessment tools/methods might you use to get more information.**

Tania should be assessed for a substance use problem with cocaine and with alcohol. Even though her mental status improved following her arrest, she should also be assessed for a mental health problem such as psychosis. The POSIT might be used to screen for substance use and concurrent mental health problems for an adolescent. The ASI could also be administered as it covers psychiatric as well as alcohol and drug treatment needs.

Tania should also be assessed for a nicotine use problem. Tania and her parents need to be aware of the possible legal consequences of her using illegal drugs and underage drinking.

2. **Do you believe that there might be a dual diagnosis? What mental health diagnosis is possible with Tania?**

It is possible that Tania may have an underlying mental health problem, such as bipolar disorder or schizophrenia, that contributes to her self-medicating with substances. On the other hand, her recent psychotic behavior could have resulted from high doses of cocaine that she had taken. Monitoring of her mental status over time by a professional clinician will assist in making an accurate differential diagnosis.

3. **Would you consider a diagnosis of a substance use disorder? Why? To which substances?**

Tania continues to use cocaine, which she started using when she was 16 years old. She also continues to use alcohol, which began at age 14. The long-term use of these substances suggests that she could have a substance use disorder. Her use could even be viewed as severe. However, more information is needed to determine the degree of severity.

Chapter 6   Case Study: Robert Lopez

1. **Mr. Lopez's history indicates a number of sociocultural issues that may need further exploration or attention in planning treatment. Identify three issues and discuss how you would approach dealing with them as his counselor.**

There are several sociocultural issues that need to be explored further. The first is how his family culture and potentially their ethnic norms affect Mr. Lopez's willingness to verbally identify and process family issues, as they may impact his substance use disorder and/or depression. This is a concern because identifying and exploring triggering events and relationships and exploring family system strategies that support using behaviors are necessary parts of treatment.

Second, because he is an Hispanic male, it is possible that he has been socialized to isolate rather than seek out support during times of stress. Given that social support is a crucial part of addiction treatment, this will present a challenge for the client's successful outcomes if he is not able to seek out and engage in social support networks. This is particularly true for this client given that his current social support systems appear to involve using drugs and alcohol, which are high-risk situations for him.

Third, he indicates that he not only does not agree with organized religion but that he also rejects any "higher power." This potentially could be an issue because the primary method for getting social support in addiction recovery is participation in 12-step groups, which are based on acknowledging a higher power and turning one's life over to that power. This may be the most challenging because many addiction professionals (both on the treatment team at the RTC and in after care) believe strongly that a client must engage in a 12-step group to be successful in recovery. Therefore, part of treatment may be helping the client learn ways to assert his needs/beliefs in treatment and how to manage distressing feelings that may arise out of these situations. Additionally, the counselor will need to be creative in helping the client identify realistic ways to find social supports that will encourage his recovery behaviors.

For each of these, it is important that the counselor be intentional about identifying them and asking the client to help him/her understand his attitudes, feelings, and beliefs related to each. For each one the counselor should try to find areas that may support the client's treatment needs and use counseling techniques such as cognitive restructuring, systemic interventions, or motivational interviewing to engage the client in treatment. However, the counselor may need to discuss how the client's cultural beliefs or attitudes are inconsistent with recovery, if supported by evidence-based practice (e.g., secrecy and isolation). The counselor will need to be vigilant about his/her own biases and/or counter-transference issues during this process and seek peer consultation or clinical supervision to assist. Additionally, using the therapeutic community and/or treatment team to assist with this process may be helpful.

2. **Mr. Lopez's family history indicates some issues that may have contributed to his substance use issues. Discuss three potential family issues impacting the client's treatment and how the treatment plan can help address these.**

The client's family history is complicated. First, the client basically experienced abandonment by his father and mother by their placing him with his grandparents to be raised while raising all of his other siblings. This isolation and probable attachment wound likely are triggers for his substance use. We also don't know what happened with his grandparents and how he experienced these relationships, or how the relationships may have impacted his using behaviors. Part of the treatment plan may be helping the client process through these potential abandonments, and how that impacts his feelings of loneliness and isolation will likely help him identify feelings, thoughts, and situations that are high risk for him.

Second, he described his maternal relationship as more like "siblings" than mother-son. This experience may result in additional issues that trigger his using behaviors. It may also indicate that because his mother had him young and had to "give him up" to be raised by her parents, she may excuse or avoid addressing high-risk situations she is aware of because she feels guilty for leaving him. So treatment planning would ideally involve a family therapy component to help not only the identified client but also his mother increase awareness of how her guilt may be driving behaviors that enable his substance use.

Third, the conflict with his wife and now his son Carlos that has been a consequence of his substance use may now become an additional trigger for his use. It is important that the family allow him to get better. So treatment planning should also address not only the client's identifying high-risk situations related to these conflicts that may contribute to his behavior but also helping the client's wife and children understand that their level of willingness to allow him to get better may impact his success in recovery. This may indicate a need for family members to work through their own feelings about his using and how it has impacted them and for the client to take responsibility for the consequences of his behavior without shaming him.

3. **Using the DSM-5 and review of the client's biopsychosocial history, what is your understanding of Mr. Lopez's alcohol use in relationship to his view of his drinking, and how does this impact treatment and how will you address it therapeutically?**

The client's biopsychosocial history indicates that he likely has an alcohol use disorder in addition to a marijuana use disorder. If he is unable to acknowledge that alcohol is a problem, he may continue to get into high-risk situations where he drinks with friends and family, ultimately leading to relapsing in smoking marijuana as well. The treatment plan should include psychoeducation about how alcohol is a depressant, how that may impact his feelings of depression, and how feeling depressed contributes to his desire to smoke marijuana. In order not to isolate the client, however, it is likely important that motivational interviewing be used as one intervention method in the treatment plan to engage the client's awareness about how alcohol may be problematic.

Chapter 7   Case Study: Jodi

1. **What stage of change is Jodi currently in?**

Jodi is currently functioning at the contemplation stage. Jodi desires recovery and is open to learning coping strategies. The motivational interviewing technique will be beneficial for Jodi to progress to the preparation and action stages.

2. **What is Jodi's extrinsic motivation to begin recovery?**

Jodi's extrinsic motivation is to begin a relationship with her three-year-old daughter, who is currently in foster care. The counselor could use the motivational interviewing techniques to evoke behavior changes toward a productive relationship.

3. **What would be positive outcomes for Jodi to begin to therapeutically process the traumatic life events?**

EMDR as a therapeutic treatment will be used to address the abandonment issues as well as the sexual assault. The positive outcome is that Jodi will process the feelings surrounding the traumatic events and become desensitized to both while minimizing relapse triggers.

Chapter 8   Case Study: Rodney

1. **What are the possible advantages and disadvantages of Rodney participating in group counseling?**

His embarrassment and shame could be a two-edged sword. It might not allow him to share in a group setting. However, being with others who are experiencing the same issues might allow him to normalize his behavior and feelings.

2. **What considerations might you have for Rodney's veteran status? What other cultural considerations would you have when matching Rodney to appropriate treatment?**

Certainly a veteran's group would be an excellent choice if available so that Rodney could discuss his experiences in war and PTSD. Also, being Black should be considered in setting up a group experience for Rodney. SES status is not mentioned but might need to be considered also.

3. **What counseling approaches might be useful to Rodney in the group modality? How would you apply specific approaches to help him in the group setting?**

Cognitive–behavioral group therapy would be an excellent choice. This approach is easily used in a group setting to allow Rodney and others to see their illogical thinking process. Each instance of working on this would enlighten each member of the group about their own thinking process. So, cross counseling and education would be achieved.

4. **What are some reasonable treatment goals for Rodney? What would be a logical course of action if Rodney is unable to make progress toward his goals in the intensive outpatient level of care?**
The first goal would be abstinence. It would be important for Rodney to sustain his sobriety for a significant amount of time before discussing underlying issues that might be leading him to continue his use. Behaviorally, Rodney should develop other friends that are not part of his drinking group. Also, as stated earlier, CBT should be used to examine his thinking process and change that process. Logically, the next step for Rodney would be inpatient care.

Chapter 9   Case Study: Amanda

1. **Based on the information Amanda gave you, what other information would you need to determine her level of drug use?**
Amanda appears to be very open about her drug use. However, as most users tend to downplay their use, as her counselor you might ask for specifics. Outside confirmation would be helpful but is probably not a possibility in this case.

2. **What dynamics in Amanda's family would you consider nature and/or nurture?**
Amanda has multiple learned behaviors: Her drinking and smoking as well as her early behavioral problems have all been modeled by her parents through the years. Her diagnosis of ADD might have a biological component, but that would need to be retested at this time. Also, with the new information on the brain and its functioning, Amanda's early use has affected her brain functioning and perhaps heredity impacts her substance use.

3. **What would be your strategy for the family therapy weekend? Who would you want to attend? What would you specifically want to know/observe?**
The counselor would like to have the whole family there—parents and brother—as well as any other individuals that Amanda may consider family. Observing the interaction of Amanda with her parents, with her brother, and the interaction between her parents would be important information. Using general systems concepts to recognize their family patterns would be helpful.

    If Amanda wanted other individuals to attend, observing her interactions with these individuals and how they are the same or different from her "nuclear family" would also give the counselor important information.

Chapter 10   Case Study: Robert

1. **Robert is facing a number of difficulties—a substance use disorder, depression, hopelessness, and alienation from the church, a previous diagnosis of HIV, unemployment, and estrangement from his family. What problem does he need to address first? Provide a rationale for your choice.**
Integrated care refers to the need for individuals with a co-occurring substance use disorder with a mental illness to receive treatment for both disorders simultaneously and in an integrated manner. If treatment is not integrated, use of a substance can exacerbate symptoms of the mental disorder, or flare-up of the mental illness can result in use of a substance to manage the symptom. Integrated treatment can be provided by a single treatment team trained to treat both disorders or can entail substance use and mental health treatment teams working closely with each other and with the client on a single treatment plan.

2. **What model/s of relapse planning and management is most relevant to Robert's situation? What, if any, self-help recovery program/s would you recommend?**
Robert seems to be losing hope that he can manage or stop his use of substances. He has also experienced rejection for being a gay man. He needs to find social supports that will respect him for who he is. Given his history of, and apparent current interest in, faith, Robert might benefit from finding an AA group that welcomes gay individuals and that accepts members who also have a mental illness.

Finding a setting where he is able to experience a higher power and fellow members who love and respect him as a gay man who experiences bouts of depression has the potential to provide the healing and affirmation that he needs.

3. **In your view, what role, if any, should spirituality have in recovery from an addiction?**

According to ASERViC, spirituality is innate and unique to each person, encompassing the search for meaning, wellness, and connecting with others (ASERViC, n.d.). Whereas religion entails beliefs and practices that the believer is required to follow to be included as a member, spirituality represents the values that the individual holds most dear to himself in his search for integrity. As successful recovery is achieved only by the person's becoming aware of oneself and one's motivations, spirituality is an essential resource in successful recovery.

4. **What should Robert do about his alienation from the church? He states that faith in God is important to him, but he has been told that homosexuality is an abomination.**

In addition to finding an AA group that welcomes individuals who are gay and who have a mental illness, Robert might be encouraged to continue to look for a church that welcomes and respects persons who are gay. The counselor should offer her/his knowledge of community resources and/or conduct research to locate a Christian church known for welcoming gay persons.

5. **How could a well-rounded life with hope become part of Robert's recovery from addiction? What could a counselor do to assist Robert to discover hope in recovery?**

The counselor could educate Robert about the CHIME model of recovery and assist him to connect with a support group whose members achieve hope through a life filled with opportunities for friendship, social engagement, affirmation, and celebrating one's uniqueness. Robert may then be able to discover his special talents that he can share in the group and beyond.

Chapter 11   Case Study: Loren

1. **Describe how you would protect Loren and ensure her negative experiences in her first treatment episode are not repeated. Keep in mind that this is a residential treatment center where Loren will be staying for a minimum of 28 days.**

- Accept her into your program and house her as you would other women in your program
- Dorm-type rooms are acceptable; single private room is also acceptable if available
- Designate appropriate time she can use group showers; if individual showers are available for women, this would be preferable
- Insist on all staff referring to her and treating her as a woman
- Assist in finding outside support for transgender individuals
- Address any client issues as you normally would, through individual counseling
- Engage in staff and client education about transgender individuals, as needed

2. **Social support is very important as an individual enters into and maintains recovery from substance use. Based on the vignette, how would you as Loren's counselor help her use and strengthen her support network?**

- Involve Loren's family, as she described them as supportive and positive (e.g., family education, family therapy)
- Consider additional supports such as friends (e.g., work with Loren to identify these individuals)
- Help connect Loren to adjunct supports such as AA/NA—be sure to research and identify a home group where LGBTQ individuals, especially transgender people, attend and are embraced
- Identify a transgender sponsor/main support/mentor who can support Loren in her early recovery
- Based on Loren's mental health history, a psychiatric evaluation should be recommended immediately with a culturally sensitive psychiatrist who is skilled in working with trans and gender-nonconforming clients
- Treatment should include individual counseling with a sensitive and skilled clinician; group counseling that provides a safe space for Loren where hostility and cisgenderism are not permitted; family education and therapy since the family is supportive of Loren and positive aspects of her recovery

- Help connect Loren to adjunct supports such as AA/NA—be sure to research and identify a home group where LGBTQ individuals, especially transgender people, attend and are embraced; identify a transgender sponsor/main support/mentor who can support Loren in her early recovery
- Treatment goals should focus on relapse prevention (triggers to use and development of coping strategies); mental health; family relationships; vocational and educational interests; and her transition as it relates to her substance use (remember to not overemphasize gender identity when it is not relevant)

Chapter 12   Case Study: The Gutierrez Family

1. **Given your reading of this chapter, identify and describe three assumptions related to Hispanic cultural values that you would make about this case.**
   1. There is often a dynamic of machismo and marianismo at play in the Latino culture. The former dictates the man/husband is the ruler, and the latter that the woman/wife is submissive. Miguel clearly has macho characteristics, and Angela for a long time assumed a submissive role. Problems erupted when she began relinquishing that role.
   2. Loyalty to family is paramount in the Latino culture. An example of this includes Angela's reluctance to report Miguel for violating his order of protection. If Angela did report Miguel, it would cause permanent disruption to the family and deny her children a relationship with their father.
   3. *Personalismo* is evident in the family' relationship to the therapist, who has consistently shown the family warmth, support, caring, and respect through all of its difficult moments.
   4. Extended family plays a huge part in this scenario and in Miguel's drinking in particular. He is very close to some of his family members who all drink heavily. Angela, on the other hand, is bereft of extended family that makes her situation as a Latina woman even more vulnerable.
2. **Identify all of the possible people who are directly and indirectly involved in this case. Briefly describe how they are—or should be—involved, and why.**
   1. All immediate members and extended family members of the Gutierrez family should be directly/indirectly involved in this case. As mentioned previously, Miguel's extended family plays a huge role in his drinking. Angela receives some support by phone from her sister in Guatemala with whom she is very close.
   2. The police and the judicial system in adjudicating Miguel's case of domestic violence should be included.
   3. School personnel who are concerned about Joaquin's academic performance and emotional welfare should be included. The therapist needs to work closely with the school after having obtained the necessary permissions from parents to talk with the school.
   4. Other, non-Latina women in the life of Angela who have provided her with a different model of an empowered female.
3. **Describe how the acculturation process produced stress for Angela and strain on the Gutierrez family.**
   This is one of the central themes of the case, and the basis for a good deal of discussion. Angela has changed by taking on more aspects of the dominant culture, especially in regard to the role of women. This, Miguel believes, is central to their marital problems. If Angela would only follow his rules, all would be fine. Angela, on the other hand, says that if Miguel would stop drinking, all would be fine. Angela has changed the rules of the marriage—rules that were very much in place when they first married. Is that fair to Miguel? Miguel wants the old rules that made everything fine. Is that fair to Angela? Angela has made it clear: Once empowered, there is no going back. Students can discuss the future of the couple's relationship and whether the dominant culture has been both an asset and a liability in the lives of Miguel and Angela.

Chapter 13   Case Study: Marci and Joey

1. **Joey and Marci are from the same family; however, their situations are different. Considering each of them, compare and contrast the risk factors and protective factors including all levels**

and domains discussed in the chapter that should be considered when determining the appropriate strategies to prevent them from developing a moderate or severe substance use disorder. At the level of agent, we know that Marci is using alcohol and marijuana and that her brother is drinking with friends. Both seem to be experimenting with substances; however, Marci's use has been going on for some time and has begun to negatively impact her social functioning, her judgment, and her academic performance.

At the host level, there are biomedical, personality/character, and behavioral/attitudinal considerations. They have the same genetic vulnerability, which seems to work in their favor based on the limited information we have that neither parent manifests a substance use disorder. They also share race/ethnicity. Marci's personality includes the following risk factors: alienation; poor coping skills for boredom and isolation; potentially a co-occurrence of depression, although this needs further assessment; increased stress from her child-care responsibilities; and low self-esteem.

In terms of protective factors, she has made good grades and been able to handle family responsibilities in the past and comes from a stable family with parents who are high achieving, so we can conclude that she has the ability to be self-disciplined and to problem-solve, and that she is more likely (based on family expectations and rearing) to have internal locus of control. Joey likely possesses the same protective factors in addition to high self-esteem, and he likely has only one risk factor in the personality category, which is risk-taking behavior.

In the behavioral/attitudinal domain, Marci is socially marginalized, whereas Joey is popular. However, Marci also seems to understand at times that her use is problematic, whereas Joey seems to demonstrate adolescent invincibility. Both demonstrate favorable attitudes toward substance use and underestimate the dangers or consequences. Both seem equally susceptible to negative peer influence, and both have friends who use. But they also both have positive relationships with their parents and positive moral values. Neither demonstrates antisocial behaviors or other types of risky behaviors that we are aware of. We need to further examine their expectations for the future.

At the environmental level, we must consider family, school, community, and other societal influences. Their family influences would be very similar, although we lack specific information about their individual relationships with other family members to determine if there are significant differences to consider. They seem to have positive family bonding, clear high expectations set by their parents, and an expectation that they are responsible for their decisions. However, in recent months they have had less supervision at home and less "quality time" to spend with parents. This likely negatively impacts Marci more, because she is more socially isolated than her brother and therefore likely depends more on parental emotional support for positive coping.

In the school domain, Marci experiences more social alienation and recent academic failure, whereas her brother is popular, achieving athletically and academically. The community domain includes certain risks that seem to impact both, such as availability of substances in spite of local ordinances prohibiting that. They appear to have opportunities for pro-social involvement and drug-free alternative coping activities available. Similarly, other societal influences such as media, the soundness of social institutions in their neighborhood, and cultural factors would be the same for Marci and Joey.

2. **Identify the levels of prevention (primary, secondary, tertiary and universal, selective, and indicated) that are most appropriate for this problem, and give examples that the PTA could develop to deal with the presenting problem.**

Primary prevention efforts might include enforcing existing laws and ordinances in order to control access; providing classroom guidance to educate students and raise awareness of the risks and to promote healthy attitudes and behaviors; providing Parent-Teacher Association (PTA) meetings with the goal of increasing awareness of the problem and helping parents learn ways to help prevent substance use behaviors with their children. These are also examples of universal prevention strategies because they target the entire community (law enforcement), student body (classroom guidance), and parents (PTA meeting).

Secondary prevention is most appropriate for both Marci and Joey because they are already demonstrating problems with substance use. This may include the school developing a program for general screening for alcohol and drug use problems. The program should include the school counselor reviewing data on attendance, grades, and behavioral issues to initially identify kids at potential risk and then meeting with these students and conducting a "quick screen" such as a CAGE to identify whether absenteeism, failing grades, or behavioral issues are attributable to substance use. The school could form a partnership with a local nonprofit agency that they could refer students to for further assessment, triage, and potential treatment if needed. These are selective prevention strategies that are targeting a subpopulation known to be at higher risk: students who demonstrate problems with attendance, grades, and behavioral issues.

3. **List and describe the five public health principles that should be considered by the prevention planning workgroup and give relevant examples.**
   1. Identifying the appropriate levels of prevention. These include primary, secondary, and tertiary. Another description of levels is that they are universal, selected, and indicated prevention measures. These were described in relation to this case in question 2 above.
   2. Epidemiology triangle is used to identify major risk factor categories. The first side is the host (community or individual at risk), next is the agent (substance or behavior targeted), and the environmental context (family, community, school, etc.). A thorough description and examples were provided in question 1.
   3. Passive and active approaches are employed. Passive approaches would not require additional effort and automatically protect everyone. Active approaches require individual action, such as implementing the assessment of data on attendance, grades, and behavioral issues to determine if students need to be further screened for selective or indicated prevention efforts.
   4. Multiple program targets are identified, possibly including individual, societal, and environmental/engineering. Prevention campaigns are more successful if there are multiple targets. The example of raising student or parent awareness of risks and consequences would be considered a strategy targeting individuals, whereas the example of enforcing laws and ordinances about selling alcohol to minors would be an example of a societal-targeted strategy.
   5. Effective strategies should be used, which means that the committee should research evidence-based practices that have been demonstrated to be successful. These can be found on the SAMHSA website.

Chapter 14   Case Study: Helen

1. **Even before evaluations, what are the physical/mental characteristics observed in the case study that are relevant to substance use disorder and compulsive buying disorder?**
   Helen's need to purchase items to make herself feel better and to "show off" her purchases to her friends is an important aspect of her diagnosis. Also, Helen admits to anxiety and depression with problems with sleeping and eating. The fact that her friends are concerned about her drinking and shopping indicates a problem, as does her divorce from her husband because of these issues.

2. **What instruments or evaluations would you use to determine what level of substance use disorder Helen has? Her mood disorder? What would you use to screen for compulsive buying disorder?**
   Using the MAST or the CAST would help with the substance use disorder. The Compulsive Buying Scale is the most frequently used to evaluate CBD. Looking at these two instruments together with an intensive interview would give you information for diagnosis of all issues.

3. **What type(s) of treatment would you recommend for Helen?**
   With multiple diagnoses, the clinician must determine which symptoms to address first. Does the client need inpatient or outpatient treatment? Is it possible to address both CBD and the substance use at the same facility? What about the reported mood disorder? How might that best be treated?

REFERENCES

Chapter 1

American Cancer Society. (2015). Cancer facts and figures. Retrieved from http://www.cancer.net/cancer-types/liver-cancer/statistics

American Psychiatric Association. (2013). *Diagnostic and statistical manual of mental disorders* (5th ed.). Washington: Author.

Basca, B. (2008). *The elderly and prescription drug misuse and abuse. Prevention tactics.* Retrieved from http://www.cars-rp.org/publications/Prevention%20Tactics/PT09.02.08.pdf

Blincoe, L., Miller, T. A., Zaloshnja, E., & Lawrence, B. A. (2014). *The economic and societal impact of motor vehicle crashes, 2010.* Washington, DC: U.S. Department of Transportation, National Highway Traffic Safety Administration.

Centers for Disease Control and Prevention. (2012). *Viral hepatitis statistics and surveillance.* Retrieved from http://www.cdc.gov/hepatitis/Statistics/2012Surveillance/Commentary.htm

Centers for Medicare & Medicaid Services. (2015). *Medicare & Medicaid statistical supplement. Retrieved from http://www.cms.gov/Research-Statistics-Data-and-Systems/Statistics-Trends-and-Reports/MedicareMedicaidStatSupp/index.html*

Chafetz, M. E. (1965). *Liquor: The servant of man.* Boston: Little, Brown.

Cherrington, E. H. (1920). The evolution of Prohibition in the United States of America. Westerville, OH: American Issue Press.

Culberson, J. W., & Ziska, M. (2008). Prescription drug misuse/abuse in the elderly. *Geriatrics, 3*(9), 22–31.

Doweiko, H. E. (2013). *Concepts of chemical dependency* (8th ed.). Pacific Grove, CA: Brooks/Cole.

Drug Enforcement Administration. (1988, September 6). In the matter of marijuana rescheduling petition, Docket 86-22 opinion, recommended ruling, findings of fact, conclusions of law, and decision of administrative law judge, September 6, 1988. Washington, DC: Author.

Drug Enforcement Administration. (2014). National drug threat assessment summary. Retrieved from http://www.dea.gov/resource-center/dir-ndta-unclass.pdf

Hanson, D. J. (n.d.). Was Prohibition really a success? Alcohol problems and solutions. Retrieved from https://www.alcoholproblemsandsolutions.org/Controversies/20070322134427.html

Kane, H. H. (1883). A hashish-house in New York. *Harper's Monthly, 67,* 944–949.

Meier, M. H., Caspi, A., Ambler, A., Harrington, H. L., Houts, R., Keefe, R. S. E., . . . Moffitt, T. E. (2012). Persistent cannabis users show neuropsychological decline from childhood to midlife. *Proceedings of the National Academy of Science of the United States of America, 109*(40), E2657–E2664.

National Drug Intelligence Center. (2011). *The economic impact of illicit drug use on American society.* Washington, DC: U.S. Department of Justice.

National Highway Traffic Safety Administration. (2013, December). *Traffic safety facts 2012: Alcohol-impaired driving.* Washington, DC: Author. Available at http://www-nrd.nhtsa.dot.gov/Pubs/811870.pdf

National Institute on Drug Abuse. (2012). *Medical consequences of drug abuse: HIV, hepatitis and other infectious diseases.* Retrieved from http://www.drugabuse.gov/publications/medical-consequences-drug-abuse/hiv-hepatitis-other-infectious-diseases

National Institute on Drug Abuse. (2014a). *DrugFacts: Marijuana.* Retrieved from http://www.drugabuse.gov/publications/drugfacts/marijuana

National Institute on Drug Abuse. (2014b). *Prescription drugs & cold medicines.* Retrieved from http://www.drugabuse.gov/drugs-abuse/prescription-drugs-cold-medicines

National Institute on Drug Abuse. (2014c). *Trends & statistics.* Retrieved from http://www.drugabuse.gov/related-topics/trends-statistics

National Institute on Drug Abuse. (2014d). DrugFacts: MDMA (Ecstasy/Molly). Retrieved from http://www.drugabuse.gov/publications/drugfacts/mdma-ecstasy-or-molly

Office of National Drug Control Policy. (2015, February). *National drug control budget: FY 2016 funding highlights.* Washington, DC: Author. Retrieved from https://www.whitehouse.gov/sites/default/files/ondcp/press-releases/ondcp_fy16_budget_highlights.pdf.

Public Broadcasting System. (n.d.). *A social history of America's most popular drugs.* Retrieved from http://www.pbs.org/wgbh/pages/frontline/shows/drugs/buyers/socialhistory.

Sifferlin, A. (2014, July 22). $23.6 billion lawsuit winner to big tobacco: "Are you awake now?" Retrieved from http://time.com/3016961/23-6-billion-lawsuit-winner-to-big-tobacco-are-you-awake-now

Simoni-Wastila, L., & Yang, H. K. (2006). Psychoactive drug abuse in older adults. *American Journal of Geriatric Pharmacotherapy, 4*(4), 380–394.

Substance Abuse and Mental Health Services Administration. (2014). *Results from the 2013 National Survey on Drug Use and Health: Summary of national findings* (NSDUH Series H-48, HHS Publication No. [SMA] 14-4863). Rockville, MD: Substance Abuse and Mental Health Services Administration. Retrieved from http://www.samhsa.gov/data/sites/default/files/NSDUHresultsPDFWHTML2013/Web/NSDUHresults2013.pdf

Weisheit, R. A., & White, W. (2010). *Methamphetamine: Its history, pharmacology, and treatment.* Center City, MN: Hazelden.

World Health Organization. (2006). Intimate partner violence and alcohol. Retrieved from http://www.who.int/violence_injury_prevention/violence/world_report/factsheets/fs_intimate.pdf

Chapter 2

American Counseling Association. (2010). *Licensure requirements for professional counselors.* Alexandria, VA: Author.

American Counseling Association. (2014). *2014 ACA code of ethics.* Retrieved from http://www.counseling.org/docs/ethics/2014-aca-code-of-ethics.pdf?sfvrsn=4

American Mental Health Counseling Association. (2010). *Code of ethics.* Alexandria, VA: Author.

American School Counselor Association. (2010). *Ethical standards for school counselors.* Alexandria, VA: Author.

Arredondo, P., Toporek, M. S., Brown, S., Jones, J., Locke, D. C., Sanchez, J., & Stadler, H. (1996). Operationalization of the Multicultural Counseling Competencies. AMCD: Alexandria, VA.

Astramovich, R. J., & Hoskins, W. J. (2013). Evaluating addictions counseling programs: Promoting best practices, accountability, and advocacy. *Journal of Addictions & Offender Counseling, 34*(2), 114–124. doi:10.1002/j.2161-1874.2013.00019.x

Broderick, E. B. (2007). *Report to Congress: Addictions treatment workforce development.* Retrieved from www.pfr.samhsa.gov/docs/Report_to_Congress.pdf

Burrow-Sanchez, J. J., Jenson, W. R., & Clark, E. (2009). School-based interventions for students with substance abuse. *Psychology in the Schools, 46*(3), 238–245.

Code of Federal Regulations, 42, 6-25. (1994). Washington, DC: U.S. Government Printing Office. (2010). E-code available at http://www.ecfr.gov/cgi-bin/text-idx?tpl=/ecfrbrowse/Title42/42tab_02.tpl

Coleman, P. (2005). Privilege and confidentiality in 12-step self-help programs: Believing the promises could be hazardous to an addict's freedom. *Journal of Legal Medicine, 26*, 435–474. doi:10.1080/01947640500364713

Corey, G., Corey, M., & Callanan, P. (2011). *Issues and ethics in the helping profession.* Belmont, CA: Brooks/Cole.

Cox v. Miller, 537 U.S. 1192 (2003).

Doukas, N., & Cullen, J. (2010). Recovered addicts working in the addiction field: Pitfalls to substance abuse relapse. *Drugs: Education, Prevention & Policy, 17*(3), 216–231. doi:10.3109/09687630802378864

Even, T. A., & Robinson, C. R. (2013). The impact of CACREP accreditation: A multiway frequency analysis of ethics violations and sanctions. *Journal of Counseling & Development, 91*, 26–34. doi:10.1002/j.1556-6676.2013.00067.x

Family Educational Rights and Privacy Act. (1974). 20 U.S.C.A. Section 1232g. [Buckley Amendment.] (1991). Implementing regulations 34 *CFR* 99.3. Fed. Reg. 56, Section 117, 28012.

Francis, P. C. & Dugger, S. M. (2014). Professionalism, ethics, and value-based conflicts in counseling: An introduction to the special section. *Journal of Counseling & Development, 92*(2), 131–134. doi:10.1002/j.1556-6676.2014.0013

Froeschle, J. G., & Crews, C. (2010). An ethics challenge for school counselors. *Journal of School Counseling, 8* (14). Retrieved from http://eric.ed.gov/?id=EJ885152

Hagedorn, W. B., Culbreth, J. R., & Cashwell, C. S. (2012). Addiction counseling accreditation: CACREP's role in solidifying the counseling profession. Retrieved from http://tpcjournal.nbcc.org/wp-content/uploads/2012/09/AddictionCounsAccreditation_Hagedorn-Manuscript-p124-133.pdf

Hanson, S. (2009). Confidentiality guidelines for school counselors. School Counseling Zone. Retrieved from http://www.school-counseling-zone.com/support-files/confidentiality-guidelines-for-school-counselors-short-version.pdf

Health Information Technology for Economic and Clinical Health (HITECH) Act, Title XIII of Division A and Title IV of Division B of the American Recovery and Reinvestment Act of 2009 (ARRA), Pub. L. No. 111-5, 123 Stat. 226 (Feb. 17, 2009), codified at 42 U.S.C. §§300jj et seq.; §§17901 et seq. (2009).

Health Insurance Portability and Accountability Act of 1996 (HIPAA), Pub. L. 104-191, Sec. 261–264.

Hendricks, B. E., Bradley, L. J., Southern, S., Oliver, M., & Birdsall, B. (2011). Ethical code for the International Association of Marriage and Family

Counselors. *The Family Journal, 19*, 217–224. doi:10.1177/1066480711400814

Herbert, P. B., & Young, K. A. (2002). *Tarasoff* at twenty-five. *Journal of the American Academy of Psychiatry and the Law, 30*, 275–281. Retrieved from www.jaapl.org/cgi/reprint/30/2/275.pdf

Hu, L. L., Sparenborg, S., & Tai, B. (2011). Privacy protection for patients with substance use problems. *Substance Abuse and Rehabilitation Training, 2*, 227–233. doi:10.2147/SAR.S27237

Illinois State Board of Education. (n.d.). *No child left behind*. Retrieved from http://www.isbe.state.il.us/nclb/htmls/ppra_ferpa.htm

Individuals with Disabilities Education Act of 1997. (1997). Pub. L. No. 105-17, 34 *CFR* 300–574.

International Association of Marriage and Family Counselors. (2011). *Ethical code of the International Association of Marriage and Family Counselors*. Retrieved from http://www.iamfconline.org/public/department3.cfm

Kaplan, D. M. (2014). Ethical implications of a critical legal case for the counseling profession: *Ward v. Wilbanks*. *Journal of Counseling and Development, 92*, 142–146. doi:10.1002/j.1556-6676.2014.00140.x

Kocet, M. M., & Herlihy, B. (2014). Decision making model for addressing value-based counseling conflicts. *Journal of Counseling of Development, 92*, 182–186. doi:10.1002/j.1556-6676.2014.00146.x

Lipari v. Sears, Roebuck & Co., 836F.2d 209 (1987).

Macy, R. J., & Goodbourn, M. (2012). Promoting successful collaborations between domestic violence and substance abuse treatment service sectors: A review of the literature. *Trauma, Violence & Abuse, 13*(4), 234–251. doi:10.1177/152483801245587

National Addiction Technology Transfer Center. (2010). Licensing and certification requirements. Retrieved from http://www.nattc.org/getCertified.asp

National Association of Alcoholism and Drug Abuse Counselors. (2011a). *Scopes of practice & career ladder for substance use disorder counseling*. Retrieved from http://www.addictioncareers.org/addictioncareers/resources/documents/PEP11-SCOPES.pdf

National Association of Alcoholism and Drug Abuse Counselors. (2011b). *Ethical standards of alcoholism and drug abuse counselors*. Retrieved from http://www.naadac.org/assets/1959/naadac_code_of_ethics_brochure.pdf

National Association of Alcoholism and Drug Abuse Counselors. (2015). *Certifications: Types and eligibility*. Retrieved from http://www.naadac.org/typeseligibility

National Board for Certified Counselors. (2011). *Exam for master of addictions counselor application*. Retrieved from http://www.nbcc.org/Certification/MasterAddictionsCounselor

National Board for Certified Counselors. (2012). *National Board for Certified Counselors code of ethics*. Retrieved from http://www.nbcc.org/Assets/Ethics/NBCCCodeofEthics.pdf

Office for Civil Rights. (2003). *Summary of the HIPAA privacy rule*. Retrieved from http://www.hhs.gov/sites/default/files/privacysummary.pdf

Olivier, C. (2009). Enhancing Confidentiality within Small Groups: The Experiences of AIDS Service Organizations. *Social Work With Groups, 32*(4), 274–287. doi:10.1080/01609510902874586

Oser, C. B., Biebel, E. P., Pullen, E. & Harp, K. L. H. (2013). Causes, consequences, and prevention of burnout among substance abuse treatment counselors: A rural versus urban comparison. *Journal of Psychoactive Drugs, 45(1):*17–27. doi:10.1080/02791072.2013.763558

Patient Protection and Affordable Care Act, 42 U.S.C. §18001 (2010).

Pearlman, S. (2013). The Patient Protection and Affordable Care Act: Impact on mental health services demand and provider availability. *Journal of the American Psychiatric Nurses Association, 19*, 6, 327–334. doi:10.1177/1078390313511852

Protection of Pupil Rights Amendment. (1994). Goals 2000: Educate America Act. 20 USC, Section 1232h.

Remley, T., & Herlihy, B. (2013). *Ethical, legal, and professional issues in counseling* (4th ed.). Upper Saddle River, NJ: Pearson Education.

Rubin, S. E., Wilson, C. A., Fischer, J., & Vaughn, B. (1992). *Ethical practices in rehabilitation: A series of instructional modules for rehabilitation education programs*. Carbondale, IL: Southern Illinois University.

Schank, J. A., Helbok, C. M., Haldeman, D. C., & Gallardo, M. E. (2010). Challenges and benefits of ethical small-community practice. *Professional Psychology, Research & Practice, 41*(6), 502–510. doi:10.1037/a0021689

Stone, C. (2001). *Ethics and law for school counselors*. ASCA: Alexandria, VA.

Sue, D., Arredondo, P., & McDavis, R. (1992, March). Multicultural counseling competencies and standards: A call to the profession. *Journal of Counseling & Development, 70* (4), 477–486. Retrieved from Academic Search Premier database.

Tarasoff v. Regents of the University of California. 17 Cal. 3d 425, 131 Cal. Rep. 14, 551 P. 2d 334. (1976).

U.S. Department of Education. (2009). Family educational right and Privacy Act regulations. Retrieved from http://www.ed.gov/policy/gen/guid/fpco/pdf/ferparegs.pdf

White, W. L. (2008). Alcohol, tobacco and other drug use by addictions professionals: Historical reflections and suggested guidelines. *Alcoholism Treatment Quarterly, 26*(4), 500–535. doi:10.1080/07347320802347228

Chapter 3

Adinoff, B., Devous, M. D. Sr., Williams, M. J., Best, S. E., Harris, T. S., Minhajuddin, A., . . . Cullum, M. (2010). Altered neural cholinergic receptor systems in cocaine-addicted subjects. *Neuropsychopharmacology, 35*, 1485–1499. doi:10.1038/npp.2010.18

Ahern, N. R., & Falsafi, N. (2013). Inhalant abuse: Youth at risk. *Journal of Psychosocial Nursing and Mental Health Services, 51*, 19–24. doi:103928/02793695-20130612-02

Allain, F., Minogianis, E., Roberts, D. S., & Samaha, A. (2015). How fast and how often: The pharmacokinetics of drug use are decisive in addiction. *Neuroscience and Biobehavioral Reviews, 56*, 166–179. doi:10.1016/j.neubiorev.2015.06.012

Alvik, A., Aalen, O. O., & Lindemann, R. (2013). Early fetal binge alcohol exposure predicts high behavioral symptom scores in 5.5 year old children. *Alcoholism: Clinical and Experimental Research, 37*(11), 1954–1962. doi:10.1111/acer.12182

American Cancer Society. (2010). *Alcohol and cancer.* Retrieved from www.cancer.org

American Psychiatric Association. (2013). *Diagnostic and statistical manual of mental disorders (5th ed.).* Washington, DC: Author.

Atluri, S., Sudarshan, G., & Manchikanti, L. (2013). Assessment of the trends in medical use and misuse of opioid analgesics from 2004 to 2011. *Pain Physician, 17*(2), E119–E128.

Baldwin, D. S., Aithchison, K., Bateson, A., Curran, H. V., Davies, S., Leonard, B., . . . Wilson, S. (2013). Benzodiazepines: Risk and benefits. A reconsideration. *Journal of Psychopharmacology, 27*, 967–971. doi:10.1177/0269881113503509

Baraona, E., Abittan, C. S., Dohmen, K., Moretti, M., Pozzato, G., Chayes, Z. W., . . . Lieber, C. S. (2001), Gender differences in pharmacokinetics of alcohol. *Alcoholism: Clinical and Experimental Research, 25*, 502–507. doi: 10.1111/j.1530-0277.2001.tb02242.x

Bartholomew, J., Holroyd, S., & Heffernan, T. M. (2010). Does cannabis use affect prospective memory in adults? *Sage Journals Online.* Retrieved from http://jop.sagepub.com/content/24/2/241.abstract

Bergin, J. E., & Kendler, K. S. (2012). Common psychiatric disorders and caffeine use, tolerance, and withdrawal: An examination of shared genetic and environmental effects. *Twin Research and Human Genetics, 15*, 473–482. doi:10.1017/thg.2012.25

Bhattacharyya, S., Fusar-Poli, P., Borgwardt, S., Martin-Santos, R., Nosarti, C., O'Carroll, C., & McGuire, P. (2009). Modulation of mediotemporal and ventrostraital function in humans by Δ9-tetrahydrocannabinol. *Archives of General Psychiatry, 66*, 442–451. Retrieved from http://archpsyc.ama-assn.org/cgi/content/abstract/66/4/442

Blanco-Gandía, M. C., García, A. M., García-Pardo, M. P., Montagud-Romero, S., Rodríguez-Arias, M., Miñarro, J., & Aguilar, M. A. (2015). Effect of drugs of abuse on social behaviour: A review of animal models. *Behavioural Pharmacology, 26*(6), 541–570. doi:10.1097/FBP.0000000000000162

Brents, L. K., & Prather, P. L. (2014). The K2/Spice Phenomenon: Emergence, identification, legislation and metabolic characterization of synthetic cannabi-noids in herbal incense products. *Drug Metabolism Reviews, 46*(1), 72–85. doi:10.3109/03602532.2013.839700

Brunt, T. M., Koeter, M. W., Hertoghs, N., van Noorden, M. S., & van den Brink, W. (2013). Sociodemographic and substance use characteristics of gamma hydroxy-butyrate (GHB) dependent inpatients and associations with dependence severity. *Drug and Alcohol Dependence, 131*, 316–319. doi:10.1016/j.drugalcdep.2012.12.023

Buttigieg, J., Brown, S., Zhang, M., Lowe, M., Holloway, A. C., & Nurse, C. A. (2008). Chronic nicotine in utero selectively suppresses hypoxic sensitivity in neonatal. *Journal of the Federation of American Societies for Experimental Biology, 22*, 1317–1326.

Cairney, S., O'Connor, N., Dingwall, K. M., Maruff, P., Shafiq-Antonacci, R., Currie, J., & Currie, B. J. (2013). A prospective study of neurocognitive changes 15 years after chronic inhalant abuse. *Addiction, 108*, 1107–1114. doi:10.1111/add.12124

Campbell, N. D. (2010). Toward a critical neuroscience of "addiction." *BioSocieties, 5*, 89–104. doi: 10.1057/biosoc.2009.2

Cannon, M. J., Guo, J., Denny, C. H., Green, P. P., Miracle, H., Sniezek, J. E., & Floyd, R. L. (2015). Prevalence and characteristics of women at risk for an alcohol-exposed pregnancy (AEP) in the United States: Estimates from the National Survey of Family Growth. *Maternal and Child Health Journal, 19*(4), 776–782. doi:10.1007/s10995-014-1563-3

Chapy, H., Smirnova, M., André, P., Schlatter, J., Chiadmi, F., Couraud, P., . . . Cisternino, S. (2015). Carrier-mediated cocaine transport at the blood-brain barrier as a putative mechanism in addiction liability. *International Journal of Neuropsychopharmacology, 18*(1), 1–10.

Cicero, T. J., & Ellis, M. S. (2015). Abuse-deterrent formulations and the prescription opioid abuse epidemic in the United States: Lessons learned from OxyContin. *JAMA Psychiatry, 72*(5), 424–429. doi:10.1001/jamapsychiatry.2014.3043

Clark, T., Marquez, C., Hare, C. B., John, M. D., & Klausner, J. D. (2012). Methamphetamine use, transmission risk behavior and internet use among HIV-infected patients in medical care, San Francisco, 2008. *AIDS and Behavior, 16*(2), 396–403. doi:10.1007/s10461-010-9869-7

Cosgrove, K. P., Batis, J., Bois, F., Maciejewski, P. K., Esterlis, I., & Staley, J. K. (2009). Beta2-Nicotinic acetylcholine receptor availability during acute and prolonged abstinence from tobacco smoking. *Archive of General Psychiatry, 66*(6), 666–676. doi: 10.1001/archgenpsychiatry.2009.41

Cowan, R. L., Haga, E., Deb Frederick, B., Dietrich, M. S., Vimal, R. L. P., Lukas, S. E., & Renshaw, P. F. (2006). MDMA use is associated with increased spatial fMRI visual cortex activation in human MDMA users. *Pharmacology Biochemistry and Behavior, 84*(2), 219–228.

Cui, C., Noronha, A., Morikawa, H., Alvarez, V. A., Stuber, G. D., Szumlinski, K. K., . . . Wilcox, M. V. (2013). New insights on neurobiological mechanisms underlying alcohol addiction. *Neuropharmacology, 67*, 223–232. doi:10.1016/j.neuropharm.2012.09.022

Dacher, M., & Nugent, F. S. (2011). Opiates and plasticity. *Neuropharmacology, 61*(7), 1088–1096. doi:10.1016/j.neuropharm.2011.01.028

Degenhardt, L., Singleton, J., Calabria, B., McLaren, J., Kerr, T., Mehta, S., . . . Hall, W. D. (2011). Mortality among cocaine users: A systematic review of cohort studies. *Drug and Alcohol Dependence, 113*(2–3), 88–95. doi:10.1016/j.drugalcdep.2010.07.026

Dingwall, K. M., & Cairney, S. (2011). Recovery from central nervous system (CNS) changes following volatile solvent use (VSU). *Substance Use and Misuse, 46*, 73–83. doi:10.3109/10826084.2011 .580221

Doherty, D., Millen, K. J., & Barkovich, A. J. (2013). Midbrain and hindbrain malformations: Advances in clinical diagnosis, imaging, and genetics. *Lancet Neurology, 12*(4), 381–393. doi:10.1016/S1474-4422(13)70024-3

Doidge, N. (2007). *The brain that changes itself.* New York, NY: Viking.

Dow-Edwards, D. (2010). Sex differences in the effects of cocaine abuse across the life span. *Physiology & Behavior, 100*(3), 208–215. doi:10.1016/j.physbeh.2009.12.017

Doweiko, H. E. (2014). *Concepts of chemical dependency*, 9th ed. Pacific Grove, CA: Brooks/Cole.

Drake, J. (2009). Fetal alcohol syndrome testing expands. *e! Science News.* Retrieved from http://esciencenews.com/articles/2009/03/19/fetal.alcohol.syndrome.testing

Drug Enforcement Administration, Office of Diversion Control. (2013). *Benzodiazepines.* Retrieved from https://www.deadiversion.usdoj.gov/drug_chem_info/benzo.pdf

Dubroqua, S., Yee, B. K., & Singer, P. (2014). Sensorimotor gating is disrupted by acute but not chronic systemic exposure to caffeine in mice. *Psychopharmacology, 231*(21), 4087–4098. doi:10.1007/s00213-014-3548-8

Durand, D., Delgado, L. L., Parra-Pellot, D. L., & Nichols-Vinueza, D. (2015). Psychosis and severe rhabdomyolysis associated with synthetic cannabinoid use. *Clinical Schizophrenia & Related Psychoses, 8*(4), 205–208. doi:10.3371/CSRP.DUDE.031513

Egan, K. L., Suerken, C. K., Reboussin, B. A., Spangler, J., Wagoner, K. G., Sutfin, E. L., . . . Wolfson, M. (2015). K2 and Spice use among a cohort of college students in southeast region of the USA. *American Journal of Drug & Alcohol Abuse, 41*(4), 317–322. doi:10.3109/00952990.2015.1043438

el-Guebaly, N., Mudry, T., Zohar, J., Tavares, H., & Potenza, M. N. (2012). Compulsive features in behavioural addictions: The case of pathological gambling. *Addiction, 107*(10), 1726–1734. doi:10.1111/j.1360-0443.2011.03546.x

Fairman, B. J. (2016). Trends in registered medical marijuana participation across 13 US states and District of Columbia. *Drug & Alcohol Dependence, 159*, 72–79. doi:10.1016/j.drugalcdep.2015.11.015

Fernández-Hernández, I., & Rhiner, C. (2015). New neurons for injured brains? The emergence of new genetic model organisms to study brain regeneration. *Neuroscience and Biobehavioral Reviews, 56*, 62–72. doi:10.1016/j.neubiorev.2015.06.021

FDA Commissioner testified: Tobacco companies spiking cigarettes to addict smokers. (2009). *eSmoke.* Retrieved from www.esmoke.net/news

Fortuna, J. L. (2010). Sweet preference, sugar addiction and the familial history of alcohol dependence: Shared neural pathways and genes. *Journal of Psychoactive Drugs, 42*(2), 147–151. doi:10.1080/02791072.2010.10400687

Friedmann, P. D. (2013). Alcohol use in adults. *New England Journal of Medicine, 368*, 365–373. doi:10.1056/NEJMcp1204714

Fukunaga, R., Bogg, T., Finn, P. R., & Brown, J. W. (2013). Decisions during negatively-framed messages yield smaller risk-aversion-related brain activation in substance-dependent individuals. *Psychology of Addictive Behaviors, 27*(4), 1141–1152. doi:10.1037/a0030633

Garland, E. L., & Howard, M. O. (2011). Adverse consequences of acute inhalant intoxication. *Experimental and Clinical Psychopharmacology, 19*, 134–144. doi:10.1037/a0022859

Geibprasert, S., Gallucci, M., & Krings, T. (2009). Addictive illegal drugs: Structural neuroimaging. *American Journal of Neuroradiology, 31*, 803–808. doi:10.3174/anjnr.A1811

Giedd, J. N. (2015). Adolescent neuroscience of addiction: A new era. *Developmental Cognitive Neuroscience, 16*, 192–193. doi:10.1016/j.dcn.2015.11.002

Gilpin, N. W. (2014). Brain reward and stress systems in addiction. *Frontiers in Psychiatry, 5*, 79.

Goldstein, R. B., Smith, S. M., Dawson, D. A., & Grant, B. F. (2015). Sociodemographic and psychiatric diagnostic predictors of 3-year incidence of DSM-IV substance use disorders among men and women in the National Epidemiologic Survey on Alcohol and Related Conditions. *Psychology of Addictive Behaviors, 29*(4), 924–932. doi:10.1037/adb0000080

Goodman, J., & Packard, M. G. (2015). The influence of cannabinoids on learning and memory processes of the dorsal striatum. *Neurobiology of Learning & Memory, 125*, 1–14. doi:10.1016/j.nlm.2015.06.008

Hanlon, C. A., Wesley, M. J., & Porrino, L. J. (2009). Loss of functional specificity in the dorsal stratum of chronic cocaine users. *Drug Alcohol Dependence, 102*(1–3), 88–94. doi:10.1016/ j.drugalcdep.2009. 01.005

Hanlon, C. A., Wesley, M. J., Roth, A. J., Miller, M. D., & Porrino, L. J. (2010). Loss of laterality in chronic cocaine users: An fMRI investigation of sensorimotor control. *Psychiatry Research: Neuroimaging, 181*(1), 15–23. doi:10.1016/j.pscychresns.2009.07.009

Harris, C. R., & Brown, A. (2013). Synthetic cannabinoid intoxication: A case series and review. *Journal of Emergency Medicine (0736-4679), 44*(2), 360–366. doi:10.1016/j.jemermed.2012.07.061

Hassan, H. E., Meyers, A. L., Lee, I. J., Chen, H., Coop, A., & Eddington, N. D. (2010). Regulation of gene expression in brain tissues of rats repeatedly treated by the highly abused opioid agonist, oxycodone:

microarray profiling and gene mapping analysis. *U.S. National Library of Medicine National Institutes of Health, 38*(1):157–167.

Hermens, D. F., Lagopoulos, J., Tobias-Webb, J., De Regt, T., Dore, G., Juckes, L., . . . Hickie, I. B. (2013). Pathways to alcohol-induced brain impairment in young people: A review. *Cortex, 49*, 3–17. doi:10.1016/j.cortex.2012.05.021

Højsted, J., Ekholm, O., Kurita, G. P., Juel, K., & Sjøgren, P. (2013). Addictive behaviors related to opioid use for chronic pain: A population-based study. *Pain, 154*(12), 2677–2683. doi:10.1016/j.pain.2013.07.046

Hood, S. D., Norman, A., Hince, D. A., Melichar, J. K., & Hulse, G. K. (2012). Benzodiazepine dependence and its treatment with low dose flumazenil. *British Journal of Clinical Pharmacology, 77*, 285–294. doi: 10.1111/bcp.12023

Howard, M. O., Bowen, S. E., Garland, E. L., Perron, B. E., & Vaughn, M. G. (2011). Inhalant use and inhalant use disorders in the United States. *Addiction Science and Clinical Practice, 6*(1), 18–31.

Huebner, S. M., Tran, T. D., Rufer, E. S., Crump, P. M., & Smith, S. M. (2015). Maternal iron deficiency worsens the associative learning deficits and hippocampal and cerebellar losses in a rat model of fetal alcohol spectrum disorders. *Alcoholism: Clinical and Experimental Research, 39*(11), 2097–2107. doi:10.1111/acer.12876

Hurd, Y. L., Michaelides, M., Miller, M. L., & Jutras-Aswad, D. (2014). Trajectory of adolescent cannabis use on addiction vulnerability. *Neuropharmacology, 76*, 416–424. doi:10.1016/j.neuropharm.2013.07.028

Johnson, P. M., & Kenny, P. J. (2010). Dopamine D2 receptors in addiction-like reward dysfunction and compulsive eating in obese rats. *Nature Neuroscience, 13*(5), 635–641. doi:10.1038/nn.2519

Johnston, L. D., O'Malley, P. M., Bachman, J. G., & Schulenberg, J. E. (2011). Monitoring the future national results on adolescent drug use: Overview of key findings in 2010. Ann Arbor, MI: Institute for Social Research, University of Michigan.

Johnston, L. D., O'Malley, P. M., Miech, R. A., Bachman, J. G., & Schulenberg, J. E. (2016). *Monitoring the Future national survey results on drug use, 1975–2015: Overview, key findings on adolescent drug use.* Ann Arbor, MI: Institute for Social Research, The University of Michigan.

Juliano, L. M., Huntley, E. D., Harrell, P. T., & Westerman, A. T. (2012). Development of the Caffeine Withdrawal Symptom Questionnaire: Caffeine withdrawal symptoms cluster into 7 factors. *Drug and*

Alcohol Dependence, 124(3), 229–234. doi:10.1016/j.drugalcdep.2012.01.009

Kamali, A., Sair, H. I., Blitz, A. M., Riascos, R. F., Mirbagheri, S., Keser, Z., & Hasan, K. M. (2015). Revealing the ventral amygdalofugal pathway of the human limbic system using high spatial resolution diffusion tensor tractography. *Brain Structure & Function.* doi:10.1007/s00429-015-1119-3

Kaplan, L. (2015). Medical marijuana. *Nurse Practitioner, 40*(10), 46–55. doi:10.1097/01.NPR.0000471361.02487.3b

Kim, H. R., Hung, M. H., Lee, S. Y., Oh, S. M., & Chung, K. H. (2013). Marijuana smoke condensate induces p53-mediated apoptosis in human lung epithelial cells. *Journal of Toxicological Sciences, 38*(3), 337–347.

Knight, K. R., Das, M., DeMicco, E., Raiford, J. L., Matheson, T., Shook, A., . . . Herbst, J. H. (2014). A roadmap for adapting an evidence-based HIV prevention intervention: Personal cognitive counseling (PCC) for episodic substance-using men who have sex with men. *Prevention Science, 15*(3), 364–375. doi:10.1007/s11121-013-0364-z

Konopka, L. M. (2014). Marijuana use: Neuroscience perspective. *Croatian Medical Journal, 55*(3), 281–283. doi:10.3325/cmj.2014.55.281

Lau, B. W-M., Yau, S-Y., & So, K-F. (2011). Reproduction: A new venue for studying function of adult neurogenesis? *Cell Transplantation, 20*(1), 21–35.

Lee, D., Schroeder, J. R., Karschner, E. L., Goodwin, R. S., Hirvonen, J., Gorelick, D. A., & Huestis, M. A. (2014). Cannabis withdrawal in chronic, frequent cannabis smokers during sustained abstinence within a closed residential environment. *American Journal on Addictions, 23*(3), 234–242. doi:10.1111/j.1521-0391.2014.12088.x

Lev-Ran, S., Le Strat, Y., Imtiaz, S., Rehm, J., & Le Foll, B. (2013). Gender differences in prevalence of substance use disorders among individuals with lifetime exposure to substances: Results from a large representative sample. *American Journal on Addictions, 22*(1), 7–13. doi:10.1111/j.1521-0391.2013.00321.x

Licata, S. C., & Renshaw, P. F. (2010). Neurochemistry of drug action: Insights from proton magnetic resonance spectroscopic imaging and their relevance to addiction. *Academic Science, 1187,* 148–171. doi: 10.1111/j.1749-6632.2009.05143.x

Liu, J. X., Zerbo, E., & Ross, S. (2015). Intensive ketamine use for multiple years: A case report. *American Journal on Addictions, 24,* 7–9. doi:10.1111/ajad.12153

Liu, Y., Han, M., Liu, X., Deng, Y., Li, Y., Yuan, J., . . . Gao, J. (2013). Dopamine transporter availability in heroin-dependent subjects and controls: Longitudinal changes during abstinence and the effects of Jitai tablets treatment. *Psychopharmacology, 230*(2), 235–244. doi:10.1007/s00213-013-3148-z

Loflin, M., & Earleywine, M. (2014). A new method of cannabis ingestion: The dangers of dabs? *Addictive Behaviors, 39*(10), 1430–1433. doi:10.1016/j.addbeh.2014.05.013

Lopez-Quintero, C., Roth, K. B., Eaton, W. W., Wu, L-T., Cottler, L. B., Bruce, M., & Anthony, J. C. (2015). Mortality among heroin users and users of other internationally regulated drugs: A 27-year follow-up of users in the epidemiologic catchment area program household samples. *Drug and Alcohol Dependence.* doi:10.1016/j.drugalcdep.2015.08.030

McCabe, S. E., Cranford, J. A., & West, B. T. (2008). Trends in prescription drug abuse and dependence, co-occurrence with other substance use disorders, and treatment utilization: Results from two national surveys. *Addictive Behaviors, 33*(10), 1297–1305. doi:10.1016/j.addbeh.2008.06.005

McCabe, S. E., West, B. T., Morales, M., Cranford, J. A., & Boyd, C. J. (2007). Does early onset of non-medical use of prescription drugs predict subsequent prescription drug abuse and dependence? Results from a national study. *Addiction, 102*(12), 1920–1930. doi:10.1111/j.1360-0443.2007.02015.x

McQueeny, T., Padula, C. B., Price, J., Medina, K. L., Logan, P., & Tapert, S. F. (2011). Gender effects on amygdala morphometry in adolescent marijuana users. *Behavioural Brain Research, 224*(1), 128–134. doi:10.1016/j.bbr.2011.05.031

Maldonado, J. R., Nguyen, L. H., Schader, E. M., & Brooks, J. I. (2012). Benzodiazepine loading versus symptom-triggered treatment of alcohol withdrawal: A prospective, randomized clinical trial. *General Hospital Psychiatry, 34*(6), 611–617. doi:10.1016/j.genhosppsych.2012.06.016

Mariani, J. J., & Levin, F. R. (2012). Psychostimulant treatment of cocaine dependence. *Psychiatric Clinics of North America, 35,* 425–439. doi:10.1016/j.psc2012.03.012

Mathern, G. W., Beninsig, L., & Nehlig, A. (2015, January). Fewer specialists support using medical marijuana and CBD in treating epilepsy patients compared with other medical professionals and patients: Result of *Epilepsia*'s survey. *Epilepsia* (Series 4), 1–6. doi:10.1111/epi.12843.

Memo, L., Gnoato, E., Caminiti, S., Pichini, S., & Tarani, L. (2013). Fetal alcohol spectrum disorders and fetal alcohol syndrome: The state of the art and new diagnostic tools. *Early Human Development, 89*(Suppl 1), S40–S43. doi:10.1016/S0378-3782(13)70013-6

Meyer, K. D., & Zhang, L. (2009). Short-and long-term adverse effects of cocaine abuse during pregnancy on the heart development. *Therapeutic Advances in Cardiovascular Disease, 3*(1), 7–16.

Naloxone "Reboots" Opioid Pain-Relief System. (2010). *Pain Treatment Topics.* Retrieved from http://updates. pain-topics.org/2010/11/naloxone-reboots-opioid-pain-relief.html

National Institute on Drug Abuse. (2012a). *NIDA DrugFacts: Inhalants.* Retrieved from: https://www. drugabuse.gov/publications/drugfacts/inhalants

National Institute on Drug Abuse. (2012b). *NIDA DrugFacts: Anabolic steroids.* https://www.drugabuse. gov/publications/drugfacts/anabolic-steroids

National Institute on Drug Abuse. (2013a). *NIDA DrugFacts: Cocaine.* Retrieved from https://www. drugabuse.gov/publications/drugfacts/cocaine

National Institute on Drug Abuse. (2013b). *NIDA DrugFacts: MDMA (Ecstasy).* Retrieved from https:// www.drugabuse.gov/publications/drugfacts/ mdma-ecstasy-or-molly

National Institute on Drug Abuse. (2014a). *Drugs, brains, and behavior—The science of addiction.* Retrieved from https://www.drugabuse.gov/publications/drugs-brains-behavior-science-addiction/preface

National Institute on Drug Abuse. (2014b). *Nationwide trends.* Retrieved from https://www.drugabuse.gov/ publications/drugfacts/nationwide-trends

National Institute on Drug Abuse. (2014c). *NIDA DrugFacts: Club drugs (GHB, ketamine, and Rohypnol).* Retrieved from https://www.drugabuse.gov/ sites/default/files/drugfacts_clubdrugs_12_2014.pdf

National Institute on Drug Abuse. (2014d). *NIDA DrugFacts: Hallucinogens—LSD, peyote, psilocybin, and PCP.* Retrieved from https://teens.drugabuse.gov/ sites/default/files/hallucinogens_df_12_2014.pdf

National Institute on Drug Abuse. (2014e). *NIDA DrugFacts: Methamphetamine. Retrieved from* https:// www.drugabuse.gov/publications/drugfacts/ methamphetamine

National Institute on Drug Abuse. (2014f). NIDA *DrugFacts: Stimulant ADHD medications: Methylphenidate and amphetamines.* Retrieved from https://www.drugabuse.gov/publications/drugfacts/ stimulant-adhd-medications-methylphenidate-amphetamines

National Institute on Drug Abuse. (2015a). *Neuroscience Consortium.* Retrieved January 5, 2016, from

http://www.drugabuse.gov/about-nida/organization/ workgroups-interest-groups-consortia/neuroscience-consortium

National Institute on Drug Abuse. (2015b). *NIDA DrugFacts: Cigarettes and other tobacco products.* Retrieved from https://www.drugabuse.gov/publications/drugfacts/cigarettes-other-tobacco-products

National Institute on Drug Abuse. (2015c). *NIDA DrugFacts: Marijuana.* Retrieved from https://www. drugabuse.gov/publications/drugfacts/marijuana

National Institute on Drug Abuse. (2015d). *NIDA DrugFacts: Synthetic cannabinoids.* Retrieved from https://www.drugabuse.gov/publications/drugfacts/ synthetic-cannabinoids

Nelson, D. E., Jarman, D. W., Rehm, J., Greenfield, T. K., Rey, G., Kerr, W. C., . . . Naimi, T. S. (2013). Alcohol-attributable cancer deaths and years of potential life lost in the United States. *American Journal of Public Health, 103*, 641–648. doi:10.2105/ AJPH.2012.301199

Ogeil, R. P., Rajaratnam, S. M. W., & Broadbear, J. H. (2013). Male and female ecstasy users: Differences in patterns of use, sleep quality and mental health outcomes. *Drug and Alcohol Dependence, 132*, 223–230. doi:10.1016/j.drugalcdep.2013.02.002

Oklan, A. M., & Henderson, S. J. (2014). Treating inhalant abuse in adolescence: A recorded music expressive arts intervention. *Psychomusicology, 241*, 231–237. doi:10.1037/pmu0000058

Paton, A. (2015). Alcohol in the body. *ABC of Alcohol, 12.*

Peciña, S., & Berridge, K. C. (2013). Dopamine or opioid stimulation of nucleus accumbens similarly amplify cue triggered "wanting" for reward: Entire core and medial shell mapped as substrates for PIT enhancement. *European Journal of Neuroscience, 37*(9), 1529–1540. doi:10.1111/ejn.12174

Pope, H. J., Kanayama, G., Athey, A., Ryan, E., Hudson, J. I., & Baggish, A. (2014). The lifetime prevalence of anabolic androgenic steroid use and dependence in Americans: Current best estimates. *American Journal on Addictions, 23*(4), 371–377. doi:10.1111/j.1521-0391.2013.12118.x

Popova, S., Stade, B., Bekmuradov, D., Lange, S., & Rehm, J. (2011). What do we know about the economic impact of fetal alcohol spectrum disorder? A systematic literature review. *Alcohol and Alcoholism, 46*, 490–497. doi:10.1093/alcalc/agr029

Quickfall, J., & Crockford, D. (2006). Brain neuroimaging in cannabis use: A review. *Journal of Neuropsychology & Clinical Neurosciences, 18*, 318–332. doi:10.1176/appi. neuropsych.18.3.318

Rais, M., Wiepke, C., Van Haren, N., Schnack, H., Caspers, E., Hulshoff, H., & Kahn, R. (2008). Excessive brain volume loss over time in cannabis-using first-episode schizophrenia patients. *American Journal of Psychiatry, 165*, 490–496. doi: 10.1176/appi.ajp2007.07071110

Raj, V., Liang, H., Woodward, N., Bauernfeind, A., Lee, J., Dietrich, M., . . . Cowan, R. (2009). MDMA (Ecstasy) use is associated with reduced BOLD signal change during semantic recognition in abstinent human polydrug users: A preliminary fMRI study. *Journal of Psychopharmacology, 24*(2), 187–201. doi: 10.1177/0269881109103203

Rasmussen, N. (2009). *On speed: The many lives of amphetamine.* New York, NY: New York University Press.

Rehm, J., & Shield, K. D. (2013). Alcohol and mortality: Global alcohol-attributable deaths from cancer, liver cirrhosis, and injury in 2010. *Alcohol Research: Current Reviews, 35*(2), 174–183.

Rio, K. (2011). MDMA—The ecstasy. *Journal of Young Investigators, 21*(5).

Rogers, P. J., Heatherley, S. V., Mullings, E. L., & Smith, J. E. (2013). Faster but not smarter: Effects of caffeine and caffeine withdrawal on alertness and performance. *Psychopharmacology, 226*(2), 229–240. doi:10.1007/s00213-012-2889-4

Sayette, M. A., Creswell, K. G., Dimoff, J. D., Fairbairn, C. E., Cohn, J. F., Heckman, B. W., . . . Moreland, R. L. (2012). Alcohol and group formation: A multimodal investigation of the effects of alcohol on emotion and social bonding. *Psychological Science, 23*, 869–878. doi:10.1177/0956797611435134

Schore, A. N. (2014). The right brain is dominant in psychotherapy. *Psychotherapy, 51*(3), 388–397. doi:10.1037/a0037083

Scott-Sheldon, L. A. J., Carey, K. B., Elliott, J. C., Garey, L., & Carey, M. P. (2013). Efficacy of alcohol interventions for first-year college students: A meta-analytic review of randomized controlled trials. *Journal of Consulting and Clinical Psychology, 82*, 177–188. doi:10.1037/a0035192

Seely, K. A., Lapoint, J., Moran, J. H., & Fattore, L. (2012). Spice drugs are more than harmless herbal blends: A review of the pharmacology and toxicology of synthetic cannabinoids. *Progress in Neuro-psychopharmacology & Biological Psychiatry, 39*(2), 234–243. doi:10.1016/j.pnpbp.2012.04.017

Sherman, C. (2006). Drugs affect men's and women's brains differently. *National Institute on Drug Abuse,* 20(6). Retrieved from http://archives.drugabuse.gov/NIDA_Notes/NNVol20N6/Drugs.html

Shi, Y. (2014). At high risk and want to quit: Marijuana use among adults with depression or serious psychological distress. *Addictive Behaviors, 39*(4), 761–767. doi:10.1016/j.addbeh.2013.12.013

Shukla, R. K., Crump, J. L., & Chrisco, E. S. (2012). An evolving problem: Methamphetamine production and trafficking in the United States. *International Journal of Drug Policy, 23*(6), 426–435. doi:10.1016/j.drugpo.2012.07.004

Smith, P. H., Homish, G. G., Leonard, K. E., & Collins, R. L. (2013). Marijuana withdrawal and aggression among a representative sample of U.S. marijuana users. *Drug & Alcohol Dependence, 132*(1/2), 63–68. doi:10.1016/j.drugalcdep.2013.01.002

Spaderna, M., Addy, P. H., & D'Souza, D. C. (2013). Spicing things up: Synthetic cannabinoids. *Psychopharmacology, 228*(4), 525–540. doi:10.1007/s00213-013-3188-4

Staff. (2009). Migraine attacks may become more frequent due to certain medications. *Daily RX Relevant Health News.* Retrieved from http://dailyrx.com/news-article/migraine-attacks

Substance Abuse and Mental Health Services Administration. (2010). *Results from the 2009 National Survey on Drug Use and Health: Volume 1. Summary of national findings.* Office of Applied Studies, NSDUH Series H-38A, HHS Publication No. SMA 10-4856. Rockville, MD: Author.

Substance Abuse and Mental Health Services Administration. (2011). *Results from the 2010 National Survey on Drug Use and Health: National Findings.* Office of Applied Studies, NSDUH Series H-41, HHS Publication No. (SMA) 11–4658. Rockville, MD: Author.

Substance Abuse and Mental Health Services Administration. (2013). *Results from the 2012 National Survey on Drug Use and Health: Summary of national findings.* NSDUH Series H-46, HHS Publication No. (SMA) 13-4795. Rockville, MD: Author.

Substance Abuse and Mental Health Services Administration. (2014). *Results from the 2013 National Survey on Drug Use and Health: Summary of national findings.* NSDUH Series H-48, HHS Publication No. (SMA) 14-4863. Rockville, MD: Author.

Tan, K. R., Brown, M., Labouèbe, G., Yvon, C., Creton, C., Fritschy, J., . . . Lüscher, C. (2010). Neural bases for addictive properties of benzodiazepines. *Nature, 463*(7282), 769–774. doi:10.1038/nature08758

Tobias, M. C., O'Neill, J., Hudkins, M., Bartzokis, G., Dean, A. C., & London, E. D. (2010). White-matter abnormalities in brain during early abstinence from methamphetamine abuse. *Psychopharmacology, 209*(1), 13–24. doi: 10.1007/s00213-009- 1761-7

U.S. Department of Health and Human Services, Office on Smoking and Health. (2014). *The health consequences of smoking: 50 years of progress. A report of the Surgeon General.* Atlanta, GA: Author. Printed with corrections, January 2014.

Ukaigwe, A., Karmacharya, P., & Donato, A. (2014). A gut gone to pot: A case of cannabinoid hyperemesis syndrome due to K2, a synthetic cannabinoid. *Case Reports in Emergency Medicine*, 1–3. doi:10.1155/2014/167098

van Noorden, M. S., van Dongen, L. C., Zitman, F. G., & Vergouwen, T. A. (2009). Gamma-hydroxybutyrate withdrawal syndrome: Dangerous but not well-known. *General Hospital Psychiatry, 31,* 394–396. doi: 10.1016/j.genhosppsych.2008.11.001

Veterinary Practice News. (2010). Generic ketamine approved by FDA. Retrieved from www.veterinarypracticenews.com/vet-breaking-news/

Volkow, N. (2005). Inhalant abuse: Danger under the kitchen sink. *National Institute on Drug Abuse, 20*(3). Retrieved from http://archives.drugabuse.gov/NIDA_Notes/NNVol20N3/DirRepVol20N3.html

Volkow, N. (2006). Steroid abuse is a high-risk route to the finish line. *National Institute on Drug Abuse, 21*(1). Retrieved from https://www.drugabuse.gov/news-events/nida-notes/2006/10/steroid-abuse-high-risk-route-to-finish-line

Volkow, N. D., & Baler, R. D. (2015). NOW vs LATER brain circuits: Implications for obesity and addiction. *Trends in Neurosciences, 38*(6), 345–352. doi:10.1016/j.tins.2015.04.002

Volkow, N. D., Koob, G. F., & McLellan, A. T. (2016). Neurobiologic advances from the brain disease model of addiction. *New England Journal of Medicine, 374*(4), 363–371. doi:10.1056/NEJMra1511480

Warren, K. R. (2015). A review of the history of attitudes toward drinking in pregnancy. *Alcoholism: Clinical and Experimental Research, 39*(7), 1110–1117. doi:10.1111/acer.12757

Weisheit, R. A., & Wells, L. E. (2014). A comparison of criminological and public health models: Geographic and social diversity associated with methamphetamine laboratory seizures. *American Journal of Criminal Justice, 39*(1), 1–21. doi:10.1007/s12103-012-9197-8

Welch, K. A., Mcintosh, A. M., Job, D. E., Whalley, H. C., Moorhead, T. W., Hall, J., . . . Johnstone, E. C. (2010). The impact of substance use on brain structure in people at high risk of developing schizophrenia. *Oxford Journals.* doi: 10.1093/schbul/sbq013

Xue, G., Lu, Z., Levin, I., Weller, J., Li, X., & Bechara, A. (2009). Functional dissociations of risk and reward processing in the medial prefrontal cortex. *Cerebral Cortex, 19*(5), 1019–1027. doi: 10.1093/cercor/bhn147

Yucel, M., Solowij, N., Respondek, C., Whittle, S., Fornito, A., Pantelis, C., & Lubman, D. (2008). Regional brain abnormalities associated with long-term heavy cannabis use. *Archives of General Psychiatry, 65,* 694–701. Retrieved from http://archpsyc.ama.assn.org/cgi.content/abstract/65/6/694

Zaniewska, M., Filip, M., & Przegaliński, E. (2015). The involvement of norepinephrine in behaviors related to psychostimulant addiction. *Current Neuropharmacology, 13*(3), 407–418. doi:10.2174/1570159X13666150121225659

Zawilska, J. B., & Wojcieszak, J. (2014). Spice/K2 drugs—More than innocent substitutes for marijuana. *International Journal of Neuropsychopharmacology, 17*(3), 509–525. doi:10.1017/S1461145713000124

Zhang, Z., & Pan, Z. Z. (2010). Synaptic mechanism for functional synergism between δ - and μ-opioid receptors. *The Journal of Neuroscience, 30*(13), 4735–4745. doi:10.1523/JNEUROSCI.5968-09.2010

Chapter 4

Agrawal, A., & Lynskey, M. T. (2006). The genetic epidemiology of cannabis use, abuse and dependence. *Addiction, 101*(6), 801–812. doi:10.1111/j.1360-0443.2006.01399.x

Agrawal, A., & Lynskey, M. T. (2008). Are there genetic influences on addiction? Evidence from family, adoption, and twin studies. *Addiction, 103*(7), 1069–1081. doi: 10.1111/j.1360-0443.2008 .02213.x

Akins, S., Smith, C. L., & Mosher, C. (2010). Pathways to adult alcohol abuse across racial/ethnic groups: An application of general strain and social learning theories. *Journal of Drug Issues, 40,* 321–351.

Alcoholics Anonymous. (1976). *Is there an alcoholic in your life?* Retrieved from www.aa.org/pdf/products/p-30_isthereanalcoinyourlife1.pdf

Alcoholics Anonymous. (2002). *The Twelve Steps of Alcoholics Anonymous.* Retrieved from aa.org/en_pdfs/smf-121_en.pdf

American Medical Association. (1966). Drug dependencies as diseases. Policy Finder. H-95.983. Chicago: Author. Retrieved from www.ama-assn.org

American Psychiatric Association. (2013). *Diagnostic and statistical manual of mental disorders (5th ed.).* Washington, DC: Author.

Andreassen, C., Griffiths, M. D., Gjertsen, S., Krossbakken, E., Kvam, S., & Pallesen, S. (2013). The relationships between behavioral addictions and the five-factor model of personality. *Journal of Behavioral Addictions, 2*(2), 90–99.

Babor, T. F., & Caetano, R. (2006). Subtypes of substance dependence and abuse: Implications for diagnostic classification and empirical research. *Addiction, 101* (Suppl. 1), 104–110. doi:10.1111/j.1360-0443. 2006.01595.x

Babor, T. F., Hofmann, M., Del Boca, F., Hesselbrock, V., Meyer, R., Dolinsky, Z., & Rounsaville, B. (1992). Types of alcoholics, I. Evidence for an empirically-derived typology based on indicators of vulnerability and severity. *Archives of General Psychiatry, 49*(8), 599–608.

Bandura, A. (1977). *Social learning theory.* Englewood Cliffs, NJ: Prentice-Hall.

Barry, C. L., McGinty, E. E., Pescosolido, B. A., & Goldman, H. H. (2014). Stigma, discrimination, treatment effectiveness, and policy: Public views about drug addiction and mental illness. *Psychiatric Services, 65*(10), 1269–1272. doi:10.1176/appi.ps.201400140

Becker, H. C. (2008). Alcohol dependence, withdrawal, and relapse. *Alcohol Research & Health, 31*(4), 348–361. Retrieved from http://www.niaaa.nih.gov

Bryson, E., & Silverstein, J. (2008). Addiction and substance abuse in anesthesiology. *Anesthesiology, 109*(5), 905–917. doi:10.1097/ALN.0b013e3181895bc1

Burrow-Sanchez, J. J. (2006). Understanding adolescent substance abuse: Prevalence, risk factors, and clinical implications. *Journal of Counseling Development, 84,* 283–290.

Calabrese, E. J. (2008). Addiction and dose response: The psychomotor stimulant theory of addiction reveals that hermetic dose responses are dominant. *Critical Reviews in Toxicology, 38,* 599–617. doi:101080/104084402026315

Calafat, A., García, F., Juan, M., Becoña, E., & Fernández-Hermida, J. R. (2014). Which parenting style is more protective against adolescent substance use? Evidence within the European context. *Drug and Alcohol Dependence, 138,* 185–192. doi:10.1016/j.drugalcdep.2014.02.705

Carbaugh, R. J., & Sias, S. M. (2010). Comorbidity of bulimia nervosa and substance abuse: Etiologies, treatment issues, and treatment approaches. *Journal of Mental Health Counseling, 32*(2), 125–138.

Chastain, G. (2006). Alcohol, neurotransmitter systems, and behavior. *Journal of General Psychology, 133*(4), 329–335. doi:10.3200/GENP.133.4.329-335

Ciesla, J. R. (2010). Evaluating the risk of relapse for adolescents treated for substance abuse. *Addictive Disorders & Their Treatment, 9*(2), 87–92. doi:10.1097/ADT.0b013e3181b8cd05

Clark, H. K., Shamblen, S. R., Ringwalt, C. L., & Hanley, S. (2012). Predicting high risk adolescents' substance use over time: The role of parental monitoring. *Journal of Primary Prevention, 33*(2–3), 67–77. doi:10.1007/s10935-012-0266-z

Cloninger, C. R., Bohman, M., & Sigvardsson, S. (1981). Inheritance of alcohol abuse: Cross-fostering analysis of adopted men. *Archives of General Psychiatry, 38*(3), 861–868.

Costa, P. T., Jr., & McCrae, R. R. (1985). *The NEO personality inventory manual.* Odessa, FL: Psychological Assessment Resources.

Daughters, S. D., Gorka, S., Matusiewicz, A., & Anderson, K. (2013). Gender specific effect of psychological stress and cortisol reactivity on adolescent risk taking. *Journal of Abnormal Child Psychology, 41*(5), 749–758.

Demetrovics, Z. (2009). Co-morbidity of drug addiction: An analysis of epidemiological data and possible etiological models. *Addiction Research and Theory, 17*(4), 420–431. doi:10.1080/16066350802601324

Dennis, M., & Scott, C. K. (2007). Managing addiction as a chronic condition. *Addiction Science and Clinical Practice, 4*(1), 45–55.

DePue, M. K. (2013). The relationship of the bottoming out experience and the cognitive shift from drinker to nondrinker on early recovery for substance use disorders in treatment settings (Unpublished doctoral dissertation). University of Central Florida, Orlando, FL.

DePue, M. K., Finch, A. J., & Nation, M. (2014). In search for rock bottom: A phenomenological study of the alcoholic's "rock bottom" and its relationship to change. *Journal of Addictions & Offender Counseling, 35*(4), 38–56. doi:10.1002/j.2161-1874.2014.00023.x

Dick, D. M., & Agrawal, A. (2008). The genetics of alcohol and other drug dependence. *Alcohol Research & Health, 31*(2), 111–118. Retrieved from http://www.niaaa.nih.gov

Dolan, S. L., Rohsenow, D. J., Martin, R. A., & Monti, P. M. (2013). Urge-specific and lifestyle coping strategies of alcoholics: Relationships of specific strategies to treatment outcome. *Drug and Alcohol Dependence, 128*(1–2), 8–14. doi:10.1016/j.drugalcdep.2012.07.010

Doweiko, H. E. (2011). *Concepts of chemical dependency* (8th ed.). Pacific Grove, CA: Brooks/Cole.

Draus, P., Roddy, J., & Greenwald, M. (2012). Heroin mismatch in the Motor City: Addiction, segregation, and the geography of opportunity. *Journal of Ethnicity in Substance Abuse, 11*(2), 149–173. doi:10.1080/1533 2640.2012.675246

du Plessis, G. P. (2012). Toward an integral model of addiction: By means of integral methodological pluralism as a metatheoretical and integrative conceptual framework. *Journal of Integral Theory and Practice, 7*(3), 1–24.

Ducci F., & Goldman, D. (2012). The genetic basis of addictive disorders. *Psychiatric Clinics of North America, 35*, 495–519.

Everitt, B. J. (2014). Neural and psychological mechanisms underlying compulsive drug seeking habits and drug memories—Indications for novel treatments of addiction. *European Journal of Neuroscience, 40*(1), 2163–2182. doi:10.1111/ejn.12644

Faulkner, C. A., & Faulkner, S. S. (2009). *Research methods for social workers: A practice-based approach* (p. 9). Chicago, IL: Lyceum Books. Retrieved from http://lyceumbooks.com/default2.htm

Ferguson, C. J., & Meehan, D. C. (2011). With friends like these. . . : Peer delinquency influences across age cohorts on smoking, alcohol and illegal substance use. *European Psychiatry, 26*(1), 6–12. doi:10.1016/j.eurpsy.2010.09.002

Foroud, T., Edenberg, H. J., & Crabbe, J. C. (2010). Genetic research: Who is at risk for alcoholism? *Alcohol Research & Health, 33*(1/2), 64–75. Retrieved from http://www.niaaa.nih.gov

Fox, H. C., Bergquist, K. L., Hong, K. I., & Sinha, R. (2007). Stress-induced and alcohol cue-induced craving in recently abstinent alcohol dependent individuals. *Alcoholism: Clinical and Experimental Research, 31*(3), 395–403. doi:10.1111/j.1530-0277.2006. 00320.x

Giordano, A. L., Prosek, E. A., Daly, C. M., Holm, J. M., Ramsey, Z. B., Abernathy, M. R., & Sender, K. M. (2015). Exploring the relationship between religious coping and spirituality among three types of collegiate substance abuse. *Journal of Counseling & Development, 93*(1), 70–79.

Glatt, M. M. (1975). Today's enjoyment—Tomorrow's dependency: The road towards the "rock bottom" and the way back. In M. M. Glatt & C. M. Idestrom (Eds.), *British Journal of Addiction to Alcohol and Other Drugs, 70*(Supplement No.1).

Gourley, M. (2004). A subcultural study of recreational ecstasy use. *Journal of Sociology, 40*(1), 59–73. doi:10.1177/1440783304040453

Graham, M. D., Young, R. A., Valach, L., & Wood, R. A. (2008). Addiction as a complex social process: An action theoretical perspective. *Addiction Research and Theory, 16*(2), 121–133. doi:10.1080/16066350701794543

Gurman, A. S., & Messer, S. B. (2003). *Essential psychotherapies: Theory and practice.* New York, NY: Guilford.

Harakeh, Z., Scholte, R. H. J., de Vries, H., & Engels, R. C. M. E. (2006). Association between personality and adolescent smoking. *Addictive Behaviors, 31*, 232–245. doi:10.1016/j.addbeh.2005.05.003

Hasin, D., Samet, S., Nunes, E., Meydan, J., Matseoane, K., & Waxman, R. (2006). Diagnosis of comorbid psychiatric disorders on substance users assessed with the psychiatric research interview for substance and mental disorders for DSM-IV. *American Journal of Psychiatry, 163*, 689–696. doi: 10.1176/appi.ajp.163.4.689

Hayatbakhsh, R., Williams, G. M., Bor, W., & Najman, J. M. (2013). Early childhood predictors of age of initiation to use of cannabis: A birth prospective study. *Drug and Alcohol Review, 32*(3), 232–240. doi:10.1111/j.1465-3362.2012.00520.

Henden, E., Melberg, H. O., & Røgeberg, O. J. (2013). Addiction: Choice or compulsion? *Frontiers in Psychiatry, 4*, 77.

Hicks, B. M., Iacono, W. G., & McGue, M. (2012). Index of the transmissible common liability to addiction: Heritability and prospective associations with substance abuse and related outcomes. *Drug and Alcohol Dependence, 123S*, S18–S23. doi:10.1016/j.drugalcdep.2011.12.017

Hopwood, C. J., Morey, L. C., Skodol, A. E., Stout, R. L., Yen, S., Ansell, E. B., . . . McGlashan, T. H. (2007). Five-factor model personality traits associated with alcohol-related diagnosis in a clinical sample. *Journal of Studies on Alcohol and Drugs, 68*(3), 455–461.

Humensky, J. L. (2010). Are adolescents with high socioeconomic status more likely to engage in alcohol and illicit drug use in early adulthood? *Substance Abuse Treatment, Prevention, and Policy, 5*, 19–29. doi:10.1186/1747-597x-5-19

Jackson, K. F., & LeCroy, C. W. (2009). The influence of race and ethnicity on substance use and negative activity involvement among monoracial and multiracial adolescents of the Southwest. *Journal of Drug Education, 39*(2), 195–210. Retrieved from http://www.ncbi.nlm.nih.gov/pubmed/19999705

Jellinek, E. M. (1946). Phases in the drinking history of alcoholics: Analysis of a survey conducted by the official organ of alcoholics anonymous. *Quarterly Journal of Studies on Alcohol, 7*, 1–88.

Jellinek, E. M., (1960). *The disease concept of alcoholism.* New Haven, CT: Hillhouse.

Johnston, L. D., O'Malley, P. M., Bachman, J. G., & Schulenberg, J. E. (2011). *Monitoring the Future: National results on adolescent drug use: Overview of key findings, 2010.* Ann Arbor, MI: Institute for Social Research, University of Michigan. Retrieved from http://monitoringthefuture.org

Kendler, K. S., Ohlsson, H., Sundquist, K., & Sundquist, J. (2014). The causal nature of the association between neighborhood deprivation and drug abuse: A prospective national Swedish co-relative control study. *Psychological Medicine, 44*(12), 2537–2546. doi:10.1017/S0033291713003048

Keyes, K. M., Li, G., & Hasin, D. S. (2011). Birth cohort effects and gender differences in alcohol epidemiology: A review and synthesis. *Alcoholism: Clinical and Experimental Research, 35*(12), 2101–2112. doi:10.1111/j.1530-0277.2011.01562.x

Kienast, T., Stoffers, J., Bermpohl, F., & Lieb, K. (2014). Borderline personality disorder and comorbid addiction. *Deutsches Ärzteblatt International, 111*(16), 280–286.

King, S. M., Keyes, M., Malone, S. M., Elkins, I., Legrand, L. N., Iacono, W. G., & McGrue, M. (2009). Parental alcohol dependence and the transmission of adolescent behavioral disinhibition: A study of adoptive and non-adoptive families. *Addiction, 104*(4), 578–586. doi: 10.1111/ j.1360-0443.2008.02469.x

Komro, K. A., Tobler, A. L., Maldonado-Molina, M. M., & Perry, C. L. (2010). Effects of alcohol use initiation patterns on high-risk behaviors among urban, low-income, young adolescents. *Prevention Science, 11*(1), 14–23. doi:10.1007/s11121-009-0144-y

Kouimtsidis, C. (2010). Cognitive theories of addiction: A narrative review. *Psychiatriki, 21*(4), 315–323.

Kovac, V. B. (2013). The more the "Merrier": A multi-sourced model of addiction. *Addiction Research & Theory, 21*(1), 19–32. doi:10.3109/16066359.2012.691581

Kornør, H., & Nordvik, H. (2007). Five-factor model personality traits in opioid dependence. *BMC Psychiatry, 7.* doi:10.1186/1471-244X-7-37

Le Moal, M., & Koob, G. F. (2007). Drug addiction: Pathways to the disease and pathophysiological perspectives. *European Neuropsychopharmacology, 17*(6–7), 377–393. doi:10.16/j .euroneuro.2006.10.006

Leggio, L., Kenna, G. A., Fenton, M., Bonenfant, E., & Swift, R. M. (2009). Typologies of alcohol dependence. From Jellinek to genetics and beyond. *Neuropsychology Review, 19*(1), 115–129. doi:10.1007/s11065-008-9080-z

Luo, X., Kranzler, H. R., Zuo, L., Wang, S., & Gelernter, J. (2007). Personality traits of agreeableness and extra-version are associated with ADH4 variation. *Biological Psychiatry, 61*(5), 599–608. doi:10.1016/j.biopsych.2006.05.017

Lynskey, M. T., Nelson, E. C., Neuman, R. J., Bucholz, K. K., Madden, P. A., Knopik, V. S., . . . Heath, A. C. (2005). Limitations of DSM-IV operationalizations of alcohol abuse and dependence in a sample of Australian twins. *Twin Research and Human Genetics, 8*(6), 574–584. doi:10.1375/183242705774860178

McLellan, A., Lewis, D., O'Brien, C., & Kleber, H. D. (2000). Drug dependence, a chronic medical illness: implications for treatment, insurance, and outcomes evaluation. *JAMA: The Journal of The American Medical Association, 284*(13), 1689–1695.

Moore, S., Montaine-Jaime, L., Carr, L., & Ehlers, C. (2007). Variations in alcohol metabolizing enzymes in people of East-Indian and African descent from Trinidad and Tobago. *Alcohol Research & Health, 30*(1), 18–21. Retrieved from http://www.niaaa.nih.gov

Moos, R. (2007). Theory-based processes that promote the remission of substance use disorders. *Clinical Psychology Review, 27*(5), 537–551. doi:10.1016/j.cpr.2006.12.006

Moss, H. B., Chen, M. C., & Yi, H. (2007). Subtypes of alcohol dependence in a nationally representative sample. *Drug and Alcohol Dependence, 9*(2–3), 149–158. doi:10.1016/j.drugalcdep.2007.05.016

National Institute on Alcohol Abuse and Alcoholism. (1995). *Diagnostic criteria for alcohol abuse and dependence.* Alcohol Alert, No. 30, PH 359. Bethesda, MD: Author. Retrieved from http://pubs.niaaa.nih.gov/publications/aa30.htm

National Institute on Alcohol Abuse and Alcoholism. (2005). Module 10-H: *Ethnicity, culture and alcohol.* Participant handout.

NIAAA: Social Work Education for the Prevention and Treatment of Alcohol Use Disorders. Updated March 2005. Retrieved from http://pubs.niaaa.nih.gov/publications/Social/Module10HEthnicity&Culture/Module10H.html

National Prohibition Act of 1919, Pub. L. No. 66-66, 41 Stat. 305 (1919). Retrieved from http://www.encyclopedia.com/history/encyclopedias-almanacs-transcripts-and-maps/national-prohibition-act-1919

Nurnberger, Jr., J. I., & Bierut, L. J. (2007). Seeking the connections: Alcoholism and our genes. *Scientific American, 296*(4), 46–53. doi:10.1038/scientificamerican0407-46

Park, S., Kim, H., & Kim, H. (2009). Relationships between parental alcohol abuse and social support, peer substance abuse risk and social support, and substance abuse risk among South Korean adolescents. *Family Therapy, 36*(1), 50–62.

Pietrzykowski, A. Z., & Treistman, S. N. (2008). The molecular basis of tolerance. *Alcohol Research & Health, 31*(4). Retrieved from http://www.niaaa.nih.gov

Riley, B. P., Kalsi, G., Kuo, P-H., Vladimirov, V., Thiselton, D. L., & Kendler, K. S. (2006). Alcohol dependence is associated with the ZNF699 gene, a human locus related to drosophila hangover, in the Irish affected sib pair study of alcohol dependence (IASPSAD) sample. *Molecular Psychiatry, 11*, 1025–1031. doi:10.1038/sj.mp.4001891

Rolison, J. J., Hanoch, Y., Wood, S., & Liu, P. (2014). Risk-taking differences across the adult life span: A question of age and domain. *Journals of Gerontology Series B: Psychological Sciences & Social Sciences, 69*(6), 870–880.

Room, R. (2005). Stigma, social inequality and alcohol and drug use. *Drug and Alcohol Review, 24*(2), 143–155. doi:10.1080/09595230500102434

Saatcioglu, O., Erim, R., & Cakmak, D. (2006). Role of family in alcohol and substance abuse. *Psychiatry and Clinical Neurosciences, 60*, 125–132.

Salas-Wright, C. P., Clark, T. T., Vaughn, M. G., & Cordóva, D. (2015). Profiles of acculturation among Hispanics in the United States: Links with discrimination and substance use. *Social Psychiatry and Psychiatric Epidemiology, 50*(1), 39–49. doi:10.1007/s00127-014-0889-x

Samel, A. N., Sondergeld, T. A., Fischer, J. M., & Patterson, N. C. (2011). The secondary school pipeline: Longitudinal indicators of resilience and resistance in urban schools under reform. *High School Journal, 94*(3), 95–118.

Schlaepfer, I. R., Hoft, N. R., & Ehringer, M. A. (2008). The genetic components of alcohol and nicotine co-addiction: From genes to behavior. *Current Drug Abuse Review, 1*(2), 124–134. Retrieved from http://www.ncbi.nlm.nih.gov/pmc/articles/PMC2600802/

Scholz, H., Franz, M., & Heberlein, U. (2005). The "hangover" gene defines a stress pathway required for ethanol tolerance development [letter]. *Nature, 436*(7052), 845–847. doi: 10.1038/nature03864

Scholz, H., Ramond, J., Singh, C. M., & Heberlein, L. (2000). Functional ethanol tolerance in *Drosophila*. *Neuron, 28*(1), 261–271. Retrieved from http://www.ncbi.nlm.nih.gov/pubmed/11086999

Schneider, S., Peters, J., Bromberg, U., Brassen, S., Miedl, S. F., Banaschewski, T., . . . Büchel, C. (2012). Risk taking and the adolescent reward system: A potential common link to substance abuse. *American Journal of Psychiatry, 169*(1), 39–46. doi:10.1176/appi.ajp.2011.11030489

Schuckit, M., Smith, T., & Danko, G. (2007). A comparison of factors associated with substance-induced versus independent depressions. *Journal of Studies of Alcohol and Drugs, 68*(6), 805–812.

Scott, D., & Taylor, R. (2007). Health related effects of genetic variations of alcohol metabolizing enzymes in African Americans. *Alcohol Research & Health, 30*(1), 18–21. Retrieved from http://www.niaaa.nih.gov

Sigvardsson, S., Bohman, M., & Cloninger, C. R. (1996). Replication of the Stockholm Adoption Study of alcoholism: Confirmatory cross-fostering analysis. *Archives of General Psychiatry, 53*(8), 681–687.

Silverman, K., DeFulio, A., & Sigurdsson, S. O. (2012). Maintenance of reinforcement to address the chronic nature of drug addiction. *Preventive Medicine, 55*(Suppl), S46–S53. doi:10.1016/j.ypmed.2012.03.013

Sinha, R., Fox, H., Hong, K. A., Bergquist, K., Bhagwagar, Z., & Siedlarz, K. M. (2009). Enhanced negative emotion and alcohol craving, and altered physiological responses following stress and cue exposure in alcohol dependent individuals. *Neuropsychopharmacology, 34*(5), 1198–1208. doi:10.1038/npp.2008.78

Sjoerds, Z., Luigjes, J., van den Brink, W., Denys, D., & Yücel, M. (2014). The role of habits and motivation in human drug addiction: A reflection. *Frontiers in Psychiatry, 5*, 8. doi:10.3389/fpsyt.2014.00008

Smirnov, A., Najman, J. M., Hayatbakhsh, R., Wells, H., Legosz, M., & Kemp, R. (2013). Young adults' recreational social environment as a predictor of Ecstasy use initiation: Findings of a population-based prospective study. *Addiction, 108*(10), 1809–1817. doi:10.1111/add.12239

Stafström, M. (2014). Influence of parental alcohol-related attitudes, behavior and parenting styles on alcohol use in late and very late adolescence. *European Addiction Research, 20*(5), 241–247. doi:10.1159/000357319

Staiger, P. K., Richardson, B., Long, C. M., Carr, V., & Marlatt, G. A. (2013). Overlooked and underestimated? Problematic alcohol use in clients recovering from drug dependence. *Addiction, 108*(7), 1188–1193. doi:10.1111/j.1360-0443.2012.04075.x

Substance Abuse and Mental Health Services Administration. (2014). *Results from the 2013 National Survey on Drug Use and Health: Summary of national findings:* NSDUH Series H-41.

Sum, A., Khatiwada, I., McLaughlin, J., & Palma, S. (2011). No country for young men: Deteriorating labor market prospects for low-skilled men in the United States. *Annals of the American Academy of Political & Social Science, 635*, 24–55.

Terracciano, A., Löckenhoff, C. E., Crum, R. M., Bienvenu, J. O., & Costa, Jr., P. T. (2008). Five-factor model personality profiles of drug users. *BMC Psychiatry, 8*, 22–32. doi:10.1186/1471-244X-8-22

Urbanoski, K. A., & Kelly, J. F. (2012). Understanding genetic risk for substance use and addiction: A guide for non-geneticists. *Clinical Psychology Review, 32*(1), 60–70. doi:10.1016/j.cpr.2011.11.002

U.S. Department of Health and Human Services. (2008). Alcohol: A women's health issue. *National Institutes of Health: The Office of Research on Women's Health. Revised 2008.* Retrieved from http://pubs.niaaa.nih.gov/publications/brochure-women/women.htm

Venner, K. L., & Miller, W. R. (2001). Progression of alcohol problems in a Navajo sample. *Journal of Studies on Alcohol, 62*(2), 158–165.

Volkow, N. D., Fowler, J. S., & Wang, G. J. (2004). The addicted human brain viewed in the light of imaging studies: Brain circuits and treatment strategies. *Neuropharmacology, 47*(1), 3–13. doi: 10.1016/j.neuropharm.2004.07.019

Walther, B., Morgenstern, M., & Hanewinkel, R. (2012). Co-occurrence of addictive behaviours: Personality factors related to substance use, gambling and computer gaming. *European Addiction Research, 18*(4), 167–174. doi:10.1159/000335662

White, W. (2009). *Long-term strategies to reduce the stigma attached to addiction, treatment, and recovery within the City of Philadelphia (with particular reference to medication-assisted treatment/recovery).* Philadelphia, PA: Department of Behavioral Health and Mental Retardation Services. Retrieved from http://www.williamwhitepapers.com/pr/2009Stigma%26methadone.pdf

Wise, R. A., & Koob, G. F. (2014). The development and maintenance of drug addiction. *Neuropsychopharmacology, 39*(2), 254–262. doi:10.1038/npp.2013.261

Wu, L.-T., Swartz, M. S., Brady, K. T., Blazer, D. G., & Hoyle, R. H. (2014). Nonmedical stimulant use among young Asian-Americans, Native Hawaiians/Pacific Islanders, and mixed-race individuals aged 12–34 years in the United States. *Journal of Psychiatric Research, 59*, 189–199. doi:10.1016/j.jpsychires.2014.09.004

Yin, H. H. (2008). From actions to habits: Neuroadaptations leading to dependence. *Alcohol Research & Health, 31*(4), 340–344.

Chapter 5

American Psychiatric Association. (2000). *Diagnostic and statistical manual of mental disorders* (4th ed.—text revision). Washington, DC: Author.

American Psychiatric Association. (2013). *Diagnostic and statistical manual of mental disorders* (5th ed.). Washington, DC: Author.

American Society of Addiction Medicine. (2007). *Second edition—revised of Patient Placement Criteria (ASAM PPC-2R).* Chevy Chase, MD: Author. Retrieved from http://198.65.155.172/PatientPlacementCriteria.html.

Babor, T., McRee, B., Kassebaum, P., Grimaldi, P., Ahmed, K., & Bray, J. (2007). Screening, Brief Intervention, and Referral to Treatment (SBIRT). *Substance Abuse, 28*(3), 7–30.

Bender, K., Tripodi, S., & Rock, J. (2013). Adolescents. In M. G. Vaughn & B. E. Perron (Eds.), *Social work practice in the addictions.* New York, NY: Springer.

Bones, T. B., Bailey, B. A., & Sokol, R. J. (2013). Alcohol use in pregnancy: Insights in screening interventions for clinicians. *Clinical Obstetrics and Gynecology, 56*(1), 114–123. doi:10.1097/GRF.0b013e31827957c0

Burck, A. M., Laux, J. M., Ritchie, M., & Baker, D. (2008). An examination of the Substance Abuse Subtle Screening Inventory-3 Correctional scale in a college student population. *Journal of Addictions & Offender Counseling, 29*, 49–61. doi:10.1002/j.2161-1874.2008.tb00043.x

Celio, M., Vetter-O'Hagen, C. S., Lisman, S. A., Johansen, Gerard, J. E., & Spear, L. P. (2011). Integrating field methodology and web-based data collection to assess the reliability of the Alcohol Use Disorders Identification test (AUDIT). *Drug and Alcohol Dependence, 119*, 142–144.

Connell, M. (2015). Expert testimony in sexual assault cases: Alcohol intoxication and memory. *International Journal of Law and Psychiatry, 42–43*, 98–105. doi:10.1016/j.ijlp.2015.08.013

Craig, R. J. (2004). Counseling the alcohol and drug dependent client. New York, NY: WW Norton & Company, Inc.

Creighton, G., Oliffe, J., Matthews, J., & Saewyc, E. (2016). Dulling the edges: Young men's use of alcohol to deal with grief following the death of a male friend. *Health Education & Behavior 43*(1), 54–60. doi:10.1177/1090198115596164.

Dailey, S. F., Gill, C. S., Karl, S. L., & Barrio Minton, C. A. (2014). *DSM-5 learning companion for counselors*. Alexandria, VA: American Counseling Association.

Dawson, D. A., Goldstein, R. B., & Grant, B. F. (2013). Differences in the profiles of DSM-IV and DSM-5 alcohol use disorders: implications for clinicians. *Alcohol Clinical Experiential Research, 37*(1), 305–313. doi:10.1111/j.1530-0277.2012.01930.x.

Di Pierro, R., Preti, E., Vurro, N., & Madeddu, F. (2014). Dimensions of personality structure among patients with substance use disorders and co-occurring personality disorders: A comparison with psychiatric outpatients and healthy controls. *Comprehensive Psychiatry, 55*, 1398–1404. doi:10.1016/j.comppsych.2014.04.005

Doweiko, H. E. (2015). *Concepts of chemical dependency* (9th ed.). Stamford, CT: Cengage Learning.

Earnshaw, V. A., Smith, L. R., Cunningham, C. O., Copenhaver, M. M. (2015). Intersectionality of internalized HIV stigma and internalized substance use stigma. *Journal of Health Psychology, 20*(8), 1083–1089. doi:10.1177/1359105313507964

Ferrari, A. J., Norman, R. E., Freedman, G., Baxter, A. J., Pirkis, J. E., Harris, M. G., . . . Whiteford, H. A. (2014). The burden attributable to mental and substance use disorders as risk factors for suicide: Findings from the global burden of disease study 2010. *PLoS One, 9*(4), 1–11.

Fureman, B., Parikh, G., Bragg, A., & McLellan, A. (1990). *Addiction severity index (5th edition): A guide to training and supervising ASI interviews based on the past ten years*. Philadelphia, PA: University of Penn/VA Center for Studies of Addiction.

Graham, J. R. (1990). MMPI-2: *Assessing personality and psychopathology*. New York, NY: Oxford University Press.

Hart, C. L., & Ksir, C. (2013). *Drugs, society & human behavior* (15th ed.). New York, NY: McGraw-Hill.

Heinemann, A. W., Moore, D., Lazowski, L. E., Huber, M., & Semik, P. (2014). Benefits of substance use disorder screening on employment outcomes in state-federal vocational rehabilitation programs. *Rehabilitation Counseling Bulletin, 57*(3), 144–158.

Hodgson, R. J., John, B., Abbasi, T., Hodgson, R. C., Waller, S., Thom, B., & Newcombe, R. B. (2003). Fast screening for alcohol misuse. *Addictive Behaviors, 28*, 1453–1463.

Hoffman, N. G., Halikas, J. A., Mee-Lee, D., & Weedman, R. D. (1991). *ASAM patient placement criteria for the treatment of psychoactive substance use disorders*. Washington, DC: American Society of Addiction Medicine.

Huber, M., Keferl, J. E., Lazowski, L. E., Heinemann, A. W., & Moore, D. (2011). A comparison of didactic and learner-centered training models for substance abuse screening: Considerations for administrators. *Journal of Rehabilitation Administration, 35*(2), 95–104.

Huntley, Z., & Young, Y. (2014). Alcohol and substance use history among ADHD adults: The relationship with persistent and remitting symptoms, personality, employment, and history of service use. *Journal of Attention Disorders, 19*(1), 82–90. doi:10.1177/1087054712446171

Hupp, S. D. A., & Jewell, J. D. (2010). Brief report on assessing common rationalizations for drinking and driving: Comparisons of a DUI court group and traffic court control group. *Impaired Driving Update, Summer*.

Kessler, F., Cacciola, J., Alterman, A., Faller, S., Souza-Formigoni, M. L., Cruz, M. S., . . . Pechansky, F. (2012). Psychometric properties of the sixth version of the Addiction Severity Index (ASI-6) in Brazil. *Revista Brasileira De Psiquiatria, 34*(1), 24–33.

Kim, Y. (2009). Korean version of the Revised Problem-Oriented Screening Instrument for Teenagers Substance Use/Abuse Scale: A validation study. *Journal of Social Service Research, 36*(1), 37–45.

Kinney, J. (2015. *Loosening the grip: A handbook of alcohol information* (11th ed.). New York, NY: McGraw-Hill.

Klein, C., di Menza, S., Arfken, C., & Schuster, C. R. (2002). Interaction effects of treatment setting and client characteristics on retention and completion. *Journal of Psychoactive Drugs, 34*(1), 39–50.

Kulesza, M., Ramsey, S. E., Brown, R., & Larimer, M. E. (2014). The relationship between treatment for substance use disorders and stigma. *Drug and Alcohol Dependence, 140*, e112–e113. doi:10.1016/j.drugalcdep.2014.02.323

Laux, J. M., Piazza, N. J., Salyers, K., & Roseman, C. P. (2012). The Substance Abuse Subtle Screening Inventory-3 and stages of change: A screening validity study. *Journal of Addictions & Offender Counseling, 33*, 82–92.

Laux, J. M., Perera-Diltz, D. M., Calmes, S. A., Behl, M., & Vasquez, J. (2016). Assessment and diagnosis of addictions. In Capuzzi & Stauffer (Eds.), *Foundations of addictions counseling* (3rd Ed.). Boston, MA: Pearson.

Lewis, J. A., Dana, R. Q., & Blevins, G. A. (2015). *Substance abuse counseling* (5th ed.). Stamford, CT: Cengage Learning.

Livingston, J. D., Milne, T., Fang, M. L., & Amari, E. (2012). The effectiveness of interventions for reducing stigma related to substance use disorders: A systematic review. *Addiction, 107*(1), 39–50. doi:10.1111/j.1360-0443.2011.03601.x

Lundin, A., Hallgren, M., Balliu, N., & Forsell, Y. (2015). The use of Alcohol Use Disorders Identification Test (AUDIT) in detecting alcohol use disorder and risk drinking in the general population: Validation of AUDIT using schedules for clinical assessment in neuropsychiatry. *Alcoholism: Clinical and Experimental Research, 39*(1), 158–165. doi:10.1111/acer.12593

Magura, S., Fong, C., Staines, G. L., Cleland, C., Foote, J., Rosenblum, A., . . . DeLuca, A. (2005). The combined effects of treatment intensity, self-help groups and patient attributes on drinking outcomes. *Journal of Psychoactive Drugs, 37*(1), 85–92.

Mancini, M. (2013). Assessment strategies for substance use disorders. In M. G. Vaughn & B. E. Perron (Eds.), *Social work practice in the addictions.* New York, NY: Springer.

Marsiglia, F. F., & Booth, J. (2013). Empirical status of culturally competent practices. In M. G. Vaughn & B. E. Perron (Eds.), *Social work practice in the addictions.* New York, NY: Springer.

Mattoo, S. K., Sarkar, S., Nebhinani, N., Gupta, S., Parakh, P., & Basu, D. (2015). How do Indian substance users perceive stigma towards substance use vis-à-vis their family members? *Journal of Ethnicity in Substance Abuse, 14*(3), 223–231. doi:10.1080/15332640.2014.980960

McCabe, P. J., Christopher, P. P., Druhn, N., Roy-Bujnowski, K. M., Grudzinskas, A. J., & Fisher, W. H. (2012). Arrest types and co-occurring disorders in persons with schizophrenia or related psychoses. *Journal of Behavioral Health Services and Research, 39*(3), 271–284. doi:10.1007/s11414-011-9269-4

Mee-Lee, D. (2014, March). What's new in DSM-5 and the new ASAM criteria? Implications in an era of health-care reform. *The Addiction Technology Transfer Center Network Messenger.* Retrieved from http://www.attc-network.org/find/news/attcnws/epubs/addmsg/ATTCmessengerMarch2014articleDSM5_ASAM.pdf.

Mericle, A. A., Park, V. M. T., Holck, P., & Arria, A. M. (2012). Prevalence, patterns, and correlates of co-occurring substance use and mental disorders in the United States: variations by race/ethnicity. *Comprehensive Psychiatry, 53*, 657–665. doi:10.1016/j.comppsych.2011.10.002

Miller, G. (1997). *The Substance Abuse Subtle Screening Inventory-3.* Bloomington, IN: SASSI Institute.

Miller, W. R., & Rollnick, S. (1991). Motivational interviewing: Preparing people to change addictive behavior. New York, NY: Guilford.

Myers, P. L., & Salt, N. R. (2013). *Becoming an addictions counselor: A comprehensive text* (3rd ed.). Boston, MA: Jones & Bartlett.

New York State Education Department. (2014). *Office of professions. Mental health practitioners.* Retrieved from http://www.op.nysed.gov/prof/mhp/article163.htm

New York State Education Department. (2015). *Office of professions. Psychology.* Retrieved from http://www.op.nysed.gov/prof/psych/article153.htm

Prochaska, J. O., & DiClemente, C. C. (1982). Transtheoretical therapy: Toward a more integrative model of change. *Psychotherapy Theory, Research, and Practice, 19,* 276–288.

Prochaska, J. O., & DiClemente, C. C. (1984). *The transtheoretical approach: Crossing traditional boundaries of therapy.* Homewood, IL: Dow Jones/Irwin.

Rahdert, E. R. (1991). *The adolescent assessment/referral system manual* (DHHS Publication No. ADM 91-1735).

Russell, M. (1994) New assessment tools for risk drinking during pregnancy. *Alcohol Health & Research World, 18,* 55–61.

Selzer, M. L. (1971). The Michigan alcoholism screening test: The quest for a new diagnostic instrument. *American Journal of Psychiatry, 127,* 1653–1658.

Shepard, D. S., Strickler, G. K., McAuliffe, W. E., Beaston-Blaakman, A., Rahman, M., & Anderson, T. E. (2005). Unmet need for substance abuse treatment of adults in Massachusetts. *Administration and Policy in Mental Health, 32*(4), 403–426.

Shields, A. L., Howell, R. T., Potter, J. S., & Weiss, R. D. (2007). The Michigan Alcoholism Screening Test and its shortened form: A meta-analytic inquiry into score reliability. *Substance Abuse and Misuse, 42,* 1783–1800.

Stone, R. (2015). Pregnant women and substance use: Fear, stigma, and barriers to care. *Health & Justice, 3*(2), 1–15. doi:10.1186/s40352-015-0015-5

Substance Abuse and Mental Health Services Administration. (2013). *Substance abuse treatment for persons with co-occurring disorders.* Treatment Improvement Protocol (TIP) Series, No. 42. HHS Publication No. (SMA) 133992. Rockville, MD: Author.

Substance Abuse and Mental Health Services Administration. (2015a). *Behavioral health trends in the United States: Results from the 2014 National Survey on Drug Use and Health.* Retrieved from http://www.samhsa.gov/data/sites/default/files/NSDUH-FRR1-2014/NSDUH-FRR1-2014.pdf

Substance Abuse and Mental Health Services Administration. (2015b). Brief strategic family therapy: Family Therapy Training Institute of Miami. *National Registry of Evidence-based Program and Practices.* Retrieved from http://legacy.nreppadmin.net/ViewIntervention.aspx?id=404

Sullivan, E., & Fleming, M. (2008). A guide to substance abuse services for primary care clinicians: Treatment improvement protocol (TIP) Series. In Treatment Improvement Protocol (TIP) Series #24 (2008) Center for Substance Abuse Treatment, SAMHSA, DHHS, http://integratedrecovery.org/wp-content/uploads/2010/08/TIP24-SA.Services.for_.Primary.Care_.Clinicians.pdf

van Weeghel, J., van Boekel, L. C., Garretsen H. F. L., & Brouwers, E. P. M. (2013). Stigma among health professionals towards patients with substance use disorders and its consequences for healthcare delivery: Systematic review. *Drug and Alcohol Dependence, 131*(1–2), 23–35. doi:10.1016/j.drugalcdep.2013.02.018

Vaughn, M. G. (2013). Etiology. In M. G. Vaughn & B. E. Perron (Eds.) *Social work practice in the addictions.* New York, NY: Springer.

Wusthoff, L., Wall. H., & Grawe, R. (2014). The effectiveness of integrated treatment in patients with substance use disorders co-occurring with anxiety and/or depression—a group randomized trial. *BMC Psychiatry, 14*, 1–12. doi:10.1186/1471-244X-14-67

Chapter 6

Affordable Care Act, 42 U.S.C. § 18031 (2010).

Allen, J. P., Crawford, E. F., & Kudler, H. (2016, February 22). Nature and treatment of comorbid alcohol problems and post-traumatic stress disorder among American military personnel and veterans. *Alcohol Research Current Reviews, 38*(1). Retrieved from http://www.arcr.niaaa.nih.gov/arcr/arcr381/article15.htm

American Society of Addiction Medicine. (2015, February 18). An introduction to the ASAM Criteria for patients and families. Retrieved from http://www.valueoptions.com/members/files/Introduction-to-The-ASM-Criteria-for-Patients-and-Families.pdf

American Society of Addiction Medicine. (2016, February 22). The ASAM criteria. Retrieved from http://www.asam.org/publications/the-asam-criteria/about

Baron, M., Erlenbusch, B., Moran, C. F., O'Conner, K., Rice, K., & Rodriguez, J. (2008). *Best practices manual for discharge planning: Mental health & substance abuse facilities, hospitals, foster care, prisons and jails.* Los Angeles Coalition to End Hunger & Homelessness. Retrieved from http://homelesshub.ca/resource/best-practices-manual-discharge-planning-mental-health-substance-abuse-facilities-hospitals

Beronio, K., Glied, S., & Frank, R. (2014). How the affordable care act and mental health parity and addiction equity act greatly expand coverage of behavioral health care. *Journal of Behavioral Health Services and Research, 41*(4), 410–428. doi:10.1007/s11414-014-9412-0.

CARF. (2016, February 20). *2016 behavioral health programs descriptions.* Retrieved from www.carf.org/programdescriptions/bh/

Carnevale Associates Strategic Policy Solutions. (2013). *Affordable Care Act: Shaping substance abuse treatment information brief.* Gaithersburg, MD: Author. http://www.carnevaleassociates.com/the_affordable_care_act-_shaping_substance_abuse_treatment_final.pdf

Dodes, L. (2014). *The sober truth.* Boston, MA: Beacon Press.

Dom, G., & Moggi, F. (Eds.) (2015). *A practice based handbook from a European perspective.* Berlin, Germany: Springer. doi:10.1007/978-3-642-45375-5_1.

Doweiko, H. E. (2015). *Concepts of chemical dependency* (9th ed.). Belmont, CA: Brooks/Cole.

Fisher, G. I., & Roget, N. A. (Eds.) (2009). *Encyclopedia of substance abuse prevention, treatment, and recovery.* Thousand Oaks, CA: Sage.

Galanter, M., Kleber, H. D., & Brady, K. T. (2014). *American Psychiatric Publishing textbook of substance abuse treatment* (5th ed.). Arlington, VA: American Psychiatric Publishing.

Grohsman, B. (2009). *In drug treatment centers: Drug treatment.* Retrieved from http://www.treatment-centers.net/drug-treatment.html

Jazeri, S. A., & Habil, M. H. B. (2012). Reviewing two types of addiction: Pathological gambling and substance use. *Indian Journal of Psychological Medicine, 34*(1), 5011. doi:10.4103/0253-7176.96147

Kaiser Family Foundation. (2015, December 28). *Key facts about the uninsured population.* Retrieved from http://kff.org/uninsured/fact-sheet/key-facts-about-the-uninsured-population/

Lieb, R. (2015). Epidemiological perspectives on comorbidity between substance use disorders and other mental disorders. In G. Dom, F. Moggi (Eds.), *A practice based handbook from a European perspective*. Berlin, Germany: Springer. doi:10.1007/978-3-642-45375-5_1.

Magellan Health Services (2016, February 29). *The what, who, when & how of treatment planning*. Retrieved from http://www.magellanofiowa.com/media/150426/txplanning_presentation.pdf

Mee-Lee, D. (2016, February 19). *Understanding and utilizing the ASAM placement criteria*. Retrieved from http://www.naadac.org/assets/1959/2012-03-14_understanding_and_utilizing_asam_webinarslides.pdf

Mee-Lee, D., & Shulman, G. D. (2011). The ASAM placement criteria and matching patients to treatment. Chapter 27 in Section 4, Overview of addiction treatment. In C. A. Cavacuiti (Ed.) *Principles of addiction medicine: The essentials*. Philadelphia, PA: Lippincott Williams & Wilkins.

Moore, G. F., Rothwell, R., & Segrott, J. (2010). An exploratory study of the relationship between parental attitudes and behavior and young people's consumption of alcohol. *Substance Abuse Treatment, Prevention, and Policy, 5*(6), 1–14.

Owen, P. (2000). Minnesota model: Description of counseling approach. In J. J. Boren, L. S. Onken, & K. M. Carroll (Eds.), *Approaches to drug abuse counseling* (NIH Publication No. 00-4151, pp. 117–125). Bethesda, MD: National Institutes of Health.

Owen, P. (2016, February 20). Minnesota model: Description of counseling approach. National Institute on Drug Abuse. Retrieved from http://archives.drugabuse.gov/ADAC/ADAC11.html

Patient Protection and Affordable Care Act, 42 U.S.C. § 18001 et seq. (2010).

Public Law 110-343 (2008). Mental Health Parity and Addiction Equity Act of 2008. Retrieved from https://www.congress.gov/bill/110th-congress/house-bill/6983

Substance Abuse and Mental Health Services Administration. (2016, February 2). *Detoxification and substance abuse treatment training manual: TIP 45*. Retrieved from https://store.samhsa.gov/shin/content/SMA09-4331/SMA09-4331.pdf

U.S. Department of Veterans Affairs. (2016). *PTSD and substance abuse in veterans*. Retrieved from http://www.ptsd.va.gov/public/problems/ptsd_substance_abuse_veterans.asp

Chapter 7

American Academy of Family Physicians. (2014). *Tobacco: Preventing and treating nicotine dependence and tobacco use*. Retrieved from http://www.aafp.org/about/policies/all/nicotine-tobacco-prevention.html

American Psychiatric Association. (2013). *Diagnostic and statistical manual of mental disorders: DSM-5*. Washington, D.C.: American Psychiatric Association.

American Society of Addiction Medicine. (2013). Retrieved from http://www.asam.org/publications/the-asam-criteria/about/

Ames, S. C., & Roitzsch, J. C. (2000). The impact of minor stressful life events and social support on cravings: A study of inpatients receiving treatment for substance dependence. *Addictive Behaviors, 25*(4), 539–547.

Anton, R. F., O'Malley, S. S., Ciraulo, D. A., Cisler, R. A., Couper, D., Donovan, D. M., . . . COMBINE Study Research Group. (2006). Combined pharmacotherapies and behavioral interventions for alcohol dependence: the COMBINE study: A randomized controlled trial. *Journal of the American Medical Association, 295*, 2003–2017.

Asberg, K., & Renk, K. (2012). Substance use coping as a mediator of the relationship between trauma symptoms and substance use consequences among incarcerated females with childhood sexual abuse histories. *Substance Use & Misuse, 47*(7), 799–808. doi:10.3109/10826084.2012.669446

Askari, J., Hassanbeigi, A., & Fallahzadeh, H. (2011). The rate of various psychological stressors, perceived mental strain due to these stressors, and coping strategies in opium addicts compared to normal individuals. *Procedia: Social and Behavioral Sciences, 30*, 654–661.

Bandura, A., & Schunk, D. A. (1981). Cultivating competence, self-efficacy, and intrinsic interest through proximal self-motivation. *Journal of Personality and Social Psychology, 41*(3), 586–598.

Brewer, J., Sinha, R., Chen, J., Michalsen, R., Babuscio, T., . . . Rounsaville, B. J. (2009). Mindfulness training and stress reactivity in substance abuse: Results from a randomized controlled stage I pilot study. *Substance Abuse, 30*(4), 306–317.

Burlew, A. K., Montgomery, L., Kosinski, A. S., & Forcehimes, A. (2013). Does treatment readiness enhance the response of African American substance users to Motivational Enhancement Therapy? *Psychology of Addictive Behaviors, 27*(3), 744–753. doi:.10.1037/a003.1274.

Carroll, K., & Onken, L. S. (2007). Behavioral therapies for drug abuse. *Focus: The Journal of Lifelong Learning in Psychiatry, 5*(2), 240–248.

Ciccocioppo, R., Economidou, D., Rimondini, R., Sommer, W., Massi, M., & Heilig, M. (2007). Buprenorphine reduces alcohol drinking through activation of the nociception/Orphanin FQ–NOP receptor system. *Biological Psychiatry, 61*(1), 4–12.

Cihan, A., Winstead, D.A., Feit, L., & Feit, M. (2014). Attachment theory and substance abuse: Etiological links. *Journal of Human Behavior in the Social Environment, 24*(5). doi.10.1080/10911359.2014.908592.

Cleveland, H. H., & Harris, K. S. (2010). The role of coping in moderating within-day associations between negative triggers and substance use cravings: A daily diary investigation. *Addictive Behaviors, 35*, 60–63.

Courbasson, C. M., & Nishikaway, Y. (2010). Cognitive behavioral group therapy for patients with co-existing social anxiety disorder and substance use disorders: A pilot study. *Cognitive Therapy and Research, 34*, 82–91.

DeFulio, A., Donlin, W. D., Wong, C. J., & Silverman, K. (2009). Employment-based abstinence reinforcement as a maintenance intervention for the treatment of cocaine dependence: A randomized controlled trial. *Addiction, 104*, 1530–1538.

Des Jarlais, D. C., McKnight, C., Goldblatt, C., & Purchase, D. (2009). Doing harm reduction better: Syringe exchange in the United States. *Society for the Study of Addiction, 104*, 1441–1446.

Dolan, S. L., Rohsenow, D. J., Martin, R. A., & Monti, P. M. (2013). Urge-specific and lifestyle coping strategies of alcoholics: Relationships of specific strategies to treatment outcome. *Drug and Alcohol Dependence, 128*, 8–14.

Doweiko, H. E. (2012). Concepts of chemical dependency (8th ed.). Belmont, CA: Brooks/Cole, Cengage.

Doweiko, H. E. (2015). Concepts of chemical dependency (9th ed.). Belmont, CA: Brooks/Cole, Cengage.

Duff, C. T., & Bedi, R. P. (2010). Counselor behaviors that predict therapeutic alliance: From the client's perspective. *Counseling Psychology Quarterly, 23*(1), 91–110.

Ekendahl, M. (2007). Will and skill—An exploratory study of substance abusers' attitudes toward lifestyle change. *European Addiction Research, 13*, 148–155.

Fareed, A., Vayalapalli, S., Casarella, J., Amar, R., & Drexler, K. (2010). Heroin anticraving medications: A systematic review. *American Journal of Drug & Alcohol Abuse, 36*(6), 332–341.

Fields, D., & Roman S. (2010). Total quality management and performance in substance abuse treatment centers. *Health Services Research, 45*, 6 Part 1, 1630–1650.

Finch, J. W., Kamien, J., & Amass, L. (2007). Two-year experience with buprenorphine-naloxone (suboxone) for maintenance treatment of opioid dependence within a private practice setting. *Journal of Addiction Medicine, 1*(2), 104–110.

Fowler, J. C., Groat, M., & Ulanday, M. (2013). Attachment style and treatment completion among psychiatric inpatients with substance use disorders. *American Journal on Addictions, 22*(1), 14–17. doi:10.1111/j.1521-0391.3013.00318x

Hassanbeigi, A., Askari, J., Hassanbeigi, D., & Pourmovahed, Z. (2013). The relationship between stress and addiction. *Procedia: Social and Behavioral Sciences, 84*, 1333–1340.

Hathaway, A. D., Callaghan, R. C., Macdonald, S., & Erickson, P. G. (2009). Cannabis dependence as a primary drug use-related problem: The case for harm reduction–oriented treatment options. *Substance Use and Misuse, 44*, 990–1008.

Korte, K., & Schmidt, N.B. (2013). Motivational enhancement therapy reduces anxiety sensitivitiy. *Cognitive Therapy Research, 37*(6), 1140–1150.

Kübler-Ross, E. (1969). *On death and dying.* New York, NY: Macmillan.

LeBeau, R. T., Davies, C. D., Culver, N. C & Craske, M. G. (2013). Homework compliance counts in cognitive-behavioral therapy. *Cognitive Behaviour Therapy, 42*(3), 171–179.

Lewis, J. A., Dana, R. Q., & Blevins, G. A. (2015). *Substance abuse counseling: An individual approach* (5th ed.). Pacific Grove, CA: Brooks/Cole.

Lightfoot, J. M. (2014). Solution Focused Therapy. *International Journal of Scientific & Engineering Research, 5*(12), 238–240.

Marlatt, G. A. (Ed.). (1998). *Harm reduction: Pragmatic strategies for managing high-risk behaviors.* New York, NY: Guilford Press.

Mee-Lee, D. (2010). *The Asam Criteria: Treatment Criteria for Addictive, Substance-Related, and Co-Occurring Conditions.* Published by "American Society of Addiction Medicine".

Melvin, A. M., Davis, S., & Koch, D. (2012). Employment as a predictor of substance abuse treatment. *Journal of Rehabilitation, 78*(4), 31–37.

Miller, W. R., & Rollnick, S. (2009). Ten things that motivational interviewing is not. *Behavioral and Cognitive Psychotherapy, 37*, 1.

Miller, W. R., & Rollnick, S. (2013). *Motivational interviewing—Helping people change* (3rd ed.). New York, NY: Guilford Press.

Moss-King, D. (2009). *Unresolved grief and loss issues related to heroin recovery. Grief and loss issues in heroin recovery.* Germany: VDM Verlag Dr. Müller.

National Institute on Drug Abuse. (2012, December). *Principles of drug addiction and treatment: A research based guide* (3rd ed.). NIH Publication No. 12–4180.

Norcross, J. C., Krebs, P. M., & Prochaska, J. O. (2011). Stages of change. *Journal of Clinical Psychology, 67*(2), 143–154. doi:10.1002/jc.lp.20758

O'Connell, O. (2009). Introducing mindfulness as an adjunct treatment in an established residential drug and alcohol facility. *The Humanistic Psychologist, 37*, 178–191.

Orman, J. S., & Keating, G. M. (2009). Spotlight on buprenorphine/naloxone in the treatment of opioid dependence. *CNS Drugs, 23*(10), 899–902.

Patra, J., Gilksman, L., Fischer, B., Newton-Taylor, B., Belenko, S., Ferrari, M., . . . Rehm, J. (2010). Factors associated with treatment compliance and its effects on retention among participants in a court mandated treatment program. *Contemporary Drug Problems, 37,* 289–313.

Redko, C., Rapp, R. C., & Carlson. R. G. (2007). Pathways of substance users linking (or not) with treatment. *Journal of Drug Issues, 37*(3), 597–617.

Rothenberg, L. (1988). The ethics of intervention. *Alcoholism & Addiction, 9*(1), 22–24.

Senbanjo, R., Wolff, K., Marshall, J., & Strang, J. (2009). Persistence of heroin use despite methadone treatment: Poor coping self-efficacy predicts continued heroin use. *Drug and Alcohol Review, 28*, 608–615.

Shapiro, F. (2013). *Getting past your past: Take control of your life with self-help techniques from EMDR therapy.* New York, NY: Rodale.

Shapiro, F. (2014). The role of eye movement desensitization and reprocessing (EMDR) therapy in medicine: Addressing the psychological and physical symptoms stemming from adverse life experiences. *The Permanente Journal, 18*(1), 71–77.

Smith, D. E., Lee, D. R., & Davidson, L. D. (2010). Health care equality and parity for treatment of addictive disease. *Journal of Psychoactive Drugs, 41*(2), 121–126.

Substance Abuse and Mental Health Services Administration. (2013). *Behavioral health treatments and services: Cognitive behavioral therapy/therapies.* Retrieved from http://www.samhsa.gov/treatment

Substance Abuse and Mental Health Services Administration: Center for Substance Abuse Treatment. (2012). *Enhancing motivation for change in substance abuse treatment.* Treatment Improvement Protocol (TIP) Series 35. HHS Publications: Rockville, MD.

Ungless, M. A., Argilli, E., & Bonci, A. (2010). Effects of stress and aversion on dopamine neurons: Implications for addiction. *Neuroscience and Behavioral Reviews, 35,* 151–156.

Verendeev, A., & Riley, A. L. (2012). Conditioned taste aversion and drugs of abuse: History and interpretation. *Neuroscience and Bio-behavioral Reviews, 36,* 2193–2205.

Walker, M. A. (2009). Program characteristics and the length of time clients are in substance abuse treatment. *Journal of Behavioral Health Services and Research, 36*(3), 330–342.

Webster, J. M., Dickson, M. F., Staton-Tindall, M., & Leukefeld, C. (2015). Predictors of recidivism among rural and urban drug-involved prisoners. *Journal of Offender Rehabilitation, 54*(8), 539–555.

Wesson, D. R., & Smith, D. E. (2010). Buprenorphine in the treatment of opiate dependence. *Journal of Psychoactive Drugs, 42*(2), 161–175.

West, S. (2008). The utilization of vocational rehabilitation services in substance abuse treatment facilities in the U.S. *Journal of Vocational Rehabilitation, 29*(2), 71–75.

Winkelstein, E. (2010). *Understanding Drug-Related Stigma: Tools for Better Practice and Social Change.* Published by Harm Reduction Coalition. Retrieved from harmreduction.org/about-us/principles-of-harm-reduction/

Witkiewitz, K., Bowen, S., Douglas, H., & Hsu, S. H. (2013). Mindfulness-based relapse prevention for substance craving. *Addictive Behaviors, 38*(2), 1563–1571.

Zarrin, S. A., Baghban, I., & Abedi, M. R. (2011). Reliability and correlation of interest inventories: Strong Interest Inventory (SII) and Self-Directed Search (SDS). *International Journal of Psychology and Counselling, 3*(7), 111–116.

Chapter 8

Allen, J. P., Babor, T. F., Mattson, M. E., & Kadden, R. M. (2003). Matching alcoholism treatment to client heterogeneity: The genesis of Project MATCH. In T. F. Babor, F. K. Del Boca, T. F. Babor, F. K. Del Boca (Eds.), *Treatment matching in alcoholism* (pp. 3–14). New York, NY: Cambridge University Press.

American Counseling Association. (2014). *ACA Code of Ethics.* Alexandria, VA: Author.

Bandura, A. (1994). Self-efficacy. In V. S. Ramachaudran (Ed.), *Encyclopedia of human behavior* (Vol. 4, pp. 71–81). New York, NY: Academic Press. (Reprinted in H. Friedman [Ed.], *Encyclopedia of mental health.* San Diego, CA: Academic Press, 1998).

Beadnell, B., Nason, M., Stafford, P. A., Rosengren, D. B., & Daugherty, R. (2012). Short-term outcomes of a motivation-enhancing approach to DUI intervention. *Accident Analysis and Prevention, 45*, 792–801. doi:10.1016/j.aap.2011.11.004

Botvin, G. J., & Griffin, K. W. (2015). Life Skills Training: A competence enhancement approach to tobacco, alcohol, and drug abuse prevention. In L. M. Scheier, L. M. Scheier (Eds.), *Handbook of adolescent drug use prevention: Research, intervention strategies, and practice* (pp. 177–196). Washington, DC: American Psychological Association. doi:10.1037/14550-011

Brook, D. W. (2015). Group therapy. In M. Galanter, H. D. Kleber & K. T. Brady (Eds.), *The American Psychiatric Publishing textbook of substance abuse treatment* (5th ed.; pp. 463–478). Arlington, VA: American Psychiatric Publishing.

Brooks, F., & McHenry, B. (2015). *A contemporary approach to substance use disorders and addiction counseling* (2nd ed.). Alexandria, VA: American Counseling Association.

Brown, N. W. (2011). *Psychoeducational groups: Process and practice* (3rd ed.). New York, NY: Routledge.

Center for Substance Abuse Treatment. (2005). *Substance abuse treatment: Group therapy* (TIP 41). DHHS Publication No. (SMA) 05-3991. Rockville, MD: Substance Abuse and Mental Health Services Administration.

Center for Substance Abuse Treatment. (2009a). *A provider's introduction to substance abuse treatment for lesbian, gay, bisexual, and transgender individuals.* Rockville, MD: Substance Abuse and Mental Health Services Administration.

Center for Substance Abuse Treatment. (2009b). *Substance abuse treatment: Addressing the specific needs of women* (TIP 51). Rockville, MD: Substance Abuse and Mental Health Services Administration.

Connors, G. J., DiClemente, C. C., Velasquez, M. M., & Donovan, D. M. (2013). *Substance abuse treatment and the stages of change: Selecting and planning interventions* (2nd ed.). New York, NY: Guilford Press.

Corey, G. (2016). *Theory and practice of group counseling* (9th ed.). Belmont, CA: Brooks/Cole-Thomson.

Council for Accreditation of Counseling and Related Educational Programs. (2016). *2016 CACREP standards.* Retrieved from http://www.cacrep.org/for-programs/2016-cacrep-standards/

Cummings, A. M., Gallop, R. J., & Greenfield, S. F. (2010). Self-efficacy and substance use outcomes for women in single-gender versus mixed-gender group treatment. *Journal of Groups in Addiction & Recovery, 5*, 4–16. doi:10.1080/15560350903543915

Dennis, M., Godley, S. H., Diamond, G., Tims, F. M., Babor, T., Donaldson, J., . . . Funk, R. (2004). The Cannabis Youth Treatment (CYT) Study: Main findings from two randomized trials. *Journal of Substance Abuse Treatment, 27*, 197–213. doi:10.1016/j.jsat.2003.09.005

Donovan, D., & Witkiewitz, K. (2012). Relapse prevention: From radical idea to common practice. *Addiction Research & Theory, 20*, 204–217. doi:10.3109/16066359.2011.647133

Donovan, D. M., Daley, D. C., Brigham, G. S., Hodgkins, C. C., Perl, H. I., Garrett, S. B., . . . Zammarelli, L. (2013). Stimulant abuser groups to engage in 12-step: A multisite trial in the National Institute on Drug Abuse Clinical Trials Network. *Journal of Substance Abuse Treatment, 44*, 103–114. doi:10.1016/j.jsat.2012.04.004

Doweiko, H. E. (2015). *Concepts of chemical dependency* (9th ed.). Belmont, CA: Thomson Brooks/Cole.

DuPont, R. L., McLellan, A. T., Carr, G., Gendel, M., & Skipper, G. E. (2009). How are addicted physicians treated? A national survey of Physician Health Programs. *Journal of Substance Abuse Treatment, 37*, 1–7. doi:10.1016/j.jsat.2009.03.010

Faragher, J. M., & Soberay, A. (2014). Group approaches for addictive behaviors. In J. L. DeLucia-Waack, C. R. Kalodner, & M. T. Riva (Eds.), *Handbook of group counseling and psychotherapy* (2nd ed., pp. 410–420). Thousand Oaks, CA: Sage.

Guerrero, E. G., Marsh, J. C., Duan, L., Oh, C., Perron, B., & Lee, B. (2013). Disparities in completion of substance abuse treatment between and within racial and ethnic groups. *Health Services Research, 48*, 1450–1467. doi:10.1111/1475-6773.12031

Harris, J., Underhill, M., & Hill, R. (2011). How do we know the group has worked?. In R. Hill, J. Harris, R. Hill, J. Harris (Eds.), *Principles and practice of group work in addictions* (pp. 127–137). New York, NY: Routledge/Taylor & Francis.

Hunter, S. B., Ramchand, R., Griffin, B. A., Suttorp, M. J., McCaffrey, D., & Morral, A. (2012). The effectiveness of community-based delivery of an evidence-based treatment for adolescent substance use. *Journal of Substance Abuse Treatment, 43*, 211–220.

Johnson, J. E., Burlingame, G. M., Olsen, J. A., Davies, D. R., & Gleave, R. L. (2005). Group climate, cohesion, alliance, and empathy in group psychotherapy: Multilevel structural equation models. *Journal of*

Counseling Psychology, 52, 310–321. doi:10.1037/
0022-0167.52.3.310

Karno, M. P., & Longabaugh, R. (2005). Less directive-
ness by therapists improves drinking outcomes of reac-
tant clients in alcoholism treatment. *Journal of
Consulting and Clinical Psychology, 73*, 262–267.
doi:10.1037/0022-006X.73.2.262

Kaskutas, L., Subbaraman, M., Witbrodt, J., & Zemore,
S. E. (2009). Effectiveness of Making Alcoholics
Anonymous Easier (MAAEZ), a group format
12-step facilitation approach. *Journal of Substance
Abuse Treatment, 37*, 228–239. doi:10.1016/j.jsat.
2009.01.004

Kelly, J. F., Magill, M., & Stout, R. L. (2009). How do people
recover from alcohol dependence? A systematic review of
the research on the mechanisms of behavior change in
Alcoholics Anonymous. *Addiction Research and
Theory, 17*, 236–259. doi:10.1080/16066350902770458

Kelly, V. A. (2016). *Addiction in the family: What every
counselor needs to know.* Alexandria, VA: American
Counseling Association.

Khantzian, E. J., Golden-Schulman, S. J., & McAuliffe,
W. E. (2004). Group therapy. In M. Galanter, H. D.
Kleber (Eds.), *The American Psychiatric Publishing
textbook of substance abuse treatment* (3rd ed.,
pp. 391–403). Arlington, VA: American Psychiatric
Publishing.

Kingree, J. B. (2013). Twelve-step facilitation therapy. In
P. M. Miller, S. A. Ball, M. E. Bates, A. W. Blume,
K. M. Kampman, D. J. Kavanagh, . . . P. De Witte
(Eds.), *Comprehensive addictive behaviors and disor-
ders, Vol. 3: Interventions for addiction* (pp. 137–146).
San Diego, CA: Elsevier Academic Press. doi:10.1016/
B978-0-12-398338-1.00015-4

Krejci, J., & Neugebauer, Q. (2015). Motivational interviewing in groups: Group process considerations.
Journal of Groups in Addiction & Recovery, 10,
23–40. doi:10.1080/1556035X.2015.999616

LeNoue, S. R., & Riggs, P. D. (2016). Substance abuse
prevention. *Child and Adolescent Psychiatric Clinics
of North America*, doi:10.1016/j.chc.2015.11.007

Margolis, R. D., & Zweben, J. E. (2011). Group therapy
and self-help groups in addiction treatment. In
*Treating patients with alcohol and other drug prob-
lems: An integrated approach* (2nd ed.; pp. 173–197).
Washington, DC: American Psychological
Association. doi:10.1037/12312-007

Marinchak, J. S., & Morgan, T. J. (2012). Behavioral
treatment techniques for psychoactive substance use
disorders. In S. T. Walters & F. Rotgers (Eds.),
Treating substance abuse, third edition: Theory

and technique (pp. 138–166). New York, NY:
Guilford.

Marmarosh, C., Holtz, A., & Schottenbauer, M. (2005).
Group cohesiveness, group-derived collective self-
esteem, group-derived hope, and the well-being of group
therapy members. *Group Dynamics: Theory, Research,
and Practice, 9*, 32–44. doi:10.1037/1089-2699.9.1.32

Marsh, J. C., Cao, D., Guerrero, E., & Shin, H. (2009).
Need-service matching in substance abuse treatment:
Racial/ethnic differences. *Evaluation and Program
Planning, 32*, 43–51. doi:10.1016/j.
evalprogplan.2008.09.003

Matano, R. A., & Yalom, I. D. (1991). Approaches to
chemical dependency: Chemical dependency and interactive group therapy: A synthesis. *International
Journal of Group Psychotherapy, 41*, 269–293.

McNair, L. D. (2005). Top 10 recommendations for treating comorbid addictive behaviors in African
Americans. *Behavior Therapy, 28*, 116–118.

Milgram, D., & Rubin, J. S. (1992). Resisting resistance:
Involuntary substance abuse group therapy. *Social
Work With Groups, 15*, 95–110.

Miller, G. (2005). *Learning the language of addiction
counseling* (2nd ed.). Hoboken, NJ: Wiley.

Miller, P. G., Curtis, A., Sønderlund, A., Day, A., &
Droste, N. (2015). Effectiveness of interventions for
convicted DUI offenders in reducing recidivism: A
systematic review of the peer-reviewed scientific literature. *The American Journal of Drug and Alcohol
Abuse, 41*, 16–29. doi:10.3109/00952990.2014.966199

Miller, W. R., & Rollnick, S. (2013). *Motivational interviewing: Helping people change* (3rd ed.). New York,
NY: Guilford Press.

Miller, W. R., Benefield, R. G., & Tonigan, J. S. (1993).
Enhancing motivation for change in problem drinking:
A controlled comparison of two therapist styles.
Journal of Consulting and Clinical Psychology, 61,
455–461. doi:10.1037/0022-006X.61.3.455

Miller, W. R., Forcehimes, A. A., & Zweben, A. (2011).
Treating addiction: A guide for professionals.
New York, NY: Guilford Press.

Mitcheson, L., & Grellier, B. (2011). Motivation and
change: The role of motivational interviewing in substance use groups. In R. Hill, J. Harris, R. Hill, J.
Harris (Eds.), *Principles and practice of group work in
addictions* (pp. 17–29). New York, NY: Routledge/
Taylor & Francis.

Morgan, R. D., Romani, C. J., & Gross, N. R. (2014). In
J. L. DeLucia-Waack, C. R. Kalodner, & M. T. Riva
(Eds.), *Handbook of group counseling and psychother-
apy* (2nd ed., pp. 441–449). Thousand Oaks, CA: Sage.

Morgan-Lopez, A. A., & Fals-Stewart, W. (2006). Analytic complexities associated with group therapy in substance abuse treatment research: Problems, recommendations, and future directions. *Experimental and Clinical Psychopharmacology, 14*, 265–273. doi:10.1037/1064-1297.14.2.265

NAADAC, The Association for Addiction Professionals. (2013). *NAADAC/NCC AP Code of Ethics*. Retrieved from http://www.naadac.org/code-of-ethics#iii

National Institute on Drug Abuse. (2012). *Principles of effective treatment: A research-based guide* (3rd ed.). (NIH No. 12-4180). Washington, DC: National Institutes of Health. Retrieved from http://www.drugabuse.gov/sites/default/files/podat_1.pdf

Norcross, J. C., Krebs, P. M., & Prochaska, J. O. (2011). Stages of change. *Journal of Clinical Psychology, 67*, 143–154. doi:10.1002/jclp.20758

Pooler, D. K., Qualls, N., Rogers, R., & Johnston, D. (2014). An exploration of cohesion and recovery outcomes in addiction treatment groups. *Social Work With Groups: A Journal of Community and Clinical Practice, 37*, 314–330. doi:10.1080/01609513.2014.905217

Prochaska, J. O., DiClemente, C. C., & Norcross, J. C. (1992). In search of how people change: Applications to addictive behaviors. *American Psychologist, 47*, 1102–1114. doi:10.1037/0003-066X.47.9.1102

Project MATCH Research Group. (1997). Matching alcoholism treatments to client heterogeneity: Project MATCH posttreatment drinking outcomes. *Journal of Studies on Alcohol, 58*, 7–29.

Project MATCH Research Group. (1998). Matching alcoholism treatments to client heterogeneity: Project MATCH three-year drinking outcomes. *Alcoholism: Clinical and Experimental Research, 22*(6) 1300–1311.

Ramchand, R., Griffin, B. A., Suttorp, M., Harris, K. M., & Morral, A. (2011). Using a cross-study design to access the efficacy of Motivational Enhancement Therapy–Cognitive Behavioral Therapy 5 (MET/CBT) in treating adolescents with cannabis-related disorders. *Journal of Studies on Alcohol and Drugs, 72*, 380–389.

Roth, J. D. (2004). *Group psychotherapy and recovery from addiction: Carrying the message*. Binghamton, NY: Hawthorne Press.

Sampl, S., & Kadden, R. (2001). *Motivational enhancement therapy and cognitive behavioral therapy for adolescent cannabis users: 5 sessions, Cannabis youth treatment (CYT) series, Volume 1*. Rockville, MD: Substance Abuse and Mental Health Services Administration.

Schimmel, C. J., & Jacobs, E. (2015). Group counseling as a therapeutic intervention for substance use. In C. S. Bhat, Y. Pillay, & P. R. Selvaraj (Eds.), *Group work experts share their favorite activities for the prevention and treatment of substance use disorders* (pp. 26–35). Alexandria, VA: Association for Specialists in Group Work.

Singh, A. A., Merchant, N., Skudrzyk, B., & Ingene, D. (2012). *Association for Specialists in Group Work: Multicultural and social justice competence principles for group workers*. Retrieved from http://www.asgw.org

Sobell, L. C., Sobell, M. B., & Agrawal, S. (2009). Randomized controlled trial of a cognitive–behavioral motivational intervention in a group versus individual format for substance use disorders. *Psychology of Addictive Behaviors, 23*, 672–683. doi:10.1037/a0016636

Stevens, S. J., Arbiter, N., & Glider, P. (1989). Women residents: Expanding their role to increase treatment effectiveness in substance abuse programs. *International Journal of the Addictions, 24*, 425–434.

Substance Abuse and Mental Health Services Administration. (2014). *National survey of substance abuse treatment services: 2013. Data on substance abuse treatment facilities*. BHSIS Series S-73, HHS Publication No. (SMA) 14-4890. Rockville, MD: Author.

Tantillo, M. (2006). A relational approach to eating disorders multifamily therapy group: Moving from difference and disconnection to mutual connection. *Families, Systems & Health, 24*, 82–102. doi:10.1037/1091-7527.24.1.82

Velasquez, M. M., Crouch, C., Stephens, N. S., & DiClemente, C. C. (2016). *Group treatment for substance abuse: A stages-of-change therapy manual* (2nd ed.). New York, NY: Guilford Press.

Wagner, C. C., & Ingersoll, K. S. (2013). *Motivational interviewing in groups*. New York, NY: Guilford Press.

Webb, C., Scudder, M., Kaminer, Y., & Kadden, R. (2002). *The motivational enhancement therapy and cognitive behavioral therapy supplement: 7 sessions of cognitive behavioral therapy for adolescent cannabis users, Cannabis youth treatment (CYT) series, Volume 2*. Rockville, MD: Substance Abuse and Mental Health Services Administration.

Weegmann, M. (2004). Alcoholics Anonymous: Group therapy without the group therapist. In B. Reading, & M. Weegmann (Eds.), *Group psychotherapy and addiction* (pp. 27–41). Philadelphia, PA: Whurr Publishers. doi:10.1002/9780470713549.ch3

Weiss, R. D., Jaffee, W. B., de Menil, V. P., & Cogley, C. B. (2004). Group therapy for substance use disorders: What do we know? *Harvard Review of Psychiatry, 12,* 339–350. doi:10.1080/10673220490905723

Wenzel, A., Liese, B. S., Beck, A. T., & Friedman-Wheeler, D. G. (2012). *Group cognitive therapy for addictions.* New York, NY: Guilford Press.

Witkiewitz, K., Hartzler, B., & Donovan, D. (2010). Matching motivation enhancement treatment to client motivation: Re-examining the Project MATCH motivation matching hypothesis. *Addiction, 105,* 1403–1413. doi:10.1111/j.1360-0443.2010.02954.x

Yalom, I. D., & Leszcz, M. (2005). *The theory and practice of group psychotherapy* (5th ed.). Cambridge, MA: Basic Books.

Chapter 9

Acheson, A., Tagamets, M. A., Rowland, L. M., Mathias, C. W., Wright, S. N., Hong, L. E., . . . Dougherty, D. M. (2014). Increased forebrain activations in youths with family histories of alcohol and other substance use disorders performing a go/nogo task. *Alcoholism: Clinical and Experimental Research.* doi:10.1111/acer.12571.

Ackerman, R. J. (1983). *Children of alcoholics: A guide book for educators, therapists, and parents.* Holmes Beach, FL: Learning Publications.

Adler, A. (1927). *The practice and theory of individual psychology.* New York, NY: Harcourt Brace.

Anda, R. F., Dong, M. X., Brown, D. W., Felitti, F. V. J., Giles, W. H., & Perry, G. S. (2009). The relationship of adverse childhood experiences to a history of premature death of family members. *BMC Public Health, 9* (article 106).

Bateson, B. (1971). *Steps toward an ecology of the mind.* New York, NY: Ballantine.

Bertalanffy, L. von (1968). *General systems theory: Foundation, development, applications.* New York, NY: Braziller.

Black, C. (1981). *It will never happen to me.* Denver, CO: MAC.

Black, C. (2010). Families and addictions: Interventions [pdf format] NASW, WV Chapter, April, 2010. Retrieved from www.claudiablack.com

Bowen, M. (1974). Alcoholism as viewed through the family systems theory and family psychotherapy. *Annals of the New York Academy of Science, 233,* 115–122.

Bowen, M. (1976). Theory in the practice of psychotherapy. In P. J. Guerin, Jr. (Ed.), *Family therapy: Theory and practice.* New York, NY: Gardner.

Capuzzi, D., & Stauffer, M. D. (2012). *Foundations of addiction counseling.* Boston, MA: Pearson Publishing.

Cherpitel, C. J., Yu Ye, K. W., Brubacher, J. R., & Stenstrom, R. (2012). Risk of injury from alcohol and drug use in the emergency department: A case-crossover study. *Drug and Alcohol Review, 31*(4), 431–438.

Cleaver, H, Unell, I., & Aldgate, J. (2010). Children's needs—parenting capacity: *Child abuse, parental mental illness, learning disability, substance misuse, and domestic violence* (2nd revised ed.). Great Britain: TSO Publishing.

Cranford, J. A., Floyd, F. J., Schulenberg, J. E., & Zucker, R. A. (2011). Husbands' and wives' alcohol use disorders and marital interactions as longitudinal predictors of marital adjustment. *Journal of Abnormal Psychology, 120*(1), 210–222.

Cruse, J., & Wegscheider-Cruse, S. (2012). *Understanding codependency: The science behind it and how to break the cycle.* Deerfield Beach, FL: Health Communications.

Doweiko, H. E. (2015). *Concepts of chemical dependence* (9th ed.). Pacific Grove, CA: Brooks/Cole.

Duke, A. A., Giancola, P. R., Morris, D. H., Holt, J. C. D., & Gunn, R. L. (2011). Alcohol dose and aggression: Another reason why drinking more is a bad idea. *Journal of Studies on Alcohol and Drugs, 72*(1), 34–43.

Erickson, C. K. (2007). *The science of addiction.* New York, NY: W. W. Norton.

Felitti, V. J. (2004). *The origins of addictions: Evidence from the Adverse Childhood Experience Study.* Retrieved from http://www.nijc.org/pdfs/Subject%20 Matter%20Articles/Drugs%20and%20Alc/ACE%20 Study%20-%20OriginsofAddiction.pdf

Gladding, S. (2014). *Family therapy: History, theory, and practice* (6th ed.). Upper Saddle River, NJ: Merrill/Prentice-Hall.

Goldenberg, I., & Goldenberg, H. (2012). *Family therapy: An overview* (8th ed.). Pacific Grove, CA: Brooks/Cole.

Goldstein, S., & Brooks, R. B. (Eds.). (2013). *Handbook of resilience in children.* Retrieved from http://link. springer.com/book/10.1007/978-1-4614-3661-4

Gorski, T. T. (1992). Diagnosing codependence. *Addiction and Recovery, 12*(7), 14–16.

Hughes, C., Payne, J., Macgregor, S., & Pockley, K. (2014). A beginner's guide to drugs and crime: Does one always lead to the other? *Of Substance: The National Magazine on Alcohol, Tobacco and Other Drugs, 12*(2), 26–29. Retrieved from http://search. informit.com.au/documentSummary;dn=38114724369 2346;res=IELHEA

Jackson, D. D. (1960). *The etiology of schizophrenia.* New York, NY: Basic Books.

Johnson, J. (2004) *Fundamentals of substance abuse practice.* Independence, KY: Cengage.

Kaufman, E. (1985). Family therapy in the treatment of alcoholism. In T. E. Bratter & G. G. Forrest (Eds.), *Alcoholism and substance abuse* (pp. 376–397). New York, NY: Free Press.

Kaufman, E., & Kaufman, P. (1992). From psychodynamic to structural to integrated family treatment of chemical dependency. In E. Kaufman & P. Kaufman (Eds.), *Family therapy of drug and alcohol abuse* (pp. 34–45). Boston, MA: Allyn & Bacon.

Leonard, K. E., & Hornish, G. G. (2008). Predictors of heavy drinking and drinking problems over the first 4 years of marriage. *Psychology of Addictive Behaviors, 22*(1). doi:10.1037/0893-164X.22.1.25

Lewis, J. A., Dana, R. Q., & Blevins, G. A. (2014). *Substance abuse counseling* (5th ed.). Belmont, CA: Brooks/Cole.

Liddle, H. A., Rowe, C. L., Dakof, G. A., Henderson, C. E., & Greenbaum, P. E. (2009). Multidimensional family therapy for young adolescent substance abuse: Twelve month outcomes of a randomized controlled trial. *Journal of Consulting and Clinical Psychology, 77*(1), 12–15.

Livingston, M. (2011). A longitudinal analysis of alcohol outlet density and domestic violence. *Addiction, 105*(5), 919–925.

Lowe, R. N. (1982). Adlerian/Dreikursian family counseling. In M. A. Horne & M. M. Ohlsen (Eds.), *Family counseling and therapy* (pp. 329–359). Itasca, IL: Peacock.

Mares, S. H. W., van der Vorst, H., Engels, R. C., & Lichtwarck-Aschoff, A. (2011). Parental alcohol use, alcohol-related problems, and alcohol-specific attitudes, alcohol-specific communication, and adolescent excessive alcohol use and alcohol-related problems: An indirect path model. Retrieved from: http://www.sciencedirect.com/science/article/pii/S0306460310003011. doi:10.1016/j.addbeh.2010.10.013

McCrady, B. S. (2011). Family and other close relationships. In W. R. Miller & K. M Carroll (Eds.), *Rethinking substance abuse: What science shows and what we should do about it* (pp. 166–181). New York, NY: Guilford.

McCrady, B. S., Epstein, E. E., Cook, S., Jensen, N. K., & Hildebrandt, T. (2009). A randomized trial of individual and couple behavioral alcohol treatment for women. *Journal of Consulting and Clinical Psychology, 77*(2), 243–256.

McNeece, C. A., & DiNitto, D. M. (2011). *Chemical dependency: A systems approach* (4th ed.). Boston, MA: Pearson Publishing.

Merriam-Webster's Online Dictionary. (2014). Definition of *system.* Retrieved from http://www.merriam-webster.com/dictionary/system

Minuchen, S. (1974). *Families and family therapy.* Cambridge, MA: Harvard University Press.

Minuchen, S. (1992). Constructing a therapeutic reality. In E. Kaufman & P. Kaufman (Eds.), *Family therapy of drug and alcohol abuse* (pp. 1–14). Boston, MA: Allyn & Bacon.

Napier, A. Y., & Whitaker, C. A. (1988). *The family crucible.* New York, NY: Harper & Row.

National Alliance on Mental Illness. (2015). *Dual diagnosis.* Retrieved from http://www.nami.org/Learn-More/Mental-Health-Conditions/Related-Conditions/Dual-Diagnosis

National Institutes of Health. (2014). What is the IRP? *Intramural Research Program.* Retrieved from http://irp.nih.gov/about-us/what-is-the-irp

Nichols, M. P. (2012). *Family therapy: Concepts and methods* (10th ed.). Boston, MA: Allyn & Bacon.

O'Connor, J., & McDermott, I. (1997). *The art of systems thinking.* London, England: Thorsons.

Powers, M. B., Vedel, E., & Emmelkamp, P. M. G. (2008). Behavioral couples therapy (BCT) for alcohol and drug use disorders: A meta-analysis. *Clinical Psychology Review, 28*(6), 952–962.

Substance Abuse and Mental Health Services Administration. (2013). Resiliency annotated bibliography: SAMHSA's partners for recovery initiative. Retrieved from http://www.samhsa.gov/sites/default/files/resiliency-annotated-bibliography.pdf

Substance Abuse and Mental Health Services Administration. (2014a). 2013 National Survey on Drug Use and Health (NSDUH). Table 5.8A—Substance Dependence or Abuse in the Past Year among Persons Aged 18 or Older, by Demographic Characteristics: Numbers in Thousands, 2011 and 2012. Retrieved from http://www.samhsa.gov/data/sites/default/files/NSDUH-DetTabs2012/NSDUH-DetTabs2012/HTML/NSDUH-DetTabsSect5peTabs1to56-2012.htm#Tab5.8A

Substance Abuse and Mental Health Services Administration. (2014b). *National Registry of Evidence-based Programs and Practices.* Retrieved from http://www.nrepp.samhsa.gov

Satir, V. (1967). *Conjoint family therapy.* Palo Alto, CA: Science and Behavior Books.

Söderpalm Gordh, A. H. V., & Söderpalm, B. (2011). Healthy subjects with a family history of alcoholism show increased stimulative subjective effects of alcohol. *Alcoholism: Clinical and Experimental Research.* doi:10.1111/j.1530-0277.2011.01478.x

Steinglass, P. (1980). A life history model of the alcoholic family. *Journal of the American Medical Association, 254,* 2614–2617.

Wilcoxon, A., & Remley, T. P. (2013). *Ethical, legal, and professional issues in the practice of marriage and family therapy.* Boston, MA: Merrill.

Zimmerman, M. A. (2013). Resiliency theory: A strengths-based approach to research and practice of adolescent health. *Health Education Behavior, 40*(4), 381–383. doi: 10.1177/1090198113493782

Chapter 10

Akins, S., Smith, C. L., & Mosher, C. (2010). Pathways to adult alcohol abuse across racial/ethnic groups: An application of general strain and social learning theories. *Journal of Drug Issues, 40*(2), 321–351. Retrieved from EBSCO*host.*

Alcoholics Anonymous. (2015). *Estimated worldwide A.A. individual and group membership.* Retrieved from http://www.aa.org/assets/en_US/smf-132_en.pdf

American Psychiatric Association. (2013). *Diagnostic and Statistical Manual of Mental Disorders, 5th Edition* (DSM-5). Arlington: American Psychiatric Publishing.

Association for Spiritual, Ethical, and Religious Values in Counseling. (n.d.). *Spirituality: A white paper.* Retrieved from http://www.angelfire.com/nj/counseling/Whitepaper1.htm

Bahr, S. J., Harris, L., Fisher, J. K., & Harker Armstrong, A. (2010). Successful reentry: What differentiates successful and unsuccessful parolees? *International Journal of Offender Therapy and Comparative Criminology, 54,* 667–692. doi:10.1177/03066240 9342435

Bahr, S. J., Masters, A. L., & Taylor, B. M. (2012). What works in substance abuse treatment programs for offenders? *Prison Journal, 92*(2), 155–174. doi:10.1177/0032885512438836

Bandura, A. (1969). *Principles of behavior modification.* New York, NY: Holt, Rinehart, & Winston.

Bandura, A. (1977). Reflections on self-efficacy. *Advances in Behavioral Research and Therapy, 1,* 237–269.

Bertrand, K., Richer, I., Brunelle, N., Beaudoin, I., Lemieu, A., & Ménard, J. M. (2013). Substance abuse treatment for adolescents: How are family factors related to substance use change? *Journal of Psychoactive Drugs, 45*(1), 28–38. doi:10.1080/02791 072.2013.76360.

Best, D. W., & Lubman, D. I. (2012). The recovery paradigm: A model of hope and change for alcohol and drug addiction. *Australian Family Physician, 41*(8), 593–597.

Brooks, A. J., & Penn, P. E. (2003). Comparing treatments for dual diagnosis: Twelve-step and self-management and recovery training. *American Journal of Drug and Alcohol Abuse, 29*(2), 359–383. doi:10.1081/ADA-120020519

Capuzzi, D., & Stauffer, M. D. (2012). *Foundations of addictions counseling.* Boston, MA: Pearson.

Clarke, P. B., & Myers, J. E. (2012). Developmental counseling and therapy: A promising intervention for preventing relapse with substance-abusing clients. *Journal of Mental Health Counseling, 34*(4), 308–321.

Collins, S. E., Clifasefi, S. L., Logan, D. E., Samples, L. S., Somers, J. M., & Marlatt, G. A. (2012). Current status, historical highlights, and basic principles of harm reduction. In G. A. Marlatt, M. E. Larimer, & K. Witkiewicz (Eds.), *Harm reduction: Pragmatic strategies for managing high-risk behaviors,* 2nd Ed. (pp. 3–35). New York, NY: Guilford Press.

Curry, S., Marlatt, G. A., & Gordon, J. R. (1987). Abstinence violation effect: Validation of an attributional construct with smoking cessation. *Journal of Counseling and Clinical Psychology, 55,* 147–149.

DiClemente, C. (2007). Mechanisms, determinants and processes of change in the modification of drinking behavior. *Alcoholism: Clinical & Experimental Research, 31*(S3), 13s–20s. doi:10.1111/j.1530-0277.2007.00489.

Di Noia, J., Mauriello, L., Byrd-Bredbenner, C., & Thompson, D. (2012). Validity and reliability of a dietary stages of change measure among economically disadvantaged African-American adolescents. *American Journal of Health Promotion, 26*(6), 381–389.

Doan, S. N., Dich, N., & Evans, G. W. (2013). Childhood cumulative risk and later allostatic load: Mediating role of substance use. *Health Psychology, 33*(11), 1402–1409. doi:10.1037/a0034790

Double Trouble in Recovery (Hazelden Publishing). (2014). Peer support is critical to co-occurring recovery. Retrieved from http://www.hazelden.org/web/go/dtr

Doweiko, H. E. (2012). *Concepts of chemical dependency* (8th ed.). Belmont, CA: Brooks/Cole.

Drazdowski, T. K., Jäggi, L., Borre, A., & Kliewer, W. L. (2015). Use of prescription drugs and future delinquency among adolescent offenders. *Journal of Substance Abuse Treatment, 48*(1):28–36. doi:http://d. doi.org/10.1016/j.jsat.2014.07.008

D'Sylva, F., Graffam, J., Hardcastle, L., & Shinkfield, A. J. (2012). Analysis of the stages of change model of drug and alcohol treatment readiness among prisoners. *International Journal of Offender Therapy and Comparative Criminology, 56*(2), 265–280.

Dunnington, K. (2011). *Addiction and virtue: Beyond the models of disease and choice*. Grove, IL: InterVarsity Press.

Fanton, M. C., Azzollini, S. C., Ayi, J. A., Sio, A. G., & Mora, G. E. (2013). Perception of control over cocaine use and stages of change. *Psychology of Addictive Behaviors, 27*(3), 841–847. doi:10.1037/a0033437

Ferrer, R., Amico, K. K., Bryan, A., Fisher, W., Cornman, D., Kiene, S., & Fisher, J. (2009). Accuracy of the stages of change algorithm: Sexual risk reported in the maintenance stage of change. *Prevention Science, 10*(1), 13–21. doi:10.1007/s11121-008-0108-7

Forcehimes, A. A., & Tonigan, J. S. (2008). Self-efficacy as a factor in abstinence from alcohol/other drug abuse: A meta-analysis. *Alcoholism Treatment Quarterly, 26*(4), 480–489. doi:10.1080/07347320802347145

Fox, H., Anderson, G., Tuit, K., Hansen, J., Kimmerling, A., Siedlarz, K., . . . Sinha, R. (2012). Prazosin effects on stress- and cue-induced craving and stress response in alcohol-dependent individuals: Preliminary findings. *Alcoholism, Clinical and Experimental Research, 36*(2), 351–360. doi:10.1111/j.1530-0277.2011.01628.

Freyer-Adam, J., Coder, B., Ottersbach, C., Tonigan, J., Rumpf, H., John, U., & Hapke, U. (2009). The performance of two motivation measures and outcome after alcohol detoxification. *Alcohol & Alcoholism, 44*(1), 77–83. doi:10.1093/alcalc/agn088

Gifford, E. V., Tavakoli, S., Weingardt, K. R., Finney, J. W., Pierson, H. M., Rosen, C. S., . . . Curran, G. M. (2012). How do components of evidence-based psychological treatment cluster in practice? A survey and cluster analysis. *Journal of Substance Abuse Treatment, 42*(1), 45–55. doi:10.1016/j.jsat.2011.07.008

Gorski, T. T. (1990). The CENAPS model of relapse prevention: Basic principles and procedure. *Journal of Psychoactive Drugs, 22*, 125–133.

Gorski, T. T. (2007). *The Gorski-CENAPS model for recovery and relapse prevention*. Independence, MO: Herald House/Independence Press.

Gorski, T. T., & Grinstead, S. F. (2010). Relapse prevention therapy workbook, Revised edition. Independence, MO: Herald Publishing House.

Gorski, T. T., & Miller, M. (1986). Staying sober: A guide for relapse prevention—Based upon the CENAPS model of treatment. Independence, MO: Independence Press.

Gossop, M., Stewart, D., & Marsden, J. (2008). Attendance at Narcotics Anonymous and Alcoholics Anonymous meetings, frequency of attendance and substance use outcomes after residential treatment for drug dependence: A 5-year follow-up study. *Addiction, 103*(1), 119–125. doi:10.1111/j.1360-0443.2007.02050.

Hagedorn, W., & Moorhead, H. (2010). The God-Shaped Hole: Addictive disorders and the search for perfection. *Counseling & Values, 55*(1), 63–78. Retrieved from Academic Search Complete database.

Hendershot, C. S., Witkiewitz, K., George, W. H., & Marlatt, G. A. (2011). Relapse prevention for addictive behaviors. *Substance Abuse Treatment, Prevention, and Policy, 6*(1), 1–17.

Horton-Parker, R. J., & Fawcett, R. C. (2010). *Spirituality in counseling and psychotherapy: The Face-Spirit model*. Denver, CO: Love.

Hunter-Reel, D., Witkiewitz, K., & Zweben, A. (2012). Does session attendance by a supportive significant other predict outcomes in individual treatment for alcohol use disorders? *Alcoholism, Clinical and Experimental Research, 36*(7), 1237–1243. doi:10.1111/j.1530-0277.2011.01719.

Jafari, E., Eskandari, H., Sohrabi, F., Delavar, A., & Heshmati, R. (2010). Effectiveness of coping skills training in relapse prevention and resiliency enhancement in people with substance dependency. *Procedia Social and Behavioral Sciences, 5*, 1376–1380.

Jellinek, E. M. (1960). *The disease concept of alcoholism*. New Brunswick, NJ: Millhouse.

Jhanjee, S. (2014). Evidence based psychosocial interventions in substance use. *Indian Journal of Psychological Medicine, 36*(2), 112–118.

Kadden, R. M., & Litt, M. D. (2011). The role of self-efficacy in the treatment of substance use disorders. *Addictive Behaviors 36*,1120–1126.

Kelly, J. F., & Hoeppner, B. B. (2013). Does Alcoholics Anonymous work differently for men and women? A moderated multiple-mediation analysis in a large clinical sample. *Drug and Alcohol Dependence, 130*, 186–193. http://d.doi.org/10.1016/j.drugalcdep.2012.11.005

Kelly, J. F., Kahler, C. W., & Humphreys, K. (2010). Assessing why substance use disorder patients drop out from or refuse to attend 12-step mutual-help groups: The "REASONS" questionnaire. *Addiction Research & Theory, 18*(3), 316–325. doi:10.3109/16066350903254775

Kinney, J. (2009). *Loosening the grip: A handbook of alcohol information.* New York, NY: McGraw-Hill.

Klingemann, H., Schläfli, K., Eggli, P., & Stutz, S. (2013). Drinking episodes during abstinence-oriented inpatient treatment: Dual perspectives of patients and therapists—A qualitative analysis. *Alcohol and Alcoholism, 48*(3), 322–328.

Leamy, M., Bird, V., Le Boutillier, C., Williams, J., & Slade, M. (2011). Conceptual framework for personal recovery in mental health: Systematic review and narrative synthesis. *British Journal of Psychiatry, 199*, 445–452. Retrieved from http://bjp.rcpsych.org/content/199/6/445

Marlatt, G. A. (1985a). Cognitive assessment and intervention procedures for relapse prevention. In G. A. Marlatt & J. Gordon (Eds.), *Relapse prevention: A self-control strategy for the maintenance of behavior change* (pp. 201–209). New York, NY: Guilford.

Marlatt, G. A. (1985b). Lifestyle modification. In G. A. Marlatt & J. Gordon (Eds.), *Relapse prevention: A self-control strategy for the maintenance of behavior change* (pp. 280–350). New York, NY: Guilford.

Marlatt, G. A., & Gordon, J. (Eds.). (1985). *Relapse prevention: A self-control strategy for the maintenance of behavior change.* New York, NY: Guilford.

Marlatt, G. A., Larimer, M. E., & Witkiewitz, K. (Eds.). (2012). *Harm reduction: Pragmatic strategies for managing high-risk behaviors* (2nd ed.): New York, NY: Guilford Press.

Marlatt, G. A., & Witkiewitz, K. (2011). Behavioral therapy across the spectrum. *Alcohol Research & Health, 33*(4), 313–319. Retrieved from http://go.galegroup.com.ezproy2.drake.brockport.edu/ps/i.do?id=GALE%7CA255840780&v=2.1&u=brockport&it=r&p=HRCA&sw=w&asid=6ed9835d485e502b298cd70883ba6b4a

Matheson, F. I., Doherty, S., & Grant, B. A. (2011). Community-based aftercare and return to custody in a national sample of substance-abusing women offenders. *American Journal of Public Health, 101*(6), 1126–1132.

Miller, W. R., & Rollnick, S. (2009). Ten things that motivational interviewing is not. *Behavioural Psychotherapy, 37*, 120–140. doi:10.1017/S1352465809005128

Miller, W. R., & Rollnick, S. (2014). The effectiveness and ineffectiveness of complex behavioral interventions: impact of treatment fidelity, *Contemporary Clinical Trials, 37*(2), 234–241. doi:10.1016/j.cct.2014.01.005

Minervini, I., Palandri, S., Bianchi, S., Bastiani, L., & Paffi, D. (2011). Desire and coping self-efficacy as craving measures in addiction: The Self-Efficacy and Desire Scale (SAD). *Open Behavioral Science Journal, 5*, 1–7. doi:10.2174/1874230001105010001

Moderation Management. (2014a). *What is Moderation Management?* Retrieved from http://www.moderation.org/whatisMM.shtml

Moderation Management. (2014b). *Suggested readings at MM meetings.* Retrieved from http://www.moderation.org/readings.shtml

Moderation Management. (2015). *Alcohol consumption limits.* Retrieved from http://moderation.org/otherlim.shtml

Moore, T. M., Seavey, A., Ritter, K., McNulty, J. K., Gordon, K. C., & Stuart, G. L. (2014). Ecological momentary assessment of the effects of craving and affect on risk for relapse during substance abuse treatment. *Psychology of Addictive Behaviors, 28*(2), 619–624. doi:10.1037/a0034127

Moos, R. H., Moos, B. S., & Timko, C. (2006). Gender, treatment and self-help in remission from alcohol use disorders. *Clinical Medicine & Research, 4*(3), 163–174. Retrieved from EBSCO*host*.

Murphy A., Taylor, E., & Elliott, R. (2012). The detrimental effects of emotional process dysregulation on decision-making in substance dependence. *Frontiers in Integrative Neuroscience, 6*, 101. doi:10.3389/fnint.2012.00101

Nattala, P., Leung, K. S., Nagarajaiah, & Murthy, P. (2010). Family member involvement in relapse prevention improves alcohol dependence outcomes: A prospective study at an addiction treatment facility in India. *Journal of Studies on Alcohol and Drugs, 71*(4), 581–587. Retrieved from http://go.galegroup.com/ps/i.do?id=GALE%7CA231504588&v=2.1&u=brockport&it=r&p=HRCA&sw=w&asid=0299e6671c180a17e4cdc629316b7035

Noël, X., Bechara, A., Brevers, D., Verbanck, P., & Campanella, S. (2010). Alcoholism and the loss of willpower: A neurocognitive perspective. *Journal of Psychophysiology, 24*(4), 240–248. doi:10.1027/0269-8803/a000037

Osten, K. A., & Switzer, R. (2014). *Integrating 12-Steps and psychotherapy.* Los Angeles, CA: Sage.

Pagano, M. E., White, W. L., Kelly, J. F., Stout, R. L., & Tonigan, J. S. (2013). The 10-year course of Alcoholics Anonymous participation and long-term outcomes: A follow-up study of outpatient subjects in Project MATCH. *Substance Abuse, 34*, 51–59. doi:10.1080/08897077.2012.691450

Petry, N. M., Barry, D., Alessi, S. M., Rounsaville, B. J., & Carroll, K. M. (2012). A randomized trial adapting contingency management targets based on initial abstinence status of cocaine-dependent patients. *Journal of Consulting and Clinical Psychology, 80*(2), 276– 285. doi:10.1037/a0026883

Post, S. G. (2014). The ontological generality: Recovery in triadic community with a Higher Power, neighbor, and self. *Alcoholism Treatment Quarterly, 32*(2–3), 120–140. doi:10.1080/07347324.2014.907031

Prochaska, J. J., & Prochaska, J. O. (2011). A review of multiple health behavior change interventions for primary prevention. *American Journal of Lifestyle Medicine, 5*(3), 208–221.

Prochaska, J. O., DiClemente, C. C., & Norcross, J. C. (1992). In search of how people change. *American Psychologist, 47*(9), 1102–1114. Retrieved from EBSCO*host*.

Rational Recovery. (2013). Retrieved from https:// rational.org/inde.php?id=1

Raylu, N., & Kaur, I. (2012). Relationships between treatment expectations and treatment Outcomes among outpatients with substance use problems. *International Journal of Mental Health & Addiction, 10*(5), 607–621. doi:10.1007/ s11469-011-9358-

Rosenberg, H., Bonar E. E., Hoffmann, E., Kryszak E., Young, K. M., Krauss, S. W., . . . Pavlick, M. (2011). Assessing university students' self-efficacy to employ alcohol-related harm reduction strategies. *Journal of American College Health, 59*(8), 736–742.

Rowe, C. L. (2012). Family therapy for drug abuse: Review and updates 2003–2010. *Journal of Marital and Family Therapy, 38*(1), 59–81. doi:10.1111/j.1752-0606.2011.00280

Rowland, B., Allen, F., & Toumbourou, J. W. (2012). Impact of alcohol harm reduction strategies in community sports clubs: Pilot evaluation of the Good Sports program. *Health Psychology, 31*(3), 323–333. doi:10.1037/a0026397

Russell, C., Davies, J. B., & Hunter, S. C. (2011). Predictors of addiction treatment providers' beliefs in the disease and choice models of addiction. *Journal of Substance Abuse Treatment, 40*(2), 150–164. doi:10.1016/j.jsat.2010.09.006

Samek, D. R., & Rueter, M. A. (2011). Considerations of elder sibling closeness in predicting younger sibling substance use: Social learning versus social bonding explanations. *Journal of Family Psychology, 25*(6), 931–941. doi:10.1037/a0025857

Secular Organizations for Sobriety. (2015). *Center for inquiry.* Retrieved from http://www.centerforinquiry. net/sos

Senbanjo, R., Wolff, K., Marshall, E., & Strang, J. (2009). Persistence of heroin use despite methadone treatment: Poor coping self-efficacy predicts continued heroin use. *Drug & Alcohol Review, 28*(6), 608–615. doi:10.1111/ j.1465-3362.2009.00064.

Shepherd, J. (2014). Combating the prescription painkiller epidemic: A national prescription drug reporting program. *American Journal of Law & Medicine, 40*(1), 85–112.

Sinha, R. (2012). How does stress lead to risk of alcohol relapse? *Alcohol Research: Current Reviews, 34*(4), 432–440.

Slesnick, N., & Prestopnik, J. L. (2009). Comparison of family therapy outcome with alcohol abusing runaway adolescents. *Journal of Marital and Family Therapy, 35*(3), 255–277. doi:10.1111/j.1752-0606.2009.00121.

SOS Fast Index. (2015). Retrieved from http://www. sossobriety.org/meetings/

The SOS Story. (2014). Retrieved from http://www. sossobriety.org/james%20christopher.htm

Substance Abuse and Mental Health Services Administration (SAMHSA). (2014). *Mental health and substance use disorders.* Retrieved from http://www. samhsa.gov/disorders

Thakker, J., & Ward, T. (2010). Relapse prevention: A critique and proposed reconceptualisation. *Behaviour Change, 27*(3), 154–175. doi:10.1375/bech.27.3.154

Tonigan, J. S. (2008). Alcoholics Anonymous outcomes and benefits. In M. Galanter & L. A. Kaskutas (Eds.), *Recent developments in alcoholism, Vol. 18, Research on Alcoholics Anonymous and spirituality in addiction recovery* (pp. 59–70). Totowa, NJ: Humana Press.

Trimpey, J. (1996). *Rational Recovery: The new cure for substance addiction.* New York, NY: Simon & Schuster.

Vanderplasschen, W., Bloor, M., & McKeganey, N. (2010). Long-term outcomes of aftercare participation following various forms of drug abuse treatment in Scotland. *Journal of Drug Issues, 40*(3), 703–728. doi:10.1177/002204261004000308

Wahab, S. (2010). Motivational interviewing and social work practice. In K. van Wormer & B. A. Thyer (Eds.), *Evidence-based practice in the field of substance abuse* (pp. 197–210). Los Angeles, CA: Sage.

Wanberg, K. W., & Milkman, H. B. (2008). *Criminal conduct and substance abuse treatment: Strategies for self-improvement and change.* Los Angeles, CA: Sage.

Ward, T., & Fortune, C. A. (2013). The Good Lives Model: Aligning risk reduction with promoting offenders' personal goals. *European Journal of Probation, 5*(2), 29–46.

White, W. L., & Kurtz, E. (2008). Twelve defining moments in the history of Alcoholics Anonymous. In M. Galanter & L. A. Kaskutas (Eds.), *Recent developments in alcoholism, Vol. 18, Research on Alcoholics Anonymous and spirituality in addiction recovery* (pp. 37–57). Totowa, NJ: Humana Press.

Willis, G. M., Ward, T., & Levenson, J. S. (2014). The Good Lives Model (GLM): An evaluation of GLM operationalization in North American treatment programs. *Sexual Abuse: A Journal of Research and Treatment, 26*(1), 58–81. doi:10.1177/1079063213478202

Witkiewitz, K., Bowen, S., Douglas, H., & Hsu, S. H. (2013). Mindfulness-based relapse prevention for substance craving. *Addictive Behaviors, 38*(2), 1563–1571.

Witkiewitz, K., Lustyk, M. B., & Bowen, S. (2013). Retraining the addicted brain: A review of hypothesized neurobiological mechanisms of mindfulness-based relapse prevention. *Psychology of Addictive Behaviors, 27*(2), 351–365. doi:10.1037/a0029258

Witkiewitz, K., & Marlatt, G. A. (2004). Relapse prevention for alcohol and drug problems: That was Zen, this is Tao. *American Psychologist, 59*(4), 224–235. doi:10.1037/0003-066.59.4.224

Witkiewitz, K., & Marlatt, G. A. (2006). Overview of harm reduction for alcohol problems. *International Journal of Drug Policy, 17*(4), 285–294. doi:10.1016/j.drugpo.2006.03.005

Zois, E. K., Vollstädt-Klein, S., Lemenager, T., Beutel, M., Mann, K., & Fauth-Buhler, M. (2014). Decision-making deficits in patients diagnosed with disordered gambling using the Cambridge Gambling task: The effects of substance use disorder comorbidity. *Brain and Behavior, 4*(4), 484–494. doi:10.1002/brb3.231

Chapter 11

Agrawal, A. (2005). *Patterns of use: Initiation to treatment.* Rockville, MD: SAMHSA's National Survey on Drug Abuse and Health.

Blank, K. (2009). Older adults & substance use: New data highlight concerns. *SAMHSA Newsletter, 17*(1).

Blustein, E. C., Munn-Chernoff, M. A., Grant, J. D., Sartor, C. E., Bucholz, K. K., Madden, P. A. F., & Heath, A. C. (2015). The association of low parental monitoring with early substance use in European-American and African-American adolescent girls. *Journal of Studies on Alcohol and Drugs, 76*, 852–861.

Brault, M. W. (2012). *Americans with disabilities: 2010.* U.S. Department of Commerce.

Brooks, M. K. (2012). Legal issues for programs treating LGBT clients. In *Center for Substance Abuse Treatment: A provider's introduction to substance use treatment for lesbian, gay, bisexual, and transgender individuals* (pp. 29–48). HHS Pub. No. (SMA) 12-4104-4104. Rockville, MD: Department of Health and Human Services.

Brooks-Russell, A., Conway, K. P., Liu, D., Xie, Y., Vullo, G. C., Li, K., . . . Simons-Morton, B. G. (2015). Dynamic patterns of adolescent substance use: Results from a nationally representative sample of high school students. *Journal of Studies on Alcohol and Drugs, 76,* 962–970.

Brown, B. (2010). *The Gifts of Imperfection: Let Go of Who You Think You're Supposed to be and Embrace Who You are.* Published by Hazelden Information & Educational Services.

Brown, S. A., Brumback, T., Tomlinson, K., Cummins, K., Thompson, W. K., Nagel, B. J., . . . Tapert, S. F. (2015). The National Consortium on Alcohol and Neuro-Development in Adolescence (NCANDA): A multisite study on adolescent development and substance use. *Journal of Studies on Alcohol and Drugs, 76,* 895–908.

Cabaj, R. P., & Smith, M. (2012). Overview of treatment approaches, modalities, and issues of accessibility in the continuum of care. In *Center for Substance Abuse Treatment: A provider's introduction to substance use treatment for lesbian, gay, bisexual, and transgender individuals* (pp. 49–60). HHS Pub. No. (SMA) 12-4104. Rockville, MD: Department of Health and Human Services.

Camarota, S. A., & Zeigler, K. (2015a, August). *Immigration population hits record 42.1 million in second quarter of 2015.* Washington, DC: Center for Immigration Studies.

Camarota, S. A., & Zeigler, K. (2015b, April). *Immigration population to hit highest percentage ever in 8 years.* Washington, DC: Center for Immigration Studies.

Capuzzi, D., & Gross, D. R. (2012). *Introduction to the counseling profession* (6th ed.). New York, NY: Pearson Education.

Carlini, B. H., Safioti, L., Rue, T. C., & Miles, L. (2015). Using Internet to recruit immigrants with language and culture barriers for tobacco and alcohol use screening: A study among Brazilians. *Journal of Immigrant Minority Health, 17,* 553–560.

Cass, V. C. (1979). Homosexual identity formation: A theoretical model. *Journal of Homosexuality, 4,* 219–235.

Cass, V. C. (1984). Homosexual identity formation: Testing a theoretical model. *Journal of Sex Research, 20,* 143–167.

Center for Substance Abuse Treatment (CSAT). (2012a). *A provider's introduction to substance abuse treatment for lesbian, gay, bisexual, and transgender individuals.* HHS Pub. No. (SMA) 12-4104. Rockville, MD: Department of Health and Human Services.

Center for Substance Abuse Treatment. (2012b). *Substance abuse among older adults.* Treatment Improvement Protocol (TIP) Series, No. 26. HHS Pub. No. (SMA) 12-3918. Rockville, MD: Substance Abuse and Mental Health Services Administration.

Choi, N. G., DiNitto, D. M., & Marti, C. N. (2014). Treatment use, perceived need, and barriers to seeking treatment for substance abuse and mental health problems among older adults compared to younger adults. *Drug and Alcohol Dependence, 145*, 113–120.

Coalition for the Homeless. (2016). *A growing crisis for single adults.* Retrieved from http://www.coalition-forthehomeless.org/wp-content/uploads/2016/08/Briefing-Paper-Single-Adult-Homelessness_FINAL.pdf

Cooper, L. (2012). Combined motivational interviewing and cognitive-behavioral therapy with older adult drug and alcohol abusers. *Health and Social Work*, 173–179.

Counselor (2006). Substance use treatment for disabled persons. *Magazine for Addiction Professionals, 7*, 62–66.

Department of Defense. (2013). Health Related Behaviors Survey of Active Duty Military Personnel. Retrieved from file:///C:/Users/Perry/Desktop/Research/Military/Final%202011%20HRB%20Active%20Duty%20Survey%20Exec%20Summary.pdf

Dunn, M. G., & Mezzich, A.C. (2007). Development in childhood and adolescence: Implications for prevention research and practice. In P. Tolan, J. Szapocznik, & S. Sambrano (Eds.), *Preventing youth substance use: Science-based programs for children and adolescents* (pp. 21–40). Washington, DC: American Psychological Association.

Ewing, B. A., Chan Osilla, K., Pedersen, E. R., Hunter, S. B., Miles, J., & D'Amico, E. J. (2015). Longitudinal family effects on substance use among an at-risk adolescent sample. *Addictive Behaviors, 41*, 185–191.

Finnegan, D. G. (2012). Clinical issues with lesbians. In *Center for Substance Abuse Treatment: A provider's introduction to substance use treatment for lesbian, gay, bisexual, and transgender individuals* (pp. 75–79). HHS Pub. No. (SMA) 12-4104. Rockville, MD: Department of Health and Human Services.

Gans, J., Falco, M., Schackman, B. R., & Winters, K. C. (2010). An in-depth survey of the screening and assessment practices in highly regarded adolescent substance abuse treatment programs. *Journal of Child & Adolescent Substance Abuse, 19*, 33–47.

Greenfield, S. F., Back, S. E., Lawson, K., & Brady, K. T. (2010). Substance Abuse in women. *Psychiatric Clinics of North America, 33*, 339–355.

Griffin, K. W., & Botvin, G. J. (2010). Evidence-based interventions for preventing substance use disorders in adolescents. *Child and Adolescent Psychiatric Clinics of North America, 19*, 505–526.

Hazle, M., Wilcox, S. L., & Hassan, A. M. (2012). Helping veterans and their families fight on! *Advances in Social Work, 13*(1), 229–242.

Ibabe, I., Stein, J. A., Nyamathi, A., & Bentler, P. M. (2014). Predictors of substance use treatment participation among homeless adults. *Journal of Substance Abuse Treatment, 3*, 374–381.

Institute of Medicine. (2012). *Substance use disorders in the U.S. armed forces: Report brief.* Retrieved from: https://iom.nationalacademies.org/~/media/Files/Report%20Files/2012/Military-SUD/SUD_rb.pdf

Institute of Medicine. (2012). *The mental health and substance use workforce for older adults. In whose hands?* Washington, DC: Institute of Medicine of the National Academies.

Johnston, L. D., O'Malley, P. M., Miech, R. A., Bachman, J. G., & Schulenberg, J. E. (2015). *Monitoring the Future national survey results on drug use, 1975–2014: Overview, key findings on adolescent drug use.* Ann Arbor: Institute for Social Research, The University of Michigan.

Kaya, A., Iwamoto, D. K., Grivel, M., Clinton, L., & Brady, J. (2015, November 9). The role of feminine and masculine norms in college women's alcohol use. *Psychology of Men & Masculinity.* Retrieved from http://dx.doi.org/10.1037/men0000017.

Kinney, J. (2009). *Loosening the grip: A handbook of alcohol information.* Boston, MA: McGraw-Hill.

Korper, S. P., & Raskin, I. E. (2008). *The impact of substance use and abuse by the elderly: The next 20 to 30 years.* Rockville, MD: Office of Applied Studies, SAMHSA.

Lanzetta, B. J. (2005). *Radical wisdom: A feminist mystical theology.* Minneapolis, MN: Fortress Press.

Lee, H. S., & Petersen, S. R. (2009). Demarginalizing the marginalized in substance abuse treatment: Stories of homeless, active substance users in an urban harm reduction based drop-in center. *Addiction Research and Theory, 17*, 622–636.

Levounis, P., Drescher, J., & Barber, M. D. (2012). *The LGBT casebook.* Washington, DC: American Psychiatric Publishing.

Li, K., & Wen, M. (2015). Substance use, age at migration, and length of residence among adult immigrants in the United States. *Journal of Immigrant Minority Health, 17*, 156–164.

Livneh, H., & Antonak, R. F. (2007). Psychological adaptation to chronic illness and disability: A primer for counselors. In A. E. Dell Orto & P. W. Power (Eds.), *The psychological and social impact of illness and disability* (pp. 125–144). New York, NY: Springer.

Mancini, M. A., Salas-Wright, C. P., & Vaughn, M. G. (2015). Drug use and service utilization among Hispanics in the United States. *Social Psychiatry and Psychiatric Epidemiology, 50*, 1679–1689.

Martin, F. S., & Aston, S. (2014). A "special population" with "unique treatment needs": Dominant representations of "women's substance abuse" and their effects. *Contemporary Drug Problems, 41*, 335–360.

McCabe, P. T. (2012). Families of origin and families of choice. In *Center for Substance Abuse Treatment: A provider's introduction to substance use treatment for lesbian, gay, bisexual, and transgender individuals* (pp. 71–74). HHS Pub. No. (SMA) 12-4104. Rockville, MD: Department of Health and Human Services.

McCabe, S. E., Bostwick, W. B., Hughes, T. L., West, B. T., & Boyd, C. J. (2010). The relationship between discrimination and substance use disorder among lesbian, gay, and bisexual adults in the United States. *American Journal of Public Health, 100*, 1946–1952.

McFarling, L., D'Angelo, M., Drain, M., Gibbs, D. A., & Rae Olmsted, K. L. (2011). Stigma as a barrier to substance abuse and mental health treatment. *Military Psychology, 23*(1), 1–5.

McNally, E. B. (2012). The coming out process for lesbians and gay men. In *Center for Substance Abuse Treatment: A provider's introduction to substance use treatment for lesbian, gay, bisexual, and transgender individuals* (pp. 63–69). HHS Pub. No. (SMA) 12-4104. Rockville, MD: Department of Health and Human Services.

Moya, E. M., & Shedlin, M. G. (2008). Treatment: Obstacles to recovery and immigrant health. *Substance Use & Misuse, 43*, 1747–1769.

National Alliance to End Homelessness. (2016a). *The state of homelessness in America.* Retrieved from http://www.endhomelessness.org/library/entry/SOH2016

National Alliance to End Homelessness. (2016b). *Snapshot of homelessness.* Retrieved from http://www.endhomelessness.org/pages/snapshot_of_homelessness.

National Center on Family Homelessness. (2016). *America's youngest outcasts: Fact sheet.* Newton, MA: Author.

National Coalition for the Homeless. (2009). *Substance use and homelessness.* Washington, DC: Author.

National Coalition for the Homeless. (2012). *Hate crimes and violence against people experiencing homelessness.* Washington, DC: Author.

National Institute on Drug Abuse. (2007a). *Message from the director: Women's Health Week.* Bethesda, MD: U.S. Department of Health and Human Services.

National Institute on Drug Abuse. (2007b). *Preventing drug use among children and adolescents: A research based guide.* NIH Pub. No. 04-4212 (B). Rockville, MD: National Clearinghouse for Alcohol and Drug Information.

National Law Center on Homelessness and Poverty. (2015). *Homeless in America: Overview of data and causes.* Washington, DC: Author.

Obando D., Trujillo, A., & Trujillo, C. A. (2014). Substance use and antisocial behavior in adolescents: The role of family and peer-individual risk and protective factors. *Substance Use and Misuse, 49*, 1934–1944.

Ojeda, V. D., Patterson, T. L., & Strathdee, S. A. (2008). The influence of perceived risk to health and immigration-related characteristics on substance use among Latino and other immigrants. *American Journal of Public Health, 98*, 862–868.

O'Sullivan, D. O., Blum, J. B., Watts, J., & Bates, J. K. (2015). SMART Recovery: Continuing care considerings for rehabilitation counselors. *Rehabilitation Counseling Bulletin, 58*, 203–2016.

Partnership for Drug-Free Kids. (2013). *The Partnership Attitude Tracking Study (PATS).* New York, NY: MetLife Foundation.

Piko, B. F., & Kovacs, E. (2010). Do parents and school matter? Protective factors for adolescent substance use. *Addictive Behaviors, 35*, 53–56.

Reivich, K. (2010, Mar/Apr). Building resilience in youth: The Penn resiliency program. *National Association of School Psychologists, Communique.*

Rosen, D., Heberlein, E., & Engel, R. J. (2013). Older adults and substance-related disorders: Trends and associated costs. *ISRN Addiction*, 1–4.

Salas-Wright, C. P., & Vaughn, M. G. (2014). A "refugee paradox" for substance use disorders? *Drug and Alcohol Dependence, 142*, 345–349.

Salas-Wright, C. P., Vaughn, M. G., Clark, T. T., Terzis, L. D., & Cordova, D. (2014). Substance use disorders among first- and second-generation immigrant adults in the United States: Evidence of an immigrant paradox. *Journal of Studies on Alcohol, 75,* 958–967.

Savage, J. E., & Mezuk, B. (2014). Psychosocial and contextual determinants of alcohol and drug use disorders in the national Latino and Asian American study. *Drug and Alcohol Dependence, 139,* 71–78.

Sharma, M. (2014). Substance use in women: Implications for research and practice. *Journal of Alcohol and Drug Education, 58,* 3–6.

Smart, J. (2009). *Disability, society, and the individual.* Austin, TX: Pro-Ed.

Stade, B. C., Bailey, C., Dzendoletas, D., Sgro, M., Dowswell, T., & Bennett, D. (2009). Psychological and/or educational interventions for reducing alcohol consumption in pregnant women and women planning pregnancy. *Cochrane Database of Systematic Reviews, 2,* CD004228.

Stevens, S. J. (2006, January). *Women and substance use: A gendered perspective.* Paper presented at the Fifth Annual Women's Mental Health Symposium, Tucson, AZ.

Stevens, S. J., Andrade, R. A. C., & Ruiz, B. S. (2009). Women and substance Abuse: Gender, age, and cultural considerations. *Journal of Ethnicity in Substance Abuse, 8,* 341–358.

Stone, A. L., Becker, L. G., Huber, A. M., & Catalano, R. F. (2012). Review of risk and protective factors of substance use and problem use in emerging adulthood. *Addictive Behaviors, 37,* 747–775.

Substance Abuse and Mental Health Services Administration. (2006). *Prevention of alcohol misuse for older adults.* Rockville, MD: Older Americans Technical Assistance Center.

Substance Abuse and Mental Health Services Administration. (2014a). *Results from the 2013 National Survey on Drug Use and Health: Summary of national findings.* NSDUH Series H-48, HHS Publication No. (SMA) 14-4863. Rockville, MD: Author.

Substance Abuse and Mental Health Services Administration. (2014b). *Veterans and military families.* Retrieved from httpww.samhsa.gov/veterans-military-families

Suicide Prevention Resource Center. (2008). *Suicide risk and prevention for lesbian, gay, bisexual, and transgender youth.* Newton, MA: Education Development Center.

Szaflarski, M., Cubbins, L. A., & Ying, J. (2011). Epidemiology of alcohol abuse among U.S. immigrant populations. *Journal of Immigrant Minority Health, 13,* 647–658.

Tran, A. G., Lee, R. M., & Burgess, D. J. (2010). Perceived discrimination and substance use in Hispanic/Latino, African-Born Black, and Southeast Asian immigrants. *Cultural Diversity and Ethnic Minority Psychology, 16,* 226–236.

Trenz, R. C., Dunne, E. M., Zur, J., & Latimer, W. W. (2015). An investigation of school-related variables as risk and protective factors associated with problematic substance use among vulnerable urban adolescents. *Vulnerable Children and Youth Studies, 10,* 131–140.

Tze, V. M., Li, J. C., & Pei, J. (2012). Effective prevention of adolescent substance use—educational versus deterrent approaches. *Alberta Journal of Educational Research, 58*(1), 122–138.

United States Conference of Mayors. (2014). *Hunger and Homelessness Survey: A status report on hunger and homelessness in America's cities.* Retrieved from http://usmayors.org/publications/

U.S. Bureau of the Census. (2010). *Population profile of the United States.* Washington, DC: U.S. Government Printing Office.

U.S. Department of Defense. (2010). *Suicide Prevention Taskforce executive summary.* Retrieved from http://www.stripes.com/polopoly_fs/1.115776.1282666756!/menu/standard/file/Suicide%20Prevention%20Task%20Force_EXEC%20SUM_08-20-10%20v6.pdf

U.S. Department of Health and Human Services. (2000, November). *Healthy People 2010: Understanding and improving health* (2nd ed.). Washington, DC: U.S. Government Printing Office. Retrieved from http://www.healthypeople.gov/2010/document/pdf/uih/2010uih.pdf

U.S. Department of Health and Human Services. (2005a, September). *National summit on recovery: Conference report.* Rockville, MD: SAMHSA/CSAT. Retrieved from http://pfr.samhsa.gov/docs/Summit-Rpt.pdf

U.S. Department of Health and Human Services. (2005b). *The Surgeon General's call to action to improve the health and wellness of persons with disabilities.* U.S. Department of Health and Human Services: Office of the Surgeon General. Retrieved from https://www.ncbi.nlm.nih.gov/books/NBK44667/pdf/Bookshelf_NBK44667.pdf

West, S. L., Graham, C. W., & Cifu, D. X. (2009). Prevalence of persons with disabilities in alcohol/other drug treatment in the United States. *Alcoholism Treatment Quarterly, 27,* 242–252.

White, W. L., & Kilbourne, J. (2006). American women and addiction: A cultural double bind. *Counselor, 7,* 46–50.

Wilsnack, S. C., Wilsnack, R. W., & Wolfgang Kantor, L. (2014). Focus on: Women and the costs of alcohol use. *Alcohol Research: Current Reviews*, 219–228.

Chapter 12

Abe-Kim, J., Takeuchi, D. T., Hong, S., Zane, N., Sue, S., Spencer, M. S., . . . Alegría, M. (2007). Use of mental health-related services among immigrant and U.S.-born Asian Americans: Results from the National Latino and Asian American study. *American Journal of Public Health*, 97(1), 91–98.

Alarcon, R. D., & Ruiz, P. (2010). Hispanic Americans. In P. Ruiz & A. Primm (Eds.), *Disparities in psychiatric care: Clinical and cross-cultural perspectives* (pp. 30–39). Baltimore, MD: Lippincott Williams & Wilkins.

American Foundation for Suicide Prevention. (2014). *Suicide statistics*. Retrieved from https://afsp.org/about-suicide/suicide-statistics/

Appleyard, K., Berlin, L. J., Rosanbalm, K. D., & Dodge, K. A. (2011). Preventing early child maltreatment: Implications from a longitudinal study of maternal abuse history, substance use problems, and offspring victimization. *Prevention Science*, 12(2), 139–149.

Bachman, J. G., Staff, J., O'Malley, P. M., & Freedman-Doan, P. (2013). Adolescent work intensity, school performance, and substance use: Links vary by race/ethnicity and socioeconomic status. *Developmental Psychology*, 49(11), 2125–2134.

Banks, J., & McGee Banks, C. (Eds). (2010). *Multicultural education: Issues and perspectives* (4th ed.). New York, NY: Wiley.

Barnes, P. M., Adams, P. F., & Powell-Griner, E. (2010). Health characteristics of the American Indian or Alaska Native adult population: United States, 2004–2008. *National Health Statistics Reports*, 20, 1–22.

Baumann, A. A., Kuhlberg, J. A., & Zayas, L. H. (2010). Familism, mother-daughter mutuality, and suicide attempts of adolescent Latinas. *Journal of Family Psychology*, 24(5), 616–624.

Beauvais, F. (2014). Substance use. In F. T. L. Leong, L. Comas-Díaz, G. C. Nagayama Hall, V. C. McLoyd, & J. E. Trimble (Eds.), *APA handbook of multicultural psychology, Vol. 2: Applications and training* (pp. 329–343). Washington, DC: American Psychological Association.

Bell-Tolliver, L., Burgess, R., & Brock, L. J. (2009). African American therapists working with African American families: An exploration of the strengths perspective in treatment. *Journal of Marital and Family Therapy*, 35(3), 293–307.

Bernal, G., Cumba-Avilés, E., & Rodriguez-Quintana, N. (2014). Methodological challenges in research with ethnic, racial, and ethnocultural groups. In F. T. L. Leong, L. Comas-Díaz, G. C. Nagayama Hall, V. C. McLoyd, & J. E. Trimble (Eds.), *APA handbook of multicultural psychology, Vol. 1: Theory and research.* (pp. 105–123). Washington, DC: American Psychological Association.

Blume, A. W., & Escobedo, C. J. (2005). Best practices for substance abuse treatment among American Indians and Alaskan Natives: Review and critique. In E. H. Hawkins & R. D. Walker (Eds), *Best practices in behavioral health services for American Indian and Alaskan Natives* (Draft). Portland, OR: One Sky National Resource Center for American Indian and Alaskan Native Substance Abuse Prevention and Treatment Services.

Boardman, J. D., Finch, B. K., Ellison, C. G., Williams, D. R., & Jackson, J. S. (2001). Neighborhood disadvantage, stress, and substance use among adults. *Journal of Health and Social Behavior*, 42(2), 151–165.

Bowser, B. P., Word, C. O., Fulliove, R. E., & Fulliove, M. T. (2014). Post-script to the crack epidemic and its links to HIV. *Journal of Equity in Health, 3*, 45–54.

Bridges, A. J., Andrews, A. R. I., & Deen, T. L. (2012). Mental health needs and service utilization by Hispanic immigrants residing in Mid-southern United States. *Journal of Transcultural Nursing*, 23(4), 359–368.

Carpiano, R. M. (2007). Neighborhood and social capital and adult health: An empirical test of a Bourdieu-based model. *Health and Place, 13*, 639–655.

Carvajal, S. C., & Young, R. S. (2009). Culturally based substance abuse treatment for American Indians/Alaska natives and Latinos. *Journal of Ethnicity in Substance use*, 8(3), 207–222.

Centers for Disease Control and Prevention. (2009). *Health, United States, 2008*. Table 61. Retrieved from http://www.cdc.gov/nchs/data/hus/hus08.pdf

Centers for Disease Control and Prevention. (2010). *Leading causes of death in males United States, 2010.* Retrieved from http://www.cdc.gov/men/lcod/2010/index.htm

Centers for Disease Control and Prevention. (2011). *CDC health disparities and inequalities report—United States, 2011. MMWR, 60* (Suppl). Retrieved from http://www.cdc.gov/mmwr/pdf/other/su6001.pdf

Chaix, B., Merlo, J., Subramanian, S. V., Lynch, J., & Chauvin, P. (2005). Comparison of a spatial perspective with the multilevel analytical approach in neighborhood studies: the case of mental and behavioral disorders due to psychoactive substance use in Malmö, Sweden, 2001. *American Journal of Epidemiology, 162*(2), 171–182.

Chang, T., & Subramaniam, P. R. (2008). Asian and Pacific Islander American men's help-seeking: Cultural values and beliefs, gender roles, and racial stereotypes. *International Journal of Men's Health, 7*(2), 121–136.

Chartier, K., & Caetano, R. (2010). Ethnicity and health disparities in alcohol research. *Alcohol Research & Health, 33*(1–2), 152–160.

Chavez, L. G. (2005). Latin American healers and healing: Healing as a redefinition process. In R. Moodley & W. West (Eds.), *Integrating traditional healing practices into counseling and psychotherapy* (pp. 85–99). Thousand Oaks, CA: Sage.

Choi, Y., Harachi, T. W., & Catalano, R. F. (2006). Neighborhoods, family, and substance use: Comparisons of the relations across racial and ethnic groups. *Social Service Review, 80*(4), 675–704.

Chou, R. S., & Feagin, J. R. (2008). *The myth of the model minority: Asian Americans facing racism.* St. Paul, MN: Paradigm.

Chou, T., Asnaani, A., & Hofmann, S. G. (2012). Perception of racial discrimination and psychopathology across three U.S. ethnic minority groups. *Cultural Diversity and Ethnic Minority Psychology, 18*(1), 74–81.

Choudhuri, D. D., Santiago-Rivera, A. L., & Garrett, M. T. (2012). *Counseling and diversity.* Belmont, CA: Cengage.

Chuang, Y.-C., Ennett, S. T., Bauman, K. E., & Foshee, V. A. (2005). Neighborhood influences on adolescent cigarette and alcohol use: Mediating effects through parent and peer behaviors. *Journal of Health and Social Behavior, 46*(2), 187–204.

Cleveland, M. J., Feinberg, M. E., & Greenberg, M. T. (2010). Protective families in high- and low-risk environments: Implications for adolescent substance use. *Journal of Youth and Adolescence, 39*(2), 114–126.

Datta, G. D., Subramanian, S. V., Colditz, G. A., Kawachi, I., Palmer, J. R., & Rosenberg, L. (2006). Individual, neighborhood, and state-level predictors of smoking among U.S. Black women: A multilevel analysis. *Social Science & Medicine, 63*(4), 1034–1044.

Denny, C. H., Floyd, R. L., Green, P. P., & Hayes, D. K. (2012). Racial and ethnic disparities in preconception risk factors and preconception care. *Journal of Women's Health, 21*(7), 720–728.

Edlin, G., & Golanty, E. (2010). *Health and wellness. Achievement gap.* Sudbury, MA: Jones & Bartlett.

Espirito Santo, D. (2010). Spiritist boundary-work and the morality of materiality in Afro-Cuban religion. *Journal of Material Culture, 15*(1), 64–82.

Falconier, M. K., Nussbeck, F., & Bodenmann, G. (2013). Immigration stress and relationship satisfaction in Latino couples: The role of dyadic coping. *Journal of Social and Clinical Psychology, 32*(8), 813–843.

Fauth, R. C., Leventhal, T., & Brooks-Gunn, J. (2007). Welcome to the neighborhood? Long-term impacts of moving to low-poverty neighborhoods on poor children's and adolescents' outcomes. *Journal of Research on Adolescence, 17*(2), 249–284.

Fortuna, L. R., Alegria, M., & Gao, S. (2010). Retention in depression treatment among ethnic and racial minority groups in the United States. *Depression and Anxiety, 27*(5), 485–494.

Furman, R., Negi, N. J., Iwamoto, D. K., Rowan, D., Shukraft, A., & Gragg, J. (2009). Social work practice with Latinos: Key issues for social workers. *Social Work, 54*(2), 167–174.

Galea, S., Ahern, J., Tracy, M., Rudenstine, S., & Vlahov, D. (2007). Education inequality and use of cigarettes, alcohol, and marijuana. *Substance and Alcohol Dependence, 90*(Suppl), S4–S15.

Galea, S., Ahern, J., Tracy, M., & Vlahov, D. (2007). Neighborhood income and income distribution and the use of cigarettes, alcohol, and marijuana. *American Journal of Preventive Medicine, 32*(6, Suppl 1), S195–S202.

Gardner, M., Barajas, R. G., & Brooks-Gunn, J. (2010). Neighborhood influences on substance use etiology: Is where you live important? In L. Scheier (Ed.), *Handbook of substance use etiology: Theory, methods, and empirical findings.* (pp. 423–441). Washington, DC: American Psychological Association.

Garrett, M., & Portman, E. F. (2011). *Counseling Native Americans.* Belmont, CA: Cengage.

Garza, Y., & Watts, R. E. (2010). Filial therapy and Hispanic values: Common ground for culturally sensitive helping. *Journal of Counseling & Development, 88*(1), 108–113.

Hall, E. T. (1984). *The dance of life: The other dimension of time.* New York, NY: Anchor Books.

Hardaway, C. R., & McLoyd, V. C. (2009). Escaping poverty and securing middle class status: How race and socioeconomic status shape mobility prospects for African Americans during the transition to adulthood. *Journal of Youth and Adolescence, 38*(2), 242–256.

Hardy, K. M. (2012). Perceptions of African American Christians' attitudes toward religious help-seeking: Results of an exploratory study. *Journal of Religion &*

Spirituality in Social Work: Social Thought, 31(3), 209–225.

Henkel, D. (2011). Unemployment and substance use: A review of the literature (1990–2010). *Current Substance Abuse Reviews, 4*(1), 4–27.

Huang, L. N. (1994). An integrative approach to clinical assessment and intervention with Asian-American adolescents. *Journal of Clinical Child Psychology, 23*, 21–31.

Hummingbird, L. M. (2011). The public health crisis of Native American youth suicide. *NASN School Nurse (Print), 26*(2), 110–114.

Indian Health Service. (2014). *Behavioral health.* Washington, DC: Author.

Ivy, W. I., Miles, I., Le, B., & Paz-Bailey, G. (2014). Correlates of HIV infection among African American women from 20 cities in the United States. *AIDS and Behavior, 18*(Suppl 3), S266–S275.

Juthani, N. V., & Mishra, A. S. (2009). Clinical insights from working with immigrant Asian Americans and their families: Focus on acculturation stressors. In N.-H. Trinh, Y. C. Rho, F. G. Lu, & K. M. Sanders (Eds.), *Handbook of mental health and acculturation in Asian American families.* (pp. 179–197). Totowa, NJ: Humana Press.

Kim, P. Y., & Lee, D. (2014). Internalized model minority myth, Asian values, and help-seeking attitudes among Asian American students. *Cultural Diversity and Ethnic Minority Psychology, 20*(1), 98–106.

Kling, J. R., Leibman, J. B., & Katz, L. F. (n.d.). Experimental analysis of neighborhood effects. *Econometrica, 75*, 83–119.

Kochanek, K. D., Xu, J., Murphy, S. L., Miniño, A. M., & Kung, H. C. (2011, March). *National Vital Statistics Report, 59*(4). U.S. Department of Health and Human Services. DHHS Publication No. (PHS) 2011-1120.

Kulis, S., Marsiglia, F. F., Sicotte, D., & Nieri, T. (2007). Neighborhood effects on youth substance use in a southwestern city. *Sociological Perspectives, 50*(2), 273–301.

Landen, M., Roeber, J., Naimi, T., Nielsen, L., & Sewell, M. (2014). Alcohol-attributable mortality among American Indians and Alaska Natives in the United States, 1999–2009. *American Journal of Public Health, 104*(Suppl 3), S343–S349. doi:10.2105/AJPH.2013.301648

Latkin, C. A., Curry, A. D., Hua, W., & Davey, M. A. (2007). Direct and indirect associations of neighborhood disorder with substance use and high-risk sexual partners. *American Journal of Preventive Medicine, 32*(6, Suppl 1), S234–S241.

Latkin, C. A., German, D., Hua, W., & Curry, A. D. (2009). Individual-level influences on perceptions of neighborhood disorder: A multilevel analysis. *Journal of Community Psychology, 37*(1), 122–133.

Le, C. N. (2011). *"14 important statistics about Asian Americans" Asian-nation: The landscape of Asian America.* Retrieved from http://www.asian-nation.org/14-statistics.shtml

Le, T. N., Goebert, D., & Wallen, J. (2009). Acculturation factors and substance use among Asian American youth. *Journal of Primary Prevention, 30*(3-4), 453–473.

Lester, K., Artz, C., Resick, P. A., & Young-Xu, Y. (2010). Impact of race on early treatment termination and outcomes in posttraumatic stress disorder treatment. *Journal of Consulting and Clinical Psychology, 78*(4), 480–489.

Lewis-Fernandez, R., Das, A. K., Alfonso, C., Weisman, M. M., & Olfson, M. (2005). Depression in U.S. Hispanics: Diagnostic and management considerations in family practice. *Journal of the American Board of Family Medicine, 18*(4), 282–296.

Mahalingam, R. (2013). Model minority myth: Engendering cultural psychology of Asian immigrants. In E. L. Grigorenko (Ed.), *U.S. immigration and education: Cultural and policy issues across the lifespan* (pp. 119–136). New York, NY: Springer.

Marsh, K., Chaney, C., & Jones, D. (2012). The strengths of high-achieving Black high school students in a racially diverse setting. *Journal of Negro Education, 81*(1), 39–51.

Matthews, T. J., & MacDorman, M. F. (2013). Infant mortality statistics from the 2010 period linked birth/infant death data set. *National Vital Statistics Reports: From the Centers for Disease Control and Prevention, National Center for Health Statistics, National Vital Statistics System, 62*(8), 1–26.

Maslowsky, J., Schulenberg, J., Chiodo, L. M., Hannigan, J. H., Greenwald, M. K., Janisse, J., . . . Delaney-Black, V. (2015). Parental support, mental health, and alcohol and marijuana use in national and high-risk African-American adolescent samples. *Substance Abuse: Research and Treatment, 9* (Suppl 1), 11–20.

Mauer, M. (2013). *The changing racial dynamics of women's incarceration.* Retrieved from http://sentencingproject.org/wp-content/uploads/2015/12/The-Changing-Racial-Dynamics-of-Womens-Incarceration.pdf

Morning Edition. (2008, May). American Indian boarding schools haunt many. *National Public Radio.* Retrieved from http://www.npr.org/templates/story/story.php?storyId=16516865

Mosher, C. J., & Akins, S. (2007). *Substances and substance use: The control of consciousness alteration.* Thousand Oaks, CA: Sage.

Mui, A. C., & Kang, S.-Y. (2006). Acculturation stress and depression among Asian immigrant elders. *Social Work, 51*(3), 243–255.

Novins, D. K., Moore, L. A., Beals, J., Aarons, G. A., Rieckmann, T., & Kaufman, C. E. (2012). A framework for conducting a national study of substance abuse treatment programs serving American Indian and Alaska native communities. *American Journal of Substance and Alcohol Abuse, 38*(5), 518–522.

Ojelade, I. I., McCray, K., Ashby, J. S., & Meyers, J. (2011). Use of Ifá as a means of addressing mental health concerns among African American clients. *Journal of Counseling & Development, 89*(4), 406–412.

Palmer, R. T., Davis, R. J., Moore, J. L., & Hilton, A. A. (2010). A nation at risk: Increasing college participation persistence among African American males to stimulate U.S. global perspectives. *Journal of African American Males in Education, 1*(2), 105–124.

Pamber, A. (2010, February). High school graduation rates low where most American Indians, Alaskan Natives live, report says. *Diverse Issues in Higher Education.* Retrieved from http://diverseeducation.com/article/13555

Peregoy, J. J., & Gloria, A. M. (2007). Applying multicultural guidelines to American Indian/Alaskan Native populations. In M. G. Constantine (Ed.), *Clinical practice with people of color: A guide to becoming clinically competent* (pp. 61–94). New York, NY: Columbia University Press.

Perez-Rodriguez, M. M., Baca-Garcia, E., Oquendo, M. A., Wang, S., Wall, M. M., Liu, S.-M., & Blanco, C. (2014). Relationship between acculturation, discrimination, and suicidal ideation and attempts among U.S. Hispanics in the National Epidemiologic Survey of Alcohol and Related Conditions. *Journal of Clinical Psychiatry, 75*(4), 399–407.

Pew Hispanic Center. (2011). Hispanics account for more than half of nation's growth in past decade. *Pew Research Center.* Retrieved from http://pewhispanic.org/reports/report.php?ReportID=140

Pollack, C. E., Cubbin, C., Ahn, D., & Winkleby, M. (2005). Neighbourhood deprivation and alcohol consumption: does the availability of alcohol play a role? *International Journal of Epidemiology, 34*(4), 772–780.

Pollard, D. T. (2011). *Blackout: Black unemployment rate rises as overall rate falls.* Retrieved from http://pollardpost.blogspot.com/2011/04/blackout-black-unemployment-rate-rises.html

Rojas, J. I., Hallford, G., Brand, M. W., & Tivis, L. J. (2012). Latino/as in substance abuse treatment: Substance use patterns, family history of addiction, and depression. *Journal of Ethnicity in Substance Abuse, 11*(1), 75–85.

Rosario-Sim, M. G., & O'Connell, K. A. (2009). Depression and language acculturation correlate with smoking among older Asian American adolescents in New York City. *Public Health Nursing, 26*, 532–542. doi:10.1111/j.1525-1446.2009.00811.x

Saxe, L., Kadushin, C., Beveridge, A., Livert, D., Tighe, E., Rindskopf, D., . . . Brodsky, A. (2001). The visibility of illicit substances: Implications for community-based substance control strategies. *American Journal of Public Health, 91*(12), 1987–1994.

Schott Foundation. (2012). *The urgency of now: The Schott 50 state report on public education and black males 2012.* Retrieved from https://www.opensocietyfoundations.org/reports/urgency-now-schott-50-state-report-public-education-and-black-males

Schwartz, S. J., Weisskirch, R. S., Zamboanga, B. L., Castillo, L. G., Ham, L. S., Huynh, Q.-L., . . . Cano, M. A. (2011). Dimensions of acculturation: Associations with health risk behaviors among college students from immigrant families. *Journal of Counseling Psychology, 58*(1), 27–41.

Seefeldt, K. S., & Graham, J. D. (2013). *America's poor and the Great Recession.* Bloomington: Indiana University Press.

Simpson, G. M., & Lawrence-Webb, C. (2009). Responsibility without community resources: Informal kinship care among low-income, African American grandmother caregivers. *Journal of Black Studies, 39*(6), 825–847.

Spillane, N. S., & Smith, G. T. (2010). Individual differences in problem drinking among tribal members from one first nation community. *Alcoholism: Clinical and Experimental Research, 34*(11), 1985–1992.

Stimpson, J. P., Ju, H., Raji, M. A., & Eschbach, K. (2007). Neighborhood deprivation and health risk behaviors in NHANES III. *American Journal of Health Behavior, 31*(2), 215–222.

Substance Abuse and Mental Health Services Administration (2013). *Results from the 2012 National Survey on Substance Use and Health: Summary of National Findings,* NSDUH Series H-46, HHS

Publication No. (SMA) 13-4795. Rockville, MD: Author.

Sue, D. W., & Sue, D. (2013). *Counseling the culturally diverse: Theory and practice (6th ed.)*. Hoboken, NJ: Wiley.

Taylor, R. D. (2010). Risk and resilience in low-income African American families: Moderating effects of kinship social support. *Cultural Diversity and Ethnic Minority Psychology, 16*(3), 344–351.

Thomas, L. R. (2005, May). *Journeys of the Circle: Canoe journey, life's journey intervention for at-risk native youth*. Presentation at the 31st School on Addictions, Anchorage, AK.

Tobler, A. L., & Komro, K. A. (2010). Trajectories or parental monitoring and communication and effects on substance use among urban young adolescents. *Journal of Adolescent Health, 46*(6), 560–568.

Trenz, R. C., Harrell, P., Scherer, M., Mancha, B. E., & Latimer, W. W. (2012). A model of school problems, academic failure, alcohol initiation, and the relationship to adult heroin injection. *Substance Use & Misuse, 47*(10), 1159–1171.

Trimble, J. E. (2010). The virtues of cultural resonance, competence, and relational collaboration with Native American Indian communities: A synthesis of the counseling and psychotherapy literature. *The Counseling Psychologist, 38*(2), 243–256.

Uhm, S. Y. (2014). Mental illness from an Asian American perspective. In J. M. Davis & R. C. D'Amato (Eds.), *Neuropsychology of Asians and Asian Americans: Practical and theoretical considerations*. (pp. 77–90). New York, NY: Springer Science + Business Media.

Unger, J. B., Schwartz, S. J., Huh, J., Soto, D. W., & Baezconde-Garbanati, L. (2014). Acculturation and perceived discrimination: Predictors of substance use trajectories from adolescence to emerging adulthood among Hispanics. *Addictive Behaviors, 39*(9), 1293–1296.

U.S. Census Bureau. (2010). *Statistical abstract of the United States 2010: Population*. Washington, DC: U.S. Bureau of Census.

U.S. Census Bureau. (2011). *The Hispanic population 2010*. 2010 Census Briefs. Retrieved from http://www.census.gov/prod/cen2010/briefs/c2010br-04.pdf

U.S. Census Bureau. (2012). *Annual Estimates of the Resident Population by Sex, Race Alone or in Combination, and Hispanic Origin for the United States, States, and Counties: April 1, 2010 to July 1, 2012*. Source: U.S. Census Bureau, Population Division.

U.S. Census Bureau. (2014a). *Facts for features: African American history month*. Retrieved from https://www.census.gov/content/dam/Census/newsroom/facts-for-features/2014/cb14-ff03_black_history_month.pdf

U.S. Census Bureau. (2014b). *As the nation ages, seven states become younger, Census Bureau reports*. Retrieved from http://www.census.gov/newsroom/press-releases/2014/cb14-118.html

U.S. Department of Health and Human Services, Office of Health Service Policy. (2006). *Data on health and well-being of American Indians, Alaskan Natives, and other Native Americans data catalog* (HHS Contract: 233-02-0087). Retrieved from https://aspe.hhs.gov/report/data-health-and-well-being-american-indians-alaska-natives-and-other-native-americans

U.S. Department of Justice, Bureau of Justice Statistics. (2011). *Criminal victimization in the United States, 2008 statistical tables* (NCJ 231173). Retrieved from http://bjs.ojp.usdoj.gov/content/pub/pdf/cvus0805.pdf

Watkins, N. L., LaBarrie, T. L., & Appio, L. M. (2010). Black undergraduates' experiences with perceived racial microaggressions in predominately White colleges and universities. In D. W. Sue (Ed.), *Microaggressions and marginality: Manifestation, dynamics, and impact*. (pp. 25–57). Hoboken, NJ: Wiley.

Whitesell, N. R., Asdigian, N. L., Kaufman, C. E., Big Crow, C., Shangreau, C., Keane, E. M., . . . Mitchell, C. M. (2014). Trajectories of substance use among young American Indian adolescents: Patterns and predictors. *Journal of Youth and Adolescence, 43*(3), 437–453.

Williams, C. T., & Latkin, C. A. (2007). Neighborhood socioeconomic status, personal network attributes, and use of heroin and cocaine. *American Journal of Preventive Medicine, 32*(6, Suppl 1), S203–S210.

Wu, L.-T., Blazer, D. G., Swartz, M. S., Burchett, B., & Brady, K. T. (2013). Illicit and nonmedical substance use among Asian Americans, Native Hawaiians/Pacific Islanders, and mixed-race individuals. *Substance and Alcohol Dependence, 133*(2), 360–367. doi:10.1016/j.substancealcdep.2013.06.008

Chapter 13

Affordable Care Act. 42 U. S. C. § 18001 (2010). Retrieved March 23, 2016 from https://www.gpo.gov/fdsys/pkg/PLAW-111publ148/content-detail.html

Al-Anon. (n.d.). *History of Al-Anon Family Groups*. Retrieved from http://www.al-anon.alateen.org/al-anon-history

American Society of Addiction Medicine. (n.d.). *About us.* Retrieved from http://www.asam.org/about-us

Anti-Drug Abuse Act of 1986. H.R. 5484 (99th). Retrieved from https://www.govtrack.us/congress/bills/99/hr5484/text/enr

Bock, G. W., Zmud, R. W., Kim, Y. G., & Lee, J. N. (2005). Behavioral intention formation in knowledge sharing: Examining the roles of extrinsic motivators, social-psychological forces, and organizational climate. *MIS Quarterly, 29*(1), 87–111.

Brickmayer, J. D., Holder, H. D., Yacoubian, G. S., & Friend, K. B. (2004). A general causal model to guide alcohol, tobacco, and illicit drug prevention: Assessing the research evidence. *Journal of Drug Education, 34*(2), 121–153. Retrieved from https://www.ok.gov/odmhsas/documents/A%20GENERAL%20CAUSAL%20MODEL%20GUIDE%20-%20PIRE.pdf

Center for the Application of Prevention Technologies. (2016). *21st century partners in prevention.* Washington, DC: SAMHSA.

Centers for Disease Control and Prevention. (2016). *Impaired driving: Get the facts.* Retrieved March 2016 from http://www.cdc.gov/motorvehiclesafety/impaired_driving/impaired-drv_factsheet.html

Child Welfare Information Gateway. (2014). *Parental substance use and the child welfare system.* Washington, DC: U.S. Department of Health and Human Services, Children's Bureau. Retrieved March 2016 from https://www.childwelfare.gov/pubPDFs/parentalsubabuse.pdf

Christopher D. Smithers Foundation, Inc. (n.d.). *Over 60 years of philanthropy in the fight against alcoholism.* Retrieved from http://www.smithersfoundation.org/history/

Cima, R. (2015). DARE: The anti-drug program that never actually worked. *Priceonomics.* Retrieved from http://priceonomics.com/dare-the-anti-drug-program-that-never-actually/

Comprehensive Alcohol Abuse and Alcoholism Prevention, Treatment, and Rehabilitation Act, Public Law 93 STAT. 1301. (1970). Retrieved March 2016 from https://www.gpo.gov/fdsys/pkg/STATUTE-93/pdf/STATUTE-93-Pg1301.pdf

Cooper, B., Eisenberg, L., Sell, H., & Bertolote, J. M. (n.d.). *Guidelines for the primary prevention of mental, neurological and psychosocial disorders.* Geneva, Switzerland: World Health Organization. Retrieved March 2016 from http://apps.who.int/iris/bitstream/10665/60992/1/WHO_MNH_MND_94.21.pdf

Correia, M. (2013). Substance abuse in child welfare. *Casey practice digest: Substance use disorders in families with young children.* Casey Family Programs, Issue 5.

Coulson, A. J. (2012). *"Zero tolerance." Causes, consequences, and alternatives.* Washington, DC: CATO Institute. Retrieved from cato.org/publications/congressional-testimony/zero-tolerance-causes-consequences-alternatives

Drug Abuse Treatment Act of 1972. Public Law 92-255. Retrieved from https://www.gpo.gov/fdsys/pkg/STATUTE-86/pdf/STATUTE-86-Pg65.pdf

Galloway, R. D. (2003). Health promotion: Causes, beliefs and measurements. *Clinical Medicine & Research, 1*(3), 249–258. Retrieved from http://www.ncbi.nlm.nih.gov/pmc/articles/PMC1069052/pdf/ClinMedRes0103-0249.pdf

Gerhard, P., & Woolley, J. T. (1980). *The American Presidency Project.* http://www.presidency.ucsb.edu/ws/?pid=45420

Harrison Narcotics Tax Act of 1914. Public Law Ch. 1, 38 Stat. 785. Retrieved March 2016 from http://legisworks.org/sal/38/stats/STATUTE-38-Pg785.pdf

Holder, H. D., & Carina, R. T. (2012). *Guide to strategic planning for environmental prevention of ATOD problems using a logic model.* Calverton, MD: Pacific Institute for Research and Evaluation. Retrieved from http://doview.com/files/other/holder-carina-2012-strategic-planning-logic-model.pdf

Horvath, T., Misra, K., Epner, A. K., & Cooper, G. M. (2016). *Public health model of addiction and recovery implications.* Retrieved from https://www.mentalhelp.net/articles/public-health-model-of-addiction-and-recovery-implications/

Institute of Medicine. (1997). *Dispelling the myths about addiction: Strategies to increase understanding and strengthen research.* Washington, DC: National Academy Press. Retrieved from http://www.nap.edu/read/5802/chapter/1

Institute of Medicine and National Research Council. (2009). *Preventing mental, emotional, and behavioral disorders among young people.* Washington, DC: National Academies Press. doi:10.17226/12480.

Institute of Medicine and National Research Council. (2013). *New directions in child abuse and neglect research.* Washington, DC: National Academies Press. Retrieved from http://www.nationalacademies.org/hmd/Reports/2013/New-Directions-in-Child-Abuse-and-Neglect-Research.aspx

Jellinek, E. M. (1960). *The disease concept of alcoholism.* London, England: Hillhouse Press.

Johnson, E. M., Amatetti, S., Funkhouser, J. E., & Johnson, S. (1988). *Theories and models supporting prevention approaches to alcohol problems among youth.* Rockville,

MD: Office for Substance Abuse Prevention. Retrieved from https://www.ncbi.nlm.nih.gov/pmc/articles/PMC1478154/pdf/pubhealthrep00167-0024.pdf

Lander, L., Howsare, J., & Byrne, M. (2013). The impact of substance use disorders on families and children: From theory to practice. *Social Work Public Health, 28*, 194–205. doi:10.1080/19371918.2013.759005.

McKelvey v. Walters, 596 F. Supp. 1317, 1321. (1984).

Mothers Against Drunk Driving. (n.d.). The history of MADD: 35 years: Saving lives, serving people. Retrieved March 2016 from http://www.madd.org/about-us/history/

National Association of Drug Court Professionals. (n.d.). History: Justice professionals pursue a vision. Retrieved March 2016 from http://www.nadcp.org/learn/what-are-drug-courts/drug-court-history

National Committee for Education on Alcoholism. (1950). [Editorial]. *New England Journal of Medicine, 242*(25), 991.

National Data Archive on Child Abuse and Neglect. (2012). *Adoption and foster care analysis reporting system.* [Data file]. Ithaca, NY: Child Welfare Information Gateway.

National Institute on Drug Abuse. (1984). *Prevention research: Deterring drug abuse among children and adolescents.* Research Monograph Series, 63. U.S. Department of Health and Human Services. Retrieved from https://archives.drugabuse.gov/pdf/monographs/63.pdf

National Institute on Drug Abuse. (2012). *Medical consequences of drug abuse.* Retrieved March 2016 from https://www.drugabuse.gov/related-topics/medical-consequences-drug-abuse

National Institute on Drug Abuse. (2015a). *Trends and statistics.* Retrieved March 2016 from https://www.drugabuse.gov/related-topics/trends-statistics

National Institute on Drug Abuse. (2015b). *Overdose death rates.* Retrieved March 2016 from https://www.drugabuse.gov/related-topics/trends-statistics/overdose-death-rates

National Minimum Drinking Age Act. (1984). Public Law 23 U.S. Code § 158. Retrieved from https://www.law.cornell.edu/uscode/text/23/158

OASAS. (n.d.). *OASAS risk and protective factors.* Retrieved March 2016 from https://www.oasas.ny.gov/prevention/documents/rpfactordictionary07.pdf

Obama, B. (2015). *National Substance Abuse Prevention Month: A proclamation.* Retrieved March 2016 from https://www.whitehouse.gov/sites/default/files/2015substanceabuse.prc_.rel_.pdf

O'Connell, M. E., Boat, T., & Warner, K. E. (Eds.). (2009). *Preventing mental, emotional, and behavioral disorders among young people: Progress and possibilities.* Washington, DC: The National Academies Press.

Office of National Drug Control Policy. (n.d.). *Prevention and the national drug control strategy.* Retrieved March 2016 from https://www.whitehouse.gov/ondcp/prevention-and-the-national-drug-control-strategy

Office of National Drug Control Policy. (1999). *Preventing drug abuse.* Retrieved March 2016 from https://www.ncjrs.gov/ondcppubs/publications/policy/99ndcs/iv-b.html

Pan, W., & Bai, H. (2009). A multivariate approach to a meta-analytic review of the effectiveness of the D.A.R.E. program. *International Journal of Environmental Research and Public Health, 6*, 267–277. doi:10.3390/ijerph6010267. Retrieved from http://www.ncbi.nlm.nih.gov/pmc/articles/PMC2672328/pdf/ijerph-06-00267.pdf

Portland Injury Prevention. (n.d.). *The 5 public health principles.* Retrieved March 2016 from http://www.npaihb.org/images/epicenter_docs/injuryprevention/PublicHealthPrinciples.pdf

Potenza, M. N. (2014). Non-substance addictive behaviors in the context of the DSM-5. *Addictive Behaviors, 39*(1), 1–4. doi:10.1016/j.addbeh.013.09.004.

Prevention Institute. (1999). The spectrum of prevention: Developing a comprehensive approach to injury prevention. Retrieved from https://www.preventioninstitute.org/sites/default/files/publications/Spectrum%20of%20Prevention_0.pdf

Prochaska, J. O., & Di Clemente, C. C. (1982). Transtheoretical therapy: Toward a more integrative model of change. *Psychotherapy: Theory, Research and Practice, 19*(3), 276–288. Retrieved from http://hbftpartnership.com/documents/uploadResources/TranstheoreticalT-Prochaska1982.pdf

Ronald Reagan Presidential Foundation & Library. (2010). *Just say no.* Retrieved March 2016 from http://www.reaganfoundation.org/details_f.aspx?p=RR1008NRHC&tx=6

Rosenbaum, D. P. (2007). Just say no to D.A.R.E. *Criminology & Public Policy, 6*(4), 815–824.

Single, E., Collins, D., Easton, B., Harwood, H., Lapsley, H., Kopp, P., & Wilson, E. (2001). *International guidelines for estimating the costs of substance abuse—2001 edition.* Retrieved from http://www.pierrekopp.com/downloads/International%20guidelines%202001%20edition-4.pdf

Students Against Destructive Decisions. (n.d.). Retrieved from http://www.bethechangenc.com/sadd-contracts-for-life.html

Substance Abuse and Mental Health Services Administration. (2010). *Focus on Prevention.* Retrieved from http://store.samhsa.gov/shin/content/SMA10-4120/SMA10-4120.pdf

Substance Abuse and Mental Health Services Administration. (2013). 6.8 million adults had both mental illness and substance use disorder in 2011. *The NSDUH Report.* Retrieved March 2016 from http://www.samhsa.gov/data/sites/default/files/spot111-adults-mental-illness-substance-use-disorder/spot111-adults-mental-illness-substance-use-disorder.pdf

Substance Abuse and Mental Health Services Administration. (2014). Evidence-based practices web guide. Retrieved from http://www.samhsa.gov/ebp-web-guide/substance-abuse-prevention

Substance Abuse and Mental Health Services Administration. (2015). *Behavioral health trends in the United States: Results from the 2014 National Survey on Drug Use and Health.* Retrieved March 2016 from http://www.samhsa.gov/data/sites/default/files/NSDUH-FRR1-2014/NSDUH-FRR1-2014.pdf

Substance Abuse and Mental Health Services Administration. (2016). *Prevention of substance abuse and mental illness.* Retrieved March 2016 from http://www.samhsa.gov/prevention

Traynor v. Turnage, 485 U.S. 535 (1988).

U.S., 56 U.S.L.W. 4319, 4324 (U.S. April 20, 1988).

Van Wormer, K., & Davis, D. R. (2013). *Addiction Treatment: A Strengths Perspective* (3rd ed.). Belmont, CA: Brooks-Cole.

Webb v. United States, 249 U.S. 96 (1919). Retrieved from https://supreme.justia.com/cases/federal/us/249/96/case.html

White, W. (2014). *The history of addiction counseling in the United States.* Alexandria, VA: Association for Addiction Professionals.

Wilson, B. (1939, 1955, 1976, 2001). *Alcoholics Anonymous* (4th ed.). New York, NY: Alcoholics Anonymous World Services, Inc.

Wulczyn, F., Ernst, M., & Fisher, P. (2011). *Who are the infants in out-of-home care? An epidemiological and developmental snapshot.* Chicago, IL: Chapin Hall at the University of Chicago.

Chapter 14

Aboujaoude, E., Koran, L. M., Gamel, N., Large, M. D., & Serpe, R. T. (2006). Potential markers for problematic Internet use: A telephone survey of 2,513 adults. *CNSSpectrums, 11,* 750–755.

Achab, S., Nicolier, M., Mauny, F., Monnin, J., Trojak, B., & Vandel, P. (2011). Massively multiplayer online role-playing games: Comparing characteristics of addict vs. non-addict online recruited games in a French adult population. *BMC Psychiatry, 11,* 144.

Ackard, D. M., Brehm, B. J., & Steffen, J. J. (2002). Exercise and eating disorders in college-aged women: Profiling excessive exercise. *Eating Disorders, 10*(1), 31–47.

American Gaming Association. (2012). Gambling revenue, 10-year trends. Retrieved February 2016, from http://www.americangaming.org/industry-resources/research/factsheets/gaming-revenue-10-year-trends

American Psychiatric Association. (2013). *Diagnostic and statistical manual of mental disorders* (5th ed.). Washington, DC: Author.

American Society of Addiction Medicine. (2011). *Definition of addiction.* Retrieved from http://www.asam.org/research-treatment/definition-of-addiction

Augustine Fellowship. (1986). *Sex and Love Addicts Anonymous.* The Augustine Fellowship. Retrieved from https://slaafws.org/english

Bamber, D. J., Cockerill, I. M., Rodgers, S., & Carroll, D. (2003). Diagnostic criteria for exercise dependence in women. *British Journal of Sports Medicine, 37*(5), 393–400.

Benson, A. L., Dittmar, H., & Wolfsohn, R. (2010). Compulsive buying: Cultural contributions and consequences. In E. Aboujaoude & L. A. Koran (Eds.), *Impulse control disorders* (pp. 23–33). Cambridge, England: Cambridge University Press. Retrieved from http://dx.doi.org/10.1017/CBO9780511711930

Benson, A. L., & Eisenach, D. A. (2013). Stopping over-shopping: An approach to the treatment of compulsive-buying disorder. *Journal of Groups in Addiction & Recovery, 8*(1), 3–24. doi:10.1080/1556035X.2013.727724

Berczik, K., Szabo, A., Griffiths, M. D., Kurimay, T., Kun, B., Urban, R., & Demetrovics, Z. (2012). Exercise addiction: Symptoms, diagnosis, epidemiology, and etiology. *Substance Use and Misuse, 47,* 403–417.

Biddle, S. J. H., & Mutrie, N. (1991). *Psychology of physical activity and exercise: A health related perspective.* London, England: Springer.

Black, D. W. (2011). Epidemiology and phenomenology of compulsive buying disorder. In J. E. Grant & M. E. Potenza (eds.), *I shop, therefore I am—Compulsive buying and the search for self* (pp. 191–216). New York, NY: Aronson.

Black, D. W., & Grant, J. E. (2015). *DSM-5 guidebook: The essential companion to the Diagnostic and Statistical Manual of Mental Disorders.* Washington, DC: APPI.

Blaydon, M. J., & Lindner, K. J. (2002). Eating disorders and exercise in triathletes. *Eating Disorders, 10*(1), 49–60.

Blaydon, M. J., Lindner, K. J., & Kerr, J. H. (2004). Metamotivational characteristics of exercise dependence and eating disorders in highly active amateur sports participants. *Journal of the American Medical Association, 252*(4), 520–523.

Carnes, P. (1983). Out of the shadows: *Understanding sexual addiction.* Minneapolis, MN: CompCare.

Carnes, P. (2004). Out of the shadows: *Understanding sexual addiction* (Rev. ed.). Center City, MN: Hazelden.

Carnes, P., Green, B., & Carnes, S. (2010). The same yet different: Refocusing the Sexual Addiction Screening Test (SAST) to reflect orientation and gender. *Sexual Addiction Compulsivity, 17*(1), 7–30.

Carnes, P. J., Green, B. A., Merlo, L. J., Polles, A., Carnes, S., & Gold, M. S. (2011) *PATHOS: a brief screening application for assessing sexual addiction.* doi:10.1097/ADM.0b013e3182251a28.

Chou, K. L., & Afifi, T.O. (2011). Pathological gamblers respond equally well to cognitive-behavioral therapy of other mental health treatment status. *American Journal of Addictions, 19*, 550–556.

Christakis, D. A., Moreno, M. M., Jelenchick, L., Myaing, M. T. & Zhou, C. (2011). Problematic Internet usage in US college students: A pilot study, *BMC Medicine, 22*(9), 77.

Cuzen, N. L., & Stein, D. J. (2014). Behavioral addiction: The nexus of impulsivity and compulsivity. In K. P. Rosenberg & L. C. Feder (Eds.), *Behavioral addictions: Criteria, evidence, and treatment* (pp. 19–34). Boston, MA: Elsevier.

Dell'Osso, B., Allen, A., Altamura, C., Buoli, M., & Hollander, E. (2008a). Epidemiological and clinical updates on impulse control disorders: A critical review. *European Archives of Psychiatry and Clinical Neurosciences, 256*, 464–475.

Dell'Osso, B., Allen, A. A., Altamura, C., Buoli, M., & Hollander, E. (2008b). Impulsive compulsive buying disorder: Clinical overview. *Australian and New Zealand Journal of Psychiatry, 42*, 259–266.

Demetrovics, Z., Urbán, R., Nagygyörgy, K., Farkas, J., Griffiths, M. D., & Pápay, O. (2012). The development of the Problematic Online Gaming Questionnaire (POGQ). *PLoS One, 7*(5), e36417.

Department of Health and Human Services. (2015). *Nutrition and exercise.* Retrieved January 2016 from http://www.hhs.gov/programs/prevention-and-wellness/nutrition-and-fitness/

Dittmar, H. (2005). Compulsive buying—A growing concern? An examination of gender, age, and endorsement of materialistic values as predictors. *British Journal of Psychology, 96*, 467–491.

Dong, G., Lu, Q, Zhou, H., & Zhou, X. (2011). Precursor or sequel: Pathological disorders in people with Internet addiction disorder. PLoS One, 6(2), e14703. doi:10.1371/journal.pone.0014703.

Engs, R. C. (2012). *What are addictive behaviors?* Bloomington, IN: Tichenor.

Faber, R. J., & O'Guinn, T. C. (1992). A clinical screener for compulsive buying. *Journal of Consumer Research, 19*, 459.

Fong, T. W. (2006). Understanding and managing compulsive sexual behaviors. *Psychiatry, 3*(11), 51–58.

Garcia, F. D., & Thibaut, F. (2010). Sexual addictions. *American Journal of Drug and Alcohol Abuse, 36*, 254–260. doi:10.3109/00952990.2010.503823

Gentile, D. A. (2009). Pathological video-game use among youths 8 to 18: A national study. *Psychological Science, 20*(5), 594–602.

Glasser, W. (1976). *Positive addiction.* New York, NY: Harper & Row.

Gooding, P., & Tarrier, N. (2009). A systematic review and meta-analysis of cognitive-behavioral interventions to reduce problem gambling: Hedging our bets? *Behavior Research and Therapy, 47*, 592–607. doi:10.1016/j.brat.2009.04.002

Gordon-Lamoureux, R. J. (2007). Exploring the possibility of sexual addiction in men arrested for seeking out prostitutes: A preliminary study. *Journal of Addiction Nursing, 18*, 21–29. doi:10.1080/10884600601174458

Grant, J. E., Kim, S. W., & Hartman, B. (2008). A double-blind placebo-controlled study of the opiate antagonist naltrexone in the treatment of pathological gambling urges. *Journal of Clinical Psychiatry, 69*, 783–789.

Grant, J. E., Odlaug, B. L., & Mooney, M. (2012). Telescoping phenomenon in pathological gambling: Association with gender and comorbidities. *Journal of Nervous & Mental Disease, 200*, 996–998.

Grant, J. E., & Potenza, M. N. (2006). Sexual orientation of men with pathological gambling: Prevalence and psychiatric comorbidity in a treatment-seeking sample. *Comprehensive Psychiatry, 47*, 515–518.

Grant, J. E., Potenza, M. N., Weinstein, A., & Gorelick, D. A. (2010). Introduction to behavioral addictions.

American Journal of Drug and Alcohol Abuse, 36, 233–241. doi:10.3109/00952990.2010.491884

Griffiths, M. D. (2005). Exercise addiction: A case study. *Addiction Research, 5*, 161–168.

Han, D. H., & Renshaw, P. F. (2012). Bupropion in the treatment of problematic online game play in patients with major depressive disorder. *Journal of Psychopharmacology, 25*(5), 689–696.

Hardoon, K. K., & Derevensky, J. L. (2002). Child and adolescent gambling behavior: Current knowledge. *Clinical Child Psychology & Psychiatry, 7*, 263–281.

Hartney, E. (2011). *Symptoms of addiction: Signs and symptoms of addiction to look out for.* Retrieved from http://addictions.about.com/od/howaddictionhappens/a/symptomslist.htm

Hartston, H. (2012). The case for compulsive shopping as an addiction. *Journal of Psychoactive Drugs, 44*(1), 64–67.

Hathaway, S., & McKinley, J. C. (1989). *Minnesota Multiphasic Personality Inventory (MMPI-2).* Columbus, OH: Merrill/Prentice-Hall.

Hausenblas H. A., & Symons Downs, D. (2002). How much is too much? The development and validation of the Exercise Dependence Scale. *Psychology of Sports and Exercise, 3*(2), 89–123.

Hook, J. N., Hook, J. P., Davis, D. E., Worthington, E. L., & Penberthy, J. L. (2010). Measuring sexual addiction and compulsivity: A critical review of instruments. *Journal of Sex and Marital Therapy, 36*, 227–260.

Hook, J. N., Hook, J. P., & Hines, S. (2008). Reach out or act out: Long term group therapy for sexual addiction. *Sexual Addiction and Compulsivity, 15*, 217–235.

Internet World Stats. (2016). Internet world stats: Usage and populations stats. Retrieved from http://www.internetworldstats.com/stats.htm

Isrealashvili, M., Kim, T., & Bukobza, G. (2012). Adolescents' over-use of the cyber world—Internet addiction or identity exploration? *Journal of Adolescence, 35*(2), 417–424.

Jazaeri, S. A., & Bin Habil, M. H. (2012). Reviewing two types of addiction—pathological gambling and substance use. *Indian Journal of Psychological Medicine, 34*(1), 5–11. doi:10 4102/0253-7176.96147

Kafka, M. P. (2010). Hypersexual disorder: A proposed diagnosis for DSM-5. *Archives of Sexual Behavior, 39*(2), 377–400.

Kaplan, M. S., & Krueger, R. B. (2010). Diagnosis, assessment, and treatment of hypersexuality. *Journal of Sex Research, 47*(2–3), 181–198.

Kessler, R. C., Hwang, I., LaBrie, R., Petukhova, M., Sampson, N. A., & Winters, K. C. (2008). DSM-IV pathological gambling in the National Comorbidity Survey Replication. *Psychological Medicine, 38*(9), 1351–1360.

Koran, L. M., Faber, R. J., Aboujaoude, E., Large, M. D., & Serpe, R. T. (2006). Estimated prevalence of compulsive buying behavior in the United States. *American Journal of Psychiatry, 163*(10), 1806–1812.

Kuzma, J. M., & Black, D. W. (2008). Epidemiology, prevalence, and natural history of compulsive sexual behavior. *Psychiatric Clinics of North America, 31*, 603–611.

Lam, L. T., Peng, Z. W., Mai, J. C., & Jing, J. (2009). Factors associated with Internet addiction among adolescents. *Cyberpsychology and Behavior, 12*(5), 551–555.

Landolfi, E. (2013). Exercise addiction. *Sports Medicine, 43*, 111–119. doi:10.1007/s40279-012- 0013-x

Lee, B. W., & Stapinski, L. A. (2012). Seeking safety on the Internet: Relationship between social anxiety and problematic Internet use. *Journal of Anxiety Disorders, 26*(1), 197–205.

McKeague, E. L. (2014). Differentiating the female sex addict: A literature review focused on themes of gender difference used to inform recommendations for treating women with sex addiction. *Sexual Addiction & Compulsivity: Journal of Treatment and Prevention, 21*, 203–224. doi:10.1080/10720162.2014.931266

Miller, W. R., Forcehimes, A. A., & Zweben, A. (2011). *Treating addiction: A guide for professionals.* New York, NY: Guilford Press.

Miller, W. R., & Rollnicj, S. (2002). *Motivational interviewing: Preparing people for change.* New York, NY: Guilford Press.

Mónok, K., Berczik, K., Urbán, R., Szabo, A., Griffiths, M. D., & Farkas, J. (2012). Psychometric properties and concurrent validity of two exercise addiction measures. A population wide study. *Psychology of Sport and Exercise, 13*(6), 739–746.

Mueller, A., Claes, L., Mitchell, J. E., Faber, R. J., Fisher, J., & de Zwaan, M. (2011). Does compulsive buying differ between male and female students? *Personality and Individual Differences, 50*, 1309–1312.

O'Brien, C. P., Volkow, N., & Li, T.-K. (2006). What's in a word? Addiction versus dependence in DSM-V. *American Journal of Psychiatry, 163*, 764–765

Ogden, J., Veale, D. M., & Summers, Z. (1997). The development and validation of the Exercise Dependence Questionnaire. *Addiction Research, 5*(4), 343–355.

Orford, J. (1978). Hypersexuality: Implications for the theory of dependence. *British Journal of Addiction, 73*, 299–303.

Pápay, O., Urbán, R. Griffiths, M. D., Nagygyörgy, K. Farkas, J., Kökönyei, G., . . . Demetrovics, Z. (2013). Psychometric properties of the Problematic Online Gambling Questionnaire Short-Form (POGQ-SF) and prevalence of problematic online gaming in a national sample of adolescents. *Cyberpsychology, Behavior and Social Networking, 16*, 340–348.

Potenza, M. N., Koran, L. M., & Pallanti, S. (2010). Relationship between impulsive control disorders and obsessive-compulsive disorder: A current understanding and future research directions. In E. Hollander, & J. Zohar (Eds.), *Obsessive compulsive spectrum disorders* (pp. 117–140). Arlington, VA: American Psychiatric Publishing.

Rosenberg, K. P., & Feder, L. C. (2014). *Behavioral addiction: Criteria, evidence, and treatment.* Boston, MA: Academic Press.

Rush, B. (1812). *Medical inquiries and observation upon the diseases of the mind.* Philadelphia, PA: Kimber & Richardson.

Saktor, T. C. (2011). How does PKMzeta maintain long-term memory? *Nature Reviews Neuroscience, 12*, 9–15.

Sharma, V., Narang, K., Rajender, G., & Bhatia, M. S., (2009). Shopaholism (compulsive buying)—A new entity. *Delhi Psychiatry Journal, 12*(1), 110–113.

Shaw, M., & Black, D. W. (2008). Internet addiction: Definition, assessment, epidemiology and clinical management. *CNS Drugs, 22*(5), 353–365.

Sohn, S. H., & Choi, Y. J. (2014). Phases of shopping addiction evidenced by experiences of compulsive buyers. *International Journal of Mental Health and Addiction, 12*, 243–254. doi:10.1007/s11469-013-9449-y

Symons Downs, D., Hausenblas, H. A., & Nigg, C. R. (2004). Factorial validity and psychometric examination of the Exercise Dependence Scale-Revised. *Measurement in Physical Education and Exercise Science, 8*(4), 183–201.

Toneatto, T. (2008) Reliability and validity of the Gamblers Anonymous Twenty Questions. *Journal of Psychopathology and Behavioral Assessment, 30*(1), 71–78.

Topf, J. L., Yip, S. W., & Potenza, M. N. (2009). Pathological gambling: Biological and clinical considerations. *Journal of Addiction Medicine, 3*(3), 111–119.

Tosto, G., Talarico, G., Lenzi, G. L., & Bruno, G. (2008). Effect of citalopram in treating hypersexuality in an Alzheimer's disease case. *Neurological Science, 29*, 269–270.

Wong, P. W., Chan, W. S., Conwell, Y., Conner, K. R., & Yip, P. S. (2010). A psychological autopsy study of pathological gamblers who died by suicide. *Journal of Affective Disorders, 120*, 213–216.

Wood, R. T., & Williams, R. J. (2009). *Internet gambling: Prevalence, patterns, problems, and policy options.* Retrieved from http://hdl.handle.net/10133/693

Wood, R. T., & Williams, R. J. (2011). A comparative profile of the Internet gambler: Demographic characteristics, game-play patterns, and problem gambling status. *New Media & Society, 13*, 1123–1141.

World Health Organization. (1992). *The ICD-10 classification of mental and behavioural disorders: Clinical descriptions and diagnostic guidelines.* Geneva, Switzerland: Author.

Young, K. S. (1998). *Caught in the net.* New York, NY: Wiley. Retrieved from http://netaddiction.com/Internet-addiction-test

Young, K. S. (2012). *Internet infidelity.* Retrieved from http://netaddiction.com

NAME INDEX

SUBJECT INDEX

Chlordiazepoxide, 60, 61
Christopher D. Smithers Foundation, 314
Christopher, James, 245
Chronic phase
  of addiction, 120–121
  Jellenik's, 94*f*
Cigarette smoking, 18. *See also* Nicotine; Tobacco
  adolescents and, 253
  e-cigarettes, 253
  prevention, 311
Cirrhosis, 59
Citalopram, 341
Clients
  confidentiality and, 32, 33*t*
  consent to disclosure of information, 34
  as drug dealers, 42
Closed group counseling, 196
Club drugs, 49, 55, 84–86
  GHB, 64–65
  ketamine (special K), 83–84
  LSD, 82
  MDMA (Ecstasy), 85–86
  PCP, 82–83
CNS (central nervous system) depressants, 4
  alcohol, 57–60
  barbiturates, 63–64
  benzodiazepines, 61–63
  GHB (club drug), 64–65
  opiates, 65–67
Coalition for the Homeless, 276
Coca-Cola, 13
Cocaine, 68–71, 176–177
  effects on the body, 69–70
  effects on the fetus, 70–71
  history of, 12–13
  incidence, 68–69
  neurotransmitters and, 54*t*
  psychoactive effects, 69
  tolerance and withdrawal, 70
Cocaine Anonymous (CA), 244
Cocaine hydrochloride, 68
Codeine, 65
Code of Federal Regulations 42, Part 2, 33–34, 37, 38, 42
  minors and, 40–41
Codependency, 216, 217
Cognitive-behavioral theory, 146
Cognitive-behavioral therapy, 275
  in group counseling, 198–199
  individuals and, 174
  for relapse prevention, 236–239, 238*f*
Cognitive behavior processes, 103
Cognitive dissonance, 321
Cognitive distortions, 268
Collaboration, in motivational interviewing, 172
Commission on Accreditation of Rehabilitation Facilities
  (CARF), 153

Communicable diseases, ethics and, 33, 33*t*, 34, 36, 38
Communication and behavior change model, 323
Community-based processes, 327
Community education and treatment efforts, 314, 317
Comorbid disorders, 257, 259, 273
Comorbidity, 100
Compassion, in motivational interviewing, 172
Comprehensive Alcohol Abuse and Alcoholism
  Prevention Treatment and Rehabilitation Act, 315
Comprehensive Drug Abuse Prevention and Control Act,
  15, 56
Comprehensive prevention, 314, 315, 319, 320, 322,
  325–329, 328*t*
Compulsive buying disorder (CBD), 343–345
  case study, 347–348
  diagnosis and assessment, 344
  terms associated with, 344
  treatment, 345
Compulsivity, 332
Confidential Alcohol Treatment and Education Pilot
  (U.S. Army), 280
Confidentiality
  Code of Federal Regulations 42, Part 2, 33–34, 37, 42
  in ethical codes, 31*t*, 32
  in group counseling, 37, 195
  imminent danger and, 38
  limits to, 32–33, 33*t*
  of minors, 37–38
  of patient records, 34, 35
  in 12-step programs, 37
Conflict
  case discussion, 225–226
  ethical, 41
  families and, 212, 214, 218
  interpersonal, 230
  values conflict, 44
Conflicting laws, 26, 37, 43
Consent
  informed, 38, 42
  written, 32–34, 45
Consent Directive, 36
Continuum of care, 201–203
Controlled Substance Act (CSA), 15
Controlled substances schedules, 56
  anabolic-androgenic steroids, 87–89
  depressants, 56–67
  hallucinogens, 81–84
  stimulants, 67–81
  volatile substances or inhalants, 86–87
Control stage, 124
Convulsive seizures, 59–60
Co-occurring disorders, 134–135. *See also* Dual-diagnosis
  inpatient hospitalization
Cooperation, as cultural value, 286
Coping skills, 260
Coping skills training, 177–179, 182